Teaching Strategies
for Ethnic Studies

Teaching Strategies

for Ethnic Studies

Fifth Edition

James A. Banks
University of Washington, Seattle

Allyn and Bacon

Boston   London   Toronto   Sydney   Tokyo   Singapore

Series Editor: *Sean W. Wakely*
Production Administrator: *Annette Joseph*
Production Coordinator: *Susan Freese*
Editorial-Production Service: *Grace Sheldrick, Wordsworth Associates*
Cover Administrator: *Linda K. Dickinson*
Cover Designer: *Suzanne Harbison*

Copyright © 1991, 1987, 1984, 1979, 1975 by Allyn and Bacon
A Division of Simon & Schuster, Inc.
160 Gould Street
Needham Heights, Massachusetts 02194

Library of Congress Cataloging-in-Publication Data

Banks, James A.
    Teaching strategies for ethnic studies / James A. Banks. — 5th
  ed.
        p. cm.
    Includes bibliographical references and index.
    ISBN 0–205–12756–8
    1. Minorities—United States—Study and teaching.   2. Ethnicity —
Study and teaching—United States.   3. United States—Ethnic
relations—Study and teaching.   I. Title.
E184.A1B24   1990
305.8′0071′073—dc20
                                                                    90–1246
                                                                    CIP

 # 22389342

Printed in the United States of America
10 9 8 7 6 5 4 3 2   95 94 93 92 91

110742

*To the memory of Bob, my brother,
who shared my dream for a better world*

*and to Mrs. Black, Mrs. Clay, Miss Curry,
Mrs. Jones, and Mrs. Wilson,
five of my elementary teachers,
whose many heroic deeds are unsung*

Brief Contents

Contents

Part II
The First Americans and African Americans: Concepts and Strategies   129

Part IV
Hispanic Americans: Concepts and Strategies   305

Part V
Asian Americans: Concepts and Strategies   401

Part VI
Multicultural Units and Evaluation   485

Appendixes

Preface

The pace of demographic changes in the U.S. population has accelerated since the fourth edition of *Teaching Strategies for Ethnic Studies* was published. Significant new trends and developments have also occurred in ethnic studies and multicultural education. The growth rate in the nation's population of people of color continues to outpace the growth of the nation's White population. These disproportionate growth rates are occurring because the birth rate exceeds the death rate among people of color and because most immigrants now entering the United States are from nations in Latin America and Asia. Between 1981 and 1986, 85% of the legal immigrants who settled in the United States were from Latin America and Asia. Only 11% came from Europe. Demographers predict that by the turn of the century, one of every three Americans will be a person of color.

The nation's changing ethnic texture is having and will continue to have a major influence on its schools and other public and private institutions. By 2020, if current growth trends continue, students of color will make up about 46% of the nation's school-age youths. To prepare our students for the multicultural world in which they will live, we must help them develop multicultural literacy and cross-cultural competency.

A major goal of this fifth edition of *Teaching Strategies for Ethnic Studies* is to help present and future teachers acquire the knowledge, concepts, strategies, and resources needed to integrate content about ethnic groups into the mainstream curriculum. This fifth edition reflects current and emerging concepts, perspectives, and issues in the field. Since the previous edition was published, an acid debate has developed over the curriculum canon that is institutionalized within the schools and colleges. Ethnic scholars as well as feminists have challenged the dominant canon and demanded that it be reconceptualized and broadened to reflect more accurately the experiences of people of color and women. During the 1980s, multicultural curriculum reformers experienced major victories at Stanford University, the University of California–Berkeley, and the University of Minnesota–Twin Cities.

In preparing this edition, I have incorporated new terms and concepts that are emerging in the field. In most instances, the phrase *people of color* rather than *ethnic minority* is used to refer to groups such as Mexican Americans, African Americans, Puerto Ricans, and Native Americans. *People of color* is used to reflect new demographic realities: These groups are majorities rather than minorities in a growing number of schools and school districts. To refer to a group that is a numerical majority within an institution as a minority is an anachronism at variance with current demographic realities. I usually refer to Blacks as *African Americans* because this term parallels terms used to refer to most other U.S. ethnic groups (e.g., Mexican Americans and Italian Americans). It also emphasizes the shared identity of people of African descent throughout the world.

In this edition, all statistics and demographic data have been updated, using U.S. Census *Current Population Reports* for 1988 and 1989, U.S. Census population projections for 1990, and *Statistical Abstract of the United States, 1989*. Throughout the book, the bibliographies have been extensively revised for readers in the 1990s. Some chapters retain few titles from the previous edition. Readers of this edition can refer to previous editions of this book for older but nonetheless important titles.

The chapters on all ethnic groups have been updated with new information and Census data. The introductory section for Part IV, "Hispanic Americans: Concepts and Strategies," has been expanded. Information on Central and South Americans has been added to this section. (These groups now make up about 12% of the Hispanic Americans.) A discussion of the new nativism and xenophobia of the 1980s and 1990s is also new to this edition, as is an appendix listing books on women of color. Appendix B has been substantially revised to include a preponderance of new and exciting videotapes on U.S. ethnic groups.

Teaching Strategies for Ethnic Studies, Fifth Edition, is divided into six parts. Part I presents a rationale for incorporating ethnic content into the total school curriculum. Goals and key concepts for the multicultural curriculum are also discussed in Part I. The main goal of the multicultural curriculum should be to help students develop the ability to make reflective decisions so that they can, through thoughtful action, influence their personal, social, and civic worlds.

Parts II through V contain chapters on the major ethnic groups in the United States. Each chapter contains (1) a chronology of key events, (2) a historical overview of the group discussed, (3) illustrative key concepts and teaching strategies, (4) an annotated bibliography for teachers, and (5) an annotated bibliography for elementary and secondary school students. Recommended grade levels are designated for the student resources. Although the bibliographies are selective, few of the books are appropriate for all purposes and settings. You should examine each book carefully before assigning it to your students. The annotations can help in this screening process.

Part VI highlights and summarizes the major points discussed in the previous chapters and illustrates how you can use the information and strategies in Parts I through V to develop and teach multicultural units and curricula that focus on two or more ethnic groups. Chapter 15 presents the major components of a sample multicultural unit to illustrate the steps in unit construction. Annotated bibliographies of multicultural resources for teachers and students are included in this chapter, as well. Techniques for evaluation are also discussed.

The appendixes are designed to help you obtain information and materials for classroom use. Appendix A is a chronology of key events in the history of ethnic groups in the United States. Appendix B lists videotapes and films. Appendix C lists books about women of color. Appendix D lists the Carter G.

Woodson Award books, and Appendix E cites twenty classic and landmark books in ethnic literature.

I am grateful to a number of colleagues and friends for help in the preparation of this fifth edition. Carlos F. Diaz contributed chapters 6 and 12. Virgie O. Chattergy updated the bibliographies in chapter 6. Jermone L. Ruderman contributed chapter 9. Cherry A. McGee Banks co-authored chapter 14.

A group of academic specialists prepared thoughtful and helpful comments after reviewing the chapters in Parts II through V. I thank them for their help and expert guidance:

Francis Femminella, State University of New York–Albany—chapter 8;

Erasmo Gamboa, University of Washington, Seattle—chapter 10;

Geneva Gay, Purdue University—chapter 7;

Sonia Nieto, University of Massachusetts–Amherst—chapter 11;

Valerie Ooka Pang, San Diego State University—chapter 13;

Vuong G. Thuy, Consultant, Jenkintown, Pennsylvania—chapter 14; and

Kathryn Vangen, University of Washington—chapter 5.

Jesus Garcia, Indiana University, reviewed the previous edition and made helpful suggestions for this new edition.

I also wish to thank Nannette McGee, for help in updating the list of Carter G. Woodson Award books in Appendix D, and Angela M. Banks, for help in preparing tables based on U.S. Census data. A special thanks is extended to Grace Sheldrick, Wordsworth Associates, for her editorial and production assistance and expert advice.

I am fortunate to be a faculty member at a university with an innovative and visionary Department of American Ethnic Studies whose members are interested in the nation's schools. Several faculty members in that department—including Professors Erasmo Gamboa, Johnnella Butler, and Joseph W. Scott—have graciously shared new books and materials.

Cherry A. McGee Banks is both a friend and a respected colleague. We have shared ideas about education and diversity for more than two decades. I am grateful to her for being a compassionate but firm critic and for locating and annotating the books for students. My daughters, Angela and Patricia, have helped me keep my eyes on the prize.

J. A. B.

Part I

Goals, Concepts,

and Instructional

Planning

Part I of this book discusses the basic instructional problems in teaching ethnic content and integrating it into the curriculum. Chapter 1 reviews some of the major trends in teaching ethnic content and argues for a need to expand the definition of ethnic studies and to include content about a range of ethnic groups in the multicultural curriculum. The problem of formulating goals for the multicultural curriculum and the interdisciplinary, conceptual approach to teaching are discussed in chapter 2. The author states that the major goal of the multicultural curriculum should be to help students develop decision-making skills so that they can become effective change agents in contemporary society.

To help students develop effective decision-making skills, the multicultural curriculum must help them master higher-level concepts and generalizations. Chapter 3 discusses key concepts that can be used to organize a sound multicultural curriculum. The final chapter in Part I, chapter 4, discusses practical ways to plan, organize, and teach multicultural units and lessons. The actual steps to follow to gain the needed content background, to identify key concepts and generalizations, and to choose ethnic content are discussed. Valuing strategies and social action projects are also discussed in chapter 4.

Chapter 1

The Multicultural

Curriculum

Rationale, Trends, and Goals

Introduction

This chapter describes the nature and complexity of ethnic diversity in U.S. society. It also discusses emerging demographic trends, current developments in multicultural education in the nation's schools, and the goals of a multicultural curriculum. An important goal of the multicultural curriculum is to help students view events, concepts, issues, and problems from diverse cultural and ethnic perspectives.

The Persistence of Ethnicity in American Society

Americans have always held tightly to the idea that ethnic cultures would melt or vanish. Consequently, a strong assimilationist idea has dominated American society since the British gained control of most American institutions early in the nation's history. The American assimilationist idea envisions a society in which ethnicity and race are not important identities. Group identities and affiliations would be based primarily on such variables as social class, politics, education, and other interests. The assimilationist idea that deeply influenced American life is symbolized by the melting pot concept. This concept was celebrated in Zangwill's play, *The Melting Pot*, staged in New York City in 1908.

Even though the strong assimilationist idea in U.S. society contributed greatly to the making of one nation out of disparate ethnic and immigrant groups, it has not eradicated ethnic and cultural differences and is not likely to do so in the future. Ethnic differences persist in U.S. society for several important reasons. Discrimination prevents many individuals and groups with particular ethnic, racial, and/or cultural characteristics from attaining full structural inclusion into U.S. society.[1] Ethnic cultures and communities often help individuals satisfy important human needs.[2] Ethnicity also persists because of continuing immigration to the United States.[3]

Immigration to the United States has increased markedly since the Immigration Reform Act, enacted in 1965, became effective in 1968. Most new immigrants are coming from Spanish-speaking Latin American nations and from Asia rather than from Europe, the continent from which most American immigrants came in the past. Between 1981 and 1986, 89% of the legal immigrants to the United States came from non-European nations; 11% came from Europe. Moreover, 85% of the immigrants to the United States during this period came from Asia (47%) and nations in the Americas (38%). Most Asian immigrants came from the Philippines, Korea, and China. Mexico and Cuba were the leading sources of immigrants from the Americas.[4]

The U.S. ethnic minority population is increasing at a much faster rate than is the general population. If current trends continue, it is projected that the Asian-American population will nearly double by the year 2000 whereas the total U.S. population will increase by 20 percent.[5] The U.S. Hispanic population is growing five times faster than is the rest of the U.S. population. On October 12, 1989, the United States Census Bureau announced that Hispanics in the United States had passed 20 million, a statistical landmark. Hispanics in the United States increased from 17.7 million in 1984 to more than 20 million in 1989.

Although frequently done in the popular media, it is misleading to view Hispanics as a single ethnic or cultural group because they speak the same language. Extensive cultural, ethnic, and racial differences exist both between and within the various Hispanic groups, such as those from Mexico, Cuba, Puerto Rico, El Salvador, the Dominican Republic, Colombia, and Venezuela. Most Hispanics view themselves as Mexicans, Puerto Ricans, or Cubans rather than as Hispanics.

The Demographic Imperative

The ethnic texture of the United States is changing greatly. The landmark report published jointly by the American Council on Education and the Education Commission of the States in 1988, *One-Third of a Nation*, states that by the year 2000 one-third of the population of the United States will consist of non-White Americans or of persons of color.[6] The changing ethnic texture of the U.S. population has major implications for all of the nation's institutions, including schools, universities, and the work force. These institutions must be restructured in order to meet the needs of the different kinds of people who will work in and be served by them. People of color will make up one-third of the net additions to the U.S. labor force between 1985 and 2000. By the year 2000, 21.8 million of the 140.4 million people in the U.S. labor force will be people of color.[7] Eighty % of the new entrants to the labor force will be women, immigrants, or people of color.[8]

The population of the nation's schools is becoming increasingly non-White and poor. Pallas, Natriello, and McDill have summarized several important demographic characteristics of the nation's future student population.[9] By the year 2020, White students will make up only 54.5% of the nation's school population. They made up 73% of the nation's student population in 1982. Hispanics will constitute about 25.3% of the nation's student population in 2020; they made up 9.3% of the student population in 1982. The number of children in poverty will grow considerably in future years. The number of children in poverty is expected to increase from 14.7 million in 1984 to 20.1% in 2020, a 37% increase. In 1989, about 1 in 5 American children lived in poverty; this constituted about 12 million children, the equivalent of a medium-sized nation.[10]

American classrooms are experiencing the largest influx of immigrant students since the turn of the century. In both 1986 and 1987, the United States received more than 600,000 legal immigrants.[11] A large but undetermined number of illegal or undocumented immigrants also enter the United States each year. The influence of an increasingly ethnically diverse population on the nation's schools is and will continue to be enormous. In 25 of the nation's largest cities and metropolitan areas, half or more of the public school students are students of color. In California, the population of students of color in the public schools exceeded the percentage of White students during the 1988/89 school year.

Students of color will make up about 46% of the nation's student population by 2020.[12] Most teachers now in the classroom or in teacher education programs are likely to have students from diverse ethnic, cultural, and racial groups in their classrooms during their careers. This is true for both inner-city and suburban teachers.

A major goal of multicultural education is to transform the challenges of ethnic, cultural, and racial diversity into educational and societal opportunities. To reach this goal teachers will need to acquire new knowledge, skills, and attitudes. A major goal of this book is to help teachers attain the knowledge, skills, and attitudes they need to be effective in multicultural classrooms and schools.

Ethnic Revival Movements: A World Development

Many Americans think of ethnic and racial diversity as something uniquely American. Yet, most Western societies are racially, ethnically, and culturally diverse. Since the 1960s, ethnic revival movements have arisen in the United States, as well as in other Western nations, such as in Canada, the United Kingdom, Australia, and several Western European nations.[13] An ethnic revival movement occurs when an ethnic group initiates organized efforts to attain equality within a society, to eliminate discrimination toward its members, to attain structural inclusion into society, to legitimize its culture within the nation, and to shape a new, positive identity. Goals of ethnic revival movements are usually political, economic, and cultural. Ethnic revival movements tend to reinforce and intensify ethnic identifications and allegiances. Table 1–1 describes the phases that usually characterize ethnic revival movements in Western societies.[14]

Ethnic revival movements tend to arise in nation-states that are ethnically diverse and in which ethnic stratification exists. Since World War II, the ethnic texture of Western European nations such as the United Kingdom, France, and the Netherlands has been enriched significantly by immigrants from their former colonies. Many immigrants from Southern and Eastern Europe have settled in nations such as Germany and Sweden in search of jobs and upward social mobility. In 1984, immigrants made up 7.1% of the population in the Federal Republic of Germany. Frankfurt/Main had the highest percentage of immigrants, 23.9%. Immigrants made up 12.4% of the population of West Berlin in 1984. There were 109,630 Turks, 30,163 Yugoslavs, 7,210 Greeks, 7,233 Italians, and 11,030 Poles living in West Berlin in 1984.[15] More than 405,000 foreign nationals were living in Sweden in 1983. The largest groups consisted of

Table 1–1   Phases in the Development of Ethnic Revitalization Movements

The Precondition Phase

This phase is characterized by the existence of a history of colonialism, imperialism, an institutionalized democratic ideology, and efforts by the nation-state to close the gap between democratic ideals and societal realities. These factors create rising expectations among victimized ethnic groups that pave the way for ethnic protest and a revitalization movement.

The First Phase

This phase is characterized by ethnic polarization, an intense identity quest by victimized ethnic groups, and single-causal explanations. An effort is made by ethnic groups to get racism legitimized as a primary explanation of their problems. Both radical reformers and staunch conservatives set forth single causal explanations to explain the problems of victimized ethnic groups.

The Later Phase

This phase is characterized by meaningful dialogue between victimized and dominant ethnic groups, multiethnic coalitions, reduced ethnic polarization, and the search for multiple-causal explanations for the problems of victimized ethnic groups.

The Final Phase

Some of the elements of the reforms formulated in the earlier phases become institutionalized during this phase. Other victimized cultural groups echo their grievances, thereby expanding and dispersing the focus of the ethnic reform movement. Conservative ideologies and policies become institutionalized during this phase, thus paving the way for the development of a new ethnic revitalization movement.

160,000 Finns and 38,000 Yugoslavs. Other groups included Turks, Greeks, Poles, Chileans, and Africans from several different nations.[16]

Australia has also become much more culturally and ethnically diverse since the 1960s. Traditionally Anglo-Celtic with a ban on the immigration of non-White groups and a policy that discouraged the immigration of individuals from Southern, Eastern, and Central Europe, Australia now has large populations of Greeks and Italians and a significant Indochinese population.[17] Melbourne, Victoria (Australia), has a larger population of Greeks than does any other city except Athens. Canada is also an immigrant society that is racially, culturally, and linguistically diverse.[18]

Diversity: An Opportunity and a Challenge

The kind of cultural, ethnic, racial, and religious diversity that the Western nations are experiencing is both an opportunity and a challenge to their society and institutions, including the schools. When groups with different cultures and values interact within a society, ethnocentrism, racism, and religious bigotry as well as other forms of institutionalized rejection and hostility occur. Ample examples of these forms of group hostility and rejection exist in every nation characterized by racial, ethnic, and cultural diversity. In several nation-states throughout the world, the incidents of bigoted attacks on ethnic and cultural minorities are on the upswing. This is true in both the United Kingdom and the United States. Some observers have linked the increase in overt bigotry to the serious economic transformations that are occurring in most Western nations.

Ethnic and cultural diversity is also an opportunity. It can enrich a society by providing novel ways to view events and situations, to solve problems, and to view our relationship with the environment and with other creatures. The exploitation of the environment is a serious problem in most developed nations, partly because of how Westerners have traditionally viewed their relationship with the earth. Traditional Indian cultures in North America viewed the earth as sacred and had deep reverence for other living creatures.

The challenge to Western societies and their schools is to try to shape a modernized, national culture that has selected aspects of traditional cultures co-existing in some kind of delicate balance with a modernized, postindustrial society. In the past, in their singular quest for modernity and a technocratic society, the Western nation-states tried to eradicate traditional cultures and thus alienated individuals and groups from their first cultures and linguistic origins. This approach to shaping a unified nation-state has created anomie and alienation and has deprived individuals and groups of some of the most important ways in which people satisfy their needs for symbolic meaning and community. It has also resulted in the political and cultural oppression of some racial and ethnic groups within society and has consequently caused them to focus on their particular needs and goals rather than on the overarching goals of the nation-state. Westernized nation-states will be able to create societies with overarching goals that are shared by diverse groups only when these groups feel that they have a real stake and place in their nation-states and that their states mirror their own concerns, values, and ethos. A multicultural curriculum, which reflects the cultures, values, and goals of the groups within a nation, will contribute significantly to the development of a healthy nationalism and national identity.

The Complexity of Ethnicity in American Society

Ethnicity is an integral but complex part of American life. To acquire a sophisticated knowledge of the United States, students must master facts, concepts, generalizations, and theories related to the intricate nature of ethnicity in American society. Although ethnicity is a significant part of American life, there is a national American culture and identity shared by all groups in the United States. This national culture resulted (and is resulting) from a series of multiple acculturations.[19] Diverse ethnic cultures, such as the Anglo-Saxon Protestant, the African, the Jewish, and the Mexican, influenced each other. The national American culture and identity consist of cultural components that have become universalized and are shared by most people within the nation. These universalized cultural components are products of the ethnic cultures in the United States and the American experience. Gleason describes the American national identity as follows:

> To affirm the existence of American nationality does not mean that all Americans are exactly alike or must become uniform in order to be real Americans. It simply means that a genuine national community does exist and that it has its own distinctive principle of unity, its own history, and its own appropriate sense of belongingness by virtue of which individuals identify with the symbols that represent and embody that community's evolving consciousness of itself. American nationality . . . does not preclude the existence of ethnicity in the subgroup peoplehood-sense, but neither does the existence of the latter preclude the former.[20]

In addition to the national American culture, there are ethnic and other subsocieties and institutions in the United States whose characteristics have not been universalized or become part of the shared national culture. The Anglo-Saxon Protestant subsociety, like other ethnic subsocieties, has cultural elements that are not universalized or shared by other Americans. Consequently, an individual American is ethnic to the extent that he or she functions within ethnic subsocieties and shares their values, behavioral styles, and cultures. An individual, however, may have a low level of ethnicity or psychological identification with his or her ethnic group or groups.

In Figure 1–1, the ruled area represents the American national culture shared by all ethnic and cultural groups. Circles A, B, C, and D represent ethnic

Figure 1–1   *Ethnicity and the National American Culture*

The shaded area represents the national American culture. Circles A, B, C, and D represent ethnic subcultures.

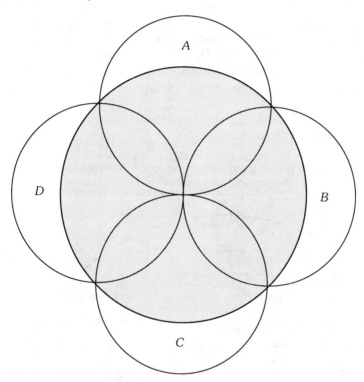

subsocieties, such as the Anglo-Saxon Protestant, African-American, Italian-American, and Mexican-American subsocieties. A major goal of the multicultural curriculum is to help students develop *cross-cultural competency*, which consists of the abilities, attitudes, and understandings students need to function effectively within the American national culture, within their own ethnic subsocieties, and within and across different ethnic subsocieties and cultures.

Ethnicity and Individuals

Ethnicity becomes even more complex when we try to determine the ethnic group affiliations and identification of individuals. Many individuals in American society not only perceive themselves as members of ethnic groups, but also are perceived as members of these groups by individuals outside their ethnic groups. This includes many, but not all, Americans who are Mexican, Polish, Jewish, and

Vietnamese. The asterisks in the closed circles in Figure 1–2 represent individuals within these ethnic groups. However, these individuals also perceive themselves and are usually perceived by others to be *American*, as well as Mexican,
Polish, Jewish, or Vietnamese, even though Mexican, for example, may be the
first and most important identity for many Mexican Americans. Mexican Americans also share a broader American identity and the overarching idealized
American values that cement the nation. Many Anglo-Saxon Protestants, such
as those who are members of the Brahmin elite in Boston, also see themselves
as members of a specific cultural group. Individuals represented by the asterisks

Figure 1–2 *Ethnicity and Individuals*

The asterisks in the closed circles represent individuals who perceive themselves and
who are perceived by other people to be members of clearly delineated ethnic
groups. The plus signs [+] represent individuals who perceive themselves and are
perceived by most other people to be merely *American*.

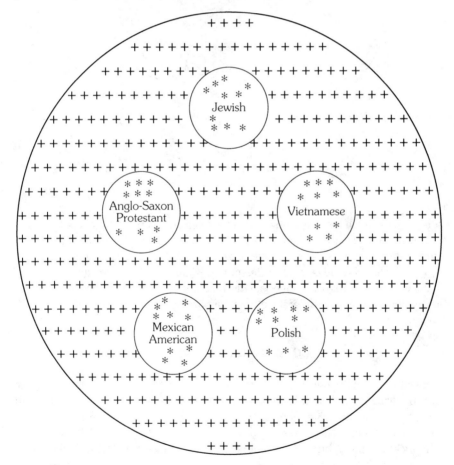

in the closed circles in Figure 1–2 are clearly ethnic, from both inside and outside points of view.

Other Americans are more difficult to characterize ethnically because of how they view themselves and how others view them. These individuals are represented by the plus signs in Figure 1–2. They perceive themselves only as *American* and do not consciously identify with a clearly defined ethnic group. This group of Americans includes many third- and fourth-generation Irish and Scandinavians, as well as individuals with multiple European heritages. These individuals can best be described as *mainstream Americans* from sociological and psychological perspectives. Culturally, however, mainstream Americans share many characteristics with Anglo-Saxon Protestants because Anglo-Saxon Protestants have influenced the national culture more than any other American subgroup.

Ethnic Studies: Assumptions and Practices

Many educators realize the importance of ethnicity in American society and the need to help students develop more sophisticated understandings of the diverse ethnic groups that make up America and a greater acceptance of cultural differences. Educational institutions at all levels have made some attempts to include more information about ethnic groups in the social studies, language arts, and humanities curricula. However, some assumptions about ethnic studies have adversely affected the integration of ethnic content into the curriculum. We need to examine and challenge these assumptions and related school practices and to formulate new assumptions and goals in order for the multicultural education movement to serve as a catalyst for curriculum reform. The greatest promise of ethnic studies is that it will serve as a vehicle for general curriculum reform. If ethnic content is merely added to the traditional curriculum, which in many ways is ineffective, efforts to modify the curriculum with ethnic content are likely to lead to a dead end. The total school curriculum should be transformed.

One pervasive assumption many educators embrace is that ethnic studies deals exclusively with groups of color, such as Asian Americans, American Indians, and African Americans. This assumption is widespread within the schools, and school programs often reflect it. In many school ethnic studies units and lessons little or no attention is devoted to the experiences of European-American ethnic groups, such as Jewish Americans, Polish Americans, and Italian Americans. This narrow conceptualization of ethnic studies emerged out of the social forces that gave rise to the ethnic studies movement in the 1960s. To conceptualize ethnic studies exclusively as the study of people of color is inconsistent with how sociologists define ethnicity.[21] It also prevents the development of broadly conceptualized comparative approaches to ethnic studies. Comparative approaches to ethnic studies are needed to help students understand fully the complex role of ethnicity in American life and culture. Conceptualizing ethnic studies exclusively as the study of ethnic groups of color also promotes a kind of *we–they* attitude among many White students and teachers. Many students think that ethnic studies is the study of *them*, whereas American studies is the study of *us*. Many educators believe that ethnic studies has no place within an all-White classroom.

A related assumption, which educators often make about ethnic studies, is that only students who are members of a particular ethnic group should study that group's history and culture. Some ethnic studies units and lessons focus on one specific ethnic group, such as Puerto Ricans, African Americans, or American Indians. The ethnic group on which the units and lessons focus is usually either present or dominant in the local school population. Significantly, specialized ethnic studies courses are rarely found in predominantly White schools and are almost always electives in schools with large populations of students of color. This fact underscores the need for content related to diverse ethnic groups to be an integral part of the curriculum experienced by all students. *Ethnic modification of the total curriculum is essential.*

All students, regardless of their race, ethnicity, or social class, should study about the cogent and complex roles of ethnicity and ethnic conflict in American society and culture. Most Americans are socialized within ethnic or cultural enclaves and are ethnically illiterate. Within their communities, people learn primarily about their own cultures and assume that their life-styles are the legitimate ones and that other cultures are invalid, strange, and different. The school should help students to break out of their cultural enclaves and to broaden their cultural perspectives. Students need to learn that there are cultural and ethnic alternatives within our society that they can freely embrace.

Many educators assume that ethnic studies is essentially additive in nature and that we can create a sound multicultural curriculum by leaving the present curriculum intact and adding ethnic heroes, such as Martin Luther King, Jr., and Cesar Chávez, to the list of Anglo-American heroes who are already studied in most schools. Conceptualizing ethnic studies as essentially additive in nature is problematical for several reasons. In too many classrooms throughout the nation teachers still emphasize the mastery of low-level facts and do not help students master higher levels of knowledge.

Modifying the school curriculum to include ethnic content provides a tremendous opportunity to reexamine the assumptions, purposes, and nature of the curriculum and to formulate a curriculum with new assumptions and goals. Merely adding low-level facts about ethnic content to a curriculum that is already bulging with discrete and isolated facts about mainstream American heroes will result in overkill. Isolated facts about Crispus Attucks and the Boston Massacre do not stimulate the intellect any more than do isolated facts about George Washington or Abraham Lincoln. To integrate ethnic content meaningfully into the total school curriculum, we must undertake more substantial curriculum reform. Adding facts about ethnic heroes and events of questionable historical significance is not sufficient. Transformation of the curriculum is essential.

An Expanded Definition of Ethnicity

Problems in teaching about ethnic groups result, in part, from the ways in which ethnicity and ethnic groups in America are often defined by teachers and curriculum specialists. They often limit their conceptualization of an ethnic group to an ethnic group of color or to an ethnic minority group. Teachers and curriculum specialists must have a more accurate and inclusive definition of an ethnic group in order to integrate ethnic content into the curriculum in more meaningful ways.

What is an *ethnic group?* Individuals who constitute an ethnic group share a sense of group identification, a common set of values, political and economic interests, behavioral patterns, and other culture elements that differ from those of other groups within a society. According to Rose, "Groups whose members share a unique social and cultural heritage passed on from one generation to the next are known as *ethnic groups.* Ethnic groups are frequently identified by distinctive patterns of family life, language, recreation, religion, and other customs that cause them to be differentiated from others. Above all else, members of such groups feel a consciousness of kind and 'interdependence of fate' with those who share the customs of the ethnic tradition."[22]

An individual is ethnic to the extent that he or she shares the values, behavioral patterns, cultural traits, and identification with a specific ethnic group. Many individuals have multiple ethnic group attachments; others consider themselves "American" rather than ethnic. Data from the 1980 United States Census indicate that most Americans, about 83% of the population (188,302,438) have an identification with at least one ancestry or ethnic group.[23] Of the remaining 17% of the population, 6% indicated that their ancestry was "American" or "United States," 1% provided a religious or unclassifiable response, and 10% did not report any ancestry.

In addition, 52% of the population reported only one ancestry, whereas 31% reported more than one ancestry. Below is a list of the most frequently reported ancestry groups:

English	50 million
German	49 million
Irish	40 million
African American	21 million
French	13 million
Italian	12 million
Scottish	10 million
Polish	8 million
Mexican	8 million
American Indian	7 million
Dutch	6 million

An individual's identity with his or her ethnic group varies significantly with the times in his or her life, economic and social status, and the encompassing situations and/or settings. Ethnicity is very important for some Americans and of little or only symbolic importance to others. Other groups, such as religious, social class, regional, or occupational groups, are more important to many individuals. As members of lower socioeconomic ethnic groups attain more economic mobility, their social class interests often become more important to them than their ethnic affiliations.

In this book, ethnic studies is conceptualized broadly, as it is in the *Harvard Encyclopedia of American Ethnic Groups.*[24] Information, materials, and strategies for teaching about White ethnic groups, such as Italian Americans and Jewish Americans, as well as about the experiences of ethnic groups of color, such as Mexican Americans, Puerto Ricans, and Indochinese Americans, are included. To conceptualize ethnic studies more narrowly will result in curricula that are too limited in scope and that will fail to help students understand fully both the similarities and differences in the experiences of the diverse groups in the United States.

The multicultural curriculum should enable students to derive valid generalizations and theories about the characteristics of ethnic groups and to learn how they are alike and different, in both their past and present experiences. Even though it is neither possible nor necessary for the curriculum of a particular school or district to include content about every ethnic group in the United States (there are more than 100), *each curriculum should focus on a range of groups that differ in their racial characteristics, cultural experiences, languages, histories, values, and current problems.* By studying a range of ethnic and cultural groups, students will be able to formulate valid comparative generalizations and theories about the nature of race, ethnicity, and culture in U.S. society. The curriculum can be transformed only when events, concepts, and issues are studied from the perspectives of a range of cultural and ethnic groups.

Ethnic Minority Groups/People of Color

Even though an ethnic group shares a common set of values, behavioral patterns, culture traits, and a sense of peoplehood, an ethnic minority group can be distinguished from an ethnic group. An ethnic minority has unique physical and/or cultural characteristics that enable people who belong to mainstream groups to identify its members easily and thus to treat them in a discriminatory way. Jewish Americans are an ethnic minority group with unique cultural and religious characteristics. African Americans are an ethnic minority group with both unique physical and cultural characteristics.

An ethnic minority group is often a numerical minority and comprises only a small percentage of the national population. In 1980, the non-White ethnic minorities in the United States made up about 17% of the national population. However, as pointed out, the non-White percentage of the U.S. population is growing at a much faster rate than is the rest of the population. By the turn of the century, demographers predict that non-Whites, or people of color, such as African Americans, Hispanics, Asians, and American Indians, will make up about one-third of the population of the United States.

In many school districts and schools, and in the school-age population of California, students of color constitute majorities. In part for this reason, educators and social scientists are increasingly referring to groups such as African Americans, Hispanics, and Asian Americans as *people of color* rather than as ethnic minorities. Educators and social scientists are becoming more aware that many terms and concepts used in the past do not accurately and sensitively describe ethnic realities today. Table 1–2 shows the population of the major ethnic groups in the United States in 1980 and the 1990 projected population.

Ethnic Studies:
A Process of Curriculum Reform

Ethnic content should not be studied only by ethnic minorities or be limited to specialized courses. Rather, ethnic studies should be viewed as a process of curriculum reform and transformation that will result in the creation of a new curriculum based on new assumptions and new perspectives. Such a transformed curriculum will help students gain novel views of the American experience and a new conception of what it means to be an American. Because the English immigrants assumed control of most economic, social, and political institutions early in U.S. national history, to *Americanize* has been interpreted to mean to *Anglicize*. During the height of nativism in the late 1800s and early 1900s, the English-Americans defined *Americanization* as *Anglicization*.[25] This notion of Americanization is still widespread within U.S. society and schools today. Thus, when we think of American history and American literature, we tend to think of Anglo-American history and of literature written by Anglo-American authors.

Reconceptualizing American Society

Because the assumption that what is Anglo-American is American is so deeply ingrained in curriculum materials and in the hearts and minds of many students and teachers, we cannot transform the curriculum by merely adding a unit or a lesson here and there about African American, Jewish American, or Italian American history or literature. Rather, we need to examine seriously the conception of American that is perpetuated in the curriculum and the basic canon, assumptions, and purposes that underlie the curriculum.

It is essential to reconceptualize how we view American society and history in the school curriculum. We should view American history, literature, art, music, and culture from diverse ethnic and cultural perspectives rather than primarily or

Table 1–2 *Population of Ethnic Groups in the United States, 1970, 1980, and Projected Population, 1990*

Ethnic Group	1970 Population	1980 Population	1990 Projected Population
Total	203,211,926	226,504,825	252,293,000
White Americans*	177,748,975	188,340,790	191,594,000
African Americans	22,580,289	26,448,218	30,915,000
Hispanics	9,072,602	14,608,673	21,854,000
Mexican Americans	4,532,435	8,740,439	13,768,020
Puerto Ricans	1,429,396	2,013,945	2,666,188
Cubans	544,600	803,226	1,180,116
Central and South Americans			2,491,356
Other Spanish Origin			1,748,320
Jewish Americans			5,814,000**
American Indians	792,730	1,361,869	1,500,000**
Eskimos		42,149	64,000**
Aleuts		14,177	
Chinese Americans	431,583	812,178	1,260,000
Filipino Americans	336,731	781,894	1,410,000
Japanese Americans	588,324	716,331	800,000
Korean Americans	69,510	357,393	810,000
Asian Indians		387,223	680,000
Vietnamese Americans			860,000
Native Hawaiians	100,179	172,346	

Sources: Based on several reports from the U.S. Census Bureau, including *National Origin and Language,* PC(2)–1A, 1973; *Race of the Population of States,* 1980, PC80–S1–3, 1981; *Projections of the Population of the U.S. by Age, Sex, and Race 1983–2080* (1989); and on projections reported in John W. Wright, ed., *The Universal Almanac 1990.* Kansas City: Andrews and McNeel, 1990.

Note: Not all of the racial and ethnic categories are mutually exclusive; for example, many Hispanic Americans are also White.
*This figure includes the roughly 53% of Hispanics who classified themselves as White.
**1989 figure

exclusively from the point of view of mainstream historians, writers, and artists. Most courses in the curriculum are taught primarily from mainstream perspectives. These types of lessons, units, and courses are based on what I call the Mainstream Centric Model, or Model A (see Figure 1–3). Ethnic studies, as a process of curriculum reform, can and often does proceed from Model A to Model B, the Ethnic Additive Model. In courses and experiences based on Model B, ethnic content is additive to the major curriculum thrust, which remains mainstream-oriented. Many school districts that have attempted ethnic modification of the curriculum have implemented Model B-type curriculum changes. Courses on specific ethnic groups, such as African Americans and Mexican

Figure 1–3 *Ethnic Studies as a Process of Curriculum Reform*

Ethnic studies is conceptualized as a process of curriculum reform that can lead from only mainstream perspectives on our history and culture (Model A—*Mainstream Centric Model*), to multiethnic perspectives as additives to the major curriculum thrust (Model B—*Ethnic Additive Model*), to a completely multicultural curriculum, in which every historical and social event is viewed from the perspectives of different cultural and ethnic groups (Model C—*Multiethnic Model*). In Model C mainstream perspectives are among several and are in no way superior or inferior to other perspectives. In Model D (*Ethno-National Model*), students study historical and social events from the perspectives of groups in several different nations. Many schools that have attempted ethnic modification of the curriculum have implemented Model B types of programs. It is suggested here that curriculum reform move directly from Model A to Model C and ultimately to Model D. However, in districts that have Model B types of programs, it is suggested that they move from Model B to Model C and eventually to Model D types of curriculum organizations.

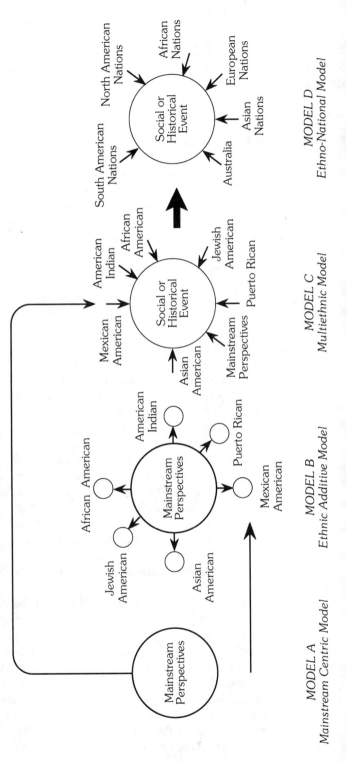

MODEL A
Mainstream Centric Model

MODEL B
Ethnic Additive Model

MODEL C
Multiethnic Model

MODEL D
Ethno-National Model

Americans, and special units on ethnic groups are examples of Model B types of curricular experiences.

Teaching Multicultural Perspectives: A Model C Curriculum

Curriculum reform should proceed directly from Model A to Model C, the Multiethnic Model. In courses and experiences based on Model C, the curriculum is transformed and students study historical, social, artistic, and literary events and concepts from several ethnic and cultural perspectives. Mainstream perspectives are only one group of several and are in no way superior or inferior to other perspectives.

I am not suggesting that we eliminate or denigrate mainstream historians, writers, and artists, or mainstream perspectives on U.S. society and culture. I am suggesting that mainstream perspectives should be among many different perspectives taught in the various content areas. Only by approaching the study of American society and culture in this way will students obtain a global, rather than an ethnocentric, view of our nation's history and culture.

A writer's or artist's experience and culture, including his or her ethnic or community culture, cogently influences his or her works and views of the past and present. However, it would be simplistic to argue that there is one mainstream view of history, art, literature, on contemporary events or one African-American view. Wide differences in experiences and perceptions exist both within and across ethnic and cultural groups.

People who have experienced a historical event or social phenomenon, such as racial discrimination or internment, often view and express the event differently than do people who have watched it from a distance. There is no one mainstream perspective on the internment as there is no one Japanese-American view of it. However, accounts written by people who were interned, such as Takashima's powerful *A Child in Prison Camp*,[26] often provide insights and perspectives that cannot be provided by people who were not interned. Individuals who viewed the internment from the outside can also provide unique and important perspectives. Hence, both insider and outsider perspectives should be studied in a sound multicultural curriculum.[27] Table 1-3 consists of a lesson that illustrates how to teach more than one perspective on an event.

Only by looking at events from many different perspectives can we fully understand the complex dimensions of American culture and society. Various ethnic and cultural groups are often influenced by events differently and perceive and respond to them differently. Important goals of the multicultural curriculum are to broaden students' conceptions of what "American" means and to present them with new ways to view and interpret American society, literature, music, and art. Any goals that are less ambitious, while important, will not result in curriculum transformation.

Table 1–3   *Teaching Multiple Perspectives*

Christopher Columbus and the Arawaks

The students are presented with the following excerpt from Christopher Columbus's diary that describes his arrival in an Arawak Indian community in the Caribbean in 1492. These are some of the observations that Columbus makes about the Arawaks:

> They took all and gave all, such as they had, with good will, but it seemed to me that they were a people very lacking in everything. They all go naked as their mothers bore them, and the women also, although I saw only one very young girl. . . . They should be good servants and quick to learn, since I see that they very soon say all that is said to them, and I believe that they would easily be made Christians, for it appeared to me that they had no religious beliefs. Our Lord willing, at the time of my departure, I will bring back six of them to Your Highnesses, that they may learn to talk. I saw no beast of any kind in this island, except parrots.

The students are then encouraged to view Columbus's statement from the perspective of the Arawaks. The Arawaks had an aural culture and consequently left no written documents. However, archaeologist Fred Olsen studied Arawak artifacts and used what he learned from them to construct a day in the life of the Arawaks, which he describes in his book, *On the Trail of the Arawaks*. The students are asked to read an excerpt from Olsen's account of a day in the life of the Arawaks and to respond to these questions:

1. Columbus wrote in his diary that he thought the Arawaks had no religious beliefs. You read about Arawak life in the report by Fred Olsen. Do you think Columbus was correct? Why?

2. Accounts written by people who took part in or witnessed (saw) an historical event are called primary sources. Can historians believe everything they read in a primary source? Explain.

Sources:
Jan, Cecil. *The Voyages of Christopher Columbus*. London: The Argonaut Press, 1930.
Olsen, Fred. *On the Trail of the Arawaks*. Norman: University of Oklahoma Press, 1974.

Ethnic Studies and Global Education

Students should also study world events, issues, and concepts from diverse cultural perspectives and points of view. The world studies program in schools is often characterized by a Model A type Eurocentric approach. Events, concepts, and issues are viewed primarily or exclusively from the perspectives of mainstream groups in European nations and cultures. Model D (the Ethno-National Model) provides rich opportunities for linking ethnic studies and global education. In this model students study global events, issues, and concepts from the perspectives of ethnic groups within different nations, as illustrated in Figure 1–4. It is important to link ethnic studies and global education because they share

Figure 1–4 *Model D—The Ethno-National Model*

This figure illustrates how an event, problem, issue, or concept can be viewed from the perspectives of ethnic groups within several nations. A study of ethnic perspectives within other nations will help students gain a global framework for viewing and studying human events and problems.

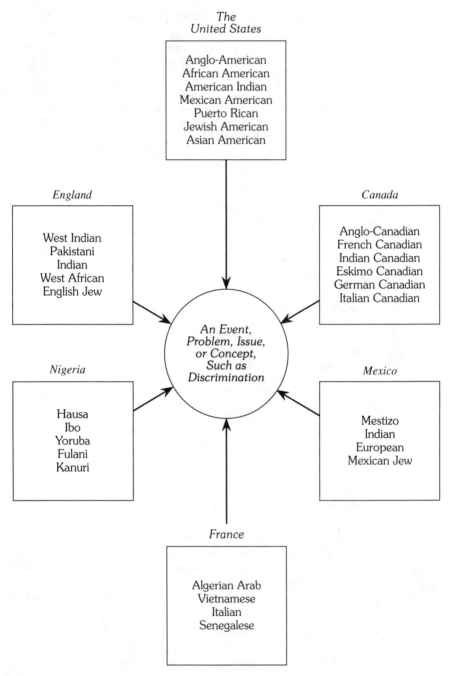

The
United States

Anglo-American
African American
American Indian
Mexican American
Puerto Rican
Jewish American
Asian American

England

West Indian
Pakistani
Indian
West African
English Jew

Canada

Anglo-Canadian
French Canadian
Indian Canadian
Eskimo Canadian
German Canadian
Italian Canadian

An Event,
Problem, Issue,
or Concept,
Such as
Discrimination

Nigeria

Hausa
Ibo
Yoruba
Fulani
Kanuri

Mexico

Mestizo
Indian
European
Mexican Jew

France

Algerian Arab
Vietnamese
Italian
Senegalese

several important goals and because the population of the United States is constantly being changed by the infusion of ethnic and immigrant groups from beyond its borders. Ethnic studies helps students better understand the lands and cultures from which these groups come.

The Battle over the Canon and Curriculum Reform

A major reason that the curriculum in U.S. schools and colleges remains Anglocentric, Eurocentric and male dominated is that the canon on which the mainstream curriculum is based is rarely made explicit, defined, or discussed. However, in recent years a vigorous debate about the canon on which the mainstream curriculum is based has taken place. The dominant canon has been questioned seriously by scholars of color and by feminists. It has been defended by mainstream scholars. During the late 1980s, mainstream scholars established two organizations to defend the dominant canon—the Madison Center and the National Association of Scholars.

A canon is a "norm, criterion, model or standard used for evaluating or criticizing."[28] It is also "a basic general principle or rule commonly accepted as true, valid, and fundamental."[29] A specific and identifiable canon is used to define, select, and evaluate knowledge in the school and university curriculum in the United States and in other Western nations. This canon is rarely explicitly defined or discussed. It is taken for granted, unquestioned, and internalized by writers, researchers, teachers, professors, and students. It is European-centric and male dominated. It often marginalizes the experiences of people of color, Third World nations and cultures, and the perspectives and histories of women.

African American scholars such as George Washington Williams, Carter G. Woodson, and W. E. B. DuBois challenged the established canon in social science and history in the nineteenth and early twentieth centuries. Their scholarship was influential in the Black academic community but was largely ignored by the White world. The ethnic studies movement, which grew out of the civil rights movement of the 1960s and 1970s, seriously challenged the European-centric canon that dominates the school and university curricula. Later, the established canon was also challenged by the women studies movement. The ethnic and women studies movements are forcing an examination of the canon used to select and judge knowledge in the school and university curricula.

Schools and universities experienced controversy and confusion when they tried to respond to the demands by students of color for ethnic studies courses and for Black and Brown teachers, administrators, and professors. Despite rough beginnings and a shaky status, ethnic studies courses are becoming institutionalized on the campuses of most major research universities. The Ethnic Studies Program at the University of California-Berkeley, for example, grants a doctoral degree.

Ethnic studies courses in the elementary and high schools have not fared as well as those on university campuses. Most school districts have tried to incorporate the history and culture of ethnic groups, as well as those of women, into the mainstream curriculum rather than to establish separate courses on ethnic groups and women. The rationale for this approach is intellectually defensible and laudable. It has, however, had mixed results. In most schools, the textbook is the curriculum. In the early 1970s, when the civil rights movement was at its apex and publishers were being pressured to integrate textbooks, large bits and pieces of ethnic content were inserted into textbooks. Because the civil rights movement has lost much of its momentum and national influence, however, the pressure on textbook publishers has lessened. Consequently, the ethnic presence in elementary and high school textbooks today is less visible than it was during the late 1970s.

University students of color are now pushing for reforms that go beyond separate ethnic studies courses and programs. They are trying to persuade university faculties to integrate ethnic content into the mainstream or core curriculum. The ugly racial incidents that occurred during the late 1980s on a number of university campuses were an important factor that stimulated curriculum reform. Acid and divisive controversies arose on several campuses over the attempt to make ethnic content a part of the mainstream university curriculum or to require all students to take ethnic studies courses. These controversies were in some ways more wrenching than those that arose when the attempt was made to establish separate ethnic studies courses and programs. This is probably because the guardians of the established canon perceive the inclusion of ethnic content into the mainstream curriculum as a more serious threat to it than are separate ethnic studies courses and programs.

On several campuses, such as the University of Minnesota-Minneapolis and Bowling Green State University, a national controversy did not develop when ethnic studies became a part of the mainstream curriculum. However, a bitter and divisive campus and national debate occurred when Stanford replaced a required freshman Western culture course with a course entitled "Culture, Ideas and Values." This course includes the study of at least one non-Western culture and "works by women, minorities and persons of color." A year-long, bitter controversy also raged at the University of California-Berkeley before the Academic Senate finally approved a required ethnic studies course on April 25, 1989. The curriculum controversies may have been especially acute at Stanford and Berkeley because they are two of the nation's most prestigious universities. Consequently, they may be considered by many Western-centric scholars and citizens as chief guardians of the established canon.

The struggle over the inclusion of ethnic content and content about women in the university mainstream curriculum can best be understood as a battle over who will participate in or control the formulation of the canon or standard used to determine what constitutes a liberal education. The guardians and defenders of the established canon believe that it serves their interests and consequently the interests of the society and nation-state. They also view it as consistent with their experiences and perspectives and their visions of the future. People who criticize the established canon, such as many ethnic and feminist scholars, believe that it marginalizes their experiences and voices and results in a curriculum that largely ignores their histories and cultures.

The people who formulate a canon or standard shape it in their own image and in ways that present their experiences, voices, and perspectives as essential parts of the human experience. The people who do not participate in formulating or shaping a canon are often marginalized or invisible in the curriculum that emanates from it. Students of color, such as African Americans and Mexican Americans, have been active voices on university campuses, demanding that the canon be transformed so that it recognizes and legitimizes their histories and cultures as essential parts of the United States and the world. Only when the canon is transformed to reflect cultural diversity will students in our schools and colleges be able to attain the knowledge, skills, and perspectives needed to participate effectively in the global society of the next century.

Approaches to Teaching Multicultural Content

Several identifiable approaches to the integration of ethnic content into the curriculum have evolved since the 1960s. The *Contributions Approach* to integration is one of the most frequently used. This approach is characterized by the addition of ethnic heroes into the curriculum. This approach to curriculum reform is usually a Model A (Mainstream centric) type of curriculum change because the ethnic heroes added to the curriculum are not only viewed from a mainstream centric perspective but are also usually selected for inclusion into the curriculum using mainstream criteria. Consequently, ethnic heroes viewed positively by the mainstream society, such as Booker T. Washington, Marian Anderson, and Sacajawea, are most often chosen for study rather than are ethnic Americans who challenged the dominant class and social structure in society, such as W. E. B. Dubois, Geronimo, and Angela Davis.

The mainstream curriculum remains unchanged in terms of its basic structure, goals, and salient characteristics. This is the easiest approach for teachers to use to integrate the curriculum with ethnic content. However, it has several serious limitations. Students do not attain a comprehensive view of the role of ethnic and cultural groups in U.S. society. Rather, they see ethnic issues and events primarily as an addition to the curriculum and thus as an appendage to the main story of the nation's development.

Content, concepts, themes, and perspectives are added to the curriculum without changing its basic structure, purpose, and characteristics in the *Additive Approach*. This approach is consistent with Model B or the Ethnic Additive Model discussed earlier in this chapter. The content, concepts, and issues added to the curriculum are viewed primarily from mainstream perspectives. This approach is often accomplished by the addition of a book, a unit, or a course to the curriculum without changing it substantially. The Additive Approach allows the teacher to put ethnic content into the curriculum without restructuring it, which takes substantial time, effort, training, and rethinking of the curriculum and its purposes, nature, and goals.

The Additive Approach can be the first phase in a more radical curriculum reform effort designed to restructure the total curriculum and to integrate it with ethnic content, perspectives, and frames of reference. However, this approach shares several disadvantages with the Contributions Approach. Its most important shortcoming is that it usually results in the viewing of ethnic content from the perspectives of mainstream historians, writers, artists, and scientists because it does not involve a restructuring of the curriculum.

The *Transformation Approach*, which incorporates Model C, the Mutliethnic Model, differs fundamentally from the Contributions and Additive Approaches. This approach changes the basic assumptions of the curriculum and enables students to view concepts, issues, themes, and problems from several ethnic perspectives and points of view. The key curriculum issue involved in the Transformation Approach is not the addition of ethnic groups, heroes, and contributions, but the infusion of various perspectives, frames of reference, and content from different groups that will extend students' understandings of the nature, development, and complexity of the United States and the world.

The *Social Action Approach* includes all of the elements of the Transformation Approach and adds components that require students to make decisions and take actions related to the concept, issue, or problem they have studied. Table 1–4 shows a list of possible actions developed by a junior high school social studies class after studying a unit on the civil rights movements of the 1960s and 1970s.

The four approaches to the integration of ethnic content into the curriculum described above are often mixed and blended in actual teaching situations (see Figure 1–5). The move from the lower to the higher levels of ethnic content integration is likely to be gradual and cumulative. An important goal of teaching about racial, cultural, and ethnic diversity should be to empower students with the knowledge, skills, and attitudes they need to participate in civic action that will help transform our world and enhance the possibility for human survival.

The Goals of the Multicultural Curriculum

Concepts, content, and teaching strategies cannot be identified and selected until goals are clearly defined. The development of *decision-making and social action skills* is the key goal for the multicultural curriculum presented in this

Table 1–4   *Student Action*

After a unit on the civil rights movement of the 1960s and 1970s, Mr. Carson's 7th-grade social studies class made this list of actions they could take to help reduce discrimination in their personal lives, their school, and community.

1. Making a personal commitment to stop telling racist jokes.
2. Making a commitment to challenge our own racial and ethnic stereotypes either before or after we verbalize them.
3. Compiling an annotated list of books about ethnic groups that we will ask the librarian to order for our school library.
4. Asking the principal to order sets of photographs that show African Americans and other people of color who have jobs that represent a variety of careers. Asking the principal to encourage our teachers to display these photographs on their classroom walls.
5. Observing television programs to determine the extent to which people of color, such as African Americans and Asian Americans, are represented in such jobs as news anchors and hosts of programs. Writing to local and national television stations to express our concern if we discover that people of color are not represented in powerful and visible roles in news or other kinds of television programs.
6. Contacting a school in the inner-city to determine if there are joint activities and projects in which we and they might participate.
7. Asking the principal or the board of education in our school district to require our teachers to attend inservice staff development workshops that will help them learn ways in which to integrate content about ethnic and racial groups into our courses.
8. Sharing some of the facts that we have learned in this unit, such as that by the year 2000, one out of every three Americans will be a person of color, with our parents and discussing these facts with them.
9. Making a personal commitment to have a friend from another racial, ethnic, or religious group by the end of the year.
10. Making a personal commitment to read at least one book a year that deals with a racial, cultural, or ethnic group other than my own.
11. Do nothing; take no actions.

book. The multicultural curriculum should help students develop the ability to make reflective decisions on issues related to ethnicity and to take personal, social, and civic actions to help solve the racial and ethnic problems in our national and world societies. Effective solutions to the enormous ethnic and racial problems in our nation and world can be found only by an active and informed citizenry capable of making reflective personal and public decisions. Chapter 4 discusses decision making and its components in more detail.

The multicultural curriculum should also help students view historical and contemporary events from diverse ethnic perspectives, clarify their ethnic identities, and function effectively within their own ethnic communities. Individuals must clarify their own ethnic and cultural identities before they can relate

Figure 1–5   *Levels of Integration of Ethnic Content*

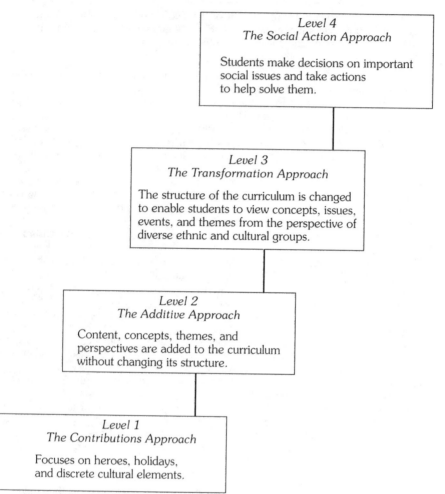

Level 4
The Social Action Approach

Students make decisions on important
social issues and take actions
to help solve them.

Level 3
The Transformation Approach

The structure of the curriculum is changed
to enable students to view concepts, issues,
events, and themes from the perspective of
diverse ethnic and cultural groups.

Level 2
The Additive Approach

Content, concepts, themes, and
perspectives are added to the curriculum
without changing its structure.

Level 1
The Contributions Approach

Focuses on heroes, holidays,
and discrete cultural elements.

positively to people who belong to different racial and ethnic groups. Educators
need to foster the development of self-acceptance, but to discourage ethnic
ethnocentrism.

The multicultural curriculum should also help individuals develop cross-
cultural competency—the ability to function within a range of cultures. Although
individuals within a pluralistic society must learn to accept their own ethnic and
cultural identities and become comfortable with them, they must also learn to
function effectively within other cultures and to respond positively to individuals
who belong to other ethnic and cultural groups. They also need to learn how to

interact with members of outside ethnic groups and how to resolve conflicts with them.

Another important goal of the multicultural curriculum is to provide students with cultural and ethnic alternatives. Both the Anglo-Saxon Protestant and the Filipino-American student should be provided with cultural and ethnic options in the school. Historically, the school curriculum has focused primarily on the cultures of Anglo-Saxon Protestants. The school was, and often is, primarily an extension of the homes and communities of Anglo-Saxon Protestant students. It rarely presents Anglo students with cultural and ethnic alternatives, thereby denying them the richness of the music, literature, art, values, life-styles, and perspectives that exist among such ethnic groups as Jews, Greeks, Puerto Ricans, and Blacks. Many behaviors and values within these ethnic groups can help mainstream Anglo students to enrich their personal and public lives.

The multicultural curriculum should also try to reduce ethnic and cultural encapsulation and enable students to understand their own cultures better. Individuals who only know, participate in, and see the world from their unique cultural and ethnic perspectives are denied important aspects of the human experience and are culturally and ethnically encapsulated. These individuals are unable to know and see their own cultures fully because of their cultural and ethnic blinders. The multicultural curriculum seeks to help individuals gain greater self-understanding by viewing themselves from the perspectives of other cultures.

The multicultural curriculum should also help students to expand their conceptions of what it means to be human, to accept the fact that ethnic minority cultures are functional and valid, and to realize that a culture can be evaluated only within a particular cultural context. Because cultures are made by people, there are many ways of being human. By studying this important generalization, students will hopefully develop an appreciation for the great capacity of human beings to create a diversity of life-styles and to adapt to a variety of social and physical environments. All students also need ethnic content to help them better understand themselves and the world in which they live. The ethnic experience is part of the human experience; education should deal with the total experience of humankind.

Another important goal of the multicultural curriculum is to help students master essential reading, writing, and computational skills. Multicultural theorists believe that ethnic content can help students master important skills in these content areas. Multiethnic readings and data, if taught effectively, can be highly motivating and meaningful. Students are more likely to master skills when the teacher uses content that deals with significant human problems, such as ethnicity within our national and world societies. Content related to ethnicity in America, in the world, and to the ethnic communities in which many students live is significant and meaningful to students, especially those who are socialized within ethnic communities. Skill goals are extremely important in an effective multicultural curriculum.

Education for Survival in the Twenty-First Century

The current school curriculum is not preparing most students to function successfully within a world community of the future. Many students grow up in middle-class, mainstream communities and attend predominantly mainstream, middle-class schools. Their world is very different from the world society in which they will be required to function in the future. The White race is a world minority. Two out of three people in the world live in poor and developing nations in regions such as Africa, Asia, and Latin America. Yet, the one out of three people in the world who live in the developed Western nations consume most of the earth's resources and exercise most of the world's political and economic power. The world is sharply divided between the few who are rich and well-fed in the Western developed nations—who are predominantly White—and the many who are poor and hungry in the developing nations, who are predominantly people of color. These sharp divisions also exist within nations.

Allport's seminal theory teaches us that people from diverse groups can work cooperatively to solve problems only when they function in equal-status situations and when they perceive their fates as shared.[30] We will not be able to substantially reduce ethnic, racial, and cultural tension in the United States and the world until most people have a decent standard of living and a modicum of political and economic power. Groups from different ethnic groups, races, cultures, and nations who have highly unequal amounts of power, influence, and wealth are rarely able to work cooperatively to solve difficult human problems. A major goal of education for survival in a multicultural global society is to help students acquire the knowledge, attitudes, and skills needed to participate in the reformation of the world's social, political, and economic systems so that peoples from diverse ethnic, cultural, and religious groups will be politically empowered and structurally integrated into their societies. Helping students to acquire the competencies and commitments to participate in effective civic action in order to create equitable national societies is the most important goal for multicultural and global education in the twenty-first century.

Summary

The ethnic texture of the United States is deepening because most immigrants entering the nation today are coming from Asia and Latin America and because the birthrate of people of color exceeds that of Whites. People of color will make up one-third of the nation's population by the turn of the century.

The curriculum within the nation's schools, colleges, and universities needs to be reformed so that it will accurately reflect the ethnic, cultural, and racial diversity within the United States. Schools, colleges, and universities are using various approaches to infuse ethnic content into the curriculum, including the contributions and additive approaches. Each of these approaches has important problems. To respond adequately to the ethnic realities within the nation and the world, the curriculum should be transformed and should help students develop decision-making and social-action skills.

Questions and Activities

1. The melting pot concept does not accurately describe the nature of ethnicity in the United States. React to this position by stating whether you agree or disagree with it, and why.

2. Make a list of the different ethnic backgrounds that constitute your ethnic heritage. Compare your list with similar lists made by other individuals in your class or workshop. What conclusions can you derive about ethnicity in U.S. society by analyzing these data?

3. Study the results of the last national or local election. Note particularly the voting patterns of predominantly ethnic communities. What generalizations can you make on the basis of these data? What are the limitations of your generalizations?

4. Interview a curriculum coordinator in one or two local school districts. Ask this individual to describe the school's efforts to implement multicultural education. If the school focuses on some ethnic groups and not on others, ask for an explanation of this practice. How do your findings compare with the trends described in this chapter?

5. According to the author, what should be the goals of the multicultural curriculum? Write, in one sentence or more, what you *think* should be the goals of the multicultural curriculum. Compare your statement with the goals listed in this chapter. In what ways are your statement and the listed goals alike and different? Why? How are your assumptions about ethnic studies and ethnicity similar to and different from those of the author?

6. Divide into small discussion groups in your class or workshop. Appoint a group leader and a reporter for each group. Discuss the following questions in your groups. When the small-group discussions have ended, the class or workshop should reassemble. Reporters should give a brief summary of each group's discussion. The large group should then react both to the reports and to the following questions:

   a. Which of the Curricular Models presented in Figure 1–3 best describes the curriculum in your school or in a school in which you have observed or attended?

   b. Do you think it would be desirable to help your school (or a school in which you have observed or attended) move from one Model to another? (For example, move from Model A to B or from B to C.)

c. What problems might you, as a teacher, encounter in trying to move your school (or a school in which you have observed or attended) curriculum from one Model to another? (For example, moving from Model A to Model C.)
d. How might these problems best be overcome?
e. What benefits might result for both you and the students if your school (or the school in which you have observed or attended) changed from one Model to another?

7. Define each of the following concepts and terms and tell why each is important:

the melting pot	Ethno-National Model
ethnic group	sense of peoplehood
ethnic minority group	contributions approach
people of color	additive approach
Mainstream Centric Model	transformation approach
Ethnic Additive Model	social action approach
Multiethnic Model	

Endnotes

1. William J. Wilson, *The Truly Disadvantaged: The Inner City, the Underclass, and Public Policy* (Chicago: The University of Chicago Press, 1987); Gerald D. Jaynes and Robin M. Williams, Jr., eds., *A Common Destiny: Blacks and American Society* (Washington, D.C.: National Academy Press, 1989).

2. Geneva Gay and Willie L. Barber, eds., *Expressively Black: The Cultural Basis of Ethnic Identity* (New York: Praeger, 1987).

3. U.S. Bureau of the Census, *Statistical Abstract of the United States: 1989*, 109th ed. (Washington, D.C.: U.S. Government Printing Office, 1989).

4. Ibid., p. 10.

5. Robert W. Gardner, Bryant Robey, and Peter C. Smith, "Asian Americans: Growth, Change and Diversity," *Population Bulletin* 40, No. 4 (Population Reference Bureau, Inc.: Washington, D.C., 1985), pp. 1–44.

6. The Commission on Minority Participation in Education and American Life, *One-Third of a Nation* (Washington, D.C.: American Council on Education and Education Commission of the States, 1988).

7. William B. Johnston and Arnold E. Packer, *Workforce 2000: Work and Workers for the 21st Century* (Indianapolis: Hudson Institute, 1987).

8. Ibid., p. xx.

9. Aaron M. Pallas, Gary Natriello, and Edward L. McDill, "The Changing Nature of the Disadvantaged Population: Current Dimensions and Future Trends," *Educational Researcher* 18, No. 5 (June–July 1989): 16–22.

10. Ford Foundation, Project on Social Welfare and the American Future, *The Common Good: Social Welfare and the American Future* (New York: Ford Foundation, 1989), p. 10.

11. U.S. Bureau of the Census, *Statistical Abstract of the United States*, p. 9.

12. Pallas, Natriello, and McDill, "The Changing Nature of the Disadvantaged Population," p. 19.

13. James A. Banks and James Lynch, eds., *Multicultural Education in Western Societies* (London: Holt, Rinehart and Winston, 1986).

14. James A. Banks, "Ethnic Revitalization Movements and Education," *Educational Review* 37, no. 2 (1985): 131–139.

15. *Foreign Nationals and Policy Matters Concerning Foreigners: Getting along Together* (Pamphlet) (Berlin: The Commissioner for Foreigners' Affairs of the Senat of Berlin, Senat Department of Health and Social Affairs, 1985).

16. The Swedish Institute, "Immigrants in Sweden," Fact Sheets on Sweden Series (Stockholm: The Institute, 1984).

17. Des Storer, editor-in-chief, *Ethnic Family Values in Australia* (Sydney: Prentice-Hall of Australia, 1985).

18. John R. Mallea and Jonathan C. Young, eds., *Cultural Diversity and Canadian Education* (Ottawa: Carleton University Press, 1984).

19. James A. Banks, *Multiethnic Education: Theory and Practice*, 2nd ed. (Boston: Allyn and Bacon, 1988), pp. 128–130.

20. Philip Gleason, "American Identity and Americanization," In *Harvard Encyclopedia of American Ethnic Groups*, eds. Stephen Thernstrom, Ann Orlov, and Oscar Handlin (Cambridge: Harvard University Press, 1980), p. 57.

21. Wsevolod W. Isajiw, "Definitions of Ethnicity," *Ethnicity* 1 (July 1974): 111–124.

22. Peter I. Rose, *They and We: Racial and Ethnic Relations in the United States*, 2nd ed. (New York: Random House, 1974), p. 13.

23. These data are from U.S. Bureau of the Census, *Ancestry of the Population by State: 1980*. Supplementary Report PC80–S1–10, April 1983, pp. 1–2.

24. Stephen Thernstrom, Ann Orlov, and Oscar Handlin, eds., *Harvard Encyclopedia of American Ethnic Groups* (Cambridge: Harvard University Press, 1980).

25. John Higham, *Strangers in the Land: Patterns of American Nativism 1860–1926* (New York: Atheneum, 1972).

26. Shizuye Takashima, *A Child in Prison Camp* (Montreal, Canada: Tundra Books, 1971).

27. Robert K. Merton, "Insiders and Outsiders: A Chapter in the Sociology of Knowledge," *The American Journal of Sociology* 78, no. 1 (July 1972): 9–47.

28. *Webster's Third New International Dictionary*, unabr. (Springfield, Mass.: Merriam-Webster, Inc., 1986), p. 328.

29. Ibid.

30. Gordon W. Allport, *The Nature of Prejudice*, 25th anniv. ed. (Reading, Mass.: Addison-Wesley, 1979).

Annotated Bibliography

Banks, James A. *Multiethnic Education: Theory and Practice*, 2nd ed. Boston: Allyn and Bacon, 1988.

> *This book discusses the historical, conceptual, and philosophical issues in the fields of multicultural and multiethnic education. It includes an important chapter on "Reducing Prejudice in Students: Theory, Research, and Strategies."*

Banks, James A., and Banks, Cherry A. McGee, eds. *Multicultural Education: Issues and Perspectives.* Boston: Allyn and Bacon, 1989.

> *Nineteen scholars in multicultural education discuss educational issues and strategies related to ethnicity and race, gender, social class, religion, and exceptionality in this introduction to multicultural education.*

Banks, James A., and Lynch, James. *Multicultural Education in Western Societies.* London: Cassell, 1986.

> *Theories, practices, and research on multicultural education in the major Western nations are described, as well as guidelines for action.*

Gibbs, Jewelle Taylor, and Huang, Larke Nahme, and associates. *Children of Color: Psychological Interventions with Minority Youth.* San Francisco: Jossey-Bass Publishers, 1990.

> *This book includes original papers that discuss various aspects of the cultures and the psychological interventions needed for youths of color.*

Katz, Phyllis A., and Taylor, Dalmas A., eds. *Eliminating Racism: Profiles in Controversy.* New York: Plenum Press, 1988.

> *A group of distinguished social scientists provide different perspectives on issues related to race and public policy in this well-crafted, edited book.*

King, Edith W. *Teaching Ethnic and Gender Awareness: Methods and Materials for the Elementary School,* 2nd ed. Dubuque, Ia: Kendall/Hunt Publishing Company, 1990.

> *This book includes a rationale for teaching ethnic and gender awareness as well as activities and teaching strategies that can be used to integrate content related to ethnic and gender awareness into the elementary school curriculum.*

Lynch, James. *Multicultural Education in a Global Society.* New York: Falmer Press, 1989.

> *The author extends his earlier work in multicultural education by linking it with global education.*

————. *Prejudice Reduction and the Schools.* New York: Nichols Publishing Company, 1987.

> *This comprehensive book discusses both theory and practice related to reducing prejudice in students and helping them to attain more democratic social attitudes.*

Multicultural Leader. Quarterly newsletter published by the Educational Materials and Services Center, 144 Railroad Avenue, Suite 107, Edmonds, Wa. 98020.

> *This quarterly newsletter helps practicing educators keep up-to-date on current theory, research, and teaching materials related to race and ethnicity, gender, social class, and exceptionality.*

Phinney, Jean S., and Rotheram, Mary J., eds. *Children's Ethnic Socialization: Pluralism and Development.* Beverly Hills, Calif.: Sage Publications, 1987.

> *This volume consists of a well-researched collection of essays that discusses the development of children's ethnic identity and racial attitudes..*

Simon, Roger I.; Brown, John; Lee, Enid; and Young, Jon. *Decoding Discrimination: A Student-Based Approach to Anti-Racist Education Using Film.* London, Ontario: Althouse Press, Faculty of Education, The University of Western Ontario, 1988.

> *In this series of interesting and creative lessons, students are taught to decode or analyze the basic assumptions and purposes of films and to view films as a type of social construction.*

Sleeter, Christine E., and Grant, Carl A. *Making Choices for Multicultural Education: Five Approaches to Race, Class, and Gender.* Columbus, Oh.: Merrill, 1988.

> *Teachers will find the five approaches to multicultural education described by Sleeter and Grant helpful in thinking about ways to devise multicultural teaching strategies.*

"Race, Racism and American Education: Perspectives of Asian Americans, Blacks, Latinos, and Native Americans, " *Harvard Educational Review* 58, no. 3 (August 1988), special issue.

> *A variety of perspectives on issues related to ethnicity and schooling are presented in this special issue of the* Harvard Educational Review. *Contributors include Angela Y. Davis, June Jordan, Lisa D. Delpit, Maria de la Luz Reyes, and Valerie Ooka Pang.*

Takaki, Ronald, ed. *From Different Shores: Perspectives on Race and Ethnicity in America.* New York: Oxford University Press, 1987.

> *The carefully selected essays that comprise this book are reprinted from other sources. They are organized into these topics: patterns, culture, class, gender, and prospects. This book contains a useful bibliography.*

Wilson, William J. *The Truly Disadvantaged: The Inner City, the Underclass, and Public Policy.* Chicago: The University of Chicago Press, 1987.

> *This is one of the most helpful and thoughtful books written within the last decade that discusses issues related to poverty and the growing underclass in U.S. society, a disproportionate percentage of whom are people of color.*

Chapter 2

Developing

a Conceptual

Multicultural Curriculum

Introduction

The key goal of the multicultural curriculum should be to help students develop decision-making and citizen-action skills. The decision-making process consists of several components, including knowledge, values, the synthesis of knowledge and values, and action designed to implement the decision made. However, the knowledge that comprises reflective decision making must have certain characteristics. It must be scientific, higher level, conceptual, and interdisciplinary. Reflective decision makers must identify the sources of their values, determine how these values conflict, identify value alternatives, and choose freely from among the alternatives. They act only after identifying alternative courses of action, ordering them according to personal values, and expressing a willingness to accept the possible consequences of their actions.

This chapter focuses on the knowledge components of decision making. A presentation of the interdisciplinary conceptual approach is followed by a discussion of the four categories of knowledge: *facts, concepts, generalizations,* and *theories.* You must be able to identify the categories of knowledge in order to structure interdisciplinary and conceptual lessons and units. Chapter 3 discusses concepts you can use to organize multicultural lessons and units. The valuing and social action components of the multicultural curriculum are discussed in chapter 4. Key issues related to the selection and evaluation of multicultural teaching materials are also discussed in chapter 4.

The Interdisciplinary-Conceptual Approach

A decision-making curriculum is not only characterized by the sequential development of higher-level ideas, but it is also *interdisciplinary.* In such a curriculum, concepts, when feasible and appropriate, are viewed from the perspectives of several disciplines and subject areas, such as the various social sciences, art, music, literature, physical education, communication, the physical and biological sciences, and mathematics.

It is necessary for students to view events and situations from the perspectives of several disciplines because any one discipline gives them only a partial understanding of issues and concepts related to ethnic and cultural diversity in society. Concepts such as *discrimination* and *pluralism* are not merely sociological; they also have multiple dimensions. They have economic, political, legal, cultural, and moral aspects. The values and experiences of people of color are reflected in their literature, art, music, drama, dance, communication styles, and foods. Dominant ethnic groups within a society also express issues related to ethnic diversity and respond to these issues in their artistic and cultural forms. Students must view concepts and issues related to ethnic groups from diverse disciplinary perspectives in order to gain a complete understanding of the experiences of the diverse cultural and ethnic groups in the United States and the world.

Studying Culture: An Example of the Interdisciplinary-Conceptual Approach

When students study a concept such as *culture*, they can gain a global understanding only by viewing ethnic cultures from the perspectives of the various social sciences and by examining the expressions of ethnic cultures in literature, music, drama, dance, art, communication, and foods. Content and insights from science and mathematics can also be incorporated into an interdisciplinary study of cultures. The next section discusses special issues involved in incorporating science and mathematics into the multicultural curriculum.

Concepts such as *culture* can be used to organize units and activities related to ethnicity that are interdisciplinary and cut across disciplinary lines. Other concepts, such as cultural assimilation, acculturation, and values, can also be analyzed and studied from an interdisciplinary perspective. However, it is neither possible nor desirable to teach each concept in the curriculum from the perspectives of all disciplines and curricular areas. Such an attempt would result in artificial relationships and superficial learnings by students.

There are many excellent opportunities within the curriculum for teaching concepts from an interdisciplinary perspective. Interdisciplinary teaching, however, requires the strong cooperation of teachers in the various content areas. Team teaching will often be necessary, especially at the high school level, to organize and implement interdisciplinary units and lessons. Table 2–1 contains key questions that students can pursue when they study cultures from an interdisciplinary perspective. Figure 2–1 illustrates the process.

Table 2–1   *Studying Ethnic Cultures from an Interdisciplinary Perspective*

Discipline or Curriculum Area	Key or Focus Question
Social Studies	In what ways are the cultures of ethnic groups such as African Americans, Jewish Americans, and Mexican Americans similar and different? Why?
Reading and Literature	How do the fiction and other literary works by American ethnic authors reveal characteristics and components of their cultures?
Music	What does the music of an ethnic group reveal about its values, symbols, and culture?
Drama	What do plays written by ethnic authors reveal about their culture?
Physical Education	How do ethnic groups express their cultures, values, aspirations, and frustrations in their dances and creative movements?
Art	What does the art of an ethnic group reveal about its life-styles, perceptions, values, history, and culture?
Communication (Language Arts)	How does the language of an ethnic group express and reflect its values and culture? What can we learn about an ethnic group by studying its symbols and communication styles, both verbal and nonverbal?
Home Economics	What do ethnic foods reveal about an ethnic group's values and culture? What can we learn about an ethnic culture by studying its foods?
Science	How do the physical characteristics of an ethnic group influence its interactions with other groups, intragroup relationships, and its total culture?
Mathematics	What is the relationship between the number system used within a society and its culture? What do the symbol systems within a culture reveal about it? Historically, what contributions have different ethnic groups made to our number system?

Incorporating Elements from Science and Mathematics into the Multicultural Curriculum

Incorporating elements from science and mathematics into the multicultural curriculum is difficult for most teachers. Issues related to science and mathematics can be incorporated into the multicultural curriculum in at least three ways: (1) ways related to content; (2) ways related to perspectives, paradigms, and concepts; and (3) ways related to equity issues.

Figure 2–1   *Studying Ethnic Cultures from an Interdisciplinary Perspective*

This figure illustrates how a concept such as *culture* can be viewed from the perspectives of a number of disciplines and areas. Any one discipline gives only a partial understanding of a concept, social problem, or issue. Thus, multicultural units and lessons should be interdisciplinary and cut across disciplinary lines.

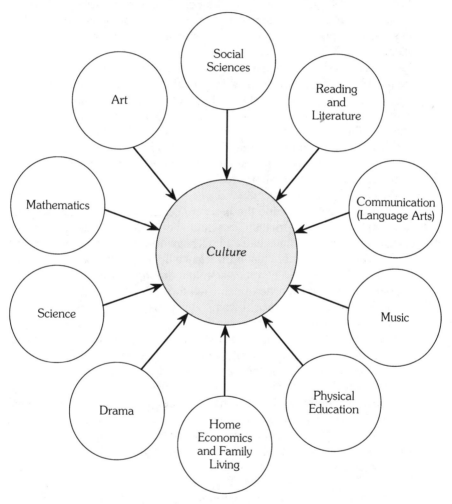

Some content related to science and mathematics can be incorporated into the multicultural curriculum. In science, the biological basis of skin color and the other physical characteristics of various racial groups can be studied. However, when the biological basis of race is studied, students should be helped to understand that race is largely a socially constructed concept or category even though scientists have attempted to formulate different racial categories. Health issues and diseases related to various ethnic groups are other appropriate subjects for science in the multicultural curriculum.

The experiences of various ethnic and cultural groups in science, in both past and contemporary society, is another appropriate study for science in the multicultural curriculum. The lives of African American scientists such as Daniel Hale Williams and Ernest E. Just should be examined in the scientific component of the multicultural curriculum. These individuals made significant contributions to science despite the blatant discrimination they experienced. Contemporary scientists from diverse groups should also be studied.

Content related to mathematics in the multicultural curriculum can highlight the role played by groups such as the Egyptians and Aztecs in the development of theory and practice in mathematics.[1] In the film *Stand and Deliver* Mr. Escalante uses his knowledge of Aztec contributions to mathematics to motivate his Mexican-American students to study calculus. Mr. Escalante reminds his students that their ancestors, the Aztecs, made significant mathematical breakthroughs. Students can also examine the experiences of mathematicians today from various cultural and racial groups.

Another important way to view science and mathematics in the multicultural curriculum is to examine the basic concepts, paradigms, and perspectives used in science and mathematics and the influence these paradigms, concepts, and perspectives have had and still have on various ethnic and cultural groups. This can be done more readily in science than in mathematics. Darwin's theory of evolution, as well as other scientific theories—such as the genetic theory of intelligence—have often been used to support scientific racism. Students can examine scientific racism from both a historical and contemporary perspective.

Levins and Lewontin, using a Marxist dialectic, argue that scientists act within a social context and from a philosophical perspective that is inherently political.[2] Students can examine the Levins and Lewontin thesis and determine the extent to which it is applicable to their science textbooks and readings. Students can also study such questions as these: What major assumptions, concepts, and perspectives do scientists use today that are related to the experiences of ethnic groups? What major influence are these assumptions, concepts, and perspectives having on the experiences of ethnic groups? Students can also examine how applied mathematics is being used to influence societal issues and practices.

A third, and perhaps the most important way in which science and mathematics teachers can include multicultural content in their curricula is by examining equity issues in science and mathematics and by modifying their teaching techniques and expectations in order to enhance the academic achievement of students of color and of women. Researchers have indicated that students of color and female students often do not achieve as well as White males in higher-level mathematics and science courses.[3] Students of color and female students also take fewer high-level mathematics and science courses than do White males. Researchers have suggested that these problems result in part from low teacher expectations and from the teaching styles used in science and mathematics courses that are inconsistent with how many students of color and female students learn.[4] To make their teaching multicultural, science and mathematics teachers should encourage their students of color and their female students to enroll in higher-level courses, provide them with support and encouragement, and modify their teaching techniques to make them more consistent with the learning styles of students of color and female students. Treisman has found that cooperative teaching and learning strategies can help students of color to learn advanced calculus.[5]

The Forms of Knowledge

I have illustrated how a key concept such as culture can be viewed from diverse disciplinary perspectives. To identify and select key concepts such as culture, you must be familiar with the nature of knowledge and its various forms— including facts, concepts, generalizations, and theories. These major knowledge forms and the contribution that each can make to an interdisciplinary and conceptual multicultural curriculum are discussed and highlighted next.

Facts

Facts are low-level, specific empirical statements about limited phenomena. Facts may be considered the lowest level of knowledge and have the least predictive capacity of all of the knowledge forms. In multicultural studies, as in all academic areas and disciplines, facts are the building blocks of knowledge. Students must master facts in order to learn higher levels of knowledge.

Examples of facts are as follows:

- The Chinese immigrants who came to San Francisco in the 1800s established the *hui kuan*.
- In 1987, 72,400 legal immigrants came to the United States from Mexico.
- Between 1981 and 1986, 384,300 legal immigrants from Europe settled in the United States.

A careful study of these facts about U.S. ethnic groups reveals several characteristics of factual statements. First, facts are empirical statements, or statements that can be tested with available data or data that can be obtained. By carefully studying and analyzing historical documents and statistical data, a social scientist can determine whether the Chinese immigrants who came to the United States in the 1800s actually established *hui kuan* societies. It is important to stress that factual statements are capable of verification or testing because many statements presented as facts, especially in multicultural studies, are on closer scrutiny normative or value statements that cannot be tested or can be tested only with great difficulty. An example of such a statement is "Indians were hostile.'' This statement is actually a misleading stereotype masquerading as a factual statement.

Because factual statements are limited in explaining causal relationships, students need to master higher levels of knowledge in addition to facts. Facts should not be the end goal of instruction because they are highly limited. Many teachers end units by testing students primarily for their mastery of facts. Because facts, in and of themselves, do not encompass a large quantity of data, they have little transfer value, are quickly forgotten by students, and do not, if they are the end goal of instruction, help students to gain in-depth understanding of society.

However, to say that facts are limited in the contribution they can make to students' understanding of social events and problems is not to say that they are not important and that they do not have a proper role in instruction—quite the contrary. Factual statements are important in teaching. If you keep their limitations in mind and use them judiciously, they can contribute to student learning. Facts are the foundations of the higher levels of knowledge: *concepts, generalizations*, and *theories*. Without learning facts, as I later illustrate, students will not be able to master concepts and generalizations. However, you are justified in teaching facts only if they are used to help students develop higher forms of knowledge or make decisions. Thus, for every fact you select for inclusion in the curriculum, you should have a concept, generalization, or theory in mind that the fact is intended to help the students develop. Facts taught randomly and in isolation have little instructional value. Yet, they can become powerful instructional tools if they are carefully selected and taught.

Concepts

Concepts are words or phrases that enable us to categorize or classify a large class of observations and thus reduce the complexity of our social environment. In structure and function, concepts differ from facts, generalizations, and theories. Both facts and generalizations are empirical *statements*; a theory consists of a system of interrelated generalizations. However, concepts are special constructs because they are necessary for the formulation of the other categories of knowledge and are contained in all facts, generalizations, and theories. Because concepts are contained in all other forms of knowledge, students cannot understand a fact, generalization, or theory unless the concepts contained within them are meaningful.

The following are some of the key concepts discussed in chapter 3:

Cultural assimilation	Culture
Structural assimilation	Immigration
Acculturation	Power
Race	Values
Economic oppression	

Even though concepts are contained in all facts, generalizations, and theories, they are unique because they can also encompass a large range of facts and generalizations, and a complete theory can be formulated about a single concept, such as discrimination. Some concepts are rather concrete, such as *street*; others are more abstract, such as *megalopolis*. Some concepts, such as *city*, are somewhere between these two extremes. We might call these kinds of concepts *intermediate-level* concepts. Thus, if we arrange these concepts into a hierarchy, it would look like this:

mègalopolis

  city

    street

In this example, megalopolis is the highest-level concept because it consists of a region made up of several cities and their surrounding areas. City is the next level because a city contains many streets. Of course, there are parallel concepts that are more concrete than *street*.

Concepts encompassing generalizations are often more abstract (or at a higher level) than are concepts that are contained in the generalizations encompassed. Also, the concepts contained in facts are often less abstract than those used to classify those facts. The same is true for theories. The example below illustrates how a higher-level concept, *immigration*, can be used to categorize a number of facts. The facts, of course, contain many concepts.

HIGHER-LEVEL CONCEPT: Immigration

Facts being categorized or grouped under concept:

- Between 1820 and 1965, millions of Europeans came to the United States.
- By 1860, there were 34,933 Chinese in the United States.
- In 1900, 24,326 Japanese lived in the United States.
- In 1987, 24,200 Vietnamese immigrated to the United States.

Higher-level concepts can also encompass or classify generalizations (see discussion below for definition of a generalization). In the example below, the concept *culture* is used to categorize a number of generalizations at varying levels of abstractions.

CONCEPT: Culture

Generalizations being categorized or grouped under concept:

- An ethnic minority group usually acquires some of the values, behaviors, and beliefs of the dominant ethnic groups within a society.
- Dominant ethnic groups usually attain some of the traits and artifacts of ethnic minority groups.
- African Americans have made a number of contributions to American music.

In many cases, some concepts are clearly at a higher level than are others. For example, *city* is a higher-level concept than *street* because a city contains many streets. However, because a concept appears in a factual statement does not necessarily mean that it is a lower-level or concrete concept. Study this factual statement:

More than 24,000 Vietnamese immigrants arrived in the United States in 1987.

This factual statement contains the higher-level concept, *immigrant*. As previously illustrated, the concept *immigration* can be used to categorize a number of facts. The distinguishing characteristic of a higher-level concept is that it is able to categorize a number of facts and generalizations. This is true even though that same concept may sometimes appear within factual statements. By identifying higher-level concepts, you will be able to help students relate discrete facts and data to form generalizations about ethnicity, which they can apply when studying ethnic and cultural groups both within the United States and in other nations. Table 2–2 illustrates how key concepts can be used to do a comparative study of ethnic groups within the United States and in other nations.

Table 2–3 illustrates one strategy for teaching a concept. This strategy is called "Lesson Plan for Attaining a Concept." Try teaching this lesson to a group of students or to a group of your classmates or colleagues in your workshop. After teaching this lesson, respond to this question: What are the advantages of using a conceptual approach to teaching?

Generalizations

A generalization contains two or more concepts and states the relationship between them. Like empirical facts, generalizations are scientific statements that can be tested and verified with data. Generalizations are useful tools in instruction because they can be used to summarize a large mass of facts and to show the relationship between higher-level concepts that students have mastered. Like concepts, generalizations vary greatly in their level of inclusiveness. There are low-level generalizations, which are little more than summary statements, and there are high-level generalizations, which are universal in applicability. To illustrate levels of generalizations, we study one fact listed earlier in this chapter and state generalizations at various levels that encompass it.

FACT: The Chinese immigrants who came to San Francisco in the 1800s established the *hui kuan.*

Lower-Level Generalization: Chinese immigrants in America established various forms of social organizations.

Intermediate-Level Generalization: All groups that have immigrated or migrated to the United States have established social organizations.

Table 2–2 A Comparative Study of Ethnic Groups in Different Nations

Key Concepts and Related Key Questions	Filipino Americans (USA)	British Pakistanis	French Canadians	Nigerian Ibos	Mexican Indians	French Algerians
Origins Is the group native or did it migrate or immigrate to its current location? If immigrant group, what caused the immigration?						
Discrimination Is the group experiencing discrimination? If so, what kinds? If not, why not?						
Culture What are the group's unique cultural and ethnic characteristics?						
Assimilation To what extent is the group assimilated both culturally and structurally?						

continued

Table 2-2 Continued

Key Concepts and Related Key Questions	Filipino Americans (USA)	British Pakistanis	French Canadians	Nigerian Ibos	Mexican Indians	French Algerians
Economic Status Is the group facing economic problems or does it have a secure economic status?						
Education Are the group's youths experiencing problems in the schools? Why or why not?						
Power What role does the group play in the political system? Has it been able to organize and to exercise political power effectively?						
Ethnic Revitalization Is the group experiencing or has it experienced an ethnic revitalization movement? Explain.						

Table 2–3 *Lesson Plan for Attaining a Concept*

1. Write "Rite of Passage" on the board. Ask the students to repeat the words.
2. List these examples of rites of passage on the board and tell the students, "These are examples of rites of passage":

Marriage ceremony
Christening ceremony
Funeral
Vision quest among the Zuni Indians
Baptism
Bar Mitzvah
Bas Mitzvah

3. Ask the students to describe what these examples of the concept have in common. Put the list on the board.
4. Help the students to identify and state the critical attributes of "rite of passage."
5. Ask the students to write a definition of "rite of passage" using the list of key attributes that they formulated above. Their definitions should be a variation of this one: "Ceremonies that mark a critical transition in the life of an individual from one phase of the life cycle to another."*

Follow-up Activity: Ask the students to interview parents and other family members to find out what rites of passages have taken place in their families. Ask them to share at least one family rite of passage in which they have participated or observed. Ask the students: "What important functions do rites of passage play for individuals, families, and societies?"

*This definition is from George A. Theodorson and Archilles G. Theodorson, *A Modern Dictionary of Sociology.* New York: Barnes and Noble, 1979, p. 350.

Highest-Level or Universal Generalization: In all human societies, forms of social organizations emerge to satisfy the needs of individuals and groups.

A study of these examples indicates that a generalization is a higher-level statement than a fact because generalization encompasses a number of facts. The fact noted above tells us only that Chinese Americans established one kind of social organization, the *hui kuan.* The lower-level generalization in our example reveals that Chinese Americans established a variety of social organizations. Thus, the lower-level generalization not only encompasses the fact about the *hui kuan,* but also the following facts:

- Chinese immigrants in America formed organizations called clans.
- The Chinese Benevolent Association is a confederation of clans and secret societies.
- Secret societies emerged within Chinese communities in the United States.
- The Chinese secret societies provided help to Chinese Americans and obtained control of gambling in Chinese-American communities.

The next generalization in the example, an intermediate-level generalization, encompasses facts not only about Chinese Americans, but also about all immigrants and migrants in the United States. Thus, this generalization is at a higher level of abstraction because it encompasses more facts than the lower-level generalization. For example, the intermediate-level generalization, in addition to encompassing the facts about Chinese-American organizations, also encompasses the following facts:

- Puerto Ricans established the Puerto Rican Forum to help solve the problems of Puerto Rican migrants in New York City.
- Jewish Americans founded the Anti-Defamation League of B'nai B'rith to help mitigate anti-Semitism in the United States.
- In 1921, Spanish-speaking Americans formed the Orden Hijos de America (Order of the Sons of America) to train its members for American citizenship.
- Japanese immigrants in America created the Japanese Association to provide services for its members.
- The National Urban League was founded in 1911 to help Black southern migrants adjust to city life.

The last generalization is the highest form of generalization possible because it encompasses all the other facts and generalizations above it, and it applies to all human societies in the past and present. Note that it does not contain a reference to any particular people, region, or culture. One way to determine whether a generalization is written at the highest possible level is to ascertain whether it is limited to a particular people, culture, or historical era. A generalization of wide applicability contains few or no exceptions and can be tested and verified, to varying degrees, within any human culture. The highest-level generalization in the example states that in every past and present human society, one can find examples of social organizations. This generalization has been tested and verified by social scientists. Whether they studied a preliterate tribe in New Zealand or the cultures in Medieval Europe, social scientists found types of social organizations such as the family and some kind of kinship system. It is true that the forms these organizations take vary greatly both within and between cultures, but nevertheless they exist.

It is necessary for you to be able to identify and write generalizations at various levels in order to incorporate ethnic content into the curriculum. During initial planning, you should identify generalizations of the highest order so that you can then select content samples from a variety of cultures to enable students to *test* them. If you start planning by identifying lower-level or intermediate-level generalizations, you will be greatly limited in the content that you can select to exemplify the generalizations. For example:

Chinese immigrants in America established various forms of social organization.

If you selected this generalization on which to organize instruction, you would not be able to help students derive generalizations related to the organizations that other ethnic groups, such as Anglo-Saxon Protestants, Mexican Americans, Jewish Americans, and African Americans, have formed in the United States.

You should begin planning by identifying high-level concepts and generalizations (often called *key* or *organizing* generalizations in this book) and then select lower-level concepts and generalizations related to the chosen *content samples*. This type of planning is necessary in order to help students develop higher-level statements—one of the ultimate goals of instruction. Chapter 4 discusses procedures you can use to identify high-level concepts and generalizations that can form the core of a sound multicultural curriculum.

We have noted that generalizations range from the concrete to those that are universal in application. A fact related to a Chinese-American institution, the *hui kuan*, was chosen to illustrate how a single fact can be encompassed by generalizations at three different levels. The choice of three levels was an arbitrary decision; generalizations at fewer or more levels could have easily been written. For example, Hilda Taba has identified four levels (or orders, as she calls them) of generalizations.[6] Because generalizations exist at many different levels, it is not necessary for you to spend undue time trying to devise elaborate schemes for classifying levels of generalizations.

However, to plan effective units and lessons, you should know that generalizations exist at many different levels, that all generalizations are at a higher level than facts, and that the highest order or level generalizations should be identified during the initial stages of unit planning.

Earlier, I said that a generalization is a statement capable of being tested or verified. This is true; but because human behavior is so complex, generalizations in the social and behavioral sciences are always *tentative* statements and can never be proven 100% correct. Almost always, social science generalizations will have some exceptions. Because social science generalizations tend to be tentative and nonconclusive, they often contain qualifying words.

Study this generalization: "When an ethnic minority group is oppressed, and it sees no legitimate ways to alleviate its problems, rebellions will sometimes occur." The word *sometimes* qualifies this generalization because in many situations an ethnic minority group may feel oppressed and see no legitimate ways to alleviate its problems, yet ethnic rebellions may not occur. Japanese Americans, when they were forced to leave their homes during World War II and were sent to internment camps, did not resist or rebel as a group, although some individuals did resist internment. One social scientist has hypothesized that most Japanese Americans cooperated with the federal government because of the norms within their culture toward authority and because they did not believe that resistance would succeed.[7] On the other hand, many African Americans who felt oppressed in our cities in the late 1960s violently rebelled. The particular times, the culture of a group, and the group's perceptions of its social and economic status greatly influence how it will respond to an oppressive situation.

This example is used merely to illustrate that students should be taught how tentative social science conclusions and generalizations are and should learn that social knowledge is constantly changing and is never absolute.

Generalizations are important in instruction because they enable students to make predictions; the predictive capacity of generalizations varies directly with their degree of applicability and amount of empirical support. Generalizations that describe a large class of behaviors and that have been widely verified are the most useful for making predictions. We have called these types of generalizations *high-level* or *organizing* generalizations. Generalizations not only enable students to predict behavior with a fairly high degree of accuracy, but also to solve problems in novel situations.

Theory

Theory is the highest form of knowledge and is the most useful for predicting human behavior. I stated that a *concept* was a word or phrase that was used to categorize or classify facts, data, and other forms of information and knowledge. A *generalization* was defined as a statement showing the relationship between two or more concepts that could be empirically verified. A review of the definitions of these terms is important because a theory consists of a number of related generalizations. The generalizations within a theory constitute a deductive system and are logically interrelated. The generalizations contained within a theory are also *high-level* and *universal-type* generalizations; they are not low-level ones. A theory is called a *deductive* system because when several generalizations within a theory are stated, the concluding ones can be logically derived. In other words, when given some propositions within a theory, a conclusion can be derived from the stated generalizations. An empirical theory has the following characteristics:

- It consists of a set of interrelated lawlike propositions or generalizations that are testable.
- The propositions must show the relationship between variables or concepts that are clearly defined.
- The propositions must constitute a deductive system and be logically consistent; unknown principles must be derivable from known ones.
- The propositions must be a source of testable hypotheses.

The following example of a theory illustrates how the deductive process works. Gordon's theory of cultural and structural assimilation has heavily influenced the field of ethnic studies. Here are the four major generalizations within this theory:[8]

1. With regard to *cultural behavior*, differences of social class are more important and decisive than are differences of ethnic group.

2. With regard to *social participation* in primary groups and primary relationships, people tend to confine these to their own social class segment within their own ethnic group—that is, the *ethclass*.
3. With a person of the same social class but of a different ethnic group, one shares behavioral similarities but not a sense of peoplehood.
4. With those of the same ethnic group but of a different social class, one shares a sense of *peoplehood* but not behavioral similarities [*emphases added*].

Gordon's theory satisfies our criterion of a theory: a system of high-level interrelated generalizations that constitute a deductive system. In the first generalization in the theory, Gordon hypothesizes that in terms of cultural behavior, social class is more important than ethnicity. By cultural behavior, he means such things as the values a person holds, his or her speech patterns, and occupational aspirations.

This generalization suggests that an upper-class African American individual's clothing, values, and foods are likely to be more similar to those of an upper-class White than to those of a lower-class African American. The second generalization in the theory suggests that an upper-class Mexican American, while sharing cultural characteristics with White Anglo-Saxons, is more likely to participate in the private clubs and cliques of other upper-class Mexican Americans than in Anglo-Saxon private clubs and social cliques. The theory hypothesizes that even though upper-status individuals within different ethnic groups share similar values and behavior, their close, primary group relationships are highly confined to members within their ethnic groups of the same social class. This is also true for lower-class members of ethnic groups. Gordon presents much compelling evidence in his book to support the generalizations that comprise his theory.

Gordon's theory meets the criterion of a theory because when given generalizations one and two of his theory (presented above), one can logically derive generalizations three and four. To do so, however, it might be necessary to know how he defines two key concepts in his generalizations: *ethclass* and *sense of peoplehood*. He defines *ethclass* as the "subsociety created by the intersection of the vertical stratifications of ethnicity with the horizontal stratifications of social class."[9] Thus, lower-middle-class Vietnamese Americans constitute an ethclass. By *sense of peoplehood*, Gordon means an individual's identification with a group that shares a common culture, religious beliefs, and values.[10] He contends, for example, that African Americans in all social classes share an ethnic identification.

To help students fully understand the ethnic experience in the United States, you should, whenever possible, help them relate generalizations to a theoretical system. Generalizations have much more meaning when they are studied within a theoretical framework than when studied in isolation.

Because of their specialized structure and function, a complete theory can be structured around a single concept. Gordon's theory of cultural and structural

assimilation is an example of a theory formed around the concept of assimilation. Cultural assimilation occurs when one ethnic group attains the values and
behavior patterns of another ethnic group. Usually the ethnic minority group
attains the cultural characteristics of the dominant ethnic group. Structural
assimilation occurs when one ethnic group participates in the primary groups,
such as private clubs and social cliques, of another ethnic group.[11] Gordon
concludes that even though widespread cultural assimilation has taken place in
American society, little structural assimilation has occurred because ethnic
groups within U.S. society, including dominant ethnic groups and people of
color, participate mainly in the primary groups of their own ethnic communities.
He maintains that our society has a high degree of cultural assimilation but is
characterized by *structural pluralism.*[12]

An Effective Multicultural Curriculum

Major goals of an effective multicultural curriculum are to help students develop
the ability to make reflective decisions on personal and public issues and to take
successful action. Integrating the curriculum with ethnic content can be viewed
as a process of curriculum reform. During this process, the entire curriculum is
transformed to enable students to view events, concepts, and issues from diverse
ethnic and cultural perspectives.

The multicultural curriculum is broadly conceptualized and includes the
study of a wide range of ethnic groups. These groups are studied using a
comparative approach. The multicultural curriculum is also conceptual and
interdisciplinary. Major concepts, when feasible and appropriate, are studied
from the perspectives of disciplines such as the various social sciences, art,
literature, communication, and the physical and biological sciences. Figure 2–2
summarizes the characteristics of an effective multicultural curriculum. The next
chapter discusses key concepts that can be used to plan and organize a multicultural curriculum.

Summary

The conceptual approach can best facilitate the integration of ethnic content into
the curriculum and into the various subject areas. Using this approach, the
teacher selects key concepts, such as culture, power, and discrimination, and
then identifies content samples that can be used to help students attain these
ideas. The conceptual approach allows the teacher to use content samples from
several different disciplines and thus to teach in an interdisciplinary way.

When identifying concepts for a conceptual multicultural curriculum, you
should make sure that a balanced approach is taken and that people of color are

Figure 2–2   *The Components of an Effective Multicultural Curriculum*

The effective multicultural curriculum must be conceptual, broadly conceptualized, interdisciplinary, comparative, decision-making and social-action focused, and viewed as a process of curriculum transformation.

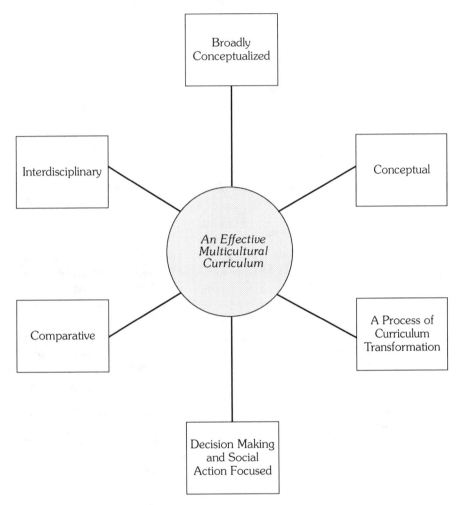

not depicted only or primarily as victims. They should also be described as people who helped to shape their own destiny, who built ethnic institutions, and who played a major role in attaining their civil rights. It is necessary to teach such concepts as prejudice, discrimination, and racism. However, it is also essential to teach such concepts as protest, empowerment, interracial cooperation, and ethnic institutions in order to portray a full and accurate view of the experiences of ethnic groups in the United States.

Questions and Activities

1. Label each of the following a *fact*, *concept*, or *generalization* and justify each label:

    a. Acculturation._____

    b. In every human society there is a conflict between unlimited wants and limited resources._____

    c. Assimilation._____

    d. In 1827 Vincente Guerrero became president of Mexico._____

    e. Ethnic cultures, values, and behavior are undergoing constant change. _____

    f. On September 22, 1862, President Lincoln issued a statement that has been called the Preliminary Emancipation Proclamation._____

    g. In 1980, 93,038 Puerto Ricans lived in the state of California._____

    h. During the 1960s and 1970s people of color strove less for cultural assimilation and more for cultural pluralism._____

    i. Cultural pluralism._____

    j. Ethnic group._____

2. Here is a higher-level generalization: "Most foreigners who voluntarily immigrated to the United States were seeking better economic, political, and social opportunities." Examine several of the books on ethnic groups contained in the bibliographies in Parts II–V and write several factual statements and lower-level generalizations that this generalization will encompass.

3. Examine several of the books in the bibliographies in Parts II–V and find a number of factual statements and generalizations that these concepts will encompass: cultural assimilation, structural assimilation, protest, discrimination.

4. Tell whether each of these statements is normative or empirical, and why:

    a. The American colonists should not have taken land away from the American Indians.

    b. Irresponsible Blacks rioted in many American cities in the 1960s.

    c. Many Mexican immigrants entered the United States illegally.

    d. Japanese Americans should not have been sent to relocation camps in 1942.

    e. Many Puerto Ricans migrate to the U.S. mainland each year.

    f. Many Chinese Americans live in ghettos in American cities.

5. What do you think should be the role of the following categories of knowledge in a sound multicultural curriculum, and why?

    a. Facts

    b. Concepts

    c. Generalizations

    d. Theories

6. Examine several books dealing with people of color (see the annotated bibliographies in Parts II–V of this book) and identify a theory related to ethnic groups. Can this theory be taught to a group of elementary or high school students? Why or why not? If you think that it can be taught to a group of students, develop a plan for teaching it. If you are a classroom teacher or a student teacher, implement your teaching plan and evaluate its effectiveness.

7. Make a list of your close friends. Note their ethnic, religious, and racial backgrounds. Compare your list with similar lists made by other individuals in your class or workshop. What conclusions can you make about structural assimilation in American society on the basis of the responses made by you and your classmates or fellow workshop participants?

8. If your parents are first- or second-generation American immigrants, make a list of their values and life-styles that are different from your own. If your parents are not first- or second-generation immigrants, interview individuals whose parents are and compare their values and life-styles with those of their parents. What tentative generalizations can you make about cultural assimilation in American society by studying these data?

9. Define each of the following terms and tell why each is important:

knowledge	ethclass
reflective decision	cultural assimilation
fact	structural assimilation
concept	intermediate-level generalization
generalization	high-level generalization
theory	high-level concept
normative statement	low-level concept
empirical statement	

Endnotes

1. Ivan Van Sertima, ed., *Blacks in Science: Ancient and Modern* (New Brunswick: Transaction Books, 1986); Stephen F. Mason, *A History of the Sciences* (New York: Collier Books, 1962).

2. Richard Levins and Richard Lewontin, *The Dialectical Biologist* (Cambridge: Harvard University Press, 1985).

3. Mary F. Belenky et al., *Women's Ways of Knowing: The Development of Self, Voice and Mind* (New York: Basic Books, 1986).

4. Ibid; Robert E. Slavin, *Cooperative Learning* (New York: Longman, 1983).

5. Rose Asera, "The Mathematics Workshop: A Description" (Berkeley: University of California, Charles A. Dana Center for Innovation in Mathematics and Science Education. March 2, 1988), unpublished paper.

6. Hilda Taba, Mary C. Durkin, Jack R. Fraenkel, and Anthony H. McNaughton, *A Teacher's Handbook for Elementary School Studies: An Inductive Approach*, 2nd ed. (Reading, Mass.; Addison-Wesley, 1971).

7. Harry H. L. Kitano, *Japanese Americans: The Evolution of a Subculture*, 2nd ed. (Englewood Cliffs, N.J.: Prentice-Hall, 1976), pp. 70–88.

8. Milton M. Gordon, *Assimilation in American Life* (New York: Oxford University Press, 1964), pp. 52–53.

9. Ibid., p. 51.

10. Ibid., p. 23.

11. Ibid., pp. 19–59.

12. Ibid.

Annotated Bibliography

Banks, James A., with Clegg, Ambrose A., Jr. *Teaching Strategies for the Social Studies: Inquiry, Valuing and Decision-Making*, 4th ed. White Plains, N.Y.: Longman, 1990.

Chapter 3 of this book is a detailed discussion, with illustrations, of the nature and teaching of concepts, generalizations, and theories. Part IV discusses value inquiry, decision making, citizen action, and evaluation strategies.

Banks, James A. "Multicultural Education: Its Effects on Students' Racial and Gender Role Attitudes" in James P. Shaver, ed. *Handbook of Research on Social Studies Teaching and Learning*. New York: Macmillan, 1991.

This chapter consists of a comprehensive review and discussion of the research related to ways to help students acquire more positive racial and gender-role attitudes.

Butler, Johnnella E., and Walter, John C., eds. *Transforming the Curriculum: Ethnic Studies and Women Studies*. Albany: State University of New York Press, 1990.

The thoughtful and provocative essays in this book explore various dimensions of integrating content about ethnic groups and women into the mainstream curriculum. Although the essays focus on the college and university curriculum, the issues, problems and solutions they identify are applicable to the K–12 curriculum.

Grant, Carl A., and Sleeter, Christine E. *Turning on Learning: Five Approaches for Multicultural Teaching Plans for Race, Class, and Disability*. Columbus, Oh.: Merrill, 1989.

A book of lesson plans for teaching multicultural content in a variety of subjects, including science and mathematics.

Lee, Enid, *Letters to Marcia: A Teacher's Guide to Anti-Racist Education*. Toronto: Cross Cultural Communications Centre, 1985.

A thoughtful and creative guide, written in the form of letters, for helping teachers to reduce racism in the classroom and school. It is written by one of Canada's most creative and effective teacher trainers.

Lightfoot, Sara Lawrence. *Balm in Gilead: Journey of a Healer*. Reading, Mass.: Addison-Wesley, 1988.

In this deeply moving and affectionate biography, a daughter describes her mother's long journey to become one of the nation's first African-American child psychiatrists. This book will help teachers gain the knowledge, insights, and sensitivities needed to teach a multicultural curriculum. A New York Times Book Review Notable Book of 1989.

Pedersen, Paul. *A Handbook for Developing Multicultural Awareness*. Alexandria, Va.: American Association for Counseling and Development, 1988.

Although this book was written for counselors, classroom teachers will find many of its insights helpful in examining their attitudes toward racial and ethnic diversity. The author presents three stages of multicultural development: awareness, knowledge, and skill.

Simonson, Rick, and Walker, Scott, eds. *The Graywolf Annual Five: Multicultural Literacy*. St. Paul: Graywolf Press, 1988.

This thoughtful and stimulating collection of essays is an antidote to the Western-centric notion of cultural literacy promoted by several noted mainstream scholars. The contributors include James Baldwin, Carlos Fuentes, and Michele Wallace.

Sertima, Ivan Van, ed. *Blacks in Science: Ancient and Modern*. New Brunswick, N.J.: Transaction Books, 1986.

African contributions to astronomy, agriculture, architecture and engineering, mathematics, medicine, and other scientific fields are discussed in the essays that comprise this book.

Sleeter, Christine E., ed. *Empowerment through Multicultural Education*. Albany: State University of New York Press, 1991.

The authors of the chapters in this book discuss a variety of issues and problems related to multicultural education and teaching in multicultural environments. The contributors include James A. Banks, Carlos E. Cortes, Lois Weis, Signithia Fordham, and Valerie Pang.

Taba, Hilda; Durkin, Mary C.; Fraenkel, Jack R.; and McNaughton, Anthony. *A Teacher's Handbook to Elementary Social Studies*. Menlo Park, Calif.: Addison-Wesley, 1971.

This is still one of the best books that describes ways to develop a conceptual curriculum, the approach to curriculum development recommended in this book.

Wurzel, James. *Toward Multiculturalism: Readings in Multicultural Education.* Yarmouth, Me.: Intercultural Press, 1988.

> *The readings in this book are in two main categories: human condition themes and cultural orientation themes. The contributors include Studs Terkel, George Spindler, Peter Farb, and Robert Kaplan.*

Chapter 3

Key Concepts for

the Multicultural

Curriculum

Introduction

The multicultural curriculum should help students to master higher levels of knowledge so that they can better understand race and ethnic relations and develop the skills and abilities needed to make reflective personal and public decisions. Sound multicultural lessons and units focus on higher-level concepts and generalizations and use facts primarily to help students to master higher forms of knowledge and to make decisions. Students must be able to make reflective decisions in order to take thoughtful personal, social, and civic action.

Criteria for Selecting Interdisciplinary Concepts

Within the various academic fields and disciplines is a wide range of concepts from which you might select when planning the multicultural curriculum. What criteria can you use when selecting concepts to organize multicultural units and lessons? First, you should consider whether the concept will help explain some significant aspect of the history, culture, and contemporary experiences of a range of ethnic groups in U.S. society. The experiences of ethnic groups in the United States have been characterized by a number of salient events, expressions, and themes, such as discrimination, protest and resistance, cultural assimilation, and acculturation. Consequently, these themes are highly appropriate organizing concepts for the multicultural curriculum.

Higher-level concepts that are capable of encompassing a wide range of data and information should also be selected for the multicultural curriculum. Culture is a more powerful concept than language because it can be used to organize and teach more information.

Concepts chosen for the multicultural curriculum should also be inter-disciplinary. Interdisciplinary concepts are capable of encompassing facts, generalizations, and examples from several disciplines and areas. It is necessary to select interdisciplinary concepts because the curriculum should help students view and interpret events and situations from the perspectives of several disciplines. When students view events and situations from the perspective of a single discipline, they can acquire, at best, only a partial understanding of the event or situation they are studying.

When social protest, for example, is studied only from the perspective of political science, students learn that social protest occurs when alienated groups within a political system organize to push for political and social change. However, students need to study protest from other disciplinary perspectives to understand it fully (see Figure 3–1). During the civil rights movement of the 1960s, African Americans expressed protest not only in politics but also in their literature, songs, dances, art, and language. Thus, students need to examine social protest in these forms of communication to understand fully Black protest in the 1960s.

Some concepts are important to the structure of a particular discipline but cannot function successfully in an interdisciplinary role. Rhythm, melody, harmony, and tone color are important concepts in music. Key concepts in art include form, line, and shape. However, because these concepts are highly specific to their particular disciplines, they are not effective interdisciplinary concepts. However, both music and art, as well as dance and language, are forms of communication and culture. Music and art also have themes or convey central messages to the perceiver; so do a play, a dance, and many examples of human behavior. Consequently, communication, culture, and theme are effective interdisciplinary concepts because they are able to help students develop generalizations by studying examples drawn from the social sciences and the humanities.

When selecting organizing concepts for multicultural lessons, you should give some attention to the developmental level of your students. Young children can understand discrimination easier than they can understand institutionalized racism, in part because almost every child has been the victim of some kind of discrimination at some time. He or she may have been the new child in the classroom, fat or thin, or had some other characteristic that other students singled out for ridicule. Young children can also understand discrimination more easily than institutionalized racism because discrimination is a more well-defined, less abstract, and less ambiguous concept than is institutionalized racism.

In the primary grades, you should focus on concepts that can be taught using *concrete* examples, such as similarities, differences, culture, race, discrimination, and ethnic group. Open-ended stories and role-playing situations, many of which are described in Parts II through V, can make these concepts real and meaningful to young children. Children's books are also a powerful tool for teaching concepts to students in the primary and intermediate grades. *A Jar of Dreams*, by Yoshiko Uchida, is a moving story that vividly describes examples of discrimination directed against 11-year-old Rinko and her family.[1] *Songs of the*

Figure 3–1   *Viewing Social Protest from an Interdisciplinary Perspective*

This figure illustrates how a concept such as social protest must be viewed from diverse disciplinary perspectives in order for students to understand its total political, social, and artistic ramifications.

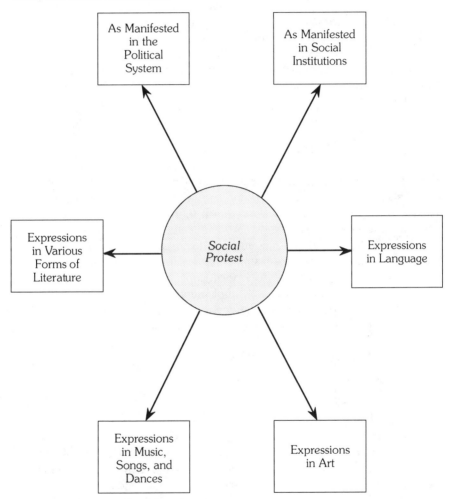

Trees by Mildred D. Taylor can also be used to teach discrimination.[2] Black language and cultural expressions are salient parts of Virginia Hamilton's *A Little Love*.[3] *Mountain Light* by Laurence Yep, which enables the reader to experience the life of Chinese immigrants, can help make the concept of immigration meaningful and real to students.[4] A number of outstanding children's books, annotated in Parts II through V, are available that you can use successfully to teach concepts such as cultural differences, prejudice, discrimination, and identity to students in the primary, intermediate, upper, and high-school grades.

The student's previous experience with concepts and content related to race and ethnicity is an important consideration when selecting concepts for study. Concepts such as institutionalized racism, ethnic separatism, ethnic revitalization movement, and colonialism are so complex and emotional that they are often inappropriate for students who are studying race and ethnicity for the first time. More concrete and less controversial concepts are appropriate for such students. A student who is not familiar with such basic concepts as ethnic group, ethnic minority group, people of color, discrimination, and prejudice will have a difficult time understanding and appreciating abstract concepts such as institutionalized racism and ethnic separatism. These concepts should be studied only after students have mastered the basic concepts in ethnic studies.

Interdisciplinary Concepts

Concepts drawn from various behavioral science disciplines that can be used effectively to organize interdisciplinary units and lessons are discussed below. The social and behavioral sciences are a rich source of interdisciplinary concepts because behavioral scientists study a wide range of human behavior. Art, music, dance, foods, language, and literature are expressions of concepts studied by behavioral scientists. Table 3–1 summarizes major concepts discussed in this chapter. Table 3–2 illustrates how key concepts such as those in the following discussion can be used to plan and implement a comparative study of ethnic groups. Table 3–3 describes nine key concepts that can be used to organize a focused study of an ethnic group in the United States.

Culture, Ethnicity, and Related Concepts

Culture

Culture is the key concept in cultural anthropology. It is an essential concept in ethnic studies because an ethnic group is a type of cultural group. Culture consists of the behavior patterns, symbols, institutions, values, and other human-made components of society. It is the unique achievement of a human group that distinguishes it from other groups. Even though cultures are in many ways similar, a particular culture constitutes a unique whole.

There is tremendous debate and controversy within anthropology about the meaning of culture. Some anthropologists contend that tools and other artifacts are not examples of culture but that the meaning and interpretation of these elements are what constitute culture. Bullivant defines culture as a program for survival that "embodies strategies by which social groups maximize their perceived advantage relative to other groups."[5] He also maintains that culture "contains not only survival instructions but also often an elaborate justification for their type and purpose."[6]

Table 3–1 *Key Concepts*

Culture, Ethnicity, and Related Concepts	Culture
	Ethnic group
	Ethnic minority group
	Stages of ethnicity
	Ethnic diversity
	Cultural assimilation
	Acculturation
	Community culture
Socialization and Related Concepts	Socialization
	Prejudice
	Discrimination
	Race
	Racism
	Ethnocentrism
	Values
	Self-concept
Intercultural Communication and Related Concepts	Communication
	Intercultural communication
	Perception
	Historical bias
	Environmental perception
Power and Related Concepts	Power
	Social protest and resistance
The Movement of Ethnic Groups	Migration
	Immigration

Note: This table contains a list of high-level concepts that can be used to develop units and lessons that draw content, examples, and information from several disciplines. These concepts are defined and illustrated in this chapter.

The U.S. culture is comprised of many smaller groups. These microcultural groups share many characteristics with the common national culture but have some distinguishing characteristics that set them apart from other groups. Thus, it is possible to describe the U.S. culture—as well as the various microcultures that constitute it, such as the Appalachian culture, the Southern culture, and the youth culture.

Ethnic Group and Ethnic Minority Group

Ethnic groups are types of microcultural groups within the United States that have unique characteristics that set them apart from other cultural groups. Many microcultural groups are voluntary groups, but an ethnic group is usually an involuntary group, although individual identification with the group may be optional.[7] An ethnic group has a historic origin and a shared heritage and tradition. The origins of the group preceded the creation of the nation state or

Table 3-2 An Interdisciplinary Study of Ethnic Groups

Key Concepts and Related Questions	American Indians	Mexican Americans	African Americans	Jewish Americans	Filipino Americans	Puerto Ricans
Culture: What ethnic cultural elements are present in the group's culture today? How is the group's culture reflected in its music, literature, and art?						
Ethnic Enclave: To what extent are members of the group concentrated within particular geographical regions?						
Racism and Discrimination: To what extent is the group a victim of racism or other forms of discrimination?						
Communication: To what extent do members of the group encounter problems when communicating with other ethnic groups?						
Self-Concept: How have the group's societal experiences affected the self-concepts of its members?						
Power: To what extent does the group exercise power within the ethnic community? Within the economic system? Within the larger society?						

Note: This table illustrates how a data retrieval chart organized around key concepts can be used by the teacher to plan and implement a comparative study of ethnic groups.

Table 3-3 *Organizing Concepts for a Focused Study of an Ethnic Group*

The experience of each ethnic group in the United States can be viewed and compared using a few key concepts and themes. Below are nine concepts that can be used to view and study the experiences of an ethnic group.

Origins and Immigration

It is important to examine the origins and immigration pattern of an ethnic group in the United States.

Shared Culture, Values, and Symbols

Most ethnic groups in the United States have unique cultures and values that resulted from an interaction of their original culture with the host culture in the United States, from ethnic institutions created partly as a response to discrimination, and from their social-class position.

Ethnic Identity and Sense of Peoplehood

A shared sense of peoplehood and ethnic identity is one of the most important characteristics of an ethnic group in the United States. This shared sense of identity results from a common history and current experiences.

Perspectives, World Views, and Frames of Reference

Members of the same ethnic group often view reality in a similar way and differently from other groups within a society. This results largely from their shared sense of peoplehood and identity described above.

Ethnic Institutions and Self-Determination

Many ethnic institutions were formed by ethnic groups in the United States in response to discrimination and segregation. Many of these institutions continue to exist today because they help ethnic groups to satisfy unique social, cultural, and educational needs.

Demographic, Social, Political, and Economic Status

When studying about a U.S. ethnic group, its current demographic, social, political, and economic status needs to be determined. The economic and educational status of an ethnic group can change. New immigration can change the demographic and economic profile of an ethnic group.

Prejudice, Discrimination, and Racism

Prejudice, discrimination, and racism have been major themes and issues in the history and contemporary experiences of U.S. ethnic groups, particularly those of color.

Intraethnic Diversity

Even though ethnic groups share culture, values, a sense of identity, and a common history, there are tremendous differences within ethnic groups. These important differences must always be kept in mind when ethnic groups are studied, or new stereotypes and misconceptions may arise.

Assimilation and Acculturation

The exeriences of ethnic groups in the United States have been and still are characterized by widespread cultural assimilation on the part of ethnic minority groups and ethnic minority cultures. The influence of ethnic minority cultures on the mainstream culture should be examined as should the assimilation of minority groups into the mainstream culture.

were external to the nation state. An ethnic group also has an ancestral tradition, and its members share a sense of peoplehood and an interdependence of fate. It has some value orientations, behavioral patterns, and interests, often political and economic, that differ from those of other groups within society. Ethnic groups tend to have an influence, often substantial, on the lives of their members. Anglo-Saxon Protestants, Italian Americans, and Irish Americans are examples of ethnic groups.

An ethnic minority group is an ethnic group with several distinguishing characteristics. Although an ethnic minority group, like an ethnic group, shares a common culture, a historic tradition, and a sense of peoplehood, it also has unique physical and/or cultural characteristics that enable individuals who belong to other ethnic groups to identify its members easily, often for discriminatory purposes. Ethnic minority groups also tend to be a numerical minority and to exercise minimal political and economic power. Vietnamese Americans are an ethnic minority group with unique physical and cultural characteristics. Non-White ethnic minority groups, such as Vietnamese Americans and African Americans, are often called *people of color.* Jewish Americans, another ethnic minority group, are distinguished on the basis of their religious and cultural characteristics.

Culture, ethnic group, ethnic minority group, and people of color are essential concepts for the multicultural curriculum and should be introduced in the primary grades. You can introduce the concept of culture by showing the students a menorah, an engagement ring, and the numeral "5." By asking the students what these objects have in common, and by class discussion and the use of more examples, you can help your students formulate a definition of culture. When introducing the concept of culture, you should emphasize the *meanings* that artifacts and cultural elements have to individuals and groups and how they use and interpret them.

After the students have studied culture, they can then be introduced to the concept of *microcultural group.* Ethnic group and later ethnic minority group can be introduced using appropriate examples. When you introduce *ethnic group,* you should help students to understand that they are members of many different groups, such as religious, kinship, and economic groups, and that an ethnic group is only one of the many groups to which individuals belong.

A person's attachment to and identity with these various groups varies with the individual, the times in one's life, and the situations and settings in which one finds oneself. Depending on experiences, social class, and many other variables, ethnicity may be important to an individual or it may be unimportant. Students should be helped to understand that just because they think an individual is a member of a particular ethnic group, that does not mean that the individual has a strong identity with his or her ethnic group or that ethnicity is important in his or her life. Ethnicity is rather unimportant in the lives of many highly assimilated and upper-status members of ethnic groups but tends to be a cogent factor in the lives of many lower-class ethnics.

Stages of Ethnicity

We often assume that ethnic groups are monolithic and have rather homogeneous needs and characteristics. Rarely is sufficient attention given to the enormous differences within ethnic groups. We also tend to see ethnic groups as static and unchanging. However, ethnic groups within modernized democratic societies are highly diverse, complex, and changing entities. I have developed a typology that attempts to describe some of the differences existing between individual members of ethnic groups. The typology assumes that individual members of an ethnic group are at different stages of ethnic development and that these stages can be identified and described.

The typology is a preliminary ideal-type construct in the Weberian sense and constitutes a set of hypotheses based on the existing and emerging theory and research, and on my observations and study of ethnic behavior.[8] The typology is presented here because it can be used as a departure point for classroom discussions of ethnicity. *However, its tentative and hypothetical nature should be emphasized in class discussions.*

Stage 1. Ethnic Psychological Captivity. During this stage, the individual has internalized negative ideologies and beliefs about his or her ethnic group that are institutionalized within the society. Consequently, the Stage-1 person exemplifies ethnic self-rejection and low self-esteem. The individual is ashamed of his or her ethnic group and identity during this stage and may respond in a number of ways, including avoiding situations that lead to contact with other ethnic groups or striving aggressively to become highly culturally assimilated.

Stage 2. Ethnic Encapsulation. Stage 2 is characterized by ethnic encapsulation and ethnic exclusiveness, including voluntary separatism. The individual participates primarily within his or her own ethnic community and believes that his or her ethnic group is superior to that of others. Many Stage-2 individuals, such as many Anglo-Saxon Protestants, have internalized the dominant societal myths about the superiority of their ethnic or racial group and the innate inferiority of other ethnic groups and races. Many individuals who are socialized within all-White suburban communities and who live highly ethnocentric and encapsulated lives may be described as Stage-2 individuals. Alice Miel describes these kinds of individuals in *The Shortchanged Children of Suburbia.*[9]

Stage 3. Ethnic Identity Clarification. At this stage, the individual is able to clarify personal attitudes and ethnic identity, reduce intrapsychic conflict, and develop positive attitudes toward his or her ethnic group. The individual learns to accept self, thus developing the characteristics needed to accept and respond more positively to outside ethnic groups. Self-acceptance is a requisite to accepting and responding positively to other people.

Stage 4. Biethnicity. Individuals within this stage have a healthy sense of ethnic identity and the psychological characteristics and skills needed to participate in their own ethnic culture, as well as in another ethnic culture. The individual also has a strong desire to function effectively in two ethnic cultures. We may describe such an individual as *biethnic* or *bicultural.*

Stage 5. Multiethnicity. Stage 5 describes the idealized goal for citizenship identity within an ethnically pluralistic nation. The individual at this stage is able to function, at least at minimal levels, within several ethnic sociocultural environments and to understand, appreciate, and share the values, symbols, and institutions of several ethnic cultures. Such multiethnic perspectives and feelings, I hypothesize, help the individual to live a more enriched and fulfilling life and to formulate more creative and novel solutions to personal and public problems.

Stage 6: Globalism and Global Competency. Individuals within Stage 6 have clarified, reflective, and positive ethnic, national, and global identifications and the knowledge, skills, attitudes, and abilities needed to function in ethnic cultures within their own nation as well as in cultures within other nations. These individuals have the ideal delicate balance of ethnic, national, and global identifications, commitments, literacy, and behaviors. They have internalized the universalistic ethical values and principles of humankind and have the skills, competencies, and commitments needed to act on these values.

Characteristics of the Typology

The emerging stages of ethnicity typology is an ideal-type construct and should be viewed as dynamic and multidimensional rather than as static and unilinear. The characteristics within the stages exist on a continuum. Thus, within Stage 1, individuals are more or less ethnically psychologically captive; some individuals are more ethnically psychologically captive than others.

The division between the stages is blurred rather than sharp. Thus, a continuum exists between as well as within the stages. The ethnically encapsulated individual (Stage 2) does not suddenly attain clarification and acceptance of personal ethnic identity (Stage 3). This process is gradual and developmental. Also, the stages should not be viewed as strictly sequential and unilinear. I am hypothesizing that some individuals may never experience a particular stage. However, I also hypothesize that once an individual experiences a particular stage that person is likely to experience the stages above it sequentially and developmentally. However, individuals may experience the stages upward, downward, or in a zigzag pattern. Under certain conditions, for example, the biethnic (Stage 4) individual may become multiethnic (Stage 5); under new conditions the same individual may again become biethnic (Stage 4), ethnically identified (Stage 3), and ethnically encapsulated (Stage 2). For example, many individual members of northern White ethnic groups became increasingly more ethnically encapsulated as busing for school desegregation gained momentum in northern cities such as Boston during the 1970s.

Figure 3–2 illustrates the dynamic and multidimensional characteristics of the development of ethnicity among individuals. Note especially the arrowed lines, which indicate that continua exist both horizontally and vertically.

Ethnic Diversity

Students should learn that there are many different ethnic cultures in our society, and that these differences are not likely to vanish. Events cause them to emerge in each new generation. This concept is the antithesis of the melting pot

Figure 3–2   *The Emerging Stages of Ethnicity: A Preliminary Typology.*

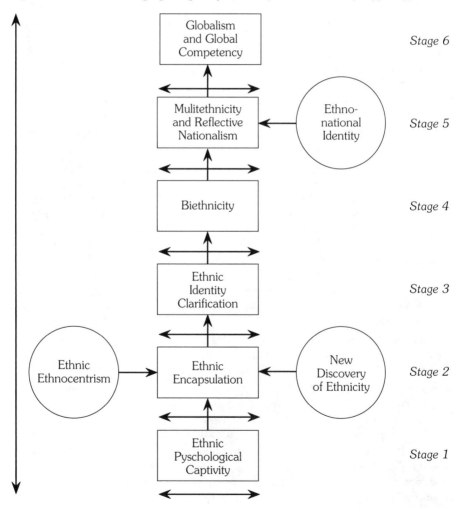

theory. When studying about ethnic differences in the United States, students should be helped to understand that even though we have not experienced a true melting pot, most ethnic groups have acquired many mainstream American cultural characteristics.

Many ethnic individuals are *bicultural*; that is, they usually acquire culture traits of mainstream American culture but also retain many of their ethnic characteristics. Even though the more upwardly mobile members of ethnic groups tend to be less ethnic than are lower-class members, this generalization is nevertheless valid. A highly acculturated Chinese American, for example, will often marry a Chinese, eat Chinese foods, and belong to Chinese social organizations. Many ethnic youths attend public schools during the day and a language or ethnic school after regular school hours or on the weekend. Most African Americans who obtain college degrees speak standard English on their jobs and in other settings where it is appropriate to conform to the dominant society's norm. However, when socializing with less assimilated relatives and friends, they often use many words and phrases that linguists call *Black English* or Ebonics. Upwardly mobile Mexican Americans will eat "Anglo-Saxon steak" at fancy Anglo restaurants with their Anglo friends, but they often drive to Spanish-speaking neighborhoods to eat foods such as enchiladas and chiles rellenos.

In other words, ethnic individuals acquire those mainstream cultural traits necessary for them to survive in the wider society but retain many of the elements of their ethnic culture. The more upwardly mobile an individual is, the more likely he or she is to acquire mainstream cultural traits. The acquisition of mainstream Anglo-American speech, behavior, and values is necessary for upward mobility in the United States because mainstream Americans control entry to most social, economic, and political institutions.

When studying about ethnic differences, students should learn that cultural differences exist within as well as between various ethnic groups. Too many Americans think of ethnic groups as monolithic, and they find it difficult to understand why conflict exists within ethnic groups. *It is very important for students to study about the differences that exist within ethnic groups.* When many mainstream Americans are introduced to an African American or an Asian American, certain stereotypic images often emerge. They often assume that all African Americans know something about the Black ghetto because of their personal experiences and can tell them how the Black community feels about busing or interracial marriage. Many people assume that all Asian Americans are stoic, shy, and have a high scientific aptitude.

It is true that we can associate certain general characteristics with the various American ethnic groups. However, within these groups, individuals embrace these characteristics to varying degrees. Some *deliberately* attempt to reject them. When we meet an individual and know only that he or she is a Mexican American, and nothing else, there are but a few conclusive statements we can accurately make about that person.

Mexican Americans, like Asian Americans and African Americans, are a highly diverse group. Some Mexicans identify strongly with this group's political movement and wish to be called Chicanos. Others, especially those in the upper classes, tend to identify more strongly with their Spanish heritage and consider the word *Chicano* pejorative and insulting. Such individuals are more likely to prefer the term *Latin American* or *Spanish American* and to reject their Indian heritage. Some Mexican Americans consider themselves Spanish, even though their biological traits may be identical to others who consider themselves Chicanos or Mexican Americans.

The tremendous differences that exist within various ethnic groups often make it difficult for many mainstream Americans to understand why many Japanese Americans are anti-Korean, why the Nisei (first-generation Japanese American) often express disappointment about the values and life-styles of the Sansei (second generation), or why some upwardly mobile Mexican Americans disdain Mexican migrant workers. Intragroup differences and conflict exist within dominant ethnic groups as well as within minority groups. However, Americans tend to understand why a German-American corporation president might disdain a German-American dishwasher. The African American, however, who openly wonders about what life is like in the Black inner-city may be considered an oddity by many mainstream Americans. During the 1980s, class differences within the African American community deepened considerably.

Cultural Assimilation

When a member of an ethnic minority group acquires the behavior patterns, life-styles, values, and language of the mainstream culture we say that he or she has become culturally assimilated. *Cultural assimilation* is the process by which an individual or group acquires the culture traits of a different ethnic or cultural group. Because the dominant group controls most of the social, economic, and political institutions in a society, members of ethnic minority groups must acquire its cultural traits to move up the social and economic ladder. When studying this concept, it is important for students to learn that although people of color may become totally assimilated culturally (i.e., in cultural characteristics they may become indistinguishable from Anglo-Saxon Protestants), they will still be victims of discrimination and racism because of their different physical characteristics.

A widespread myth is that Mexican Americans and African Americans experience discrimination because they often have meager educations and live in barrios and ghettos. Even though it is true that many Mexican Americans and African Americans are members of the lower socioeconomic classes, and that all lower-class individuals are treated differently than middle- and upper-class people, it is also true that Mexican Americans and African Americans with high educational levels and incomes frequently experience discrimination *because of their color*. Because American racism is based largely on skin color, no degree of cultural assimilation eliminates it.

Some discussion of forced assimilation and cultural genocide should take place when students study cultural assimilation. Assimilation often occurs when a minority group "voluntarily" acquires the behavior patterns and life-styles of the dominant group in order to attain social mobility and occupational success. I use the word *voluntarily* here somewhat reluctantly because without some degree of cultural assimilation, a group that is very different culturally may not be able to survive in a particular culture. However, in the history of the United States, some forms of cultural assimilation that took place were totally nonvoluntary and might be called *forced assimilation* because the cultures of certain groups were deliberately destroyed (*cultural genocide*). These groups were forced to acquire the language, life-styles, and values of the dominant culture.

Individuals and groups who refused to accept the dominant culture were sometimes the victims of severe punishments, such as death. The cultures of African groups were deliberately destroyed by the slave masters. This cultural destruction began on the slave ships. It seems that systematic and deliberate attempts were made to destroy Indian cultures. These efforts were highly successful. Many of the cultural elements of these groups now exist only in the pages of history, and sometimes not even there because they were often destroyed before they could be recorded.

Acculturation

When an Anglo-Saxon Protestant eats chow mein and a Chinese American sees a Shakespearean play, we say that *acculturation* is occurring because two different ethnic groups are exchanging cultural elements and complexes. Although the exchange of cultural traits is widespread within U.S. society, we often think of the cultural traits that ethnic minorities acquire from dominant ethnic groups, but we hear too little about the cultural traits that dominant groups have acquired from ethnic minorities. Since this is the case, you should highlight the ethnic minority cultural traits that have been acquired by mainstream Americans.

Students should study about the contributions African Americans have made to American music, especially their spirituals, blues, and jazz.[10] American culture traits of Indian origin are rarely mentioned in schoolbooks. As Vogel has noted, "As Rome hid its debt to the Etruscans, we have obscured our inheritance from the red men. Anthropologists know that acculturation proceeds in both directions when two societies are in any kind of contact, and that even a conquered people helps to shape the destiny of their overlords."[11] Indian contributions to American culture include the selection of sites for many American cities, as well as dress styles, tobacco, foods, and values related to the veneration and preservation of the earth.

All American ethnic groups, including people of color, have contributed material elements (such as foods and fashions), as well as nonmaterial traits (such as values and norms), to mainstream American culture. Students can use a *data retrieval chart* similar to the one illustrated earlier in Table 3–2 to record examples of contributions that various groups have made to American life. This type of chart is a convenient tool for studying cultural contributions as well as other aspects of ethnic group life in the United States.

Community Culture

Most Americans grow up in communities in which ethnic and cultural values, life-styles, language patterns, and behavior patterns differ from those of many other groups. This is as true for Puerto Ricans who grow up in East Harlem as it is for Anglo-Saxon Protestants who are raised in wealthy suburban neighborhoods such as Mercer Island, Washington, or Forest Park, Illinois. We usually do not think that middle-class or wealthy White suburbs have a unique culture because the culture within them constitutes the dominant one in the United States. However, Alice Miel in *The Shortchanged Children of Suburbia*, and Jules Henry in *Culture against Man* and *Pathways to Madness*, delineate some of the unique cultural traits of middle-class mainstream American communities.[12]

Because most Americans grow up in ethnic or cultural enclaves, they are *culturally encapsulated*. Ethnic minority groups, in order to attain social and economic mobility, are usually forced out of their ethnic encapsulation. However, mainstream Americans, who control entry to most social, economic, and political institutions, often spend their entire lives within their own unique cultural communities. The cultures of other groups remain foreign, nonhuman, and exotic to them. African Americans who grow up in small southern rural communities often think that everyone eats sweet potato pie, chitterlings, and hog head and black-eyed peas to celebrate New Year's Day. Without this kind of New Year's meal, bad luck will be imminent. When these African Americans migrate to northern and western cities and begin to participate in social institutions that have other norms and values, they discover, sometimes abruptly, that their world is not the entire world, and that not only do many people not eat sweet potato pie, but they have serious questions about people who eat hog intestines!

A sound multicultural curriculum should help all students—from both majority and minority groups—to break out of their cultural and ethnic enclaves and learn that there are many ways to live and survive and that because an individual has a different life-style, he or she is not inferior or superior. Many youths of color tend to devalue their ethnic cultures when they begin to participate in the mainstream society. Mainstream students should learn that there are different ways of living that are as legitimate and functional as their own. I am not suggesting that the school should attempt to force different life-styles on students. However, the school should help release students from *cultural* and *ethnic captivity* so that they can learn to appreciate cultural differences and thus learn how to live with people who speak a different dialect, eat different foods, and value things they may not value. We can learn to respect and appreciate different cultures without choosing to participate in them. Participation should be an individual decision. However, cultural understanding and empathy for other people should be fostered by the school.

Socialization and Related Concepts

Socialization

Socialization describes the process by which people become human. Sociologists, who use socialization as their central concept, assume that even though people are born with the physical capacities to become human, they are capable of becoming many things, including animal-like. Sociologists assume that people acquire human traits and characteristics only by interacting with the human group. The group makes use of norms and sanctions to ensure that the individual acquires the attitudes, values, and behavior patterns it deems appropriate.

Socialization and related concepts, such as values and norms, are important in multicultural education because they provide useful insights that help us understand how individuals acquire prejudices and ethnocentric values, and how people learn to discriminate against other groups. Socialization theory teaches us that children are not born with racial antipathies. Children learn these attitudes from the adults in their environment early in life.[13] Modern sociological research and theory dispel old notions, such as the racial and cultural difference theory, which held that individuals have an instinctive fear and dislike of people who are physically and culturally different from them. Also discredited is the traumatic experience theory, which states that "racial prejudice emerges in an individual following a traumatic experience involving a member of a minority group during early childhood."[14] Negative attitudes toward certain ethnic groups are institutionalized within our society. Children acquire them by interacting with "significant others" in their environment and reading books in school, watching television, and going to their place of worship. Most institutions within our society, including the schools, reinforce and teach negative lessons about America's ethnic minority groups. Students need to understand the relationship between socialization, prejudice, racism, and discrimination.

Prejudice and Discrimination

Prejudice is a set of rigid and unfavorable attitudes toward a particular group or groups that is formed in disregard of facts. The prejudiced individual responds to perceived members of these groups on the basis of his or her preconceptions, tending to disregard behavior or personal characteristics that are inconsistent with his or her biases. Individuals who are anti-Semitic will argue that Jews are loud and rudely aggressive no matter how many Jews they meet who do not have these characteristics. Prejudiced people see the world through a set of blinders and refuse to perceive people, incidents, and groups that do not reinforce their negative attitudes and stereotypes.

Although prejudice and discrimination are highly related and are usually associated, they are different concepts. Prejudice is a set of *attitudes*, whereas discrimination consists of differential *behavior* directed toward a stigmatized group. Rose has defined discrimination "as the differential treatment of individuals considered to belong to particular groups or social categories."[15]

Merton has developed a useful typology of discrimination that you can use with students in the middle, upper, and high school grades.[16] Merton's typology makes it clear that a prejudiced individual will not necessarily discriminate and that an individual who is not prejudiced may discriminate. Merton's typology clarifies the extent to which discrimination is contextual, situational, and related to the social settings in which individuals function. Merton identifies four types of persons:

> *Type I: The unprejudiced nondiscriminator or all-weather liberal.* This individual believes in racial equality and acts on his or her beliefs.
>
> *Type II: The unprejudiced discriminator or fair-weather liberal.* This is a person of expediency. He or she does not have personal prejudices but will discriminate when it is easier or more profitable to do so.
>
> *Type III: The prejudiced nondiscriminator or fair-weather illiberal.* This person does not believe in racial equality but does not discriminate because of laws or external factors that negatively sanction racial discrimination.
>
> *Type IV: The prejudiced discriminator or the all-weather illiberal.* This is the bigot who is not ashamed of his or her attitudes and who acts on his or her prejudices and beliefs.

When using Merton's typology with students, point out that it is an ideal-type conceptualization. This means that no actual individual is a pure type of any of Merton's four types. Rather, the typology can be used to think of and to classify individuals who approach one of the types. Students can also use Merton's typology to describe individuals they encounter in their readings, media presentations, or in their social settings. They can use it to analyze and think about their own behavior and attitudes toward other racial and ethnic groups.

Race

Physical anthropologists attempt to divide the human species into subgroups on the basis of biological traits and characteristics. They use the concept of *race* to differentiate between the various human subgroups. However, anthropologists have had considerable difficulty in trying to structure valid racial categories because of the wide variety of traits and characteristics that human groups share, the extensive mixture among groups, and because the racial categories they have formulated have been largely arbitrary. Consequently, the schemes they have developed for classifying human races vary greatly in number and in characteristics.

Montagu classifies humankind into four major groups: Negroid or Black, the Archaic White or Australoid, the Caucasoid or White, and the Mongoloid.[17] Oliver presents a scheme with seven major races: Early Mongoloid, Late Mongoloid, Negro, Bushmen, Australian, Pygmy Negroids, and White.[18] Nine different racial types are identified in *Encyclopaedia Britannica*.[19] There is considerable inconsistency in how physical anthropologists classify human racial groups.

Montagu, who calls race "man's most dangerous myth," believes that the four categories he identifies can best be regarded as major *human groups* rather than as races. He seriously questions the validity of the concept of race and believes it has been a highly destructive factor in the history of humankind. He writes, "It is impossible to make the sort of racial classifications which some anthropologists and others have attempted. The fact is that all human beings are so . . . mixed with regard to origin that between different groups of individuals . . . 'overlapping' of physical traits is the rule."[20]

In most societies, the social significance of race is much more important than the presumed physical differences among groups. The social definitions of race also reveal the arbitrariness of the concept and why it might well be humankind's most dangerous myth. In the United States, any person with any acknowledged Black African blood is classified as Black, regardless of that person's phenotype. Many such persons, of course, look completely Caucasian and classify themselves as White. The majority of them accept the racial category imposed on them by society. We have no reliable statistics of how many such persons "pass" as White.

In early Mexico, the Spaniards invented so many concepts and terms for different types of racial mixtures that the cumbersome system of racial classification eventually became so complex and dysfunctional that it died of its own weight.[21] Partly as a result, the attitudes toward differences in skin color and in physical characteristics are considerably more flexible in former Spanish America than they are in the United States. In contemporary Puerto Rican society, for example, individuals with a wide range of skin colors are regarded as White. Other variables, such as social status, income, education, and hair texture are important in determining an individual's racial designation.[22] In Mexico, the rural Indian can become a Mestizo by moving from the village to the city, becoming assimilated into the dominant Mestizo culture, and learning to speak Spanish.[23] By exploring the complex ramifications of the social meaning of race in both the United States and in other nations, students will be able to gain a better understanding of both the arbitrariness and political implications of the concept of race.

Racism

Racism is closely related to the idea of race. Racism is a belief that human groups can be validly grouped on the basis of their biological traits and that these identifiable groups inherit certain mental, personality, and cultural characteristics that determine their behavior. A corollary belief is that some biological groups, such as Caucasians, have superior mental and behavioral traits and that others, such as African Americans and Indians, are mentally and culturally inferior. Van den Berghe defines racism as "any set of beliefs that organic, genetically transmitted differences (whether real or imagined) between human groups are intrinsically associated with the presence or the absence of certain socially relevant abilities or characteristics, hence that such differences are a legitimate basis of invidious distinctions between groups socially defined as races."[24]

Racism, however, is not merely a set of beliefs but is practiced when a group has the power to enforce laws, institutions, and norms, based on its beliefs, which oppress and dehumanize another group. Gay stresses the behavioral aspects of racism: "It is an extension of an attitude into an action. Although the focus of attention is on *behavior,* attitudes are of crucial importance for they are the motivating forces which determine the nature of the actions one takes."[25] In a racist society, the political, economic, and social systems reflect and perpetuate racism; thus, racism is institutionalized.

Even though ethnocentrism is found in all human societies, racism is not. The kind of racism that exists in the modern world is a rather recent historical development. In the ancient world, different groups and peoples were often the victims of oppression or were enslaved. However, discrimination was rarely done on the basis of racial characteristics. Rather, it was usually based on religious, cultural, political, and social-class differences. Social scientists have noted that with few exceptions racism as we know it today was not practiced up through the seventeenth century.[26] According to van den Berghe, however, racism "has been independently discovered and rediscovered by various peoples at various times in history."[27] However, he notes that it was not until the nineteenth century that racism became an elaborate ideology distinguishable from ethnocentrism.[28] Racism developed in the modern world to justify the exploitation and enslavement of aboriginal peoples by Europeans when they began their explorations into Africa, the Caribbean, and the Americas.

The European explorers and slave owners were Christians who needed an ideology to justify slavery when it began to be attacked. They needed an ideology they could view as consistent with both their religious beliefs and economic institutions. The arguments they structured eventually blossomed into an elaborate racist ideology. According to van den Berghe, "Racism was congruent with prevailing forms of capitalist exploitation, notably with slavery in the New World and incipient colonial expansion in Africa. There is no question that the desire to rationalize exploitation of non-European peoples fostered the elaboration of a complex ideology of paternalism and racism."[29] Montagu echoes the same point: "The idea of 'race' was, in fact, the deliberate creation of an exploiting class which was seeking to maintain and defend its privileges against what was profitably regarded as an inferior social caste."[30]

When students study racism, they can try to determine the extent to which it is institutionalized within American society, such as in the mass media or within schools and churches, and how racism is manifested in employment and in housing. The students can also discuss whether they are unconscious participants within an institutionalized racist system and what they might be able to do to change the system. Geneva Gay has distinguished *institutionalized, individual,* and *cultural racism.*[31] Fruitful activities for students are to attempt to formulate working definitions for each of these concepts and to identify examples of them.

Ethnocentrism

Most ethnic groups within a society tend to think that their culture is superior to the culture of other groups. This is especially true of the most powerful and dominant groups. In our society, Anglo-Saxon Protestants are the dominant group. Many of them feel that their culture is superior to the cultures of other groups and define *culture* as those aspects of *their* culture that they value highly, such as classical music and paintings by the European masters.

Students must understand *ethnocentrism* to comprehend fully the complex dimensions of American racism and the separatist movements that have emerged within ethnic minority groups. Although some minority persons, because of their socialization, tend to have low self-concepts and value the mainstream culture over their own, ethnocentrism among people of color escalated in the late 1960s. Some African Americans, Mexican Americans, and Asian Americans extolled the virtues of their cultures and demanded *separatism* and independent institutions. It may be that some degree of ethnocentrism is necessary for a group to attain cohesion and a strong identity, and that separatism is, as Sizemore has suggested, a necessary step toward inclusion within the larger society.[32] However, you can ask students this question: How much cultural and political separatism can a society experience and remain cohesive? If this question is raised, several related ones should also be posed: If a society needs some common goals in order to survive, what groups within it should determine these goals? How might we change our society so that each ethnic group can influence policy that shapes common societal goals? At present, dominant groups determine both societal goals and the means to attain them. However, ethnic groups of color made it clear during the 1960s and 1970s that they will not accept this kind of power arrangement without protest and conflict. These kinds of questions and problems, related to ethnocentrism, should constitute a vital part of the multicultural curriculum.

Values

Those elements within a culture to which individuals and groups attach a high worth are called *values.* Within a social system are values that influence the group's feelings toward foods, human life, behavior patterns, and attitudes toward people who belong to outgroups. Sociologists have studied how values develop within societies and how they are inculcated by individuals in a community. Values, like attitudes and beliefs, are learned from the groups in which the individual is socialized; we are not born with a set of values and do not derive them independently. Groups use norms and sanctions to assure that individuals inculcate the pervasive values within their culture or microculture.

Even though there are some common values embraced by most American communities (such as a respect for the lives of those regarded as human beings and kind treatment of children), these shared values are often defined and perceived differently within various ethnic microcultures, or they take diverse forms. Other values are important in some ethnic communities and largely absent in others.

The Nisei usually endorse many traditional Japanese values, including etiquette, personal control, the samurai ethic, a high respect for authority, the achievement ethic, and a strong sense of family obligation. Family obligation in traditional Japanese cultures was often considered more important than personal freedom. Although many of the Nisei values have eroded among the Sansei because the Sansei are highly culturally assimilated, important vestiges of these values remain in Japanese communities today, especially among the aged. Some of these values, such as a high respect for authority and a strong sense of family obligation, conflict with mainstream American values. In mainstream American society, authority is often challenged. It is rarely concentrated in one family member. Mainstream Americans also tend to be highly individualistic rather than group oriented.

Values in ethnic minority communities are often different from those in mainstream American society. In the traditional Puerto Rican family, the girl was highly protected, and father was the undisputed head of the family. The family was also a highly interdependent unit. Uncles, aunts, and other relatives were often considered integral parts of the family unit. This type of extended family was also common among African Americans in the deep South. As African Americans and Puerto Ricans become more urbanized and more heavily represented in the middle classes, these aspects of their cultures diminish. However, the extended family is still a part of these ethnic cultures. Puerto Rican girls in New York City often do not have the same freedom to come and go with boys as do their Anglo-American peers.

When American Indians are studied in school, students are often introduced to certain stereotypic components of their cultures, such as tipis, baskets, canoes, or moccasins. These physical elements were parts of the cultures of certain American Indian groups, but they were by no means the most essential parts of them. Thus, students gain a superficial view of Indian cultures when they study only tangible cultural elements. *The essence of a culture can be understood only by studying its central values and their relationships to the daily lives of the people.*

The Indian view of people and their relationship to the universe must be studied to understand Indian values toward people and nature. Indian groups tended to look on the universe as a whole, with every object having a sacred life;

to separate people from nature was antithetical to the Great Spirit, for to the Great Spirit all was life.

It is the values and related life-styles of ethnic communities that constitute their essence, not chow mein, basket weaving, sombreros, or soul food. These values and related behavioral characteristics and perspectives should be emphasized in the curriculum, not exotic cultural elements whose major outcome is the reinforcement of stereotypes. However, I am not suggesting that tangible cultural elements should not be studied, but that they should not be emphasized. Even though the study of ethnic values should constitute a large part of the multicultural curriculum, it is important to realize, however, that the values of all of America's ethnic groups are slowly changing, especially in urban areas. People of color are becoming urbanized at a faster rate than mainstream Americans. It is also important to remember that highly assimilated and higher-status members of ethnic minority groups may share few, if any, characteristics with their more humble brothers and sisters. Despite these caveats, ethnic values are an integral part of American life. They add strength and diversity to the U.S. national culture. This significant message should be communicated to students in all grades.

Self-Concept

An individual's feelings, attitudes, and evaluations of self constitute his or her self-concept.[33] Each individual has a total picture of self that is largely a product of the individual's interactions within his or her social environment. How a person views himself or herself is cogently influenced by significant persons within his or her social world. Often individuals who exercise power over a person's life, such as parents and teachers, are important influences on the development of an individual's self-concept.

Many of the messages that youths of color receive from significant individuals and institutions within American society regarding their ethnic groups are negative and dehumanizing. This fact has led some social scientists to hypothesize that youths of color internalize the negative images of themselves perpetuated by the larger society and thus have lower self-concepts than do White children. Prior to the 1960s, studies by researchers such as the Clarks, Goodman, and Trager and Yarrow consistently concluded that most Black children had lower self-concepts than did most White children.[34] This research also indicated that African-American youths make more incorrect racial self-identifications than do White children.

Some researchers have seriously questioned the negative self-concept hypothesis.[35] These researchers argue that the self-concepts of African-American youths tend to be as positive as, and in some cases more positive than, the self-concepts of White children. Baughman argues that the African-American child's positive self-concept is formed prior to his or her experiences with the White world. The research on the self-concepts of children of color is contradictory and inconclusive.

Intercultural Communication and Related Concepts

Communication

Social science literature is replete with definitions of communication. An actor whose behavior and symbols are perceived and interpreted by another individual are common to these many definitions. When an individual communicates, he or she uses symbols that are interpreted by the perceiver. Successful communication occurs when both the sender and receiver of the symbols interpret them in a similar way. Communication is unsuccessful when the sender and receiver of the symbols interpret them differently.

Individuals who are socialized within the same culture or microculture are more likely to have shared meanings of symbols than are individuals who are socialized within different microcultures, cultures, and nations. The wider the differences in cultures or microcultures between individuals, the more ineffective communication is likely to be. A middle-class Australian is less likely to interpret correctly the symbols made by a lower-class African American than is a middle-class mainstream American.

Intercultural Communication

In response to the increased communication between nations and world cultures (caused in part by new technological developments and a heightened interest in ethnic minorities in the United States), a new field, *intercultural communication*, has emerged. This field draws concepts and generalizations from various disciplines and studies the variables involved in communication across cultures. The field is also known as cross-cultural communication, inter-ethnic communication, and transracial communication. Samovar and Porter state, *"Intercultural communication occurs whenever a message producer is a member of one culture and the message receiver is a member of another."*[36] Communication often fails across cultures because the message producer and the receiver have few shared symbols and have been socialized within environments in which the same symbols are interpreted differently.

Intercultural communication is an important concept in multicultural studies. It helps explain many of the conflicts and misunderstandings that often occur between ethnic groups in the United States. During the 1960s, many African Americans interpreted Black power symbols positively and viewed them as symbols of racial pride and political efficacy. Whites often viewed Black power negatively and considered it threatening and a form of Black racism.

Cross-cultural communication can be improved when individuals from different cultures begin to interpret symbols in similar ways and when they have a strong desire to communicate effectively. When teaching about intercultural communication, you can identify many examples of barriers to effective communication across ethnic boundaries on radio and television news programs and in local and national newspapers and magazines. The class can use role-playing and discussion techniques to explore ways in which cross-ethnic and cross-racial communication can be improved.

Perception

Social scientists define *perception* as the "complex process by which people select, organize, and interpret sensory stimulation into a meaningful and coherent picture of the world."[37] This concept helps us better understand the factors that influence how individuals come to know and interpret their physical and social environments. Many factors influence how people view their world. Social and cultural factors are cogent variables. In our society, race, ethnic group membership, and social class often influence how people see and interpret events, situations, and social issues. An African American civil rights leader and a mainstream American corporation president are likely to view the high unemployment rate among African American youths quite differently.

Cultural, ethnic, and racial variables affect the perception of the historian, the writer, and the artist, as well as the layperson. Culture and ethnicity may have a cogent impact on a particular ethnic historian, writer, or artist, or practically no influence. The individual's level of identification with his or her cultural or ethnic group will highly influence whether his or her work will be affected by culture or ethnicity. Ethnicity tends to be a strong factor in people's lives in a society characterized by inequality and high levels of ethnic discrimination; it tends to be a less important factor in a society in which the various ethnic groups experience social and economic equality. The United States is highly stratified along racial, social class, and ethnic lines. Consequently, culture, ethnicity, and race are cogent factors that often influence members of both dominant and minority groups, including the members of these groups who are historians, writers, and artists.

Historically, American history and literature written by mainstream Americans have been mainstream-centric and have interpreted events and situations primarily from mainstream perspectives. Often, minority group cultures were not regarded as worthy of inclusion in literature anthologies, American history textbooks, and in music and art textbooks. Since the 1960s many mainstream American historians and writers have attempted to include more about ethnic groups in their works. However, often their interpretations of the experiences of other ethnic groups are mainstream-centric—although more benign than in the past. Since the 1970s, more historical, sociological, and artistic works by people of color have been produced. Many of the perspectives presented in these works are refreshing. They add a vital component to our academic, artistic, literary, and social worlds.

Historical Bias

The social, cultural, and ethnic variables that influence how historians perceive their data result in *historical bias*. A historian's view of the past is influenced by his or her culture, personal biases, purposes for writing, availability of data, and the times in which he or she lives and writes. Because the historian can never totally reconstruct past events and is unable to report all the data he or she uncovers about particular events, he or she must use some criteria to determine which aspects of an event to report. The historian must also interpret historical events. History cannot be written without presenting interpretations and points of view. Because this is the case, it is important for you to teach students about the biases inherent in all historical writing and how to recognize and analyze them.

It is especially important for you to teach students how to analyze historical materials that are related to America's ethnic minority groups. The histories of minority groups have been written largely by members of the mainstream groups. They often write histories of ethnic minorities that legitimize the dominant social and economic structure and that often depict minorities negatively. Mainstream American writers and social scientists often perpetuate myths and stereotypes about ethnic minorities to explain why they "deserve" the low status in society to which they are most often assigned. Such stereotypes and myths are widespread within U.S. society; for example, African Americans were enslaved because they were uncivilized and lazy; slavery would not only civilize them, but would also deliver their souls to God; Indians were savages who had to be civilized by Whites in order to survive; Japanese Americans were a threat to national survival during World War II and thus had to be confined to relocation camps for national security. Some social scientists and other scholars are gatekeepers of the status quo; they generate research legitimizing the myths and stereotypes that dominant groups create about powerless groups to justify their status.[38]

Throughout human society, history has been written by the victors and not by the vanquished. Thus, most students in our schools study histories of American Indians and African Americans that were written by American mainstream historians who most often had little empathy or understanding of those cultures. Since this is the case, you should help students view the experiences of ethnic minority groups from *their perspectives.* I am not suggesting that the histories of ethnic minorities written by mainstream writers should be banned from the schools. However, the study of America must also be seen through the eyes of the vanquished, since students now study it primarily from the viewpoints of the victors. Even though both views can add to our understanding of the American experience, we must stress other viewpoints because mainstream views of American history are so widespread within our schools and the larger society. Only by trying to see this nation from the viewpoints of victimized peoples will we be able to understand fully its complexity.

Histories and social science accounts written by ethnic minority writers, like the writings of dominant groups, reflect particular points of view and biases. However, students need to study these writings seriously in order to gain a "balanced" perspective on U.S. life and history.

Environmental Perception

The attitudes, feelings, and ideas that people have about their physical and cultural environment are referred to as *environmental perception.* When studying this concept, you should help students discover how different people who inhabit various regions often have different and conflicting perceptions of the same geographical regions. Many people who live in the outlying regions of a metropolitan area often consider the barrio a dilapidated and dangerous slum that should be avoided if at all possible. Many such people, on their way to other parts of the city, will take routes around the barrio because they consider it dangerous. The Spanish-speaking people who live in the barrio may have positive feelings toward their neighborhood and consider it a safe place in which to live and work. Many people, whose entire lives have been confined within their ethnic communities, might be surprised to learn that other people consider their home neighborhoods a ghetto and even more surprised to learn that some believe that it is a dangerous place in which to live.

When studying about the various perceptions that different people have of the same geographical locations, the students might explore what causes divergent perceptions. Many Puerto Ricans who live in the barrio know little about any other world and have had few experiences that would cause them to feel that their community is deviant or dangerous. On the other hand, many mainstream Americans who live in suburbs obtain most of their information about the barrio from the news media, which tend to publish highly sensationalized stories about life in the barrio and to emphasize the criminal events that take place within it. Even though it is true that certain kinds of crimes occur more often in lower-class neighborhoods than in higher-status ones, it is also true that many inhabitants of ethnic neighborhoods feel relatively safe in them. Unlike the stranger in the neighborhood, they know how best to survive in their communities.

Power and Related Concepts

Power

The ethnic experience within the United States cannot be understood without considering the role that the struggle for power among competing ethnic groups has played in shaping American history. History and contemporary social science teach us that in every past and present culture individuals have had, and still have, widely unequal opportunities to share fully in the reward systems and benefits of their society. The basis for unequal distribution of rewards is determined by elitist groups in which power is centered.

Almost every decision made by people in power, including economic policy, is made to enhance, legitimize, and reinforce their power. Powerful groups not only make laws, but they also determine which traits and characteristics are necessary for full societal participation. They determine necessary traits on the basis of the similarity of such traits to their own values, physical characteristics, life-styles, and behavior. At various periods in history, powerful groups have used celibacy, gender, ethnicity, race, religion, as well as many other variables, to determine which individuals and groups would be given or denied opportunities for social mobility and full societal participation.

In colonial America, male Anglo-Saxon Protestants with property controlled most social, political, economic, and military institutions. These were the men who wrote the Declaration of Independence and the United States Constitution. They excluded from full participation in decision making those people such as African Americans and American Indians who were different from themselves. Our founding fathers had a deep suspicion of and contempt for individuals who were culturally and racially different. They invented and perpetuated stereotypes and myths about excluded groups to justify their oppression.[39] The United States, like all other nations, is still controlled by a few powerful groups who deny individuals opportunities to participate in society on the basis of how similar such individuals are to themselves.

When studying about power relationships in American society, students can be asked to hypothesize about how we can make our nation an open society and thus more consistent with our national ideology. They can define an *open society* as one in which rewards and opportunities are not necessarily evenly distributed, but are distributed on the basis of the knowledge and skills that each person, regardless of his or her ethnic characteristics, can contribute to the fulfillment of the needs of society. Students should be asked to discuss which of their hypotheses are most sound, how actions based on them might be implemented, and to state their limitations. When studying about power, students should also be introduced to the related concepts: oppression, political alienation, colony, colonized, and separatism.

Some civil rights leaders and social scientists compare the social and political conditions of people of color in the United States to the situations of developing nations that were colonies of Western empires. Such writers argue, with some validity, that ethnic minority communities, like colonized nations, are economically and politically powerless and are almost totally dependent on powerful groups in America in order to survive.[40] To gain more political and economic power, separatist movements emerged within some ethnic minority communities in the 1960s. The primary goal of such movements was to create social, economic, and political institutions that were controlled by the ethnic group, thus making it less dependent on other groups for jobs, shelter, and the satisfaction of other survival needs. One of the most researched of such movements is the Nation of Islam.[41]

Social Protest and Resistance

Throughout U.S. history, movements have emerged within ethnic communities to protest social conditions, political policies, and economic practices that ethnics considered unjust and unconstitutional. The types of protest have varied widely, from the actions of individual Japanese Americans to resist the internment during World War II to the race riots that occurred in U.S. cities in the 1960s. Groups tend to resort to extreme methods of protest such as riots and rebellions when they feel that the political system is oppressive, that there are no legitimate channels for the alleviation of their grievances, that there is some cause for hope, or that their protest movement might succeed. When studying about social protest, it is important for students to understand that such movements occur only when oppressed people feel that there is a cause for *hope*. For example, students can derive this generalization when studying the Black protest movements of the 1960s. This movement emerged partly because prior policies aimed at reducing discrimination had occurred. These included the desegregation of the armed forces by President Harry S Truman, the laws that desegregated many southern state universities, and the historic *Brown* v. *Board of Education* Supreme Court Decision in 1954, which legally outlawed de jure school segregation. These events were necessary precedents to the Black civil rights movement of the 1960s.

Many people think the ethnic protests of the 1960s were the first of their kind in U.S. history. Even though it is true that ethnic protests reached their zenith during these years, ethnic groups have protested discrimination and racism throughout U.S. history. Black protest actually began on the slave ships—on the journeys from West Africa to the Americas. Slave uprisings and mutinies often occurred on these ships. Many slaves also committed suicide by throwing themselves into the Atlantic rather than acquiescently accepting bondage. Protest by African Americans continued during and after slavery. Slave uprisings, led by such individuals as Denmark Vesey, Gabriel Prosser, and Nat Turner, sometimes resulted in the mass murder of Whites.

Around the turn of the century, Black organizations emerged to fight systematically for civil rights, including the National Association for the Advancement of Colored People (NAACP) and the National Urban League. Other ethnic groups have also continually fought for their rights. Such organizations as the Anti-Defamation League of B'nai B'rith, the Japanese American Citizenship League, the League of United Latin-American Citizens, and the Puerto Rican Forum were organized to work for the civil rights of various ethnic groups in a systematic way. Oppression of any human group is likely to lead to organized protest and resistance. Such protest and resistance have emerged within all of America's ethnic minority groups, although the forms and styles of that protest have reflected the unique cultural values and life-styles of the particular groups.

The Movement of Ethnic Groups

Migration and Immigration

When individuals or groups move within a nation in which they are natives or citizens, we say that they are *migrants*. Individuals or groups who settle in a foreign country are called *immigrants*. Thus, migration describes the movement of individuals and groups within a nation, and immigration describes the settlement of people in a foreign nation. These two concepts must be studied in the multicultural curriculum because all groups that comprise the United States, except for a few such as American Indians, Eskimos, Aleuts, and Native Hawaiians, immigrated to this country from a foreign nation or migrated from Puerto Rico. We call Puerto Ricans migrants rather than immigrants because they became U.S. citizens with the passage of the Congressional Jones Act of 1917. Archeological theories and evidence indicate that American Indians immigrated to the Americas from Asia via the Bering Strait. Although this evidence is strongly endorsed by anthropologists, it is inconclusive. Many American Indians believe that they were created in the Americas by the Great Spirit.

When studying these two concepts, students can formulate hypotheses about why masses of immigrants entered the United States in the nineteenth century. Between 1820 and 1930, about 38 million immigrants came to the United States, most of them from Europe.[42] Students might hypothesize that many individuals and groups came to the United States to avoid religious and political persecution and to improve their economic conditions. When studying statistics on immigration to the United States, students can be asked to note the countries from which most immigrants came and why. For example, between 1820 and 1979 6,985,000 German immigrants entered the United States. During the same period, only 3,038,000 immigrants came from the entire continent of Asia, and 36,267,000 came from Europe. Only 142,000 came from Africa. An investigation into why many more immigrants came from Europe than from Asia and Africa will lead students to discover that our immigration policies, until they were reformed in 1965, were designed to keep this nation largely White and to keep out non-Whites. Table 3–4 gives the numbers and countries of origin of people immigrating to the United States between 1820 and 1979. This table can be the source of numerous inquiry exercises like the one suggested above.

A study of immigration to the United States since the Immigration Reform Act of 1965 reveals that the source of immigration to the United States has changed substantially since that time (see Table 3–5). Nearly 60% of the immigrants to the United States between 1951 and 1960 were from nations in Europe. Europeans comprised only 11% of the immigrants to the United States between 1981 and 1986. Asian immigrants to the United States increased from about 6% between 1951 and 1960 to 47% between 1981 and 1986.

During their study of the immigration and migration of ethnic groups, students can profitably compare and contrast the reasons that various groups migrated and the kinds of experiences they had in their new country. The special case of African immigrants to the United States should be highlighted. This group differed from all the other immigrant groups because their immigration was *forced*. They were also the only group enslaved on their arrival in the Americas. All the other groups of immigrants voluntarily came to the Americas, although many were escaping abject poverty, religious persecution, and dehu-

Table 3–4 Immigrants, by Country of Last Permanent Residence: 1820–1979

Country	1820–1979, total	1951–1960, total	1961–1970, total	1971–1979, total	1975	1976	1977	1978	1979	Percentage 1820–1979	1961–1970	1971–1979
Total	**49,124**	**2,515.5**	**3,321.7**	**3,962.5**	**386.2**	**398.6**	**462.3**	**601.4**	**460.3**	**100.0**	**100.0**	**100.0**
Europe	**36,267**	**1,325.6**	**1,123.4**	**728.2**	**72.8**	**73.0**	**74.0**	**76.2**	**64.2**	**73.8**	**33.8**	**18.4**
Austria	4,316	67.1	20.6	9.1	.5	.5	.5	.5	.5	8.8	.6	.2
Hungary		36.6	5.4	5.8	.6	.6	.5	.6	.5		.2	.1
Belgium	204	18.6	9.2	4.7	.4	.5	.5	.6	.6	.4	.3	.1
Czechoslovakia	138	.9	3.3	5.0	.3	.3	.3	.4	.5	.3	.1	.1
Denmark	364	11.0	9.2	3.9	.3	.4	.4	.4	.4	.7	.3	.1
Finland	33	4.9	4.2	2.3	.2	.2	.2	.3	.3	.1	.1	.1
France	754	51.1	45.2	22.7	1.8	2.0	2.7	2.7	2.9	1.5	1.4	.6
Germany[1]	6,985	477.8	190.8	67.9	5.9	6.6	7.4	7.6	7.2	14.2	5.7	1.7
Great Britain[2]	4,914	195.5	210.0	121.5	12.2	13.0	14.0	16.4	15.5	10.0	6.3	3.1
Greece	661	47.6	86.0	87.7	9.8	8.6	7.8	7.0	5.9	1.3	2.6	2.2
Ireland[3]	4,724	57.3	37.5	10.6	1.1	1.0	1.0	.9	.8	9.6	1.1	.3
Italy	5,300	185.5	214.1	123.9	11.0	8.0	7.4	7.0	6.0	10.8	6.4	3.1
Netherlands	360	52.3	30.6	9.5	.8	.9	1.0	1.2	1.2	.7	.9	.2
Norway	856	22.9	15.5	3.5	.4	.3	.3	.4	.4	1.7	.5	.1
Poland[1]	520	10.0	53.5	32.5	3.5	3.2	3.3	4.5	3.9	1.1	1.6	.8
Portugal	453	19.6	76.1	93.3	11.3	11.0	10.0	10.5	7.1	.9	2.3	2.4
Soviet Union[14]	3,376	.6	2.3	28.4	4.7	7.4	5.4	4.7	1.9	6.9	.1	.7
Spain	262	7.9	44.7	37.4	2.6	2.3	5.6	4.3	3.3	.5	1.3	.9
Sweden	1,273	21.7	17.1	5.8	.5	.6	.6	.6	.8	2.6	.5	.1
Switzerland	350	17.7	18.5	7.7	.7	.8	.8	.9	.9	.7	.6	.2
Yugoslavia	116	8.2	20.4	28.5	2.9	2.3	2.3	2.2	1.9	.2	.6	.7
Other Europe	310	10.8	9.2	16.4	1.3	2.0	2.0	2.5	1.8	.6	.3	.4

Asia[5]	**3,038**	**153.3**	**427.8**	**1,352.1**	**129.2**	**146.7**	**150.8**	**243.6**	**183.0**	**6.2**	**12.9**	**34.1**
China[5]	540	9.7	34.8	96.7	9.2	9.9	12.5	14.5	12.3	1.1	1.0	2.4
Hong Kong	[6]200	15.5	75.0	109.5	12.5	13.7	12.3	11.1	16.8	.4	2.3	2.8
India	182	2.0	27.2	141.4	14.3	16.1	16.8	19.1	18.6	.4	.8	3.6
Iran	[6]48	3.4	10.3	34.9	2.2	2.6	4.2	5.9	8.3	.1	.3	.9
Israel	[6]90	25.5	29.6	34.2	3.5	5.2	4.4	4.5	4.3	.2	.9	.9
Japan	411	46.3	40.0	45.4	4.8	4.8	4.5	4.5	4.5	.8	1.2	1.1
Jordan	[6]41	5.8	11.7	24.0	2.3	2.4	2.9	3.2	3.2	.1	.3	.6
Korea	[6]276	6.2	34.5	235.4	28.1	30.6	30.7	28.8	28.7	.6	1.0	5.9
Lebanon	[6]58	4.5	15.2	37.3	4.0	5.0	5.5	4.8	4.8	.1	.5	.9
Philippines	[7]431	19.3	98.4	312.7	31.3	36.8	38.5	36.6	40.8	.9	3.0	7.9
Turkey	386	3.5	10.1	11.1	1.1	1.0	1.0	1.0	1.3	.8	.3	.3
Vietnam	[8]133	2.7	4.2	129.3	2.7	2.4	3.4	87.6	19.1	.3	.1	3.3
Other Asia	244	9.0	36.7	140.3	13.2	16.2	14.1	22.0	20.3	.5	1.2	3.5
America	**9,248**	**996.9**	**1,716.4**	**1,778.3**	**174.7**	**169.2**	**223.2**	**266.5**	**197.1**	**18.8**	**51.7**	**44.9**
Argentina	[9]97	19.5	49.7	27.2	2.8	2.7	3.1	4.1	3.1	.2	1.5	.7
Brazil	[9]59	13.8	29.3	16.4	1.4	1.4	1.9	2.2	1.8	.1	.9	.4
Canada	4,125	378.0	413.3	156.2	11.2	11.4	18.0	23.5	20.2	8.4	12.4	3.9
Colombia	[9]156	18.0	72.0	66.0	6.4	5.7	8.2	10.9	10.5	.3	2.2	1.7
Cuba	[10]539	78.9	208.5	249.7	25.6	28.4	66.1	27.5	14.0	1.1	6.3	6.3
Dominican Republic	[10]235	9.9	93.3	130.8	14.1	12.4	11.6	19.5	17.5	.5	2.8	3.3
Ecuador	[9]91	9.8	36.8	44.0	4.7	4.5	5.2	5.7	4.4	.2	1.1	1.1
El Salvador	[9]50	5.9	15.0	28.4	2.4	2.4	4.4	5.9	4.5	.1	.4	.7
Guatemala	[9]44	4.7	15.9	22.2	1.9	2.0	3.7	4.1	2.6	.1	.5	.6
Haiti	[10]89	4.4	34.5	49.8	5.0	5.3	5.2	6.1	6.1	.2	1.0	1.3
Honduras	[9]37	6.0	15.7	14.8	1.4	1.3	1.6	2.7	2.5	.2	.5	.4
Mexico	2,177	299.8	453.9	583.7	62.6	58.4	44.6	92.7	52.5	4.4	13.7	14.7
Panama	[9]51	11.7	19.4	19.8	1.7	1.8	2.5	3.3	3.5	.1	.6	.5
Peru	[9]52	7.4	19.1	25.1	2.3	2.6	3.9	5.1	4.0	.1	.6	.6

Continued

Table 3-4 Continued

Country	1820–1979, total	1951–1960, total	1961–1970, total	1971–1979, total	1975	1976	1977	1978	1979	Percentage 1820–1979	Percentage 1961–1970	Percentage 1971–1979
Other West Indies	758	29.8	133.9	237.4	22.3	19.6	27.1	34.6	33.5	1.5	4.0	6.0
Other America	695	99.2	106.2	106.9	8.9	9.3	16.1	18.6	16.4	1.4	3.2	2.7
Africa	142	14.1	29.0	66.7	5.9	5.7	9.6	10.3	11.2	.3	.9	1.7
Australia and New Zealand	123	11.5	19.6	21.6	1.8	2.1	2.5	2.6	2.5	.3	.6	.5
All other	309	14.0	5.7	15.8	1.8	1.9	2.2	2.2	2.3	.6	.2	.4

Source: U.S. Immigration and Naturalization Service, *Annual Report.* Reprinted from U.S. Bureau of the Census, *Statistical Abstract of the United States, 1982–83* (Washington, D.C.: U.S. Government Printing Office, 1982), p. 89.

[In thousands, except percent. For years ending June 30 except, beginning 1977, ending September 30. Data prior to 1906 refer to country from which aliens came. Because of boundary changes and changes in list of countries separately reported, data for certain countries not comparable throughout. See also *Historical Statistics, Colonial Times to 1970,* series C 89–119.]

[1] 1938–1945, Austria included with Germany; 1899–1919, Poland included with Austria-Hungary, Germany, and Soviet Union.

[2] Beginning 1952, includes data for United Kingdom not specified, formerly included with "Other Europe."

[3] Comprises Eire and Northern Ireland.

[4] Europe and Asia.

[5] Beginning 1957, includes Taiwan.

[6] Prior to 1951, included with "Other Asia."

[7] Prior to 1951, Philippines included with "All other."

[8] Prior to 1953, data for Vietnam not available.

[9] Prior to 1951, included with "Other America."

[10] Prior to 1951, included with "Other West Indies."

Table 3–5 *Immigrants, by Country of Birth: 1961–1987*

Country of Birth	1961–1970, total	1971–1980, total	1981–1986, total	1987
All countries	**3,321.7**	**4,493.3**	**3,466.1**	**601.5**
Europe[1]	**1,238.6**	**801.3**	**384.3**	**61.2**
Austria	13.7	4.7	2.4	.5
Belgium	8.5	4.0	3.2	.6
Czechoslovakia	21.4	10.2	6.2	1.4
Denmark	11.8	4.5	3.1	.5
Finland	5.8	3.4	1.9	.3
France	34.3	17.8	12.6	2.5
Germany	200.0	66.0	41.6	7.3
Greece	90.2	93.7	18.8	2.7
Hungary	17.3	11.6	4.7	1.0
Ireland	42.4	14.1	7.4	3.1
Italy	206.7	130.1	20.9	2.8
Netherlands	27.8	10.7	6.9	1.2
Norway	16.4	4.0	2.3	.3
Poland	73.3	43.6	44.8	7.5
Portugal	79.3	104.5	25.2	3.9
Romania	14.9	17.5	22.0	3.8
Soviet Union[2]	15.7	43.2	42.1	2.4
Spain	30.5	30.0	9.2	1.6
Sweden	16.7	6.3	5.8	1.1
Switzerland	16.3	6.6	3.9	.8
United Kingdom	230.5	123.5	85.4	13.5
Yugoslavia	46.2	42.1	10.1	1.8
Asia[1]	**445.3**	**1,633.8**	**1,644.5**	**257.7**
Cambodia	1.2	8.4	83.6	12.5
China: Mainland } Taiwan	96.7	202.5	219.4	{ 25.8 { 11.9
Hong Kong	25.6	47.5	30.7	4.7
India	31.2	176.8	145.9	27.8
Iran	10.4	46.2	79.0	14.4
Iraq	6.4	23.4	14.2	1.1
Israel	12.9	26.6	20.1	3.7
Japan	38.5	47.9	24.0	4.2
Jordan	14.0	29.6	18.0	3.1
Korea	35.8	272.0	201.8	35.8
Laos	.1	22.6	105.2	6.8
Lebanon	7.5	33.8	21.0	4.4
Pakistan	4.9	31.2	31.8	6.3
Philippines	101.5	360.2	273.8	50.1
Thailand	5.0	44.1	32.5	6.7
Turkey	6.8	18.6	13.2	1.6
Vietnam	4.6	179.7	264.8	24.2

Continued

Table 3–5   Continued

Country of Birth	1961–1970, total	1971–1980, total	1981–1986, total	1987
North America[1]	**1,351.1**	**1,645.0**	**1,093.4**	**216.6**
Canada	286.7	114.8	66.6	11.9
Mexico	443.3	637.2	401.7	72.4
Caribbean[1]	519.5	759.8	473.2	102.9
Barbados	9.4	20.9	11.0	1.7
Cuba	256.8	276.8	92.0	28.9
Dominican Republic	94.1	148.0	130.8	24.9
Haiti	37.5	58.7	56.6	14.8
Jamaica	71.0	142.0	120.1	23.1
Trinidad and Tobago	24.6	61.8	19.9	3.5
Centra! America	97.7	132.4	151.5	29.3
El Salvador	15.0	34.4	53.8	10.7
Guatemala	15.4	25.6	25.1	5.7
Nicaragua	10.1	13.0	17.1	3.3
Panama	18.4	22.7	17.6	2.1
South America[1]	**228.3**	**284.4**	**225.9**	**44.4**
Argentina	42.1	25.1	12.4	2.1
Brazil	20.5	13.7	11.0	2.5
Colombia	70.3	77.6	63.0	11.7
Ecuador	37.0	50.2	26.7	4.6
Guyana	7.1	47.5	53.1	11.4
Peru	18.6	29.1	26.7	5.9
Africa	**39.3**	**91.5**	**94.5**	**17.7**
Egypt	17.2	25.5	17.2	3.4
Australia	**9.9**	**14.3**	**8.0**	**1.3**
New Zealand	**3.7**	**5.3**	**3.8**	**.6**
Other countries	**5.5**	**17.7**	**11.7**	**2.0**

Source: U. Bureau of the Census, *Statistical Abstract of the United States* (109th ed.) (Washington, D.C.: U.S. Government Printing Office, 1989), p. 10.
Note: [In thousands. For fiscal years ending in year shown.]
[1]Includes countries not shown separately.
[2]Europe and Asia.

manization. When studying about the southern and eastern European immigrants to the United States, students can note how each group experienced discrimination, lived in urban ghettos, and how many of them eventually became culturally assimilated, attained social mobility, and moved to the suburbs of cities such as New York, Boston, and Chicago. Groups like Italians and Poles discriminated against African Americans and Mexican Americans when these groups started migrating to large cities after the two world wars.

European immigrant groups, especially the southern and eastern ones, were often the victims of discrimination and racist ideologies, but the racism they experienced never reached the proportions it did in the South against African Americans or on the West Coast when Asian immigrants started arriving there in the 1800s. It is important for students to realize that even though certain classes of European immigrants, such as lunatics, convicts, and idiots, were prevented from entering the United States in the 1800s, the first national group that was totally excluded from the United States was non-White. The Chinese Exclusion Act of 1882 completely stopped Chinese immigration to the United States for several decades. In the 1920s, the number of southern and eastern European immigrants entering the United States was reduced to a trickle because discrimination against them became intense and widespread. Non-White groups were virtually excluded from the United States. Only groups from northern and western Europe were favored by the "national origins" quota system that was set up by Congress in 1921 and tightened in 1924. The quota was based on percentage of residents of a particular nationality in the United States in 1920. The McCarran Act of 1952 relaxed some of the earlier restrictions but made the national origin parts of the law even more severe. Immigration reform did not occur until the Immigration Act of 1965, which became effective in 1968. The 1965 act removed the national origin quotas and liberalized American immigration policy.

Summary

This chapter has discussed a number of high-level concepts that can be used effectively to organize and teach multicultural units and lessons. I suggested that key concepts selected for the multicultural curriculum should be able to function successfully in an interdisciplinary role, should help explain some significant aspects of the cultures and experiences of ethnic groups, and should be able to encompass a wide range of data and information. When choosing concepts for the multicultural curriculum, you should also consider your students' developmental levels and their prior experiences with content related to race and ethnicity. Chapter 4 discusses ways in which the multicultural curriculum can be planned and organized.

Questions and Activities

1. Identify an ethnic problem in your community, such as a controversy over busing for school desegregation or affirmative action, the question of open housing, or discrimination in employment. List concepts and generalizations from several disciplines

that might help students understand the problem. What strategies and materials would you use to teach the problem to students?

2. State the advantages of interdisciplinary multicultural lessons and units. What problems might you encounter in trying to structure these kinds of lessons and units? How might you resolve them?

3. Examine several of the books dealing with specific ethnic groups listed in the bibliographies of this book. Identify and list *culture traits* that are unique to different ethnic communities. What is the origin of these culture traits? Why do they continue to exist? Are they unique to particular ethnic groups or merely associated with lower-class status or a certain region? Explain your responses.

4. After reading a book on each of the major ethnic groups, make a list of the types of cultural and physical *differences* existing *within* them. Explain why these differences emerged and why they still exist.

5. Make a list of the major occupations in which most American Indians, Mexican Americans, Asian Americans, Puerto Rican Americans, and African Americans work. Note the percentages of each group working in the major occupations identified. Carefully study the data you have gathered. What generalizations and conclusions can you make about the occupational status of ethnic groups of color in U.S. society? What factors explain their occupational status?

6. Using a map of your city or community, pinpoint the regions in which the various ethnic groups live, with different colored markers to represent each major ethnic group. What conclusions and generalizations can you make about where different ethnic groups are concentrated in your community? What factors explain their location patterns?

7. Conduct a small-scale field study to gather data about how people within an ethnic community view their neighborhood and how outsiders view it. What conclusions can you make? What factors explain your findings?

8. Locate several conflicting accounts of slavery or the U.S.–Mexican War and develop an inquiry lesson to teach students how personal biases influence the writing of history.

9. Study the treatments of the major ethnic groups in your basal social studies, language arts, or other textbooks. What conclusions can you make? What materials and strategies can you use to extend textbook treatments of ethnic groups? How?

10. List examples of racial and ethnic discrimination you have seen and/or experienced. Why did the discrimination occur? How might this type of discrimination be reduced? How did you respond to it? Explain.

11. Watch several television programs during the week that have ethnic minority characters. Also study the treatment of ethnic groups such as African Americans and Mexican Americans in a newspaper or news magazine for a one-week period. Write a three- to five-page paper summarizing your observations about the treatment of ethnic minorities on television and in the printed sources you examined. Did you find any examples of racism? Explain.

12. Try to think of several examples of problems that result from communicating across different ethnic cultures. Develop and write a lesson plan for teaching the concept of intercultural communication to students.

13. Define each of the following terms and tell why each is important:

high-level concept	microculture
interdisciplinary	ethnic group
conceptual curriculum	socialization
culture	intercultural communication
macroculture	power

Endnotes

1. Yoshiko Uchida, *A Jar of Dreams* (New York: Atheneum, 1982).
2. Mildred D. Taylor, *Song of the Trees* (New York: Dial, 1975).
3. Virginia Hamilton, *A Little Love* (New York: Philomel Books, 1984).
4. Laurence Yep, *Mountain Light* (New York: Harper and Row, 1985).
5. Brian M. Bullivant, *Pluralism: Cultural Maintenance and Evolution* (Avon, England: Multilingual Matters Ltd., 1984), p. 2.
6. Ibid.
7. For my definition of ethnic groups presented here, I have relied on: James A. Banks, Carlos E. Cortés, Geneva Gay, Ricardo L. Garcia, and Anna S. Ochoa, *Curriculum Guidelines for Multiethnic Education* (Arlington, Va.: National Council for the Social Studies, 1976).
8. This typology is discussed more extensively in James A. Banks, *Multiethnic Education: Theory and Practice*, 2nd ed. (Boston: Allyn and Bacon, 1988), pp. 193–202.
9. Alice Miel, with Edwin Kiester, Jr., *The Shortchanged Children of Suburbia* (New York: American Jewish Committee, 1967).
10. Eileen Southern, *The Music of Black Americans: A History* (New York: W. W. Norton, 1971).
11. Virgil J. Vogel, "The Indian in American History," *Social Education* 33 (February 1969): 200.
12. Miel, with Kiester, *The Shortchanged Children*; Jules Henry, *Culture against Man* (New York: Vintage Books, 1963); and Jules Henry, *Pathways to Madness* (New York: Random House, 1971).
13. David Milner, *Children and Race* (Beverly Hills: Sage Publications, 1983).
14. Arnold M. Rose, "The Causes of Prejudice," in *American Cultural Minorities: A Textbook of Readings in Intergroup Relations*, ed. Milton L. Barron (New York: Alfred A. Knopf, 1962), pp. 77–80.
15. Peter I. Rose, *They and We: Racial and Ethnic Relations in the United States*, 2nd ed. (New York: Random House, 1974), p. 102.
16. Robert K. Merton, "Discrimination and the American Creed," in *Majority and Minority: The Dynamics of Race and Ethnicity in American Life*, 3rd ed., eds. Norman R. Yetman, with C. Hoy Steele (Boston: Allyn and Bacon, 1982).
17. Ashley Montagu, *Man's Most Dangerous Myth: The Fallacy of Race*, 5th ed. (New York: Oxford University Press, 1974), p. 9.
18. Douglas L. Oliver, *An Invitation to Anthropology: A Guide to Basic Concepts* (Garden City, N.Y.: The National History Press, 1964), p. 14.
19. *The Encyclopaedia Britannica*, s.v. "Macropaedia" (Chicago: Encyclopaedia Britannica, 1976), p. 350.
20. Montagu, *Dangerous Myth*, p. 7.

21. Charles L. Hunt and Lewis Walker, *Ethnic Dynamics: Patterns of Intergroup Relations in Various Societies* (Homewood, Ill.: The Dorsey Press, 1974), pp. 128–159.

22. Melvin M. Tumin, with Arnold S. Feldman, *Social Class and Social Change in Puerto Rico,* 2nd ed. (Indianapolis: Bobbs-Merrill, 1971).

23. Pierre L. van den Berghe, *Race and Racism: A Comparative Perspective,* 2nd ed. (New York: John Wiley, 1978).

24. Van den Berghe, *Race and Racism,* p. 11.

25. Geneva Gay, "Racism in America: Imperatives for Teaching Ethnic Studies," in *Teaching Ethnic Studies: Concepts and Strategies,* ed. James A. Banks (Washington, D.C.: National Council for the Social Studies, 1973), p. 30.

26. Montagu, *Dangerous Myth,* p. 31.

27. Van den Berghe, *Race and Racism,* p. 21.

28. Ibid., p. 17.

29. Ibid.

30. Montagu, *Dangerous Myth,* p. 39.

31. Gay, "Racism in America: Imperatives for Teaching Ethnic Studies," pp. 31–34.

32. Barbara A. Sizemore, "Is There a Case for Separate Schools?" *Phi Delta Kappan* 53 (January 1972): 281–284.

33. Henry Clay Lindgren, *An Introduction to Social Psychology,* 2nd ed. (New York: John Wiley, 1973), pp. 228–229.

34. Kenneth B. Clark and Mamie P. Clark, "Skin Color as a Factor in Racial Identification of Negro Pre-School Children," *Journal of Social Psychology* 11 (1940): 159–167; Mary Ellen Goodman, *Race Awareness in Young Children* (New York: Collier Books, 1964); and Helen G. Trager and Marian Radke Yarrow, *They Learn What They Live* (New York: Harper, 1952).

35. E. Earl Baughman, *Black Americans: A Psychological Analysis* (New York: Academic Press, 1971); R. W. Larkin, "Class, Race and Preadolescent Attitudes," *California Journal of Educational Research* 23 (1972): 213–223.

36. Larry A. Samovar and Richard E. Porter, *Intercultural Communications: A Reader,* 2nd ed. (Belmont, Calif.: Wadsworth, 1976), p. 4.

37. Bernard Berelson and Gary A. Steiner, *Human Behavior: An Inventory of Scientific Findings* (New York: Harcourt, Brace and World, 1964), p. 88.

38. Arthur R. Jensen, "How Much Can We Boost IQ and Scholastic Achievement?" *Harvard Educational Review* 39 (Winter 1969): 1–123; Edward C. Banfield, *The Unheavenly City* (Boston: Little, Brown, 1970).

39. John Hope Franklin, *Racial Equality in America* (Chicago: University of Chicago Press, 1976).

40. See, for example, Robert Blauner, *Racial Oppression in America* (New York: Harper, 1972); Martin Carnoy, *Education as Cultural Imperialism* (New York: David McKay, 1974); and Robert L. Williams, *Educational Alternatives for Colonized People: Models for Liberation* (New York: Dunellen, 1974). Many of the individuals who write from the colonialist perspective have been influenced by Albert Memmi, Paulo Freire, and Frantz Fanon. See Albert Memmi, *The Colonizer and the Colonized* (New York: Orion Press, 1965); Paulo Freire, *Pedagogy of the Oppressed* (New York: Herder and Herder, 1972); and Frantz Fanon, *The Wretched of the Earth* (New York: Grove, 1968).

41. E. U. Essien-Udom, *Black Nationalism: A Search for an Identity in America* (New York: Dell, 1962); and C. Eric Lincoln, *The Black Muslims in America* (New York: Beacon, 1961).

42. *Statistical Abstract of the United States, 1982–83.* (Washington, D.C.: U.S. Government Printing Office, 1982), p. 89.

Annotated Bibliography

Alba, Richard D., ed. *Ethnicity and Race in the U.S.A.: Toward the Twenty-First Century.* New York: Routledge, 1988.

The essays in this book focus on important aspects of the experiences of African Americans, American Indians, Hispanics, Asian Americans, Jews, and Italians.

Allen, James P., and Turner, Eugene J. *We the People: An Atlas of America's Ethnic Diversity.* New York: Macmillan, 1988.

This comprehensive atlas of the nation's ethnic population includes excellent maps, rich statistics, and a readable text. It can serve as a springboard for many inquiry activities by students.

Allport, Gordon W. *The Nature of Prejudice.* 25th anniv. ed. Reading, Mass.: Addison-Wesley, 1979.

This is a classic and seminal study of the origin and nature of prejudice.

Cole, Johnnetta B., ed. *All American Women: Lines That Divide, Ties That Bind.* New York: The Free Press, 1986.

An excellent collection of essays that discuss the hopes, dreams, and problems of women of color.

———, ed. *Anthropology for the Nineties: Introductory Readings.* New York: The Free Press, 1988.

A number of the readings in this anthology deal with ethnic groups in the United States, including "Black American English," "American Catalogues of Asian Brides," and "Indians and the Economy."

Crawford, James. *Bilingual Education: History, Politics, Theory and Practice.* Trenton, N.J.: Crane Publishing, 1989.

A skillfully written and comprehensive discussion of the development and nature of bilingual education in the United States.

Davis, Larry E., and Proctor, Enola K. *Race, Gender, and Class: Guidelines for Practice with Individuals, Families and Groups.* Englewood Cliffs, N.J.: Prentice-Hall, 1989.

Although this book focuses on counseling, the insights provided by the authors are very helpful to teachers.

Fass, Paula S. *Outside In: Minorities and the Transformation of American Education.* New York: Oxford University Press, 1989.

This is a partial history of minorities in American education. It focuses on European immigrants, the New York schools in the 1930s and 1940s, Black education in the 1930s and 1940s, and the education of women, 1945–1963.

Hampton, Henry, and Fayer, Steve. *Voices of Freedom: An Oral History of the Civil Rights Movement form the 1950s through the 1980s.* New York: Bantam Books, 1990.

This excellent and comprehensive documentary history of the civil rights movement is a companion to the acclaimed television series Eyes on the Prize. This is an excellent source to use with students.

Milner, David. *Children and Race.* Beverly Hills, Calif.: Sage Publications, 1983.

The author discusses ways in which children acquire prejudices from society. He focuses on the racial situation in Britain but draws much of his research data from the United States.

Mindel, Charles H., Habenstein, Robert W. and Wright, Roosevelt, Jr., eds. *Ethnic Families in America: Patterns and Variations,* 3rd ed. New York: Elsevier, 1988.

This comprehensive collection of original essays discusses 17 kinds of U.S. ethnic families, including Cuban, Vietnamese, and Mormon families.

Omi, Michael, and Winant, Howard. *Racial Formation in the United States: From the 1960s to the 1980s.* New York: Routledge and Kegan Paul, 1986.

In this theoretical book, the authors contend that race is an organizing principle of social action.

Simpson, George E., and Yinger, J. Milton. *Racial and Cultural Minorities: An Analysis of Prejudice and Discrimination,* 5th ed. New York: Plenum Press, 1985.

This comprehensive and classic text in the field of race relations discusses the major concepts, topics, and issues in race and ethnic relations in the United States. The meaning of race and the nature of prejudice and discrimination are among the major concepts discussed in considerable detail.

Sollors, Werner, ed. *The Invention of Ethnicity.* New York: Oxford University Press, 1989.

This interesting anthology includes essays that discuss a wide range of issues related to ethnicity, culture, and identity. The contributors include Richard Rodriguez, Thomas Ferraro, and Shawn Wong.

Thernstrom, Stephan; Orlov, Ann; and Handlin, Oscar, eds. *Harvard Encyclopedia of American Ethnic Groups.* Cambridge: Harvard University Press, 1980.

This standard reference contains major essays on general issues and topics in ethnic studies as well as historical descriptions of the major ethnic groups in the United States.

Wilson, Anne. *Mixed Race Children: A Study of Identity.* Boston: Allen and Unwin, 1987.

An interesting study of the racial identity and categorization of a group of racially mixed children in Britain.

Chapter 4

Planning the

Multicultural

Curriculum

Introduction

The multicultural curriculum should help students develop the ability to make reflective personal and public decisions. A curriculum focused on decision making must be conceptual, interdisciplinary, and based on higher levels of knowledge. The preceding chapter, "Key Concepts for the Multicultural Curriculum," presents criteria and examples of concepts that you can use to organize multicultural units and lessons.

This chapter discusses ways to organize a decision-making curriculum after you have selected appropriate concepts and content. It also presents other components of an effective multicultural curriculum, including valuing and personal, social, and civic action. Steps you can take to master ethnic content and to select and evaluate instructional materials are also discussed.

Identifying Key Concepts and Organizing Generalizations

When planning multicultural lessons and units that have a comparative approach and focus, you or a curriculum committee should start by identifying key concepts. These concepts should be higher-level ones that can encompass numerous facts and lower-level generalizations. They should have the power to organize a great deal of information and to explain significant aspects of the experiences and histories of ethnic groups. These concepts should also be able to function successfully in an interdisciplinary role.

After you or a curriculum committee has selected key concepts from several disciplines, at least one organizing generalization related to each concept should be identified. Each organizing generalization should be a higher-level

Table 4–1   Key Concepts and Organizing Generalizations

Key Concept	Organizing Generalization
Acculturation	Whenever ethnic groups have extended contact, exchange of cultural traits occurs between minority and majority groups, as well as between different ethnic groups.
Intercultural communication	Individuals and groups socialized within different ethnic cultures are often unable to communicate effectively because they interpret the meanings of symbols differently. Ineffective communication frequently results in conflict between ethnic groups.
Perception	In a society stratified along racial and ethnic group lines, ethnicity and race tend to influence cogently how individuals see and interpret events, situations, and public issues.
Racism	Powerful groups that hold racist beliefs usually structure institutions, laws, and norms that reflect their beliefs and oppress the victims of racism.
Power	Within an ethnically stratified society, individuals and groups struggle for power and influence. Power struggles often lead to social change.
Immigration–migration	In all cultures, individuals and groups have moved to seek better economic, political, and social opportunities. However, movement of individuals and groups has been both voluntary and forced.

statement that explains some aspects of human behavior in all cultures, times, and places. It should not contain references to any particular culture or group but should be a universal type of statement capable of being scientifically tested. Table 4–1 presents a list of key concepts and related organizing generalizations that can be used to plan a multicultural conceptual curriculum incorporating the experiences of a range of ethnic and cultural groups.

Identifying Intermediate-Level Generalizations

After an organizing (universal-type) generalization is identified for each key concept chosen, an intermediate-level generalization that relates to each organizing generalization should be formulated. An intermediate-level generalization applies to a nation, regions within a nation, or to groups comprising a particular culture. Table 4–2 presents an intermediate-level generalization for immigration–migration, a key concept listed in Table 4–1. In an actual curriculum, intermediate-level generalizations would be identified for each organizing generalization selected and shown in Table 4–1. However, the example in Table 4–2 is limited to save space.

Table 4–2   *Generalizations Related to Immigration–Migration*

Key Concept

Immigration–migration

Organizing Generalization

In all cultures, indivduals and groups have moved to seek better economic, political, and social opportunities. However, movement of individuals and groups has been both voluntary and forced.

Intermediate-Level Generalization

Most individuals and groups who immigrated to the United States and who migrated within it were seeking better economic, political, or social opportunities. However, movement of individuals and groups to and within the United States has been both voluntary and forced.

Low-Level Generalizations

Indians: Most movement of Indians within the United States was caused by forced migration and genocide.

Mexican Americans: Mexicans who immigrated to the United States came primarily to improve their economic condition by working as migrant laborers in the western and southwestern states.

European Americans: Most southern and eastern Europeans who immigrated to the United States came primarily to improve their economic status.

African Americans: Large numbers of Blacks migrated to northern and western cities in the early 1900s to escape lynchings and economic and political discrimination in the South.

Asian Americans: Most Asian immigrants who came to the United States in the 1800s expected to improve their economic conditions and return to Asia. During World War II, Japanese Americans were forced to move from their homes to federal internment camps.

Puerto Ricans: Puerto Ricans usually come to the U.S. mainland seeking better jobs; they sometimes return to the island of Puerto Rico because of American racism and personal disillusionment experienced on the mainland.

Indochinese Americans: Most Indochinese Americans, unlike most American immigrant groups, came to the United States because of political developments in their native lands.

Determining Which Ethnic Groups to Study

Selecting a Range of Groups

When an intermediate-level generalization has been identified for each key concept, you must decide which ethnic groups will be selected for study. A range of groups should be included in comparative multicultural units and lessons in order to teach significant concepts related to American ethnic groups and to illustrate both the differences and similarities in their experiences, cultures, and histories. Groups that differ in racial characteristics, levels of assimilation, social-class status, and in the periods and circumstances of immigration to or migration in the United States should also be studied in the multicultural curriculum.

Units that include ethnic groups that have been successful educationally and economically, such as Jewish Americans and Japanese Americans, and those who still face massive social and economic problems, such as American Indians and Mexican Americans, can illustrate the enormous range in the experiences of ethnic groups in the United States. However, when ethnic groups such as Jewish Americans and Japanese Americans are studied, you should help students understand that although Jewish Americans and Japanese Americans have experienced tremendous educational and social mobility, members of these groups are often victims of discrimination and sometimes face identity problems related to their ethnicity. Thus, these groups share characteristics with lower-status ethnic groups such as American Indians, African Americans, and Mexican Americans.

Studying ethnic groups such as Chinese immigrants and Cuban Americans can illustrate the differences and similarities of two ethnic groups who came in large numbers to the United States at different points in history and for different reasons. The first Chinese immigrants came to the United States in the 1800s hoping to get rich quickly and return to their homeland. Most of the Cubans who settled in the United States after 1959 came to escape a communist form of government. African Americans provide an interesting contrast to these groups. They were the only ethnic group that was forced to come to America. They came in chains.

The experiences of Jewish Americans in the United States have also been rather unique. Jews comprise a White ethnic, cultural, and religious group that has experienced high levels of educational and economic mobility but still retain significant aspects of their ethnic culture and identity. Most Jews still marry other Jews. Usually White ethnic groups become mainstream Americans when they attain high levels of educational and economic mobility. American Indians, Eskimos, Aleuts, and Native Hawaiians differ from most other ethnic groups because they can claim America as their native land. Indochinese Americans can be studied to illustrate the problems faced by ethnic groups displaced by a modern war and relocated in an alien and highly industrialized society.

Studying Groups That Illustrate Key Concepts

No single multicultural curriculum can include a study of each American ethnic group. The number is much too large to be manageable. There are more than 100 ethnic groups in the United States.[1] In addition to the groups of color who, since the 1960s, have urged educators to include more information about their histories and cultures in the curriculum, some White ethnic groups are also urging teachers to include the study of their experiences and histories in the school curriculum.

A major goal of the multicultural curriculum is to help students master key concepts that will help them make better decisions and become more effective citizens in a pluralistic democratic society. *Thus, the focus should be on helping students master key concepts that highlight major themes in the experiences of ethnic and cultural groups in the United States.* Within a conceptual curriculum, which particular ethnic groups are selected for study becomes a secondary, though important, consideration. The experiences of the ethnic groups selected for study should be the best examples of particular concepts.

It is essential that students master certain concepts, such as race, racism, prejudice, and discrimination, if they are to gain a full understanding of American society and history. Racism has been a decisive force in our nation since its beginning and is still a major force in America today. Consequently, students must study this concept in a sound multicultural curriculum. When studying racism, students will need to examine the histories and contemporary experiences of ethnic groups of color such as African Americans, Indians, Mexican Americans, and Asian Americans. Racism emerged to justify the enslavement of African Americans and was later developed into a full-blown ideology used to defend the exploration and exploitation of America and its native peoples.

Racism is still a major problem in American society. A study of various ethnic groups that are victimized by institutionalized racism will help students develop a better understanding of this enormous social problem and the ability to reason about it more intelligently. The different forms of prejudice and discrimination that exist in U.S. society also merit serious study by students in all grades, kindergarten through the university level. Research by Glock et al. indicates that students who are more cognitively sophisticated and who can reason more logically about prejudice are likely to express fewer prejudices than are less cognitively sophisticated students.[2]

A study of the experiences of Jews in the United States can facilitate an examination of the forms of prejudice and discrimination in contemporary American society. Research indicates that anti-Semitism is widespread in the United States.[3] It warrants open examination by students within an uncoerced classroom atmosphere.

Concepts such as cultural assimilation and structural assimilation are also important in the multicultural curriculum. A study of groups of color, such as African Americans and Filipino Americans, can illustrate how some members of these groups have become culturally assimilated but have been denied structural assimilation or the ability to participate freely in most American institutions because of their physical characteristics. However, the study of White ethnic groups such as Irish Americans and German Americans can illustrate how these groups have attained high levels of cultural and structural assimilation. Often members of these groups are indistinguishable from other mainstream Americans.

When studying cultural and structural assimilation, students can also examine such groups as Polish Americans and Italian Americans. By studying these groups, students can see how some White ethnic groups are experiencing particular levels of cultural and structural assimilation but still retain many ethnic institutions. Individuals within these ethnic groups often participate in ethnic communities and institutions.

Other factors will also influence which ethnic groups you or the curriculum committee selects for study, including your interests and academic background and the ethnic groups represented in the class, school, and local community. However, units and lessons should not be limited to a study of local ethnic groups. Puerto Rican students should have the opportunity to study their own ethnic culture. They also need to learn about other ethnic cultures in order to understand more fully their own ethnic culture and the total human experience. Learning only about one's own culture is encapsulating and restricting. As Edward T. Hall has perceptively stated, "The future depends on [humankind's] transcending the limits of individual cultures."[4]

Identifying Low-Level Generalizations

When key concepts and organizing generalizations have been selected and the ethnic groups to be studied have been identified, low-level generalizations related to each ethnic group selected for study should be stated. Identifying a low-level generalization for each group will ensure that specific information about each group will be included in the teaching units and lessons that will be developed later. Table 4–2 presents low-level generalizations related to seven major ethnic groups and to the key concept, immigration–migration.

Organizing generalizations are universal statements that omit references to specific peoples, cultures, and places. Intermediate-level generalizations refer to a particular nation, regions within a nation, and to a particular culture. Low-level generalizations differ from both organizing and intermediate-level generalizations. They apply to specific groups or microcultures within a culture and a nation.

Concepts and Generalizations in the Multicultural Curriculum

To help you plan the multicultural curriculum, I have identified five key concepts related to ethnic groups and related intermediate-level generalizations. To save space, related organizing generalizations are not stated. However, these can be inferred from the generalizations given. For example, the first concept is conflict. The related organizing generalization, which encompasses the two statements below it, is: *Throughout history, conflict has arisen between and among groups in all cultures.* Although organizing generalizations are not given below, they are important because they enable you to incorporate content from other nations for comparative purposes and to help students appreciate the power of high-level ideas. Table 4–3 shows how the students may use a data retrieval chart to study the key concepts below and immigration–migration, which is in Table 4–2.

Table 4–3 Using Selected Key Concepts for a Comparative Study of American Ethnic Groups

Key Concepts	American Indians	Mexican Americans	African Americans	Jewish Americans	Vietnamese Americans	Puerto Ricans	Cuban Americans
Conflict: Within group: With other groups:							
Cultural Diversity: Within group:							
Values: Unique: Shared with others:							
Social Protest: Types used: Results of:							
Immigration– Migration: Reasons for: When: Results of:							
Assimilation: Cultural: Structural:							

CONFLICT: (The words and phrases in italic capitals are concepts; the statements that follow them are related generalizations.) Conflict exists between different generations and subgroups within ethnic minority groups. These conflicts are especially evident in values, goals, and methods of protest.

CULTURAL DIVERSITY: There is wide diversity between and within various ethnic groups. The extent of group identification by members of ethnic groups varies greatly and is influenced by many factors, such as skin color, social class, and personal experiences.

VALUES: Many values within ethnic minority communities differ from those of mainstream Americans, even though their values are changing, especially as people of color become more culturally assimilated.

SOCIAL PROTEST: At various times in history, movements within ethnic minority groups emerge to develop more pride in their groups, to shape new identities, to gain political power and control of institutions, and to shatter stereotypes. The intensity, scope, and type of movements have varied widely from group to group and have been influenced by the unique histories, values, cultures, and life-styles of ethnic groups.

ASSIMILATION: As ethnic groups become more assimilated and attain higher socioeconomic status, they tend to abandon certain elements of their traditional cultures. However, they sometimes reclaim aspects of their cultural heritage once they are secure in middle- or upper-class status. This assimilation usually occurs in the third generation.

Teaching Strategies and Materials

Once you or the curriculum committee has identified the key concepts and generalizations that can serve as a framework for a multicultural curriculum or unit and has stated lower-level generalizations related to the experiences of ethnic groups in the United States, you (or the committee) can then identify the materials and teaching strategies necessary to help students derive the concepts and their related generalizations. A wide variety of teaching strategies, content, and materials can be used to teach ethnic content. The sample generalization about immigration–migration in Table 4–2 can be effectively taught by using content related to the forced westward migration of the Cherokee, which occurred in 1838 and 1839. This poignant migration is often called "The Trail of Tears." When teaching about Puerto Rican migrants, you can use such excellent books as Elena Padilla's *Up from Puerto Rico* and Stan Steiner's *The Islands: The World of the Puerto Ricans.* Oscar Handlin's compassionate and sensitive book, *The Uprooted,* and Irving Howe's *World of Our Fathers* will give students useful overviews of the frustrations and problems encountered by the southern and eastern European immigrants to the United States. Vincent Harding in

There Is a River describes the forced migration of Africans to North America. *Roots* by Alex Haley powerfully conveys the human dimension of the slave's journey from Africa to America. Simulation, role playing, as well as other strategies described in Parts II through V can be used to teach effectively about immigration and other key concepts identified in this chapter.

The six key concepts and organizing generalizations presented in Table 4–1 can be taught at every level within a spiral conceptual curriculum and developed at increasing levels of complexity with different content samples. At each level, K–12, materials related to a range of ethnic groups should be used as content samples to teach students key social science concepts and generalizations. Figure 4–1 illustrates how six key concepts can be spiralled within a

Figure 4–1   *Six Key Concepts Spiralled within a Conceptual Curriculum at Eight Different Levels*

This diagram illustrates how information related to America's ethnic groups can be organized around key concepts and taught at successive levels at an increasing degree of complexity.

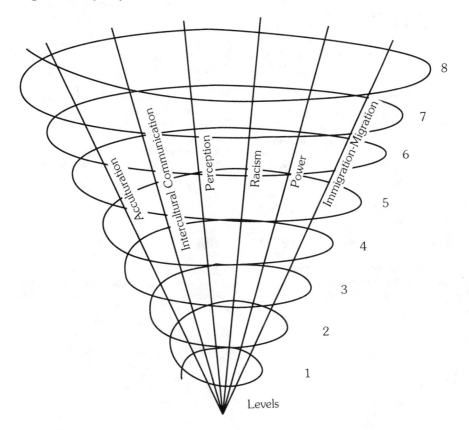

conceptual curriculum at eight different levels. This same curriculum design, of course, can be used in a K–12 program, an 8–12 curriculum, or with any levels.

Planning Lessons

To assure that every lower-level generalization identified in the initial stages of planning is adequately developed within a unit, the teacher can divide a sheet of paper in half and list the key concepts, and the organizing, intermediate-level, and lower-level generalizations on one side of it, and the strategies and materials needed to teach the ideas on the other half (see Table 4–4).

Table 4–4   Key Ideas and Teaching Strategies

Key Ideas	Activities
Key Concept: Immigration–Migration *Organizing Generalization:* In all cultures, individuals and groups have moved to different regions in order to seek better economic, political, and social opportunities. However, movement of individuals and groups has been both voluntary and forced. *Intermediate-Level Generalization:* Most individuals and groups who have immigrated to the United States and who have migrated within it were seeking better economic, political, and social opportunities. However, movement of individuals and groups within the United States has been both voluntary and forced. *Lower-Level Generalization:* During World War II, Japanese Americans were forced to move from their homes to internment camps.	1. Reading aloud selections from Takashima, *A Child in Prison Camp.* 2. Discussing how Shichan, Yuki, and Mother felt when David and Father were taken away. 3. Viewing and discussing the drawings in *A Child in Prison Camp.* 4. Viewing and discussing the photographs in Conrat and Conrat, *Executive Order 9066: The Internment of 110,000 Japanese Americans.* 5. Hypothesizing about why Japanese Americans were interned. 6. Comparing textbook accounts of the internment with accounts in *Executive Order 9066* and *Within the Barbed Wire Fence: A Japanese Man's Account of His Internment* by Takeo U. Nakano. 7. Reading selections from the novel, *Journey to Topaz*, by Yoshiko Uchida, and discussing the experiences of the Sakane family during internment. 8. Viewing and discussing the videotape, *Family Gathering* (New York: New Day Films). In this videotape, a Japanese-American woman comes to terms with her family's World War II internment. 9. Summarizing and generalizing about the forced migration (internment) of Japanese Americans during World War II.

The Value Component
of the Multicultural Curriculum

Although higher-level, scientific knowledge is necessary for reflective decision-making on ethnic and racial problems, it is not sufficient. To make reflective decisions, social actors must also identify and clarify their values and relate them to the knowledge they have derived through the process of inquiry.

Because many ethnic and racial problems within our society are rooted in value confusion, the school should play a significant role in helping students to identify and clarify their values and to make moral choices reflectively. Although the school has a tremendous responsibility to help students make moral choices reflectively, there is abundant evidence that teachers have largely failed to help students deal with moral issues reflectively.

Some teachers treat value problems like the invisible person; that is, they deny their existence. They assume that if students know all the "facts," they can resolve value problems. Such teachers may be said to practice the cult of false objectivity. Other teachers use an evasion strategy: when value problems arise in the classroom, they try to change the subject to a safer topic. Probably the most frequently used approach to value education in the elementary and high school is the inculcation of values considered "right" by adults or the indoctrination of these values. Such values as honesty, justice, truth, freedom, equality, and love (as defined by teachers) are taught with legendary heroes, stories, rituals, and patriotic songs. This approach to value education is unsound and inconsistent with a culturally pluralistic ideology.

Although the school should promote the values inherent within the American creed, such as human dignity, justice, and equality, these values cannot be taught in a didactic fashion. Didactic approaches to moral education, which many teachers use, are unsound because they fail to help students learn a *process* for handling value conflicts and dilemmas. Often, individuals must choose between two equally "good" values, such as between freedom and equality. In a democratic pluralistic nation such as the United States, values such as freedom and equality are often interpreted differently by different individuals and groups. The values themselves are also often in conflict.

In the 1980s many northern Whites argued that court-mandated busing for school desegregation violated their individual freedoms. The National Association for the Advancement of Colored People (NAACP) argued that busing for school desegregation was necessary for Black students to have equal educational opportunities. Many African Americans, Mexican Americans, Indians, and women argued that affirmative action programs were necessary for them to attain equal employment opportunities because of past discrimination. White males often opposed affirmative action and felt that it denied them equality and justice.

Because of the different ways in which various ethnic and racial groups often interpret the same values, such as justice, equality, and freedom, and because of the conflicts inherent in these values, teaching students in a didactic manner that they should value honesty, freedom, or justice is ineffective. Rather, students should be taught a process for identifying value conflicts, analyzing them, and for resolving value conflicts and dilemmas.

Students should also be helped to make reflective moral choices and learn how to justify their moral decisions. All values are not equally valid. Some values, such as inequality, racism, and oppression, are clearly inconsistent with human dignity and other American creed values that are set forth in the basic legal and constitutional documents of the United States. Although standards that guide a person's life must be freely chosen from alternatives after thoughtful consideration of their consequences, students who choose or hold values that conflict with human dignity and other American creed values should be helped to see how their values conflict with democratic values and ideologies.

Students should also be helped to understand and predict the possible consequences of the values they embrace. The major goal of moral education should be to help students develop a process for identifying value conflicts, resolving them, and rationally choosing and defending their moral choices. This is the only approach to value education that is consistent with our democratic ideology and that is educationally sound. Serious value problems arise in the classroom when ethnic groups are studied. Students of color often have important value questions about their ethnic cultures, their identities, and about effective strategies to use to effect social and political change. Public issues such as busing for school desegregation, affirmative action, and discrimination in housing and employment pose controversial and complex moral dilemmas.

Approaches to Moral Education

A number of models, approaches, and theories related to value education have been developed that you can use to organize and teach value inquiry lessons. These include the public issues approach developed by Oliver and Shaver, and Newmann,[5] the values clarification approach conceptualized by Raths and his colleagues,[6] and the cognitive-developmental approach developed by Lawrence Kohlberg.[7] The next section presents a brief summary of the cognitive-developmental approach developed by Kohlberg and a value inquiry model that I have developed.

The Cognitive-Developmental Approach to Moral Education

Kohlberg hypothesized that an individual's ability to reason morally develops sequentially in a series of definite stages and that these stages are found in all nations and cultures. He identified three levels of moral development: (1) the preconventional, (2) the conventional, and (3) the postconventional. Each level has two stages. The six stages constitute a hierarchy: each higher stage is a more sophisticated and more rational form of moral reasoning (see Table 4–5).[8]

The theory assumes that an individual's stage of moral development can be determined and that moral education must be based on the student's stage of moral reasoning. A major goal of moral education, according to Kohlberg, is to stimulate students, by using moral dilemmas, to move to the next higher stage of moral development.

Table 4–5 *A Summary of Kohlberg's Stages of Moral Development*

Level 1: Pre-Conventional

At this level an individual's moral reasoning results from the consequences of actions (punishment, reward, exchange of favors) and from the physical power of those in positions of authority.

Stage 1: Decisions result from a blind obedience to power, an attempt to avoid punishment, or an attempt to seek rewards

Stage 2: Decisions result from a desire to satisfy one's own needs and occasionally the needs of others. Individuals view reciprocity as a matter of "You scratch my back and I'll scratch yours." Reasoning involves little consideration of loyalty, gratitude, or justice.

Level 2: Conventional

At this level an individual's moral reasoning involves consideration of the interest of others (family and peers) and a desire to maintain, respect, support, and justify the existing social order.

Stage 3: Decisions result from a desire to please and help others and receive their approval in return. Behavior is frequently judged by intention—"He means well" becomes important for the first time.

Stage 4: Decisions result from a desire to maintain the existing authority, rules, and social order. Right behavior consists of doing one's duty.

Level 3: Post-Conventional

At this level an individual's moral reasoning incorporates moral values and principles that have validity and application beyond the authority of groups. Moral reasoning becomes more comprehensive and reflects universal principles.

Stage 5: Decisions result from recognition of an individual's rights within a society that has a social contract. As a result the individual's reasoning emphasizes the "legal point of view," but with an emphasis on the possibility of changing laws.

Stage 6: Decisions result from an obligation to universal ethical principles that apply to all [human-] kind. The universal principles of justice, reciprocity and equality of human rights, and respect for the dignity of human beings as individuals serve as a basis for individual reasoning.

Source: From "An Application of Kohlberg's Theory of Moral Development to the Social Studies Classroom" by Ronald E. Galbraith and Thomas M. Jones, 1975, *Social Education, 39,* p. 17. Copyright 1975 by National Council for the Social Studies. Reprinted by permission.

Kohlberg believed that students are not able to understand levels of moral reasoning that are more than one stage higher than their own. However, instruction below a student's stage of moral development will not stimulate him or her to think at the next higher stage. Kohlberg's research indicated that when students are engaged in discussions about moral dilemmas in which they are required to reason at one stage above their current stage, moral development and growth occur. Two basic assumptions of Kohlberg's theory are that an individual must proceed through the stages sequentially and that none can be skipped.

The theory assumes that there is an indirect relationship between chronological age and level of moral development. Very young children, according to the theory, tend to reason at the lower levels. As individuals grow older, they tend to reason at the higher levels. However, Kohlberg found that most individuals he studied were not able to reason beyond Stage 4. Kohlberg used open-ended stories that present moral dilemmas, and discussion related to the dilemmas, to stimulate students to think at higher stages of moral development. The nature and quality of the subsequent discussion are an extremely important part of this teaching strategy. Kohlberg used stories similar to the following one:

What Should the Vinsons Do?

Mr. and Mrs. Vinson are strong advocates of civil rights in the local community. Mr. Vinson testified in favor of school desegregation when the U.S. Commission on Civil Rights held hearings on school desegregation in Northtown two years ago. A year ago the Northtown Public Schools were ordered by a federal judge to implement immediately a plan for desegregating its public schools. The plan was implemented when school opened in September. Lincoln School, which had been an all-White school, was the first school that African American students attended. These students are bused from the Vinsons' neighborhood.

The Vinsons' daughter, Tessie Mae, who is 8, is one of the students being bused to the Lincoln School each day. Tessie Mae gets up at 6:30 A.M. so that she can catch the bus in front of her house at 7:30 A.M. Last week, just one month after school opened, a 10-year-old African American girl was beaten by a White mob at Lincoln School. Rumors say that some White parents are coming to school with guns. The climate of the school is tense and hostile. A racial incident occurs at the school almost daily. Several days last week White parents greeted the buses bringing Black children to Lincoln School by throwing rocks and eggs at them. Anti-Black graffiti are on the walls of Lincoln's halls.

The Vinsons are worried about their daughter and are seriously considering taking her out of Lincoln School. However, the leaders of the National Association for the Advancement of Colored People (NAACP), who initiated the legal suit that resulted in the court order forcing the Northtown schools to desegregate, are strongly urging African Americans to keep sending their children to Lincoln. These leaders feel that if African American parents stop sending their children to Lincoln they will be doing exactly what many of the Whites want them to do and that they will be defeating the desegregation plan. The NAACP is urging the African-

American community to stand up for what it believes in: an equal education for African-American children.

Question: Should the Vinsons take Tessie Mae out of Lincoln School?

A Value Inquiry Model

I have developed a value inquiry model that is presented in detail in my book, *Teaching Strategies for the Social Studies*, 4th edition,[9] that you can use to help students identify value conflicts, resolve them, and reflectively choose and defend their moral choices. The model is reprinted below (in list form), along with sample exercises illustrating how it can be used when discussing value problems related to race and ethnicity.

1. Defining and recognizing value problems: *observation-discrimination.*
2. Describing value-relevant behavior: *description-discrimination.*
3. Naming values exemplified by behavior described: *identification-description, hypothesizing.*
4. Determining conflicting values in behavior described: *identification-analysis.*
5. Hypothesizing about sources of values analyzed: *hypothesizing* (citing data to support hypotheses).
6. Naming alternative values to those exemplified by behavior observed: *recalling.*
7. Hypothesizing about the possible consequences of the values analyzed: *predicting, comparing, contrasting.*
8. Declaring value preference: *choosing.*
9. Stating reasons, sources, and possible consequences of value choice: *justifying, hypothesizing, predicting.*

Value Inquiry Lessons: Examples

For value inquiry lessons, you can use case studies clipped from the daily newspaper, such as incidents involving controversy between police officers and various ethnic groups or cases related to busing, open housing, and affirmative action. Ethnic literature is an excellent resource for value inquiry. I use two examples to illustrate its use. Photographs, roleplaying activities, and open-ended stories related to ethnic events can also be used effectively.

Example 1: Literature

A Child in Prison Camp by Shizuye Takashima is a powerful and poignant autobiographical account of a young girl's experiences in a Canadian internment camp during World War II. When the internment of the Japanese is studied, you can read aloud the following section from the book about the family conflict that occurred when the family was trying to decide whether to stay in Canada or return to Japan. You can then ask the questions that follow.

Spring 1944

The war with Japan is getting very bad. I can feel my parents growing anxious. There is a lot of tension in the camp; rumors of being moved again, of everyone having to return to Japan. Kazuo and his family leave for Japan. Many are angry they have left us. Some call them cowards, others call them brave! I only feel sad, for I like Kazuo so much, so very much.

Father shouts at mother, "We return to Japan!"

"But what are we going to do? You have brothers and sisters there. I have no one. Besides, the children. . . ."

"Never mind the children," father answers. "They'll adjust. I'm tired of being treated as a spy, a prisoner. Do what you like: I'm returning!"

I can see Mrs. Kono looks confused.

"My husband is talking of returning to Japan, too. I think it's the best thing. All our relatives are still there. We have nothing here."

Yuki stares at her. "It's all right for you, Mrs. Kono, you were born there, but we weren't. I am not going. That's all!"

And she walks out of the house.

Mother gets very upset. I know she wants to cry.

"I don't want to go to Japan, either," I say. "They're short of food and clothing there. They haven't enough for their own people. They won't want us back."*

Questions

1. What problem does the family face? (Defining and recognizing value problems)
2. What does mother want to do? What does father want to do? What does Shichan want to do? (Describing value-relevant behavior)
3. What does the behavior of mother, father, and Shichan tell us about what each thinks is important? (Naming values exemplified by behavior described)
4. How are mother's, father's, and Shichan's beliefs alike? Different? (Determining conflicting values in behavior described)
5. Why do you think that mother feels the way she does? Father? Shichan? (Hypothesizing about sources and values analyzed)
6. What are some other things that the family might have been able to do? Why? (Naming alternative values to those exemplified by behavior observed)
7. What might happen to the family if it stays in Canada? Goes to Japan? Why? (Hypothesizing about the possible consequences of the values analyzed)
8. What would you do if you were mother? Father? Shichan? Why? (Declaring value preference)
9. Why would you do what you said you would do? What might happen to you as a result of your decision? (Stating reasons, sources, and possible consequences of value choice)

---

*Reprinted from Shizuye Takashima, *A Child in Prison Camp* © 1971 by Shizuye Takashima, published in Canada by Tundra Books and in the U.S. by William Morrow.

Example 2: An Open-Ended Story

Open-ended stories present problem situations. If carefully chosen or written, they are excellent tools for stimulating class discussions of issues related to race and ethnicity, as well as other human relations problems After reading an open-ended story to the class, you can have the students identify the problems within it, the values of the characters, the courses of action they might take to resolve the problems, and the possible consequences of the proposed solutions. The students can also act out or roleplay solutions to the problems.

Role-Playing in the Curriculum by Fannie R. Shaftel and George Shaftel includes several open-ended stories that deal with race relations problems. The story reprinted below is from this book. Questions that can be used with the story are also provided.

Seed of Distrust

Betty was all excited when she ran into the apartment. "Mother, will you iron my green dress tonight?"

"I was planning to do it Saturday night, honey, so you'd have it for Sunday School."

"But I'll need it!"

"What's the rush?"

"Nora's invited me to a party tomorrow after school."

"Oh, I see," her mother said slowly, as if thinking hard. "Nora's the little girl on the second floor?"

"Yes. She's real nice."

Betty's sister Lucy, who was a sophomore in high school, asked, "Does her mother know?"

"Know what?" Betty asked.

"Nora's White, isn't she?"

"Sure!"

"Does her mother know she's invited you?"

"Of course! I m-mean, I guess so."

"Does her mother know you're Black?" [Or Mexican, or Puerto Rican, etc.]

"Sure!"

"You mean you think so?"

"Y–Yes," Betty stammered.

"Better make sure," Lucy said, and turned back to the math she was studying.

"I'll iron your dress, honey," Betty's mother said reassuringly. "You'll look real nice."

"Uh-huh," Betty said dully. "Thanks, Mom."

And then, next day, after lunch, the thing happened—Nora met Betty in the hall, outside the fifth-grade room.

"Betty, I've been hunting for you," Nora said urgently. "Listen. My Aunt Dorothy phoned last night. She's arriving today for a visit. My grandma's coming over to see her, and mother's making a dinner for the whole family, cousins and all.

You see? We've got to postpone my party. Until next week, maybe. I'll let you know!''

Betty looked at her, blank-faced.

"Don't bother," Betty said. "Don't bother at all." And Betty turned and walked away, her back very straight. For an instant Nora just stood and stared. Then she ran. She caught Betty's arm and stopped her.

"Betty, what's the matter? Why're you talking like that?"[10]

Questions

1. What is the main problem in this story?
2. What do you think of these characters: Betty, Lucy, Nora? Why? What kinds of things and people do you think are important to each of them? Why?
3. Do you think that Lucy should have asked Betty if Nora's mother knew that she was Black? Why or why not?
4. Do you think Nora told the truth about the family dinner? Why or why not?
5. What are some courses of action that Betty can take? What should Betty do? Why? What would you do if you were Betty? Why? What might be the consequences of your action? Why?

Providing Opportunities
for Personal, Social, and Civic Action

People of color in all regions of the United States are victims of institutionalized racism, poverty, and political powerlessness. When you identify concepts and generalizations, you should select those that will help students to make decisions and to take personal, social, or civic actions that reduce prejudice and discrimination in their personal lives, in the school, and, when possible, in the other social settings in which they function. Primary grade students cannot take actions that will reduce discrimination in the larger society. However, they can make a commitment to not tell or laugh at racist jokes, to play with and make friends with students from other racial, ethnic, and religious groups, and to read books that describe children from other racial and ethnic groups. Middle, upper grade, and high school students can also take personal and social actions within the school community to improve race and ethnic relations.

Teachers must play an active role in getting students to undertake personal and social action to improve race relations in their personal lives and in the institutions in which they function. To improve race relations in the classroom, you can structure interracial work and study groups, making sure that students of color have equal-status roles in these groups. Research has indicated that when students from different races and social classes have equal status within interracial work and study groups, these groups can improve interracial attitudes and help students of color to increase their academic achievement.[11] A number of researchers, such as Johnson and Johnson, Slavin, and Cohen, have written publications that will help you to structure cooperative groups that will help students develop more positive intergroup and interracial attitudes.[12] If you structure groups within the classroom that improve students' interracial and ethnic attitudes, the students will be more likely to take actions in their personal lives outside of the classroom that will make their lives more interracial and intercultural.

After they have mastered higher-level knowledge related to racial and ethnic problems and have clarified their values, you can ask your students to list *possible actions* they can take to help improve race relations in their personal lives, in the school, and in the other institutions in which they function. Also ask them to list the *possible consequences* of each action they identify. Students should participate in action activities and projects only after they have studied the issues related to the action from the perspectives of the social sciences and humanities, analyzed and clarified their values regarding them, identified the possible consequences of their actions, and expressed a willingness to accept them.

Figure 4–2 is a graphic you can use when asking students to list possible actions and consequences they can take when planning action and participation projects and activities.

Gaining the Content Background

Most teachers, like most other Americans, have large gaps in their knowledge of ethnic and racial groups because content about these groups has not been thoroughly integrated into the mainstream school, college, and university curricula. Ethnic studies courses are often electives in high schools, colleges, and universities. Only a few American colleges and universities now require all students to take ethnic studies courses or have integrated ethnic content into the core curriculum required for all students. Consequently, many future teachers will have studied little more about ethnic and racial groups than teachers now in the classroom. Some teachers who have taken ethnic studies courses have not studied about ethnic groups within a comparative framework. They have taken one or two courses on a single ethnic group, such as African Americans or Mexican Americans.

You need a working knowledge of the role of ethnicity in American life and about the histories and the problems of the various ethnic groups before you can implement a sound multicultural curriculum. Even for the most ambitious teacher, acquiring the minimal knowledge needed to teach a multicultural curriculum is a challenging task. Although attaining information about American ethnic groups is challenging, it is equally rewarding. Ethnic content deals with the conflicts and dilemmas that have decisively shaped American life. It sometimes evokes anger and shame, but just as often compassion, admiration, and *hope*.

You should begin a reading program with one or two general books giving an overview of ethnicity in the United States. This type of book can provide you with a conceptual framework for interpreting and comparing the experiences of

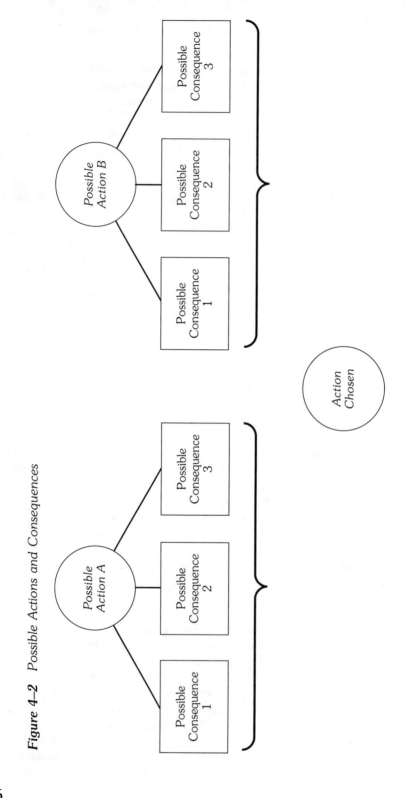

Figure 4–2 Possible Actions and Consequences

116

the various ethnic groups, as well as serve as an excellent source for concepts and generalizations that can be taught to students.

You should also read at least one general survey book on each of the major U.S. ethnic groups. This book should be a high-quality sociological or historical survey written from the perspectives of the group being studied. To become sensitive, you must learn to view events from the viewpoints of the victims of discrimination because for too long we have viewed American history and sociology primarily from mainstream American perspectives. Most teachers are familiar with mainstream perspectives on American history and society. They need to become more aware of other ways to view American life and culture. The bibliography at the end of this chapter contains recommended books that give a general overview of ethnicity in the United States, as well as survey books on each of the major American ethnic groups. Annotations for most of these books are found at the end of appropriate chapters in Parts II through V.

Finding Students Resources

Prior to the 1960s, the paucity of books for children and young people that dealt with ethnic groups was a serious problem for teachers and librarians. The number of books on ethnic groups increased significantly during the period between the late 1960s and the late 1970s. However, during the 1980s, the number of children's books published with ethnic themes and issues decreased, perhaps reflecting the general conservative mood in the nation during that decade. There are more books available on some groups than on others. A reasonable number of books on Jewish Americans and African Americans are still published each year. However, there is a paucity of new books for children and young people each year on Puerto Ricans, Mexican Americans, and Filipino Americans.

Evaluating books with ethnic themes is still a major problem; it is discussed later. How can you locate published books? The children's librarian in the public library and at the curriculum center of the local college or university are excellent resource people, as is the school librarian. Children's librarians receive a number of book lists and books from a wide variety of sources. They are usually willing and able to help you find books on a particular topic such as ethnic studies.

Hundreds of children's books are published each year. Consequently, you will find it necessary to rely on bibliographies published periodically by professional and ethnic organizations to locate the most recent books. Some of the best bibliographies that list books on ethnic groups are published by public and private organizations, such as state departments of education, school systems, civil rights organizations, public libraries, and professional organizations. Two of the best publications that list and critically discuss books on ethnic groups are *Multicultural Leader*, published quarterly by the Educational Materials and Services Center, and *The Bulletin*, published by the Council on Interracial

Books for Children. The Educational Materials and Services Center also markets multicultural materials for both teachers and students. The Center's periodic catalog contains a comprehensive collection and description of multicultural materials, including books, simulation games, and audiovisual materials. The Council on Interracial Books for Children issues periodic special publications that contain critical essays on books for young people dealing with ethnic groups.

The Japanese American Curriculum Project and the Anti-Defamation League of B'nai B'rith also issue periodic bibliographies. The bibliographies issued by the Anti-Defamation League deal with a range of ethnic groups. Other ethnic organizations, such as the National Association for the Advancement of Colored People, the Puerto Rican Forum, and the American Indian Historical Society, also publish periodic bibliographies.

Social Education, the official journal of the National Council for the Social Studies, publishes an annual supplement on notable children's books. *The Booklist*, published by the American Library Association, the *Bulletin of the Center for Children's Books*, published by the University of Chicago Press for the University's Graduate School of Librarianship, *School Library Journal*, published by the R. R. Bowker Company, and *Horn Book* are periodic publications that contain reviews of children's books. *The Language Arts*, published by the National Council of Teachers of English, occasionally publishes articles that discuss children's books. The Council periodically issues special publications on books dealing with ethnic groups.

Magazines and newspapers, such as *Ebony* and the *New York Times*, also publish book lists and reviews of children's books periodically. You should check these sources. Finally, browsing in the children's section of local bookstores in large cities can lead to the discovery of a gold mine of recent children's books. The salesperson in charge of children's books is usually willing and able to help the browsing educator or school librarian.

Guidelines for Evaluating and Selecting Multicultural Materials

Many of the books and other materials on each ethnic group are insensitive, inaccurate, and written from mainstream and insensitive perspectives and points of view. Nevertheless, good materials on each group do exist. Identifying them requires a considerable amount of time and careful evaluation and selection. The criteria and examples of books below are offered to help teachers, curriculum specialists, and librarians evaluate and select ethnic studies resources for classroom use.

One useful way to select excellent books on ethnic themes for children and young adults is to examine carefully the new works of authors who have established reputations for writing sensitive and excellent books for children and young adults. African American authors, such as Lucille Clifton, Virginia Hamilton, Walter Dean Myers, and Mildred D. Taylor, have written excellent books that accurately depict African-American culture in sensitive ways. Other authors of color have also written sensitive and powerful books about their particular groups, such as Yoshiko Uchida (Japanese American), Laurence Yep (Chinese American), Byrd Baylor (American Indian), Virginia Driving Hawk Sneve (American Indian), and Pura Belpré (Puerto Rican). Some writers who are not members of the ethnic groups they write about have also established excellent reputations for writing and editing outstanding books. Both Dorothy Sterling and Milton Meltzer have edited outstanding books on African Americans.

Books and other materials should accurately portray the perspectives, attitudes, and feelings of ethnic groups. Certain values, aspirations, and viewpoints are prevalent in American ethnic communities. Books should honestly and accurately reflect these perspectives and feelings, both through characters and in the interpretations of events and situations. *My Heart Soars* by Chief Dan George powerfully depicts the Native American view that human beings exist in harmony with Mother Earth and other creatures. *We Are Sisters: Black Women in the Nineteenth Century,* edited by Dorothy Sterling, is a rich and powerful collection of documents that present the rage and dreams of African-American women in the nineteenth century. *America Is in the Heart* by Carlos Bulosan, *Mountain Light* by Laurence Yep, *Bless Me Ultima* by Rudolfo Anaya, and *The Sacred Pipe* by Black Elk also faithfully portray ethnic feelings and aspirations.

Fictional works should have strong ethnic characters. Many books have characters of color who are subservient, weak, and ignorant. Papa, Mama, Aunt Waka, and Rinko are strong characters with whom the reader can empathize in *A Jar of Dreams* by Yoshiko Uchida. The reader learns about the further adventures of Rinko in the sequels to this book, *The Best Bad Thing* and *The Happiest Ending.* Drawing on Black legend, myth, and folklore, Virginia Hamilton creates strong and convincing characters in *The Magical Adventures of Pretty Pearl.*

Books should describe settings and experiences with which all students can identify and yet accurately reflect ethnic cultures and life-styles. *Let the Circle Be Unbroken* by Mildred D. Taylor, *Child of the Owl* by Laurence Yep, *A Little Love* by Virginia Hamilton, and *Barrio Boy* by Ernesto Galarza faithfully portray ethnic cultures in such a way that mainstream American students can learn a great deal about them.

The protagonists in books with ethnic themes should have ethnic characteristics but should face conflicts and problems universal to all cultures and groups. The characters in *Dragonwings* by Laurence Yep, *The Best Bad Thing* by Yoshiko Uchida, and *The Friendship* by Mildred D. Taylor have authentic ethnic characteristics and values yet describe universal human problems.

The illustrations in books should be accurate, ethnically sensitive, and technically well done. Many books have beautiful photographs or drawings that are inaccurate. Two of several excellent books that discuss ethnic themes and contain accurate and moving photographs are *The Chinese in San Francisco: A Pictorial History* and *Manzanar.* Photographs in the first book give a comprehensive history of the Chinese in San Francisco. The latter book consists of poignant and deeply moving photographs about the internment.

The illustrations by Susan Meddaugh in *Bimwili and the Zimwi* are captivating and significantly enhance the appeal of this enchanting Tanzanian tale. The woodcuts by Ashley Bryan in *I'm Going to Sing: Black American Spirituals* add a powerful and somber quality to this song book. It is said that one picture is worth a thousand words. There is much truth in this adage. Teachers and librarians should carefully study the illustrations in books and other materials and check them for authenticity, accuracy, and sensitivity. Students can learn either stereotypes or facts from illustrations. Pictures often speak louder than words.

Ethnic materials should not contain racist concepts, clichés, phrases, or words. Many books contain words, phrases, and statements that have negative connotations even though these books might have many other strengths. Books on Eskimos sometimes present them as carefree, happy people who have no serious human problems. Some books on Indians either state or imply that all Indians lived in tepees, were hostile to European settlers, and were savages. Words such as *savage, hostile, primitive,* and *uncivilized* can alert you to a possibly insensitive book or resource, although their use in a book does not necessarily mean that it is insensitive. An author might use these words for the sake of historical accuracy, to depict the language of bigots, or for other justifiable reasons. The teacher or librarian must judge the use of words and phrases within the total context of the book or resource. Nevertheless, you should watch for these kinds of words when evaluating instructional materials. You should also be sensitive to stereotypes of ethnic groups that are subtle. Subtle ethnic stereotypes are more frequent in books today than are blatant ones.

Factual materials should be historically accurate. Books that present inaccurate information about ethnic groups confuse students and reinforce stereotypes. They can also be the source of misconceptions and stereotypes. Examples of accurate informational books about ethnic groups are *Never to Forget* by Milton Meltzer, *Walking the Road to Freedom* by Jeri Ferris, and *Hispanic Voters* by Judith Harlan.

Multiethnic resources and basal textbooks should discuss major events and documents related to ethnic history. Events such as the removal of Indians to Indian Territory in the 1800s and the large migrations of Puerto Ricans to the U.S. mainland that began in the 1920s should be included in every multiethnic and U.S. history textbook. Key legal documents such as the Treaty of Guadalupe Hidalgo (1848) and the Chinese Exclusion Act of 1882 should be included. To be able to determine which key events and documents should be included in basic factual sources, you will need to read at least one general book on each of the major ethnic groups, as suggested earlier.

In addition to the guidelines suggested above, you should determine the age level for which a particular book might be appropriate. Both interest and reading level should be considered. Some books are excellent for adult reading but are inappropriate for school use; others are fine for older readers but inappropriate for young children. The type of classroom situation should also be considered when selecting multicultural materials. A particular book might be appropriate for use with some classrooms but not with others. You should bear in mind whether your class is, for example, all African American, all American Indian, all Asian, all White, or ethnically integrated. You should also consider how you will use each resource. Some books are excellent for basic information but will not give the students a feeling for the ethnic group. Other books have excellent illustrations but poor and distorted texts. Some excellent books, like *A Little Love* by Virginia Hamilton and *My Special Best Words* by John Steptoe, are not appropriate for all students, all purposes, and in all kinds of settings. You must exercise sound judgment, sensitivity, integrity, and insight when selecting and evaluating multicultural materials for class use. In the final analysis, only you can determine which materials can best help to achieve your instructional goals.

Summary

This chapter has delineated the steps you must take to structure a multicultural curriculum focused on decision making. These steps include (1) the identification of key concepts and generalizations, (2) the formulation of intermediate-level generalizations, and (3) the identification of lower-level generalizations related to the ethnic groups selected for study. Once these steps are completed, you can then proceed to structure lessons and gather materials. When formulating lessons, you should make sure that lessons include value inquiry exercises as well as social-action and participation activities when these are appropriate. Examples of value inquiry lessons and social participation activities were discussed.

Prior to implementing a multicultural curriculum, you should plan a reading program that includes (1) one or two general books on ethnicity in the United States, and (2) at least one survey book on each of the major ethnic groups. Recommended books in both categories are in the bibliography of this chapter. The selection and evaluation of student materials are your most challenging tasks. Guidelines and resources for completing this task were given.

Part I of this book deals with the goals of the multicultural curriculum and procedures for planning and organizing instruction. Parts II through V present historical overviews of ethnic groups in the United States and strategies and materials for teaching about them.

Questions and Activities

Respond to the following Ethnic Literacy Test and discuss your responses, giving reasons for them, with your classmates or colleagues. Determine your Ethnic Literacy Score by comparing your responses with the answers given at the end of the test. How might you use this test with your students to stimulate research and discussion? What sources might they use to check their responses? Administer this test, in part or whole, to your class. Adapt it to your students' reading and grade levels. How well did they do on the test? Why?

Ethnic Literacy Test

Directions: Indicate whether each of the following statements is TRUE or FALSE by placing a "T" or "F" in the space preceding it.

1. _____ The percentage of Whites in the United States, relative to non-Whites, decreased between 1970 and 1980.
2. _____ The first Chinese immigrants who came to the United States worked on the railroads.
3. _____ In 1990, there were more than 30 million African Americans in the United States.
4. _____ Puerto Ricans on the island of Puerto Rico became U.S. citizens in 1920.
5. _____ In 1989, Mexican Americans made up about 63% of the Hispanics in the United States.
6. _____ Between 1820 and 1930, 15 million immigrants came to the United States.
7. _____ White Anglo-Saxon Protestants are the most powerful ethnic group in the United States.
8. _____ Rosh Hashanah, which in Hebrew means "end of year," is a Jewish holiday that comes early in the fall.
9. _____ Between 1820 and 1971, Germans were the largest European group immigrating to the United States.
10. _____ The first law to limit immigration to the United States was passed in 1882 to restrict the number of African immigrants.
11. _____ Puerto Ricans in New York City tend to identify strongly with African Americans in that city.
12. _____ Between 1820 and 1971, more individuals from Canada and New-foundland immigrated to the United States than from Mexico.
13. _____ Most African Americans came from the eastern parts of Africa.
14. _____ The internment of the Japanese Americans during World War II was opposed by President Franklin D. Roosevelt.
15. _____ In 1989, there were about 20 million Hispanic Americans in the United States.
16. _____ More than 323,000 immigrants came to the United States from the Philippines between 1981 and 1987.

17. _____ Congress passed a Removal Act that authorized the removal of Indians from east to west of the Mississippi in 1830.
18. _____ A Japanese settlement was established in California as early as 1869.
19. _____ The United States acquired a large part of Mexico's territory under the terms of the Treaty of Guadalupe Hidalgo in 1848.
20. _____ Agriculture dominates the economy of the island of Puerto Rico.
21. _____ The first Africans to arrive in North America came on a Dutch ship that landed at Jamestown, Virginia, in 1619.
22. _____ Demographers predict that one out of every three United States citizens will be a person of color by the year 2000.
23. _____ *Paper sons* is a custom that is associated with Chinese Americans.
24. _____ In 1980, there were about one and one-half million American Indians, Eskimos, and Aleuts in the United States.
25. _____ Some of the bloodiest riots involving African Americans and Whites occurred in the early 1900s.
26. _____ About 289,000 Vietnamese immigrated to the United States between 1981 and 1987.
27. _____ The United States acquired the island of Puerto Rico from Spain in 1898.
28. _____ There are only 438 Japanese surnames.
29. _____ Chinese immigrants to the United States became distinguished for their outstanding work on truck farms.
30. _____ The only large Puerto Rican community on the U.S. mainland is in New York City.
31. _____ A third-generation Japanese American is called a *Sansei.*
32. _____ More than 93,000 Iranians immigrated to the United States between 1981 and 1987.
33. _____ More than one-half of American Indians lived in central cities in 1980.
34. _____ Most Chinese immigrants to the United States came from western China.
35. _____ Eleven Italian Americans were lynched in New Orleans in 1892.
36. _____ Nativism directed against southern and eastern European immigrants was intense when the Statue of Liberty was dedicated in 1886.
37. _____ In 1989 there were more than one million Cubans living in the United States.
38. _____ More than 71,000 Haitians immigrated to the United States between 1971 and 1980.

Answers to Ethnic Literacy Test

1. **T**	2. **F**	3. **T**	4. **F**	5. **T**	6. **F**	7. **T**	8. **F**	9. **T**
10. **F**	11. **F**	12. **T**	13. **F**	14. **F**	15. **T**	16. **T**	17. **T**	18. **T**
19. **T**	20. **F**	21. **F**	22. **T**	23. **T**	24. **T**	25. **T**	26. **T**	27. **T**
28. **F**	29. **F**	30. **F**	31. **T**	32. **T**	33. **T**	34. **F**	35. **T**	36. **T**
37. **T**	38. **T**							

3

3

Endnotes

1. More than 100 ethnic groups are identified and described in Stephan Thernstrom, Ann Orlov, and Oscar Handlin, eds., *Harvard Encyclopedia of American Ethnic Groups* (Cambridge: Harvard University Press, 1980).
2. Charles Y. Glock, Robert Wutnow, Jane A. Piliavin, and Metta Spencer, *Adolescent Prejudice* (New York: Harper and Row, 1975).
3. Ibid.
4. Edward T. Hall, *Beyond Culture* (Garden City, N.Y.: Doubleday, 1977).
5. Donald Oliver and James P. Shaver, *Teaching Public Issues in the High School* (Boston: Houghton Mifflin, 1966); and Fred N. Newmann, with the assistance of Donald W. Oliver, *Clarifying Public Controversy: An Approach to Teaching Social Studies* (Boston: Little, Brown, 1970).
6. Louis E. Raths, Merrill Harmin, and Sidney B. Simon, *Values and Teaching: Working with Values in the Classroom*, 2nd ed. (Columbus, Oh.: Charles E. Merrill, 1978).
7. Lawrence Kohlberg and Elliot Turiel, "Moral Development and Moral Education," in *Psychology and Educational Practice*, ed. Gerald S. Lesser (Glenview, Ill.: Scott, Foresman, 1971).
8. Lawrence Kohlberg, "Moral Education for a Society in Moral Transition," *Educational Leadership* 33 (October 1975): 46–54.
9. James A. Banks, with Ambrose A. Clegg, Jr., *Teaching Strategies for the Social Studies*, 4th ed. (New York: Longman, Inc., 1990), pp. 435–445.
10. From *Role-Playing in the Curriculum*, 2nd ed. (pp. 383–384) by Fannie R. Shaftel and George Shaftel, 1982. Englewood Cliffs, N.J.: Prentice-Hall. Copyright 1982 by Prentice-Hall. Reprinted by permission.
11. Elliot Aronson and Alex Gonzalez, "Desegregation, Jigsaw, and the Mexican-American Experience," in *Eliminating Racism: Profiles in Controversy*, eds. Phyllis A. Katz and Dalmas A. Taylor (New York: Plenum Press, 1988), pp. 301–314.
12. David W. Johnson and Roger T. Johnson, *Learning Together and Alone: Cooperative, Competitive, & Individualistic Learning*, 2nd ed. (Englewood Cliffs, N.J.: Prentice-Hall, 1987); Robert E. Slavin, *Cooperative Learning* (New York: Longman, 1983); Elizabeth G. Cohen, *Designing Groupwork: Strategies for the Heterogeneous Classroom* (New York: Teachers College Press, 1986).

Books Cited in Chapter Text

Aardema, Verna. *Bimwili and the Zimwi*. Illustrated by Susan Meddaugh. New York: Dial, 1985.
Anaya, Rudolfo. *Bless Me Ultima*. Berkeley, Calif.: Tonatiuh International, 1972.
Armor, John, and Wright, Peter. *Manzanar*. Photographs by Ansel Adams. Commentary by John Hersey. New York: Vintage, 1988.
Black Elk. *The Scared Piple*. Edited by John Epes Brown. Baltimore: Penguin, 1971.
Bryan, Ashley. *I'm Going to Sing: Black American Spirituals*. Vol. 2. New York: Atheneum, 1982.
Bulosan, Carlos. *America Is in the Heart*. Seattle: University of Washington Press, 1973 (Reprint).

Chief Dan George. *My Heart Soars.* Illustrated by Helmut Hirnschall. Buffalo, N.Y.: Hancock House Publishers, 1974.

Dicker, Laverne Mace. *The Chinese in San Francisco: A Pictorial History.* New York: Dover, 1979.

Ferris, Jeri. *Walking the Road to Freedom.* Minneapolis: Carolrhoda Books, 1988.

Galarza, Ernesto. *Barrio Boy.* South Bend, Ind.: University of Notre Dame Press, 1971.

Hamilton, Virginia. *A Little Love.* New York: Philomel, 1984.

————. *The Magical Adventures of Pretty Pearl.* New York: Harper and Row, 1983.

Harlan, Judith. *Hispanic Voters.* New York: Franklin Watts, 1988.

Meltzer, Milton. *Never to Forget: The Jews of the Holocaust.* New York: Harper and Row, 1976.

Steptoe, John. *My Special Best Words.* New York: Viking Press, 1974.

Sterling, Dorothy, ed. *We Are Sisters: Black Women in the Nineteenth Century.* New York: Norton, 1984.

Taylor, Mildred D. *The Friendship.* Pictures by Max Ginsburg. New York: Dial, 1987.

————. *Let the Circle Be Unbroken.* New York: Dial, 1981.

Uchida, Yoshiko. *The Best Bad Thing.* New York: Atheneum, 1985.

————.*The Happiest Ending.* New York: Atheneum, 1985.

————. *A Jar of Dreams.* New York: Atheneum, 1981.

Yep, Laurence. *Child of the Owl.* New York: Harper and Row, 1977.

————. *Dragonwings.* New York: Harper and Row, 1975.

————. *Mountain Light.* New York: Harper and Row, 1985.

Bibliography

Multiethnic References

Mindel, Charles H.; Habenstein, Robert W.; and Wright, Roosevelt, Jr., eds. *Ethnic Families in America,* 3rd ed. New York: Elsevier, 1988.

Rimers, David M. *Still the Golden Door: The Third World Comes to America.* New York: Columbia University Press, 1985.

Rose, Peter I. *They and We: Racial and Ethnic Relations in the United States,* 4th ed. New York: Random House, 1990.

African Americans

Blackwell, James E. *The Black Community: Diversity and Unity.* New York: Harper and Row, 1985.

Franklin, John Hope, and Moss, Alfred A., Jr. *From Slavery to Freedom: A History of Black Americans,* 6th ed. New York: Knopf, 1988.

Jaynes, Gerald D., and Williams, Robin M., Jr. *A Common Destiny: Blacks and American Society.* Washington, D.C.: National Academy Press, 1989.

Landry, Bart. *The New Black Middle Class.* Berkeley: University of California Press, 1987.

American Indians

Calloway, Colin G., ed. *New Directions in American Indian History.* Norman: University of Oklahoma Press, 1988.
Trenton, Patricia, and Houlihan, Patricia T. *Native Americans: Five Centuries of Changing Images.* New York: Harry N. Abrams, Inc. Publishers, 1989.
Waldman, Carl. *Atlas of the North American Indians.* Maps and illustrations by Molly Braun. New York: Facts on File Publications, 1985.

Asian Americans

Caplan, Nathan; Whitemore, John K.; and Choy, Marcella H. *The Boat People and Achievement in America: A Study of Family Life, Hard Work, and Cultural Values.* Ann Arbor: The University of Michigan Press, 1989.
Cordova, Fred. *Filipinos: Forgotten Asian Americans.* Dubuque, Ia.: Kendall/Hunt Publishing Company, 1983.
Kitano, Harry H. L., and Daniels, Roger. *Asian Americans: Emerging Minorities.* Englewood Cliffs, N.J.: Prentice-Hall, 1988.
Takaki, Ronald. *Strangers from a Different Shore: A History of Asian Americans.* Boston: Little, Brown, 1989.
Tsai, Shih-Shan Henry. *The Chinese Experience in America.* Bloomington: Indiana University Press, 1986.

Hispanic Americans

Acuña, Rodolfo. *Occupied America: A History of Chicanos,* 3rd ed. New York: Harper and Row, 1988.
Bean, Frank D., and Tienda, Marta. *The Hispanic Population of the United States.* New York: Russell Sage Foundation, 1987.
Boswell, Thomas D., and Curtis, James R. *The Cuban-American Experience: Culture, Images and Perspectives.* Totowa, N.J.: Rowman and Allanheld, 1984.
Moore, Joan, and Pachon, Harry. *Hispanics in the United States.* Englewood Cliffs, N.J.: Prentice-Hall, 1985.
Rodriguez, Clara E. *Puerto Ricans: Born in the USA.* Boston: Unwin Hyman, Inc., 1989.

European Americans

Battistella, Graziano, ed. *Italian Americans in the 80s: A Sociodemographic Profile.* Staten Island, N.Y.: Center for Migration Studies, 1989.
Cordasco, Francesco, ed. *A Dictionary of American Immigration History.* New York: Garland Publishing Company, 1989.
Dinnerstein, Leonard, and Reimers, David M. *Ethnic Americans: A History of Immigration,* 3rd ed. New York: Harper and Row, 1988.
Shapiro, Mary J. *Gateway to Liberty: The Story of the Statue of Liberty and Ellis Island.* New York: Vintage, 1986.

Jewish Americans

Bletter, Diana, and Grinker, Lori. *The Invisible Thread: Portraits of Jewish American Women.* Philadelphia: Jewish Publication Society, 1989.

Hertzberg, Arthur. *The Jews in America, Four Centuries of an Uneasy Encounter: A History.* New York: Simon & Schuster, 1989.

Johnson, Paul. *A History of the Jews.* New York: Harper and Row, 1987.

Part II

The First Americans

and African Americans

Concepts and Strategies

T his part consists of content, concepts, teaching strategies, and materials for teaching about American Indians, Native Hawaiians, and African-Americans. Although different in many ways, these groups share some important experiences. American Indians and Native Hawaiians are native to the land that is now the United States. African Americans were one of the first groups to come to America from a distant land. They were the only group to come in chains. Each of these groups has deep roots in America.

American Indians and Native Hawaiians are two of the nation's smallest ethnic groups (1980 population—1,361,869 and 172,346, respectively). African Americans are the nation's largest ethnic minority group (1988 population—29.3 million). African Americans comprised about 12.2% of the nation's population in 1980. Despite the tremendous differences in the sizes of the populations of African Americans, Indians, and Native Hawaiians, the experiences of these groups have often been characterized by common concepts and themes, such as racism, discrimination, protest, and resistance. A study of these three ethnic groups will help students better understand the long journey toward freedom in the United States. It might also help them renew their commitment to justice and equality.

Chapter 5

American Indians

Concepts, Strategies, and Materials

The earth was created by the assistance of the sun, and it should be left as it was. . . . The earth and myself are of one mind.

—Chief Joseph, Nez Perce

Introduction

Popular images about American Indians and Eskimos are widespread in the United States. These images are often stereotypic. They contribute to students' misunderstandings of Indian and Eskimo cultures. Older Western movies shown on television contribute greatly to the stereotypic image of American Indians within U.S. society. Statements made in schools by educators, such as "Sit like an Indian," also contribute to the perpetuation of Indian stereotypes. Even though textbooks in the 1990s do not include the blatant stereotypes of the "hostile" Indian often found in textbooks in the past, they usually present history from a Western-centric point of view and perspective. Textbooks often call the Americas *The New World*, imply if not state that Columbus "discovered" America, and describe the migration of European Americans from the eastern to the western part of the United States as "The Westward Movement."

These approaches to the study of U.S. history and culture are Eurocentric and mainstream-centric because they imply that American civilization did not exist until the Europeans first arrived in the late fifteenth century. They consequently deny the existence of the Native American cultures and civilizations that had existed in the Americas for centuries before the Europeans came.

Archaeologists estimate that human beings have lived in the Americas for at least 40,000 years. These peoples had established complex civilizations before the Europeans arrived in the fifteenth century. These cultures included elaborate irrigation works and massive artificial mounds crowned with temples. The Olmec in Mexico, the Chavin in Peru, and the civilizations of Teotihuacan, the Maya, the Toltecs, and Aztecs were important American civilizations before the Europeans arrived in the Americas.[1]

A major goal of American Indian curriculum content should be to help students to view the development of the Americas—and of U.S. society in particular—from the point of view of the Native Americans. For example, the movement of the European Americans from the eastern to the western part of the United States was not, from the Indian point of view, a westward movement. The Lakota Sioux did not consider their homeland the west but the center of the universe. Students should be helped to understand key events, concepts, and issues from different ethnic and cultural perspectives. The "Westward Movement" had very different meanings for the migrating European Americans and for the Indians whose homeland was being invaded. To the Indians, it could more appropriately be called, "An Age of Doom" or "The Great Invasion," rather than "The Westward Movement." By helping students to view concepts, events, and issues from diverse cultural and ethnic perspectives, we can help them become critical thinkers and more compassionate citizens of the nation-state. Content about American Indians can contribute greatly to these important and generic educational goals.

American Indians: Historical Perspective

Important Dates

1513	Juan Ponce de León landed on the Florida peninsula while on route from Puerto Rico. The relationship between Europeans and North American Indians began.
1565	The Spaniards established the St. Augustine colony in Florida, the first settlement organized by Europeans in present-day United States.
1637	Connecticut colonists killed more than 500 Indians when the Pequot tribe tried to stop the colonists from invading their territory. This event is known as the Pequot War.
1675–76	King Philip, a Wampanoag chief, led a coalition of Indian troops that nearly defeated the English colonists. However, his forces were eventually beaten and his body dismembered by the colonists.
1680	The Pueblos rebelled against the Spaniards and drove them from Pueblo territory. Many Spaniards were killed during the uprising.

Important Dates	
1754–63	The French and Indian War occurred. It was one of a series of wars in which the French and the British struggled for control of the eastern part of North America. Each nation vied for Indian support.
1784	A group of Indians suffered a crushing defeat at Fallen Timbers in Ohio on August 20. In 1795, they were forced to sign a treaty that ceded large segments of their lands in the Northwest Territory to Whites.
1812	The War of 1812, a war between the United States and Britain, caused deep factions among the Indian tribes because of their different allegiances. The Indian allies of the British were severely punished by the United States when the war ended.
1824	The Bureau of Indian Affairs was established in the War Department.
1830	Congress passed a Removal Act that authorized the removal of Indians from east to west of the Mississippi and stated conditions under which removal could be legally undertaken.
1831	The Supreme Court recognized Indian tribes as "domestic dependent nations" within the United States. In an 1832 decision, the Court declared that such nations had a right to self-government.
1838–39	The Cherokee were forcefully removed from Georgia to Indian Territory in present-day Oklahoma. Their poignant journey westward is recalled as the "Trail of Tears."
1864	The Colorado militia killed nearly 300 Cheyennes in a surprise attack at Sand Creek, after the Cheyenne leaders had negotiated an armistice. This incident is known as the Sand Creek Massacre.
1871	A congressional act prohibited the making of further treaties with Indian tribes.
1876	Sioux tribes, under the leadership of Sitting Bull, wiped out Custer's Seventh Cavalry at Little Big Horn. This was one of the last victories for Indian tribes.
1881	Helen Hunt Jackson's *A Century of Dishonor* was published. It was the first influential book to dramatize the plight of Indian peoples in the United States.
1886	The brave Apache warrior, Geronimo, surrendered to U.S. forces in September 1886. His surrender marked the defeat of the southwest tribes.

Important Dates	
1887	Congress passed the Dawes Severalty Act, which was designed partially to terminate the Indian's special relationship with the U.S. government. It proved to be disastrous for Indians.
1890	Three hundred Sioux were killed at Wounded Knee Creek in South Dakota.
1924	The Snyder Act made American Indians citizens of the United States.
1928	The Meriam Survey recommended major changes in federal policy related to Indian affairs. Many of its recommendations were implemented in subsequent years.
1934	The Wheeler-Howard Act made it possible for Indians to reestablish aspects of their traditional cultures, including tribal lands and governments.
1944	The National Congress of American Indians was organized by Indians.
1946	The Indian Claims Commission was established to hear cases related to possible compensations due Indians for loss of land and property.
1948	Indians were granted the right to vote in New Mexico and Arizona.
1953	A congressional act enabled nonreservation Indians to purchase alcohol. Reservations were authorized to determine local policy with regard to the sale of alcohol.
1954	Congressional acts terminated the relationship between the federal government and several Indian tribes, including the Klamath tribe in Oregon, the Menominee of Wisconsin, and the California Indians.
1961	The National Indian Youth Council was organized.
1969	*Custer Died for Your Sins: An Indian Manifesto* by Vine DeLoria, Jr., was published. This book represented a significant point in the Indian civil rights movement. N. Scott Momaday won the Pulitzer Prize for *House Made of Dawn.*
1970	President Richard M. Nixon made a statement advocating Indian self-determination.
1972	Congress restored the Menominee tribe of Wisconsin to federal-trust status.

Important Dates	
1973	Members of the American Indian Movement and other Indians occupied Wounded Knee, South Dakota, to dramatize the Indian's condition in the United States.
1975	The Indian Self-Determination Act recognized the autonomy of Indian tribes and their special relationship with the federal government.
1978	The Indian Freedom of Religion Act was passed. This act granted Indians the right to practice their religious beliefs.
1979	The Supreme Court upheld the fishing rights claims of the Indian tribes of Washington state.
1980	The Passamaquoddy and Penobscot tribes of Maine received a settlement of their land claims after a long and difficult legal battle.
1989	Native American tribal groups were successful in convincing the Smithsonian Institution to develop a policy that will allow it to return the remains of their ancestors to them. Native American tribes felt that the remains of their ancestors were being desecrated by the Smithsonian as well as by other museums.

Early Life in the Americas

When the European explorers arrived in the Western Hemisphere in 1492, it was populated by many different cultures and groups that became collectively known as "Indians" to Europeans. Columbus thought that he had reached India when he landed in San Salvador in 1492. This misnaming of the aboriginal peoples of the Americas by the Europeans foreshadowed the misunderstandings, distrust, and hostility that later developed between the two groups.

The early history of American Indians is still somewhat of a mystery to scientists. Archaeologists are trying to unravel their early history by digging up fossils that give clues to early human life in the Americas. Occasionally, landmark archaeological discoveries are made, enabling scientists to learn more about early people in the Western Hemisphere. In 1927, near Folsom, New Mexico, scientists found a point embedded between the ribs of a Pleistocene bison that early Americans used to kill. This finding proved that men and women were in the Americas when Ice Age animals were roaming freely on this continent. Similar points were found at a dig near Clovis, New Mexico, in 1932. Scientists were able to date the points to 9200 B.C. by using Carbon 14.[2]

The Origins of American Indians

We do not know exactly when people first came to the Americas. However, archaeologists have ruled out the possibility that human beings evolved in the Western Hemisphere because no fossils of pre-Homo Sapiens have been found on the American continent.[3] No remains of the closest cousins of human beings, the great apes, have been found in the Americas, either. Despite these theories, however, many Indian groups believe that they were created by the Great Spirit in the Americas. Archaeologists believe that the ancestors of American Indians originally came from Asia. However, when they came is a topic of tremendous controversy. In the late 1960s, a few American archaeologists accepted dates before 13,000 B.C. In the early 1980s, some archaeologists put the date as far back as 100,000 years. In the 1990s, the dates accepted by archaeologists range from 16,000 to 40,000 years ago, with few accepting a date greater than 40,000 years ago.[4]

Most archaeologists use the Bering Strait theory to explain how people first reached the Western Hemisphere. The body of water separating Siberia and Alaska today is called the Bering Strait. Archaeologists believe that at various times in prehistory this water receded and a landmass bridged present-day Siberia and Alaska. This land bridge is called *Beringia*. The early ancestors of the Native Americans crossed this stretch of land while hunting animals and plants to eat. (See Figure 5–1.)

The Indian Population before the Europeans Came

There is as much controversy about the size of the Indian population when the Europeans arrived in the Americas in the fifteenth century as there is about when the Indians crossed Beringia to reach the Americas. The population estimates vary greatly. In 1924, Rivet estimated the Western hemisphere population to have been 40 to 50 million and the North American population to have been 2 to 3.5 million when the Europeans arrived. Mooney, in 1928, estimated the Indian North American pre-Columbian population to be 1,153,000. In 1939, Kroeber estimated the Western hemisphere population to be 8,400,000 and the North American continent population to be 900,000.[5]

In the 1960s and 1970s researchers such as Dobyns and Denevan seriously challenged the estimates by Mooney and Kroeber. They have given much higher estimates. Dobyns believes that the Americas were heavily populated when the Europeans arrived. In 1966, Dobyns estimated that the Western hemisphere population at contact was 90,043,000 and that the North American population was 9,800,000 (see Table 5–1).[6] Dobyns and Denevan estimate that the population north of the Rio Grande was at least 10 million when the Europeans first came to the Americas.[7]

Figure 5–1 *The Bering Strait Land Bridge and the Migration of Early Indians*

Siberia

Bering Strait Land Bridge

Ice Cap during Wisconsin Glaciation

Possible Coastline during Glaciation

Possible Migration Routes of Early Indians

Source: From *Atlas of the North American Indian*, by Carl Waldman, Maps and illustrations by Molly Braun. Copyright© 1985 by Carl Waldman. Reprinted with the permission of Facts on File, Inc., New York.

Table 5–1   *Estimates of the Indian Population at Contact with Europeans*

Date of Estimate	Author	Western Hemisphere	North America
1910	Mooney	–	1,150,000
1924	Rivet	40–50,000,000	1,148,000
1924	Supper	40–50,000,000	2–3,500,000
1928	Spinden	50–75,000,000	–
1928	Mooney	–	1,153,000
1931	Wilcox	13,101,000	1,002,000
1939	Kroeber	8,400,000	900,000
1945	Rosenblat	13,385,000	1,000,000
1945	Steward	13,170,000	1,000,000
1949	Steward	15,490,800	1,000,000
1964	Borah	100,000,000	–
1966	Dobyns	90,043,000	9,800,000
1976	Ubelaker	–	2,171,125
1981	Thornton and Marsh-Thornton	–	7,705,000
1983	Dobyns	–	18,000,000

Sources: Henry Dobyns, *Their Number Became Thinned: Native American Population Dynamics in Eastern North America* (Knoxville: University of Tennessee Press, 1983), pp. 33–45; Russell Thornton and Jeanne Marsh-Thornton, "Estimating Prehistoric American Indian Population Size for United States: Implications of the Nineteenth Century Population Decline and Nadir," *American Journal of Phyiscal Anthropology* 55 (1981): 47–53; and Douglas H. Ubelaker, "Prehistoric New World Population Size: Historical Review and Current Appraisal of New World Estimates," *American Journal of Physical Anthropology* 45 (1976): 661–666.

Table Source: Paul Stuart, *Nations within a Nation: Historical Statistics of American Indians* (Greenwood Press, Westport, CT, 1987), p. 51. Copyright © 1987 by Paul Stuart. Reprinted with permission of Greenwood Publishing Group, Inc.

The Diversity of Indian Cultures

Although the word *Indian* often connotes a stereotypic image in the popular mind, Indian peoples were quite diverse, both physically and culturally. Their skin color ranged from dark to light. Their height, hair texture, and facial features varied greatly.

It is not possible to determine exactly how many languages were spoken in the Americas before the Europeans came or to determine how many people spoke each language. Two frequently accepted estimates of the number of languages spoken are 1,800 and more than 2,000.[8] Anthropologists have tried with great difficulty to categorize Indian languages into six major language families.

How Indians survived also varied widely. Some groups, like the tribes of the subarctic, did not practice agriculture, but obtained food by fishing and hunting. Agriculture was the basis of the sedentary communities and complex cultures of the southwest Indians.

Political institutions in Indian cultures were also quite diverse. Highly sophisticated confederations were common among the northeast tribes, such as the Creek Confederacy and the League of the Iroquois. These confederations contrasted strikingly with political life within the California tribes. These tribes usually had no formal political institutions, but were organized into small family units that were headed by men who had group responsibilities but little authority over others. Warring and raiding were important aspects of the Apache culture. However, the Hopi, who called themselves "the peaceful ones," were one of the most tranquil people on earth. Social class had little meaning among the southwest tribes, but was extremely important in the northwest Pacific Coast cultures. Food, hunting methods, house types, clothing, tools, and religious ceremonies also varied greatly among and within various American Indian cultural groups.[9]

Similarities in Indian Cultures

Although American Indian cultures were highly diverse, they were similar in many ways. Some of their similar traits, especially those related to core values, make up "Indianness" or what is uniquely "Indian." Most American Indians were deeply religious and spiritual people. Religion greatly influenced all aspects of their lives. Because Indians saw people existing within a spiritual world that included all other living things, animal spirits often played major roles in their religions. They viewed the universe as a harmonious whole, with every object and being having a sacred life; to separate human beings from nature was antithetical to the Great Spirit, for to the Great Spirit all was life.

The tribes of the northwest Pacific Coast believed in many spirits, such as those of the eagle, beaver, and whale. They sought the protection of these spirits through various ceremonies and rituals. The shaman, who played a key role in many Indian religions, helped them gain contact with the spiritual world.

The southwest tribes had a rich and elaborate year-round sequence of ceremonials including songs, dances, and poetry. American Indians often called on the help of the spirits in their daily lives. The Hopi performed dances to bring rain. The Apaches engaged in special dances and ceremonies to gain the support of the spirits before undertaking raids or going into war. Tribes in the Plains and the northwest Pacific Coast often sought contact with the spirits by going on a vision quest. Religious beliefs and rituals permeated every aspect of Indian life.

American Indians had a deep respect and reverence for the earth and for all other living things. They believed that people must not harm the earth and should regard it as sacred. Many Indian religious leaders were often shocked by the ways in which the White people's agriculture defiled the Mother Earth. Forbes has summarized these beliefs: "The Earth our Mother is holy and should be treated as such . . . all forms of life are our brothers and sisters and have to be respected. . . . Life itself is a holy, sacred experience . . . we must live our lives as a *religion*, that is, with constant concern for spiritual relationships and values . . . we must live lives that bring forth both physical and spiritual 'beauty.' All life has the potentiality of bringing forth Beauty and Harmony, but [humans] in particular [have] also the ability to bring forth ugliness and disharmony."[10]

In their literature and speeches, American Indians often bemoaned how the Whites destroyed and defiled the earth, as in this passage by an old Winto woman: "The White people plow up the ground, pull down the trees, kill everything. The tree says, 'Don't. I am sore. Don't hurt me.' But they chop it down and cut it up. The spirit of the land hates them. They blast our trees and stir it up to its depths. . . . How can the spirit of the earth like the White man? . . . Everywhere the White man has touched it, it is sore."[11]

The Indian conception of the earth and their relationship to the land differed greatly from the Europeans' and was a source of conflict between the two cultures. The Indians believed that people could use the earth as long as they treated it with respect, but they could not sell it anymore than they could sell the air or the sea. When, in exchange for gifts, American Indians gave Europeans permission to use their lands, many did not realize that from a European viewpoint they were also giving up their own rights to use the lands. The European regarded the earth as a commodity that could be broken into parts and owned by individuals. To the American Indian, the earth was sacred and consequently could never be owned by human beings.

The Indian also had a deep respect for the rights and dignity of the individual. Decisions in Indian councils and confederacies were usually based on group consensus. Deliberations were often long and decisions of governing bodies slow because consensus had to be attained. The Creek Confederacy reached all of its decisions by consensus. However, each nation within the confederacy maintained its autonomy and was not bound to a decision with which it did not agree. The Europeans learned a great deal from the American Indians about representative government and the rights and dignity of the individual, which they incorporated into the major constitutional documents on which U.S. democracy is based.

Leaders of groups within the subarctic tribes had little authority over their followers. This was characteristic of Indian societies. Leaders were rarely deified as they were in Europe, the Middle East, and Asia. There were few hierarchical political organizations in the Americas. Leaders often had to earn the respect of others by becoming outstanding warriors, acquiring a special ability to communicate with the spirits, or learning to perform some other service the community needed and valued. Communities were usually democratic, with no kings or other kinds of rulers. However, there were important exceptions to these generalizations. The Inca Empire of Peru was one of the most totalitarian states that ever existed in human history.

Because of their feudalistic background, the Europeans looked for kings among the Indians and assumed that Indian chiefs had absolute authority over their tribes. The European settlers created tremendous problems by imposing their conceptions of the nation-state on Indian societies. They made treaties with chiefs and assumed that they were binding to their tribes. They did not understand that the chief's authority was usually limited by the tribal council. He had little power that the tribe did not grant him. This cultural conflict between the Europeans and the Indians haunted their relationships for centuries.

Early Contact with Europeans

The Indians' earliest contacts with the Europeans were usually friendly and generally involved trade. The French, the English, and the Dutch exchanged European goods and tools for furs. This exchange of goods was initially beneficial for both groups. The furs greatly increased the Europeans' wealth; the European goods and tools made life easier for the Indians. Eventually, the Indians began to consider the European goods necessities rather than luxuries. What had begun as a mutually beneficial trade relationship was destined to cause disaster for the Indians.

Indians acquired rum, guns, gunpowder, horses, and other goods from the Europeans. Tribes that wanted European goods but had depleted the supply of fur-producing animals on their lands began to invade the territories of other tribes to obtain furs for trade. These invasions led to skirmishes and eventually to wars. European goods made intertribal warring more likely and possible. It was rather easy for the tribes that had European guns and gunpowder to defeat tribes lacking these supplies. Thus, the Europeans, through trade and other schemes (discussed later), initiated divide-and-conquer tactics among the Indian tribes in New England. Indian wars, raids, and attacks were greatly intensified by the presence of the Europeans.

The League of the Iroquois began an aggressive campaign to gain a monopoly of the European trade and to dominate competing tribes. The League had eliminated hundreds of Hurons and forced those remaining into captivity in 1649. The Iroquois were feared by tribes throughout New England. They eventually dominated the Delawares, the Nanticokes, and other groups of Algonkian-speaking tribes by 1680. The League became so powerful that the British regarded it as power to be reckoned with.

Indian and European Wars

From about 1540 to the 1790s, no one power was dominant in the Indian territory that had been invaded by the Europeans in the Northeast. The Swedes and the Dutch had been driven from the area before 1700. However, the Frenchmen, Spaniards, and Englishmen struggled for control of the region. The Indians also tried to maintain their power. The power struggle became more intricate and intense when the British colonies entered the contest. Until the

American Revolution, the Indians were unable to tell which of the warlike European nations, if any, would become the dominant power. The Indians probably thought that a balance of power would eventually be established in the region, in which they would be a major participant.

The European wars and struggles for power deeply influenced Indian policy and political institutions. In each war with European people, the Indians had to decide which group, if any, they would support. Each of the powers competed for Indian alliance and support. Although the Indians often tried to maintain a policy of neutrality, this became increasingly difficult as the European nations aggressively vied for their support. The Creeks and the Cherokees fought on the side of the French, against the British, in the French and Indian War. The French were defeated and their Indian allies were severely punished by the British for helping the enemy. The Indians were also weakened by their severe losses during the war.

The European wars caused deep factionalism within the Indian tribes and confederations. In the War of 1812, the various tribes became deeply divided over whether they should support the United Sates or the British. The treaties ending the American Revolution and the War of 1812 stunned and angered Britain's Indian allies. Neither treaty acknowledged the decisive roles the Indians had played in these wars. After the American Revolution, the British granted the colonists lands that were occupied by these Indian allies. The British had pitted Indian tribes against each other and then ignored these allies' self-interests when the fighting stopped. In time, the Indians began to see the futility of becoming involved in the European wars. They became increasingly committed to a policy of neutrality. Alexander McGillivray, the Creek diplomat, used the Europeans' tactics and pitted the colonists against the Spaniards by astutely negotiating.

The Decline of the League of the Iroquois

The League of the Iroquois was deeply affected by the European wars and was eventually destroyed by the factionalism caused by the wars. The League, the French, and the British were the three major powers in the Northeast in the first decades of the 1700s. Factionalism developed within the League over the positions it should take in the European wars. One of the nations, the Senecas, fought on the side of the French in the French and Indian War. The other nations supported the British. Even greater disunity developed within the League when the American Revolution began. Some of the nations supported the British; others were sympathetic to the colonists. Internal splits developed within several of the nations over the issue. The colonists looted and burned Iroquois villages after the Revolution and flaunted their newly gained power.

The fate of the Iroquois was later experienced by other tribes. The Iroquois had warred against other Indian tribes to obtain furs to trade and had fought as allies in the European wars. Their confederation was later destroyed because of splits caused by the European wars. The Indian nations did not realize that they had a common fate in the Northeast, and that the future of one Indian nation was intricately tied to the future of all Indian tribes. Culturally and politically, the Indians were separate and distinct people. However, the Whites saw them as a group that had to be pushed west of the Mississippi and ultimately conquered or destroyed.

Treaties and Indian Removal

The relationship between Indians and European settlers had developed into a pattern by the time of the American Revolution. The initial contact usually involved trade, whereby Indians acquired tools and firearms and the Europeans obtained furs. These initial events usually pitted Indian tribes against each other as they competed for the European trade and for the lands containing fur-producing animals. When the furs had been depleted, the Europeans began an aggressive drive to obtain the lands the Indians occupied. The Indians often formed confederations and alliances to fight back the European invaders or extended the functions of existing confederations. Ironically, however, the Indians' involvement in the White people's wars usually disrupted these confederations. Indians adamantly resisted the attempts by the Whites to displace them. They fought defensive wars, such as the King Philip's War in 1675 and the Black Hawk War in 1832. Indian uprisings also occurred, like the Sioux uprising in 1862 and the Little Crow uprising in 1863.

Despite their aggressive and bold resistance, the Europeans were destined to win the struggle. The Whites retaliated with shocking massacres, like Sand Creek in 1864, biological warfare, and massive wars in which men, women, and children were killed and often dismembered and scalped. After Indian resistance was crushed, whites legitimized the taking of Indian lands by convincing their leaders to sign treaties. Indian chiefs were frequently offered gifts or other bribes to sign treaties. Once an Indian group had signed a treaty, the Whites schemed to remove them from their land. Often the Indians were forced west of the Mississippi into Indian Territory (present-day Oklahoma), land the Whites considered uninhabitable. If only a few Indians remained after the conquest, they were often absorbed by local tribes or forced onto reservations.

This cycle was repeated many times as the White settlers pushed westward. When Whites went farther west, Indians were forced to sign new treaties granting Whites the lands earlier treaties had assured them. Some Indian groups, like the Winnebagos, were forced to move as many as six times. The Winnebagos were shifted from location to location for 30 years. No aspects of U.S. history are more poignant than the accounts of the making and breaking of Indian treaties by Whites and the forced removal of Indians across the United States. This prediction by a Cherokee newspaper describing how Whites would obtain Indian land in Texas highlights how treaties were often made: "A Commissioner will be sent down to negotiate, with a pocket full of money and his mouth full of lies. Some chiefs he will bribe, some he will flatter, and some he will make drunk; and the result will be . . . something that will be called a treaty."[12]

The Westward Journeys

Some Indian tribes, realizing the futility of resistance, accepted their fate and moved westward without force. Others, however, bitterly resisted removal and were removed by military troops. Generally, the tribes that had to be removed at gunpoint suffered the most. However, they all suffered greatly. The Winnebagos, who offered little resistance, were shifted from place to place between 1829 and 1866. About half of them perished during the perpetual sojourn. The Seminoles, who signed a removal treaty in 1832, violently resisted removal. Hostilities began in 1835 and continued for 7 years. The United States lost nearly 1,500 men and spent more than $50 million in its attempts to crush the Seminoles' resistance. Most of the Seminoles were eventually forced to Indian Territory. However, several hundred remained in the Florida Everglades, where their descendants live today.

The Georgians began an aggressive drive to remove the Cherokees from their homeland when gold was discovered on Cherokee land in 1829. The Cherokees initiated a court battle against removal. In 1832, the Supreme Court ruled that the Cherokees had a right to remain on their land. However, this ruling by the high court did not halt the determined efforts of the Georgians and President Andrew Jackson to remove the Cherokees. Harassed and pressured, part of the tribe finally signed a removal treaty in 1835. Even though only a minority of the tribe's leaders signed the treaty, the Cherokees were forced to move to Indian Territory. During the long march from Georgia to Oklahoma in 1838 and 1839, almost one-fourth of the Cherokees died from starvation, diseases, and the perils of the journey. Their long westward journey is recalled as the "Trail of Tears." The Creeks were forced to sign a treaty in 1832, which gave the Whites rights to their lands east of the Mississippi. Nearly half of the Creeks perished during the migration to and their early years in the West.

Like the White people's wars, removal caused deep factions within the various Indian tribes and nations. Some leaders felt that it was in their best interests to cooperate with the White authorities; others believed that removal should be resisted until the bitter end. These splits within the tribes intensified when the Indians arrived in the West and hastened the disintegration of their institutions that had begun before removal.

In retrospect, it is clear that the fate of the Indians was doomed and that they either had to relocate or be exterminated. The federal government legitimized Indian removal with the Removal Act of 1830. This act legalized Indian removal and specified the conditions under which Indians could be removed legally. The act provided funds for removal and authorized an exchange of lands for displaced Indians. The act stipulated that the tribe's consent must be obtained. It made little difference in the actual removal of Indians. Local officials continued to use any possible tactics to convince Indians to sign treaties and to move westward.

Indians in the West

Much tension developed in the West when the eastern tribes reached their destinations. Many of the eastern tribes were forced to settle in territories occupied by the plains Indians. The plains tribes had acquired the White people's guns and horses and were tough fighters when the eastern tribes began to settle in their territories. When competition for the buffalo became acute, they fought and raided the eastern tribes. The U.S. government failed to provide the eastern tribes military protection as it had promised when they were forced to settle in the West.

The conquering and displacement of tribes that took place in the East later occurred west of the Mississippi. However, the conquest of the plains tribes and other western tribes took place in a shorter period of time. The powerful Sioux nation of the northern plains was defeated and forced onto reservations within 27 years. The Comanche of the southern plains had been conquered by the White settlers by 1873. Writes Spicer, "The other plains tribes presented about the same picture as the Comanche or the Sioux: a 20 or 25 year period of intensive warfare both with other tribes and the Americans, a period of unsettled and sometimes desperate conditions as they were forced on reservations and finally unhappy acceptance of the new way."[13]

When the United States acquired most of the territory that now comprises the Southwest from Mexico in 1848 (see the chapter on Mexican Americans), the fate of the Indians living in that area was doomed. The southwestern tribes quickly learned that their new conquerors were enemies, not friends. The Spaniards had never completely conquered the southwestern tribes; they had retained a great deal of their culture and many institutions. Indians such as the Pueblos and the Pimas had hoped that the United States would protect them from the Navajos and the Apaches. However, the new government's goals were to conquer all of the tribes and to place them on reservations. The California gold rush of 1849 hastened the defeat of the western tribes. A congressional act in 1871 that prohibited further treaties with the Indian tribes indicated that Indian resistance had been broken and that they were now a conquered and defeated people. The act declared that in the future, "no Indian nation or tribe within . . . the United States shall be acknowledged or recognized as an independent nation, tribe, or power."[14] This act represented a major change in federal policy in Indian affairs and reversed the policy declared by the Supreme Court in 1831. The Court ruled in 1831 that the "Cherokees and other Indians were dependent domestic nations . . . definable political entities within the United States."[15] The 1871 Congressional act closed an important chapter in Indian history. When he surrendered in 1877, Chief Joseph of the Nez Perce said, "Hear me, my chiefs, I am tired; my heart is sick and sad. From where the sun now stands, I will fight no more forever."

Messianic Movements: The Utopian Quests

Indians had been conquered by the late 1880s, and vigorous efforts to eradicate their cultures, values, and ways of life were already under way. Many were forced to live on reservations that were operated by superintendents and government agents who ruled the Indians with an iron hand and stifled all their efforts for self-initiative. Confined to reservations (some of which were fenced in), many of the proud Indian warriors were forced to farm, which they considered women's work. In their desperation, Indians turned to religious prophets who promised a return to the traditional ways and the extermination of Whites and their life-styles. Messianic leaders who heralded the end of White domination emerged within many of the eastern and western tribes.

As early as the 1760s, a prophet arose among the Delawares. He urged his followers to reject European goods and return to their old way of life. Tenskwatawa, a Shawnee, experienced a revelation in 1805 that told him that White Americans would be destroyed by a natural catastrophe. Tenskwatawa and his brother, Tecumseh, taught the Shawnees to hold firm to their lands and refuse to relinquish them to the Whites. Handsome Lake began preaching among the Senecas around 1800 after the League of the Iroquois had been broken up. He urged the Senecas to remain neutral in the White people's wars, not to indulge in the White vices, and to live by his moral code. Handsome Lake became important to those Senecas who were trying to resist cultural domination by the Whites.

As Whites began to conquer Indian tribes in the West, prophets who envisioned a utopian future emerged among the western tribes. In 1855, a prophet called Smohalla began preaching among the Wanapum Indians in the Oregon Territory. Like the eastern prophets, Smohalla preached that the White people would be eliminated and that their way of life was detrimental. He believed that the way the White people farmed harmed Mother Earth.

A Paiute prophet named Wovoka began having visions in 1885. He preached that a natural catastrophe would destroy White people and that the Indians' ancestors would return. The White authorities became alarmed about Wovoka's religion and its ritualistic dance. The religion became known to Whites as the "Ghost Dance." It spread rapidly among the Indians and eventually reached the Sioux on the Pine Ridge Reservation in South Dakota. A frightened Indian agent called soldiers to the reservation in 1890. When a misunderstanding arose between the soldiers and the worshipers, the soldiers killed 300 Sioux at Wounded Knee Creek. This incident shocked the nation and wiped out the Ghost Dance among most Indian tribes. The Wounded Knee "episode marked the completion of the White man's conquest of the Indian in the United States."[16]

American Indians and Federal Policy

When the Indians had been thoroughly conquered and placed on reservations, White authorities began efforts to "civilize" them; *civilize* meant to make them as much like Whites as possible. The goal of federal policy was to assimilate the Indians quickly into the mainstream society. No attempt was made to give them a choice or to encourage them to retain elements of their cultures. Efforts were made to make Indians farmers and to give their children the White people's education. Indian children were sent to boarding schools far away from the reservations so that the authority of their parents would be undermined. The schools were a dismal failure. When Indian children left them, they were unable to function well either in their ethnic communities or within the mainstream society. What the schools tried to teach had almost no relevance to life on the reservations. The schools also failed to teach Indian children the White people's culture. The quality of the teachers and the curricula were very poor.

Policymakers felt that they had to break up the Indians' tribal lands and make individual allotments to family heads in order to make Indians independent and successful farmers. That this would violate Indian cultures and traditions was not a major concern. In 1887 Congress passed the Dawes Severalty Act. Designed to make Indians independent and to terminate their special relationship with the federal government, the act was destined to have the opposite effect. The act authorized the president to break up tribal lands and to make individual allotments to family heads. Each family head was to receive 160 acres; minors, 80 acres each. "Surplus" land was to be sold on the open market. The government was to hold the land in trust for 25 years. Citizenship was to be granted to family heads when they received their allotments. Many tribes adamantly opposed the act from the beginning.

The results of the act were disastrous for Indians. Many Whites bought or leased lands from Indians at outrageously low prices or obtained land from them in extralegal ways. Some Whites persuaded their Indian friends to will them their lands. Indians who made such wills often turned up mysteriously dead shortly after finalizing the will. A 1906 Congressional act gave the federal government more authority to supervise the administration of the Dawes Act. However, schemes for obtaining the Indians' lands developed more rapidly than government policies to safeguard it. Many Indians became poverty stricken during the period in which the act was in effect. They lost about 90 million out of a total of 138 million acres of land between 1887 and 1932.

It was clear by the late 1920s that the Dawes Act had failed. It had not only resulted in the loss of millions of acres of tribal land but had also increased rather than decreased the role of the federal government in Indian affairs. The Meriam Report, published in 1928, recommended major reforms in federal Indian policy, including the abandoning of the allotment plan and the consolidation of Indian land for use by the tribes. John Collier, who became commissioner of Indian affairs in 1933, believed that tribal land should be reestablished, as well as

Indian government and other aspects of Indian culture. In 1934 Congress passed an act sanctioning the new federal policy. Termination had failed; the government would now take a more active role in Indian affairs and urge Indians to reestablish aspects of their cultures. The Wheeler-Howard Act of 1934 brought a halt to the allotment of Indian lands, made it possible for tribes to acquire additional lands, and granted American Indians the right to local government based on their traditional cultures.

By the 1950s, advocates for the termination of the federal government's role in Indian tribal affairs were again dominant in the nation's capital. In 1953, the federal government stated its intent to abolish the federal role in tribal affairs and to treat Indians the same as other Americans in House Concurrent Resolution 108. During the 1950s, Congress passed several laws that gave the states additional responsibilities for Indian affairs. A 1954 termination bill ended the relationship between the federal government and the Klamath tribe in Oregon. The tribe and its reservation were abolished. However, the termination was disastrous for the Klamaths because they had not achieved economic independence when it began. The Menominee Reservation in Wisconsin was also terminated during the 1950s.

Self-Determination and the Challenge to Termination

Most Indians are strongly committed to their tribal groups and to the continuation of their special legal relationship with the federal government. They feel that only in this way can they, a relatively small group, acquire their political rights and justice. Indians believe that they are too few to exercise significant political power. Most Indian leaders remained strongly committed to self-determination and against termination during the period of the 1950s and 1960s, when a termination policy was pursued by the federal government. However, termination received a severe blow when President Richard Nixon stated his Indian policy in 1970. He said

> Self-determination among the Indian people can and must be encouraged without the threat of eventual termination. . . . This is the only way that self-determination can effectively be fostered. This, then must be the goal of any new national policy toward the Indian people: to strengthen the Indians' sense of autonomy without threatening the sense of community . . . we must assure the Indian that he can assume control of his own life without being separated involuntarily from the tribal group. And we must make it clear that Indians can become independent of federal control without being cut off from federal concern and federal support.[17]

The challenge to termination and the support of Indian self-determination continued throughout the 1970s. According to the U.S. Commission on Civil Rights, "The executive branch repudiated the policy of termination and successive administrations adopted a policy of Indian self-determination—a policy favoring Indian control over decision-making and promoting tribal interest."[18] In 1975, the Indian Self-Determination Act made it clear that Indians could "con-

trol their relationships both among themselves and with non-Indian governments, organizations, and persons." The 1978 Indian Child Welfare Act provides for tribal jurisdiction and Indian community involvement in the adoption
and foster placement of Indian children.

Fishing Rights and Land Claims

Tremendous controversies developed during the 1970s over both Indian fishing
rights in the state of Washington and the land claims of Indian tribes in the states
that originally made up the 13 colonies. The fishing-rights controversy arose
because of treaties signed by the federal government and Indians in the Washington Territory in the 1850s. The Indians gave up vast land claims in return for
specific federal promises. One was a recognition of Indian fishing rights. The
Indians were promised that they "could continue to fish where they always had
fished, exclusively on reservation and in common with the citizens of the territory
at the Indians' usual and accustomed grounds and stations off reservation."[19]

As the supply of fish grew smaller, the state of Washington began to
regulate fishing in a way that favored non-Indian fishing and violated the
Indians' treaty promises. Some Indians were jailed for fishing that violated state
law. However, these Indians felt that their fishing was legal because of the terms
of the nineteenth-century treaties. When the Indians took their cases to the
courts, they won major legal victories. In 1974, Judge George Boldt ruled in a
federal District Court that the Indians had separate rights to a significant share of
the fish and that the state should protect their rights and not interfere with them.
The Boldt decision evoked a storm of controversy among the non-Indians of
Washington state and personal attacks on Judge George Boldt.

The non-Indian fishermen strongly rejected the Boldt decision and worked
to get the case to the Supreme Court. They hoped that the high court would
reverse the Boldt decision. The Supreme Court ruled on the controversial case
on July 2, 1979. It upheld the decision made by Judge Boldt.

In 1790, the U.S. Congress enacted the Indian Trade and Intercourse Act,
also known as the Nonintercourse Act of 1790. This act, which is still in effect,
requires the federal government to supervise the transfer of Indian lands to non-
Indians in states that formerly made up the original 13 colonies. This act was
designed to maintain friendly relationships between Whites and Indians. Most of
the land in these states was transferred from Indians to non-Indians without the
required federal supervision. During the 1970s, a number of eastern Indian
tribes went to court to claim that their lands had been transferred illegally and to
demand redress and compensation for the illegal transfer of their lands.

The Passamaquoddy and Penobscot tribes of Maine took legal actions to
regain more than 10 million acres of land in the state of Maine. Their claim made
up one-half of the state and was inhabited by 350,000 non-Indians. This

property was valued at $25 million. After a long and difficult battle, these tribes received a settlement of their claim in 1980.

Other tribes that have made land claims with varying results include the Oneidas in New York state, the Mashpee tribe in Massachusetts, the Schaghiticoke tribe in Connecticut, and the Narrangansetts in Rhode Island. The Narragansetts received a rather rapid settlement of their claim. They made their claim in 1976 and received a settlement in 1978. Congress provided the funds to carry out the 1,800-acre settlement.

American Indians Today

The Indian Population

Once known as the "vanishing Americans," the American Indian population has increased at every Census count since 1940. The Indian population in 1940 was 345,000. The first complete census of American Indians was conducted in 1890. There were 248,000 Indians counted that year. The biggest increase in the Indian population since 1890 occurred between the 1970 and the 1980 Censuses. The Indian population increased 42% during that 10-year period, from 793,000 to 1,364,000.[20] A number of factors other than the increase in the number of births over deaths may have accounted for this dramatic increase in the Indian population. These factors may have included improvements in the way the Census Bureau counted people in 1980, the wider use of self-identification to obtain information about ethnic group membership, and the greater tendency for people to identify as Indian in 1980 than in 1970.[21]

The 1980 Census identified about 500 American Indian tribes and bands. These tribes and bands varied greatly in size. The Cherokee and the Navajo were the only tribes that included more than 100,000 people. About 16% of all Indians identified as Cherokee; about 11% identified as Navajo. Figure 5–2 shows the 10 largest American Indian tribes in 1980 and their populations. The four states with the largest Indian populations in 1980 were California (198,275), Oklahoma (169,292), Arizona (152,498), and New Mexico (105,976).

Indians in Urban Communities

American Indians have become increasingly urbanized since the 1950 Census. In 1950 about 56,000 Indians, or 16% of the total population, lived in urban areas and cities. That number had increased to 146,000, or 28% of the population, in 1960. Most American Indians lived in cities and in urban areas in 1980. In 1980, 25% of American Indians lived on reservations, 9% lived in the historic areas of Oklahoma (excluding urban areas), and 67% lived off reservations, mostly in urban areas (see Figure 5–3).

Figure 5–2   Ten Largest American Indian Tribes: 1980

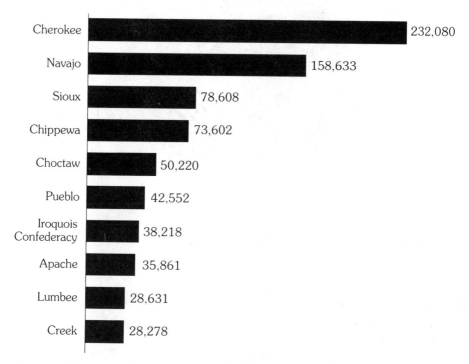

Source: U.S. Bureau of the Census. *We, The First Americans*. Washington, D.C.: U.S. Government Printing Office, December, 1988, p. 3.

Even though about 67% of American Indians live off reservations, mostly in urban areas, many reports, statistical sources, and other kinds of informational sources focus on the minority of Indians who live on reservations. Detailed studies of urban Indians are scarce. Wax includes a chapter, "Indians in the Cities," in his dated but informative book, *Indian Americans: Unity and Diversity*.[22] After a general discussion of Indians in cities, Wax discusses several case studies of urban Indian communities, including the Sioux in Rapid City, Iowa, the Tuscarora (a branch of the Iroquois) in New York state, and the Indians in Minneapolis.

Wax, as well as other authors, such as Sorkin and Bolt, point out that many Indians have a difficult time adjusting to life in urban communities.[23] Often cut off from families and reservation benefits, they have trouble getting jobs, health and medical care, and good schooling for their children. Reservation Indians who migrate to urban areas tend to settle in towns and cities near reservations and to maintain contacts with their kin on the reservation. They

Figure 5–3   *Distribution of the 1.4 Million American Indians: 1980*

American Indian
Reservations
25%

Historic Areas of
Oklahoma (Excluding
Urbanized Areas)
9%

Remainder of
United States
67%

Source: U.S. Bureau of the Census. *We, the First Americans*. Washington, D.C., December, 1988, p. 9.

frequently settle near reservations, such as in Gallup, New Mexico, Rapid City, South Dakota, and Ponca City, Oklahoma.

When teaching about Indians in the cities, you should not gloss over the enormous problems that urban Indians often have. However, you should remember that there is tremendous diversity within Indian urban communities. White, in a study summarized by Wax,[24] identified three social classes among Indians in his study of the Indians in Rapid City, South Dakota. He called one group "middle class mobiles." These individuals constituted what White called "the Mixedblood elite." They were upwardly mobile and not highly identified with the fullblood Indians who lived on the reservation. He called another group "upper middle class White Indians." These individuals were descendants of upwardly mobile mixedblood families. They occasionally identified with a female Indian ancestor. The final group of urban Indians that White identified were lower-class, rural, and reservation Indians who faced tremendous problems in the urban environment.

Despite the problems they face, most American Indian families were two-parent families in 1980. Seven out of 10 Indian families were married couples living together.

The Social and Economic Characteristics of American Indians

In 1980, the percentage of American Indians 25 years or older who had completed 4 years of high school or more was considerably below that of the general population, but much higher than the Indian percentage in 1970. In 1980, the Indian percentage was 55.8 compared to 66.5 for the total population. The Indian percentage in 1970 was 33. The median family income for American Indians in 1979 was only 68.6% of the median family income for the total population, $13,678.00, compared to $19,917.00. The percentage of Indian families living below the poverty level in 1979 was substantially above the percentage for the total population, 23.7%, compared to 9.6%. A large percentage of the Indian families in 1979 that were below the poverty level lived on reservations. About 45% of the 336,280 American Indians that lived on reservations in 1979 were living below the poverty level.

Indians Face the Future

As we approach the final years of this century, American Indians are in a unique population, cultural, legal, and historical situation. In 1980, Indians numbered more than 1 million. They are the increasing rather than vanishing Americans. However, they are never likely to be a powerful political force because of their relatively small population in a nation that numbers more than 250 million people. Yet, they have treaty rights to land and a special relationship with the federal government that no other ethnic group has. Consequently, they are able to exercise considerable power within the courts. When they do, however, as with fishing rights and land claims, they often evoke considerable hostility among non-Indians.

By most measures, Indians are one of the nation's poorest and least educated ethnic groups. Yet they own lands that contain rich resources that are of enormous value to this nation.[25] The challenge that Indians face in the final decade of this century is how to marshal their legal claims and rich resources in ways that will help them to attain the full benefits of U.S. citizenship.

Teaching Strategies

To illustrate how content related to Indians can be used to integrate the curriculum, exemplary strategies are identified for teaching these concepts at the grade levels indicated: *family relationships* (primary grades), *cultural diversity and similarity* (intermediate and upper grades), and *federal policy* (high school grades).

Primary Grades

CONCEPT: Family Relationships

Generalization: Sometimes we must learn to live without family members with whom we have strong positive relationships.

1. Ask the children: "Has one of your parents ever gone away for a long or short trip?" Did you miss your parent?" "How do we feel when someone we like very much goes away?" "Why do we feel that way?" Record the children's responses on the board or butcher paper. Through further questioning and discussion, bring out that we often feel lonely and sad when certain family members are away because we have strong positive feelings toward them.

2. Ask the pupils: "What do you think life would be like for you if mother went away forever?" "If father went away forever?" "How would you feel?" "Why?" "How do you think you would feel if your sister or brother went away forever?" "Why would you feel that way?" "How do you think members of your family would feel if you went away forever?" "Why would they feel that way?" Through further questioning and discussion, help the students to understand how emotionally difficult it might be if they no longer had one of their family members.

3. Say to the class: "Today we will read a story about an Indian girl named Annie and her grandmother, the Old One." Show the students the picture of Annie and her grandmother on page 7 of *Annie and the Old One* by Miska Miles. This is a beautiful and cogent story of a young Navajo girl who tries to halt time to delay her beloved grandmother's death. Her grandmother teaches her how to face life and to accept death. Say: "Grandmother lives with Annie and her parents. She is a member of Annie's family." Ask: "Do grandmothers live with any of you?" "Do any relatives beside your father, mother, brothers, and sisters live with any of you?" Discuss the pupils' responses. Say: "There are many different types of families in the United States. Many families have only mother, father, brothers, and sisters. However, other families have other members like Annie's family, such as grandmother, grandfather, and cousins. Other families have a mother and no father. Some have a father and no mother." Ask: "Why do you think there are different kinds of families?" Discuss the children's responses. Help them to understand why there are many different types of families in our society.

4. Focus the students' attention on the picture of Annie and her grandmother again. Ask, "What do you think this story is about?" List the students' responses on the board or butcher paper. Read the book to the class, stopping at various points to discuss the following questions:

   a. How did Annie know her grandmother would soon die?
   b. How did Annie feel when she learned that her grandmother would go to Mother Earth? Have you ever felt that way? When? Why?
   c. What did Annie do to try to stop time to delay her grandmother's death? Was she able to stop time? Why or why not?
   d. How did Annie learn to accept her grandmother's death? How did what her grandmother told her help? How did her grandmother's actions help her? What did Annie learn from her grandmother about life? About death?

Summarize the lesson by helping the children understand how we sometimes have to learn to live without family members with whom we have strong, positive relationships. Personalize the lesson by giving an example from your own life. Tell the children how you faced the problem and eventually dealt with it successfully, like Annie in the story.

Intermediate and Upper Grades

CONCEPT: Cultural Diversity and Similarity

Generalization: Indian cultures used both different and similar means to satisfy common human needs and wants.

1. Ask the students to name some things they think all human beings need in order to survive and satisfy unique human wants. Their responses will probably include "food," "a place to live in," and "clothing." Probing questions might be necessary to bring out that people also have such needs as the need to explain unknown phenomena in the universe, for government, and for self-esteem.

2. List the student responses on the board and, with the class, group them into specific categories, such as food, shelter, clothing, government, family, religion, and economy.

3. Ask the students to name some institutions and means used in our society to meet the needs they have identified and categorized. Write their responses, in abbreviated form, on the board. Tell the class that in this unit they will be studying about how four earlier cultures in North America satisfied these same human needs in ways different from the ways in which we usually satisfy them today.

4. Before introducing the four cultures, develop, with the class, key questions related to each category. The students will use the questions as guides when studying the four cultures. Examples are as follows:

a. Food
   (1) What kinds of foods did the people eat?
   (2) Were they primarily hunters and gatherers or farmers?
   (3) How was the food usually prepared? By whom?

b. Government
   (1) Who or what group made major decisions and laws?
   (2) How were major decision-makers chosen?
   (3) How were rules and laws enforced?

c. Economy
   (1) What goods and services were produced?
   (2) How were they produced? By whom? For whom?
   (3) How were goods and services exchanged? Was some form of money used? Barter?

5. The students should record the key questions in their notebooks. They will use them as guides when examining the four cultures.

6. Introduce the four cultures the class will study. When selecting four Indian

cultures for the unit, try to select cultures (1) that have both similarities and differences that the students will be able to see rather clearly and (2) for which you have adequate and high-quality student books and resources. To assure cultural diversity, select the four groups from four different geographical areas, such as the Southeast, the Northwest, the Southwest, and California. This unit could be taught with as few as two groups. However, generalizations are more powerful when they are developed from a larger content sample. On the other hand, it is difficult for elementary students to study more than four cultures in one unit. In our example, we have chosen the Iroquois (a northeastern Indian group), the Haida (Northwest), the Hopi (Southwest), and the Pomo (California). These four groups clearly illustrate both the similarities and diversity that existed within Indian cultures.

7. Ask the students to construct a data retrieval chart (like the one illustrated in Table 5–2) that includes (1) the categories and key questions they identified earlier and (2) the names of the four groups. As they read and discuss each group, they should complete the blank spaces in the chart. When the chart is completed, ask the students key questions that will enable them to formulate this generalization: "Indian cultures used both different and similar means to satisfy common human needs and wants."

8. Show the students the videotape, *Weave of Time: The Story of a Navajo Family 1938–1986*. This film shows four generations of change in one Navajo family. The videotape covers nearly 50 years. Ask the students to compare the changes over the four generations in the Navajo family with changes over the generations in their own families.

Valuing Activity

Speeches and selections that highlight traditional Indian values can evoke reflective value discussion and reasoning in the classroom. Rich and powerful sources of Indian speeches and statements are found in *I Am the Fire of Time: The Voices of Native American Women*, edited by Jane B. Katz, and *Touch the Earth: A Self-Portrait of Indian Existence*, edited by T. C. McLuhan. The following statement was made by Chief Standing Bear, a Sioux born in 1868. The teacher can read this statement to the class and/or project it using an overhead or opaque projector. He or she can then ask the questions that follow the selection and discuss them with the class. The teacher should encourage the students to give reasons for their responses and to defend rationally their moral choices.

The Lakota Was a True Naturalist—A Lover of Nature

He loved the earth and all things of the earth, the attachment growing with age. The old people came literally to love the soil and they sat or reclined on the ground with a feeling of being close to a mothering power. It was good for the skin to touch the earth and the old people liked to remove their moccasins and walk with bare feet on the scared earth. Their [tepees] were built upon the earth and their altars were made of earth. The birds that flew in the air came to rest upon the earth and it was the final abiding place of all things that lived and grew. The soil was soothing, strengthening, cleansing, and healing.

That is why the old Indian still sits upon the earth instead of propping himself

Table 5–2   *Data Retrieval Chart for Comparing and Contrasting Four Cultures*

Categories and Related Questions	Iroquois	Haida	Hopi	Pomo
Food (Questions)				
Shelter (Questions)				
Clothing (Questions)				
Government (Questions)				
Family (Questions)				
Religion (Questions)				
Economy (Questions)				

up and away from its life-giving forces. For him, to sit or lie upon the ground is to be able to think more deeply and to feel more keenly; he can see more clearly into the mysteries of life and come closer in kinship to other lives about him. . . .

Kinship with all creatures of the earth, sky, and water was a real and active principle. For the animal and bird world there existed a brotherly feeling that kept the Lakota safe among them and so close did some of the Lakotas come to their feathered and furred friends that in true brotherhood they spoke a common tongue.

The old Lakota was wise. He knew that a man's heart away from nature becomes hard; he knew that lack of respect for growing, living things soon led to lack of respect for humans too. So he kept his youth close to its softening influence.[26]

Questions

1. What are the main values of the Lakota (tribal name for the Sioux) that are revealed in this statement by Chief Standing Bear?
2. In what ways might these values of the Lakota have conflicted with the values of the Europeans who settled in North America?
3. What problems do you think developed between the Lakota and the Europeans because of their value differences? Why?
4. How do traditional Lakota values, as revealed in the statement by Chief Standing Bear, conflict with many modern-day American values?
5. Do you think it is possible for individuals who endorse traditional Lakota values,

such as those revealed in Chief Standing Bear's statement, to function successfully within a highly modernized nation such as the United States? Why or why not? What conflicts might such individuals experience? How might they resolve them?

6. Do you think that traditional Lakota values, as revealed in the Chief's statement, could help strengthen a modernized nation such as the United States? Why or why not? If so, in what ways?

7. Which of the traditional Lakota values revealed in Chief Standing Bear's statement do you personally endorse? Which do you reject? Are you willing to act on those that you endorse? Why or why not?

8. When did you last act on the values in the statement that you endorse? When do you plan to act on them again?

High School Grades

CONCEPT: Federal Policy

Generalization: Most federal policy on Indian affairs was made without Indian input and usually sought Indian assimilation and termination of federal-tribal relationships.

1. To gain an understanding of the legal relationship Indian tribes have with the federal government, the students should examine some of the Indian treaties made between the United States government and Indian tribes. These treaties were usually made when Indian tribes were forced to cede their territories and to relocate on reservations. They were granted reservation land in exchange for their land. Several such treaties are reprinted in chapter 2 of *Of Utmost Good Faith*, edited by Vine Deloria, Jr.

2. Shortly after Indians had been conquered and forced onto reservations in the late 1800s, efforts were begun by the federal government to terminate its special relationship with the tribes, to force them to give up most aspects of their cultures, and to force assimilation into the dominant culture. These goals of federal policy were implemented in the Dawes Severalty Act of 1887. Ask the students to research the arguments, both pro and con, that preceded the passage of the act.

a. Although many White liberals favored the passage of the act, most Indian tribes opposed it. When the bill was being debated in Congress, representatives of the Five Civilized Tribes sent a strong message to Congress opposing its passage. Ask the class to read and discuss this statement, which is reprinted in *Of Utmost Good Faith*, edited by Vine Deloria, Jr.

b. White allies of Indians strongly supported the passage of a bill, such as Dawes, that would break up tribal lands and allot them to individual household heads. They felt that such a bill would enable Indians to assimilate into the dominant culture. In 1884, the Indian Rights Association of Philadelphia, whose members were White friends of the Indian, issued a pamphlet strongly advocating the passage of an allotment bill. Ask the students to read and discuss excerpts from this pamphlet, reprinted in *The Indian and the White Man*, edited by Wilcombe

Washburn. The class should then compare the statement sent to Congress by the Five Civilized Tribes and the excerpt from the pamphlet. They should discuss the merits and weaknesses of the two positions.

3. Ask several students to roleplay a debate between those who favored the Dawes bill and those who opposed it.

4. Ask the students to research these questions: "What effects did the Dawes Severalty Act have on Indian people?" "On White society?" "How do you think Indian life might be different today if the bill had failed in Congress?" "Why?" Two books— Alvin M. Josephy, Jr., *The Indian Heritage of America,* and Edward H. Spicer, *A Short History of the Indian in the United States*—contain good discussions of the disastrous effects of the act on Indian tribes.

5. Because of the loss of millions of acres of tribal lands and the severe poverty of Indians, it was clear by the 1920s that the Dawes Act had been a colossal failure. John Collier, who became Commissioner of Indian Affairs in 1933, outlined a new federal policy for Indians. Ask the students to read and discuss his statement, "A New Deal for the Red Men," in Washburn and the federal act of 1934 that embodied the new federal policy, the Wheeler-Howard Act, in Deloria.

6. Ask the class to research the effects the Wheeler-Howard Act has had on Indian life and on the larger society. They can share their research findings by using roleplaying, debates, or group discussion techniques.

7. Heated arguments for the termination of federal-tribal relationship surfaced again in the 1950s. Ask the class to prepare research reports on these topics:

    a. The House Concurrent Resolution 108, 83rd Congress, lst session, passed on August 1, 1953, which called for the termination of the federal role in Indian affairs.

    b. How termination policy affected these tribes and the conditions of the termination policy in each case:

        (1) the Klamaths of Oregon

        (2) the Menominees of Wisconsin

        (3) the Alabamas and the Coushattas in the South

8. Ask the class to study the various debates on termination that took place in the 1960s and 1970s among Indians and federal officials. An interesting argument against termination by an Indian is Earl Old Person (Blackfoot), "Testimony against Proposed Congressional Legislation, 1966," reprinted in *Great Documents in American Indian History,* edited by Moquin and Van Doren.

9. To terminate this unit, ask the students to divide into three groups and pretend that they are three different reservation tribes that have legal relationships with the federal government. Each tribe must unanimously decide, in the Indian tradition, whether they will terminate or maintain their legal relationship with the federal government. When the roleplaying is over, the class should reassemble and discuss the decisions of each tribe and the process and arguments they experienced in reaching them.

Endnotes

1. *Hammond Past Worlds: The Times Atlas of Archaeology* (Maplewood, N.J.: Hammond Inc., 1988), p. 205.
2. C. W. Ceram, *The First Americans: A Story of North American Archaeology.* (New York: Mentor Books, 1971), p. 304.
3. Alvin M. Josephy, Jr., *The Indian Heritage of America* (New York: Bantam Books, 1969), p. 36.
4. *The World Atlas of Archaeology* (New York: Portland House, 1985), p. 324.
5. Paul Stuart, *Nations within a Nation: Historical Statistics of American Indians* (New York: Greenwood Press, 1987), p. 51.
6. Ibid.
7. James M. Mooney, *The Aboriginal Population of America North of Mexico.* ed. John R. Swanton, Smithsonian Miscellaneous Collections, Vol. 80, no. 7 (Washington, D.C., 1928); Alfred L. Kroeber, "Native American Population," *American Anthropologist,* 36 (1934): 1–25. Henry F. Dobyns, *Native American Demography: A Critical Bibliography* (Bloomington, Ind.: Indiana University Press, 1976); William M. Denevan, *The Native Population of the Americas in 1492* (Madison: The University of Wisconsin Press, 1976).
8. William H. Harris and Judith S. Levey, eds., *The New Columbia Encyclopaedia* (New York: Columbia University Press, 1975), p. 85.
9. Ruth M. Underhill, *Red Man's America,* rev. ed. (Chicago: University of Chicago Press, 1971).
10. Jack D. Forbes, "Teaching Native American Values and Cultures," in *Teaching Ethnic Studies: Concepts and Strategies,* ed. James A. Banks (Washington, D.C.: National Council for the Social Studies, 1973), pp. 208–209.
11. T. C. McLuhan, ed., *Touch the Earth: A Self-Portrait of Indian Existence* (New York: Pocket Books, 1971), p. 15.
12. William T. Hagan, *American Indians* (Chicago: University of Chicago Press, 1961), p. 99.
13. Edward H. Spicer, *A Short History of the Indians in the United States* (New York: Van Nostrand Reinhold, 1969), p. 87.
14. Josephy, *Indian Heritage,* pp. 339–340.
15. Spicer, *Short History,* p. 66.
16. Josephy, *Indian Heritage,* p. 343.
17. Quoted in Edward Spicer, "American Indians: Federal Policy Toward," in *Harvard Encyclopedia of American Ethnic Groups,* eds. Stephan Thernstrom, Ann Orlov, and Oscar Handlin (Cambridge: Harvard University Press, 1980), p. 120.
18. U.S. Commission on Civil Rights, *Indian Tribes: A Continuing Quest for Survival* (Washington, D.C.: The Commission, June 1981), p. 180.
19. Ibid., p. 182.
20. The Census data reported in this section are from U.S. Bureau of the Census, *We, The First Americans* (Washington, D.C.: U.S. Government Printing Office, December, 1988); and U.S. Bureau of the Census, *Statistical Abstract of the United States: 1989,* 109th ed. (Washington, D.C.: U.S. Government Printing Office, 1989), p. 39.
21. Bureau of the Census, *We, The First Americans.*
22. Murray L. Wax, *Indian Americans: Unity and Diversity.* (Englewood Cliffs, N.J.: Prentice-Hall, 1971).
23. Ibid.; Alan L. Sorkin, *The Urban American Indians.* (Lexington, Mass.: D.C. Heath, 1978); Christine Bolt, *American Indian Policy and American Reform: Case Studies of the Campaign to Assimilate the American Indians.* (London: Allen and Unwin, 1987).

24. White, Robert A., "The Urban Adjustment of the Sioux Indians in Rapid City, South Dakota," unpublished paper, summarized in Wax, *Indian Americans*, pp., 166–169.

25. Michael A. Dorris, "The Grass Still Grows, the Rivers Still Flow: Contemporary Native Americans," *Daedalus* 110 (Spring 1981): 63–64.

26. Chief Luther Standing Bear, *Land of the Spotted Eagle* (Boston: Houghton Mifflin, 1933), pp. 192–197.

Annotated Bibliography

Books for Teachers

Especially Recommended

Caduto, Michael J., and Bruchac, Joseph. Foreword by N. Scott Momaday. *Keepers of the Earth: Native American Stories and Environmental Activities for Children.* Golden, Colo.: Fulcrum, Inc., 1988.

> *This excellent teaching resource includes traditional Indian stories that deal with a range of topics such as creation, fire, earth, wind and weather, water, sky, seasons, and plants and animals. Activities for using the stories with children are described. A teacher's guide for this book is also published.*

Dorris, Michael. *A Yellow Raft in Blue Water.* New York: Warner Communications, 1987.

> *A highly acclaimed novel about three women: 15-year-old and part Black Rayona, her American Indian mother, Christine, and mysterious Ida. A Booklist Editors Choice for 1987 in both the Adult and Young Adult categories.*

O'Brien, Sharon. *American Indian Tribal Governments.* Norman: University of Oklahoma Press, 1989.

> *A comprehensive introduction to Indian tribal governments and the legal relationship between Whites and Indians.*

Snipp, C. Matthew. *American Indians: The First of This Land.* New York: Russell Sage Foundation, 1989.

> *A comprehensive, book-length analysis of the American Indians based on data from the 1980 U.S. Census. This is one volume in "The Population of the United States in the 1980s" monograph series.*

Trenton, Patricia, and Houlihan, Patricia T. *Native Americans: Five Centuries of Changing Images.* New York: Harry N. Abrams, Inc., Publishers, 1989.

> *Written by an anthropologist and an art historian, this interesting book compares actual artifacts from Native American cultures with their depictions in the art of non-Indians. This is a strikingly illustrated and engrossing book.*

Waldman, Carl. *Atlas of the North American Indian.* Maps and illustrations by Molly Braun. New York: Facts on File Publications, 1985.

> *This useful resource for teaching about American Indians includes historical overviews and a valuable appendix that contains such lists as "Chronology of North American Indian History," "The Indian Tribes of the United States and Canada with Historical and Contemporary Locations," and "Federal and State Indian Reservations, Trust Areas, and Native Villages in the United States." It also contains excellent maps.*

Weatherford, Jack. *Indian Givers: How the Indians of the Americas Transformed the World.* New York: Crown, 1988.

> *An anthropologist describes how social, cultural, and political practices of the American Indians have changed life throughout the world. About 60% of the foods eaten in the world today were first harvested by the Indians of the Americas.*

Other References

Barlett, Mary Dougherty, ed. *The New Native American Novel: Works in Progress.* Albuquerque: The University of New Mexico Press, 1986.

> *The literary excerpts in this anthology represent Native American writers from many tribes and parts of the United States. Among the authors included are Louise Erdrich, Linda Hogan, N. Scott Momaday, Michael Dorris, and Paula Gunn Allen.*

Bataille, Gretchen M., and Sands, Kathleen Mullen. *American Indian Women Telling Their Lives.* Lincoln: University of Nebraska Press, 1984.

> *The authors discuss several autobiographies in terms of what they reveal about the lives of American Indian women. This book includes a comprehensive annotated bibliography on Indian women in the United Sates.*

Bruggmann, Maximilien, and Gerber, Peter R. *Indians of the Northwest Coast.* New York: Facts on File, 1989.

> *This informative and striking book is illustrated with beautiful photographs, many in color. It contains some excellent examples of modern American Indian art.*

Ehle, John. *Trail of Tears: The Rise and Fall of the Cherokee Nation.* New York: Doubleday, 1988.

> *A moving and informative account of the tragedy of the Cherokees and their Trail of Tears.*

Erdoes, Richard. *Crying for a Dream: The World through Native American Eyes.* Santa Fe, N.M.: Bear and Company Publishing, 1990.

> *Important slices of Native American life are illustrated in this colorful book that is replete with color photographs. The book's text is informative.*

Fixico, Donald L. *Termination and Relocation: Federal Indian Policy, 1945–1960.* Albuquerque: University of New Mexico Press, 1986.

> *A scholarly and comprehensive account of federal policy and the American Indian.*

Forbes, Jack, et al. *Multicultural Education and the American Indian.* Los Angeles: American Indian Studies Center, University of California, Los Angeles, 1979.

> *The essays in this book provides some unique and interesting perspectives on multicultural education and the American Indian. Among the essays are "Traditional Native American Philosophy and Multicultural Education," "National Patterns in Contemporary Indian Studies Programs," and "Indian Portrayal in Teaching Materials."*

Gilbert, Bil. *God Gave Us This Land: Tekamthi and the First American Civil War.* New York: Atheneum, 1989.

> *An informative and well-researched biography of Tekamthi (Tecumseh), the Shawnee warrior, orator, and political strategist.*

Gilliland, Hap, and Reyhner, Jon. *Teaching the Native American*. Dubuque, Ia.: Kendall/ Hunt Publishing Company, 1988.

> *Some useful information about American Indian culture as well as tips for teaching American Indian students are contained in this book.*

Galloway, Colin G., ed. *New Directions in American Indian History*. Norman: University of Oklahoma Press, 1988.

> *This excellent resource includes bibliographic essays that describe problems, issues, and references for studying different aspects of Native American life and culture. Among the essays included are "American Indian Women: Reaching beyond the Myth," and "Scholars and Twentieth-Century Indians: Reassessing the Recent Past."*

Heinerman, John. *Spiritual Wisdom of the Native Americans*. San Rafael, Calif.: Cassandra Press, 1989.

> Chapters in this book include "The Maya Philosophy of Life," "Traditional Indian Food and Medicine," "A Love Affair with Nature," and "Raising Children and the Indian Way."

Jonaitis, Aldona. Color photographs by Stephen S. Myers. *From the Land of the Totem Poles: The Northwest Coast Indian Art Collection at the American Indian Museum of Natural History*. New York: American Museum of Natural History; and Seattle: University of Washington Press, 1988.

> *A beautifully illustrated book with an informative text.*

Josephy, Alvin M., Jr. *Now That the Buffalo's Gone: A Study of Today's American Indians*. Norman: University of Oklahoma Press, 1984, 1989.

> *A highly readable and informative account of the experiences of Indians in the United States.*

Katz, Jane B., ed. *I Am the Fire of Time: The Voices of Native American Women*. New York: Dutton, 1977.

> *This is an informative and powerful collection of songs, poetry, prose, prayer, narrative, and oral history by American Indian women.*

Kirk, Ruth. *Tradition and Change on the Northwest Coast: The Makah, Nuu-Chah-Nulth, Southern Kwakiutl and Nuxalk*. Seattle: University of Washington Press, 1986.

> *"Today's Elders," "Kinship, Rank and Privilege," and "Today and Tomorrow" are among the informative chapters in this descriptive account of Northwest Coast Indians.*

Moore, John H. *The Cheyenne Nation: A Social and Demographic History*. Lincoln: University of Nebraska Press, 1987.

> *This is a scholarly, comprehensive, and richly documented history. It contains some excellent photographs, maps, and figures.*

Niethammer, Carolyn. *Daughters of the Earth: The Lives and Legends of American Indian Women*. New York: Collier, 1977.

> *An informative and well-written book, this source deals with diverse aspects of the lives and cultures of historical Indian women.*

Olsen, Fred. *On the Trail of the Arawaks.* Norman: University of Oklahoma Press, 1974.

   The Arawaks were living in the Caribbean island on which Columbus landed on October 12, 1492. This book tells about the Arawaks and their culture. Their story needs to be told when students study about Columbus.

Silman, Janet (as told to). *Enough Is Enough: Aboriginal Women Speak Out.* Toronto, Ontario: The Women's Press, 1987.

   A group of Indian women from the Tobique Reserve in New Brunswick (Canada) tell their candid stories in this interesting book.

Szasz, Margaret C. *Indian Education in the American Colonies, 1607–1783.* Albuquerque: University of New Mexico Press, 1988.

   A scholarly, well-researched, and comprehensive educational history of the schooling of American Indians during the colonial period. Also see by the same author: Education and the American Indian, 1928–1973. Albuquerque: University of New Mexico Press, 1974.

Turner, Frederick W. III, ed. *The Portable North American Indian Reader.* New York: Penguin Books, 1977.

   Myths and tales, poetry and oratory, and documents about cultural contact are included in this comprehensive anthology.

Utley, Robert M. *The Indian Frontier of the American West 1846–1890.* Albuquerque: University of New Mexico Press, 1984.

   The final half-century of conflict between Indians and Whites is told in this scholarly book.

Vecsey, Christopher. *Imagine Ourselves Richly: Mythic Narratives of North American Indians.* New York: Crossroad, 1988.

   An interesting and useful guide for studying the oral traditions of American Indians.

Walters, Anna Lee. *The Spirit of Native America: Beauty and Mysticism in American Indian Art.* San Francisco: Chronicle Books, 1989.

   Using a combination of beautiful color photographs and text, this striking book illustrates the beauty and mysticism in Native American art.

Washburn, Wilcomb E., ed. *Handbook of North American Indians,* Vol. 4, "History of Indian-White Relations." Washington, D.C.: Smithsonian Institution, 1988.

   The most recent addition to this excellent and comprehensive handbook on the American Indians. This large volume (838 pages) is carefully researched and contains a score of articles by leading scholars. It also has an excellent bibliography and an index.

Books for Students

(Note: These designations are used throughout this book: **Primary, grades 1–3; Intermediate, 4–6; Middle School, 7–8; High School, 9–12.**)

Ashabranner, Brent. *To Live in Two Worlds.* New York: Dodd, Mead, 1984.

   Contemporary American Indians from different tribes throughout the United States tell how they are working to maintain their identity and cultural heritage. This book can help young readers understand how the past experiences of ethnic minorities are impacting their present condition. (Middle School) Morning Star, Black Sun: The Northern Cheyenne Indians and America's Energy Crisis *(Dodd, 1982) is another book by Ashabranner.*

Beck, Mary L. *Heroes and Heroines in Tlingit-Haida Legend.* Seattle: Alaska Northwest Books, 1989.

These allegories, parables, and metaphoric expressions of cultural values are drawn from the oral literature of Southeast Alaskan Native peoples. They discuss significant events in clan history, misadventures of folk heroes, and interchanges between human beings and supernatural forces. (High School)

Bierhorst, John (as retold by). *Doctor Coyote: A Native American Aesop's Fables.* New York: Macmillian, 1987.

According to Bierhorst, sometime during the sixteenth century a Spanish conquistador brought a copy of Aesop's fables to Mexico. The Aztecs recast the tortoise, hare, and other European animals in the fables into the coyote and puma. The tales were eventually written in the Aztec language by an Aztec scribe. (Primary/Intermediate)

Cameron, Anne (as retold by). *How Raven Freed the Moon.* Madeira Park, British Columbia, Canada: Harbour Publishing Company, 1987.

An entrancing Northwest Indian myth about how Raven used magic tricks to free the moon and carry it to its rightful place in the heavens. (Primary/Intermediate)

Esbensen, Barbara Juster (as retold by). *Ladder to the Sky: How the Gift of Healing Came to the Ojibway Nation.* Boston: Little, Brown, 1989.

This beautifully illustrated Ojibway Indian legend recreates the time when the Ojibway people learned how to heal themselves with herbs and flowers. (Primary) Other books by Esbensen include The Star Maiden *(Little, Brown, 1988).*

Fradin, Dennis B. *The Pawnee.* Chicago: Children's Press, 1988.

This history, values, customs, and contemporary experiences of the Pawnee Indians are discussed in this book. Color photographs help communicate the information discussed in the text. This book is part of a series that includes books on other Native American tribes. (Primary/Intermediate)

Freedman, Russell. *Buffalo Hunt.* New York: Holiday House, 1988.

This beautifully illustrated book chronicles an important chapter in Native American history, when the buffalo was both revered by Native Americans and a key factor in their survival. (All Ages). Other books by Freedman include Indian Chiefs *(Holiday House, 1987).*

Globe, Paul. *Her Seven Brothers.* New York: Bradbury, 1988.

A young Indian girl makes shirts and moccasins decorated with porcupine quills for seven brothers she has not met. This Cheyenne legend suggests that humans have a special relationship with nature and implies the existence of things that we cannot explain. (Intermediate/Middle School) Other books by Globe include Death of the Iron Horse *(Bradbury, 1987), and* Star Boy *(Bradbury, 1983).*

Harlan, Judith. *American Indians Today: Issues and Conflicts.* New York: Franklin Watts, 1987.

This informative book examines current legal, economic, health, and civil rights concerns of Native Americans. (Middle School/High School)

Hilts, Len., *Quanah Parker: Ambassador for Peace.* San Diego: Harcourt, Brace, Jovanovich, 1987.

> *Quanah Parker was a great Comanche Indian chief who led his people into battle for their homeland. This biography is based on historical fact and eyewitness accounts. (Middle School/High School)*

Hirschfelder, Arlene. *Happily May I Walk: American Indians and Alaska Natives Today.* New York: Scribner, 1986.

> *The languages, ceremonies, sports, and employment status of the Inuits, Aleuts, and American Indians are discussed in this book. (Middle School/High School)*

Jenness, Aylette, and Alice Rivers. *In Two Worlds: A Yup'ik Eskimo Family.* Boston: Houghton Mifflin, 1989.

> *This photographic essay traces the last 50 years in the life of the Rivers family, who has faced tremendous change with dignity and wisdom and adopted modern ways without giving up their traditional values. (High School)*

Martin, Bill, Jr., and Archambault, John. *Knots on a Counting Rope.* New York: Henry Holt, 1987.

> *A beautifully written and illustrated story about the love between a blind Native American boy and his grandfather. (Primary)*

Miles, Miska. *Annie and the Old One.* Illustrated by Peter Parnall. Boston: Little, Brown, 1971.

> *This beautiful and touching story is about a young Navajo girl's attempt to stop time to delay her beloved grandmother's impending death. The excellent drawings greatly enhance the text. It is a Caldecott Honor book. (Primary)*

O'Dell, Scott. *Black Star, Bright Dawn.* Boston: Houghton Mifflin, 1988.

> *Bright Dawn, a determined and courageous young Eskimo girl, takes her father's place in the Iditarod, a challenging dogsled race. The reader travels with Bright Dawn on an exciting and remarkable journey from Anchorage to Nome. During the journey, Bright Dawn confronts blizzards and risks injury and frostbite. (Middle School/High School)*

Seals, David. *The Powwow Highway.* New York: Plume, 1990.

> *Two childhood friends who are Cheyenne Indians meet again after one has become a Vietnam War hero and the other a Yale University graduate. Together they begin a journey of self-discovery in which they prove that they are modern spirit warriors. (High School)*

Wolfson, Evelyn. *From Abenaki to Zuni: A Dictionary of Native American Tribes.* New York: Walker, 1988.

> *This reference book will be a useful addition to school library collections. It contains cultural information and historical overviews on more than 68 Native American tribes. (Intermediate/Middle School)*

Yue, Charlotte, and Yue, David. *The Igloo.* Boston: Houghton Mifflin, 1988.

> *This book explains how to build and live in an igloo. The text and illustrations give a contemporary as well as a historical view of Eskimo people. (Intermediate)*

Chapter 6

Native Hawaiians

Concepts, Strategies, and Materials

You must not think that this is anything like olden times, that you are the only chiefs and can leave things as they are. Smart people have arrived from the great countries that you have never seen. They know our people are few in number and living in a small country; they will eat us up.

—David Malo, 1837

Introduction

The experiences of Native Hawaiians parallel those of other indigenous peoples whose cultures and traditional life-styles were drastically altered by European contact. Like the American Indian, the numbers of Native Hawaiians were sharply reduced in the past two centuries. Their culture was initially modified and finally overwhelmed by European and American settlers.

Native Hawaiians often found it difficult to assume a viable role in a Hawaiian society in which Western practices were foreign to them. Values that, for centuries, had been hallmarks of Native Hawaiian culture were often counterproductive in a Hawaiian society run by foreigners. This conflict inevitably led to helplessness and despair for some of Hawaii's original inhabitants.

Yet, the culture of Hawaii has shown remarkable resiliency despite the great odds against its survival. The Hawaiian Renaissance of the 1970s indicated that a new consciousness of what it means to be Hawaiian had developed. For some Native Hawaiians, the American dream has borne fruit. For most, it has been largely deferred. Students should be aware that, although small in number, Native Hawaiians have made unique and lasting contributions to the American saga.

This chapter was contributed by Carlos F. Diaz, Assistant Professor of Education, Florida Atlantic University, Boca Raton, Florida. The bibliographies at the end of this chapter were revised by Virgie O. Chattergy, Professor of Education, University of Hawaii at Manoa.

In 1778, Captain James Cook's expedition landed on the islands that he named the Sandwich Islands, now called the state of Hawaii. There, Cook found nearly 300,000 people living in relative isolation. Since that time, Hawaiian history has been fraught with benevolent paternalism by Europeans and Americans, to the detriment of Native Hawaiians. This story is one of broken promises and exploitation of the Native Hawaiians by foreigners, which, in some ways, is similar to the poignant plight of American Indians.

Until foreigners started coming to Hawaii, the Native Hawaiians did not have a word for *race*. There were two groups, Hawaiians and strangers. They called themselves *kanakas* and referred to strangers as *haoles*. This total unimportance of race was to change with the European influence. The word *haole* acquired the meaning of White instead of stranger, as Whites became more prevalent on the islands. The Hawaiian people were forced to deal with an alien White economic, social, and legal system that they did not understand.

Native Hawaiians: Historical Perspective

Important Dates

1778	The beginning of European contact. Captain James Cook's expedition landed on the Hawaiian Islands.
1795	The rise to power of King Kamehameha I, who united the Hawaiian people under one ruler. This marked the beginning of the Kamehameha dynasty.
1820	The breaking of eating *kapu* by King Kamehameha II, which signaled the end of the ancient Hawaiian religion as a state religion. The first missionaries arrived in Hawaii from New England.
1835	King Kamehameha III granted an American firm the first long-term lease for a sugar plantation.
1845	The Great Mahele; all the land on the islands was divided among the king and 245 chiefs.
1893	Queen Liliuokalani was overthrown in a bloodless revolution led by American planters. The Republic of Hawaii was established, with Sanford B. Dole as president. This government lasted until annexation by the United States.
1920	The Hawaiian Homes Commission was started to benefit the native Hawaiians. Very little of this land was used for its stated purpose. (By the 1930s, the commission was leasing half of its land to corporations or to non-Hawaiians.)

Important Dates	
1954	For the first time since Hawaii became a territory, the Democratic party captured a majority in both houses of the legislature.
1959	Hawaii became the fiftieth state of the United States.
1974	George Ariyoshi was the first non-*haole* elected governor of Hawaii.
1975	The U.S. Congress passed a law recognizing Native Hawaiians as a Native-American group.
1976	The voyage of the Hawaiian canoe Hokule'a from Hawaii to Tahiti reinforced pride in the Polynesian roots of Hawaiian culture. Daniel Akaka became the first Native Hawaiian member of the U.S. House of Representatives.
1977	The first edition of the newsletter *Native Hawaiian* was published, marking a growing Hawaiian consciousness movement.
1978	The Office of Hawaiian Affairs was established by the state government to help Native Hawaiians secure their rights.
1980	The Hawaiian tourist industry suffered its first decline since 1949. This fueled debate about diversification of the Hawaiian economy.
1984	Hawaii celebrated twenty-five years of statehood.
1986	John D. Waihee, the first Hawaiian governor of Hawaiian ancestry, took office. Hawaii's population was 1.06 million.
1987	Visitors spent 6.6 billion dollars in Hawaii.
1988	Japanese investors spent 3.3 billion dollars on Hawaiian real estate.

Native Hawaiians: Before European Contact

In the early subsistence economy of Hawaii, the survival of Hawaiians depended on a communal effort to reap the maximum benefits from the islands' scarce resources. The Hawaiians were an agricultural and fishing people with a complex socioreligious structure. The islands were governed by the *ali'i*, who were powerful chiefs. The power of these chiefs was legitimized by the priest, or *kahuna*, who interpreted the religious doctrine set forth in the *kapu*. The common people, or *maka'ainana*, were extremely devoted to their chiefs. The high chief or *ali'inui* was the supreme ruler over his territory and was expected to provide protection for his people. The people had the freedom to move to the district of another chief, but rarely did so. Although sharing was a predominant practice, there was a considerable difference between the life-styles of the chiefs and the common people.

There were two Hawaiian customs that would lead to inevitable conflict with *haoles* in the future. One was a system of sharing and bartering, in which products were exchanged from one island to another. The Hawaiians did not use currency and therefore the accumulation of wealth in a market economy as we know it was unknown. The other custom was the notion that the land belonged to the gods, and, therefore, in a sense, belonged to everyone and could not be owned. The earliest visitors to the islands found the natives willing to share whatever they had. After all, that was the Hawaiian way.

European Contact

The propensity of Hawaiians to share eventually helped to seal their demise. Besides providing provisions for ships, Hawaiians were quite willing to share their women, and Whites were eager to become intimate with them. These casual contacts over a long period of time had a decimating effect on the islands' population. The venereal diseases introduced by European and American sailors found little natural resistance among the Hawaiians and, along with measles, cholera, and alcoholism, took a deadly toll.

An estimated 300,000 people inhabited the Hawaiian Islands at the time of European contact. By 1840, only about 100,000 Hawaiians remained. Many Native Hawaiians were naturally alarmed at what was taking place due to contact with the *haoles*. According to David Malo, a Native Hawaiian writer who espoused this viewpoint, "The ships of the White man have come and smart men have arrived from the great countries. . . . They know our people are few in number and living in a small country; they will eat us up."[1] His prophecy came true eventually, but at that time it fell on deaf ears. When David Malo died, he was buried at his request in Lahaina, next to a school where he had received his education from missionaries.

The paternalism of *haoles* began with sea captains, who needed the islands as a place to replenish supplies and repair their ships. Often, chiefs were given a few metal items in return for supplies. As commercialism grew and the chiefs saw more European goods, there began to be a desire for these items. Sandalwood, which was plentiful on the islands, was in great demand for carving as well as for its aromatic qualities. It could be bought in Hawaii for 1¢ per pound and sold lucratively in Canton, China, for 34¢ per pound.[2] As the Yankee traders increased their demands for sandalwood, many chiefs forced their subjects to cut more of the mountain trees and haul the lumber down steep slopes. Some chiefs also became fervent consumers of Western goods and kept their subjects away from their own food-producing activities in order to satisfy the sandalwood trade and their own avarice. This continued until the slopes of Hawaii were nearly denuded of sandalwood trees. Today, they are scarce on the islands.

The ascension to power of King Kamehameha I marked the rise of the Kamehameha dynasty. According to one historian, "One of Kamehameha's greatest qualities was his ability to attract many White men to his service and retain their loyalty for years or even a lifetime."[3] Even though Kamehameha was skillful in retaining power, this practice proved disastrous in the long run for his heirs, because often the *haole* advisers held their own interests ahead of the people they represented.

Kamehameha I is often regarded as one of the greatest Hawaiian monarchs because he conquered populations of other islands and unified the entire island chain under one rule. The weapons and technology he had obtained through contact with Westerners were of great assistance in this campaign.

After the death of Kamehameha I in 1819, he was succeeded by his son, Liholiho. During the reign of Liholiho (Kamehameha II), he was pressured into abolishing the *kapu* system of taboos. This had far-reaching effects on Hawaiian society. Although the *kapu* system was often oppressive and sometimes abused, its elimination began an erosion of Native Hawaiian culture with no satisfactory substitutes provided.

Besides the traders and the confidants of chiefs, another group entered the Hawaiian scene to lend its paternalistic hand. In 1820, the first groups of missionaries arrived in the islands from New England. Their goal was to "Christianize" the natives, but in most cases their influence far surpassed the religious realm. According to Jacobs and Landau, "Under increased influence of the missionaries of the king, more *haoles* were given the right to lease land for commercial enterprises. But these men did not want merely to lease the land, they wanted to own it outright so they could sell or lease it to others."[4]

A further blow to the survival of Hawaiian culture was dealt in 1848, when King Kamehameha III took the suggestions of his foreign advisors and decided to redistribute the land of the Hawaiian islands. This act by the king was known as the *Great Mahele*. Kent notes that, under its provisions, "60% of the land (2,479,000 acres) was allocated to the crown and government, 29% (1,619,000 acres) to the 208 chiefs, and less than 1% to 11,000 commoners."[5]

After the Great Mahele, there was a steady decline in subsistence farming among the Native Hawaiian people. Alien concepts like land deeds and property taxes clashed with the traditional Hawaiian view that land was for the use and enjoyment of all the people. Slowly, even small plots of land owned by Native Hawaiians passed into the hands of the *haoles*. This loss of control over their land by Native Hawaiians somewhat parallels the saga of Native Americans on the mainland.

As the sandalwood trade faded, the Hawaiian economy began to rely more on supplying whaling ships with meat, vegetables, and water. Hawaii also became a convenient location to make any repairs needed by whaling vessels on their long voyages. With the income earned from these activities, Hawaii imported manufactured goods, mainly from the United States. When whaling in the Pacific began to decline, the Hawaiian economy shifted to plantation agriculture.

During each of these phases, the Hawaiian economy was being controlled by forces thousands of miles away from the islands. The interests and needs of the Native Hawaiian population were inconsequential when compared to the potential for large profits.

The plantation system began to flourish in the latter part of the nineteenth century. Native Hawaiians worked in the cane fields as laborers but were not as productive as plantation owners had expected. The dawn-to-dusk labor in the cane fields and rigid production quotas were difficult adjustments for Native Hawaiians. Lacking a significant economic niche on their islands, and slowly losing political control, the Native Hawaiian population continued to decline.

From a population of 71,019 in 1853, the Hawaiian population, including those of mixed ancestry, dropped to 39,504 by 1896.[6] During this period, planters were importing field labor to the Hawaiian islands from nearly the entire world. The first major group was the Chinese, soon followed by the Japanese, Portuguese, Koreans, Puerto Ricans, and other nationalities.

The planters' strategy was to keep any one nationality of laborers from becoming too numerous and thus to thwart any type of labor organization. George H. Fairfield, manager of the Makee Sugar Company, stated the planters' strategy as follows: "Keep a variety of laborers, that is of different nationalities, and thus prevent any concerted action in case of strikes, for there are few, if any, cases of Japanese, Chinese, and Portuguese entering into a strike as a unit."[7] Largely as a result of these methods, Hawaii's population was transformed into a multiethnic one.

As the plantation economy matured, a Big Five emerged among planters that would eventually dominate the Hawaiian economy for decades: Hackfield and Company (AMFAC), C. Brewer and Company, Theo Davis Company, Castle and Cooke, and Alexander and Baldwin.

The nature of the sugar and pineapple plantations of the nineteenth and early twentieth centuries required a large concentration of land and capital, as well as a disciplined work force. Such large-scale operations also required that the political climate of Hawaii be conducive to the interests of planters.

The practice of surrounding the Hawaiian monarch with *haole* advisors became a facade of political sovereignty in the latter part of the nineteenth century. In 1873, the Hawaiian throne was denied to Queen Emma by a group of planters who bribed, cajoled, and threatened electors into giving the crown to David Kalakaua. Pro-Emma supporters stormed the courthouse to register their outrage. This group was dispersed by U.S. Marines and British sailors whose assistance was requested by planter Charles Bishop to "quell the riotous mob."[8]

In 1877, the planter oligarchy rewrote the Hawaiian constitution and presented it to King Kalakaua for his signature under a state of armed siege. The constitution the king signed became known as the *bayonet constitution* to Hawaiians. It made the king a ceremonial monarch, disenfranchised most Native Hawaiians through strict property requirements, excluded all Asians from voting by declaring them aliens, and gave the vote only to U.S. citizens. After this action, the remaining days of pretended sovereignty were numbered.

Annexation

To paint a picture of something other than imperialistic motives by the United States in annexing Hawaii would be doing a severe injustice to the facts. American military minds saw Hawaii as a coaling station for the Pacific fleet. As Jacobs and Landau note, "The strength and influence of the pro-annexation Americans grew in Hawaii and on the mainland, where the concepts of expansion and 'manifest destiny' were attracting a growing number of adherents."[9] The latter doctrine, having reached the Pacific shore, seemed to have its sights set on Hawaii. The American planter oligarchy saw annexation as an opportunity to guarantee in perpetuity the largest market for Hawaiian agricultural products. Expansionist, military, and economic motives worked to end the last vestiges of Hawaiian autonomy.

The first attempt at the deposition of the monarchy came on January 17, 1893. This coup was supported by American troops (although not officially) and was led by Lorrin P. Thurston, a Honolulu publisher. The overthrow of Queen Liliuokalani was an event from which Hawaiians never recovered. The queen did not order her troops to battle the insurgents because the odds were overwhelmingly against her and she trusted the fairness of the United States. After losing her throne, the queen wrote a desperate plea to President Cleveland to have it restored, but it was ignored. The Republic of Hawaii was established, with Sanford B. Dole as its first and only president. Annexation by the United States was imminent. In 1898, the islands became part of the territorial possessions of the United States. Manifest Destiny had triumphed again. The *haoles* who had once come as guests had managed to usurp the entire kingdom.

Richard Olney, the secretary of state at that time, summarized the situation: "Hawaii is ours," he said, "But as I look back upon the first steps in this miserable business and as I contemplate the means used to complete the outrage, I am ashamed of the whole affair."[10]

From Territory to State

Once Hawaii became a territory of the United States, its political and economic affairs were managed by forces on the mainland or by island elites responding to powerful people on the mainland. The territorial governorship of Hawaii was a powerful position. The governor was appointed by the president of the United States. This appointment was heavily influenced by the recommendation of the

Hawaiian elite. The economy of the territory depended on favorable legislation from the U.S. Congress to subsidize Hawaiian sugar and other agricultural products. The opening of the Panama Canal made it much easier for Hawaiian products to reach markets on the East Coast of the United States. Favorable subsidies and market shares from the U.S. Congress made Hawaii nearly totally reliant on sugar.

The Big Five corporations ran the economy of the islands through a variety of interlocking directorates and the vertical integration of business. To the average Native Hawaiian, this world of Merchant Street was alien and remote. The original inhabitants of Hawaii found themselves on the bottom rung of a plantation society with little hope of improving their situation.

Prince Jonah Kuhio Kalanianaole became the territorial delegate to the Congress by serving the interests of plantation owners. However, his frustrations would sometimes emerge, as they did in 1912, when he told a Hawaiian audience, "Under the political conditions in the territory, a man doesn't own his soul."[11]

Native Hawaiians' need for land was supposed to be reconciled in 1921 with the passage of the Hawaiian Rehabilitation Act. Under the auspices of the Hawaiian Homes Commission, 200,000 acres of land were to be distributed to landless Hawaiians for small-scale farming. Most of the land actually distributed was not suitable for farming. Eventually, it passed into the hands of large plantation interests.[12] The large amount of acreage devoted to export crops like sugar and pineapples meant that the traditional small-scale farming of the Native Hawaiian was nearly a relic from the past. Hawaii had become a major importer of food from the mainland, although historically it had been self-sufficient in food. Once again, actions intended to improve living conditions for Native Americans resulted in benefits for other groups.

The plantation economy continued earning large profits with the support of the Republican party, which had dominated island politics for the first 50 years of the twentieth century. On some plantations, managers monitored the actions of their workers by hanging pencils by strings from the ceilings of the voting booths. By noting in which direction the string moved, party preference could be determined. Anyone voting for a Democrat would be fired.[13]

After World War II, political leaders in Hawaii began seriously to discuss seeking statehood from the U.S. Congress. It was argued that becoming a state would guarantee the large U.S. market for Hawaiian products. Hawaiian leaders also believed that statehood would significantly increase the tourist industry and that many new construction and service jobs would be created.

While economic predictions turned out to be in general correct, Native Hawaiians did not share proportionately in the new prosperity. As Joseph Keoloha, Chairman of the State Office of Hawaiian Affairs, observed, "Statehood was the final act following the confiscation of our land and the overthrow of our Queen, and Native Hawaiians have mixed feelings about it."[14]

The Hawaiians Today

Social Class and Politics

Present-day Hawaii is a polyglot of peoples with varied backgrounds. There are sizable communities of Chinese Americans and Japanese Americans. There is a Korean-American population that originally came to work in the pineapple and sugar cane estates. Filipinos and Portuguese also came as agricultural workers. There are also a few thousand African Americans in Hawaii, as well as the still powerful *haoles*. Americans of Japanese ancestry have been especially successful in the political arena, and Chinese Americans have become business leaders in many areas.

Upward mobility by Asian Americans contrasts sharply with their status as primarily agricultural workers one or two generations ago. This change in status has caused some interethnic discords and ill feelings. Many Native Hawaiians who perceived the *haoles* as the holders of all-powerful positions often see Japanese Americans in their place. Other groups besides Hawaiians who find themselves disproportionately represented in the lower-economic classes realize the ethnic caste system of the big plantation era still exists in a modified form.

Dissatisfaction bred by this earlier caste system caused the major political movement of this century. Organizers tried to convince workers that their future would best be served by identifying politically with their working-class brethren regardless of their ethnic origin. This movement achieved its first major success in 1954, when the Democratic party broke the traditional Republican control in both houses of the territorial legislature. The man given a major share of the credit for this triumph was John A. Burns, who would play an important role in Hawaii's future politics by lobbying vigorously for statehood and by becoming governor.

The 1954 victory was viewed generally as the beginning of a progressive movement in island politics. By 1970, the Democrats were the solidly entrenched party, and John Burns was a candidate for a third term as governor. The main opposition within the Democratic party came from Tom Gill, who had been lieutenant governor under Burns. Gill charged that what may have started out as progressive political forces in 1954 had now become a power structure that was working together with the business and economic interests they originally opposed. The Gill campaign had a strong issue orientation capitalizing on respect for Hawaii's fragile environment. Governor Burns, with a network of loyal supporters on several islands, relied primarily on a media campaign and was successful in gaining a third term.

In 1974, George Ariyoshi became the first non-*haole* governor of Hawaii. He was later reelected to second and third terms of office. Governor Ariyoshi was followed by John D. Waihee in 1986. Governor Waihee became the first person of Hawaiian ancestry to hold this office. Neither major political party in

Hawaii has a homogeneous political base. To make a viable appeal to a diverse society, each party has had leaders who represent most of Hawaii's major ethnic groups.

The issues that are likely to dominate Hawaiian politics in the foreseeable future are land use, tourism, economic diversification, and the preservation of Hawaii's fragile natural environment. Today, 55% of all land in Hawaii is privately owned, and 95% of that land is held by 70-odd corporations or individuals.[15] The zoning and distribution of land are likely to evoke strong feelings among many Hawaiians. Tourism is clearly Hawaii's largest source of income. In 1959, Hawaii had only 243,000 visitors. By mid-1980, that number had exceeded 4 million. Tourism had become a business worth nearly $4 billion annually.[16]

Some critics of the tourist-dependent economy note that visitors cannot be relied on as a stable source of income. There are many viewpoints but no clear consensus on exactly how to diversify Hawaii's economy. Agricultural land is too expensive for farming to ever gain its former prominence. Transportation and labor costs work against Hawaii's becoming a manufacturing center. Meanwhile, tourism remains the mainstay of the economy, while Hawaiians attempt to reach a consensus on new directions for the islands' economic future.

Adapting Native Hawaiian Values

The Hawaiian spirit of *Aloha Aina* (love for the land) has had a resurgence in response to growing developments. A governor's conference in the early 1970s produced three possible scenarios for Hawaii's future: Hawaii unleashed, Hawaii primeval, and a balance between the two.[17] The balanced approach was the option recommended.

The traditional value of *'ohana* is a cooperative system of social relation-ships found within an extended family. A study in a Hawaiian community near Honolulu found that the spirit of *'ohana* still permeates the lives of Native Hawaiians. This study noted the following: "Our research continually affirmed that the overwhelming proportion of the people find gratification in their life-style. If wages were higher, most would continue to invest in a life-style similar to the one they are currently leading."[18]

This value of *'ohana* is sometimes counterproductive to Hawaiian children attending school where cooperation on academic work may be perceived as "cheating." Also, Hawaiian youngsters do not particularly relish the peer com-petition engendered in many school situations, and consequently they do not respond well to competitive tasks.

The Hawaiian value of *kokua* undergirds a traditional economic system based on cooperation with some element of competition. Under this system, one expression of *kokua* (cooperation) should be repaid with another expression of *kokua*. In this manner, the status of the individual is enhanced.[19] As the trend toward development continues in a state with limited natural resources, the spirit of *kokua* might point the way toward an accommodation among competing groups.

Another Hawaiian value that could prove helpful in a multiethnic and growing society is *ho'oponopono*. Literally, it means "setting to right of wrongs."[20] In early Hawaii, ho'oponopono meant that all people had an opportunity to speak out on a problem until a solution was reached that would be binding on all parties. This ancient tradition could be adapted to modern Hawaii and prove to be a valuable tool for building a consensus on a difficult issue.

The Hawaiians Today and Tomorrow

Proper classification of Native Hawaiians is difficult because the overwhelming majority of them are part Hawaiian. Today, about 1% (approximately 10,000 people) of the Hawaiian population can be classified as pure-blooded Hawaiian. Estimates vary as to the number of part-Hawaiians. In 1990 approximately 170,000 people claimed some Hawaiian ancestry. These figures contrast sharply with the estimated 300,000 Native Hawaiians on the islands when Captain Cook first visited them in 1778.

Under current law, only people with 50% or more Hawaiian blood are entitled to land and to medical and legal benefits. Perhaps no more than 60,000 of the state's 1 million people can prove that pedigree.[21] An issue in Hawaii is whether to lower the 50% requirement in order to qualify for any program designated for Native Hawaiians. Even if the current policy is followed, the matter of establishing Hawaiian lineage to meet the 50% requirement often leaves the Office of Hawaiian Affairs in a quandary.

The average Native Hawaiians fall far below their White counterparts in the area of economic prosperity. They generally live in a community whose facilities are substandard. They comprise a disproportionately high percentage of school dropouts and police arrests.

The Native Hawaiians have generally not adapted to the competitive nature of the dominant society. They are affiliation rather than competitively oriented. Friendship and family harmony are prized possessions not to be traded for economic status. Perhaps this refusal to compete has been the only way at their disposal to retain an ethnic identity in a society that rewards competition. Hawaiian school children seem to achieve much better when they are evaluated collectively rather than individually.

During the 1970s there was a rise of Hawaiian nationalist groups whose primary purpose was to return lost economic and political power to people of Hawaiian ancestry. Along with those movements there has been a revision in Hawaiian history that does not consider the whole era of Hawaiian monarchy to be a glorious age of benevolent rule. Among some of these Hawaiian nationalists, Kamehameha III is seen as a ruler who broke up the traditional system of land ownership and started the islands on their steady slide toward *haole* control. Queen Liliuokalani is seen as a great monarch who tried to retain power in the hands of Hawaiians while facing insurmountable odds.

This militancy is reflected in the formation of such groups as the *Kokua* and the Hawaiians. Membership in the *Kokua* is limited to non-*haoles*, and they espouse a Third World outlook. The Hawaiians limit their membership to people with at least some Hawaiian blood. Their ideology is more moderate than the *Kokua*. The existence of these two groups has had little impact on the economic status of most Native Hawaiians.

A manifestation of this militancy was the Free Kahoolawe movement in the mid-1970s. Kahoolawe, a small island owned by the military six miles off the coast of Maui, had been used for bombing practice since World War II. The movement began with an occupation of the island by a group of Hawaiians joined by people from nearly all segments of Hawaii's population. The goal of the Free Kahoolawe movement was the return of the island to state government jurisdiction and public access.[22] Movements like this indicate a shift in the attitudes of Native Hawaiians toward greater political activism.

There can be little doubt that a true Hawaiian Renaissance occurred in the 1970s. This trend represented a sharp contrast to predictions that the Hawaiian culture was slowly being extinguished. The renaissance had gone beyond a renewal of interest in cultural activities. It resulted in a new economic and political consciousness, as well as increasing involvement with other Pacific Island peoples.[23] How long this ethnic revitalization movement lasts remains an open question. It can be said, however, that the Hawaiian Renaissance arrived at a propitious time, when Native Hawaiian culture was being practiced less and less.

As Native Hawaiians look to the twenty-first century, they are vitally concerned with the future of their islands' natural environment. High real estate prices in Hawaii promote vertical expansion of new dwellings, but the environment of the islands is particularly fragile. Foreign investment is playing an ever-increasing role in Hawaii's economy. Will absentee landlords be appropriately concerned with the environmental impact of development, particularly if such measures reduce profit margins? These quality of life issues are important to all Hawaiians and are particularly salient to Native Hawaiians, whose culture is inextricably tied to the land.

Hawaii is sometimes presented as the personification of the *aloha* spirit. This is a misrepresentation to some degree. Hawaii is more ethnically harmonious than some societies. However, it is not an ethnic or a racial paradise. The future of racial and ethnic distinctions in Hawaii is unclear. The Native-Hawaiians' outmarriage rate is the highest of any group on the islands.[24] In a strictly biological sense, it appears that the Native Hawaiian population is being slowly dissolved into other groups. Perhaps a more optimistic outlook is that the culture of the Native Hawaiian is, to some extent, enriching the lives of all of the inhabitants of these beautiful islands.

Teaching Strategies

The concept of *expansion* can be illustrated in many ways. The Native Hawaiians provide a classic case of the displacement of a native population because they were an obstacle to the expanding forces. Their story can be related to other native inhabitants who suffered a similar fate.

CONCEPT: Expansion

Generalization: As a nation expands to obtain territory, often the rights of the native population are not protected.

1. After giving the students sufficient background information about the Native Hawaiian, ask them to make a list of factors that apply to the Native Hawaiian and the American Indian. These factors can include both past and present situations. Afterwards, these points can be grouped, classified, and discussed.

2. Organize your students into small groups. Present them with this hypothetical situation. One person in the group would be chosen to supervise and control the financial affairs of all the members. What problems may develop with such an arrangement? A tape could be made of their reactions. Later, this tape could be replayed and compared to what occurred between American advisors and Hawaiian rulers.

3. Roleplay the following situation, which occurred in Hawaii in 1845. The *haole* advisor to the King is trying to persuade him to grant some land to Mr. Farmer, a prospective planter. Kaeo opposes the entire proposition. After the roleplaying situation, ask the students the questions that follow. The role descriptions are as follows:

King Kamehameha III: He is indecisive over what to say to the planter. Yet, he greatly respects the advice of his *haole* counsel, Mr. George Bennett.

George Bennett: Advisor to the king and a good friend of Mr. Farmer, whose interests he protects. He has been a missionary for nearly 20 years.

Floyd S. Farmer: Planter and business tycoon. He intends to start sugar plantations in Hawaii because of the predictably warm weather.

Kaeo: A Native Hawaiian and a member of the king's court. He vehemently opposes the granting of any more land to *haoles*.

Questions

1. Did George Bennett succeed in persuading the king to grant the land to Mr. Farmer? If so, why? If not, why?
2. Was Kaeo successful in his opposition to the land deal? Why or why not?
3. Did Mr. Farmer tell the king his plans for using native labor? Why or why not?
4. Did the king decide to grant the land lease to Mr. Farmer? If he did, what were his reasons? If he did not, why not?
5. Did Mr. Bennett use his position as a missionary to help his argument? Why or why not?

CONCEPT: Adaptation

Generalization: When a native culture finds itself surrounded by a dominant culture, it becomes increasingly difficult to maintain the native culture.

1. Read the following story to the class and ask the questions that follow.

A Hawaiian Dilemma

The old ramshackle house had stood relatively unchanged since the family had obtained it more than 40 years ago from the Hawaiian Homes Commission. Around it were the two acres of vegetables that had provided subsistence for the Panui family during that time. Mary Panui lived on the property along with her sons, George and Eddie. Mr. Panui had died five years before and since that time things had not been the same.

One afternoon George was weeding one of the vegetable patches when Eddie returned from a day in town. Feeling that he deserved some help, George asked his brother, "Hey, aren't you going to help out around here?"

Eddie answered, "No, I have gotten a job in town with the tourist agency. I will drive the mainland *haoles* around during the day, and in the evenings I will dance at the luaus."

George couldn't believe his ears. After all of those years that their father had taught them to respect their Hawaiian heritage, his brother was suddenly changing. "Eddie, how can you do a thing like this?" George wondered. "It would have broken Dad's heart, and anyway, what will mother say?"

Eddie looked at his brother casually and said, "I have been weeding taro root all of my life and I'm tired of it. I know Dad would probably say that I'm putting our culture up for sale but it's the only way to get ahead!"

The two brothers entered the home where Mary Panui was cooking dinner and told her of their conversation. The old woman with the creased brow was also unhappy about what Eddie was considering. However, she could not deny that the vegetable gardens would never provide more than a subsistence living.

Seeing his mother caught up in the dilemma, George tried one last time, "Eddie, can you imagine yourself in one of those flowered shirts selling shell necklaces to the tourists? Where is your pride?"

Eddie thought for a moment and answered smugly, "Pride doesn't fill your wallet; when will you realize that?"

With that, George started out of the door but stopped short and told his brother, "I may never have much money to my name, but I'll never be a practicing Hawaiian!"

Questions

1. What would you have done if you had been Eddie Panui?
2. Do you feel Eddie's brother is justified in calling him a practicing (commercialized) Hawaiian?
3. Can you think of other ethnic groups in other settings that have had their culture commercialized? If so, how much was this trend sanctioned or resisted by the group?

Endnotes

1. Paul Jacobs and Saul Landau, with Eve Pell, *To Serve the Devil,* Vol. 2: *Colonials and Sojourners* (New York: Vintage, 1971), p. 22.
2. Noel J. Kent, *Hawaii: Islands under the Influence* (New York: Monthly Review Press, 1983), p. 18.
3. A. Grove Day, *Hawaii and Its People* (New York: Meredith Press, 1968), p. 44.
4. Jacobs and Landau, with Pell, *To Serve the Devil,* p. 26
5. Kent, *Hawaii,* p. 31
6. Andrew Lind, *Hawaii's People* (Honolulu: The University Press of Hawaii, 1980), pp. 20, 21.
7. Ronald Takaki, *Pau Hana: Plantation Life and Labor in Hawaii* (Honolulu: The University Press of Hawaii, 1983), p. 24.
8. Kent, *Hawaii,* p. 45.
9. Jacobs and Landau, with Pell, *To Serve the Devil,* p. 29.
10. Theon Wright, *The Disenchanted Isles* (New York: Dial Press, 1972), p. 21.
11. Kent, *Hawaii,* p. 75
12. For a more detailed comparison of Native American and Native Hawaiian land appropriation, see Linda S. Parker, *Native American Estate: The Struggle over Indian and Hawaiian Lands* (Honolulu: The University Press of Hawaii, 1989).
13. Robert Shaplen, "A Reporter at Large: Islands of Disenchantment," *New Yorker,* 6 September 1982, p. 85.
14. K. M. Chrysler, "Hawaii: Youngest State Finds Its Place in the Sun," *U.S. News and World Report,* 27 August 1984, p. 40.
15. Shaplen, "A Reporter at Large," p. 53.
16. Chrysler, "Hawaii," p. 39
17. Ruth Tabrah, *Hawaii: A Bicentennial History* (New York: W. W. Norton, 1980), p. 217.
18. Alan Howard, *Ain't No Big Thing: Coping Strategies in a Hawaiian American Community* (Honolulu: The University Press of Hawaii, 1974), p. 226.
19. Dennis Ogawa, *Kodomo No Tame Ni* (Honolulu: The University Press of Hawaii, 1978), p. 570.
20. Ibid.
21. Timothy Egan, "Blood and Benefits: Hawaii to Vote on Ancestral Rights," *Miami Herald,* 20 January 1990, p. 29A.
22. Tabrah, *Hawaii,* p. 220.
23. George Kanahele, *Hawaiian Renaissance* (Honolulu: Project WAIAHA, 1982), p. 27.
24. William L. Abbott, "Trapped in Mystique," *Nation* 208 (3 February 1969): 147.

Annotated Bibliography

Books for Teachers

Most of the information about Native Hawaiians is found in general sources about Hawaii. With perseverance, their story can be pieced together.

Allen, Helena. *The Betrayal of Liliuokalani: Last Queen of Hawaii 1838–1917.* Glendale, Calif.: Arthur H. Clark Co., 1982.

A detailed biography of the Hawaiian queen whose reign was interrupted by the overthrow of the monarchy. It is instructive and reveals the intrigues and joys of courtly life and displays the drama of power as these unfold in the telling of her life story.

Bailey, Paul. *Those Kings and Queens of Old Hawaii.* Los Angeles: Westernlore, 1975.

One of the best available sources on the Hawaiian monarchy. This text is well organized and highly readable.

Barratt, Glynn. *The Russian Discovery of Hawaii.* Honolulu: Editions Limited, 1987.

Translated from Russian manuscripts, this English version of a historical and ethnographtic record of eight of the men on an early Russian exploration to Hawaii is an addition to the many perspectives Europeans held of early Hawaii.

Bell, Roger, *Last among Equals: Hawaiian Statehood and American Politics.* Honolulu: University Press of Hawaii, 1984.

An incisive analysis of the struggle to gain equality and autonomy as a state. Useful reference for historians, as well as for any scholar studying the patterns of support and opposition generated by the process of becoming a state whose population was predominately non-White.

Bell, Susan. *Unforgettable True Stories of the Kingdom of Hawaii.* Van Nuys, Calif.: Delta Lithographic Co., 1986.

A personalized and episodic version of Hawaiiana that began as a curiosity for the author and ended as an investigative search to understand some of the enigmas she came across while living in Hawaii. A worthwhile trip for the reader to discover Hawaii from both an insider and an outsider perspective.

Bingham, Hiram. *A Residence of Twenty-One Years in the Sandwich Islands.* Rutland, Vt.: Charles E. Tuttle and Co., 1981.

This text is a reprint of a missionary's experiences in Hawaii in the early part of the nineteenth century. It is a valuable primary historical source.

Boggs, Stephen. *Speaking, Relating and Learning: A study of Hawaiian Children at Home and at School.* Norwood, N.J.: Ablex Publishing Corporation, 1985.

A scholarly study of those aspects of speaking and relating to others, peers or adults, by Hawaiian children within the context of the home and the school environments. The author addresses the relationship of school success or failure to the consequences resulting from the congruences or incongruences between the manner and function of speech learned at home against those required and rewarded at school.

Bosserant, d'Anglade, M. G. Translated by Alfons L. Korn. *A Tree in Bud: 1889–1893.* Honolulu: University Press of Hawaii, 1987.

A period of Hawaiian history from the perspective of a French gentleman whose observations though uniquely personal draw the reader's participation so that you see what the author sees and feel what he feels as you relive life in the Island during those years.

Charlot, John. *Chanting the Universe: Hawaiian Religious Culture.* Honolulu: Emphasis International Ltd., 1983.

A refreshing and excellent portrayal of the Hawaiian world view as expressed by the beauty and power of poets. The appeal is universal even as the reader is introduced to the basic concepts and sentiments underlying the Hawaiian culture.

Coffman, Tom. *Catch a Wave.* Honolulu: University Press of Hawaii, 1973.

This is a well-written study of Hawaiian politics with a case study on the 1970 gubernatorial election.

Cooper, George, and Daws, Gavan. *Land and Power in Hawaii: The Democratic Years,* Honolulu: Benchmark Books, Inc., 1985.

Research regarding the political developments in Hawaii during three decades, from the mid-1950s just prior to the Island's becoming the 50th state and through the 1980s. Extensively researched, the authors relate economic and political power in an island environment, where land has a high premium.

Daws, Gavan. *Shoal of Time.* Honolulu: University Press of Hawaii, 1976.

This is a complete interpretive history of Hawaii from European contact to statehood.

Day, Grove A. *History Makers of Hawaii.* Honolulu: Mutual Publications of Hawaii, 1984.

This is a rich resource for anyone inquiring into the lives of individuals who have made an impact on the shaping of cosmopolitan Hawaii. It includes a chronology of significant events presented within the context of U.S. historical development.

du Plessix Gray, Francine. *Hawaii: The Sugar-Coated Fortress.* New York: Vintage Books, 1973.

This brief but excellent book was written with great empathy for Hawaii's underprivileged groups.

Fuchs, Lawrence H. *Hawaii Pono.* New York: Harcourt, Brace and World, 1961.

Perhaps the most highly regarded book on the social history of Hawaii, it covers the period from annexation through statehood.

Gallimore, Ronald; Boggs, Joan; and Jordan, Cathie. *Culture, Behavior and Education: A Study of Hawaiian Americans.* Beverly Hills, Calif.: Sage Publications, 1974.

This sociological study of the adaptation of the community of 'Aina Pumehena contains chapters on socialization, schools, and culture conflict.

Hazama, Dorothy. *Okage Sama De: The Japanese in Hawaii, 1885–1985.* Honolulu: The Bess Press, 1986.

A historical account of the 100 years of the Japanese experience in Hawaii presented through personal anecdotes. The narrators capture the dilemma and tensions experienced by a generation of Japanese immigrants who bridged or tried to bridge the traditions of ethnic roots with present realities.

Howard, Alan. "Hawaiians." In *Harvard Encyclopedia of American Ethnic Groups,* edited by Stephan Thernstrom, Ann Orlov, and Oscar Handlin. Cambridge: Harvard University Press, 1980.

This book contains an interesting summary of circumstances surrounding Native Hawaiians.

————. *Ain't No Big Thing: Coping Strategies in a Hawaiian American Community.* Honolulu: University Press of Hawaii, 1974.

> *This book is an excellent source on conflicts between traditional Hawaiian values and modern Hawaiian society written from a sociological perspective.*

Kanahele, George. *Ku Kanaka (Stand Tall): A Search for Hawaiian Values.* Honolulu: University Press of Hawaii, 1986.

> *Kanahele has long been in the forefront of searching and expressing for himself and others the core values and traditions of the Hawaiian people. This book is a valuable first attempt to deal with a complex subject. Anyone interested in Hawaii and its people will find this book informative and provocative.*

Kent, Noel J. *Hawaii: Islands under the Influence.* New York: Monthly Review Press, 1983.

> *The author elaborates on the thesis that the Hawaiian Islands have been controlled by external forces from the period of the sandalwood trade under the Hawaiian monarchy to the tourism economy present today. This source provides a well-researched geopolitical perspective.*

Kimura, Yukiko. *Issei: Japanese Immigrants in Hawaii:* Honolulu: University Press of Hawaii, 1988.

> *This sociohistorical account of the first generation of Japanese immigrants to Hawaii, covers 15 years of retelling, from 1970 to 1985. Each of the four parts focuses on a particular aspect of the Issei's experience. It is a comprehensive and informative presentation told primarily from the Issei's (first generation) point of view.*

Kittelson, David J. *The Hawaiians: An Annotated Bibliography.* Honolulu: Social Science Research Institute, University of Hawaii, Series No. 7, 1985.

> *This comprehensive and useful guide to Hawaiian sources includes books, articles, and other publications. Recent publications, as well as classic ones, are included in this extremely valuable resource. Indexed, with 384 pages.*

Kodama, Nishimoto Michi; Nishimoto, Warren; and Oshiro, Cynthia H. *Hanahana: An Oral History—Anthology of Hawaii's Working People.* Honolulu: Ethnic Studies Oral History, University of Hawaii, 1984.

> *A compilation of stories gleaned from documents and interviews depicting the lives of 12 working individuals. An informative account of part of Hawaii's social history.*

Kotani, Roland. *The Japanese in Hawaii—A Century of Struggle.* Honolulu: Hawaii Hochi, Ltd., 1985.

> *This valuable piece of history instills ethnic pride. Although the book is not about Native Hawaiians, it is illustrative and informative of the social development of the earliest and largest group of immigrants to Hawaii, who had an indelible impact in shaping modern Hawaii.*

Lind, Andrew W. *Hawaii's People.* Honolulu: University Press of Hawaii, 1980.

> *This volume describes social patterns based on statistical evidence gathered about Hawaii's diverse population during the twentieth century. It would be particularly useful for the student of social trends.*

McDermott, John F., Jr.; Tseng Wen-Shing; and Maretzki, Thomas, eds. *People and Cultures of Hawaii.* Honolulu: University Press of Hawaii, 1980.

Hawaii's population is a story of blending—the mixing of biological, sociocultural, and psychological features. The book highlights the sociocultural aspect. Leading the articles on various ethnic groups is a discussion of Hawaiians, including their value systems, coping strategies, and a historical perspective on Hawaiian society.

Mitchell, Don Kilolani. *Resource Units in Hawaiian Culture.* Honolulu: The Kamehameha Schools, 1972.

This rich teaching resource includes a goldmine of information about Native-Hawaiian culture and society.

Nordyke, Eleanor C. *The Peopling of Hawaii,* 2nd ed. Honolulu: University Press of Hawaii, 1989.

This book contains important demographic data about Hawaii's multiethnic population.

Ogawa, Dennis M. *Kodomo No Tame Ni; For the Sake of the Children.* Honolulu: University Press of Hawaii, 1978.

This text, devoted primarily to Hawaiians of Japanese origin, also contains sections that concern Native Hawaiian culture and language.

Parker, Linda S. *Native American Estate: The Struggle over Indian and Hawaiian Lands.* Honolulu: University Press of Hawaii, 1989.

This source is particularly useful for anyone interested in the process by which Native Hawaiians lost control of their lands. The author also discusses the Hawaiian Homes Commission and the long and difficult process of land restitution.

Pukui, Mary Kawena. *Olelo No 'Eau: Hawaiian Proverbs and Poetical Sayings.* Honolulu: Bernice Pauahi Bishop Museum, 1983.

This book contains a rich source of Hawaiian sayings compiled, translated, and explained succinctly. The collection presents a wide variety of literary styles (metaphors, allegory, personifications, puns, etc.) and reflects the wisdom, beauty, and wit of cultural expressions not only of Hawaiians but also of all who wish to understand the human condition.

Research Committee. *Study of Honolulu Residents and Their Attitudes in Multi-Ethnic Perspectives: Toward a Theory of the American National Character.* Honolulu: University Press of Hawaii, 1980.

Interest in what happens to the Japanese immigrants provided the impetus to study the people of Honolulu as a whole. This monograph, conducted largely by Asian social scientists, is not only informative but also provides an insight into one type of theoretical and methodological approach to cross-cultural studies examining national character.

Shaplen, Robert. "A Reporter at Large: Islands of Disenchantment," *New Yorker,* 6 September 1982, pp. 50–91.

This article contains a thorough discussion of political and economic issues that have dominated Hawaii from the period of annexation to the present. This would also be a good overview for high school students who want a concise overview of the past 90 years in Hawaii.

Stewart, Frank, ed. *Passages to the Dream Shore.* Honolulu: University Press of Hawaii, 1987.

An anthology of short stories written about contemporary Hawaii by people of all ages and from all walks of life. Each story contributes to the socially diverse patchwork quilt and unique evolution of the Islands through the writers' experiences.

Tabrah, Ruth M. *Hawaii: A Bicentennial History.* New York: W. W. Norton, 1980.

This text about the history of Hawaii was written in conjunction with the U.S. bicentennial celebration. The last chapter provides useful information on contemporary Hawaii.

Takaki, Ronald. *Pau Hana: Plantation Life and Labor in Hawaii.* Honolulu: University Press of Hawaii, 1983.

This work examines the experiences of plantation workers who came from many nations to work in the fields of Hawaii. The author also examines the world of corporate power and the formation of the Big Five in the sugar industry.

Weinstein, Michael, ed. *Social Process in Hawaii.* Vol. 29. Honolulu: University Press of Hawaii, 1982.

The entire volume is useful for its contribution to our knowledge about the major ethnic groups in Hawaii. The overview of race and ethnic relations in Hawaii is recommended for any student of race relations.

Wichinan, Frederick. *Kauai Tales.* Honolulu: Bamboo Ridge Press, 1985.

A collection of 18 stories on a variety of subjects about the island of Kauai. Some stories explain old trails and ancient roadways. Others talk of mythical figures. All entertain and present tales of Kauai to amuse.

Whittaker, Elvi. *The Mainland Haole: The White Experience in Hawaii.* New York: Columbia University Press, 1986.

The only book that studies the haole or White population. This contribution will be welcomed by scholars in the social sciences.

Books for Students

Apple, Russ and Peg. *Land, Liliuokalani and Annexation.* Honolulu: Topgallant Publishing Co., 1979.

This collection of brief essays by the authors, which appeared in the Honolulu Star-Bulletin *over several years, covers a wide range of subjects related to the land, events, people, and politics. (Intermediate)*

Bagamery, Anne. "Extra! Capitalism Breaks Out in Hawaii!" *Forbes,* 22 April 1983, pp. 48–49.

This source discusses compromises being made between Hawaii's political and business interests to try to diversify the economy of the islands. (High School)

Beamer, Winona Desha. *Talking Story with Nona Beamer.* Honolulu: The Bess Press, 1984.

A collection of selected favorite stories of Hawaii told by a well-known and popular Hawaiian composer and choreographer. A unique feature is the author's original, easy-to-learn chants created to capture the essence of some of the stories. (Primary/Intermediate)

Bianchi, Lois. *Hawaii in Pictures*, rev. ed. New York: Sterling, 1971.

> *This book is divided into sections on the land, people, history, and economy of Hawaii. It has many illustrations. (Intermediate)*

Brown, Marcia. *Backbone of the King: The Story of Paka'a and His Son Ku*. New York: Scribner, 1966.

> *This is a well-researched and exciting story. (Intermediate)*

Buffet, Guy. *Kahala: Where the Rainbow Ends*. Norfolk Island, Australia: Island Heritage Books, 1973.

> *A romantic Hawaiian folktale, this book explains the reason for the rainbow in Manoa Valley. (Intermediate)*

Chrysler, K. M. "Hawaii: Youngest State Finds Its Place in the Sun," *U.S. News and World Report*, 27 August 1984, pp. 39–40.

> *This brief informative article on economic conditions in Hawaii includes an interview with Governor George Ariyoshi. (Middle School/High School)*

Cieply, Michael. "East of Eden," *Forbes*, 31 January 1983, pp. 34–36.

> *This article discusses land distribution in the Hawaiian Islands and the politics involved in changing zoning from agricultural to other uses. It also contains useful data on Hawaii's economy. (High School)*

Dunford, Betty. *The Hawaiians of Old*. Honolulu: The Bess Press, Inc., 1987.

> *A revised edition of the author's earlier book on selected segments of Hawaiian lifestyles. The book introduces various occupations of early Hawaiians, the islands themselves and their flora and fauna. She details the varied ways in which early Hawaiians entertained themselves through sports, music, and talk stories about their mythical heroes. The glossary and reference list are useful additions to the book. (Middle School/High School)*

Gomes, Bernadette. *Maile and the Marvelous One*. Taiwan: Press Pacifica, 1984.

> *This imaginative and fanciful story is about a Hawaiian mongoose, Maile, who is teased for being a dreamer. She becomes the pride of the family when she meets and befriends the "Aumakua," the Marvelous One, protector of Hawaii's land and people. The Aumakua is disguised as a snake to test the mongoose's ability to trust. (Primary)*

Guard, David. *Hale-Mano: A Legend of Hawaii*. Milbrae, Calif.: A Dawne-Leigh Book, 1984.

> *This charming Hawaiian legend is about Hale-Mano's adventures, foremost of which was winning the love of a princess. (Intermediate)*

Hazama, Dorothy. *Ancient Hawaiians: Who Were They? How Did They Live?* Honolulu: Hogarth Press, 1973.

> *The text describes how houses were built, as well as social structure and family system as they affected the use of houses. (Intermediate)*

Kamae, Lori. *The Empty Throne*. Honolulu: Topgallant Publications Co., 1980.

> *This biography is about a Hawaiian prince who would have been a king if the island had successfully forestalled the loss of the sovereignty. This book details the life of Prince Kuhio and is informative, albeit sentimental in tone. (High School)*

Kanahele, George, *Hawaiian Renaissance.* Honolulu: Project Waiaha, 1982.

> *This is the first in a series of essays dealing with traditional and modern Hawaiian values. Topics include perceptions of young Hawaiians about being Hawaiian and features Hawaiian values regarding courage and hospitality. (Intermediate)*

Kane, Herb Kawainui. *Pele.* Honolulu: The Kawainui Press. 1987.

> *Accompanied by attractive drawings and illustrations, this book presents various aspects of the mythology of Pele, the goddess of Hawaii's volcanoes. The book also provides some background information on the Island of Hawaii's formation and the Volcano National Park. (Primary/Intermediate)*

Kelly, John M., ed. *Folk Songs Hawaii Sings.* Rutland, Vt.: Charles E. Tuttle, 1962.

> *This book includes folk songs of Hawaii, Samoa, Japan, the Phillipines, China, and Korea. (All Levels)*

Kikukawa, Cecily. *Ka Mea Ho' Ala—The Awakener.* Honolulu: Bess Press, 1982.

> *This biography is about Henry Obookiah, who lived around the turn of the nineteenth century. Spared from death several times in his young life, Obookiah, then called Opukaha'ia, sailed, in his teens, to the East Coast, where he was converted to Christianity. He was instrumental in starting a Christian mission to Hawaii. (Intermediate)*

McBarnet, Gill. *Fountain of Fire.* Puunene, Hawaii: Ruwanga Trading, 1987.

> *A simple and charming story about a young girl who lives in a community threatened by volcanic eruptions. Easy to read and attractively presented with many pictures, the author gives his readers a feel for what life is like when a volcano erupts in Hawaii. (Primary)*

Summers, Catherine C. *The Hawaiian Grass House in Bishop Museum.* Honolulu: Bishop Museum Press, 1988

> *An informative description of the style of house people in Hawaii built and lived in before the turn of the century. This replica of the hale pili or grass house is useful as a take-off point for comparing and contrasting the types of housing, materials used, and construction of dwellings and for drawing inferences on the skills and use of resources applicable to one's surroundings in a given time and place. (Intermediate)*

Titcomb, Margaret. *The Ancient Hawaiians: How They Clothed Themselves.* Honolulu: Hogarth Press, 1983.

> *A simple and easy-to-follow explanation of how the early Hawaiians made garments for themselves prior to the arrival of the Whites. Numerous drawings show how tapa, the inner bark of a cloth plant, was prepared and treated with dye and made into loincloths for men and skirts for women. (Middle School/High School)*

Tuen, Ching Suelyn. *How Maui Slowed the Sun.* Honolulu: University Press of Hawaii, 1988.

> *A delightfully retold story of the legend of Maui, the boy who forced the sun to slow down to help his people accomplish more with a longer day. This version is appealing to young children because the story line is simple, vocabulary is at their level, and the colorful drawings accompanying the story are attractive. (Primary)*

Westervelt, W. D. *Myths and Legends of Hawaii: Ancient Lore Retold.* Honolulu: Mutual Publishing Co., 1987.

   Selected folk tales from ancient Polynesian lore retold for the enjoyment of today's readers. (High School)

Chapter 7

African

Americans

Concepts, Strategies, and Materials

Prejudice is a burden which confuses the past, threatens the future, and renders the present inaccessible.

—Maya Angelou

Introduction

Africans have had a unique experience in the Americas. They came with the earliest European explorers and settlers and were gradually enslaved in the North American colonies in the 1600s. When the eighteenth century began, slavery was flourishing in North America. The African experience in the United States has strikingly revealed the gross discrepancies between American ideals and reality. Throughout their history, African Americans have called on America to make its dream a reality. Their cries have usually fallen on deaf ears. African-American history and culture must be studied to enable students to understand and appreciate fully the great conflicts and dilemmas in American society and to develop a commitment to help make America's ideals a reality.

African Americans: Historical Perspective

Important Dates

1565   Africans helped to establish a colony in St. Augustine, Florida.

Important Dates

1619	The first Africans arrived in the English North American colonies.
1808	The slave trade was legally ended, but illegal slave trading began.
1829	David Walker published his *Appeal*, in which he harshly denounced slavery and urged slaves to take up arms and rebel.
1831	Nat Turner led a slave revolt in which nearly 60 Whites were killed.
1850	The Fugitive Slave Act, which authorized the federal government to help capture runaway slaves, was enacted. It helped pave the way to the Civil War.
1857	The Supreme Court ruled in the *Dred Scott Decision* that slaves did not become free when they moved to free territory. It also held that African Americans were not and could not be citizens.
1861–62	Congress enacted several Confiscation Acts designed to prevent the Confederacy from using slaves in its war effort.
1863	Many African Americans in New York City were attacked and killed by largely Irish mobs that were protesting the draft laws and expressing anti-Black feelings. On January 1, 1863, President Lincoln issued the Emancipation Proclamation, which freed slaves in those states fighting the Union.
1865	Slavery was legally abolished throughout the United States by the enactment of the Thirteenth Amendment to the Constitution.
1866	The Fourteenth Amendment, which made African Americans United States citizens, was enacted. The Civil Rights Act of 1866 was enacted. It extended the African American's civil liberties in several areas.
1870	The Fifteenth Amendment was enacted. It enabled many African Americans to vote.
1876	In the disputed Hayes-Tilden election, Hayes's supporters promised that he would remove the remaining federal troops from the South. This bargain symbolized the extent to which northern Whites had abandoned the southern African Americans.
1896	In a historic decision, *Plessy* v. *Ferguson*, the Supreme Court ruled that "separate but equal" facilities were constitutional.

Important Dates	
1905	W. E. B. DuBois and a group of African American intellectuals organized the Niagara Movement to promote civil rights for African Americans.
1910	The National Association for the Advancement of Colored People (NAACP) was organized. It successfully fought for African American legal rights.
1911	The National Urban League was founded to help the Black urban migrant adjust to city life and find jobs.
1914	Marcus Garvey organized the Universal Negro Improvement Association. Garvey urged African Americans to return to Africa.
1917	One of the worst riots in U.S. history occurred in East St. Louis, Illinois. Thirty-nine African Americans were killed.
1919	A series of riots occurred in a number of cities during the "Red Summer" of 1919. One of the most serious occurred in Chicago, in which 38 people lost their lives.
1943	White violence directed at African Americans led to a serious riot in Detroit, in which 34 people were killed.
1954	In a landmark decision, *Brown v. Board of Education*, the Supreme Court ruled that school segregation was inherently unequal.
1955	African Americans in Montgomery, Alabama, began a boycott of the city's buses that ended bus segregation there in 1956.
1957	Martin Luther King, Jr., and a group of Baptist ministers organized the Southern Christian Leadership Conference (SCLC). National guardsmen were required to help integrate Central High School in Little Rock, Arkansas.
1960	On February 1, 1960, the sit-in movement, which desegregated public accommodation facilities throughout the South, began in Greensboro, North Carolina.
1961	The Congress of Racial Equality (CORE) led Freedom Rides through the South to desegregate interstate transportation.
1963	More than 200,000 people participated in a "March on Washington for Freedom and Jobs." In a Birmingham demonstration, led by Martin Luther King, Jr., civil rights demonstrators were violently attacked by the police.

Important Dates	
1964	The Civil Rights Act of 1964, the most comprehensive civil rights bill in U.S. history, was enacted by Congress and signed by President Lyndon B. Johnson. An antipoverty act launched the War on Poverty.
1965	Partly in response to civil rights demonstrations, the Voting Rights Act of 1965 was enacted.
1965–68	A racial rebellion in the Watts district of Los Angeles in 1965 launched one of the most serious series of racial disturbances in U.S. history. Some of the most tragic riots occurred in Newark and Detroit in 1968. A new wave followed the assassination of Martin Luther King, Jr., in 1968.
1966	Stokely Carmichael issued a call for "Black Power" during a civil rights demonstration in Greenwood, Mississippi. The Black Panther party was organized in Oakland, California.
1968	Martin Luther King, Jr., was assassinated in Memphis, Tennessee, while there to help striking garbage workers. A Poor People's Campaign was staged in Washington, D.C., to dramatize the plight of the American poor.
1972	More than 8,000 delegates attended the first National Black Political Convention in Gary, Indiana. President Richard M. Nixon signed a bill that was designed to end busing for racial integration of the schools.
1973	African Americans were elected mayors of Detroit, Atlanta, Los Angeles, and other cities.
1976	The votes of African Americans were decisive in the election of President Jimmy Carter.
1980	Feeling that neither of the major political parties was responsive to their needs, Blacks organized the Black Independent Political Party in Philadelphia.
1983	Lieutenant Colonel Guion S. Buford, Jr., served as a crew member aboard the space shuttle *Challenger* and became the first African American astronaut to travel into outer space. President Ronald Reagan signed a bill establishing a federal holiday in honor of Dr. Martin Luther King, Jr., the first national holiday named for an African American. Rev. Jesse Jackson launched his campaign as a Democrat for the U.S. presidency in his hometown of Greenville, South Carolina.

Important Dates	
1988	Jesse Jackson made an impressive bid for the Democratic presidential nomination. He won a number of important primaries and commanded national attention.
1989	David Dinkins was elected mayor of New York City. Douglas Wilder was elected governor of Virginia.

African Explorers in America

Africans have been in America for many centuries. Inconclusive evidence suggests that they established a colony in Mexico long before Columbus's voyage in 1492. Africans were with the first Europeans who explored America. Africans had been living in Europe for many years when European explorations to America began. The Moors, a North African people, invaded Europe in 711. They eventually conquered and ruled Spain. Other Africans were brought to Europe as slaves beginning in the 1400s. These Africans worked in private homes as servants, in banks, shipyards, and in mercantile establishments.

Diego el Negro was with Columbus on his last voyage to America in 1502. When Balboa arrived at the Pacific Ocean in 1513, his crew included a Black man, Nuflo de Olano. Africans explored present-day Kansas in 1541 with Coronado. Africans were also with many of the other early Spanish expeditions to the Americas. Estevanico, a Moor, is one of the most famous early Black explorers. Arriving in America in 1529, he explored present-day New Mexico and Arizona and paved the way for later Spanish explorations of the Southwest.

In addition to exploring America, Africans were among its first non-Indian settlers. Some of the settlers of the ill-fated South Carolina colony in 1526, San Miguel de Gauldape, were African. Africans helped to establish St. Augustine, Florida, in 1565, which is the oldest non-Indian settlement in the United States. A number of colonies were established by Africans and Frenchmen. These groups settled in the Mississippi Valley in the seventeenth century.

The Slave Trade

The Arabs invaded Africa and enslaved Africans long before Europeans arrived on the continent. The European nations became involved in the African slave trade when they started trading with Africa in the 1400s. In the mid-fifteenth century, European monarchs sent explorers to Africa to obtain goods such as skins and oils. Many of these explorers took back these wares as well as African slaves and gold as gifts for their rulers. These gifts greatly pleased the European monarchs. As more and more Europeans explored Africa and took Africans back to Europe, the slave trade gradually gained momentum. However, Black slavery never became widespread in Europe, but it grew by leaps and bounds when Europeans started settling in America in the 1600s. Europeans developed large plantations in the West Indies that grew crops such as sugar, indigo, cotton, and tobacco. Sugar production reigned supreme over all other crops. To produce increasing amounts of sugar, the Europeans brought thousands of Africans to the West Indies.

The slave trade became highly lucrative. European nations competed aggressively to monopolize it. At first, the Portuguese dominated the slave trade. Portugal was eventually challenged by the Dutch. Gradually, more and more nations gained a toehold in Africa. However, England was dominating the slave trade when it peaked in 1700. The European nations greatly benefited from the slave trade. They obtained many raw materials from Africa that helped them to attain high levels of industrial growth. The ships that left Europe carried small items to use for exchange with the Africans. While in Africa, they picked up wares such as gold, ivory, and dyewood as well as captives. The ships usually traveled from Africa to the West Indies, where the captives were sold and exchanged goods acquired. The goods were taken back to Europe. The journey from the West Coast of Africa to the West Indies was known as the "Middle Passage" because it was only part of a route that eventually led back to Europe.

When the slave trade in the West Indies began, European nations granted monopolies to a few favorite companies, such as the Dutch West India Company and the Royal African Company of England. Later, when these nations realized that they could make more money by allowing companies to compete, the monopoly system was abandoned. Before the monopolies ended in the late 1600s, the European colonists in North America were not able to obtain nearly as many Africans as they wanted. The major companies sold most of their Africans on the more profitable markets on the West Indian sugar plantations. However, the North American colonists were able to buy as many Africans as they wished when monopolies ended. The smaller companies were eager to trade with them.

Whereas the slave trade was profitable for European nations and contributed to their industrial growth and development, it was disastrous for the West African nations. When the trade first began, African rulers sold captives and criminals. Most of the captives had been taken from other tribes during warfare. However, as the Europeans sought more and more Africans, these sources became inadequate. The African rulers were so fascinated with the trinkets, rum, firearms, and other items they received in exchange for captives that they started warring to obtain captives, using the firearms they received from Europeans. Warring became increasingly frequent and destructive as the Europeans' desire for captives soared. As warring increased, some groups had to sell captives to acquire the firearms they needed to protect themselves. These wars adversely affected African political stability. The slave trade also drained off many of Africa's strongest and most productive young men and women. The slave traders wanted only healthy captives who could survive the horrible middle passage and the backbreaking work on the plantations in America.

The Beginning of Bondage

The captive's life was terrifying, brutal, and shocking. Slave catchers, who were usually Africans, raided the interior of the West African coast looking for captives. When Africans were caught, they were chained together and marched long distances, often hundreds of miles, to the European forts near the coast. Here they waited, sometimes for months, to be forced onto ships headed for America. The captives adamantly resisted bondage. Some of them escaped on the long march to the forts. Others jumped overboard once the ships were at sea. Mutinies occurred, both on the African shore and in mid-ocean. In 1753 a group of captives seized a ship bound for America, killed the White crew, and forced the ship back to Africa.

Conditions on the slave ships were degrading and dehumanizing. The captured Africans were packed into the ships like sardines. They were chained together with iron ankle fetters. The space for each slave was so small that they were forced to lie down in the ship. Because of the crowded and filthy conditions on the ships, diseases were rampant and took many lives. Many Africans died from scurvy, dysentery, and smallpox. Sometimes everyone on a ship was blinded by ophthalmia. Africans who became very sick were dumped into the ocean, because dead Africans were worthless on the American slave market. More than half of the Africans sometimes died during the journey. Some historians estimate that one out of every eight captives died in the middle passage and never reached the Americas. This painful trip usually took from 40 to 60 days.

Slavery in North America

The first Africans to arrive in the English North American colonies came in 1619 on a Dutch ship. These 20 Africans were not slaves but, like most of the Whites who came to the colonies during this period, were indentured servants. To pay for their passage to America, indentured servants agreed to work for their sponsors for a specified period of time. When they had completed their period of service, they became free. At first, the English colonists met their labor needs with indentured servants.

Increasingly the colonists began to feel that they were not obtaining enough workers with this system and that slavery had many more advantages. For one thing, indentured servitude was more expensive than slavery. The servants had to be provided certain goods and services. Eventually they became free. With slavery, the worker received few benefits and remained a servant for life. Also, the slaves' children would also be slaves. Clearly, slavery was a more profitable system than indentured servitude. The colonists deliberately decided to replace indentured servitude with African slavery for economic reasons.

Slavery existed in practice in most of the colonies long before it acquired legal status. The legal institutionalization of slavery was a gradual process. By

1630 in Virginia, laws and legal cases were beginning to evolve that would culminate in the legalization of slavery. In that year, a court sentenced a White man to a whipping for having sex with an African woman. The Virginia House of Burgesses passed a law in 1643 limiting the years for White indentured servants but not for African servants. The House enacted a law in 1662 that declared that children would inherit their mother's status. This law reversed English common law, which held that children inherited their father's status. A 1667 law enacted by the House enabled Christians to be slaves. A law passed in Maryland in 1664 openly declared that Blacks and their children would be slaves in that colony. By the end of the seventeenth century, slavery existed in fact as well as in law in Colonial America.

American slavery was a unique institution in human history that was designed to dehumanize Africans and to convince them that they were inferior and deserved the treatment they received. It was also designed to enable Whites to make maximum profits from African labor and to reinforce ideals of White supremacy. All of the laws, customs, and norms that developed around slavery reflected and reinforced its major goals. Slaves were regarded as property who should cater to the whims and wishes of their masters. A number of arguments and traditions emerged to justify slavery and to ensure its continuation. Because of their treatment of Blacks, and because of constant attempts by the captives to resist bondage, Whites developed a chronic fear of slave rebellions and retaliation. Sometimes, especially after a slave rebellion or when one was rumored, White fears of slave insurrections and uprisings became chronic, paranoid, and widespread. Consequently, the slave codes were made more severe and the institutions and norms supporting bondage were revitalized.

Attempts by Whites to deny the African captives humanity and to oppress them are reflected in the numerous slave codes enacted in colonies from New York to Georgia. These codes varied from colony to colony but tended to be most severe in the southern colonies and mildest in New England. However, all of them were degrading and designed to reinforce bondage. In some colonies, slaves could not form groups without the presence of a White; they could not carry or own firearms, testify in court against a White person, or be taught to read or write. Some colonies prevented them from owning property or drinking liquor and did not recognize their marriages as legal. They were forbidden from leaving the plantation unless they had a special pass. Punishment for crimes was severe, although some planters did not welcome the death penalty because it deprived them of profitable workers. Slaves were subject to the death penalty for such crimes as rape, arson, and robbery.

Slaves worked in a wide variety of occupations, especially in the northern colonies. They worked as laborers and house servants in New England, and also as skilled artisans. Many skilled slaves in the North hired themselves out and saved enough money to buy their freedom. Few skilled slaves in the South were allowed to keep the money they earned hiring themselves out. Although slaves in the South worked in many different jobs, especially in the cities where many were skilled artisans, most worked on the large plantations owned by a few rich members of the southern aristocracy. Life on these large plantations, which specialized in such crops as tobacco and cotton, was arduous and poignant. Often driven by a merciless overseer and a driver, the slaves worked from sunup to sundown. They usually lived in mud-floor shacks on the plantation that were cold in the winter and hot in the summer. Their food consisted mostly of hominy and fatback. Their clothing was limited. Men usually had little more than two shirts and two pairs of trousers.

Even though Whites tried to deny the slaves a human existence, Africans succeeded in developing a sense of community and a social life quite apart from the world of Whites. Slaves had stable marriages, even though they were not legally recognized by White society. These marriages usually occurred after long courtships. The family was important to the slaves. Family members taught the child how to survive the harsh White environment, as well as how never to submit totally to the whims of the master. Black fathers openly disapproved of the ways Whites treated their families. However, these men usually obeyed the master so that they could avoid severe punishment or death. Many slave families that had developed strong bonds of love and kinship were broken up when their master sold family members to different buyers or sold only some members of the family. Some slaves escaped to search for members of their families when they were sold.

Most African captives never totally submitted to slavery or accepted it. They resisted it in both covert and blatant ways. To avoid work, slaves would sometimes feign illness. They sometimes destroyed farm equipment deliberately or cut up the plants when they were hoeing crops. A few slaves maimed themselves to avoid work. Some domestic slaves put poison in their masters' foods and killed them. Other slaves escaped. The number of runaways increased greatly when the Civil War began and when the Emancipation Proclamation was issued in 1863. Many slaves were helped to the North and Canada by a loosely organized system known as the Underground Railroad. Free Blacks, many of whom were escaped slaves, made numerous trips to the South to help Blacks escape. Africans such as Harriet Tubman and Josiah Henson helped hundreds of slaves follow the North Star to freedom. The slaves traveled by night, and were helped by "conductors" of the Underground Railroad. Although some slaves were helped by Underground Railroad conductors, many of them escaped alone. These lone and brave captives were determined to escape bondage at any cost.

African captives also resisted slavery by rebellion. Even though most slave uprisings were unsuccessful, partly because of slave informers, historical records indicate that at least 250 occurred.[1] One of the most ambitious slave uprisings was planned by Gabriel Prosser in 1800. Prosser and a group of about 1,000 slaves armed themselves and headed for Richmond, Virginia. A heavy rainstorm stopped the rebels; and the authorities in Richmond, who had been alerted, were armed and waiting for them. Gabriel Prosser and 30 of the other captives died at the end of a rope. Denmark Vesey, a free Black in Charleston, South Carolina, planned an insurrection in 1882. The group he led armed themselves and were prepared to take Charleston's two arsenals. The revolt was crushed before it got started and the participants were hanged. The most successful slave revolt of the antebellum period was led by Nat Turner in 1831. Turner was a highly imaginative African American preacher who felt that he was destined by God to free his people from bondage. Turner organized and armed a crew that killed about 60 Whites, including his master and family. The Turner rebels caught their victims by surprise. Whites crushed the rebellion after it had raged for 48 hours. When they were seized, Turner and 19 other rebels were hanged.

The Abolitionists

The first societies organized to agitate for the abolition of slavery were formed during and after the American Revolution. The earliest was founded in Philadelphia in 1775. The Quakers were the leading figures in this society. Other abolitionary societies were formed during this period. Most of the members of these early societies were propertied men who were sympathetic to the South. They spoke kindly of the South, were soft spoken, and felt that slave owners who freed their slaves should be compensated. They advocated a gradual abolition of slavery. Because of the tactics they used, many Southerners supported these societies. These abolitionists did not believe in or practice social equality. Women and African Americans were excluded from their organizations.

The abolitionary societies organized in the 1800s were much more militant and aggressive than the earlier ones. They harshly denounced slavery and slave owners and demanded an immediate end to slavery. These groups were unpopular in both the North and the South. They became known as militants and extremists. Both Whites and Blacks participated in these societies, although the Whites, who did not believe in racial equality, tried to keep the African Americans in the background. Frederick Douglass, Robert Purvis, and Sojourner Truth were some of the leading African American abolitionists.

One of the most militant societies was the American Anti-Slavery Society, organized in 1833. Although this society vigorously denounced slavery, it kept Blacks in the shadow. In its early years, it had no African American lecturers. Most of the policy was made by Whites. Members of the society discouraged African Americans when they started editing their own newspapers and lecturing. They wanted only a few Blacks to be visible in the organization for symbolic purposes. The African American abolitionists harshly condemned the White abolitionists, accusing them of discriminating against Blacks in their businesses and their daily lives.

The African American abolitionists often went their separate ways. They edited newspapers and gave moving speeches giving Black views of abolition. Despite objections from White abolitionists such as William Lloyd Garrison,

Frederick Douglass edited and published a paper, the *North Star*. Black abolitionists also expressed their views in the series of conventions they held in the antebellum period. At the National Negro Convention in 1843, Henry Highland Garnet gave a controversial speech in which he urged slaves to rise up and fight for their freedom. He later worked with William G. Allen to edit a newspaper, *The National Watchman*. Sojourner Truth and Harriet Tubman were also important African-American abolitionists. Truth worked with other abolitionists such as William Lloyd Garrison and Frederick Douglass. She also became active in the women's rights movement. Harriet Tubman was one of the most successful "conductors" on the Underground Railroad. She helped to free more than 300 slaves.

As was to be the case in later years, African American and White participants in Black liberation movements in the 1800s often had different goals and aims, and they used different approaches. These divergent goals and methods inevitably led to conflict and hostility between these groups.

The Colonization Movement

In the early nineteenth century, an intense movement developed among Whites to deport African Americans to another country. The motives of the advocates of colonization varied. Some saw themselves as humanitarians and felt that because of White racism African Americans would never be able to achieve equality in America. They believed that Blacks would have a much better chance in another nation. Other advocates of colonization were supporters of slavery and wanted to deport *free* Blacks because they felt that nonslave Blacks were a threat to slavery. Many southern Whites eagerly supported the American Colonization Society, organized in 1816 by a group of eminent White Americans.

Many influential Whites, such as Francis Scott Key and Henry Clay, supported colonization. A region in West Africa, named Liberia, was acquired by American colonizationists in 1822. Despite the enthusiastic support for the movement, it did not succeed. Fewer than 8,000 African Americans had immigrated to Liberia by 1852. Many of these were slaves who had been granted their freedom on the condition that they immigrate to Africa. The colonization movement failed primarily because most African Americans were adamantly against it. The American Colonization Society made its plans and solicited support from eminent White Americans but ignored the feelings of African Americans. African-American leaders denounced the society, which often condoned racist practices, in loud terms. They argued that they would not leave the United States because their parents had helped to build this nation and because they had a right to live in America by birthright. The free African Americans who strongly opposed colonization saw it as an attempt by slaveowners to get rid of them and thus make slavery more safe and secure. These leaders argued that their fate rested with the fate of their enchained brothers and sisters.

A few African Americans who became disillusioned with the United States began to advocate colonization. However, some of the leaders, such as Martin Delany, strongly criticized the American Colonization Society. Delany felt that the society's members were "arrogant hypocrites." He correctly perceived the White colonizationists' motives as being quite different from his. African-American colonizationists wanted to leave the United States because they had become disillusioned and frustrated. Most White colonizationists hoped to deport African Americans so that they could get rid of a racial group they did not want in the United States.

From time to time, small groups of despairing African Americans thought seriously about colonization and sometimes took concrete actions to realize their aspirations. Paul Cuffe took 38 Blacks to Sierra Leone in 1815. In 1859, Martin D. Delany obtained a piece of land in Africa for an African American settlement. A Black colonization group, the African Civilization Society, was organized by a group of eminent African Americans in 1858. Despite these attempts, African-American colonizationists had no more success than White colonizationists because most African Americans were determined to remain in the United States. Back-to-Africa advocates emerged later in the nineteenth and twentieth centuries, but their cries continued to fall on deaf ears. Marcus Garvey was a strong advocate of African colonization in the 1930s.

Nonslave African Americans

Not all African Americans were slaves, either in the North or South, during the antebellum period. Many African Americans in the North hired themselves out and earned their freedom. Some in New England sued for their freedom in courts and won it. Some bondsmen were awarded their freedom after service in the Revolutionary War. A few African Americans were descendants of Black indentured servants and thus were never slaves. In the South, some slave masters left wills freeing their slaves on their deaths. Often these slaves were their children or other blood relatives. Some southern slaves were given their freedom after meritorious service to their communities. Others obtained their freedom by escaping. In both the North and the South, the nonslave Black was harassed and demeaned and was often treated like he or she was a slave. When Whites saw African Americans, they assumed that they were slaves. Nonslave Blacks had to prove that they were free. Free Blacks had to carry papers, which they usually had to purchase, that certified their freedom. However, they were often captured and enslaved whether they carried "free" papers or not.

Many of the legal limitations imposed on the slave also governed the nonslave African American. In many parts of the South, nonslave Blacks were forbidden from forming groups without the presence of a White, were prohibited from testifying against a White, and were not allowed to own a gun or a dog. In the North, they were denied the franchise and prohibited by law from migrating to such states as Illinois, Indiana, and Oregon. The free African American could settle in other old northwest states only after paying bonds up to a thousand dollars. Southerners regarded free African Americans as a nuisance and a threat to slavery. They blamed them for most of the slave rebellions and for encouraging slaves to escape. For these reasons, many southern Whites eagerly supported the move to deport free Blacks to Africa.

Nonslave northern Blacks played an extremely important role in African American life. They strongly protested the racism and discrimination Blacks experienced. The Negro Convention Movement served as an important protest forum. Black conventions were held from 1830 up to the beginning of the twentieth century. At most of them, the delegates issued cogent statements demanding an end to racism in various areas of American life. The colonization movement, discrimination in northern schools, and segregation in the church were targets of Black protest.

Free African Americans also organized significant institutions, including the numerous self-help and mutual-aid societies from which most of today's Black insurance companies grew. One of the earliest mutual-benefit societies, the African Union Society, was organized in Newport, Rhode Island, in 1780. Like many similar societies organized later, it helped its members when they were out of work, gave them decent burials, and set up an apprentice program that trained young Blacks to be skilled artisans. Other mutual-aid societies included the Masonic Order organized by Prince Hall in 1787 and the Grand United Order of Odd Fellows, established in 1843. These organizations were extremely important within the Black community.

African Americans also organized their own churches. African Americans were forced to sit in separate pews in White churches and were sometimes interrupted in the middle of prayers if they were seated in the "wrong" sections. These kinds of indignities led Blacks such as Richard Allen and Absalom Jones to organize independent Black churches. In 1794, two Black Methodist churches were founded in Philadelphia, St. Thomas Protestant Episcopal Church and the Bethel African Methodist Episcopal Church. African American Methodist churches soon spread to many other cities. African American Baptists also established independent churches. The Black church became an extremely important institution in African American life. It trained most Black protest leaders, opened schools for Black children, and gave Blacks practice in self-governance and increased their self-respect. The church and the fraternal orders, which were affiliated with the church, were the key institutions within Black America. Today, the African-American church still performs many of its historic functions and remains an important institution.

The Civil War and Reconstruction

African Americans viewed the Civil War as the god-sent conflict that would emancipate them from bondage. However, they were virtually alone in this view. Most White Americans, including President Lincoln and the U.S. Congress, viewed the war as a conflict to preserve the Union. When news of the war spread, northern Blacks rushed to recruiting stations and tried to enlist in the armed forces. Their services were rejected. Leaders thought that the war would last only 90 days. The war dragged on for 4 long years. When it became evident that the war would last much longer than was originally thought, the Union, and later the Confederacy, reluctantly allowed African Americans to take up arms.

Congress and President Lincoln took a number of steps to weaken the Confederacy. They realized that the slaves were being used to help the Confederate forces to maintain their strength. Consequently, Congress enacted a number of laws that undermined the Confederacy. In 1861, Congress enacted legislation enabling it to free slaves who were used to help the Confederate forces. In the summer of 1862, Congress passed a bill that freed slaves who had escaped and authorized the president to use Black troops. President Lincoln also used his authority to weaken the Confederacy. On September 22, 1862, he announced that slaves in rebel states would be freed on January 1, 1863. Lincoln kept his promise and issued the Emancipation Proclamation freeing those slaves in rebel states on January 1, 1863. Although African Americans and abolitionists rejoiced when the Emancipation Proclamation was issued, legally it did no more than the act that was passed by Congress in 1862. The thousands of slaves in states not fighting the Union were not freed. However, the proclamation did give African Americans a moral uplift and motivated more slaves to escape. However, captives had been escaping in large numbers ever since northern soldiers started coming to the South.

After 4 bitter years and the bloodiest war in U.S. history up to that time, Lee surrendered at Appomattox on April 9, 1865, and the Civil War ended. On April 14, 1865, Lincoln was assassinated by John Wilkes Booth. Andrew Johnson became president. President Johnson, like Lincoln, favored a lenient plan for readmitting the southern states back into the Union. However, the Republican Congress wanted to gain a toehold in the South so that the Republican party could win future presidential elections. To obtain their objective, they franchised the newly freed African Americans so that they would develop an allegiance to the Republican party. In a series of acts, Congress gave Blacks the right to vote, extended their civil rights, and endeared them to the Republicans. In 1865, it enacted the Thirteenth Amendment, which abolished slavery throughout the United States. Congress passed a Civil Rights Act in 1866 that made African Americans citizens and granted them certain legal rights. The Fourteenth Amendment, enacted in 1866, also recognized Blacks as citizens. The Reconstruction Act of 1867 divided the South into five military districts and required the Confederate states to enact constitutions that would be approved by Congress and to ratify the Fourteenth Amendment before they could be readmitted into the Union. The South considered the Reconstruction Act especially galling.

Because they could now vote and run for public office, a number of African Americans held elected offices for brief periods during Reconstruction. Most of them held minor local offices. However, 22 served in the U.S. Congress.

Two of these were U.S. senators. Black elected officials were too few in number and their tenure too brief for them to play a leading role in shaping policy. However, the South obtained its most enlightened state constitutions during Reconstruction and enacted some of its most humane social legislation. For years after Reconstruction, southern apologists justified southern violence by arguing that the South was reacting to the former Black control of the southern states. However, African Americans never controlled any of the states' legal bodies and none were elected governors.

The Rise of White Supremacy

The Republicans' plan to grab the Black man's vote was successful. Blacks in large numbers voted for the Republican presidential candidate in the election of 1868. However, by 1876, the Republicans, who were dominated by northern industrial interests, had new interests and no longer needed the Black man to attain them. In fact, African Americans stood in their way. Northern industrialists were now interested in extending their trade in the South and consequently wanted to court the southern Whites. To appease southern Whites, northern Whites decided to leave the question of the Black person's fate up to the South. The handling of the Hayes–Tilden election in 1876 indicated the extent to which northern Whites had abandoned African Americans. In that disputed election, an Electoral Commission named the Republican candidate, Hayes, president. To placate the South, Hayes's supporters promised White southerners that when he became president, Hayes would remove all of the remaining federal troops from the South.

Hayes kept this promise when he became president. By the time that the last federal troops were removed from the South, southern Whites were reestablishing their control of state governments throughout the South and had aggressively begun their campaigns to make African Americans chattels even though slavery had been legally abolished. One of the first acts of the state legislatures was to disenfranchise African Americans. A motley collection of ingenious methods were used to keep Blacks from voting. The Democratic primary, the grandfather clause, literacy tests, and the poll tax were among the many ways in which African Americans, and inadvertently some poor Whites, were prevented from voting.

Determined to "put Blacks in their place," violence against African Americans became rampant. The goals of this violence were to intimidate African Americans to keep them from voting and to reestablish the caste system that had existed before the Civil War. African Americans became victims of a rash of riots that swept throughout the South between 1866 and 1898. When African Americans tried to obtain the right to vote in New Orleans in 1866, a riot erupted in which 48 Blacks were killed. A riot broke out in Savannah, Georgia, in 1872 when Blacks tried to end segregation on the city's streetcars. Thirty African Americans were killed in a riot that erupted in Meridian, Mississippi, in 1871.

Forty-six died in a Memphis riot in 1866. Even though Blacks were usually innocent victims in these riots, they struck back at Whites in the Charleston Riot of 1876.

The Ku Klux Klan was reorganized in 1915. It became a prime leader of anti-Black violence. The lynching of African Americans also became wide-spread. About 100 Blacks met their death each year at the end of a rope during these difficult years.

Southern state legislatures also enacted most of their Jim Crow laws during this period. Laws were passed requiring segregation in schools, parks, restaurants, theaters, and in almost all other public accommodation facilities. Tennessee passed a Jim Crow railroad car act in 1881. Most of the other southern and border states soon followed Tennessee's lead. In a series of cases, the Supreme Court upheld and legitimized the South's Jim Crow laws. In 1883, it ruled that the Civil Rights Act of 1875 was unconstitutional. In the *Plessy* v. *Ferguson* case of 1896, it upheld a Louisiana law that required segregation in railroad cars. The Court ruled that literacy tests and poll taxes required for voting were constitutional. It stripped the Fourteenth and Fifteenth Amendments of all their meaning as far as African Americans were concerned and encouraged White southerners to enact more racist laws.

Many African Americans expected to receive 40 acres and a mule after the Civil War. However, most of the land confiscated from southern plantation owners was either given back to them or to other members of the southern aristocracy. Few African Americans were able to obtain land. Most of them became bound to the land and to White landowners in the sharecropping system. The sharecropper's life was similar to that of a slave's. In theory, a sharecropper received a share of the crop. However, Black sharecroppers, who had to buy their merchandise from their boss's store, were severely cheated. Each year when the crops were harvested, they found themselves further and further in debt and required to stay on the land until they paid their bill. The sharecropper's status was little better than that of a slave's and in some ways worse.

To make the system even more like slavery, southern state legislatures enacted a series of laws between 1865 and 1866 that became known as the *Black Codes*. These laws were similar to the old slave codes. In some states, Blacks could not testify in court against Whites, carry guns, or buy some types of property. African Americans who were unemployed could be arrested. Those who were unable to pay their fines were hired out. In some places, Black workers could not leave the farm without permission. By the beginning of the twentieth century, White southerners had totally succeeded in reestablishing White supremacy and reducing the African American to the status of peons. Black hopes born during the Civil War had been almost completely shattered. When the twentieth century opened, African Americans were deeply disillusioned and saw little hope for the future. They attempted to solve their problems by migrating North, still in search of the American Dream.

Migration and City Life

After the Civil War, large numbers of African Americans began to migrate to urban areas in the South and to settle in the Southwest. Because of the widespread discrimination they faced in America, some African Americans established all-Black towns. Nearly 30 such towns were established near the turn of the century, including Mound Bayou, Mississippi, in 1887 and Langston, Oklahoma, in 1891. Many African Americans also wanted to make Oklahoma an all-Black state, but this idea never materialized.

Although many African Americans settled in the South and Southwest, most who migrated near the turn of the century settled in large cities in the Midwest and East. New York City's Black population doubled between 1900 and 1910. During the same period, Chicago's increased by more than 30%. African Americans migrated to northern cities in large numbers in the early 1900s because of the severe economic, political, and social conditions in the South. Southern states had stripped African Americans of most of their legal rights. Disastrous floods, the boll weevil, and the sharecropping system combined to make life on the southern plantations nearly intolerable. The beginning of World War I had nearly stopped immigration from southern and eastern Europe. Consequently, northern manufacturers badly needed laborers. Some of them sent agents to the South to lure Blacks to the North. Black newspapers such as the *Chicago Defender* described the North as a land of milk and honey and urged African Americans to leave the South. These forces led nearly one-half million southern Blacks to head for the North during and immediately after World War I. This mass migration to the North greatly disturbed southern Whites because it deprived them of a cheap source of labor. They tried to stop Blacks from going North, but their efforts were useless.

When the African Americans arrived in midwestern and eastern cities, they had a rude awakening. Life in these cities was extremely difficult. African Americans were the victims of White violence and experienced gross discrimination in housing and employment. Many Blacks who moved into White communities were beaten and their homes were bombed. Because of a variety of techniques used by real estate agents, Blacks were excluded from many neighborhoods. Consequently the Black urban community grew by leaps and bounds because African Americans were forced to live in areas that were predominantly Black. Also, many Blacks preferred to live in communities that had established Black churches, clubs, and fraternal orders.

As African Americans competed with Whites for housing and jobs, conflict and tension developed between them. Whites were determined to keep Blacks from their jobs and out of their communities. White aggression and violence in the early 1900s led to some of the bloodiest riots that the United States had experienced. One of the worst riots occurred in East St. Louis in 1917. The riot was started when a group of Whites fired into a Black neighborhood and Blacks retaliated. Thirty-nine African Americans and nine Whites were killed. During the same year, riots also occurred in Philadelphia and Chester, Pennsylvania. More than 20 riots occurred in cities throughout the United States in 1919. The gifted writer James Weldon Johnson called that summer the "Red Summer" because of the blood that ran in city streets. The most tragic riot that summer occurred in Chicago. The riot started when a Black youth was drowned after being chased by a group of Whites at a segregated beach on Lake Michigan. The riot lasted for almost two weeks. When it ended, 38 people had been killed, 23 of them Black. More than 1,000 homes were destroyed and 537 people were injured. In 1919, riots also occurred in such cities as Washington, D.C., and Longview, Texas.

World War I

As with other wars, African Americans enthusiastically supported World War I and were impressed with President Wilson's high-sounding rhetoric about fighting the war to "make the world safe for democracy." African Americans took Wilson seriously and joined the armed forces in massive numbers. However, it was not long before they realized that White Americans intended for African Americans to be second-class citizens in the military. The discrimination that Black soldiers experienced during the war was blatant. When the United States first entered the war, no training camps were established for African American soldiers. Many Black professionals, like doctors, were made privates in the army. Most Black soldiers were given noncombatant assignments, although some fought on the battlefield. A tragic incident that occurred in Houston, Texas, in 1917 symbolized to African Americans more than anything else the status of the Black soldier. When a group of Black soldiers tried to board a segregated street car, a fight occurred in which 12 civilians died. Thirteen of the soldiers were sentenced to die and 14 were sent to prison for life. The fate of these soldiers shocked and dismayed the African American community.

Organizations

During these trying times a number of African American institutions and organizations emerged to help African Americans adjust to city life and to fight racism and discrimination in the courts. W. E. B. DuBois, a militant spokesman for Black rights, and a group of Black intellectuals founded the Niagara Movement in 1905. The men in this movement issued a strong statement denouncing American racism. The Niagara movement was short-lived. However, the National Association for the Advancement of Colored People (NAACP), organized in 1910, was an outgrowth of it. Although most of the officers of the NAACP were White, Black people strongly supported it. The NAACP concentrated on improving the African American's legal status. Under its leadership, the legal status of Blacks greatly improved. A group of social workers founded the National Urban League in 1911 to help Black migrants adjust to city life and to find employment. The Urban League worked against enormous odds because of job discrimination. However, it experienced some gains.

Whereas the NAACP and the National Urban League appealed greatly to middle-class and upwardly mobile African Americans, Marcus Garvey's Universal Negro Improvement Association (UNIA), organized in 1914, was a movement that strongly attracted the Black poor. Garvey preached Black pride and urged African Americans to return to Africa because they would never have equality in the United States. He also urged Blacks to establish businesses and to improve their own communities. The UNIA operated a number of businesses, including restaurants, grocery stores, and a hotel. Garvey was contemptuous of light-skinned and middle-class African Americans and felt that they wanted to associate with Whites instead of other Blacks. The leading Black spokesmen and organizations were threatened by Garvey. Partly as a result of their efforts, he was jailed for irregularities in the handling of his Black Star Line. More than any other leader during this period, Garvey helped the lower-class African American to feel proud of being Black.

The Harlem Renaissance

During the 1920s and 1930s, African American artists, writers, and musicians produced some of their best work. Like their counterparts in the 1960s, they deliberately tried to reflect the African American cultural heritage in their works. They emphasized Black pride and strongly protested racism and discrimination. Gifted poets, such as Claude McKay and Countee Cullen, penned angry poems that reflected Black aspirations and frustrations. Other African American writers during this period, such as Langston Hughes, Jean Toomer, and Zora Neale Hurston, wrote outstanding novels. African-American musicians further developed blues and jazz. These two types of music became recognized throughout the world.

World War II

African Americans did not expect World War II to bring them any great gains. Their memories of World War I were still too vivid and poignant. However, the war created additional jobs in the large cities, and masses of southern Blacks migrated during and after the war years. Many Blacks migrated to the West Coast as well as to the North. More than 150,000 African Americans left the South each year between 1940 and 1950.

Black city migrants encountered problems similar to those experienced by African Americans who had migrated in earlier decades. Segregation in housing was still increasing. Many manufacturers with government contracts to make war-related materials refused to hire Blacks or hired them only for the lowest-paying jobs. President Roosevelt refused to take action to stop job discrimination until A. Philip Randolph threatened to march on Washington with 100,000 African Americans. To prevent the march, Roosevelt issued an executive order that outlawed discrimination in defense-related jobs and set up a federal committee on fair employment.

Violence and riots also erupted in the cities. The most serious one during this period occurred in Detroit in the summer of 1943. The riot lasted for more than 30 hours. When it was over, 34 people were dead, 25 of them Black. During the same summer, riots also occurred in Los Angeles and the Harlem district of New York City. These riots, especially the one in Detroit, greatly alarmed American politicians. Mayors in many cities formulated commissions to study the causes of the racial outbreaks and to recommend ways to eliminate their causes.

President Truman

President Harry S Truman, who won the presidential election in 1948 with heavy Black support, took a number of steps to improve race relations and helped to pave the way for the civil rights movement that reached its height in the 1960s. With the use of executive orders, he desegregated the armed forces and created a Committee on Civil Rights that investigated the condition of African Americans. The committee's publication, *To Secure These Rights*, recommended total integration in American society. Truman also ordered industries doing business with the federal government to end discrimination. These measures were mainly symbolic and did not seriously affect the African American's status in the United States. However, they contributed significantly to setting an atmosphere of racial tolerance and to the rising expectations of African Americans.

The Supreme Court

More important than Truman's action in improving race relations during the 1940s and 1950s were the actions of the U.S. Supreme Court. During the decades after the Civil War, the Supreme Court had consistently made decisions that denied African Americans civil liberties and legitimized and legalized racist practices. It now began to rule in favor of civil rights. In a series of cases, most of which were led or supported by the NAACP, the Court ruled for greater civil liberties for African Americans, thus reversing its racist tradition. In 1946, the Court ruled against segregation in interstate commerce. It made a negative ruling regarding the restrictive covenants in 1948. In a number of cases related to African Americans attending segregated White universities in the southern and border states, it consistently ruled that Black Americans should be provided a higher education equal to that of Whites in their home states. These rulings forced many states to integrate their state universities. However, many of them created "instant" professional schools for African Americans. The landmark decision of this period was the *Brown* v. *Board of Education of Topeka* decision of 1954, which ruled that school segregation is inherently unequal. Perhaps more than any other single event, this decision by the high court helped pave the way for the civil rights movement of the 1960s and 1970s.

The Civil Rights Movement of the 1960s and 1970s

In the 1960s, African Americans began a fight for their rights that was unprecedented in the nation's history. However, the civil rights movement of the 1960s was intimately related to the heritage of Black protest in America, marked by the slave rebellions and uprisings. Black Americans have always protested, and in ways consistent with the times in which they lived. David Walker, W. E. B. DuBois and Ida B. Wells are a few of the many eminent African Americans who strongly protested against American racism through the years. Individuals like Martin Luther King, Jr., Stokely Carmichael, and Fannie Lou Hammer joined this long family of protest leaders in the 1960s. The Black protest in the 1960s was unique in our history because the times were different. Black protest tends to reflect the times in which it occurs.

During the late 1940s and 1950s, events that occurred to elevate Black people's hopes for a better life in America included the actions of President Truman, the Brown decision of 1954, and the Civil Rights Act of 1957. As African Americans saw more and more signs indicating that social, economic, and political conditions were improving, they became increasingly impatient with their caste status. Signs of the African American's second-class status were rampant throughout the South when the Montgomery bus boycott began in 1955. The boycott started when Rosa Parks, a tired Black seamstress, was jailed for refusing to move to the back of a city bus. Montgomery Blacks decided that they had taken enough and that they would fight the city's bus company until it eliminated segregation. They began a boycott of the bus line that did not end until a federal court outlawed racial segregation on Montgomery buses a year later. Martin Luther King, Jr., the young Black preacher who led the boycott, became America's most influential civil rights leader and remained so until he was assassinated in 1968. Under his leadership and influence, the civil rights movement used direct-action and nonviolent tactics to protest racism and discrimination in housing, education, politics, and in other areas.

The civil rights movement actually began when four African American students, who sat down at a segregated lunch counter at a Woolworth's store in Greensboro, North Carolina, on February 1, 1960, refused to leave when they were not served. They had launched the sit-in movement. Within a short time, the sit-in movement had spread throughout the South, and African American college students were desegregating lunch counters and other public accommodation facilities in many cities below the Mason-Dixon line. African American student activists formed the Student Nonviolent Coordinating Committee (SNCC) in 1960 to coordinate their protest activities.

The student protests stimulated other civil rights groups to become more active. The Congress of Racial Equality (CORE), which had been organized since 1942, sponsored a number of freedom rides to Alabama and Mississippi in 1961 to test interstate transportation laws. The CORE riders were the victims of much hostility and violence. Many of them were beaten and jailed, and some of the buses in which they rode were burned. In 1957, King and a group of Black ministers organized the Southern Christian Leadership Conference (SCLC). SCLC trained its volunteers to use civil disobedience tactics and led numerous mass demonstrations. In 1963, King led a demonstration in Birmingham to protest racism and discrimination. The demonstrators were the victims of blatant police violence that was viewed throughout the United States and the rest of the world on television. Mass demonstrations culminated in the summer of 1963, when more than 200,000 people participated in the March on Washington for Freedom and Jobs.

These demonstrations resulted in some small but significant legal gains for African Americans. The historic March on Washington helped to rally public opinion for support of the Civil Rights Act, which finally passed in 1964 after much filibustering in Congress. A voting rights act was enacted in 1965 after King led demonstrations in Selma, Alabama. As a result of this act, which authorized federal workers to oversee elections in the South, the number of African American voters increased sharply in some southern states and counties. However, the mass of African Americans remained poor and without political power. By 1965, many young African-American leaders, such as Stokely Carmichael and H. Rap Brown, who had been staunch supporters of nonviolent resistance, began to raise serious questions about this approach and to urge for more militant action and different goals.

During a civil rights demonstration in 1966, Carmichael issued a call for "Black Power," and both the phrase and the ideas it signified spread throughout Black America like wildfire. Carmichael had coined a term that described a mood already pervasive within Black America. The concept of Black Power emerged during a time when the civil rights movement was losing momentum and when African Americans were becoming increasingly frustrated with the gains they had acquired using civil disobedience tactics. Black Power had different meanings for most Whites than for most African Americans. To most African Americans, it meant political power, pride in Blackness, Black control of schools and communities, and Black self-help organizations. To most Whites, the concept meant retaliatory violence and "Black racism." Malcolm X candidly articulated the concept to the Black masses. Black organizations such as the Black Panther party, which was organized in Oakland, California, in 1966, tried to implement the concept. The Panthers attempted to protect the Black community and organized free lunch programs for African American children. The

Nation of Islam (Black Muslims) also reflected the concept in its businesses, farms, schools, and weekly newspaper.

Black frustrations, which reached new highs in the mid- and late 1960s, were manifested in a series of tragic race riots in American cities. Unlike the earlier riots in which Whites attacked Blacks, these riots were different because they involved little contact between Whites and Blacks. Rather, urban Blacks directed their attacks toward the symbols of white society within their communities. They burned buildings owned by absentee landlords and looted stores run by merchants who they believed cheated them. The prestigious Kerner Commission, which was appointed by President Johnson, concluded in 1968 that the riots were caused by the White racism that was endemic in American life. Riots occurred in cities from New York to Los Angeles. Two of the most serious occurred during the summer of 1967 in Newark and Detroit. Twenty-three people lost their lives in the Newark riot; 43 died in the Detroit outbreak. As in all of the riots during the 1960s, most of the victims were African Americans killed by White law officials. The Kerner Commission concluded in its massive report on the rebellions, "Our nation is moving toward two societies, one White, one Black—separate and unequal"[2]

Toward the Twenty-First Century

Several major trends can be identified in the social, economic, and political condition of African Americans since the civil rights movement of the 1960s. African Americans experienced significant economic gains relative to Whites during the 1960s.[3] However, the economic condition of Blacks relative to Whites since the early 1970s has stagnated or deteriorated. In 1987, the median income for African American families was $17,604, compared to $30,809 for Whites and $19,995 for Hispanics.[4] African American family median income was only 57% of White median family income in 1987. It was 88% of Hispanic family median income. In 1986, unemployment rates were substantially higher for Blacks than those for Whites. The rate was 14.5% for Blacks and 6% for Whites. The unemployment rate was 39.2% for young Blacks, ages 16 to 19.[5]

Another important index of the status of African Americans is the percentage of Black persons living below the poverty level compared to Whites. In 1987, about 8,983,000 Blacks, or 31% of the population, were living below the official government poverty level. This figure compared to 22,183,000 White persons, or 11% of Whites, who lived below the poverty level. About 27% of Hispanics lived below the poverty level in 1987.[6]

A number of factors have contributed to the stagnating or deteriorating conditions of African Americans since the 1970s. An important factor has been substantial changes in the economy. Most low-skilled workers were able to obtain well-paying jobs a generation ago. However, as the U.S. economy has become transformed, fewer low-skilled jobs are available. Increasingly, available jobs require technical skills and knowledge. Black workers are disproportionately concentrated among low-skilled workers. The movement of many jobs out of the central cities and into the suburbs, as well as racial discrimination, are additional factors that have slowed the economic progress of African Americans since the 1970s.

Conservative economic policies that favored the middle and upper classes rather than the poor shaped by the Reagan administration also slowed Black progress during the 1980s. The Reagan administration also took a number of legal steps to limit national affirmative action policies. A faltering national commitment to racial equality and to include people of color into the structure of the nation was also evident during the 1980s.

The economic situation of Blacks since the 1970s has not been entirely bleak. A substantial number of African Americans have been able to enter the middle class as a result of opportunities and possibilities that resulted from the civil rights movement of the 1960s and 1970s. One of the most important developments in the social and economic situation of Blacks since the 1960s has been the development of substantial social class differences within the African-American community and the increase of class differentiation.[7] Significant social class variation has existed within the African American community for many decades.[8] However, class variation within the African American community has never been as steep, nor have African Americans ever been as separated as much in terms of neighborhoods and communities on a social class basis. New careers, opportunities, and possibilities opened up for African Americans as a result of the civil rights movement and affirmative actions policies that followed it. Many of the African Americans who had the education and other skills to take advantage of these opportunities are now functioning in mainstream institutions as physicians, college professors and administrators, business people, and corporation heads. Many of these individuals, like their White peers, have joined the exodus to the suburbs and are sending their children to predominantly White suburban public schools or to elite private schools.[9]

Any accurate and sophisticated description of the status of African Americans on the threshold of the twenty-first century must describe not only the large percentage of Blacks who are members of "the underclass," but also the smaller and significant percentage of African Americans who have entered the middle and upper classes and who function in the mainstream society. Many of the children of the new middle class are not only unacquainted with poverty, but also have been socialized in mainstream middle- and upper-class communities. They have little first-hand experience with African American culture.

African Americans from all cultures, social classes, and walks of life experience institutional racism and discrimination. A new wave of racism swept through predominantly White college campuses as well as through the wider society during the late 1980s. The shared experiences of African Americans reinforce their sense of identity and peoplehood. Also, most middle- and upper-class African Americans want their children to know and to feel comfortable with other Blacks and with Black culture. Consequently, a number of middle- and upper-class African Americans encourage their children to attend historically Black colleges such as Fisk, Spelman, Morehouse, Howard, and Hampton.

Little careful work has been done on social class variation within the African American community. Most articles and research on African Americans focus on the bulk of African Americans who are living below the poverty level. Blackwell has developed a typology that conceptualizes social class variation within the African American community (See Figure 7–1).[10] One example can indicate the importance of a class analysis when studying the African American community. Overall, the fertility rate of Black women is greater than that for White women—2.3 children compared to 1.7 for White women. However, the birthrate for African American women who have graduated from college is lower than that of their White counterparts.[11]

Figure 7–1   *The Social Structure of the Black Community*

Solid lines denote relatively stable divisions between classes whereas broken lines indicate that demarcations between substrata are often blurred.

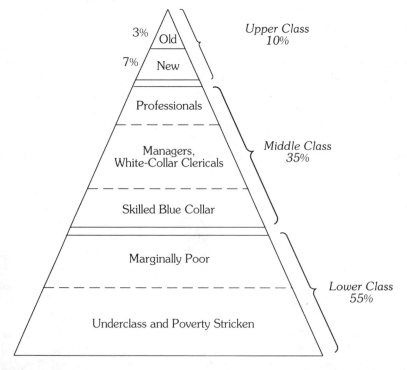

Source: Figure from *The Black Community: Diversity and Unity* by James E. Blackwell. Copyright © by Harper & Row, Publishers, Inc. Reprinted by permission of the publisher.

African Americans have made substantial gains in politics since the voting rights legislation that resulted from the civil rights movement of the 1960s and 1970s. Their progress in politics is a direct result of African Americans' being able to vote and run freely for office. Elected African American officials increased from a few dozen in 1940 to more than 6,800 in 1988.[12] In 1990, there were 300 African-American mayors, 10% of whom were mayors of cities with at least 400,000 people.[13] African Americans witnessed several significant election victories in 1988 and 1989, including the election of Douglas Wilder as governor of Virginia, the nation's first Black elected governor, and the election of the first African American mayor in New York City, David Dinkins. Norm Rice was elected mayor of Seattle in 1989 by a predominantly White electorate, with less than 10% African American voters.

As the turn of the century approached, African Americans were deeply troubled about the erosion of their social, economic, and educational status. However, a consensus was developing within the African American community that Blacks must and could take the leadership for its own improvement and that it had the resources to do so. These resources have to be mobilized. African Americans have a significant middle class that functions in many of the nation's leading institutions; Black colleges that have a distinguished record of academic excellence; and a strong tradition of self-help that has built impressive institutions and businesses. As the twenty first century approached, Blacks organized to help themselves and thought deeply about their future—and their children's future—in this land.

Teaching Strategies

To illustrate how content related to African Americans can be used to integrate the curriculum, exemplary strategies are identified for teaching these concepts at the grade levels indicated: *tradition* (primary grades), *Black protest* (intermediate and upper grades), and *separatism* (high school grades).

Primary Grades

CONCEPT: Tradition

Generalization: African-American and African folktales, like all ethnic folktales, reflect the cultural traditions of the people and explain how things in the world began.

1. There are many excellent collections of ethnic folktales that can be used to teach children about the fantasies, hopes, and fears of the cultures of people of color. One such collection is *Black Folktales* by Julius Lester. Some of the tales in this book are still heard by African children. "The Girl with the Large Eyes," reprinted here from *Black Folktales*, can be used to teach students how some early Africans explained the origin of water lilies. Tell the students what folktales are and why they are a part of the cultural traditions of

ethnic groups. Tell the class the story of "The Girl with the Large Eyes." For best effect, memorize the events in the story and re-create them in your own words.

The Girl with the Large Eyes

Many years ago in a village in Africa, there lived a girl with large eyes. She had the most beautiful eyes of any girl in the village, and whenever one of the young men looked at her as she passed through the marketplace, her gaze was almost more than he could bear.

The summer she was to marry, a drought came upon the region. No rain had fallen for months, and the crops died, the earth changed to dust, and the wells and rivers turned to mudholes. The people grew hungry, and when a man's mind can see nothing except his hunger, he cannot think of marriage, not even to such a one as the girl with the large eyes.

She had little time to think of the wedding that would have been had there been no drought. She had little time to daydream of the hours of happiness she would have been sharing with her new husband. Indeed, she had little time at all, for it was her job each day to find water for her family. That was not easy. She spent the morning going up and down the river bank, scooping what little water she could from the mudholes, until she had a pitcher full.

One morning, she walked back and forth along the river bank for a long while, but could find no water. Suddenly, a fish surfaced from the mud and said to her, "Give me your pitcher and I will fill it with water."

She was surprised to hear the fish talk, and a little frightened. But she had found no water that morning, so she handed him the pitcher, and he filled it with cold, clear water. Everyone was surprised when she brought home a pitcher of such clear water, and they wanted to know where she had found it. She smiled with her large eyes, but she said nothing.

The next day she returned to the same place, called the fish, and again he filled her pitcher with cold, clear water. Each day thereafter, she returned, and soon she found herself becoming fond of the fish. His skin was the colors of the rainbow and as smooth as the sky on a clear day. His voice was soft and gentle like the cool, clear water he put in her pitcher. And on the seventh day, she let the fish embrace her, and she became his wife.

Her family was quite happy to get the water each day, but they were still very curious to know from where she was getting it. Each day they asked her many questions, but she only smiled at them with her large eyes and said nothing.

The girl's father was a witch doctor, and he feared that the girl had taken up with evil spirits. One day he changed the girl's brother into a fly and told him to sit in the pitcher and find out from where she was getting the water. When she got to the secret place, the brother listened to the girl and the fish and watched them embrace, and he flew quickly home to tell his father what he had heard and seen. When the parents learned that their daughter had married a fish, they were greatly embarrassed and ashamed. If the young men of the village found out, none of them would ever marry her. And if the village found out, the family would be forced to leave in disgrace.

The next morning, the father ordered the girl to stay at home, and the brother took him to the secret place beside the river. They called to the fish, and, when he came up, they killed him and took him home. They flung the fish at the girl's feet and said, "We have brought your husband to you."

The girl looked at them and then at the fish beside her feet, his skin growing dull and cloudy, his colors fading. And her eyes filled with tears.

She picked up the fish and walked to the river, wondering what was to become of the child she was carrying inside her. If her parents had killed her husband, would they not kill her child when it was born?

She walked for many miles, carrying her husband in her arms, until she came to a place where the waters were flowing. She knew that suffering could only be cured by medicine or patience. If neither of those relieved it, suffering would always yield to death.

Calling her husband's name, she waded into the water until it flowed above her head. But as she died, she gave birth to many children, and they still float on the rivers to this day as water lilies.[14]

Questions

1. What happened in the village when the girl with large eyes was to marry?
2. What was her job each day?
3. Who filled her pitcher with cold, clear water each day?
4. How did the girl feel when she first met the fish?
5. What did the fish look like?
6. Why did the girl marry the fish?
7. How did her family feel about the marriage?
8. What happened to the fish? Why?
9. What happened to the girl? Why?
10. According to this story, why do we have water lilies?
11. Why do you think stories like these were made up and told?

Summarize the lesson by helping the students to understand the purposes of folktales in all cultures.

2. Help the pupils prepare a dramatization of "The Girl with the Large Eyes." Make sure that each child has a role in the pageant. Most of the students can play village people who have heard that the girl has married a fish. The students might want to invite another class or their parents to see their pageant. Other tales in *Black Folktales*, as well as in other books, can be used to extend this lesson.

Intermediate and Upper Grades

CONCEPT: Black Protest

Generalization: African Americans have protested against racism and discrimination throughout their history in America. The forms of protest reflected the times in which they occurred.

1. Begin this unit by showing and discussing with the students Part I of the videotape series, *Eyes on the Prize* (or a similar one). In the discussion, focus on the reasons Black protest emerged and the forms that it took during the years covered in this videotape, 1954–1956.

2. Tell the students the story of the slave mutinies that occurred both on the West African coast and in mid-ocean. Herbert Aptheker, *American Negro Slave Revolts*, is a well-researched and highly regarded source of information on slave rebellions. Ask the students to act out, in roleplaying situations, the stories they have heard. After the roleplaying situations, ask them to hypothesize by responding to the following questions. Write their responses on the board.

    a. Why do you think the slaves were captured?
    b. Why do you think they started mutinies?
    c. Why didn't the mutinies end the slave trade?
    d. Do you think it was right for slaves to be captured? Why or why not?
    e. Do you think it was right for slaves to rebel? Why or why not?

After the students have responded to these questions, read to them, or ask them to read, selections on the slave trade so that they can test their hypotheses.

3. Ask three different groups of students to research the following three topics:

    a. The Gabriel Prosser revolt of 1800
    b. The Denmark Vesey revolt of 1822
    c. The Nat Turner revolt of 1831

To help them guide their research, ask the groups to focus on the following questions:

    a. Where did the revolt occur?
    b. Why did the revolt occur?
    c. Who led the revolt?
    d. Was the revolt successful? Why or why not?
    e. How were the rebels punished? Why were they punished?

Discuss the questions above with the entire class when the groups have presented their research. List the students' responses on the board. Through questioning, help the student see how the slave insurrections were both alike and different, and whys of the three rebellions, only the Turner revolt was successful. After the class discussion, ask each group to plan and present to the class a dramatization showing the sequence of events in the rebellion they studied.

4. African Americans were active in the abolitionary movement and in the Underground Railroad, a loosely organized system that helped many slaves escape to the North and to Canada. Ask individual students to research the lives of and to "become" in a dramatization, the following people.

    a. David Walker
    b. Henry Highland Garnet
    c. Robert Purvis
    d. Sojourner Truth
    e. James Forten
    f. Frederick Douglass
    g. Harriet Tubman

When the dramatizations are presented, discuss the following questions with the class:

a. Why did African-American abolitionists oppose slavery? How did their views differ from those of White abolitionists? Why did White abolitionists discriminate against Black abolitionists?

b. What was the Underground Railroad? How did it help slaves escape? Who were some of the outstanding "conductors" on the railroad? What risks did captives take when they escaped? Why did they take them? If you had been a slave, would you have tried to escape? Why or why not?

5. Ask individual students or groups of students to research the following organizations and movements and to describe ways in which they protested racism and discrimination.

a. The Negro Convention movement (1800s)
b. The Niagara Movement (1905)
c. The National Association for the Advancement of Colored People (1910)
d. The National Urban League (1911)
e. The Universal Negro Improvement Association (1914)
f. The Black church in the 1800s

When their research is complete, the students should share it with the class. The class should discuss how these organizations and movements expressed discontent with the African-American's plight, the actions they took to improve it, and the successes and failures they experienced and why.

6. Have the class roleplay a civil rights conference in 1966 in which leaders of the organizations listed below debate the future directions of the movement. Each organizational representative should be thoroughly familiar with his or her organization's philosophical position in 1966. By that year, the civil rights movement was becoming increasingly radicalized and deep factions had developed between the various organizations.

a. Southern Christian Leadership Conference (SCLC)
b. National Association for the Advancement of Colored People (NAACP)
c. National Urban League
d. Congress of Racial Equality (CORE)
e. Student Nonviolent Coordinating Committee (SNCC)
f. Black Panther party
g. Revolutionary Action Movement (RAM)

7. Have the students roleplay a meeting of the following people after a serious racial rebellion in a major city in 1967. These people have met to decide what can be done to eliminate the causes of city riots. Ask individual students to play specific roles. To structure this activity more tightly, write a role description for each character on a three-by-five-inch index card and give the cards to the student roleplayers.

Roles are as follows:

a. The mayor of the city
b. An SCLC spokesperson
c. An NAACP spokesperson
d. A National Urban League spokesperson
e. A CORE spokesperson

    f. A SNCC spokesperson

    g. A Black Panther party spokesperson

    h. A RAM spokesperson

    i. A young person who has participated in a riot

    8. To enable the students to summarize this unit and to derive the key generalizations stated above, have them complete the data retrieval chart in Table 7–1.

Valuing Activity

Read the following story to the class and ask the questions that follow.

Trying to Buy a Home in Lakewood Island

About a year ago, Joan and Henry Green, a young African American couple, moved from the West Coast to a large city in the Midwest. They moved because Henry finished his Ph.D. in chemistry and took a job at a big university in Midwestern City. Since they have been in Midwestern City, the Greens have rented an apartment in the central area of the city. However, they have decided that they want to buy a house. Their apartment has become too small for the many books and other things they have accumulated during the year. In addition to wanting more space, they also want a house so that they can receive breaks on their income tax, which they do not receive living in an apartment. The Greens also think that a house will be a good financial investment.

    The Greens have decided to move into a suburban community. They want a new house and most of the houses within the city limits are rather old. They also feel that they can obtain a larger house for their money in the suburbs than in the city. They have looked at several suburban communities and have decided that they like Lakewood Island better than any of the others. Lakewood Island is an all-White community, which is comprised primarily of lower-middle-class and middle-class residents. There are a few wealthy families in Lakewood Island, but they are the exceptions rather than the rule.

    Joan and Henry Green have become frustrated because of the problems they have experienced trying to buy a home in Lakewood Island. Before they go out to look at a house, they carefully study the newspaper ads. When they arrived at the first house in which they were interested, the owner told them that his house had just been sold. A week later they decided to work with a realtor. When they tried to close the deal on the next house they wanted, the realtor told them that the owner had raised the price $10,000 because he had the house appraised since he had put it on the market and had discovered that his selling price was much too low. When the Greens tried to buy a third house in Lakewood Island, the owner told them that he had decided not to sell because he had not received the job in another city that he was almost sure that he would receive when he had put his house up for sale. He explained that the realtor had not removed the ad about his house from the newspaper even though he had told him that he had decided not to sell a week earlier. The realtor the owner had been working with had left the real estate company a few days ago. Henry is bitter and feels that he and his wife are victims of racism and discrimination. Joan believes that Henry is paranoid and that they have been the victims of a series of events that could have happened to anyone, regardless of their race.

Table 7–1 Black Protest: Data Retrieval Chart

Form of Protest, Organization, or Movement	Goal of Protests	Ways of Protests	Results of Protests
Slave mutinies			
Slave rebellions (in USA)			
Black abolitionary movement			
Underground Railroad			
Niagara Movement			
NAACP			
National Urban League			
SCLC			
CORE			
SNCC			
Black Panther party			
RAM			

Questions

1. Do you think that the Greens were discriminated against in Lakewood Island? Why or why not?
2. What should the Greens do? Why?
3. If you were the Greens, what would you do? Why?
4. What can the Greens do to determine whether they are victims of discrimination?

High School Grades

CONCEPT: Separatism

Generalization: Black separatist movements emerge when African Americans experience acute discrimination and a heightened sense of racial pride.

1. Either through choice or force, Black separatism has always existed in America. Most of the social life of the slaves was confined to community. One of the earliest manifestations of Black separatism was the colonization movement led by African Americans. To begin this unit, ask several students to prepare and present research reports on the following topics:

a. Martin R. Delany
b. Paul Cuffe
c. The African Colonization Society

When the reports are presented to the class, the following questions should be discussed:

a. Why did colonization movements emerge among African Americans?
b. Were these movements popular and successful? Why or why not?
c. Why did back-to-Africa movements fail to appeal to most African Americans?
d. If early Black-led colonization attempts had succeeded, how do you think the subsequent history of African Americans would have differed?

2. Because of discrimination and the need for group solidarity, a number of African American organizations emerged in the 1800s. Ask a group of students to prepare short papers on the following topics and present them to the class in a panel discussion on separate Black institutions in the 1800s.

a. The Black church
b. Black fraternal and self-help organizations
c. Black businesses
d. Black schools and colleges
e. The Negro Convention Movement

Roleplay a Negro Convention in the 1800s in which the participants draft a position statement stating their major grievances about the plight of African Americans and a plan of action for social change. All of the delegates to the simulated convention must reach agreement on the position statement they prepare. The student roleplayers will need to be thoroughly familiar with the Negro Convention Movement and the various points of view that were presented in the series of Negro Conventions held in the 1800s.

3. The Niagara Movement was a Black protest organization organized in 1905 by W. E. B. DuBois and a group of Black intellectuals. Ask a group of students to prepare a research report on this movement and present it to the class.

4. Most of the national civil rights organizations in the early 1900s were interracial. Ask the students to do required readings on the history and development of the NAACP and the National Urban League. When they have completed the readings, they should compare and contrast these two organizations with the Niagara Movement and earlier Black protest movements and organizations such as the Negro Convention Movement. Particular attention should be paid to (1) reasons that the organizations emerged, (2) who made major policy decisions and held key positions within them, (3) types of problems that arose within the organizations, (4) the major goals of the organizations, and (5) ways in which the organizations succeeded or failed and why. While studying these organizations, the students should compare and contrast the ideas and actions of Booker T. Washington and W. E. B. DuBois. To conclude this activity, ask two students to roleplay a debate between Washington and DuBois on the kind of education needed by African Americans. Two excellent references for this last exercise are *Up from Slavery* by Booker T. Washington, and *The Souls of Black Folk* by W. E. B. DuBois.

5. Ask a group of students to prepare a panel discussion on the ideas and actions of Marcus Garvey and the Universal Negro Improvement Association. Ask them to focus on the following questions:

    a. What social, economic, and political conditions made Garvey's movement particularly appealing to poor African Americans?

    b. How did Garvey's ideas help to improve the poor Blacks' feelings about themselves?

    c. Why was Garvey's back-to-Africa movement unsuccessful?

    d. Why did conflict develop between Garvey and other Black leaders?

    e. Why was Garvey ultimately crushed as a leader?

    f. What was the main significance of Garvey's movement?

The classic biography of Garvey is *Black Moses* by E. D. Cronon. Another excellent book for this activity is *Marcus Garvey and the Vision of Africa,* edited by John Henrik Clarke.

6. When the Black Revolt emerged in 1960, its major goal was to desegregate public accommodation facilities and other institutions. Action tactics and court battles achieved much desegregation. However, by 1965, many African Americans, especially young Black activists, were disillusioned with the attainments of the movement and realized that integration alone would not eliminate the African American's major social, economic, and political problems. These young activists felt that both the goals and tactics of the movement should be changed. They issued a call for Black Power.

Ask the entire class to read excerpts from *Black Power: The Politics of Liberation in America* by Stokely Carmichael and Charles V. Hamilton. Discuss each excerpt with the class. The following questions and exercises can help guide class discussion and student research.

    a. What did the concept *Black Power* mean? Did it mean the same things to African Americans and White Americans?

    b. Compare and contrast the goals of the Black Power movement and the goals of civil rights organizations like SCLC and the NAACP in the early 1960s.

   c. What kinds of economic, political, and social institutions are implied by the concept of Black Power?

   d. Compare and contrast the views of the following people:
     (1) David Walker
     (2) Martin R. Delany
     (3) Richard Allen
     (4) Prentice Hall
     (5) Paul Cuffe
     (6) Marcus Garvey
     (7) W. E. B. DuBois
     (8) Stokely Carmichael
     (9) Malcolm X
     (10) Angela Y. Davis
     (11) Jesse Jackson
     (12) Fannie Lou Hamer

   7. Conclude the unit by asking the students to present a dramatization that shows how Black separatism has developed and changed from the 1700s to the 1990s.

Endnotes

   1. Herbert Aptheker, *American Negro Slave Revolts* (New York: International Publishers, Inc.), 1963.

   2. *Report of the National Advisory Commission on Civil Disorders* (New York: Bantam Books, 1968), p. 1.

   3. Gerald D. Jaynes and Robin M. Williams, Jr. *A Common Destiny: Blacks and American Society* (Washington, D.C.: National Academy Press), p. 6.

   4. U.S. Bureau of the Census, *Statistical Abstract of the United States: 1989*, 109th ed. (Washington, D.C.: U.S. Government Printing Office, 1989), p. 38.

   5. U.S. Bureau of the Census, *Statistical Abstract of the United States: 1988*, 108th ed. (Washington, D.C.: U.S. Government Printing Office, 1988), p. 368.

   6. *Statistical Abstract: 1989*, p. 38.

   7. William J. Wilson, *The Declining Significance of Race: Blacks and Changing American Institutions* (Chicago: The University of Chicago Press, 1978); William J. Wilson, *The Truly Disadvantaged: The Inner City, the Underclass, and Public Policy* (Chicago: The University of Chicago Press, 1987).

   8. St. Clair Drake and Horace R. Cayton, *Black Metropolis: A Study of Negro Life in a Northern City* (New York: Harcourt, Brace and Company, 1945).

   9. James A. Banks, "Black Youths in Predominantly White Suburbs: An Exploratory Study of Their Attitudes and Self-Concepts," *The Journal of Negro Education*, 53, 1 (Winter 1984): 3–17.

   10. James A. Blackwell, *The Black Community: Diversity and Unity*, 2nd ed. (New York: Harper and Row, 1985), pp. 117–149.

   11. Robert Staples, "The Black American Family," in *Ethnic Families in America: Patterns and Variations*, eds. Charles H. Mindel, Robert W. Habenstein, and Roosevelt Wright, Jr. (New York: Elsevier, 1988), p. 311.

   12. Jaynes and Williams, *A Common Destiny*, p. 15.

13. Lloyd Shearer, "The Rise of Black Mayors," *Parade*, 7 January 1990, p. 14.
14. From *Black Folktales* (pp. 57–61) by Julius Lester, 1969. New York: Grove Press. Copyright 1969 by Julius Lester. Reprinted by permission.

Annotated Bibliography

Books for Teachers

Especially Recommended

Berry, Gordon L., and Asamen, Joy K., eds. *Black Students: Psychosocial Issues and Academic Achievement.* Newbury Park, Calif.: Sage Publications, 1989.

An excellent and informative collection of papers that discuss various aspects of the education of African-American students.

Branch, Taylor. *Parting the Waters: America in the King Years 1954–63.* New York: Simon and Schuster, 1988.

A widely acclaimed, Pulitzer Prize winning account of the civil rights movement. Attention is given to many of the civil rights' movement unsung participants.

Franklin, John Hope, and Moss, Alfred A., Jr. *From Slavery to Freedom: A History of Negro Americans*, 6th ed. New York: Knopf, 1988.

This is the classic general survey history of African Americans. It is well written and researched.

Hale-Benson, Janice E. *Black Children: Their Roots, Culture, and Learning Styles*, rev. ed. Baltimore: The John Hopkins University Press, 1982.

This book describes the unique culture of African-American children and its educational and teaching implications.

Hine, Darlene Clark, ed. *The State of Afro-American History: Past, Present, and Future.* Baton Rouge: Louisiana State University Press, 1986.

This book contains an important collection of papers that discuss various aspects of teaching African-American history in schools and colleges.

Jackson, George F. *Black Women Makers of History: A Portrait.* Oakland: GRT Book Print, 1977. (Available from: National Women's History Project, 7738 Bell Road, Windsor, CA 95492-8515.)

The journeys of more than 120 women who have made significant contributions in a variety of fields are chronicled in this book. Scientists and businesswomen, freedom fighters, entertainers, and artists are among the women included. The readings will need to be supplemented by more recent sources, such as the book by Brian Lanker annotated below.

Jaynes, Gerald D., and Williams, Robin M., Jr., eds. *A Common Destiny: Blacks and American Society.* Washington, D.C.: National Academy Press, 1989.

An excellent and comprehensive study that includes chapters on racial attitudes and behavior, political participation, Blacks in the economy, the schooling of Black Americans, Black Americans' health, and children and families.

Jones, Jacqueline. *Labor of Love, Labor of Sorrow: Black Women, Work, and the Family, from Slavery to the Present.* New York: Vintage Books, 1986.

This outstanding scholarly book, winner of the Bancroft Prize, is an essential reference for the study of the experiences of African American women.

Landry, Bart. *The New Black Middle Class.* Berkeley: University of California Press, 1987.

This is an important and sympathetic study of the African American middle class that doubled in size between 1960 and 1970.

Lanker, Brian. *I Dream a World: Portraits of Black Women Who Changed America.* Foreword by Maya Angelou. New York: Steward, Tabori and Chang, 1989.

The excellent photographs and interesting biographical profiles make this book an excellent teaching resource.

Logan, Rayford W., and Winston, Michael R., eds. *Dictionary of American Negro Biography.* New York: Norton, 1982.

Every school and college library should have this book. It contains a gold mine of information about the lives of African Americans who have shaped the nation's history.

Other References

Baker, Houston A., Jr., and Redmond, Patricia. eds. *Afro-American Literary Study in the 1990s.* Chicago: The University of Chicago Press, 1989.

This book contains an important and informative collection of essays on African-American literary criticism.

Bates, Daisy. *The Long Shadow of Little Rock: A Memoir.* Fayetteville: The University of Arkansas Press, 1987.

An insightful, poignant, and moving account of the nine African-American children who desegregated Little Rock's Central High School in 1957 by the woman who lead the desegregation effort.

Bell, Derrick. *And We Are Not Saved: The Elusive Quest for Racial Justice.* New York: Basic Books, 1987.

The incisive and powerful analysis of race in the United States by Bell is enhanced by the innovative way in which he writes the book—he uses a series of dialogues.

Bernal, Martin. *Black Athena: The Afroasiatic Roots of Classical Civilization.* Vol. 1: *The Fabrication of Ancient Greece 1785–1985.* London: Free Association Books, 1987.

In this comprehensive and seminal book, Bernal argues that classical Western civilization has deep roots in Afroasiatic cultures and that these influences have been ignored, denied, or suppressed since the eighteenth century, largely for racist reasons.

Blackwell, James E. *The Black Community: Diversity and Unity,* 2nd ed. New York: Harper and Row, 1985.

This sociological treatment of the African-American community is especially value-able because it discusses the important social class differences within the Black community.

Blassingame. John W., ed. *Slave Testimony: Two Centuries of Letters, Speeches, Interviews, and Autobiographies.* Baton Rouge: Louisiana State University Press, 1977.

This excellent and comprehensive collection of slave primary resources is edited by a veteran African-American historian who is a specialist in research on U.S. slaves. Also see his book The Slave Community, *New York: Oxford, 1979.*

Drake, St. Clark. *Black Folk Here and There: An Essay in History and Anthropology:* Vol. 1. Los Angeles: University of California, Center for Afro-American Studies, 1987.

The important chapter in this book on "White Racism and the Black Experience" is thoughtful and reflective. This book is an important contribution by a veteran African-American scholar.

Farmer, James. *Lay Bare the Heart: An Autogiography of the Civil Rights Movement.* New York: Arbor House, 1985.

An important biography of the civil rights movement by one of its chief architects.

Franklin, John Hope. *Race and History: Selected Essays 1938–1988.* Baton Rouge: Louisiana State University Press, 1989.

An informative and interesting collection of essays by the eminent African–American historian.

Franklin, John Hope, and Meier, August, eds. *Black Leaders of the Twentieth Century.* Urbana: University of Illinois Press, 1982.

Biographies of leaders such as Mary McLeod Bethune, W. E. B. DuBois, and Martin Luther King, Jr., are included in this well-researched and written book.

Garrow, David J. *Bearing the Cross: Martin Luther King, Jr., and the Southern Christian Leadership Conference.* New York: Vintage Books, 1986.

This comprehensive and well-researched biography of King was a Pulitzer Prize recipient. A more compassionate biography of King is still awaited.

Gates, Louis Henry, Jr. *The Signifying Monkey: A Theory of African-American Literary Criticism.* New York: Oxford University Press, 1988.

This seminal book, winner of a 1989 American Book Award, explores the relationship between African-American vernacular traditions and Black literature. It is a pathbreaking book in Black literary criticism.

Gay, Geneva, and Baber, Willie L., eds. *Expressively Black: The Cultural Basis of Ethnic Identity.* New York: Praeger, 1987.

The expressiveness of African-American culture in communication, the visual arts, theater, film, poetry, and in other cultural forms are ably discussed by the authors who contributed to this book.

Gibbs, Jewelle Taylor, ed. *Young, Black and Male in America.* Dover, Mass.: Auburn House Publishing Company, 1988.

Education, employment, crime, teenage fatherhood, and health and mental health are among the topics discussed in this well-researched book.

Hampton, Henry; Fayer, Steve; and Flynn, Sara, eds. *Voices of Freedom.* New York: Bantam, 1990.

This informative documentary history of the civil rights movement was designed to accompany the popular television series, Eyes on the Prize, *Part II.*

Hughes, Langston, and Bontemps, Anna, eds. *The Poetry of the Negro 1746–1970*. Garden City, N.Y.: Doubleday, 1970.

> *A rich collection of African-American poetry by two giants in Black literature.*

Hurston, Zora Neale. *Their Eyes Were Watching God*. Urbana: University of Illinois Press, 1978.

> *First published in 1937, this novel about the love between an African-American man and woman has become a classic.*

Jackson, Blyden. *A History of Afro-American Literature*. Vol. 1: *The Long Beginning, 1746–1895*. Baton Rouge: Louisiana State University Press, 1989.

> *In this important literary history, the author conceptualilzes literature broadly and includes poetry, slave narratives, and early Black historians.*

Litwack, Leon, and Meier, August, eds. *Black Leaders of the Nineteenth Century*. Urbana: University of Illinois Press, 1988.

> *Well-researched and informative biographies of leaders such as Harriet Tubman, Mary Church Terrell, Nat Turner, and Frederick Douglass are included in this book.*

Marks, Carole. *Farewell—We're Good and Gone: The Great Black Migration*. Bloomington: Indiana University Press, 1989.

> *An important historical study that compares Black migration from the South to the North from the period 1910 to 1930 to the period from 1940 to 1960. Marks uses a neo-Marxist perspective to view African-American migration.*

Morrison, Toni. *Beloved*. New York: Knopf, 1987.

> *The author received a Pulitzer Prize for this outstanding novel about an escaped slave who has risked death in order to free herself from a living death.*

Rampersad, Arnold. *The Life of Langston Hughes*, Vol. 1 and 2. New York: Oxford University Press, 1986, 1988.

> *The most comprehensive and definitive biography of Hughes to date.*

Rogers, J. A. *World's Great Men of Color*, Vol. 1: *Asia and Africa*. Vol. 2: *Europe, South and Central America, the West Indies and the United States*. New York: Macmillan, 1972.

> *These two important and comprehensive books are important resources for integrating the contributions of Africans and African Americans into world history.*

Shockley, Ann Allen, ed. *Afro-American Women Writers 1746–1933*. New York: New American Library, 1988.

> *An excellent and comprehensive account of African-American women's literature.*

Troup, Quincy, ed. *James Baldwin: The Legacy*. New York: Touchstone Books, 1989.

> *Reflections about Baldwin by Toni Morrison, Amiri Baraka, Maya Angelou, and other contemporaries of Baldwin are included in this anthology.*

Van Sertima, Ivan, ed. *African Presence in Early Europe*. New Brunswick, N.J.: Transaction Publishers, 1985.

> *An important collection of articles about the African presence in early Europe are included in this book.*

————, ed. *Great Black Leaders: Ancient and Modern.* New Brunswick, NJ: Rutgers University, Africana Studies Department, Journal of African Civilizations, 1988.

> *"Great Black Leaders of America," "Great Black Leaders of Africa," and "Great Black Leaders of the Caribbean" constitute the major sections of this edited book.*

Williams, Chancellor. *The Destruction of Black Civilization: Great Issues of a Race from 4500 BC to 2000 AD.* Chicago: Third World Press, 1987.

> *This book focuses on African contributions to world civilization and how this history has been lost or hidden.*

Wintz, Cary D. *Black Culture and the Harlem Renaissance.* Houston: Rice University Press, 1988.

> *An informative and scholarly cultural history of the Harlem Renaissance.*

Books for Students

Adler, C. S. *Always and Forever Friends.* New York: Ticknor & Fields, 1988.

> *A compassionate story about a young African American girl who feels very lonely when her best friend moves away. (Intermediate)*

Adler, David A. *Martin Luther King, Jr.: Free At Last.* New York: Holiday House, 1986.

> *This biography can help young readers understand the role Martin Luther King, Jr., played in the civil rights movement and the events leading up to his assassination. (Intermediate)*

Banks, James A., and Banks, Cherry A. *March toward Freedom: A History of Black Americans,* 2d ed., rev. Belmont, Calif.: Fearon, 1978.

> *This illustrated history of Black Americans is written especially for teenagers. (Intermediate)*

Barrow, Joe Louis, Jr., and Mander, Barbara. *Joe Louis: 50 Years an American Hero.* New York: McGraw-Hill, 1988.

> *Written by his son, this compelling and comprehensive biography reveals the private side of a public sports legend. (High School)*

Busnar, Gene. *The Picture Life of Whitney Houston.* New York: Watts, 1988.

> *This photographic biography explores the family life and career of the popular singer. (All Levels)*

Graham, Lorenz, *I, Momolu.* Claremont, Calif.: Graham Books, 1987.

> *Set in Liberia, this story gives the reader a view of urban life in Africa through the eyes of a young boy named Momolu. (Middle School)*

Greenfield, Eloise. *Grandpa's Face.* New York: Philomel, 1988.

> *This beautifully illustrated book tells a heart-warming story about the love between a grandfather and his grandchild. (Primary) Other books by Greenfield include Nathaniel Talking (Black Butterfly Children's Books, 1988); Mary McLeod Bethune (Cromwell, 1977); Honey I Love (Crowell, 1977); First Pink Light (Crowell, 1969); Good News Formerly "Bubbles" (Coward, McCann and Geoghegan,*

1977); Paul Robeson (Crowell, 1975); Sister *(Crowell, 1974); and* She Come Bringing Me That Little Baby Girl *(Lippincott, 1974).*

Hamilton, Virginia. *Anthony Burns: The Defeat and Triumph of a Fugitive Slave.* New York: Alfred A. Knopf, 1988.

> *Set in the 1850s, this book is an historically accurate account of the escape and trial of a 20-year-old slave named Anthony Burns. (Middle School/High School) Other books by Hamilton include:* Junius over Far *(Harper, 1985);* A Little Love *(Philomel, 1984);* The Magical Adventures of Pretty Pearl *(Harper, 1983);* M. C. Higgins the Great *(Macmillan, 1974), a Newbery Medal Book;* Paul Robeson: The Life and Times of a Free Man *(Harper, 1974);* The People Could Fly: American Black Folktales *(Knopf, 1985);* Sweet Whispers, Brother Rush *(Philomel, 1982);* W. E. B. DuBois: A Biography *(Crowell, 1972); and* The Writings of W. E. B. DuBois *(Crowell, 1975).*

Hansen, Joyce. *Out of This Place.* New York: Walker, 1988.

> *This fictional account of a woman named Easter examines how she faced challenges during the Civil War in her quest for independence. (Middle School).*

Haskins, James. *Black Music in America: A History through Its People.* New York: Thomas Y. Crowell, 1987.

> *Beginning with early slave songs and spirituals, this book profiles African-American men and women who created "America's first truly original cultural gift." (High School) Other books by Haskins include* Winnie Mandela: Life of Struggle *(Putnam, 1988);* Lena Horne *(Coward-McCann, 1983);* Barbara Jordan: Speaking Out *(Dial, 1977);* Fighting Shirley Chisholm *(Dial, 1975);* Ralph Bunche: A Most Reluctant Hero *(Hawthorn, 1974); and* Katherine Dunham *(Coward-McCann, 1982).*

Howard, Elizabeth Fitzgerald. *Chita's Christmas Tree.* New York: Bradbury Press, 1989.

> *This delightful story describes the Christmas experience of a middle-class African-American family in 1908. (Primary) Another book by Howard is* The Train to Lulu's *(Bradbury Press, 1988).*

Hughes, Langston; Meltzer, Milton; and Lincoln, C. Eric. *Four Centuries of Black Life: African American History.* New York: Scholastic, 1990.

> *Originally published in 1956 as* A Pictorial History of Black Americans *by Langston Hughes and Milton Meltzer, this updated volume includes information on Africa and covers 400 years of African-American history. (High School)*

Humphrey, Kathryn Long. *Satchel Paige.* New York: Watts, 1988.

> *This informative biography covers the period when Paige played in the Negro League and played major league baseball for the Cleveland Indians. (Middle School/High School)*

Humphrey, Margo. *The River That Gave Gifts: An Afro-American Story.* San Francisco: Children's Book Press, 1987.

> *This story was inspired by Caribbean folktales and explores traditional African-American values such as sharing and caring for older adults. (Intermediate)*

Jones, Lessie Little. *Children of Long Ago.* New York: Philomel, 1988.

> This heart-warming collection of poems captures the simplicity of farm life for African Americans in the early 1900s. (All Ages)

Katz, William Loren. *Black People Who Made the Old West.* New York: Thomas Y. Crowell, 1989.

> This informative and inspirational book profiles African Americans who left their mark on the old West. (High School) Another book by Katz is Black Indians (Atheneum, 1986).

McKissack, Patricia C. *Mirandy and Brother Wind.* New York: Knopf, 1988.

> The lively and colorful illustrations in this book capture the magic of this enthralling Caldecott Honor Book about a young girl who tries to catch the wind. (Primary)

Meyer, Carolyn. *Denny's Tapes.* New York: Margaret K. McElderry Books, 1987.

> A thought-provoking novel about a 17-year-old's attempt to reconcile his Black and White heritages. (High School)

Milton, Joyce. *Marching to Freedom: The Story of Martin Luther King, Jr.* New York: Dell, 1987.

> This book includes an overview of the civil rights movement and the life of Martin Luther King, Jr. (Intermediate/Middle School)

Mitchell, Barbara. *A Pocketful of Goobers: A Story about George Washington Carver.* Minneapolis: Carolrhoda Books, 1986.

> An informative biography of a well-known African-American scientist. (Primary). Another book by Mitchell is Shoes for Everyone: A Story about Jan Matzeliger. (Carolrhoda, 1986).

Myers, Walter Dean. *Fallen Angels.* New York: Scholastic, 1988.

> In 1967, 17-year-old Richie Perry enlisted in the army and spent a devastating year on active duty in Vietnam. (High School) Another book by Myers is Crystal (New York, 1987).

Reynolds, Barbara. *And Still We Rise: Interviews with 50 Black Role Models.* Washington, D.C.: Gannett News Media Services, 1988.

> This book includes interviews with Marian Wright Edelman, Alex Haley, Carol Rowan, Nikki Giovanni, and other outstanding African Americans. The interviews are powerful, moving, and inspirational. (High School)

Steptoe, John. *Mufaro's Beautiful Daughters.* New York: Lothrop, Lee and Shepard, 1987.

> A beautifully illustrated African Cinderella tale that originated in Zimbabwe. (Primary)

Taylor, Mildred D. *The Gold Cadillac.* New York: Dial, 1987.

> Set in the 1950s in Ohio, Taylor tells the story of an African-American family who returns to the South driving a gold-colored Cadillac. (Intermediate) Other books by Taylor include Let the Circle Be Unbroken (Dial, 1981); Roll of Thunder, Hear My Cry (Dial, 1976), the 1977 Newbery Medal book; and Song of the Trees (Dial, 1975).

Terry, Wallace III, ed. *Bloods: An Oral History of the Vietnamese War.* New York: Random House, 1985.

   Twenty African-American veterans from officers to enlisted men tell about their personal experiences in Vietnam. (High School)

Walker, Alice. *To Hell with Dying.* New York: Harcourt, Brace and Jovanovich, 1988.

   In this beautifully written book, Walker recounts how she and her brother were called on to revive frail Mr. Sweet with hugs and kisses. (Primary)

Part III

European

Americans

Concepts and Strategies

Part III consists of content, concepts, teaching strategies, and materials for teaching about European Americans. Most Americans are of European origin and descent. In 1990, the White population of European ancestry in the United States numbered about 191.5 million people and comprised about 76% of the nation's population. However, the percentage of the nation's population of European ancestry had declined significantly since 1900, when it comprised 87.7% of the population. Demographers predict that the percentage of European Americans in the U.S. population will continue to decline in future years. It is predicted that they will make up about 66% of the general population by the turn of the century and 54.5% of the school-age population by 2020.

White Americans of European descent are increasing at a slower rate than are other ancestry groups. Hispanic Americans increased by about 50% between 1980 and 1990, but the White population increased by about only 2%. This difference resulted primarily because a disproportionate number of Whites were middle-class (and therefore have fewer children) and because Europeans comprised only 11% of the immigrants to the United States between 1981 and 1986. Even though they are becoming a smaller percentage of the nation's population, Americans of European origin and descent still comprise the overwhelming majority of the nation's population and have the most influence on its culture, values, and ethos. A study of the sojourn of European immigrants across the Atlantic and of their journey in America is essential to a sound multicultural curriculum.

Chapter 8

European

Ethnic Groups

Concepts, Strategies, and Materials

The poorest, the most miserable came here because they had no future over there. To them, the streets of America were paved in gold. They had what the Finns called kuume, *the American fever.*

—Andy Johnson, an immigrant
From Studs Terkel, *American Dreams: Lost and Found*

Introduction

Between 1820 and 1978, more than 48 million immigrants entered the United States. Most of them (74.4%) were Europeans who belonged to many different religious, political, and cultural groups. The making of one society from so many different ethnic and nationality groups is one of the most amazing chapters in human history. Yet, social scientists, and therefore classroom teachers, have largely ignored the role of ethnicity in U.S. history and modern society. American social scientists have been preoccupied with theories of assimilation and the melting pot concept. Nevertheless, scholars in the United States have given more attention to ethnicity as a variable in American life since the ethnic protest movements in the 1960s. However, a significant gap exists between scholarship and the school curriculum. The European ethnic experience is infrequently taught in the schools.

European ethnic groups should be included in a sound multicultural curriculum because the processes of acculturation and assimilation, which they have experienced and which many European ethnic groups are still experiencing, must be considered when students formulate concepts and generalizations about ethnicity and race in U.S. society. European Americans, like other Americans, often experienced ethnic rage, changed their names, and denied their ethnic heritages to gain social and economic mobility and to realize the American dream.

It is also important for students to study European ethnic groups because individuals of European origin comprise the bulk of the nation's population (about 76%) and Europeans continue to make up a significant proportion of the immigrants to the United States. Between 1981 and 1987, more than four million (4,067,699) immigrants entered the United States. Of these, about 11% (445,500) were Europeans. Even though 11% is a significant drop in the percentage of European immigrants that settled in the United States in the decades prior to 1968, the number of European immigrants still settling in the United States is sizable.

The European immigrants who have entered the United States since 1981 are diverse in national origins and cultures. Table 8–1 shows the number of European immigrants that entered the United States between 1981 and 1987. As this table indicates, a significant proportion of them came from the Soviet

Table 8–1   *European Immigrants to the United States from Selected Nations (1981–1987)*

Country of Birth	Number
United Kingdom	98,900
Poland	52,300
Germany	48,900
Soviet Union	44,500
Portugal	29,100
Romania	25,800
Italy	23,700
Greece	21,500
France	15,100
Yugoslavia	11,900
Spain	10,800
Ireland	10,500
Netherlands	8,100
Czechoslovakia	7,600
Sweden	6,900
Hungary	5,700
Switzerland	4,700
Belgium	3,800
Denmark	3,600
Austria	2,900
Norway	2,600
Finland	2,200

Source: Based on data from U.S. Bureau of the Census, *Statistical Abstract of the United States, 1989,* 109th ed. (Washington, D.C.: U.S. Government Printing Office, 1989), p. 10.

Table 8–2 *Immigrants from Canada, Australia, and New Zealand (1981–1987)*

Country of Birth	Number
Canada	78,500
Australia	9,300
New Zealand	4,400

Source: Based on data from the U.S. Bureau of the Census, *Statistical Abstract of the United States,* 1989, 109th ed. (Washington, D.C.: U.S. Government Printing Office, 1989), p. 10.

Union and nations in Southern and Eastern Europe, such as Poland, Portugal, and Romania. Large numbers of immigrants also came from the United Kingdom and Germany. Because of the revolutionary changes that have occurred in nations such as Poland, Romania, and East Germany since 1989, it is possible that the number of immigrants entering the United States from these nations in future years may increase. Freedom to emigrate from these nations is likely to be more possible in the future than it was in the past under the old regimes.

Table 8–2 shows the number of immigrants that entered the United States between 1981 and 1987 from three other predominantly White nations: Canada, Australia, and New Zealand. Canada was second only to the United Kingdom as a source of White immigrants to the United States during these years.

European Ethnic Groups: Historical Perspectives

Important Dates

1565   Pedro Menéndez Avilés founded St. Augustine, Florida, on the site of an Indian village.

1607   English immigrants established their first permanent American colony at Jamestown, Virginia.

1620   The Pilgrims came to America from England on the *Mayflower* and established a settlement at Plymouth, Massachusetts.

1623   The Dutch West India Company settled New Netherland as a trading post.

1683   The first German immigrants to North America settled in Pennsylvania.

Important Dates	
1718	The Scots-Irish began immigrating to the American colonies in large numbers.
1729	The Pennsylvania Colony increased the head taxes charged to entering immigrants to discourage further foreign settlement.
1798	A Federalist-dominated Congress enacted the Alien and Sedition Acts to crush the Republican party and harass aliens.
1803	The British Passenger Act was enacted to discourage immigration.
1825	Great Britain repealed laws that prohibited immigration. The first group of Norwegian immigrants arrived in the United States.
1845–49	A series of potato blights in Ireland caused thousands of its citizens to immigrate to the United States.
1855	The antiforeign Know-Nothing movement reached its zenith and had a number of political successes in the 1855 elections. The movement rapidly declined after 1855. Castle Garden immigrant depot opened in New York.
1863	The Irish working-classes expressed discontent with the Civil War and hostility toward urban Blacks in the New York draft riots, which lasted for four days.
1882	A congressional immigration act established a head tax of 50¢ and excluded lunatics, convicts, idiots, and people likely to become public charges.
1883–85	An economic depression escalated nativistic feelings in the United States.
1885	The Foran Act outlawed the immigration of contract laborers.
1886	The Haymarket Affair in Chicago significantly increased fear of foreign "radicals" and stimulated the growth of nativistic sentiments in the United States. The Statue of Liberty was dedicated as nativism soared in the United States.
1891	Eleven Italian Americans were lynched in New Orleans during the height of American nativism after being accused of murdering a police superintendent.
1892	Ellis Island opened and replaced Castle Garden as the main port of entry for European immigrants.

Important Dates	
1894	The Immigration Restriction League was organized in Boston by intellectuals to promote the passage of a bill that would require entering immigrants to pass a literacy test. The passage of the bill was urged to restrict immigration from southern and eastern Europe.
1899	William Z. Ripley's *The Races of Europe* was published. Ripley divided European peoples into three major racial groups, thus giving the nativists intellectual justifications for their movement.
1901–10	Almost 9 million immigrants entered the United States, most of whom came from southern and eastern Europe. This mass immigration intensified significantly the activities of nativistic groups.
1907	A congressional act extended the classes of immigrants excluded from the United States. Victims of tuberculosis and individuals who had committed certain kinds of crimes were added to the list.
1911	The Dillingham Commission, formed in 1907, issued its forty-one volume report in which it strongly recommended a literacy test for entering immigrants and made a marked distinction between the "old" and "new" immigrants.
1916	Madison Grant, a well-known naturalist, published *The Passing of the Great Race in America*. This popular book gave the nativists more ammunition.
1916–19	The movement to Americanize aliens was widespread and intense.
1917	A comprehensive immigration bill was enacted that established the literacy test for entering immigrants, added to the classes of those excluded, and increased the head tax from $4 to $8. This act was a major victory for the nativists.
1919–20	During the height of antiradical attitudes in America, hundreds of alien radicals were captured and deported in a movement led by A. Mitchell Palmer.
1921	The Johnson Act signaled a turning point in American history. It set up a nationality quota system and imposed the first numerical limits on European immigration to the United States.
1924	The Johnson-Reed Act established extreme quotas on immigration and blatantly discriminated against southern and eastern European and non-White nations.

Important Dates	
1927	Two Italian radicals, Nicola Sacco and Bartolomeo Vanzetti, were executed during a period of extreme antiradical sentiment in America. Their execution set off a wave of reactions throughout the Western world.
1952	The McCarran-Walter Act, which allegedly removed racial barriers to immigration, essentially continued the policy established in 1924 and was in some ways more restrictive.
1954	The closing of Ellis Island marked the end of mass European immigration to the United States.
1965	A new immigration act, which became effective in 1968, abolished the national origins quota system and liberalized significantly American immigration policy.
1981	66,700 European immigrants entered the United States, and 264,300 and 210,400 entered the United States from Asia and other North American nations, respectively.
1984	Presidential and vice-presidential candidates of both major political parties appeared at the National Italian American Foundation dinner, indicating the continued importance of ethnicity to U.S. politicians.
1986	The Centennial of the Statue of Liberty was commemorated.

Spaniards in the Americas

Spain was the first European nation to establish permanent settlements in the Americas. Spanish ships arrived in the Americas in 1492 under the leadership of Christopher Columbus. In 1496, Columbus and his brother Bartholomew founded the city of Santo Domingo on the island of Hispaniola. Santo Domingo was the first permanent continuing European settlement in the Americas. A number of Spanish explorers, including Coronado, Cortez, Cabeza de Vaca, and Ponce de León, followed Columbus. These and other Spaniards explored and settled in the Americas. In 1526, San Miguel de Gualdape, a Spanish colony in South Carolina, was established by Lucas Vasquez de Ayllon. Another Spaniard named Pedro Menéndez de Avilés founded the oldest permanent city in the United States, St. Augustine, Florida, in 1565. These early Spaniards influenced the language, religion, and other cultural aspects of the Americas.

Even though their influence in the Americas was great, few Spaniards came to the Americas. It has been estimated that no more than 300,000

Spaniards came to the Americas during the entire three colonial centuries. Many of these people stayed only a short time. Many of the Spaniards who remained in America fathered children with Indian women. These unions produced a new ethnic group in the Americas, the *mestizos* (see the chapter on Mexican Americans). Today, the number of Spanish-born Americans is still small. Between 1961 and 1987, about 73,300 people immigrated to the United States from Spain.

More Europeans Come to America

Europeans began settling in America in significant numbers in the 1600s. The economic, social, and political conditions existing in Europe caused many of its inhabitants to cross the Atlantic searching for a new home. The main causes of the waves of immigrations were the drastic economic and social changes occurring in Europe. Serfdom had been the basis of European society for centuries. Most people were peasants who earned their living by farming. Throughout Europe, the old relationships between peasants and the land were changed and the peasants suffered severely. The land owned by the village was divided into individual plots. With each succeeding generation, the land was further divided. Eventually, the plots of land became so small that younger sons were unable to make a living. Some peasants suffered when land holdings were consolidated by the landlords.

The peasant became landless and thus lost his place in the social order. He was attached to the land. Without it, he was unable to make a living or maintain a sense of being. The tremendous population growth Europe experienced in the seventeenth and eighteenth centuries increased the peasants' problems. Famine and crop failures also caused many to immigrate.

The early settlers were a diverse group, although most of them were peasants. Many were unable to pay for their passage and became indentured servants in order to make the journey. However, merchants, artisans, professionals, and laborers comprised a small but significant part of the immigrants during the entire colonial period. Vagrants and convicts, who were unwanted by European nations, were also among the first settlers. However, there were never as many criminals and paupers among the colonists as is often believed.

Although the bulk of the first European immigrants came to North America primarily for economic reasons, some came for religious and political reasons. Most European nations had established churches associated with the state. Religious dissenters who wanted to practice other religions sometimes immigrated to America. The Separatists who arrived in the colonies in 1620 on the *Mayflower* were seeking a place where they could freely practice their religion. The Jewish immigrants who settled in North America during the colonial period also were seeking religious and political freedom.

Once the European immigrations were under way, the movement itself produced forces that stimulated it. The letters settlers sent back to friends and relatives in Europe extolling the wonders of America were a cogent factor that pulled more Europeans to America. Guidebooks about wages and living conditions in America were distributed in Europe by travel and shipping agents. These books helped to motivate thousands of Europeans to immigrate.

The rise of the industrial revolution and scientific farming in the nineteenth century also stimulated European immigration to America. The development of industry put many artisans out of work. Modern farming methods displaced many farmers. These displaced workers tried to solve their problems by immigrating to America. Ship companies eager to get passengers and U.S. states and railroad companies that wanted to settle sparsely populated areas in the nation recruited European immigrants. European governments either discouraged or legally prohibited immigration in the 1600s and 1700s. However, these obstacles to immigration were largely removed in the nineteenth century. This, too, encouraged Europeans to immigrate. The development of more efficient and inexpensive ocean transportation also stimulated European immigration in the nineteenth century.

Although all of these factors contributed to European immigration to America, it was the search for a chance to earn a better living that caused most European immigrants to come to the United States. The tide of immigration rose and fell with economic conditions in the United States. When times were good, the immigrants came in great numbers. When depression set in, immigration dropped significantly. During some brief periods, the number of immigrants returning to Europe actually exceeded the number that arrived. The key role that economic factors played in the European immigrations to North America make them similar to other mass movements to the United States from such nations as Canada, Mexico, the Philippines, China, and Japan.

Although some religious and political dissenters came to America so that they could freely practice their beliefs, this aspect of European immigration has been greatly exaggerated and oversimplified in textbooks and in the popular mind. Most came mainly for economic reasons. Most who were religious and political dissenters also hoped to improve their economic lot. The widespread belief that most of the first European settlers in America loved freedom and liberty has also been grossly exaggerated. The Puritans and other religious dissenters who settled in North America were not liberty-loving people, but were provincial groups who believed that their religions were the only true and valid ones. They were as intolerant of religious differences as those who protected the official churches in Europe.[1] Their aim was to find a place where they could practice *their* religions freely, and not to build a nation in which all religions would be tolerated.

Religious freedom and toleration developed in North America not because of the goals and wishes of the early colonists, but because the motley collection of religious groups that came to America competed for and won the right to practice their beliefs. The same is true about American democracy and the colonists. The colonists were Europeans in mind and spirit. They tried hard to establish European institutions and beliefs on American soil. They were not liberty-loving citizens who had a deep belief in democracy. Quite the contrary was true. They were the products of a hierarchical and class-structured society and had internalized these beliefs.[2] That they failed to establish a highly stratified society in America was not due to the fact that they did not try. Rather, a form of democracy emerged in the United States because the social and economic conditions that developed in North America made it impossible to establish a new Europe and fostered the development of a more open society. Thus, American democracy did not stem primarily from the vision the colonists brought from Europe but resulted mainly from the social and economic forces that evolved in North America.

The Passage to America

Especially in the seventeenth century, the journey from the peasants' European homes to the American port cities was hard and hazardous.[3] The peasants made the decision to come to America only after much thought. Often, only the threat of starvation or the loss of status compelled them to attempt the difficult journey. The trip was also expensive, especially during the first immigrations. Thus, even after they made the decision to come to America, they often had to save money for a long time before they could begin the trip.

The peasants' first step in the journey to America was taking a long trip, usually by foot, to a European city that had a seaport from which ships sailed to America. Not everyone who started out was able to complete this stage of the journey. Many of those who made it to the European port cities were tired and battered. Once they arrived in the port city, the peasants had to wait for weeks and sometimes months before the ship departed for America. The ship captains waited until the ships were full of goods and human cargo before they sailed for North America because the fuller ship was more profitable. During the long wait, the peasants became restless and tired. Some were not able to board the ship when it was finally ready to depart. As each day went by during the long wait for the American departure, the food the peasants had stored for the journey steadily dwindled. Renting a room at the European port city also took a large part of the meager funds they had saved up for the trip.

Finally the day came when the ship headed for America. The peasants' joy at the departure was to be short-lived. The conditions on the ships were depressing and harsh. To maximize his profits, the ship captain packed the people like sardines. Each family was assigned an extremely small space on the ship. The family spent most of its time in these dark, crowded compartments. Diseases were rampant on the vessels and took many lives. Dysentery, cholera, yellow fever, and smallpox were some of the more common ship diseases. The journey was long, often more than a month. Many families barely had enough food to last throughout the journey. Eventually, European nations passed laws requiring peasants to take a certain amount of food for the trip. However, ship captains who wanted to profit from selling food on the ships thought of many ingenious ways to evade these weakly enforced laws.

The Atlantic journey, especially before the time of the steamship, was a tremendous shock to the peasants. The family disruption that continued when they reached America began on the ship. Almost wholly dependent on the ship's crew, the father was unable to exercise his traditional role as leader and master of the family. The mother could not function in her traditional role either. When food was getting scarce, she had to try to keep the family fed. These transatlantic conditions severely strained family relationships.

The peasants who survived the journey eventually landed at an American port city. The landing was eagerly awaited and celebrated. However, the peasants still had some hurdles to overcome. They had to be checked and questioned by American immigration officials before they could travel freely in America. Wrong answers to questions or poor health could mean further questioning by officials and boards, a stay in a hospital, or even a trip back to Europe. In the earliest years, the inspection focused on physical health and ability to work. Gradually, questions related to the immigrant's morals and political beliefs were added. In 1917, Congress enacted a law requiring immigrants to demonstrate literacy in some language before they could enter the United States.

Most of the immigrants were broken, both financially and physically, when they arrived at American seaport cities. Some were the sole survivors in their families. Broken and lonely, some found asylum in poorhouses. Many immigrants who had planned to settle elsewhere never left the port cities in which their vessels landed. Thousands who had planned to settle elsewhere stayed in cities like Milwaukee, Chicago, and St. Louis. Some of the first settlers found work on construction projects in cities. Later, railroad construction provided work for immigrants. When the industrial revolution began, factory work became available. In all these lines of work, the immigrants were paid low wages and were outrageously exploited by their employers. Few immigrants became successful farmers or settled in the West. Farming required resources and capital most of the peasants did not have. American farming was also different from agriculture in the European village. Few of the immigrants were able to settle on the frontier. They lacked both the resources and the ability to push the Indians off their land like many of their American-born contemporaries.

The Urban Ghetto

Most European immigrants settled in cities, like most migrants from rural areas today. They had neither the means nor the desire to settle in rural areas. Like their modern counterparts, the new immigrants settled in blighted and dilapidated areas that became ethnic ghettos. Irishtowns, Germantowns, and Little Italys developed in most of the cities in the Northeast and Midwest. Ethnic organizations, like schools, newspapers, and churches, emerged within these communities. The immigrants, especially the more recent arrivals, usually lived in rundown housing near the business and manufacturing districts that had been vacated by suburban-bound upwardly mobile residents when the manufacturing district sprawled outward into their communities.

When the upwardly mobile left the inner city, their old mansions were converted into multiple family dwellings for the immigrants. The multiple dwelling units became a source of quick profit for the owners. Little was done to make these dwellings comfortable. Profit, not comfort, was what the slum landloard sought. When these neighborhoods were deserted by the old residents, they were also forsaken by the street cleaners and sanitation crews. The smells from the garbage were pungent. The immigrants' habit of throwing garbage out of the window and keeping animals in their backyards made these communities even more unpleasant. High-rise apartments went up in some of the ethnic communities. Most of these buildings were crowded and uncomfortable. Many did not have interior plumbing or central heating. Some of the earliest ones had no toilets. There were only two toilets on each floor in some later apartments. To help pay the rent, some families took in lodgers.

The immigrants looked forward to the day when their income would permit them to leave the ghetto and join the exodus to the suburbs. For most ethnic groups, this day eventually came. However, as one ethnic group vacated the ghetto, another group replaced it. In New York City, Italians took over old Irish communities. Jews from Russia and Poland occupied districts where the Germans had lived. After World War II, many of the urban communities that had been occupied by European ethnic groups received a large number of African Americans from the South, Mexican Americans from the Southwest, and migrants from Puerto Rico.

Immigrant Political Action

The participation of the immigrants in the urban political machines, though significant, was not the total of their importance in the American political process. Early in American political history, when the number of immigrants in American cities became substantial, and their votes had the power to sway or determine election outcomes, politicians became increasingly sensitive to the concerns and wishes of immigrant groups. Even politicians like Theodore Roosevelt and Woodrow Wilson, who felt rather negatively about the "new" immigrants, were forced on occasion to say positive things about them publicly. However, it was difficult for President Wilson to convince the southern and eastern European immigrants that he had had a change of heart.

Nevertheless, the major political parties began to vie aggressively for immigrant support and to include references to immigrants in their political platforms that reflected the specialized concerns of America's ethnic groups. These groups had many special concerns and aspirations, usually related to American foreign policy and the ways in which the United States was treating their "Mother" countries. Although many European immigrants did not have much of a sense of nationality when they arrived in America, intense nationalist movements developed among them. According to Jones, "There was a tendency among Irish political refugees as well as German Forty-eighters, to look upon themselves as exiles and to use the United States simply as a base for promoting European causes. . . . [These movements] afforded a means of group identification and self-assertion."[4]

Although the actions of these political refugees were probably extreme, most European immigrant groups did continue to see themselves as Europeans. The immigrants formed many groups to campaign aggressively for European causes and to sway American foreign policy. In World War I, German Americans criticized Wilson's actions toward Germany and the Irish Americans became bitter because of Wilson's pro-British actions. The Irish voted strongly against Wilson in the subsequent election. The militant actions by some European-American groups, especially German Americans, caused many Americans to question seriously their loyalties to the United States. However, even though some of these movements were radical and aggressively nationalistic, the most radical ones were unable to attract mass support because of the deep conservatism of most immigrants.

Anglo-Saxon Cultural Dominance

The early European settlements were highly ethnically mixed. English, Scots-Irish, Germans, French Huguenots, Africans, and Jews were among the earlier colonists (see Table 8–3). Writes Bailey, "The population of the thirteen colonies, though basically Anglo-Saxon, was perhaps the most mixed that could be found anywhere in the world. Counting [Africans], nearly 40% was of non-English origin, although New England boasted more native born and persons of English blood than the other sections. Of the 56 signers of the Declaration of Independence in 1776, 18 were non-English, and 8 of these had been born outside the colonies."[5]

Ethnic conflict also developed early in the colonies. The English were dominant during the first years of colonial settlement. Consequently, they shaped the basic social and political institutions of Colonial America. The English cultural dominance of the colonies was challenged by the subsequent groups, but it remained the dominant social and political force in American life. Because of English political and cultural dominance, Anglo-Saxon culture became the ideal by which all subsequent ethnic groups were judged and by which levels of assimilation and acculturation were judged. To become *acculturated* became synonymous with acquiring Anglo-Saxon Protestant life-styles, values, and language. The English language was dominant in almost every American colony by 1775.

Table 8–3   *Estimated Ethnic Population of the 13 Colonies, 1790*
(based on family names)

	Number	Percentage
English and Welsh	2,605,699	82.1
Scotch (including Scotch-Irish)	221,562	7.0
German	176,407	5.6
Dutch	78,959	2.5
Irish	61,534	1.9
French	17,619	0.6
All other whites	10,664	0.3
	3,172,444	100.0
[African]	757,181	19.2 of total
Grand Total	3,929,625	

Source: From *The American Pageant: A History of the Republic* (p. 67) by Thomas A. Bailey, 1961. Boston: D.C. Heath and Company. Copyright 1961 by D.C. Heath and Company. Reprinted by permission.
Note: Rossiter, *A Century of Population Growth* (1909). Later estimates by Barker and Hansen (1931) are not here used because they are confused by the inclusion of Spanish and French elements *later* a part of the United States.

Early in American colonial life, non-English groups began to be evaluated negatively. The New England colonies, which were predominantly English, took steps to bar the settlements of Roman Catholics. The French Huguenots became the focal point of English hostility. Later, the Scots-Irish and the German immigrants were the victims of English antagonism. An English mob prevented a group of Irish immigrants from landing in Boston in 1729. Several years later, another mob destroyed a new Scots-Irish Presbyterian church in Worcester. The attitude that English culture and institutions were superior to all others profoundly shaped American life and was extremely significant in the nativistic movements that emerged after the Civil War. However, when the southern and eastern European immigrants began their mass exodus to America in the late 1800s, public opinion leaders extended the "superior" traits of the English to all northern and western European "races." (In the eighteenth century, Europeans were considered to belong to several races, such as the Teutonic, the Alpine, and the Mediterranean. The races of northern and western Europe were considered superior to the races in southern, central, and eastern Europe.) This was necessary to enable the "old" immigrants to band together to condemn the "new" immigrants. However, race assumed a new meaning when the southern and eastern European groups attained "acceptable" levels of assimilation in the twentieth century. All White races became one. Racial hostilities could now focus on non-White ethnic groups, such as African Americans, Asian Americans, Mexican Americans, and American Indians. Whites of southern and eastern

European descent joined former adverse White ethnic groups to exclude people of color from full participation in American life.

The Southern and Eastern European Immigrants

Before 1812, most European immigrants who came to America were from northern and western European nations, such as England, Germany, France, and Scandinavia. Northern and western Europeans exceeded the number of immigrants from other parts of Europe up to the last decades of the nineteenth century. However, by 1896, a major change had taken place in the source of European immigrants to the United States. Most European immigrants to America now came from southern, eastern, and central Europe. Austria-Hungary, Italy, and Russia sent the largest number of new immigrants. However, substantial numbers also came from such countries as Greece, Romania, Bulgaria, Armenia, and Finland. Fifteen million European immigrants arrived in the United States between 1890 and 1914. Most of them came from southern and eastern Europe.

When immigrants from southern and eastern Europe began coming to the United States in significant numbers, a number of arguments evolved that were designed to distinguish them from immigrants who had come earlier from the northern and western parts of Europe. The southern and eastern immigrants became known as the "new" immigrants; the earlier immigrants were referred to as the "old" immigrants. The mass media, intellectuals, and politicians perpetuated the myth that the new immigrants were inferior to the older ones, that they caused major problems in the cities, and that steamship companies and American industries eager for unskilled labor were the main causes of the new traffic. The Dillingham Commission, which was formed to investigate immigration in 1907, concluded that there was a fundamental difference in both the character and the causes of the new and old immigrations.

Repetition of this myth became evidence of its validity. It was eagerly embraced by writers, historians, and policymakers and significantly influenced the racist immigration legislation enacted in the 1920s. The nativistic movements reached their zenith in the 1920s and chose the southern and eastern European immigrants as their chief targets. Only the Asian immigrants in California were more harshly criticized. The distinctions made between the old and the new immigrants were artificial and based on inaccurate information and false assumptions. The southern and eastern European immigrants came to the United States for the same reasons that the earlier immigrants had come: to improve their economic conditions and to seek religious and political freedom. Steamship lines and American industries played no greater role in stimulating immigration from southern and eastern Europe than they had played in stimulating immigration from other parts of Europe. In both cases, their influence was rather meager and has been grossly exaggerated.

The types of new immigrants who came from southern and eastern Europe, like the older immigrants, were highly diverse. Some southern and eastern Europeans came to the United States for temporary work, not because of something unique about them, but because the new steamship lines had so greatly reduced the length of the Atlantic trip that it was practical and possible to come to the United States for seasonal work.

Southern and eastern European immigrants were judged as being innately inferior to older Americans partly because they started coming to the United States when the notion that the United States should be an asylum for the oppressed peoples of Europe was beginning to wane. When the Statue of Liberty was dedicated in New York City in 1886, many Americans had lost faith in the poetic words penned by Emma Lazarus about Europe's "huddled masses." They had also begun to question the melting pot theory and to raise serious questions about whether Europeans could be as readily assimilated as they had originally believed. The doubts about the new immigrants were not caused by their inability to be assimilated, but by the conditions and conceptions of foreigners emerging within American life. Thus, the rush of southern and eastern European immigrants to the United States was poorly timed. The internal conditions in America were giving birth to distinctly antiforeign attitudes. A scapegoat was needed to blame for urban blight, political corruption in the cities, and economic recession. The new immigrants were vulnerable and convenient targets. Consequently, they were judged intellectually and culturally inferior to the old immigrants and declared unassimilable. That they were an inferior "race" became widely accepted both in the intellectual community and in the popular mind.

Nativistic Movements

As early as 1727, nativistic feelings toward the Germans in Pennsylvania ran high. (Nativism was a movement designed to restrict immigration to America and to protect the interests of the native-born. It was an extreme form of nationalism and ethnocentrism.) To discourage further foreign settlement in the colony, Pennsylvania passed a statute in 1729 increasing the head tax on foreigners, allegedly to prevent persons likely to become public charges from entering the colony. Other antiforeign legislation emerged in the eighteenth century. In 1798, Congress, dominated by the Federalists, passed the Alien and Sedition Acts to crush the Republican party by destroying its large base of immigrant support. These acts were also designed to silence criticism of the Federalists and to harass European immigrants. The Alien and Sedition Acts lengthened the time required to become an American citizen from five to fourteen years and gave the president almost unlimited control over the behavior of immigrants. They virtually nullified the freedoms of speech and the press.

Nativistic sentiments continued to ebb and flow during the eighteenth and nineteenth centuries, although their most violent expressions did not arise until the late nineteenth and early twentieth centuries. Nativism reached its zenith in the 1920s, culminating with the passage of the Johnson-Reed Act in 1924. The Know-Nothing movement, which emerged in the 1840s and reached its climax in 1855, was one of the most successful nativistic movements in the nineteenth century. The various secret organizations constituting this movement, such as the Order of United Americans and the Order of the Star-Spangled Banner, were strongly anti-Catholic and agitated for an extension of the period required for an immigrant to become an American citizen and for the election of only "Americans" to political office. The movement, which became less secretive in 1855 and openly called itself the American party, enjoyed tremendous political successes in a number of states in the 1855 elections. However, the Know-Nothing movement died as quickly as it had emerged. Conflict over slavery within the American party severely strained and weakened it. Nativistic sentiments in America in the 1850s were not strong enough to sustain the Know-Nothing movement.

By the late 1800s, anti-Chinese agitation on the West Coast was virulent and race ideologies emerged to justify it. The concept of the inferiority and superiority of various races became rampant in the West. In 1882, Congress passed the Chinese Exclusion Act, the first immigration bill specifically designed to exclude a particular race. Although many Americans viewed the case of the Chinese as separate from European immigration, the anti-Chinese act gave impetus to antiforeign attitudes throughout U.S. society. Three months after the anti-Chinese bill was passed, Congress enacted a bill further restricting the classes of Europeans who could enter the United States. Convicts, idiots, and lunatics, as well as those who might become public charges, were excluded.

Nativism grew more and more intense as the fear of a Catholic takeover of the federal government and of foreign radicals soared. The big jump in the number of southern and eastern European immigrants entering the United States in the 1800s added fuel to the fire. Cries of "100% Americanism" and "America for Americans" became widespread. Agitations for antiforeign legislation became intense, especially legislation that would exclude foreign "radicals" and require immigrants to pass a literacy test.

Congress, responding to pressure in 1885, passed the Foran Act, which prohibited the importation of contract labor from Europe. Violence also erupted during these turbulent times. Italians and Jews were frequently the victims of violent and outrageous acts. Eleven Italians were murdered in a mass lynching in New Orleans in 1891 when they were accused of killing a police superintendent. Riots directed at Jews in Chicago increased public paranoia about foreign "radicals." Congress further extended the classes of immigrants excluded from the United States in 1907. Imbeciles and victims of tuberculosis were now added to the list.

Nativistic movements, which were directed against most foreign-born groups in the 1850s, began to focus increasingly on southern and eastern European immigrants, as masses of them arrived in American cities. The intellectual community legitimized the racist myths about the innate inferiority of southern and eastern Europeans. William Z. Ripley was one of the leading intellectual nativists. His book, *The Races of Europe*, published in 1899, divided Whites into three major races: the Teutonic, the Northern blondes; the Alpine, the central race of stocky roundheads; and the Mediterranean, dark and slender longheads.[6] The Teutonic was the superior race. Ripley warned against a racial mixture that would pollute the superior race with southern and eastern European racial groups.

Madison Grant, a well-known naturalist, also argued for racial purity in his popular book, *The Passing of the Great Race in America*, published in 1916. Ripley and Grant, as well as other intellectuals and writers in the early twentieth century, provided the nativists with the scientific and intellectual justifications for their movements and issued a ringing plea for restrictive legislation.[7] As in other periods of mass hysteria in America, social and physical scientists justified and legitimized prevailing social attitudes and myths.

When the twentieth century opened, nativist sentiments and attitudes had gained tremendous momentum in American life. They did not subside until they culminated in the extreme restrictive legislation enacted in the 1920s. The Dillingham Commission, which issued its report in 1911, noted that the new European immigrants were essentially different from the old and strongly recommended the passage of a bill that would require immigrants to pass a literacy test. Agitation for a literacy test bill became intense, but the advocates of the bill faced repeated opposition in Congress and from President Wilson. As the United States prepared to enter World War I, nativism—directed especially at German Americans—became intense. Patriotic groups demanded that all aspects of German culture, including music and the names of streets and schools, be eradicated in the United States. Although most German Americans were loyal citizens during this period, they were often the victims of harassment. However, the abuses they endured were mild compared with those suffered by Japanese Americans during World War II (see chapter 13).

Just before the United States entered World War I, the literacy bill advocates finally mustered enough congressional votes to override a second Wilson veto, and the literacy bill was passed on February 5, 1917. Adult immigrants now had to be able to read a passage in some language before they could enter the United States. The bill was comprehensive. It codified existing legislation and added vagrants, chronic alcoholics, and psychopaths to the list of excluded aliens. The head tax was increased from $4 to $8.[8] Although nativists celebrated their victory, they began immediately to plan strategies to restrict further immigration to the United States.

Although America's entry into World War I diverted attention from nativistic concerns, campaigns to "Americanize" aliens already in the United States became a national passion during the war. When the war ended, again Congress was pressured to enact restrictive legislation. The law requiring immigrants to pass a literacy test did not halt immigration as the nativists had thought. In fact, it reduced it very little. Consequently nativists pushed for a quota system to restrict immigration. Antiforeign groups and organizations experienced tremendous growth in memberships. The Ku Klux Klan grew enormously in the South and Midwest. It had more than 2½ million members by 1923. The phenomenal growth of the Klan was symptomatic of pervasive antiforeign attitudes in American life.

Eventually, the nativistic forces gained congressional victories. The Johnson Act, enacted in 1921, marked a turning point in the history of American immigration. The Johnson Act established a nationality quota system and imposed the first numerical limits on immigration from European nations. The quota system was based on the various nationality groups in the United States. The most important immigration bill of this period was enacted in 1924—the Johnson-Reed Act. The quotas this act set were severe and blatantly discriminated against southern and eastern European and non-White nations. It halted Japanese immigration completely. After 1927, the act allowed only 150,000 Europeans to enter the United States each year, and they were "parceled out in ratio to the distribution of national origins in the White population of the United States in 1920." Because Europeans from the North and West represented the largest percentages of Whites in the United States in 1920, the authors of the Johnson-Reed Act had thought of an ingenious way to limit severely the number of immigrants from southern and eastern Europe, while assuring that a significant number were allowed to enter from the North and West. Nativism had triumphed, and an important chapter in U.S. history had been closed.

Subsequent Immigration Acts

There was little change in American immigration policy from 1924 until the outbreak of World War II. A number of Europeans were displaced by the events of World War II and sought asylum as refugees in the United States. After much debate, a Displaced Persons Act was passed in 1948, which permitted about 400,000 refugees to enter the United States during a four-year period. The McCarran-Walter Act, passed in 1952, allegedly to remove racial barriers to immigration, essentially continued the policy established in 1924 and was in some ways more restrictive. In 1953, Congress passed a temporary measure, the Refugee Relief Act, to enable refugees from Communist nations to settle in the United States. However, major reform in U.S. immigration policy was not made until 1965. President John F. Kennedy strongly urged Congress to pass an enlightened immigration act. After much discussion and vigorous debate, the bill finally became a reality during the Johnson administration on July 1, 1968. This act abolished the national origins quota system and allowed 170,000 persons to enter the United States each year from the Eastern Hemisphere and 120,000 from the Western Hemisphere.[10] Technical skill and kinship, rather than country of origin, became the major criteria for admitting immigrants to the United

States. This bill was a major victory for liberal-thinking Americans and is a tribute to the ideals that many Americans profess.

European Ethnic Groups in American Society

The mass settlement of Europeans in North America was one of the most unique phenomena in human history. More than 48 million immigrants entered the United States between 1820 and 1978. Most came from Europe. The European immigrants represented many religious, political, and cultural groups. Yet the United States, by forcing the immigrants to acquire the culture of the dominant society, was able to prevent the Balkanization of America and establish a unified society. The immigrants paid a heavy price for cultural assimilation and acculturation. Nevertheless, a rather culturally homogeneous society emerged, although ethnicity is still a viable but complex force in U.S. life.

When European immigrants arrived on America's shores, their thoughts, feelings, aspirations, and attitudes were decidedly European. Many immigrants aggressively tried to structure European institutions in America. They tried to maintain their religious life by building churches similar to those in Europe. They established parochial schools, ethnic newspapers, ethnic theaters, and self-help organizations in their futile attempts to hold onto the old order. Some groups such as the German Americans tried to create ethnic colonies where their European cultures and ethnic kinships could flourish. Despite the concerted efforts by the immigrants to establish European institutions in the United States, these attempts were by and large destined to fail. Forces within American life worked against them and eventually eroded or greatly modified most European cultures in the United States.

The public schools, the American press, and American political institutions played key roles in mitigating the attempts to establish and maintain European institutions on American soil. By the beginning of the nineteenth century, the English dominated most American institutions, such as the schools, the courts, and the popular press. The immigrants and their children often found it necessary to acquire Anglo-Saxon cultural traits before they were allowed to participate fully in American society. School teachers demeaned foreign languages; employers often preferred to hire assimilated immigrants. European Americans, especially the second generation, often responded to these cogent forces by becoming ashamed of their ethnic cultures, deliberately denying them, such as by Anglicizing or changing their surnames, and actively seeking to assimilate. Many second- and third-generation immigrants became—in mores, values, and outlook—similar to Anglo-Saxon Protestants. These immigrants paid a tremendous psychological price for denying their cultures, languages, and identities. However, as William Greenbaum has perceptively written, the larger society shamed the immigrants into abandoning their ethnic cultures, but held out to them the hope of economic and structural inclusion into the mainstream society.[11] White ethnic groups, unlike people of color, were able to attain full inclusion into the mainstream society once they were culturally identical to Anglo-Saxon Protestants.

The New Ethnicity

During the 1950s, social scientists expected most ethnic characteristics eventually to disappear in the United States and a modernized shared culture to evolve. In this common national culture, social class would persist but factors such as race and ethnicity would be largely unimportant.

Glazer and Moynihan, in their 1963 pathbreaking book, *Beyond the Melting Pot*,[12] presented one of the first theoretical arguments that the melting pot conception of the United States was inaccurate and incomplete. They argued that ethnicity in New York was important and that it would continue to be important for both politics and culture.[13] Significantly, they included case studies of the persistence of ethnicity among three White ethnic groups: the Jews, Italians, and Irish of New York City. They described how ethnicity persisted among these groups in politics and family structure.

During the 1960s, the civil rights movement emerged. This movement made ethnicity more legitimate. African Americans made claims on the federal government and other institutions because of their historic discrimination in the United States. The Black civil rights movement stimulated ethnic revitalization movements among other ethnic groups, such as American Indians and Mexican Americans, and among White ethnic groups, such as Jews, Poles, Italians, and Greeks. Southern, eastern, and central European ethnic groups were the most active participants in the White ethnic revitalization movements that emerged in the early 1970s.

These ethnic groups, through leaders and organizations, began to articulate ways in which they had been victims of ethnic stereotypes and discrimination, and how their histories and cultures had been omitted from history books and the school curriculum. They argued that, like Blacks, Indians, and Mexican Americans, they needed public policies that would enable them to acquire more equity and cultural democracy. Michael Novak, an articulate theologian and humanist, became the most prolific speaker and writer for what he called the "unmeltable ethnics." His book, *The Rise of the Unmeltable Ethnics*, published in 1971, signaled the birth of the "new pluralism" among White ethnic groups.

In this widely reviewed and quoted book, Novak identified the "unmeltable ethnics" (Poles, Italians, Greeks, and Slavs), tried to explain how they were both different from and culturally alienated from Anglo-Saxon Protestants, and described how they were victims of discrimination, cultural arrogance, and the intellectual community. In moving prose, Novak also described how he and other Slavs were forced to deny their cultural identities. He wrote, "The estrangement I have come to feel derives not only from a lack of family history.

Early in life, I was made to feel a slight uneasiness when I said my name. . . . Liberal education tends to separate children from parents, from their roots, from their history, in the cause of a universal and superior religion."[14]

Novak urged opinion leaders and politicians to recognize and respect the cultures of the White ethnics and predicted that they would be a powerful political force during the 1970s. He called the 1970s "the decade of the White ethnics." While Novak was arguing for the civil rights of White ethnics and attempting to mobilize them politically, researchers, such as Andrew M. Greeley and William C. McCready, were studying the extent to which ethnicity had survived among White ethnic groups, including the Irish Americans. In an article published in 1974, they described significant differences among the Anglo-Saxons, the Irish, and the Italians on personality variables, political participation, and attitudes toward sexuality and drinking.[15] Publications that focused on the new ethnicity of White ethnic groups also emerged. *Ethnicity*, a journal published between 1974 and 1982, included a number of articles describing the cultural differences among White ethnic groups.

The ethnic revitalization movements among White ethnic groups during the 1970s evoked considerable controversy. Some scholars argued that the White ethnic movement was not genuine but was a racist political movement designed to divert attention from the legitimate needs of ethnic groups of color, such as African Americans and Mexican Americans. Other critics argued that the movement was a "me-too," contrived movement. Critics of the new ethnic movements included scholars such as Orlando Patterson,[16] a Harvard sociologist, and the distinguished historian, Arthur Mann. Wrote Mann, "The White-ethnic revival was the product of a seriously divisive movement in history. Like previous revivals in America and elsewhere, secular as well as religious, the 1960s–1970s movement rested on the belief that the only way out for a troubled people lay in the return to a previous but languishing heritage."[17] Two anthropologists, Stein and Hill, published a book-length work on the White ethnic movement in which they harshly criticized it. They wrote: "The New Ethnicity, then, is both a symptomatic expression of a disintegrated life and an attempt to cope with this sense of personal disintegration through regression to an earlier stage in individual development."[18]

Scholars and civil rights leaders who defended the White ethnic movement argued that it was a genuine movement that had emerged in response to cultural assaults, discrimination, and epithets used to describe White ethnics by the liberal press. White ethnic leaders argued that those who dismissed the new pluralism as a "racist movement" had completely misunderstood its nature and complexity and were using a code word to dismiss it summarily.

White Ethnic Groups Today: Into the Twilight of Ethnicity?

As we entered the last decade of this century, most of the fervor of the ethnic revival movement of the 1970s had disappeared. Most European Americans, as they were in the 1970s, were continuing down the road toward assimilation into the mainstream society. The ethnic movement among White ethnic groups during the 1970s involved primarily ethnic leaders and intellectuals and not the common man and woman. As Alba indicates, the fact that ethnic leaders and intellectuals were able to articulate their rage and concerns in the mainstream media and intellectual community indicated that White ethnic groups had attained a significant level of structural inclusion into the mainstream society.[19]

A lasting legacy of the White ethnic movement, and of the ethnic movements in the 1970s, is that ethnicity is more legitimate in the United States today than it was before the 1970s. Many Poles, Italians, and Yugoslavs no longer feel that they need to change their names or to become completely alienated from their ethnic culture in order to realize the American dream and attain economic and social mobility. Many social, political, and scholarly organizations are working to secure visibility and rights for European ethnic groups, including organizations such as the Illinois Consultation on Ethnicity in Education and the American Italian Historical Association. While many members of White ethnic groups are becoming more assimilated into the mainstream society, continuing immigration from Europe infuses some European ethnic groups, such as Greeks and Italians, with heavy doses of ethnic culture each year. Even though groups like Greeks and Italians might well have entered the twilight of ethnicity as Alba claims,[20] new infusions of immigrants and various political and social events continue to fuel the dim ethnic flame.

Teaching Strategies

To illustrate how content related to European Americans can be used to integrate the curriculum, exemplary strategies are identified for teaching these concepts at the grade levels indicated: *cultural contributions* (primary grades), *immigration* (intermediate and upper grades), and *nativism* (high school grades).

Primary Grades

CONCEPT: Cultural Contributions

Generalization: Our ancestors came from many different nations and belonged to many ethnic groups. All these groups made outstanding contributions to American life.

1. To collect the information needed for this unit, duplicate the following letter and give each child one to take home. Tell the pupils to ask their parents to complete the form and return it to you the next day.

Dear parents:

To help our students understand and appreciate the contributions all ethnic groups have made to American life, we are studying about ethnic groups and their role in America. I want to make sure that we study the ethnic heritages of all of my students. To do this, I need your help. Would you please study the list below and place an "X" by the group indicating your child's ethnic heritage. If your child has a mixed heritage, such as "English" and "Russian," please check both of these. However, please try to limit your checks to three by checking only the *main* strains in your child's ethnic heritage. The list below is based on the categories used by the U.S. Bureau of the Census. They represent the largest ethnic groups in the United States. However, many American ethnic groups are not included. If your child's ethnic heritage is not listed, please check "Other" and fill in the name(s) of your child's ethnic group(s), such as "Spanish" or "French."

Name of Child _____

Ethnic Groups

English _____	Jewish _____
Scottish _____	(Specify nation)
Welsh _____	African American _____
German _____	American Indian _____
Irish _____	Mexican American _____
Italian _____	Asian American _____
Polish _____	(Specify group)
Russian _____	Puerto Rican _____
	Other(s) (Please specify) _____

Please send this form back to me tomorrow morning. Thank you very much for your cooperation. I am sure that your response will help us to have a much better unit.

Sincerely,
Mrs. Mildred Jones
Third Grade Teacher

2. When you have received the forms back from the parents, make a table showing the ethnic groups represented in your class. Put the table on butcher paper and list the children's names under the appropriate ethnic categories. Your table might look like Table 8–4.

Table 8–4   *Our Ethnic Heritages*

English	Irish	Italian	German	African American	Polish
Susie	Cathy	Roy	*Pete	Jack	Linda
John	*Pete	Pat	Ray	Sam	Terry

*Pete has both Irish and German ancestors. Some of the children might be listed under several categories.

Table 8–5   *Famous Ethnic Americans*

English	Italian	African American	Polish
George Washington, *President*	Joe DiMaggio, *Baseball player*	Benjamin Banneker, *Scientist*	Helena Modjeska, *Actress*
Benjamin Franklin, *Scientist*	Frank Sinatra, *Singer*	Martin L. King, *Civil rights leader*	Edmund S. Muskie, *U.S. Senator*

3. Discuss the table with the students, noting that our ancestors came from many different nations. Using a primary globe, locate and write the names of some of the nations and continents from which the children's ancestors came, such as Great Britain, Africa, and Germany. Discuss these nations and continents with the students.

4. Using the photographs in a book such as *Gateway to Liberty: The Story of the Statue of Liberty and Ellis Island* by Mary J. Shapiro (New York: Vintage Books, 1986), tell the students the story of the great immigrations from Europe. Point out some of the reasons the immigrants came, how they came, and how they settled in the United States. The special case of the African Americans, as well as immigrants from other nations of color, should also be discussed.

5. Make another table on butcher paper listing the major ethnic groups represented in your class and other major U.S. ethnic groups. Under each major group, list some famous Americans and the fields in which they have made outstanding contributions to American life. Your table might look like Table 8–5. Many books contain information about the ethnic backgrounds of famous Americans (see the annotated bibliographies in this chapter and in other chapters in Parts II through V of this book). The "In America Series," published by Lerner Publications Company in Minneapolis, Minnesota, is a comprehensive series that includes many books on various U.S. ethnic groups, such as Germans, Greeks, Hungarians, and Koreans.

6. After you have completed the Famous Ethnic Americans table, making sure that all the children's ethnic heritages are represented, discuss the table with the students and help them to formulate, in their own words, the following generalization: Our ancestors came from many different lands and groups, and all these groups made many outstanding contributions to American life. Make sure that each child knows at least one famous person who belongs to his or her ethnic group. This exercise must be modified in classrooms in which there is only one ethnic group. Use some famous Americans from the students' own ethnic group, but also select heroes and heroines from at least five or six other ethnic groups not represented in your classroom.

Intermediate and Upper Grades

CONCEPT: Immigration

Generalization: Europeans immigrated to the United States for various economic, political, and social reasons. Their experiences in the United States were both similar and different.

1. To help the students gain the needed content background to study American immigration, assign appropriate readings that will enable them to answer the following questions about the first or old immigrants to America:

    a. What European nations did the first immigrants to America come from during the colonial period?

    b. Why did they come?

    c. Was America like they expected? If so, in what ways? If not, why not? Explain.

2. After the students have completed their reading assignments, discuss the three questions above with the class. During the discussion, list on the board the reasons that various groups immigrated to the United States. When the reasons have been listed, group them, with the class, into three or four categories, such as "economic," "political," and "social" reasons.

3. Ask the students to read about the new immigrants who came to the United States from Europe in the late 1800s and early 1900s. These immigrants came primarily from southern and eastern Europe and included Ukrainians, Russians, Poles, Italians, Greeks, and many other groups from southern and eastern Europe. The students should discuss the same three questions about these immigrants that they had discussed after reading about the old immigrants.

4. After the students have read and discussed the old and new immigrants, they should compare and contrast these groups. The following questions can be used to guide discussion:

    a. Did the old and new immigrants come to the United States for similar or different reasons? Explain.

    b. How did the new immigrants differ from the old? Why?

    c. How did American life differ at the times when the old and new immigrants came to America? How did this difference affect the adjustment of the newly arrived immigrants?

    d. Both the old and the new immigrants experienced problems on the trip across the Atlantic. How were these problems similar and different?

    e. How were the problems of settlement and finding jobs in America similar and different for the two groups of immigrants?

    f. Ethnic conflict developed early during the settlement of European nationality groups in America. What problems of prejudice and discrimination were experienced by the various groups? Which groups of immigrants were discriminated against the most? The least? Why?

The students can summarize this phase of the unit by making a data retrieval chart to summarize and compare information about major ethnic groups representing old and new immigrants, similar to Table 8–6.

5. To help the students gain a feeling for the harshness of the journey across the Atlantic that the immigrants experienced, read aloud to them Chapter 2, "The Crossing," in Oscar Handlin, *The Uprooted*. The class can develop a dramatization of the passage as described in Handlin and present it in a school assembly. The entire class should be involved in writing and presenting the dramatization.

Table 8–6 *Generalizing about the Old and New European Immigrants*

	Old Immigrants			New Immigrants Southern and Eastern		
	English	Irish	Germans	Italians	Jews	Poles
Reasons for immigrating						
Kinds of people in group						
Problems on Atlantic journey						
Problems of settlement						
Prejudice and discrimination experienced						
Immigration laws in European country of origin						
Relationships *within* the nationality group						

6. European immigrants in the United States often wrote to their friends and relatives in Europe describing the wonders of America and occasionally their problems. Three such letters are reprinted in *America's Immigrants: Adventures in Eyewitness History* by Rhoda Hoff. "A Letter to His Wife in England" by John Dwone and "A Letter to a Friend at Home" by a Norwegian immigrant tell about the greatness of America. "A Letter to Her Mother and Daughter in Norway" by Guri Endresen talks about tragic encounters her family had with American Indians. Read and discuss these letters (or similar ones) with the class. Ask the students to pretend that they are new European immigrants in America in the 1800s. They should write a letter to a friend or relative in Europe telling about their experiences. This activity can be correlated with the language arts.

7. Have the students roleplay the situation below, which involves a poor Italian farmer and an agent of a steamship company who tries to persuade the farmer to immigrate to the United States. After the roleplaying situation, ask the students the questions that follow.

Mr. Pareto, a Poor Italian Farmer in Southern Italy in the 1800s

Mr. Pareto is in his thirties. He is a hard worker and is close to his family, which includes his wife, eight children, and both of his parents. For the past three years, Mr. Pareto has been unable to feed and clothe his family well because of severe crop failures. He has heard about the greatness of America and has often thought about going there. However, he knows that his father feels he should stay in Italy so that he can depend on him in his old age. He also realizes that if he goes to America he will have to leave his wife and children in Italy.

Mr. Rossi, an Agent for a Steamship Company That Makes Trips to America

Mr. Rossi tries to persuade Italian men to immigrate to America. The more men that he can persuade to go to America on his company's steamship line, the more money he makes. He goes up to Mr. Pareto at the village market and tells him about the wonders of America and why he should go there. He tells him that he can obtain a job quickly in America and become a wealthy man. He knows that if Mr. Pareto goes to America he will not be able to carry his family. However, Mr. Rossi tells Mr. Pareto that he will be able to send for his family within two or three months after he arrives in America.

Questions

1. Did Mr. Rossi persuade Mr. Pareto to go to America? Why or why not?
2. If Mr. Pareto goes to America, what do you think will happen to his family?
3. If Mr. Pareto stays in Italy, how do you think he will take care of his family?
4. How do you think his wife, parents, and children will react if Mr. Pareto goes to America? Why?
5. What else can Mr. Pareto do besides stay in his Italian village or immigrate to America?

6. If you were Mr. Pareto, would you immigrate to America? Why or why not? Explain.

7. Conclude this unit by viewing and discussing a videotape or filmstrip about European immigration. See Appendix B for complete citations for videotapes, films, and filmstrips.

Valuing Activity

Many European immigrants, especially those from southern and eastern Europe, changed their names and adopted Anglo-American culture characteristics so that they could assimilate more quickly into the dominant society and experience rapid social, economic, and political mobility. Other immigrants, however, even though they were the victims of affronts by the larger society, tried to hold onto their names and ethnic culture characteristics in America. In the following selection, written in 1939, a Polish American tells why he did not want to change his name. Read the selection to your students and ask them the questions that follow the selection.

I Was Ashamed of My Name

Twenty-odd years ago I was ashamed of my Polish name and heritage. To the boys in the neighborhood I was the lone "dirty Polack." This rankled, burned, and developed in me a bitter sense of inferiority. There was no Poland . . . I was no Polack! I was American! I didn't want to be a Polack! I would not go to a Polish school! If my parents spoke to me in Polish, I would answer in English. I dreamed of going West, changing my name to Edward R. Edwards, and being American. The end of the war and the Versailles Treaty brought some consolation. Now there was a Poland! True, we didn't hear much about it, but we knew it was there. We had found peace.

In high school, a teacher who had trouble with my name started calling me Scott. Others followed suit. I tried to convince people my name wasn't Scott Kostyra. Some refused to accept the more difficult name. Mail came to my home for me addressed to Scott. My parents soundly berated me, because they considered the pseudonym an insult to them. I was in a quandary.[21]

Questions

1. What problems did Kostyra face?
2. Why do you think it was difficult for his family to accept a new name for him?
3. Why was Kostyra ashamed of his Polish name?
4. Why do you think some Americans refused to call Kostyra by his Polish name?
5. Do you feel that an individual should change his or her name under any circumstances? Why or why not? If so, under what circumstances?
6. What are some things that Kostyra could have done to solve his problems? What were probable consequences of each course of action?
7. What do you think Kostyra should have done? Why?
8. If you had been Kostyra, what would you have done? Why?
9. Have you ever been in a situation similar to the one that Kostyra was in? If so, what did you do? Why?

High School Grades

CONCEPT: Nativism

Generalization: Negative feelings toward immigrant groups emerged early in colonial America. However, American nativism did not become widespread until the late nineteenth and early twentieth centuries. It eventually led to a virtual halt to European immigration.

1. Ask the students to read Chapter 2, "Ethnic Discord and the Growth of American Nationality," in Maldwyn Allen Jones, *American Immigration;* and Chapter 1, "The Age of Confidence," in John Higham, *Strangers in the Land: Patterns of American Nativism 1860–1925;* and be able to discuss the following questions when they have finished the reading:

   a. Antiforeign attitudes were present in the early American colonies. What groups were the main victims of these negative feelings?
   b. What forms did nativism take in colonial America? What acts and laws were passed in colonial America that reflected antiforeign attitudes?

When the students have completed these readings, discuss the above questions with the class. They will discover that the Irish, French, Huguenots, Catholics, and Germans were the main targets of early antiforeign attitudes in America. Record their responses to the questions above, in summary form, on the board.

2. Ask individual students or groups of students to prepare reports on the following topics and present them to the class.

   • The Know-Nothing movement in the 1850s
   • The Chinese Exclusion Act of 1882
   • The Immigration Act of 1882, which excluded certain classes of European immigrants
   • The Immigration Restriction League, formed in 1884
   • The Foran Act of 1885
   • The Haymarket Affair, 1886
   • The lynching of eleven Italians in New Orleans, 1891
   • William Z. Ripley's *The Races of Europe*, published in 1899
   • The Dillingham Commission, which issued its report in 1911
   • The 1917 Immigration Act
   • Madison Grant, *The Passing of the Great Race in America*, published in 1916
   • The Johnson Act of 1921
   • The Johnson-Reed Act of 1924
   • The McCarran-Walter Act of 1952
   • The Immigration Act of 1965

The books by Jones and Higham, cited above, are two excellent sources for information about the above topics. When the students are sharing their reports, help them identify some causes of nativistic movements. These causes should be noted on the board and in the students' notebooks. They include anti-Catholic attitudes, fear of foreign "radicals," domestic recession and depression, the mass of new immigrants that arrived in the United States in the late 1800s and early 1900s, the belief that aliens were taking jobs away from American citizens, and the popularity of beliefs about the innate inferiority of southern and eastern European immigrants perpetuated by such writers as William Z. Ripley and the well-known naturalist, Madison Grant.

3. Heated debates took place in Congress, as well as in other public forums, about the passage of a bill that would require immigrants to pass a reading test before they could enter the United States. Two opposing views of the literacy test are found in Chapter 8 of Oscar Handlin, ed., *Immigration as a Factor in American History*. Samuel Gompers defends the test and President Woodrow Wilson opposes it. Read these two accounts to the class. Ask the students to roleplay a session of Congress in 1917 in which the bill is discussed. Different students should argue for and against the bill. After the speeches on the floor, the students should vote for or against the bill. After the voting, they should discuss why their final vote was similar to or different from the Congressional vote in 1917.

4. Anthropologists and physical scientists divided Whites into various "races" in the 1800s. William Z. Ripley and Madison Grant popularized these views and argued that southern and eastern European immigrants were innately inferior to immigrants from the northern and western parts of Europe. Ask the class to compare the views of these writers with the racial views of contemporary scientists such as Arthur R. Jensen and William Shockley.

5. Social and physical scientists blamed the new immigrants for political corruption, urban blight, crime, and large welfare rolls. Ask the students to study writings about the immigrants during the 1800s and to compare these writings with writings today about ethnic minorities such as African Americans, Mexican Americans, and Puerto Ricans. The class can discuss the ways in which the old and new criticisms are alike and different, and why they are alike and different. Oscar Handlin, *The Uprooted*, Maldwyn A. Jones, *American Immigration,* John Higham, *Strangers in the Land,* contain information and references that will help students to carry out this activity.

6. The Johnson-Reed Act of 1924 marked the end of an era in the history of American immigration because it put a virtual end to immigration and discriminated blatantly against southern and eastern European immigrants and non-White nations. Duplicate a copy of this act for the class and ask them to discuss its legal, moral, and political implications. The students can then compare the Johnson-Reed Act with the McCarran-Walter Act of 1952 and the Immigration Act of 1965. Students can also compare nativism near the turn of the century directed against southern, central, and eastern European immigrants with the nativism today that is directed against Asians and Hispanics. For example, a number of states with large Hispanic populations have passed referenda that make English the official state language. Students should also discuss the legal, political, and moral implications of the 1965 act. You can conclude this unit by asking the students to write a five- to ten-page paper on "Nativism as a Factor in American History." This activity can be correlated with English or the language arts.

Endnotes

1. Maldwyn Allen Jones, *American Immigration* (Chicago: University of Chicago Press, 1960), pp. 6–38.

2. Ibid., pp. 141–142.

3. Oscar Handlin, *The Uprooted: The Epic Story of the Great Migrations That Made the American People* (New York: Grosset and Dunlap, 1951), pp. 37–62.

4. Jones, *American Immigration*, pp. 141–142.

5. Thomas A. Bailey, *The American Pageant: A History of the Republic*, 2nd ed. (Boston: D.C. Heath and Company, 1961), p. 67.

6. John Higham, *Strangers in the Land: Patterns of American Nativism 1860–1925* (New York: Atheneum, 1972), p. 154.

7. Ibid., pp. 155–156.

8. Ibid., pp. 203–204.

9. Ibid., p. 324.

10. Luman H. Long, ed., *The World Almanac and Book of Facts*, 1970 ed. (New York: Newspaper Enterprise Association, 1969), p. 449.

11. William Greenbaum, "America in Search of a New Ideal: An Essay on the Rise of Pluralism," *Harvard Educational Review* 44 (August 1974): 411–440.

12. Nathan Glazer and Daniel P. Moynihan, *Beyond the Melting Pot: The Negroes, Puerto Ricans, Jews, Italians, and Irish of New York City*, 2nd ed. (Cambridge: The M.I.T. Press, 1970).

13. Ibid., p. vii.

14. Michael Novak, *The Rise of the Unmeltable Ethnics: Politics and Culture in the Seventies* (New York: Macmillan, 1973), pp. 64, 69.

15. Andrew M. Greeley and William C. McCready, "Does Ethnicity Matter?" *Ethnicity* 1 (April 1974): 91–108.

16. Orlando Patterson, *Ethnic Chauvinism: The Reactionary Impulse* (New York: Stein and Day, 1977).

17. Arthur Mann, *The One and the Many: Reflections on the American Identity* (Chicago: The University of Chicago Press, 1979), pp. 41–42.

18. Howard F. Stein and Robert F. Hill, *The Ethnic Imperative: Examining the New White Ethnic Movement* (University Park: The Pennsylvania State University Press, 1977).

19. Richard D. Alba, *Italian Americans: Into the Twilight of Ethnicity* (Englewood Cliffs, N.J.: Prentice-Hall, 1985).

20. Ibid.

21. *Polish American Review*, July 1939.

Annotated Bibliography

Books for Teachers

Especially Recommended

Alba, Richard D. *Italian Americans: Into the Twilight of Ethnicity.* Englewood Cliffs, N.J.: Prentice-Hall, 1985.

> *This sociological and historical study of the experiences of Italians in the United States is written from an assimilationist perspective. The author emphasizes how European ethnic groups, including the Italians, are becoming part of the American mainstream and consequently entering the "twilight" of ethnicity.*

Bodnar, John. *The Transplanted: A History of Immigrants in Urban America.* Bloomington: Indiana University Press, 1985.

In this important scholarly history, Bodnar challenges the central thesis set forth in Oscar Handlin's award-winning book, The Uprooted: The Epic Story of the Great Migrations That Made the American People *(New York: Grosset and Dunlap, 1973).*

Casey, Daniel J., and Rhodes, Robert E., *Modern Irish-American Fiction: A Reader.* Syracuse, N.Y.: Syracuse University Press. 1989.

This anthology includes a range of Irish-American writers, including F. Scott Fitzgerald, John O'Hara, Mary McCarthy, Joseph Dever, and Mary Gordon.

Cordasco, Francesco, ed. *A Dictionary of American Immigration History.* New York: Garland Publishing, 1989.

A comprehensive and informative reference book with more than 2,500 entries by social scientists that discuss diverse aspects of American immigration history. Helpful bibliographical citations are included.

Cordasco, Francesco. *The Immigrant Woman in North America: An Annotated Bibliography of Selected References.* Methuchen, N.J.: The Scarecrow Press, 1985.

This valuable reference book contains more than 1,100 annotated bibliographic sources that deal with the experiences of immigrant women in the United States. Sections include, "Autobiographies, Biographies and Reminiscences," "The Workplace and Political Encounters," and "The Family, Immigrant Child and Educational Influences."

Dinnerstein, Leonard, and Reimers, David M. *Ethnic Americans: A History of Immigration,* 3rd ed. New York: Harper and Row, 1988.

This is an excellent introduction to the history of European ethnic groups in the United States. It is well written and includes useful appendices, such as "Jewish Immigration to the United States," and "Ethnic Background of the American Population." Ethnic groups of color who voluntarily immigrated to America after 1607 are also treated in the book.

Kivisto, Peter, ed. *The Ethnic Enigma: The Salience of Ethnicity for European-Origin Ethnic Groups.* Philadelphia: The Balch Institute Press, 1989.

This book, which consists of case studies of various European-origin ethnic groups in the United States, contains an excellent theoretical overview essay on ethnicity in America by the editor.

Thernstrom, Stephan; Orlov, Ann; and Handlin, Oscar, eds. *Harvard Encyclopedia of American Ethnic Groups.* Cambridge: Harvard University Press, 1980.

This comprehensive and scholarly reference book includes historical and sociological survey discussions of more than 100 ethnic groups, including Italians, Poles, Greeks, Czechs, and Danes in the United States.

Other References

Alfonsi, Ferinando P. *Dictionary of Italian-American Poets.* New York: Peter Lang, 1989.

This reference book contains 1,000 Italian American poets, including a short biography of each, a list of his or her books, and available published criticisms that have been given of each book.

Archdeacon, Thomas J. *Becoming American: An Ethnic History.* New York: The Free Press, 1983.

This carefully researched and readable history contains informative chapters on the "old" and "new" European immigrants to the United States.

Barolini, Helen, ed. *The Dream Book: An Anthology of Writings by Italian American Women.* New York: Schocken Books, 1985.

This collection of writings by Italian-American women includes one play, prose and poetry, oral history, and fiction. This book also includes an informative introductory essay by the editor.

Battistella, Graziano, ed. *Italian Americans in the 80s: A Sociodemographic Profile.* Staten Island, NY: Center for Migration Studies, 1989.

This book is rich in detailed demographic data about Italian Americans. Cultural aspects, education, family, economic characteristics, and geographical distribution of Italian Americans are among the topics treated.

Bukowczyk, John J. *And My Children Did Know Me: A History of Polish Americans.* Bloomington: Indiana University press, 1987.

An informative and scholarly history of Poles in the United States.

Callahan, Bob, ed. Art direction by Dennis Gallagher. *The Big Book of American Irish Culture.* New York: Viking Penguin, Inc., 1987.

Illustrated with black-and-white photographs, this interesting book gives an overview of the Irish contribution to U.S. culture. F. Scott Fitzgerald, John Barrymore, and Speaker Tip O'Neill are among the Irish Americans included.

Cordasco, Francesco. *The New American Immigration: Evolving Patterns of Legal and Illegal Emigration: A Bibliography of Selected References.* New York: Garland Publishing, Inc., 1987.

A bibliographic guide to the literature on immigration that has developed since the Hart-Cellar Immigration Act of 1965. Major divisions of the book are "American Immigration before 1965: History and Background," "American Immigration after 1965: General Studies and Related References," "Illegal Immigrants in the United States," and "Miscellanea." This valuable reference book also has an informative introductory essay written by the editor.

Diner, Hasia. *Erin's Daughters in America.* Baltimore: The John Hopkins University Press, 1983.

A scholarly treatment of the Irish experience in the United States.

Dolan, Jay. *The American Catholic Experience.* Garden City, N.Y.: Doubleday and Company, 1985.

An informative treatment of the sojourn of Catholics in the United States.

Fanning, Charles, ed. *The Exiles of Erin: Nineteenth-Century Irish-American Fiction.* Notre Dame, Ind.: University of Notre Dame Press, 1989.

A useful source of fiction written by the Irish in the United States.

Femminella, Francis X., ed. *The Italians and Irish in America.* New York: The American Italian Historical Association, 1985.

The economic, political, religious, educational, family, and recreational life of the Italians and the Irish are described in this edited volume.

di Franco, Philip. *The Italian American Experience.* New York: Tom Doherty Associates, 1988.

> *This general treatment of the Italian experience in the United States includes chapters on labor, farming, sports, government and politics, the professions, and science and engineering. It includes a foreword on the "Italian American Identity" by Francis X. Femminella.*

Greene, Victor R. *American Immigrant Leaders 1800–1910: Marginality and Identity.* Baltimore: The Johns Hopkins University Press, 1987.

> *A scholarly and comparative study of leadership in these U.S. ethnic groups: the Irish, the Germans, the Norwegians and the Swedes, the Jews, the Poles, and the Italians. The author formulates generalizations about ethnic leadership in the United States.*

Hale, Frederick, ed. *Danes in North America.* Seattle: University of Washington Press, 1984.

> *This book contains a collection of letters that Danish immigrants in the United States wrote home. The letters portray their hopes, dreams, and problems in their new land. They are excellent teaching sources.*

Handlin, Oscar. *The Uprooted: The Epic Story of the Great Migrations That Made the American People.* Rev. ed. New York: Grosset and Dunlap, 1973.

> *In this landmark book, the author chronicles the story of European immigrants to the United States from their peasant life in Europe to the nativistic movements in the late nineteenth and early twentieth centuries. It was the recipient of the Pulitzer Prize in history in 1952.*

Higham, John. *Strangers in the Land: Patterns of American Nativism 1860–1925.* New York: Atheneum, 1972.

> *This is a perceptive and pioneering study of nativistic movements in U.S. society in the late nineteenth and early twentieth centuries. In this interpretive work, the author views economic events as major determinants of nativistic forces. This highly readable and copiously documented book contains a useful bibliographic essay.*

Images: A Pictorical History of Italian Americans. Staten Island: Center for Migration Studies, 1986.

> *This pictorial history of Italian Americans has color photographs and a text in both English and Italian.*

Lieberson, Stanley, and Waters, Mary C. *From Many Strands: Ethnic and Racial Groups in Contemporary America.* New York: Russell Sage Foundation, 1988.

> *One of the volumes in "The Population of the United States in the 1980s" monograph series, this volume includes rich data on White ethnic groups from the 1980 Census. "The Ethnic and Racial Composition of the United States," "Economic Attainment," and "Intermarriage" are three of the chapters.*

McCormick, E. Allen, ed. *Germans in America: Aspects of German-American Relations in the Nineteenth Century.* New York: Columbia University Press, 1983.

> *This book contains a scholarly collection of essays that discuss various aspects of the experiences of Germans in the United States in the nineteenth century.*

Miller, Kerby A. *Emigrants and Exiles: Ireland and the Irish Exodus to North America.* New York: Oxford University Press, 1985.

  This is a scholarly and important study of Ireland and the exodus of Irish immigrants to Norh America.

Moquin, Wayne, ed. *Makers of America.* 10 Volumes. Chicago: Encyclopedia Britannica Educational Corporation, 1971.

  This 10-volume documentary history of ethnic groups in the United States is an excellent source for teaching and inquiry activities.

Moskos, Charles, Jr. *Greek Americans: Struggles for Success.* Englewood Cliffs, NJ: Prentice-Hall, 1980.

  This sociological study of Greek Americans is an informative introductory source.

Olson, James S. *Catholic Immigrants in America.* Chicago: Nelson-Hall, 1987.

  This historical treatment of Catholic immigrants includes separate chapters on the Irish, the East-European, the Mediterranean, and the Hispanic Catholics. It also has a comprehensive and helpful bibliography.

Psomiades, Harry J., and Scourby, Alice, ed. With a Bibliographic Guide by John G Zenelis. *The Greek American Community in Transition.* New York: Pella Publishing Company, 1982.

  This collection of papers includes such essays as "Greek American Studies," "Three Generations of Greek Americans: A Study in Ethnicity," and "The Role of the Church in the Evolving Greek American Community." This book also includes a comprehensive and useful bibliographic guide.

Seller, Maxine. *Immigrant Women.* Philadelphia: Temple University Press, 1980.

  This is an informative and valuable reference on immigrant women.

Shapiro, Mary J. *Gateway to Liberty: The Story of the Statue of Liberty and Ellis Island.* New York: Vintage Books, 1986.

  The more than 200 photographs and illustrations in this book, as well as its text, makes it an excellent teaching resource.

Swierenga, Robert P., ed. *The Dutch in America: Immigration, Settlement, and Cultural Change.* New Brunswick, NJ: Rutgers University Press, 1985.

  The scholarly chapters in this book discuss diverse aspects of the Dutch experience in the United States, such as "Dutch Literary Culture in America 1850–1950," and "The Reformed Churches and Acculturation."

Tomasi, Lydio F., ed. *Italian Americans: New Perspectives in Italian Immigration and Ethnicity.* New York: Center for Migration Studies, 1985.

  This book contains some excellent and scholarly papers on the Italian-American experience, such as "Italian Americans and the Media: An Agenda for a More Positive Image," by Joseph Giordano, "Italian Americans in Contemporary America," by Humbert S. Nelli, and "The Search for an Italian American Identity: Continuity and Change," by Rudolph J. Vecoli.

Tynan, Daniel J., ed. *Biographical Dictionary of Contemporary Catholic America.* New York: Greenwood Press, 1989.

> *In addition to being a biographical dictionary of Catholic writers in the United States, this book contains an informative introductory essay, "The Catholic Church in Chicano Literature."*

Books for Students

Angelini, George. *Martina Navratilova: Tennis Power.* New York: Viking, 1988.

> *This book chronicles the life of the woman who changed the face of women's tennis. It follows her from her childhood in Czechoslovakia to her phenomenal success as a U.S. tennis star. (Intermediate)*

Benton, Barbara. *Ellis Island: A Pictorial History.* New York: Facts on File, 1986.

> *This book chronicles the history of Ellis Island. At one time, Ellis Island served as the principal receiving station for more than 16 million people who immigrated to the United States. (Middle School/High School)*

Bober, Natalie S. *Breaking Tradition: The Story of Louise Nevelson.* New York: Atheneum, 1984.

> *This is a biography of a remarkable woman who rose from humble beginnings in Russia to become one of the foremost sculptors of our time. (Middle School/High School)*

Costabel, Eva Deutsch. *The Pennsylvania Dutch: Craftsmen and Farmers.* New York: Atheneum, 1986.

> *The first German-speaking colonists arrived in North America in 1683 and settled in William Penn's colony of Pennsylvania. Eva Costabel introduces her readers to a typical farm family who lived during that time and to German American crafts, including quilting, pottery-making, tombstone-carving, woodworking, calligraphy, glassblowing, and gunsmithing. (Primary/Intermediate)*

di Franco, Philip. *The Italian American Experience.* New York: Tom Doherty, 1988.

> *This book includes an interesting historical overview of Italian Americans. (Middle School)*

Eubank, Nancy. *The Russians in America.* Minneapolis: Lerner, 1986.

> *This book includes an overview of the Russian experience in the United States and profiles of Russian Americans who have made important contributions to American society. (Intermediate/Middle School)*

Fisher, Leonard Everett. *The Statue of Liberty.* New York: Holiday House, 1985.

> *An interesting account of the building of the Statue of Liberty and its history as a beacon of freedom. (Intermediate)*

Franck, Irene M., and Brownstone, David M. *America's Ethnic Heritage: The Scandinavian-American Heritage.* New York: Facts on File, 1988.

> *This book provides an overview of Scandinavian immigrants from the midseventeenth century until 1920. It chronicles their experiences as they traveled from their European homeland to the United States and their experiences in the United States. Finnish settlements in Alaska, Danish Mormons in Utah, and Scandinavian*

settlements in the Midwest are described. The authors also discuss Scandinavian religious beliefs and occupations of early Scandinavian immigrants. Another book by Franck is The German-American Heritage *(Facts on File, 1988). (Middle School)*

Helgadóttir, Gudrún. *Flumbra: An Icelandic Folktale.* Minneapolis: Lerner, 1989.

This beautifully illustrated book tells a poignant tale that explains why some natural catastrophes occur. (Primary/Intermediate)

Howell, Troy. *Peter and the North Wind.* New York: Scholastic, 1989.

This Norwegian folk tale is written in simple vocabulary for beginning readers and is illustrated with full-color paintings. (Primary)

Kherdian, David. *The Road from Home: The Story of an Armenian Girl.* New York: Viking, 1989.

This Newbery Honor Book tells a young girl's story of survival and courage during 1915, when Armenians were attacked by Turkish forces. (High School)

Kuropas, Myron B. *The Ukranians in America.* Minneapolis: Lerner, 1985.

This book contains a survey of Ukranian immigration to the United States and the contributions Ukranians have made to American life. (Intermediate/Middle School)

Lavallee, Barbara. *The Snow Child.* New York: Scholastic, 1989.

This Russian folk tale describes how a girl built out of snow comes to life. (Primary)

Lawson, Don. *Geraldine Ferraro.* New York: Julian Messner, 1985.

This book is a biography of the first woman to run for vice-president on the Democratic ticket. (Middle School)

Levinson, Riki. *Watch the Stars Come Out.* Illustrated by Diane Goode. New York: Dutton, 1985.

This beautifully illustrated book tells the story of a long journey to America. A little girl and her brother are going alone to join their parents in America during the time of the great migrations. (Primary)

Magnus, Erica. *The Boy and the Devil.* Minneapolis: Lerner, 1989.

This Norwegian folktale tells the story of a boy who was able to capture the devil by tricking him. Another book by Magnus is Old Lars *(Lerner, 1985). (Primary)*

Mednikov, Vera. *Count Your Way through Russia.* Minneapolis: Carolrhoda, 1988.

Young children can use this book to learn to count in Russian. The book also contains information on the culture, history, and climate of Russia. (Primary)

Montaufier, Poupa. *One Summer at Grandmother's House.* Minneapolis: Lerner, 1989.

Full-color paintings illustrate this delightful story about a summer in the 1950s when the author went to visit her grandmother in the Alsace region of France. (Intermediate)

Parnell, Helga. *Cooking the German Way.* Minneapolis: Lerner, 1988.

This book is part of a series of cookbooks that include easy-to-cook recipes from various countries. In addition to recipes and menus, the cookbooks include information about the history and culture of people in the country. Other books in the series include Cooking the English Way, Cooking the French Way, Cooking the Greek Way, Cooking the Hungarian Way, Cooking the Italian Way, Cooking the Norwegian Way, Cooking the Polish Way, *and* Cooking the Russian Way.

Pellegrimi, Angelo. *An Immigrant Quest: American Dream.* San Francisco: North Point Press, 1986.

An immigrant who becomes a college professor chronicles his journey from Italy to the Pacific Northwest and his life in the United States. (High School)

Petersen, Peter L. *The Danes in America.* Minneapolis: Lerner, 1987.

The Danish-American way of life and the contributions of the Danes to their new country are discussed in this book. (Intermediate/Middle School)

Tenzythoff, Gerrit J. *The Dutch in America.* Minneapolis: Lerner, 1985.

An overview of Dutch immigration to the United States and the contributions of the Dutch to various areas of American life are included in this book. (Intermediate/ Middle School)

Chapter 9

Jewish Americans

Concepts, Strategies, and Materials

The twentieth-century ideals of America have been the ideals of the Jew for more than twenty centuries.

—Louis D. Brandeis

Introduction

About 5.8 million Jewish Americans live in the United States, comprising about 2.4% of its population.[1] They constitute a religious, cultural, and ethnic minority group that originated in the land that is today Israel. They are a diverse group, living in each of the fifty states, with about two-thirds in the Northeast and North Central parts of the country. However, a shift to the South and West, following general population trends, is evident.[2]

Jewish Americans have been an integral part of American history since the days of Columbus and have contributed significantly in the arts and sciences, medicine, education, law, and other fields. American culture has been enriched by the works of Jewish novelists, playwrights, and critics who write from a Jewish perspective and on Jewish themes.[3]

Yet the role of Jews in U.S. history clearly transcends a mere listing of their contributions. Their presence is intimately intertwined with many fundamental themes and concepts that have characterized U.S. history, such as religious freedom, the achievement of civic equality, and the struggle of a group to maintain its ethnic identity while assimilating into the U.S. mainstream.

This chapter is contributed by Jerome L. Ruderman, Department Head, Social Studies, Frankford High School, Philadelphia, Pennsylvania. Mr. Ruderman's books include *Jews in American History: A Teacher's Guide* (1974), and *The American Experience: An Educational Guide for Teachers and Librarians* (1988).

Jewish Americans:
Historical Perspective

*Important
Dates*

1492   The Jews were expelled from Spain. Jews accompanied
              Columbus on his first voyage to America.

1654   Twenty-three Jewish immigrants from Brazil arrived in
              New Amsterdam. They established the first Jewish settle-
              ment in North America.

1730   The first synagogue in North America was completed in
              New Amsterdam.

1740   An act of Parliament exempted Jews from saying the
              words, "on the true faith of a Christian," in the naturaliza-
              tion oath, enabling them to become citizens in English
              colonies.

1774   Francis Salvador was elected to the South Carolina Pro-
              vincial Congress. He was the only Jewish delegate to any
              representative assembly in colonial times.

1786   The Virginia Statute of Religious Freedom was passed. It
              guaranteed religious equality to Jews in Virginia and
              became a model for other colonies.

1787   The Constitution of the United States barred religious
              tests for federal office.

1791   The First Amendment of the Bill of Rights prohibited
              congressional establishment of religion in the United
              States.

1809   Jacob Henry, a Jew, was allowed to retain his seat in the
              North Carolina House of Commons despite a state law
              limiting office holding to Protestants.

1815   The Congress of Vienna nullified the rights of German
              Jews, causing thousands to immigrate to the United
              States.

1826   The Maryland "Jew Bill" was passed. It ended religious
              tests against Jews in Maryland.

1848   The Revolution of 1848 in Europe caused many German
              Jews to come to America as political refugees.

1862   Rabbis were permitted to serve as U.S. military chaplains.
              General Ulysses S. Grant issued General Order No. 11,
              which expelled Jews as a class from the Department of
              the Tennessee.

Important Dates	
1868	The Fourteenth Amendment was adopted. Subsequent court decisions broadened it to guarantee religious equality in the states.
1877	Joseph Seligman, a Jewish manufacturer, and his family, were excluded from a resort hotel, foreshadowing the pattern anti-Semitism was to take in the United States.
1881–82	Discriminatory legislation and *pogroms* (government-sponsored attacks) against Russia's Jews spurred wholesale immigration to America.
1885	The Pittsburgh Platform was enunciated by Reform Jews. It stated their principles and beliefs.
1886	The Jewish Theological Seminary was founded by leaders of Conservative Judaism.
1914	Louis D. Brandeis became the leader of the American Zionist movement.
1915	Leo Frank, a Jew, was lynched in Georgia, a result of anti-Semitic hatred.
1924	The Johnson-Reed National Origins Quota Act drastically curtailed Jewish immigration to the United States.
1930–40	Anti-Semitism, stimulated by Nazi propaganda, reached alarming levels in the United States.
1939–46	Six million Jews were killed by the Nazis during World War II.
1948	President Harry S Truman recognized the State of Israel immediately after its establishment.
1967	Jewish Americans strongly supported Israel during the Six Day War.
1973	Jewish Americans contributed huge sums of money to Israel when the Yom Kippur War broke out.
1976	Jews throughout the world took pride in the heroic Israeli commando raid on Entebbe airfield in Uganda. This action freed hostages held by Palestinian terrorists.
1979	Egypt's President Anwar el-Sadat and Israel's Premier Menachem Begin signed a peace treaty, together with President Carter, in a White House ceremony a few months after a thirteen-day conference at Camp David.
1981	Pressure generated by the New Right and Christian Right troubled many Jewish Americans as the "moral majority" and similar groups challenged the concept of separation of church and state.

Important Dates	
1982	Many Jewish Americans were privately critical of Israel's military thrust into Lebanon to end PLO terrorism, which thus reflected a shift from unquestioned support to criticism of the Begin government.
1985	American Jews were shocked by President Reagan's visit to a military cemetery in Bitburg, Germany, which contains the graves of forty-seven members of the Waffen SS (Hitler's armed elite guard).
1989	Jewish groups object to a Carmelite convent on the site of the Auschwitz death camp because its presence detracts from the camp's significance as the central symbol of Nazi genocide against the Jews during World War II.
	American Jews expressed concern over a shift in the State Department's attitude toward Jewish immigration from the Soviet Union.

Historical Roots

Jewish history, from Biblical times to the settlement of the first Jews in America, is a vast, complicated story, woven into nearly 4,000 years of Western civilization. In the year 70 A.D., conquering Romans crushed the Jewish state in Palestine, driving most, but not all, of its inhabitants into exile. Many fled to Babylonia, where they established a community that soon outshone Palestine as a center of Jewish life. By the ninth century, the hub of the Jewish world had shifted to Spain, where cooperative attitudes of the Moors encouraged a golden age of Jewish scholarship, literature, and science. It lasted until the thirteenth century, when Christian brutality against Jews replaced the tolerant Moorish rule. Entire Jewish communities were decimated, and countless numbers of Jews were forced or frightened into the Catholic church. Many professed Christianity but secretly adhered to Judaism. They were derisively referred to by the Spanish as *Marranos* (pigs). In 1492, the Spanish monarchs expelled the entire Jewish community. Nearly 150,000 Jews left Spain. A few made their way to America, where they laid the foundations of the Jewish community in America, which in time was to become the largest Jewish population in the world. In 1989 approximately 32% of the world's Jews lived in the United States, compared with 21% in Israel.[4]

The earliest Jews (*Marranos*) to reach America arrived with Christopher Columbus in 1492. By the sixteenth century, *Marranos* were prominent in Portuguese Brazil, particularly in the city of Recife. In 1630, that city fell to the liberal Dutch, and *Marranos* joyfully abandoned the mask of Christianity. In 1654, when the Portuguese reconquered the city, they gave Jews the choice of baptism or exile. Most chose exile. Twenty-three of them found their way to the Dutch colony of New Amsterdam. Since then, Jewish immigration to the United States has been nearly continuous. The exact number in recent years is difficult to determine because a Jewish category is not included in the U.S. Census nor in the records of the U.S. Immigration and Naturalization Service. A clue may be found in the records of the Hebrew Immigrant Aid Society, which alone helped more than 137,000 Jewish immigrants between the years 1975 and 1988.[5]

The Colonies

In New Amsterdam, Governor Peter Stuyvesant wished to expel the Jews, but the Dutch West India Company disagreed. He was ordered to permit them to remain as long as they did not become a burden on the colony. However, Stuyvesant confined them to homes in a narrow street that came to be known as "Jews' Alley." He denied them equality with other people in New Amsterdam, even refusing them permission to build a synagogue. The Jews, nonetheless, formed a congregation (1656) and worshipped in private homes. With the transfer of power to the British in 1664 their status gradually improved. A synagogue was permitted; it was completed in 1730. Ten years later, Parliament exempted Jews from saying the words, "upon the true faith of a Christian," in the oath required for naturalization in the English colonies.

Jews were welcomed in other colonies such as Rhode Island, Pennsylvania, Georgia, and South Carolina. There, under the enlightened leadership of men like Roger Williams, William Penn, James Oglethorpe, and John Locke, Jewish communities were established. But even in these colonies, Jewish participation in civic life was limited. Throughout the entire colonial period only one Jew, Francis Salvador of South Carolina, was elected (1774) to a representative congress or assembly. Nonetheless, Jews slowly gained the rights of domicile, trade, and religious organization. Where restrictions against them existed, they were usually ignored.

In some colonies, however, Jews were barred altogether. No Jewish community developed in Massachusetts, for example, until after the American Revolution. Virginia and Maryland, too, were unfriendly to Jews. Maryland was actually one of the last states to lift restrictions against Jews (1826).

Biblical Influence

Ironically, though few Jews lived in New England, Jewish influence there was pervasive and penetrating. The Puritan theocracy was modeled after that of ancient Israel, its early legal codes were patterned after the Law of Moses, and daily life and religious practices were influenced by the Hebrew Bible and the Judaic tradition. In New England, as was true throughout the colonies, there was considerable interest in the Hebrew language. Intelligent laymen studied it and frequently assembled collections of Hebraica. At Harvard and Yale, proficiency in Hebrew was required for graduation. In the eighteenth century the New England clergy, often in the forefront of the drive for independence, frequently referred to the democratic principles in the Hebrew Bible, as did political pamphleteers like Thomas Paine. In their hands it became a political, as well as a religious, text.

The American Revolution

At the outbreak of the Revolution, Jewish Americans numbered about 2,000 of a total population of 2 million. Many were merchants and traders. Others were doctors, manual laborers, candlemakers, watchmakers, shoemakers, silversmiths, wigmakers, bakers, or butchers. Like other colonists, Jews participated in a wide range of professions and occupations. The notion of Jews as a homogeneous population was as erroneous then as it is today.

When fighting broke out, most Jews participated in the struggle for independence, even those of the merchant-shipowner class, whose commercial interests were in England. A few Jews were loyalists, but the majority participated as enlisted men and officers in the American army. Bernard Gratz of Philadelphia and other Jewish merchants signed nonimportation agreements. Aaron Lopez of Newport donated much of his personal fortune to the Continental cause. He and other shipowners outfitted their vessels with cannons and dispatched them against British ships. In Philadelphia, Haym Salomon was undoubtedly the most competent bill broker in America. As Broker to the Office of Finance, he sold bills of exchange and government notes for the highest possible prices and the lowest commissions. His son and the sons and grandsons of numerous Jews of the Revolutionary period served in the War of 1812.

Uriah Phillips Levy is perhaps the best known of these men. He ultimately reached the rank of Commodore in the U.S. Navy, despite a lifetime struggle to overcome anti-Semitism. Levy is best remembered for his crusade to end corporal punishment in the navy and for preserving Thomas Jefferson's home, Monticello, as a national shrine.

A result of the Revolution was that the colonists were no longer subjects of a king, but enfranchised citizens of their own country. Important as that was for the colonists in general, it was even more important for the Jews because it legitimized the rights and privileges they had won. It was the first time in the history of Western civilization that they had been a legitimate part of the body politic, no longer excluded from the civic life of the community because of their religion. This transformation was eloquently expressed in 1790 by George Washington in a letter to the Jews of Newport, Rhode Island, in which he wrote "happily the government of the United States, which gives to bigotry no sanction, to persecution no assistance, requires only that they who live under its protection should demean themselves as good citizens."

Equality in the States

Constitutional guarantees of freedom of religion implicit in the Revolution were not automatically or universally guaranteed by the federal Constitution. Its protections were limited to suffrage and office-holding at the federal level. The states were as free as ever to impose religious tests that, in some cases, remained on the statute books long after the adoption of the Constitution. In Pennsylvania, state office-holding was limited to Christians; in New Jersey and North Carolina, it was restricted to Protestants. Not until the adoption of the Fourteenth Amendment in 1868 was a significant attempt made to limit the power of the states in this regard. Even then, it was many years before the Supreme Court wrote interpretations of the Fourteenth Amendment supporting the rights of religious minorities in the states. Thus, the struggle for full equality was thrown back to the states. In Virginia, Jefferson and Madison led the way with the Virginia Statute of Religious Freedom in 1786. By 1790, New York, Georgia, Pennsylvania, and South Carolina, states with established Jewish communities, had passed similar laws. Others tarried well into the nineteenth century.

In North Carolina in 1809, Jacob Henry, a Jew, was reelected to the state House of Commons. He was challenged on the grounds that his election violated a state requirement that all public officials be Protestant and accept the divine authority of the Christian Bible. After a spirited defense, he was permitted to retain his seat, but only by a legal subterfuge. The law itself was not changed regarding Jewish Americans until 1868, when the North Carolina state constitution, which also enfranchised Blacks, was adopted by a Reconstruction government.

Similarly, the Maryland Constitution of 1776 required "a declaration of belief in the Christian religion" in order to hold state office. A protracted struggle by Maryland Jews, with the aid of a gentile, Thomas Kennedy, who was a member of the state legislature, resulted in the Maryland "Jew Bill" in 1826. It provided that any citizen could qualify for any public office by declaring "his belief in a future state of rewards and punishments." Though still a religious test of sorts, it was not specifically aimed at Jews. By the end of the Jacksonian period, the few religious disabilities that remained were largely unenforced and a friendly attitude toward Jewish Americans prevailed.

German-Jewish Immigration

Though German Jews had predominated in the colonies since 1728, the years from 1820 to 1880 are considered the period of German-Jewish immigration. During those sixty years, about 200,000 Jews came to America from Germany and neighboring countries, where for centuries Jews had been vulnerable to recurring outbursts of mass hysteria and violence by the surrounding Christian population. Often confined to ghettos and forbidden to enter many skilled trades and farming, Jews had developed a close-knit society that emphasized study of the Bible and frequently turned to trade and commerce. In the eighteenth century, the Enlightenment and the reforms of Napoleon battered down their civic disabilities, and the Jews entered the secular worlds of France and Germany. However, their emancipation was short-lived. In 1815, the Congress of Vienna sought to nullify their newly won rights, causing thousands to depart for America. They were actually part of an exodus of about 5 million Germans who sought political freedom and economic opportunity in the United States. After the Revolution of 1848, the number who came as political refugees increased.

The German immigrants spread out across the country, though most settled in the Ohio and Mississippi valleys. Many of them, Christians as well as Jews, turned to peddling, an occupation that required no training and little capital and that served the needs of rural and frontier America. From these humble beginnings, some peddlers managed to accumulate enough capital to acquire a cart, then a horse and wagon, and finally a small store, which in some cases evolved into modern department stores. Some stores founded by Jewish peddlers are Bamberger's, Bloomingdale's, Filene's, Magnin's, Gimbel's, and Macy's (a dry goods business that Isidor and Nathan Straus turned into a giant department store). Other Jewish immigrants remained in the growing cities of the East and were frequently engaged in tailoring or shoemaking or dealt in secondhand clothing or dry goods.

A small number of Jews went West and became part of the saga of the frontier as buffalo hunters, ranchers, newspaper men, mayors (Galveston, Texas, had a Jewish mayor in 1850), miners, explorers, traders, artists, and photographers. Solomon Nunes Carvalho was a prominent Jewish artist and photographer. He traveled with John Charles Fremont. Levi Strauss manufactured strong, copper-riveted denim trousers (Levi's) for the gold miners in California. By the mid-1850s, San Francisco had about 4,000 Jews.

The German-Jewish community in the nineteenth century was characterized by the multitude and variety of voluntary, self-help organizations that it established to meet a variety of social and political needs. A "Hebrew Benevolent Society" usually served many purposes in small communities. In larger cities, specific societies met specific needs, such as care of orphans or the poor. Five Jewish fraternal orders were born. The best known was B'nai B'rith in 1843. The Young Men's Hebrew Association (YMHA) was established at this time, as were a number of Jewish hospitals that provided kosher food to Jewish patients and training for Jewish medical students. During the Civil War, they admitted so many non-Jewish casualties that they became nonsectarian and have remained so to the present day.

Early attempts at Jewish schools met with little success. As public schools became popular, Jewish students attended them during the day and Jewish religious schools in the late afternoon or on Saturday or Sunday morning. This is still the most common form of Jewish education in the United States.

In 1843, the Reverand Isaac Leeser of Philadelphia founded a monthly publication. *The Occident.* Other Jewish periodicals appeared; the most important was that of Rabbi Isaac Mayer Wise, an outstanding Jewish leader and the father of Reform Judaism in America.

Reform Judaism

Most German Jews established their own congregations rather than join the existing Spanish congregations whose ritual and liturgy differed somewhat from their own. Consequently, between 1850 and 1870 the number of congregations in America rose from 37 to 189.

Among the new congregations, demands were soon heard for shorter religious services, elimination of Sabbath observance, the use of English rather than Hebrew for prayer, modified dietary laws, and elimination of many traditional restrictions that had been part of Jewish tradition for centuries. Their demands were answered by the Reform movement, which, having begun in Germany, found fertile ground in America. Its leader, Rabbi Isaac Mayer Wise, preached that Judaism must adapt to the American environment or it would die. Notwithstanding the bitter opposition of traditionalists, who felt it wrong to tamper with sacred law and tradition, the new movement had become so much a part of Jewish life in America by 1885 that a panel of Reform rabbis met in Pittsburgh to codify their principles and beliefs. While adhering to the moral teachings of Judaism, the "Pittsburgh Platform" rejected traditional practices "not adapted to the views and habits of modern civilization."

The Civil War

Before and during the Civil War, Judaism took no common position on the question of slavery. Then, as now, individual Jews and congregations were entirely free of hierarchical control. Pronouncements by individuals, even rabbis, represented no more than their personal opinions, which varied from those of fanatical abolitionists like Michael Heilprin of Philadelphia to champions of slavery like Judah P. Benjamin, Secretary of State in the Confederate government and an intimate and influential adviser of Jefferson Davis.

In general, geography determined the allegiance of American Jews, whose attitudes toward slavery reflected the culture in which they lived. A large proportion of southern Jews, native to the soil and steeped in its traditions, embraced the Confederate cause promptly and enthusiastically. In the North, many Jews were recent immigrants from Germany whose experience with persecution usually pitted them against slavery. When the fighting broke out, Jews in the North and South flocked to their respective colors. More than 6,000 Jewish soldiers and officers served in the Union forces, and several thousand Jews fought for the Confederacy, including twenty-four known staff officers.

Of greater significance than the number of Jewish participants in the war was the growth of anti-Semitism during this period. Though anti-Semitism had been present in American society since 1654, when the first Jews arrived in New Amsterdam, it was not until the Civil War that it became a national issue. The first incident occurred early in the war as Jewish soldiers in the Union army sought to have rabbis ordained as military chaplains. A furor of protest ensued as certain Protestant groups objected. In December 1861, the Reverend Arnold Fischel visited President Lincoln, who rectified the injustice.

But anti-Semitism would not be stilled. In December 1862, Ulysses S. Grant issued General Order No. 11. It expelled "the Jews, as a class" from the Department of the Tennessee without trial or hearing (The Department of the Tennessee was the district controlled by Grant's armies.) Violators would be jailed until they could be deported as prisoners. Jews sent letters and telegrams to Jewish leaders all over the country. Cesar Kaskel, one of those deported, visited President Lincoln in Washington to protest. Lincoln was sympathetic. He directed Grant to cancel the infamous order.

The press of the country was divided. Newspapers supporting the administration generally defended Grant. Some printed anti-Jewish invective previously unheard in America. The *New York Times* condemned the order as "one of the deepest sensations of the war." Jewish Americans were stunned when the Senate and House of Representatives failed to pass resolutions castigating Grant's action. Partisan arguments in both houses obscured the moral and legal aspects of the matter. Grant never apologized for the order, but as president he displayed no antagonism toward Jewish Americans. Rather, he supported Jewish causes on a number of occasions and appointed Jews to public office.

In the Confederacy, verbal attacks against Jews were widespread. Jews were frequently accused of speculating in all manner of merchandise, thereby causing the horrendous wartime inflation that paralyzed the South. A Jewish stereotype became the Confederacy's scapegoat, whereas the real causes of inflation, insufficient industrial base, heavy wartime demands on industry, and a successful Union blockade, were ignored.

Postwar Anti-Semitism

The years following the Civil War witnessed the emergence of the chief forms of anti-Semitism that Jewish Americans have had to contend with: discrimination in certain professions and occupations and exclusion from certain residential areas, social clubs, fashionable resorts, private schools, and universities, particularly medical schools. Such anti-Semitic discrimination became more striking in the 1920s, 1930s, and 1940s.

As early as 1867, attempts by a number of insurance companies to deny Jews fire insurance became a public issue. Ten years later, Joseph Seligman, an eminent Jewish clothing manufacturer and his family, were excluded from a fashionable hotel in Saratoga, New York. At about the same time, the president of the Long Island Railroad declared, "We do not like Jews as a class." These incidents and the pattern of discrimination they foreshadowed must be viewed against a background of the improved social and economic status of Jews in America. By 1877, most Jews had left the ranks of the working-class. But their rapid rise from humble origins made them abhorrent to high society. Moreover, thousands of eastern European Jews began immigrating to America after 1880. Their foreignness undoubtedly stimulated nativist tendencies and added to the determination of the White Anglo-Saxon Protestants in America to exclude all Jews from their ranks.

Although anti-Semitism has never been an instrument of governmental policy in the United States, as has been the case in Europe, and though violence has never been a serious problem for Jewish Americans—even Grant's order produced no physical violence against them—the pattern of bigotry and hatred that characterized the post–Civil War years did lead to the Georgia lynching in 1915 of a Jew named Leo Frank.

Conservative and Orthodox Judaism

By 1885, Reform Judaism had deviated drastically from received Jewish tradition. Even before that year, traditionalists, alarmed at its growing strength, had organized a countermovement that became known as Conservative Judaism. By 1886, it was strong enough to found the Jewish Theological Seminary in New York City. Though it made some concessions to the modern world, Conservative Judaism remained faithful to the core of Jewish law and ancestral traditions.

The early organizational efforts of Conservative Judaism were unimpressive, but with the arrival of one-half million Orthodox eastern-European Jews by the end of the century, its prospects improved greatly. To many of the American-born children of the Orthodox, the Conservative movement offered an attractive compromise between their middle-class desire for social integration and their attachment to traditional Jewish culture. In 1901, Jewish philanthropists financed the reorganization of the Jewish Theological Seminary, which soon began graduating American-trained rabbis to satisfy the flourishing Conservative movement.

But it was Orthodox Judaism that benefited most from the immigration of eastern European Jews. By 1900, most of the 850 congregations in the United States were Orthodox. Two years later, the Union of Orthodox Rabbis was organized to "place Orthodox Judaism in America on a firm basis." One of the educational institutions it supported became the nucleus of Yeshiva University.

Despite the growth of both the Reform and Conservative movements, Orthodox Judaism has maintained a significant place in the American-Jewish community. Its numbers were augmented after World War I with the influx of thousands of Orthodox Jews from eastern Europe, many of whom settled in New York City.

The New Immigration

Between 1881 and 1924, more than 2 million Jews left eastern Europe because of anti-Jewish legislation and *pogroms* (government-sponsored attacks) against them. In some years, they came to the United States at the rate of more than 100,000 per year. The vast majority, as was true of other immigrant groups, settled in the northeastern states, particularly in the port cities of New York, Boston, Philadelphia, and Baltimore. Others crowded into the great cities of the Midwest. The Jews moved into densely populated ethnic neighborhoods such as New York's Lower East Side, South Philadelphia, or Chicago's West Side. Data from 1908 to 1924 indicate that only 5% of Jews arriving in the United States returned to Europe, compared to 33% of the general immigration.[6] Many found work in the new ready-to-wear clothing industry. They were attracted to it, not because of an inherent proclivity for tailoring, but because of the constant demand for cheap labor and the fact that many had had garment experience in Europe. Working conditions were deplorable. The highly competitive "contract system" and the sweatshops it generated regularly exploited the workers. The sweatshops were dark, airless, unsanitary firetraps in which whole families often worked to meet production quotas. Tuberculosis and other diseases were rampant. Laborers worked from 4:00 A.M. to 10:00 P.M. Men earned $6 to $10 a week; women and children much less.

Such conditions led to the formation in 1888 of the United Hebrew Trades in New York. It was the first organization to introduce Jewish immigrants to the trade union movement. After the turn of the century, Jewish clothing workers organized the powerful International Ladies' Garment Workers Union and the Amalgamated Clothing Workers of America. In 1911, a tragic fire at the Triangle Shirtwaist Factory in New York City underscored the need for better working conditions in the industry. Over the years, the International and the Amalgamated improved conditions and benefits and broke new ground in employer-employee relations. Since the end of World War I there has been a steady exodus of Jewish workers from the garment industry, but the legacy of the once largely Jewish unions remains an important chapter in the history of American labor.

Yiddish

Yiddish was the daily language of most of the eastern European Jews. Hebrew, the holy tongue, was reserved for prayer and study of the Bible. Though both use the Hebrew alphabet and are written from right to left, they are not the same. Yiddish is similar to German; Hebrew is a Semitic language.

Daily newspapers in Yiddish appeared in several American cities, most notably in New York. They taught the immigrants American history and civics in the language they understood best. Many read Yiddish fiction in America. The stories of Sholom Aleichem, one of the better known Yiddish writers, inspired the hit Broadway musical *Fiddler on the Roof.* Yiddish theater, too, flourished and attained a high literary and dramatic level, producing a host of Yiddish dramatists. But the flowering of Yiddish was a phenomenon of the immigrant generation. By mid-twentieth century, it had fallen into disuse. Gifted writers like Waldo Frank, Ben Hecht, Ludwig Lewisohn, Michael Gold, and Abraham Cahan wrote about the Yiddish experience in English. The stories of one contemporary Yiddish writer, Isaac Bashevis Singer, are enjoyed in their English translations. Singer was awarded the Nobel Prize for Literature in 1978.

Courses in Yiddish are offered in universities and adult education programs today in an attempt to preserve and revitalize Yiddish culture. The National Yiddish Book Center, founded in 1980, oversees the recovery, collection, and cataloguing of Yiddish books around the world that would otherwise be lost when their elderly owners die and the children and grandchildren, unable to read Yiddish, throw them away. The center has instituted a Yiddish library development program, a Yiddish books-on-tape program, and Yiddish musical projects.

The Interwar Period

Following World War I, America's traditional hospitality toward immigrants suddenly changed. Undoubtedly, anti-Semitic factors account in part for the series of restrictive immigration laws that, by 1924, virtually stopped Jewish immigration. In that year, the Johnson-Reed National Origins Quota Act blatantly curtailed immigration from eastern Europe, where most Jews lived, from southern Europe, and from non-White countries. Its system of national quotas remained in effect until 1965.

The prosperity of the war years enabled many Jewish Americans to move to newer, middle-class neighborhoods, foreshadowing a later exodus to the suburbs. The less affluent, often more religious Jews, tended to remain in older neighborhoods, where eastern European orthodoxy survived in its purest forms. Kosher restaurants flourished, late afternoon Jewish schools, Yiddish publications, and Orthodox synagogues were abundant. In the newer neighborhoods, indifference, even skepticism, toward Jewish ritual was a common attitude. It seemed to foreshadow the demise of Judaism in America, yet that is not what happened. Instead, most Jewish Americans felt an overriding desire to preserve their Jewish cultural identity and pass it on to their children. This can be seen in their high rate of endogamous marriage and in the growth of congregations and Jewish schools in the newer Jewish neighborhoods during these years.

By 1940, Jewish Americans had transformed themselves from a working-class to a middle-class community of commercial, white-collar, and professional people who established an excellent record of achievement in the sciences, medicine, and other fields of endeavor.

For many, education was a calculated means of social and economic improvement. But a more likely explanation of their drive for education is to be found in Jewish culture itself, which places a high priority on knowledge and learning for its own sake. Education was part of the value system that the Jewish immigrants brought with them, as well as part of the value system that sustained generations of pious Jews in their perpetual study of the Bible.

During these years, anti-Semitism assumed an ominous hue. The Ku Klux Klan reappeared. It burned fiery crosses in front of synagogues and smashed store windows of Jewish merchants. By 1925, it had more than 4 million members. In 1920, Henry Ford reprinted *The Protocols of the Elders of Zion* in his weekly newspaper, *The Dearborn Independent*. It was a clumsy fabrication, originally published in 1904 in Russia, purporting to be the minutes of a secret meeting of Jewish leaders in Prague in the last years of the nineteenth century, who plotted the overthrow of the world. Many Americans were prepared to believe it. During the Great Depression, Jewish bankers were accused of controlling world finance. A *Fortune Magazine* survey in 1936 proved conclusively that Jews played, at best, a minimal role in national and international banking, yet the myth persisted. Later, in the 1930s, as the influence of Nazism was increasingly felt in the United States, and attempts to prove that Jews were biologically inferior were imported, anti-Jewish propaganda intensified. Hatemongers like Father Charles E. Coughlin, the Detroit "radio priest," revived the myth of a Jewish take-over of the world. But they made little headway in the United States, and with the end of World War II, when the full dimensions of the Nazi holocaust were revealed, anti-Semitism ebbed to its lowest level in years. A 1981 public opinion poll showed anti-Semitism in the United States had declined significantly during a seventeen-year period and that stereotyping of Jews by non-Jews was at an all-time low.[7]

Zionism

The two most important events in the history of the Jewish people since their dispersion 2,000 years ago have been the Nazi holocaust and the creation of the State of Israel in 1948. Modern political Zionism, as the proposal for the return of the Jewish people to Zion (Palestine) is known, is considered to have begun in 1897, when Theodore Herzl convened the first Zionist Congress in Basle, Switzerland. The Zionist movement in the United States drew its greatest support from the eastern-European Jewish immigrants. A major factor in its growth was the emergence of Louis D. Brandeis as its leader, a role he held at the time of his appointment as associate justice of the U.S. Supreme Court in 1916. Yet, it was the Nazi holocaust that brought the Zionist goal to fruition.

Six million of Europe's Jews and five million other people were killed by the Nazis in World War II. The majority were systematically murdered in specially built death camps. The commander of Auschwitz estimated that two and one-half million victims were executed at that camp alone, and another one-half million died there of starvation and disease. Had it not been for America's restrictive immigration laws during these years, many lives could have been saved. Only a pitifully small number of Jewish refugees reached the United States in the 1930s. The best known was Albert Einstein. Ships carrying refugees from Germany were actually turned away from American shores and sent back to the Nazi crematoria. The consistent refusal of the United States and other Western nations to accept Jewish refugees led to the near fanatical determination of Zionists the world over to reestablish a homeland in Palestine as a haven for persecuted Jews from any land. It also accounts for the passionate support of contemporary Jews for Israel. After the war, when the culpability of the Western nations in not accepting more refugees became evident, the general public endorsed the Zionist program. When the State of Israel was proclaimed, President Harry S Truman recognized the new nation immediately. Though few Jewish Americans have moved to Israel, their emotional attachment to their homeland remains undiminished, as witnessed by their large outpouring of support during the Six Day War in 1967 and the Yom Kippur War in 1973. Nonetheless, Jewish Americans had mixed feelings about Israel's military push into Lebanon in 1982 to end PLO terrorism and were unwilling blindly to support the Begin government. Today, even though they feel discomfort over Israel's response to the *intifada* (Palestinian uprising on the West Bank), there has been no broad-based decline in pro-Israel feeling.

Jewish Americans Today

Today, Jewish Americans are enjoying another "golden age." Yet, as notable as their gains have been, there are a few important qualifications to be made. A sizable Jewish working-class population still exists in New York City. There and in other American cities, substantial numbers of Jews still live in poverty. A 1984 study by the Federation of Jewish Agencies of Greater Philadelphia revealed that more than 27% of Jewish families in that area have annual incomes of less than \$15,000 and 7%, less than \$5,000 a year.

Until the early 1970s few Jews occupied positions of genuine power in America's largest corporations. However, in 1982 a study of Jews on corporate boards and Jews listed in *Who's Who* found no evidence of gross anti-Semitism. Another study, commissioned by the American Jewish Committee in the mid-1980s, concluded that today there is no significant climate of corporate discrimination against Jewish executives.[8]

The changed corporate environment for Jewish Americans was dramatically symbolized by the appointment in 1973 of Irving Shapiro, the Yiddish-speaking son of a poor Lithuanian Jewish immigrant, as chairman and chief executive officer of E. I. du Pont de Nemours and Company.[9]

Most Jews live in or near big cities, are middle-class, and are self-employed or in the professions. Postwar prosperity and the end of educational quotas and social barriers after World War II opened up opportunities for Jews. A large number entered the academic world. The proportion of Jewish students and Jewish teachers in colleges and in graduate and professional schools is much higher than that of the general population. By the 1970s, more than 80% of college-age Jews attended college, and 71% of all Jews between the ages of twenty-five and twenty-nine had college degrees. By 1970, more than 10% of American professors were Jewish. In the most prestigious universities, the proportion reached 30%.[10]

Even more symbolic of Jewish acceptance is the explosive growth in the number of Jewish-studies programs in American colleges and universities. Today more than 300 offer courses in Judaic studies, at least 40 have Jewish-studies majors, and 27 offer graduate degrees. It is interesting that a number of these institutions have a relatively small Jewish enrollment.[11]

In political life, Jewish Americans have traditionally occupied a left-of-center position and have supported Democratic Party candidates more frequently than all other White ethnic or religious groups.[12] Since the early 1970s, as the American political center has moved right, Jews have moved accordingly, but the center of the Jewish political spectrum remains left of the national center. It is true that a somewhat larger percentage of Jews vote Republican today than when Roosevelt, Truman, and Humphrey headed the Democratic ticket, but even at these levels, two-thirds of Jewish Americans vote for Democratic candidates. In 1984, for example, the Jewish vote was approximately 70% to 30% in favor of Mondale over Reagan, and in 1988 Michael Dukakis drew an even larger percentage of Jewish votes.[13] Moreover, the Jewish Republican vote today is smaller than it was in the 1950s, when Dwight Eisenhower won 36% of the Jewish vote in 1952 and 40% in 1956. Notwithstanding a slight shift to the right, the facts remain that over the years, the level of Jewish support for Democratic candidates has far exceeded the general vote and American Jews have been dramatically more liberal than the general population.[14] Although the reasons for their liberal attitudes are unclear, their commitment to the reformist tradition, no doubt, has deep roots in the religious, economic, and political history of the Jewish people and is related to their own struggle for equality and security from persecution. It may also be a concomitant of a highly educated people as much concerned with values as with economic interest.

The generation of Jews that came of age after World War II was in the forefront of the civil-rights movement and in liberal and radical politics. Students, professors, and rabbis were especially prominent in the demonstrations, marches, sit-ins, and voter-registration campaigns of the 1960s.

Today, Jewish Americans are unquestionably more secure in American society and more willing to demonstrate, protest, and lobby in their own self-interest than ever before. Nonetheless, disturbing manifestations of bigotry and anti-Semitism by such organizations as the revived Ku Klux Klan and the American Nazi Party are cause for anxiety, as are signs of a worldwide increase in anti-Semitism.

Since the 1960's, the number of Jews allowed to leave the Soviet Union and settle in the United States or Israel has fluctuated greatly. It has varied from a high of 51,000 in 1979 to as few as 1,000 in 1984. Then, under *glasnost*, the number spurted to more than 30,000 in 1989.[15]

As it had done in the past with earlier immigrant groups, the American-Jewish community mobilized to aid the newcomers, whose adjustment was particularly difficult as they made the transition from the planned economy of the USSR to the free-market conditions of the United States. Of even greater concern, however, is the shift in U.S. government policy toward continued Jewish immigration from the Soviet Union. In 1988, under the Reagan administration, the Immigration and Naturalization Service began to deny many Soviet Jewish emigrés status as political refugees. Heretofore, they had been granted a presumption of eligibility as refugees on the basis of their collective experience during the last 70 years of Communist rule. A year later the Bush administration formalized the change, which greatly reduced the number of Soviet Jews able to come to this country. As a result, at the end of April 1989, more than 12,000 Soviet Jews were in Europe awaiting admission to the United States.[16]

Another source of Jewish immigration is the state of Israel. Since its founding in 1948, more than 300,000 Jews have left for the United States. The majority of them settled in New York and Los Angeles and have established themselves in the business, professional, and cultural life of those communities.[17] Some remain a part of the working-class but maintain the traditional immigrant dream that their children will have greater economic opportunities than they had.

Teaching Strategies

To illustrate how content related to Jewish Americans can be used to integrate the curriculum, exemplary strategies are identified for teaching these concepts at the grade levels indicated: *values* (primary grades), *anti-Semitism* (intermediate and upper grades), and *identity* (high school grades).

Primary Grades

CONCEPT: Values

Generalization: The values of Jewish Americans, like those of other ethnic minority groups, are often reflected in their literature.

1. The obligation to help the poor and needy is one dominant value of Judaism. The Bible and rabbinic literature teach that charity is not a favor to the poor, but something to which they have a right and the donor an obligation. It is a duty usually equated with righteousness or justice. Ask the class: Which is better, to give charity or to

receive it? Ask students to explain their answers and to give examples from their own experience.

2. A great Jewish philosopher, Maimonides, listed eight increasingly virtuous ways of giving charity. People are to give as follows:

a. But grudgingly.
b. Less than is fitting, but willingly.
c. Only after being asked to.
d. Before being asked to.
e. In such a way that the giver does not know to whom he or she is giving.
f. In such a way that the one who receives does not know who has given to him or her.
g. In such a way that neither the giver nor the one who receives knows the identity of the other.
h. The highest form of charity is to help the poor become self-supporting by lending them money, taking them into partnership, or giving them work, for in this way there is no loss of self-respect.

3. Put Maimonides's eight steps on the chalkboard in scrambled order (or reproduce as a handout). Ask the class to arrange them in the proper order, from least to most virtuous. Ask students to explain the order of their lists. Then show the eight steps according to Maimonides. Discuss and ask for student examples of charity at each level.

4. Tell the class that Jewish stories, like those of other people, often reflect the ideas that they think are important, that is, their values. "If Not Still Higher," a story by Isaac L. Peretz, deals with charity. It is in *The Case against the Wind and Other Stories* by I. L. Peretz (New York: Macmillan, 1975). Read or tell the story to the class and ask the questions that follow.

If Not Still Higher

The Rabbi of Nemirov disappeared every morning during High Holy Days Selichoth prayers (prayers asking for forgiveness). Some people thought he went to heaven each morning. One day a Jew from Lithuania came to town. He laughed and assured the people that no one could go to heaven while still alive. But he decided to find out for himself where the rabbi went.

Early the next morning he followed the rabbi to a nearby forest. The rabbi was dressed as a workman. He saw the rabbi chop down a small tree, cut it into sticks, make a bundle of them, and sling them over his shoulder. He then walked to a broken-down hut where a sick, old woman lived.

"Who is it?" called the woman.

"Vassili," answered the disguised rabbi, "I have wood for sale for only six cents." He entered the house without waiting for an answer. The Lithuanian stole in behind him.

"How can a poor widow afford even six cents?" asked the old woman.

"I trust you," replied the rabbi.

"And who will light the fire?" lamented the widow. "I am too weak to get up."

"I will," said the rabbi.

As he lit the fire, the rabbi recited the Selichoth prayers. The Lithuanian watched in silence. From that moment on, he became a follower of the Rabbi of Nemirov. Later, when the people would say their rabbi flew to heaven during Selichoth prayers, he would add quietly, "If not still higher!"

Questions

1. What puzzled the people of Nemirov?
2. Where did they think their rabbi went each morning during Selichoth prayers? What does this tell about their opinion of him?
3. Was it right for the Lithuanian to follow the rabbi the next day?
4. What did the Lithuanian find out? How did it influence him? Why?
5. What does the title of the story mean?
6. Why didn't the Rabbi of Nemirov give the old woman the wood for nothing? At which level of Maimonides's list does the rabbi's deed belong? Explain.
7. What important Jewish idea does the story bring out?

Intermediate and Upper Grades

CONCEPT: Anti-Semitism

Generalization: Anti-Semitism has been and remains a serious concern of most Jewish Americans.

1. Read the following letter to the class. It was written to the editor of the *Jewish Daily Forward* in 1932. It is reprinted from *A Bintel Brief*, edited by Isaac Metzker (Garden City, N.Y.: Doubleday, 1971). After reading, ask the questions that follow.

Dear Editor,

I am an immigrant from Russia, my wife is American-born, and we are both freethinkers. We have two grown children, a son and a daughter, who know they are Jews but never saw any signs of religion or holidays in our home. Even *Yom Kippur* is just another day to us. For the last twenty years we've lived among Christians and we socialize with them. Our children also go around with Gentiles.

Some time ago a Christian girl began to come to our house, seemingly to visit our daughter, but it was no secret to us that she was after our twenty-three-year-old son, with whom she was friendly. We said nothing about it, because we wouldn't have minded having her for a daughter-in-law.

Once the girl invited our son to a party at her house where all the other guests were Gentiles. They were all having a good time until one of the guests, whether in jest or earnest, began to make fun of Jews. I don't know what happened there, but I am sure they didn't mean to hurt my son, because none of them, not even his girlfriend, knew that he is Jewish. But he was insulted and told the girl so. Then he told her that he is Jewish and this was a surprise to her.

My son left the party immediately and from that day on he is changed. He began to ask questions about religion, debated with me about things that formerly hadn't interested him. He wanted to know where I was born, how many Jews there are in the world, why the religious don't eat pork, where the hatred of Jews came from, and on and on. He was not satisfied with my short answers but began to read books looking for more information. My son also berated me for not giving him a Jewish upbringing.

His Gentile girlfriend came to beg him to forgive her. She cried and explained that it was not her fault, but he didn't want to have anything to do with her because, it seems, he was deeply insulted. His head was filled with one thought, Jewishness. He found Jewish friends, he was drawn into a Zionist club and they worked on him so that he has come to me with a suggestion that I give up the business and we all go to Palestine. And since he sees that I am not about to go, he's getting ready to go alone.

At first we took it as a joke, but we see now that he's taking it very seriously. Well, my going is out of the question. I am not that crazy. But what can be done about him? I'm willing to give in to his whim. I'm sure that in Palestine he'll sober up and realize that not everyone who is Jewish must live in Palestine. My wife is carrying on terribly; what do I mean, allowing my son to travel to a wild country [where there is conflict between Arabs and Jews]? She says we should not give him the money for the trip. But our son says he will find a way to reach the Jewish Homeland.

My wife and I are very anxious to hear your opinion.

Respectfully,
A Reader*

Questions

1. How would you advise the writer of the letter? (The editor replied: "Your son is a very sensitive and thinking person. Since he is an adult you must let him go his way and do what he wants to do.")
2. Did the son overreact to the anti-Jewish insult? Explain. How else might he have reacted? How would you react if someone insulted you because of your race, religion, or ethnic group?
3. Where and how do people learn anti-Semitism (or any kind of prejudice)? What can you do to help combat it?
4. If someone in your family made anti-Semitic jokes with which you disagreed, what could you do? What would you do?

2. Ask students to prepare a short report accounting for Jewish survival after centuries of persecution in Europe. Ask them to find out what Jews did to survive (e.g., developed strong Jewish communities and families, became *Marranos*, emigrated, etc.).

3. Write to any of the following Jewish organizations to learn how they combat anti-Semitism in the United States. (Consult your telephone directory for local offices.)

American Jewish Committee, 165 East 56th Street, New York, NY 10022

American Jewish Congress, 15 East 84th Street, New York, NY 10028

Anti-Defamation League of B'nai B'rith, 823 United Nations Plaza, New York, NY 10017

*From *A Bintel Brief* by Isaac Metzker. Copyright © 1971 by Isaac Metzker. Reprinted by permission of Doubleday & Company, Inc.

National Conference of Christians and Jews, 71 Fifth Avenue, Suite 1100, New York, NY 10003

National Jewish Community Relations Advisory Council, 443 Park Avenue South, New York, NY 10016

4. Assign reports on any of the following topics:

a. The Leo Frank case in 1915 (a rare case of a Jewish lynching in the United States).
b. The revived Ku Klux Klan of the 1920s.
c. The revived Ku Klux Klan and American Nazi Party today.
d. Grant's Order No. 11, during the Civil War.
e. *The Protocols of the Elders of Zion.*
f. Nazi-inspired hate organizations in the United States during the 1930s (e.g., The German-American Bund, The Silver Shirts, The Order of '76).
g. Father Charles E. Coughlin, the Detroit radio priest.

5. Obtain a class set of *The Holocaust* by Bea Stadtler or *Never to Forget: The Jews of the Holocaust* by Milton Meltzer. (Both are listed in the student bibliography of this chapter.) After reading, discuss with the class how anti-Semitism led to the Nazi holocaust. Ask: Could it happen again? Could a holocaust happen in the United States? To minority groups other than Jews? Why or why not?

6. Ask students to compare anti-Semitism to racism and other forms of discrimination and prejudice in the United States. Ask what can be done to combat them.

7. Assign research reports about anti-Semitism in the United States in any of the following periods:

a. Colonial
b. 1776–1860
c. 1860–1924
d. 1924–1948
e. 1948–Present

Valuing Activity

Read the following story to the class and ask the questions that follow.

Mr. Cohen and the Christmas Tree

Mr. and Mrs. Cohen live in Chicago where Mr. Cohen owns a small business. The Jewish religion is an important part of their family life. They are members of a synagogue and attend religious services every week. They observe Jewish holidays and customs, and Mrs. Cohen keeps a traditional Kosher home and lights Sabbath candles every Friday evening. Their only son is a college professor. His wife is Jewish but she is from a nonreligious background. They do not follow the Jewish religion closely. They have two children, a girl, eight, and a son, four. They live in a suburb not far from Mr. and Mrs. Cohen.

Last Christmas the Cohens were in their son's neighborhood and dropped in for a surprise visit. When they entered the living room they saw their son trimming a Christmas tree and his two children helping him. Mr. Cohen was furious. His two grandchildren greeted him with "Merry Christmas."

Mr. Cohen did not answer. He did not even take off his coat. He looked at his son and said, "Jews do not have Christmas trees." He took his wife by the arm and they turned to leave. Their son and daughter-in-law begged them to stay, but Mr. Cohen would not change his mind. Mrs. Cohen was confused. She felt her place was with her husband and returned home with him.

Mr. Cohen's son says he had the Christmas tree only for the sake of his children, so they would not feel different from their non-Jewish friends. He assured his father the Christmas tree had nothing to do with religion. He did not consider it wrong having a Christmas tree and felt his father had no right to be angry about it.

Mr. Cohen says his grandchildren are different from Christian children and should feel the difference. He argues that Jews and Gentiles should observe national American holidays, but Christmas is the most important religious holiday of the Christians, and Jews have nothing to do with it. They should not have Christmas trees.

He refuses to visit his son's home and Mrs. Cohen cannot convince him to change his mind.

Questions

1. Who is right, Mr. Cohen or his son?
2. Do you think Mr. Cohen is being unfair to his wife, his son, his daughter-in-law, his grandchildren?
3. What alternatives are open to Mr. Cohen? To his son?
4. Do you think Mr. Cohen's son should be concerned that his children feel that they are different from other children?
5. Do you think Christians should send or expect to receive Christmas cards from their Jewish friends? Justify your answer.

High School Grades

CONCEPT: Identity

Generalization: Jewish Americans have become highly assimilated in American society, yet many maintain a strong Jewish identity that they are anxious to perserve and transmit to their children.

1. Jewish Americans are frequently referred to as American Jews. This reversal of noun and adjective is generally not true of other ethnic minority groups. Ask students to explain the difference and tell its significance. Have students ask a sample of Jewish Americans which they prefer. Have them report their findings to the class.

2. Ask the class: "Are the Jews a nation, an ethnic group, a religious minority, a people, a race, all of these, some of these, or none of these?" (The answer is, "some of these." Jews are not a race.) Tell the class that the government of Israel in 1958 established a special committee to provide an answer to the perplexing question, "Who is a Jew?" The results were inconclusive. Have students conduct a survey of their own to see if they can provide an answer. Ask if other ethnic minority groups have trouble defining themselves. Why? Why not?

3. Have students read and report on a book about Jews by a Jewish-American author. Reports should tell how the individuals or families they read about reconcile their desire to become Americanized with the desire to preserve their Jewish heritage. Some Jewish authors are as follows:

Sholom Aleichem	Bernard Malamud
Mary Antin	Chaim Potok
Sholom Asch	Leo Rosten
Saul Bellow	Henry Roth
Abraham Cahan	Irwin Shaw
Edna Ferber	Leon Uris
Alfred Kazin	Herman Wouk
Ludwig Lewisohn	Israel Zangwill

4. Jews, like other ethnic minorities, have been concerned with maintaining their identity in America. One way they have done this is by establishing numerous Jewish institutions and organizations. Have the students complete the following chart by listing parallel institutions of other ethnic minority groups in column 2 and similarities and differences in column 3.

1. Jewish Institutions	*2. Non-Jewish Institutions*	*3. Similarities, Differences*
YMHA		
Jewish Social Centers		
Synagogues		
Jewish Hospitals		
Yiddish Theater		
Yiddish Press		
Jewish Publication Society		
Fraternal Organizations		
Fund-Raising Organizations		

5. Since 1948, Jewish Americans have become passionate supporters of Israel, despite the fact that few of them or their immediate ancestors were born there or plan to live there. Assign essays comparing Jewish attitudes toward Israel with those of another ethnic minority group to its country of origin. What similarities and differences exist? How do students account for them?

6. Many Jewish Americans consciously object to their children marrying non-Jews. The rate of intermarriage is lower for Jewish Americans than for many other ethnic and religious groups. Ask students to conduct an informal survey among Jewish friends and their families to determine what accounts for this attitude. Then discuss or debate the pros and cons.

7. Read the letter quoted earlier from *A Bintel Brief* to the class (or distribute as a handout) and ask the following questions:

a. Does the family described in this letter maintain a strong Jewish identity? Do they attempt to preserve and transmit it to their children? What evidence can you find in this letter to support your answer?

b. Should the son have been angry with his father for failing to give him a Jewish upbringing? Should parents teach their children to think of themselves as members of their particular ethnic group?

c. Why does the son join a Zionist club and want to go to Palestine? How will this solve his problem?

d. In what ways could the son satisfy his need to identify as a Jew without moving to Palestine?

8. Have students contact an office of the Allied Jewish Appeal of the Federation of Jewish Charities to learn through what institutions Jewish Americans financially support their own community and Israel. Have them report their findings to the class.

9. If possible, visit an observant Jewish home on a Friday evening or on a Jewish holiday. Or invite a rabbi to speak to the class. Try to learn what customs, traditions, and values have helped the Jewish family to withstand many of the disruptive influences of history and of contemporary life.

Endnotes

1. Mark S. Hoffman, ed. *The World Almanac and Book of Facts, 1989* (New York: Newspaper Enterprises, 1988), pp. 532, 591.

2. Milton Himmelfarb and David Singer, eds., *American Jewish Yearbook*, vol. 84 (New York: American Jewish Committee; and Philadelphia: Jewish Publication Society, 1984), p. 162.

3. Abraham J. Karp, "American Jewry: 1954–1971." Epilogue in *The Jews in America: A History*, ed. Rufus Learsi (New York: KTAV, 1972), p. 360.

4. Hoffman, *World Almanac*, pp. 591, 686.

5. H.I.A.S. Annual Report, 1988 (New York: Hebrew Immigrant Aid Society, 1988), p. 36.

6. Stephan Thernstrom, Ann Orlov, and Oscar Handlin, eds., *Harvard Encyclopedia of American Ethnic Groups* (Cambridge: Harvard University Press, 1980), p. 581.

7. Yankelovich, Skelly, and White (an opinion research company), "Anti-Semitism in the United States," prepared for the American Jewish Committee, mimeograph, 1981, in a study cited in *American Jewish Year Book*, vol. 83, eds. Milton Himmelfarb and David Singer (New York: American Jewish Committee; and Philadelphia: Jewish Publication Society, 1983), pp. 67, 98.

8. Samuel Z. Klausner, "Anti-Semitism in the Executive Suite, Yesterday, Today and Tomorrow," *Moment*, September 1989, pp. 33–39, 55.

9. Charles E. Silberman, *A Certain People* (New York: Summit Books, 1985), p. 83–88.

10. Thernstrom, Orlov, and Handlin, *Harvard Encyclopedia*, p. 593.

11. Silberman, *A Certain People*, pp. 226–27.

12. Steven M. Cohen, *The 1984 National Survey of American Jews: Political and Social Outlooks* (New York: American Jewish Committee, 1985), p. 3.

13. Seymour Martin Lipset, "Jewish Disunity Is Good for Us," *Moment*, September 1988, p. 59.

14. Leonard Fein, "Why Jews Vote Their Values, Not Their Economic Interests: A Defense of Liberalism," *Moment*, October 1988, p. 39.

15. "A Troublesome Exodus," *Newsweek*, 25 September 1989, p. 52.

16. *H.I.A.S. Annual Report, 1988*, p. 1.

17. Thernstrom, Orlov, and Handlin, p. 597; Hoffman, *World Almanac*, p. 541.

Annotated Bibliography

Books for Teachers

Especially Recommended

Dawidowicz, Lucy S. *On Equal Terms: Jews in America 1881–1981*. New York: Holt, Rinehart and Winston, 1984.

> This book is an overview of American-Jewish history from the beginning of the Jewish mass migrations from eastern Europe in 1881 to the present.

Feingold, Henry. *Zion in America*. Boston: Twayne, 1974.

> This is a comprehensive study of the Jewish experience in America from colonial times to the present.

Howe, Irving. *World of Our Fathers: The Journey of the East European Jews to America and the Life They Found and Made*. New York: Simon and Schuster, 1976.

> This social and cultural history of the eastern European Jewish immigrants in New York City was a national bestseller and winner of the National Book Award.

Johnson, Paul. *A History of the Jews*. New York: Harper & Row, 1987.

> Perhaps the best examination of Judaism and Jewish history in the English language by a non-Jew.

Karp, Abraham J. *Haven and Home: A History of the Jews in America*. New York: Schocken Books, 1985.

> Professor Karp explores the Jewish experience from colonial times to the present day. The book is enhanced by a wide variety of source documents.

Marcus, Jacob Rader, ed. *The American Jewish Woman: A Documentary History*. New York: KTAV Publishing House, 1981.

> This comprehensive anthology includes documents that span several centuries (1700s–1980). This book is a rich source for teachers and researchers.

Sanders, Ronald. *Shores of Refuge: A Hundred Years of Jewish Emigration*. New York: Henry Holt and Company, 1988.

> This book gives a clear picture of the great migration of East European Jews to the United States from 1881 to the present.

Singer, David, ed. *American Jewish Yearbook*, Vol. 89. New York: American Jewish Committee; and Philadelphia; Jewish Publication Society, 1989.

> *This annual yearbook, in continuous publication since 1889, is an excellent source of information about the American Jewish community. Yearly editions include a compendium of issues of concern to Jews, directories of national and community Jewish organizations, welfare funds, community councils, and other vital information.*

Other References

Belth, Nathan C. *A Promise to Keep: A Narrative of the American Encounter with Anti-Semitism*. New York: Times Books, 1979.

> *This is a thorough study of anti-Semitism in America from colonial times to the 1960s.*

Birmingham, Stephen. *"The Rest of Us": The Rise of America's Eastern European Jews*. Boston: Little, Brown, 1984.

> *This book is the third in which the author examines particular segments of Jewish-American life. (The previous two are* Our Crowd *and* The Grandees.*) It tells the story of the eastern European Jews who came to North America between 1882 and 1915 and their role in American business and society.*

Bletter, Diane, and Grinker, Lori. *The Invisible Thread: Portraits of Jewish American Women*. Philadelphia: Jewish Publication Society, 1989.

> *Through probing interviews and stunning photographs, the authors provide a collection of intimate portraits of Jewish women that shatter the narrow stereotypes of the Jewish mother and the Jewish American princess.*

Cohen, Naomi W. *Encounter with Emancipation: The German Jews in the United States, 1830–1914*. Philadelphia: Jewish Publication Society, 1984.

> *This well-documented study portrays the "Americanization" of the Jews who came to this country in the nineteenth century and, as the author maintains, set the stage for the great wave of eastern-European Jewish immigrants who came later.*

Dimont, Max I. *The Jews in America: The Roots, History and Destiny of American Jews*. New York: Simon & Schuster, 1978.

> *This book touches every facet of Jewish life in America from 1654 to the present, with predictions about the future of the Jews in America.*

Einstein, Stephen J., and Kukoff, Lydia. *Every Person's Guide to Judaism*. New York: Union of American Hebrew Congregations, 1989.

> *This book provides an introduction to Judaism as a civilization. It is organized into four sections: "The Cycle of the Year," "The Cycle of Life," "Aspects of Faith," and "Contemporary Jewish Life."*

Kolatch, Alfred J. *The Second Jewish Book of Why*. Middle Village, N.Y.: Jonathan David, 1985.

> *Written in a question-and-answer format, this book contains a great deal of information on such topics as "Who is a Jew?" "Judaism and Christianity," and "Death and Dying."*

Korn, Bertram W. *American Jewry and the Civil War*. New York: Altheneum, 1970.

> *Originally published in 1951, this is a scholarly history of the American-Jewish community during the Civil War, emphasizing the broad picture while not ignoring important details.*

Libo, Kenneth, and Howe, Irving. *We Lived There Too: A Documentary History of Pioneer Jews and the Westward Movement of America, 1630–1930*. New York: St. Martin Press, 1984.

> *This is a story of pioneer Jews told in their own words and pictures.*

Quinley, Harold E., and Glock, Charles Y. *Anti-Semitism in America*. New Brunswick, N.J.: Transaction Books, 1983.

> *The authors of this carefully researched and highly informative study draw their conclusions from a specially designed nationwide survey on anti-Semitism conducted by the Survey Research Center at the University of California, Berkeley, and from other public polls.*

Ruderman, Jerome. *Jews in American History: A Teacher's Guide*. New York: Anti-Defamation League of B'nai B'rith, 1974.

> *A basic handbook for social studies teachers, this book includes a survey of American-Jewish history, an annotated bibliography and filmography, discussion questions, and student activities.*

Schappes, Morris U., ed. *A Documentary History of the Jews in the United States 1654–1875*, 3rd ed. New York: Schocken Books, 1971.

> *This is a valuable collection of source documents.*

Schoener, Allon. *The American Jewish Album: 1654 to the Present*. New York: Rizzoli, 1983.

> *This is a lavish pictorial history of American Jews, complemented by a clear accompanying narrative.*

Silberman, Charles E. *A Certain People: American Jews and Their Lives Today*. New York: Summit Books, 1985.

> *In this examination of American Jewish life today the author repudiates the prophets of doom and decline and maintains that contemporary society offers Jews and other ethnic groups opportunities heretofore undreamed of.*

Wyman, David S. *The Abandonment of the Jews: America and the Holocaust, 1941–1945*. New York: Pantheon Books, 1984.

> *This is a documented account of the precise degree to which all segments of the U.S. population failed to do the least they could have done in order to save some of the 6 million Jewish victims of the Nazi holocaust.*

Books for Students

Adler, David A. *Our Golda: The Story of Golda Meir*. New York: Viking Press, 1985.

> *This is a biography of the Israeli prime minister and world leader, emphasizing her early childhood and youth in Russia and America. (Intermediate)*

Antin, Mary. *The Promised Land,* 2d ed. Boston: Houghton Mifflin, 1969.

> *This autobiography of a Russian-Jewish girl who came to the United States was originally written in 1911. The foreword is by Oscar Handlin. (High School)*

Arrick, Fran. *Chernowitz!* Scarsdale, N.Y.: Bradbury Press, 1981.

> *This story raises some important issues in contemporary society as tenth-grader Bobby Chemo is the victim of anti-Semitic harassment. (Middle School)*

Asher, Sandra F. *Daughters of the Law.* Beaufort, S.C.: Beaufort Books, 1980.

> *A Jewish child of parents who grew up and suffered in Nazi Germany tries to come to terms with her own identity with the aid of a compassionate gentile friend (Middle School)*

Bernbaum, Israel. *My Brothers' Keeper: The Holocaust through the Eyes of an Artist.* Illustrated by the author. New York: G. P. Putnam's Sons, 1985.

> *This beautifully designed book provides a moving account of the holocaust through an examination of five large canvasses collectively entitled "Warsaw Ghetto, 1943." (Intermediate)*

Bluestein, Gene. *Anglish-Yiddish in American Life and Literature.* Athens: University of Georgia, 1989.

> *This is a lexicon of Yiddish words that have come into use in American English and American expressions that have their origins in Yiddish phrases. (Middle School)*

Brooks, Jerome. *Make Me a Hero.* New York: Dutton, 1980.

> *An absorbing novel of a twelve-year-old child who comes of age in 1943. (Intermediate)*

Bunting, Eve. *Terrible Things: An Allegory of the Holocaust.* Illustrated by Stephen Gammell. Philadelphia: Jewish Publication Society, 1989.

> *This story of the animals of the forest to whom terrible things happen is an excellent way of teaching the meaning of the holocaust to children. (Middle School)*

Bush, Lawrence. *Rooftop Secrets and Other Stories of Anti-Semitism.* New York: Union of American Hebrew Congregations, 1986.

> *Each of the eight short stories in this book describes a Jewish child's bout with anti-Semitism, from the Spanish Inquisition to modern times. (Middle School)*

Cahan, Abraham. *The Rise of David Levinsky.* New York: Harper and Row, 1966.

> *A reprint of a classic novel, this book deals with the adjustment of the eastern European Jewish immigrants. It is set in New York City's garment industry. (High School)*

Chaikin, Miriam. *Feathers in the Wind.* New York: Harper and Row, 1989.

> *This is a thoughtfully written chapter in a boy's development. Black-and-white drawings mirror the Orthodox Jewish milieu in which the author roots her story. (Intermediate)*

———. *Sound the Shofar: The Story and Meaning of Rosh Hashanah and Yom Kippur.* Illustrated by Erika Weihs. Boston: Houghton Mifflin/Clarion Books, 1986.

> *This book deals with the themes and evolution of the holiest of Jewish holidays. (Intermediate)*

————. *Yossi Asks the Angels for Help.* Illustrated by Petra Mathers. New York: Harper & Row, 1985.

> *Yossi is shocked when he finds that the eight quarters he has to buy Hanukkah presents have disappeared through a hole in his pocket. This book gives a good picture of Orthodox Jewish family life. (Primary)*

Charing, Douglas. *The Jewish World.* Morristown, N.J.: Silver Burdett, 1984.

> This is one of a series of three large-format books entitled, Religions of the World. It gives a clear overview of Jewish practices and traditions with attractive, full-color illustrations. (Intermediate)

Cohen, Barbara. *The Carp in the Bathtub.* New York: Lothrop, Lee, and Shepard, 1972.

> *This is a humorous story that gives a feeling for Jewish family life in New York City. (Primary)*

————. *Tell Us Your Secret.* New York: Bantam Books, 1989.

> *An involving story of second-generation survivor guilt set in the context of high school philosophizing about religion, writing, and self-determination. (Middle School)*

Coleman, Hila. *Rachel's Legacy.* New York: William Morrow, 1978.

> *This is the story of a seventeen-year-old Jewish girl and her family's struggle during the Depression of the 1930s. It is an excellent introduction to the mass eastern European immigration to America at the turn of the century. The story continues in the sequel,* Ellie's Inheritance *(New York: William Morrow, 1979). (High School)*

Dolan, Edward F. *Anti-Semitism.* New York: Franklin Watts, 1985.

> *This book is as much a general history of the Jewish people as it is a history of anti-Semitism. (Middle School)*

Drucker, Malka. *Passover: A Season of Freedom.* New York: Holiday, 1981.

> *A clear text and pleasant format introduce the elaborate rituals of Passover and the reasons behind them. The book tells the story of Exodus and includes a glossary and reading list. (Intermediate)*

Gold, Michael. *Jews without Money.* New York: Avon Books, 1968.

> *A classic novel of immigrant poverty on New York's Lower East Side, this book was originally published in 1930. It includes an afterword by Michael Harrington. (High School)*

Hurwitz, Johanna. *The Rabbi's Girls.* New York: William Morrow, 1982.

> *The tender story of eleven-year-old Carrie Levin, whose family moves in 1923 to an Ohio town where her father, who is a rabbi, dies. By the author of* Once I Was a Plum Tree *(New York: William Morrow, 1980). (Intermediate)*

Kerr, M. E. *Gentlehands.* New York: Bantam, 1979.

> *The story of a present-day teenager in a small town on eastern Long Island who comes face to face with Nazi atrocities when his grandfather is suspected of murdering a large number of Jews in Auschwitz. (High School)*

Lasky, Kathryn. *Pageant.* New York: Macmillan/Four Winds, 1986.

> *The story of a Jewish girl in Indianapolis in 1960 and her slow process of self-discovery. (Middle School)*

Levitin, Sonia. *Silver Days*. New York: Atheneum, 1989.

> *The story of a Jewish immigrant family that moves to California during World War II. (Middle School)*

Meltzer, Milton. *The Jewish Americans: A History in Their Own Words, 1650–1950*. New York: Thomas Y. Crowell, 1982.

> *In this book, Jews from all parts of the country relate what the experience of being an American has meant to them. It includes excerpts from diaries, letters, and memoirs. By the author of* Taking Root: Jewish Immigrants in America *(New York: Farrar, Straus, and Giroux, Inc., 1976). (Middle School and High School)*

———— *Never to Forget: The Jews of the Holocaust*. New York: Harper and Row, 1976.

> *This is an outstanding and sensitive account of the Nazi holocaust. (Middle School)*

Metter, Bert. *Bar Mitzvah, Bat Mitzvah: How Jewish Boys and Girls Come of Age*. New York: Clarion Books, 1984.

> *This illustrated little book describes what happens in the bar mitzvah, bat mitzvah ceremony and explains the historical background of the event. (Intermediate)*

Peretz, I. L. *The Case against the Wind and Other Stories*, trans. and adapted by Esther Hautzig. New York: Macmillan, 1975.

> *This collection of classic Jewish tales by a master storyteller is rich in Jewish tradition and is suitable for reading to primary students. (Intermediate)*

Pliskin, Jacqueline Jacobson. *The Jewish Holiday Game and Workbook*. New York: Shapolsky Publishers, 1989.

> *A collection of challenging and educational Jewish theme games, puzzles, trivia brainteasers, and other activities. (Intermediate)*

Postal, Bernard, and Koppman, Lionel. *Guess Who's Jewish in American History*, 2nd ed. New York: Shapolsky Publishers, 1988.

> *This book gives vivid, fascinating stories of more than 100 Jewish men and women who for more than 300 years have played vital roles in the making of our nation. (Middle School)*

Prager, Dennis, and Telushkin, Joseph. *The Nine Questions People Ask about Judaism*. New York: Simon & Schuster/Touchstone Books, 1988.

> *Suitable for anyone who wants to understand the meaning of Judaism. (Middle School)*

Provost, Gary, and Levine-Freidus, Gail. *Good If It Goes*. Scarsdale, N.Y.: Bradbury Press, 1984.

> *This is the story of a twelve-year-old who must juggle the demands of baseball with his upcoming bar mitzvah, his girlfriend, and his family. (Middle School)*

Rosenblum, Richard. *My Bar Mitzvah*. Pen-and-ink drawings by the author. New York: William Morrow & Co., 1985.

> *A nostalgic description of an important occasion in a Jewish boy's life presented from a child's perspective. (Primary)*

————. *The Old Synagogue*. Illustrated by the author. Philadelphia: Jewish Publication Society, 1989.

> *This is a heart-warming story of the renovation of an old synagogue. (Intermediate)*

Roth, Henry. *Call It Sleep.* Paterson, N.J.: Pageant Books, 1960.

> *Originally published in 1934, this book presents a vivid picture of the Jewish immigrant experience. The language and style are difficult. (High School)*

Schappes, Morris U., ed. *The Jews in the United States, A Pictorial History: 1654 to the Present,* rev. ed. New York: Marzani and Munsell, 1965.

> *This is a profusely illustrated history. (High School)*

Stadtler, Bea. *The Holocaust: A History of Courage and Resistance.* New York: Behrman House, 1974.

> *This is a well-told, absorbing story of the Nazi holocaust. (Middle School)*

Stern, Ellen Norman. *Elie Weisel: Witness for Life.* New York: KTAV, 1982.

> *This compelling biography provides an evocative and sensitive portrait of Wiesel from his youth in Hungary, to his struggle for survival at Auschwitz, and later, his writings on the holocaust. (High School)*

Tamar, Erika. *Good-Bye Glamour Girl.* New York: Lippincott, 1984.

> *The story of a young Jewish refugee who yearns to be famous and glamorous, coming of age in Manhattan during World War II. (Middle School)*

Weilerstein, Sadie R. *The Best of K'tonton.* Philadelphia: Jewish Publication Society, 1980.

> *This anthology of 16 stories about a Jewish Tom Thumb offers an introduction to Jewish celebration. (Primary)*

Weisel, Elie. *The Fifth Son.* New York: Simon & Schuster, 1985.

> *This is the story of a young American who seeks revenge on a brutal SS officer who becomes a prosperous German businessman in postwar Germany. In the process he is assailed by agonizing moral choices. By the author of* Night *(New York: Hill and Wang, 1960). (High School)*

Wolff, Ferida. *Pink Slippers, Bat Mitzvah Blues.* Philadelphia: Jewish Publication Society, 1989.

> *This realistic novel captures the dilemmas and agonies of a busy, concerned eighth grader following her Bat Mitzvah. (Middle School)*

Part IV

Hispanic

Americans

Concepts and Strategies

P art IV consists of content, concepts, teaching strategies, and materials for teaching about three major Hispanic groups in the United States: Mexican Americans, Puerto Ricans, and Cuban Americans. Hispanics are one of the nation's fastest growing ethnic groups. The number of Hispanics in the United States grew from 14 million in 1980 to more than 20 million in 1990. Mexican Americans are the largest Hispanic group in the United States, and this group is growing faster than are Cubans or Puerto Ricans. Between 1980 and 1990, Mexican Americans increased about 58%, compared to a 47% increase of Cubans and a 32% increase of Puerto Ricans. The Hispanic population is growing about five times faster than the rest of the U.S. population. The rapid growth of Hispanics is due primarily to massive immigration and to a high birthrate.

Central and South Americans

A substantial number of immigrants from Central and South America have entered the United States since 1970. Between 1971 and 1987, 313,200 Central American and 554,700 South American immigrants settled in the United States. A significant number of these immigrants have come from El Salvador, Guatemala, Colombia, Guyana, and Ecuador. Central and South Americans made up 12% of the Hispanic population of the United States in 1988 (see Figure A). It is misleading, however, to conceptualize these diverse groups of immigrants as one people because they have wide cultural, racial, and ethnic differences.

Demographic Characteristics of Hispanics

The Hispanic population, compared to the rest of the U.S. population, is young. The median age of Hispanics in 1988 was 25.5, compared to 32.9

Figure A   *Hispanics, by Type of Origin: 1988 (in percent)*

Mexican 62%

Puerto Rican 13%

Central and
South American 12%

Cuban 5%

Other Hispanic 8%

Source: Bureau of the Census, Current Population Reports, Special Studies Series
P–23, No. 159, *Population Profile of the United States.* Washington, D.C.: U.S.
Government Printing Office, 1989, p. 38.

for the non-Hispanic population.[1] The Hispanic population is also highly
concentrated in the Southwestern United States. In 1988, 63% of all Hispanics lived in five states: Arizona, California, Colorado, New Mexico, and
Texas (see Figure B). Fifty-five percent of all Hispanics lived in two states:
Texas and California.

Hispanics continue to lag behind the rest of the population in educational and income status. In 1988, 51% of Hispanics and 78% of non-
Hispanics had completed four years of high school or more. Ten percent of
Hispanics and 21% of non-Hispanics had completed four or more years of
college. Hispanics, as well as other students of color, are becoming a larger
proportion of the nation's school-age population. Hispanics were 9.3% of
the nation's school-age population (0 to 17-year-olds) in 1982. Demographers predict that they will make up about 25.3% of the nation's school-age
population by the year 2020.[2]

In 1987, about 27.3% of Hispanic persons were living below the poverty level, compared with 13.6% for the total population, 11% for Whites,
and 31.1% for African Americans. The poverty rates for different Hispanic
groups varied. The rate was 28.4% for Mexican Americans and 39.4% for
Puerto Ricans.

Figure B Geographic Distribution of the Hispanic Population: March 1988

Arizona, Colorado, and New Mexico 8%

New York 11%

Florida 8%

Illinois 4%

New Jersey 3%

Remainder of the United States 11%

Texas 21%

California 34%

Source: U.S. Bureau of the Census. Current Population Reports. Series P–20, No. 438, *The Hispanic Population in the United States: March 1988*. Washington, D.C.: U.S. Government Printing Office, 1989, p. 3.

Diversity within Hispanics

It is misleading to consider Hispanics one ethnic group. Even though the various Hispanic groups share a past influenced significantly by Spain and the Spanish language, there are tremendous historical, racial, and cultural differences between and within them. Most Mexican Americans are *mestizos*, whereas some Cubans and Puerto Ricans are Black. Some Mexican Americans are native to the United States; others, as well as some other Hispanics, arrived in the United States quite recently. The multicultural curriculum should help students understand the ways in which the various Hispanic groups are both alike and different.

Endnotes

1. The Census data reported in this section are from these reports: U.S. Bureau of the Census. Current Population Reports. Series P–20, No. 438, *The Hispanic Population in the United States: March 1988*. Washington, D.C.: U.S. Government Printing Office, 1989; U.S. Bureau of the Census, Current Population Reports, Special Studies Series P-23, No. 159, *Population Profile of the United States*. Washington, D.C.: U.S. Government Printing Office, 1989; and U.S. Bureau of the Census, *Statistical Abstract of*

the United States: 1989 (109th ed.). Washington, D.C.: U.S. Government Printing Office, 1989.
    2. Aaron M. Pallas, Gary Natriello, and Edward L. McDill, "The Changing Nature of the Disadvantaged Population: Current Dimensions and Future Trends," *Educational Researcher* (June–July, 1989) pp. 16–22.

Annotated Bibliography

Bean, Frank D., and Tienda, Marta. *The Hispanic Population of the United States.* New
    York: Russell Sage Foundation, 1987.

> *This excellent reference book, part of "The Population of the United States in the 1980s" monograph series, contains chapters that undertake a detailed and comprehensive analysis of the 1980 Census data. The opening chapter, "The Structuring of Hispanic Ethnicity: Theoretical and Historical Considerations," is especially valuable.*

Borjas, George J., and Tienda, Marta, eds. *Hispanics in the U.S. Economy.* New York:
    Academic Press, 1985.

> *This book consists of a well-researched collection of papers that examine a range of topics related to Hispanics in the economy, including earnings and labor supply, youth employment and school enrollment, labor supply and occupational allocation of women, and labor market studies.*

Hispanic Policy Development. *The Hispanic Almanac.* New York: The Project, 1990.

> *This valuable book is packed with a gold mine of information from the U.S. Census, as well as from statistical analyses undertaken by the staff of the Hispanic Policy Development Project.*

Kanellos, Nicolas, ed. *Hispanic Theatre in the United States.* Houston: Arte Publio Press,
    1984.

> *This book includes chapters on Mexican-American, Puerto Rican, and Cuban-American theatre.*

Moore, Joan, and Pachon, Harry. *Hispanics in the United States.* Englewood Cliffs, N.J.:
    Prentice-Hall, 1985.

> *This readable book is an integrated historical survey of the major Hispanic ethnic groups in the United States.*

Olson, James S. *Catholic Immigrants in America.* Chicago: Nelson-Hall, 1987.

> *This book contains an informative chapter on "The Hispanic Catholics," pp. 147–167.*

San Juan Cafferty, Pastora, and McCready, William C., eds. *Hispanics in the United States: A New Social Agenda.* New Brunswick, N.J.: Transaction Books, 1985.

> *This book contains a collection of papers that discuss the historical, demographic, and cultural aspects of Hispanic groups in the United States.*

U.S. Bureau of the Census. Current Population Reports, Series P–20, No. 438. *The Hispanic Population in the United States: March 1988.* Washington, D.C.: U.S. Government Printing Office, 1989.

This monograph consists of a detailed demographic summary of the Hispanic population. A number of useful tables and figures are included.

Chapter 10

Mexican Americans

Concepts, Strategies, and Materials

It would be a disservice to portray the future in idealistic terms. Hope is important, but the falsification of reality can immobilize a community.

—Rodolfo Acuña, 1988

Introduction

Mexican Americans are the second largest ethnic group of color in the United States. (African Americans are the largest group.) They are also the largest Hispanic group. Mexican Americans comprised about 62% of the Hispanics in 1988. They are increasing at a much faster rate than are the other two major Hispanic groups, Puerto Ricans and Cubans. The number of documented Mexicans living in the United States increased from 8,740,439 in 1980 to a projected 13,768,020 in 1990.[1] The difference between the documented Mexican-American population in the United States in 1980 and the projected population in 1990 indicates an increase of about 58% between these years.

The rapid growth in the Mexican-American population results primarily from a higher birthrate, compared to other ethnic and racial groups, and a significant and continuing immigration from Mexico. Between 1971 and 1987, 1,111,300 legal immigrants arrived in the United States from Mexico.[2] A large, but unknown, number of undocumented Mexican aliens in the United States are not reflected in these Census figures. There is little agreement on how many undocumented Mexican aliens are living in the United States. It is also difficult to determine the extent to which the Immigration Reform and Control Act of 1986, designed to reduce the number of undocumented immigrants who enter the United State each year, has been successful. The act imposes severe penalties on employers who knowingly hire illegal aliens. Under the conditions of this act, employers are required to ask job applicants for proof of citizenship.

The Mexican-American population is highly concentrated in the West and Southwest, particularly in California and Texas. In 1980, 41.6% of Mexican-Americans lived in California, and 31.5% lived in Texas. More than 73.1% of

Table 10-1 *Population of Mexican Americans in Selected States (1980)*

California	3,367,466
Texas	2,752,487
Illinois	408,325
Arizona	396,410
New Mexico	233,772
Colorado	207,204
Michigan	112,183
Washington	81,112
Florida	79,392
Indiana	57,625
Ohio	53,318
Kansas	49,917
Oregon	45,170
Wisconsin	41,067
Oklahoma	38,974
New York	38,755
Utah	38,021
Nevada	32,681
Missouri	32,036
Louisiana	28,558
Idaho	28,143
Georgia	27,647

Source: Based on data in the U.S. Census, 1980

them lived in Texas and California. Illinois and Arizona had the next largest concentrations of Mexican Americans, 4.7% and 4.5%, respectively. In 1980, 82.3% of Mexican Americans lived in the following four states: California, Texas, Illinois, and Arizona (see Table 10-1).

Even though Mexican Americans are highly concentrated in California, the Southwest, and Illinois, pockets of them are found throughout the United States, including the South and the Northwest. More than 38,000 lived in Oklahoma in 1980. Washington state, in the Northwest, had (in 1980) the eighth largest population of Mexican Americans—81,112. Mexican Americans are also becoming increasingly urbanized. Significant numbers are concentrated in large cities, such as Los Angeles, Chicago, Milwaukee, and Detroit.

Mexican Americans were in the land that is now the United States before all other American groups, except the American Indians, Aleuts, Eskimos, and Native Hawaiians. Their ancestors had settled in the region that is now the southwestern United States before Jamestown was settled by the English colonists in 1607. They became an ethnic minority when Texas was annexed by the United States in 1845. More of their territory was conquered by the United States during the Mexican-American War, which lasted from 1846 to 1848. Their property, civic, and cultural rights were guaranteed by the treaty of

Guadalupe Hidalgo, the treaty ending the war in 1848. In the decades after 1848, the treaty was blatantly disregarded and Mexican Americans were made second-class citizens by Anglo-Americans who migrated and settled in the Southwest. There were about 80,000 Mexicans living in the territory Mexico ceded to the United States in 1848. Most modern Mexican-American communities were formed by Mexican immigrants who came to the United States after 1910. The study of the conquest and subjugation of Mexican Americans and their resistance, which greatly intensified in the 1960s, is necessary to understand the nature of U.S. society and the genesis of the ethnic conflict and tensions in American life.

Mexican Americans: Historical Perspective

Important Dates

1519	Hernán Cortés, the Spanish conquistador, and a group of Spaniards arrived in the region that is now Mexico.
1521	Cortés, with the support of thousands of Indian allies, seized the Aztec capital city, Tenochtitlán, and the empire fell.
1598	Juan de Oñate established the first Spanish settlement in what is today New Mexico. The Spanish colonial period began.
1718	New Spain founded the mission and presidio of San Antonio.
1769	Fray Junípero Serra and Gaspar de Portolá established the mission and presidio of San Diego, the first in Upper California.
1810	On September 16, 1810, Father Miguel Hidalgo sounded a battle cry known as the *El Grito de Dolores*, which signaled the beginning of the Mexican revolutionary era that eventually resulted in Mexican independence from Spain in 1821.
1836	Mexico's President Santa Anna and his troops defeated the rebelling Texans at the Alamo. Six weeks later, Santa Anna was defeated by Sam Houston and his Texan troops at San Jacinto. Texas declared itself independent and formed the Lone Star Republic.

Important Dates	
1845	The United States annexed Texas, which had declared itself independent from Mexico in 1836. This was one key event leading to the Mexican-American War.
1846	On May 13, 1846, the United States declared war on Mexico and the Mexican-American War began.
1848	The United States and Mexico signed the Treaty of Guadalupe Hidalgo, which ended the Mexican-American War. Mexico lost nearly one-third of its territory, and the United States acquired most of the territory that comprises the southwestern states.
1853	James Gadsden, representing the United States, purchased from Mexico 45,532 square miles of additional land, which was rich in copper, and opened a railroad route.
1859	Juan N. Cortina, who became a U.S. citizen under the provisions of the Treaty of Guadalupe Hidalgo, led a series of rebellions against Anglo-Americans in the Lower Rio Grande Valley of South Texas.
1862	On May 5, 1862, French forces that had invaded Mexico were defeated at Puebla by Mexican forces led by Ignacio Zaragosa, a Texas Mexican. May 5 (*Cinco de Mayo*) is an important holiday observed by Mexican Americans.
1877	The El Paso Salt War occurred, in which Mexicans organized and rebelled against Anglos because of a dispute over rights to salt beds.
1910	A revolution starting in Mexico caused thousands of Mexicans to immigrate to the United States looking for jobs and to escape political turmoil and persecution.
1924	Congress established the Border Patrol to monitor traffic across the Mexican-U.S. border. This border had previously been primarily open.
1929	The League of United Latin American Citizens was formed in Harlingen, Texas. Like other earlier Mexican-American civil rights organizations, the League stressed U.S. citizenship and assimilation.
1929–35	Thousands of Mexican immigrants and their families were repatriated to Mexico, most without legal proceedings.
1942	The United States and Mexico made an agreement that authorized Mexicans to work temporarily in the United States. This project is known as the bracero program.

Important Dates	
1943	The anti-Mexican "zoot-suit" riots occurred in Los Angeles during the summer of 1943.
1954	The U.S. Immigration and Naturalization Service began "Operation Wetback," a massive program to deport illegal Mexican immigrants to Mexico.
1965	A grape strike led by César Chávez and the United Farm Workers Association began in Delano, California, a town in the San Joaquin Valley. Rodolfo "Corky" Gonzales formed the Crusade for Justice in Denver. This important civil rights organization epitomized the Chicano movement that emerged in the 1960s. The U.S. Congress passed an immigration act limiting the number of Mexican immigrants to the United States to 20,000 annually.
1970	La Raza Unida party was organized by José Angel Gutiérrez in Crystal City, Texas.
1976	Jerry Apodaca and Raul Castro were elected governors of New Mexico and Arizona, respectively.
1979	Luis Valdez' play, *Zoot Suit*, was the first Mexican-American play produced on Broadway.
1982	Toney Anaya was elected governor of New Mexico.
1986	The Immigration Reform and Control Act of 1986 was passed. Designed to control the entry of undocumented (illegal) immigrants to the United States, it imposed severe penalties on employers who knowingly hired illegal immigrants.
1988	President Ronald Reagan appointed Dr. Lauro F. Cavazos, a university president, Secretary of Education. He was the first Hispanic appointed to the Cabinet. Bush kept Cavazos as Secretary of Education when he became president in January 1989.

The Spanish Conquest

More than 25 million Indians were living in the Western Hemisphere when the Spanish conquistadores arrived in 1517. There were a wide variety of Indian cultures and groups in the region that is now Mexico. The Mayas and the Aztecs

developed some of the most complex societies in the region. Mayan domestica-
tion and cultivation of corn significantly influenced agriculture in the Americas. A
powerful military state and the most impressive contemporary cities were built
by the Aztecs. Tenochtitlán, their capital city, has been called "the most modern
city in the world" at the time of the Spanish conquest.[3]

Hernán Cortés, a Spanish explorer, led an expedition into Mexico in 1519.
Before he reached the Aztec capital, he gained military help from other Indian
civilizations by negotiating and conquering. After a two-year intermittent struggle
with the Aztecs, Cortés finally seized Tenochtitlán on August 13, 1521, and the
Aztec empire fell. Despite the Aztecs' military strength, the Spaniards were able
to defeat them because they were helped by other Indian nations and had
superior firearms and horses. Although the Spaniards were eventually successful
in their conquest of much of the land stretching from southern South America to
most of what is today the southwestern United States, this task was not easily
accomplished. The Indians living in these areas fought hard to maintain their
power and started many rebellions after the Spanish conquest. The Spaniards
defeated most Indian groups only gradually and with the loss of many of their
men.

The Spanish settlements in Mexico and what is today the southwestern
United States differed in several significant ways from the English colonies in the
eastern parts of North America. Most English colonists considered themselves
permanent settlers in North America. Consequently, they usually brought their
families. Most Spanish settlers in the Americas were adventurous men who came
to the Americas hoping to find gold and other treasures. They rarely brought
their wives. Many more settlers came from England than from Spain. It is
estimated that only about 300,000 Spaniards came to the Americas during three
centuries of settlement.[4]

These unique characteristics of the Spanish settlers significantly influenced
the physical and cultural development of the new "race" that was formed in the
Americas. Because the Spaniards brought few women with them, most had
Indian concubines or wives. The offspring of these ethnically mixed unions were
known as *mestizos*. The biological and cultural heritage of the Mexican American includes African strains although it is primarily Spanish-Indian. When they
came to the Americas, the Spaniards had had long contact with a group of
Africans called Moors. Moors came with the conquistadores to the Americas.
Estevan is perhaps the most famous. Nearly 200,000 African slaves were also
brought to Mexico. They were so thoroughly mixed with the Spaniards and
Indians by 1900 that they were no longer distinguishable as a separate racial
group.[5] The Mexican's biological heritage is more Indian than Spanish. Although
the Spaniards imposed their culture and religion on the Indian nations, many
Indian culture elements survived and highly influenced the development of
Mexican culture. Thus, both the physical traits and culture of the Mexicans are
primarily blends of Spanish and Indian influences. "To attempt to unravel any

single strand from this pattern and label it 'Spanish' is to do a serious injustice to the Mexican and Indians . . . through whom . . . Spanish cultural influences survived.[6]

The Texas Revolt

At the beginning of the nineteenth century, Mexico was in a perpetual state of political turmoil. Greatly concerned about the declining population in Texas, the Spanish and later the Mexican government encouraged Anglo-Americans to settle there by making *empresario* land grants. The Spanish government gave an empresario grant to Moses Austin in 1821. His son Stephen received a reconfirmation of the original grant from the Mexican government in 1823. Because Texas was geographically close to the United States, it attracted a large number of Anglo immigrants. They were interested in Texas's rich resources and open territory. Most Anglo settlers in Texas failed to keep the terms of their land-grant agreements with the Mexican government, such as becoming loyal citizens and Catholics, learning Spanish, and giving up their slaves. They were not interested in Mexican culture but wanted to establish Anglo institutions in the Mexican province and to control it.

Texas Mexicans were angry about President Santa Anna's attempts to centralize his power over the northern Mexican territories. The Anglo immigrants in Texas added fuel to the fire because of their disdain for the Mexican government. By permitting and encouraging U.S. citizens to settle in sparsely inhabited Texas, Mexico had inadvertently set the stage for revolt in the province and its eventual loss to the United States.

By the time Mexico realized that Anglo-Mexicans were gaining control in Texas and took steps to undermine their power, antigovernment forces in Texas had already been firmly established. The Mexican government attempted to undermine Anglo power in Texas by abolishing slavery in 1829, by restricting Anglo immigration into Texas, and by enforcing customs regulations at the Texas-U.S. border. These actions greatly angered the Texas Anglo-Mexicans and evoked attacks against the central government. Mexican federal troops arrived in Texas in 1835 after Texas proclaimed itself "conditionally independent." These troops were badly defeated. In 1836, President Santa Anna led several thousand Mexican troops into Texas. His army killed 187 Texans at a Franciscan mission in San Antonio called the Alamo. The Mexican army had another victory at Goliad but experienced a crushing defeat by Sam Houston and his "Remember the Alamo!" shouting Texas troops at San Jacinto on April 21. After this victory, Texas sought world recognition of its independence and started the chain of events that eventually led to its annexation by the United States in 1845.

The Mexican-American War

When the Mexican government took serious steps to halt Anglo immigration to the Southwest, the United States had begun, in the name of Manifest Destiny, an aggressive campaign to annex all of Mexico's northern territories. The United States began a military conquest when negotiations failed and then angered Mexico by annexing Texas in 1845. The United States declared war on Mexico in 1846 when a boundary dispute developed between the two nations. The United States defeated Mexico within two years and occupied California and New Mexico by the end of 1846. Mexico's northern provinces had little allegiance to the nation's capital. Anglo settlers who had a strong toehold in Mexican provinces such as California and New Mexico actively sought Mexico's defeat. Mexico was also greatly weakened by internal strife and its inability to rally internal support for the war.

The Treaty of Guadalupe Hidalgo

After Mexico was defeated by the United States, representatives of the two nations signed a treaty on February 2, 1848, in the Mexican village of Guadalupe Hidalgo. The United States forced Mexico to surrender its claim to Texas, which the United States had annexed in 1845, and to cede about one-third of its territory to the United States. This chunk of land included most of the territory now comprising the states of the U.S. Southwest, including Arizona, California, New Mexico, Utah, Nevada, and a section of Colorado. The United States paid Mexico $15 million for this large piece of land.

All Mexicans who remained in this newly acquired territory received the right to become U.S. citizens. Only about 3,000 of the nearly 80,000 people living in the area chose to leave their homes and move to the Mexican side of the border. The treaty guaranteed Mexican Americans "all the rights of citizens of the United States . . . [and] the free enjoyment of . . . liberty and property."[7] "By this treaty the United States gained not only an immense new territory but also a large group of new citizens. Although they were left in their same geographic and cultural setting, these new citizens were now exposed to unfamiliar legal, political, and social institutions. . . . Guaranteed full protection of property rights, they soon became enmeshed in a web of confusing Anglo laws which required proof of ownership unfamiliar to them."[8]

After the Conquest: Oppression and Conflict

After 1848, forces were set in motion that were destined to make the Mexicans in the United States a conquered, powerless, and alienated ethnic minority. Although they were guaranteed property and citizenship rights by the Treaty of Guadalupe Hidalgo, it was only a matter of time before Anglo-Americans, through a series of legal and financial maneuvers, had obtained control in all of the southwestern territories and reduced the native Mexicans to the status of second-class citizens.

The pattern of conquest differed somewhat in the various southwestern territories. Before the Anglos came to New Mexico, a rigid class structure existed that sharply divided the rich and the poor. The Anglos in New Mexico pitted the rich against the poor in order to gain control of the territory. Anglo dominance emerged more gradually in New Mexico than in California and Texas. A mass of Anglos immigrated to California during the gold rush of 1849 and in subsequent years. Mexicans were completely outnumbered. Anglos thoroughly dominated northern California by 1851, but domination of southern California was somewhat delayed because most Anglo immigrants first settled in the northern part of the territory. However, they eventually settled in the south and within a few years expanded their dominance over the entire state. There were more than 30,000 Anglos and only 5,000 native Mexicans in Texas as early as 1834. Anglos had controlled Texas since it became independent as the Lone Star Republic in 1836. This dominance continued after U.S. annexation in 1845.

The Anglo-Americans were able to obtain most of the land owned by the Mexicans by imposing a series of legal and financial restraints. Land boundaries in Mexico had been rather loosely and casually defined. Many Mexicans had to appear in Anglo courts to defend their rights to the land they owned. Often they did not have the legal papers proving ownership of their land, and Mexican legal papers did not conform to superimposed U.S. law. In many cases they had to sell their land to pay taxes imposed by the new government or exorbitant fees to Anglo lawyers to argue their cases in court. Legal battles over land titles often dragged out in the courts for years and became expensive. Tactics such as these and the Congressional Land Act of 1851, which required U.S. recognized proof of land ownership, had the ultimate effect of making the Mexican largely landless and poverty stricken.

Rioting, lynchings, burnings, vigilante action, and other forms of violence were directed at America's "newest aliens" during this period of turmoil and Hispanic defeat in the Southwest. Moore contends that "No other part of the United States saw such prolonged intergroup violence as did the Border States from 1848 to 1925."[9] Many Anglo outlaws and social misfits settled in the Southwest during this period. They declared "open season" on Mexicans and often attacked them "just for fun." There was little or no law enforcement in many parts of the Southwest during this period. In 1850, California passed a Foreign Miner's Tax that was designed to drive Mexicans out of the mines.

The Mexican Revolution of 1910 contributed to this atmosphere of hostility and violence. Banditry and filibustering (filibustering is pursuing military activity in a foreign nation for adventure) occurred on both sides of the border. Mexican-Anglo hostility reached new highs. Mexicans considered Anglo-Americans "gringos," and Anglos called Mexicans "greasers." By the turn of the century, the Mexicans had been conquered and made foreigners within their homeland. Culturally, politically, and economically they were second-class citizens. Mexican Americans faced the beginning of the twentieth century suffering from a crushing second defeat in the Southwest.

North from Mexico

Early Immigrants

During the early development of agriculture in the Southwest, agribusinessmen depended on a large and cheap labor supply. This labor need was met in the late 1800s by the Chinese immigrants and later by immigrants from Japan and the Philippines. (See chapter 13.) The expansion of irrigated farming in the Southwest at the turn of the century coincided with the Mexican Revolution of 1910. Many Mexicans were displaced by the Revolution. They came north to the U.S. Southwest seeking job opportunities. They found jobs in truck farming, in cotton and sugar beet fields, in mines, in industry, and on the railroads. Hundreds of Mexican immigrants worked on the construction of railroad lines that crossed the West. Many Mexican-American communities in the Southwest grew up around railroad campsites.

There was no legal agreement between Mexico and the United States that protected the rights of these immigrants. Consequently, they were often exploited blatantly by their employers. They were paid the lowest wages, given the worst jobs, and were forced to live in the crudest shacks. Many became migrant workers who followed the crops. The mass of Mexican immigrants to the Southwest depressed wages so drastically that many native Mexican Americans migrated to midwestern cities, such as Detroit, Gary, and Chicago, to obtain higher wages. The large number of Mexican immigrants who came to the Southwest between 1910 and 1930 laid the foundations for most modern Mexican-American communities.

Many Anglo groups in the Southwest became alarmed by the large numbers of Mexicans who were entering the United States in the 1920s. Between 1920 and 1929, 498,900 Mexican immigrants entered the United States. Vigorous efforts were made to halt their immigration. Although the legal attempts to stop their immigration failed because of the powerful opposition from agribusinessmen who wanted them for cheap labor, other efforts were successful. The U.S.-Mexican border had historically been an open border, with Mexicans and U.S. citizens crossing it at will. The Border Patrol was established in 1924 by Congress to control traffic across the border.

When the Great Depression hit in 1929, and many Mexicans, like other Americans, lost their jobs and found it necessary to obtain welfare to survive, loud cries were heard against the Mexicans. Mexicans were regarded as "foreigners" who did not deserve welfare benefits. As with other non-White immigrants who came before them, attempts were made to deport the Mexicans when their labor was no longer needed. Jobs became increasingly scarce as the "dust bowl" White immigrants fled to the Southwest to compete for the few available jobs. The U.S. Immigration Service, as well as state, county, and local governments, began an aggressive drive to repatriate immigrants.

In the eagerness to rid the United States of Mexicans in order to cut back on welfare rolls, many Mexican-American citizens were "encouraged" or forced to go to Mexico. The civil rights of U.S. citizens of Mexican descent were violated seriously in this unfortunate repatriation movement. More than 64,000 Mexican aliens were returned to Mexico between 1930 and 1934 without the benefits of legal proceedings. The Mexican population in the United States declined from 639,000 to 377,000 from 1930 to 1940.[10]

The Bracero Program

When World War II began, a new demand for unskilled labor developed in the United States. Agribusiness leaders spoke vigorously about their desperate need for Mexican labor. Partly as a gesture to help with the war effort, Mexico agreed to a seasonal work program with the United States. The two nations signed an agreement in July 1942, which enabled Mexican citizens to work in the United States during work seasons. They were to return to Mexico when the work season ended. Unlike the earlier Mexican immigrants, these workers came under an agreement that guaranteed them specific conditions relating to such problems as wages, working conditions, transportation, and worker rights.

Although these contract stipulations helped reduce some of the extreme conditions experienced by earlier Mexican immigrants, their wages and living conditions were often depressing. The bracero program formally ended in December 1947. When it terminated, the number of undocumented immigrants crossing the U.S.-Mexican border soared. Smuggling undocumented immigrants across the border became a highly profitable business in which many "men snatchers" engaged and profited.[11]

In 1954, the U.S. Immigration and Naturalization Service began a massive drive known as "Operation Wetback" to deport undocumented immigrants to Mexico. Operation Wetback grossly violated the civil rights of many Mexicans as did the repatriation project in the 1930s. Hundreds of Mexican-American citizens were arrested and harassed. They were threatened and forced to produce "proof" of their citizenship. Only a few of the thousands of Mexicans deported had formal hearings. Operation Wetback successfully attained its goal but alienated and outraged many Mexican-American citizens. When the project ended, more than a million people had been deported to Mexico.

In 1951, the United States and Mexico jointly accepted a Migratory Labor Agreement known as Public Law 78. This agreement set forth conditions for a new bracero program. It contained conditions similar to the earlier bracero agreement. Public Law 78 was extended for various periods until it ended in December 1964. In 1965, the United States Congress passed a new immigration act, which became effective in 1968, that limited the annual immigration from Western Hemisphere nations to 120,000. Each nation, including Mexico, was given an annual quota of 20,000. This new act solved, at least for the time, problems concerning the number of Mexican nationals that could legally enter the United States.

Because of the chronic economic and population problems in Mexico, large numbers of undocumented Mexican immigrants enter the United States each year. The U.S. Census indicated that more than 20 million Hispanics lived in the United States in 1990. However, the actual number of Hispanics who lived in the United States in 1990 was much higher than this figure because of the large numbers of undocumented immigrants that enter the United States from Mexico each year.

Violence and Race Riots

In the 1940s, anti-Mexican feelings and stereotypes were rampant in the Southwest. The stereotypes, which depicted the Mexican American as criminal and violent, were perpetuated by the established Anglo press, especially the Hearst newspapers. The anti-Mexican press propaganda enflamed racial feelings and antagonisms toward the Mexican Americans. Anti-Mexican racism was the basic cause of the case of the Sleepy Lagoon and the zoot-suit riots that occurred in Los Angeles in the summer of 1943.

The Sleepy Lagoon Case

A young Mexican American, José Diaz, died mysteriously on August 2, 1942, apparently from a fractured skull. Without seriously seeking the facts of the case, the Los Angeles police immediately arrested twenty-four young men who were thought to be members of a Mexican "gang" accused of killing Diaz. All of them were charged with murder. A gravel pit, which became a central focus in the case, was dubbed "The Sleepy Lagoon" by a Los Angeles reporter. When seventeen of the twenty-four youths were convicted, the Sleepy Lagoon Defense Committee was organized. The committee, headed by journalist Carey McWilliams, successfully appealed the case. The case was dismissed because of insufficient evidence when the district court of appeals reversed the convictions on October 4, 1944.

The Zoot-Suit Riots

On June 3, 1943, eleven sailors were allegedly attacked by a group of boys in a predominantly Mexican neighborhood in Los Angeles. After this incident, the Los Angeles police conducted a "raid" that enflamed the community but failed to find the attackers. This incident kicked off a chain reaction resulting in one of the most serious series of race riots that has occurred in the United States. Encouraged by the actions of the police and the pervasive anti-Mexican attitudes in Los Angeles, about 200 sailors began to attack violently Mexican-American youths on the night of June 4.

The police responded by arresting the victims of the attacks and keeping their hands off the sailors. The Los Angeles press played its usual role in the conflict; it warned that the dangerous "zoot-suiters" would retaliate the next night. Some Mexican-American youths were referred to as "zoot-suiters" because of their style of dress during the 1940s. The press succeeded in alarming the public and in stirring up anti-Mexican feelings. On the night of June 7, hundreds of Anglos went into the streets and began a massive attack on Mexican-American youths. Many "zoot-suiters" were beaten and stripped naked in the streets. This ruckus continued until military authorities intervened late on the night of June 7. Other riots occurred in cities as far away as Philadelphia, Chicago, and Detroit in the summer of 1943.

The Chicano Movement

Prior to the civil rights movement of the 1960s, *Chicano* was a negative term used to refer to lower-class Mexican immigrants from rural areas and small towns. During the 1960s, leaders of the Mexican-American protest and civil rights movement used the term in a positive way to describe their new quest for political, social, economic, cultural, and educational equality. *Chicano* was also used to link Mexican-American political activists and intellectuals to their Mexican-Indian heritage. In the past, their Spanish heritage was usually emphasized. The Chicano movement was broad in scope: it had economic, educational, religious, and cultural goals. The push for bilingual education in the schools was one of its major goals. Including more Mexican-American priests and other church officials in the Catholic church hierarchy was another.

The Chicano movement was also political. Its leaders saw political clout as one of the best ways to attain the other goals of the movement. Its leaders, who often differed on tactics, had a variety of goals. Many believed that Chicanos would be able to overcome oppression in the United States only when they had political power and control over the institutions, such as schools and courts, that influenced their lives and destinies. It is inaccurate to interpret the Chicano movement as a protest force that suddenly arose in the 1960s, or to refer to

Chicanos as the "awakening minority." Often this was done in the 1960s. To understand the Chicano movement fully, we must view it as an important link in the long chain of resistance activities in which Chicanos have been involved since 1848. The movement cannot be viewed in isolation. As historian Rodolfo Acuña pointed out in the 1970s, "Men like Juan Patron and J. J. Herrerra were the precursors of today's breed of rebels or insurrectionists. In understanding them . . . and others of their kind, we shall better understand the present, and the words of Reis Lopez Tijerina will take on more significant meaning."[12]

Early Resistance to Anglo Dominance

Mexican Americans have resisted Anglo oppression and colonization since Anglo-Americans conquered and occupied the Southwest. Chicanos such as Juan N. Cortina, Juan José Herrerra, and Juan Patron led organized resistance efforts in the 1800s. Cortina issued a "declaration of grievances" and urged Mexican Americans to "exterminate" their oppressors. Many Mexicans responded to the revolutionary calls issued by Cortina, Herrerra, and Patron.[13] Mexican-American organizations, such as Las Gorras Blancas, fought Anglo leaders who were illegally taking land owned by Mexican Americans in New Mexico.

Unions and Strikes

In the first decades of the twentieth century, most Mexican Americans worked in agriculture, although many worked in mines, industry, and on the railroads. Farm workers were highly exploited by rich and powerful agribusinessmen. Mexican-American workers aggressively opposed their conditions and organized unions and strikes, thus shattering the myth that they were docile workers. The period from 1900 to 1940 was characterized by active Chicano involvement in strikes and union organization. In 1927 the Confederacion de Uniones Obreras Mexicanas was organized in California. This union organized a strike in 1928 in the Imperial Valley. Farm owners and law officials, which formed coalitions, responded violently to the strike. They broke it up by deporting some strikers to Mexico and assaulting and intimidating others.

This pattern was used extensively by farm owners to crush strikes by Mexican Americans. However, strikes and union activities continued in the midst of these oppressive tactics. Meier and Rivera summarize this period: "Although Mexican Americans gained much labor union experience from 1900 to 1940, their organizations achieved only limited success. Some gains were made in wages and working conditions; however, the hopes and aspirations of Mexican-American workers continued to be frustrated by repression and discrimination."[14]

Civil Rights Organizations

A number of civic, service, and political organizations have been organized since the late nineteenth century to promote the civil rights and interests of Mexican Americans. One of the first was a mutual aid organization formed in Arizona in 1894, the Alianza Hispano-Americana. These early societies restricted membership to individuals of Mexican descent who were citizens of the United States. They were made up primarily of the middle- and upper-classes and promoted assimilation by urging their members to become loyal U.S. citizens. Cuellar argues that these organizations pursued a "politics of adaptation," rather than aggressively pushing for their political rights.[15] They included the Order of the Sons of America, organized in San Antonio in 1921, and the League of United Latin-American Citizens, formed in Corpus Christi, Texas, in 1929.

Mexican Americans became more politicized in the post–World War II period. The organizations emerging during these years reflected acute political awareness and skill. The Community Service Organization, which was formed in Los Angeles in 1947, stressed political involvement and broad political participation. It organized a number of successful voter registration drives. The American G.I. Forum, founded in 1948, the Mexican American Political Association, organized in 1959, and the Political Association of Spanish-Speaking Organizations, formed in 1960, stressed political involvement. These organizations were direct predecessors of the Chicano movement that emerged in the 1960s.

The Militant Chicano Movement

Mexican-Americans' protest activities, which had been going on historically, were intensified in the 1960s and 1970s and became collectively known as the "Chicano movement." In addition to being more intense than earlier Mexican-American movements, the Chicano movement had other unique characteristics. It was more militant and often used forms of direct confrontation. It included a large range of individuals among its ranks, such as intellectuals, students, and community activists. Its goals were more ambitious than the goals of traditional Mexican-American civil rights groups. It sometimes demanded Chicano control of institutions within the Mexican-American community. Some of its leaders argued that Chicanos in the United States were a colonized people who had been culturally and politically oppressed. They demanded redress of these grievances.

Chicano leaders also gave more attention to their mixed Mexican heritage than did earlier leaders. Their unique heritage, they argued, was to be celebrated and not denied, as was often done in the past by Mexican Americans who insisted on being viewed as "Spanish" instead of "Mexican." Much emphasis was placed on Mexican culture, values, foods, and especially on the speaking of

Spanish. They demanded the right to speak Spanish in all American institutions such as the school and church. Some Chicano leaders argued that "revolution" was necessary to liberate them.

Of the many local Chicano civil rights leaders, four young men epitomized the movement in the public vision. They were César Chávez, Reies López Tijerina, Rodolfo "Corkey" Gonzales, and José Angel Gutiérrez. Chávez headed the United Farm Workers Organizing Committee, unionized farm workers, and successfully led the famous Delano grape strike in 1965, as well as many subsequent farm strikes. Tijerina demanded that Anglos in New Mexico return the lands they had taken from Mexican Americans in the 1800s. He formed the Federal Alliance of Free Cities in 1963 to push for the return of New Mexico lands to Chicanos or compensation to Chicanos for the loss of these lands. An important and militant civil rights group, the Crusade for Justice, was organized in Denver in 1965 by Gonzales. The crusade initiated successful projects related to improved education, better housing, and the elimination of police brutality in the Mexican American community. As a result of the activities of the political party, La Raza Unida, which was organized in 1970 by Gutiérrez, Chicanos exercised unprecedented political power in Crystal City, Texas, in the 1970s, which spread throughout the lower Rio Grande Valley. These four charismatic leaders embodied the hopes and aspirations of millions of Mexican Americans.

Mexican Americans Today

Mexican Americans, like African Americans and other people of color, made important educational and economic gains during the 1960s. However, many of these gains faded during the 1970s and 1980s. The loss of gains during the 1970s and 1980s was caused by a number of factors, including the conservative national policies during the Reagan years and important changes in the U.S. economy. In previous decades, when industrial manufacturing was an important part of the U.S. economy, groups with few skills that were highly concentrated in the lower and working classes—such as Mexican Americans and African Americans—could move to large cities and obtain manufacturing jobs that paid well. There has been a substantial decrease in such jobs in the United States during the last 20 years as the United States and other major Western nations have increasingly become societies characterized by high technology and service occupations. These developments in the economy have had a disproportionately negative influence on job availability for groups heavily concentrated in the lower rungs of the economic and educational ladder, such as Mexican Americans, Puerto Ricans in the United States, and African Americans.[16]

At the beginning of the 1990s, and despite some progress in education and income status, Mexican Americans lagged behind Whites and the U.S. total population. In 1987, 27.3% of Mexican Americans 25 years old and over had completed four years of high school. This compared to 31.4% for Puerto Ricans, 29% for all Hispanics, 39.2% for Whites, and 38.7% for the total U.S. population.[17] Almost 6% (5.8%) of Mexican Americans 25 years old and over had completed four years or more of college in 1987. This compared to 8% for Puerto Ricans, 8.6% for all Hispanics, 10.7% for African Americans, 20.5% for Whites, and 19.9% for the total U.S. population.

The median income for Mexican Americans in 1987 was $19,326, compared to $14,584 for Puerto Ricans, $19,995 for all Hispanics, $17,604 for African Americans, $30,809 for Whites, and $29,458 for the total U.S. population. The percentage of Mexican Americans living below the official poverty level was considerably above the percentage for Whites and that for the total population in 1987. The percentages were 27.3 for Mexican Americans, 39.4 for Puerto Ricans, 31.1 for all Hispanics, 31.1 for African Americans, 11 for Whites, and 13.6 for the total population.

By the late 1980s, the militant Chicano movement of the 1960s had been transformed into more pragmatic forms of political organization. The various Hispanic groups, such as Mexican Americans, Puerto Ricans, and Cubans, were working cooperatively to form political, cultural, and business organizations to push for their collective rights and to improve the economic and educational status of U.S. Hispanics. These organizations included the National Association of Latino Elected and Appointed Officials, the Congressional Hispanic Caucus (comprised of Hispanics in the U.S. Congress), the National Hispanic Chamber of Commerce, the League of United Latin American citizens, and the Hispanic Policy Development Project, an organization that gathers data and analyzes public policy related to U.S. Hispanic groups. Many Mexican-American organizations also remained viable, such as the Mexican-American Legal Defense and Education Fund. This organization was making tremendous strides in size, scope, and influence.

Mexican Americans were also reaping benefits in local and state elections and were becoming more conscious of their potential political clout. In 1984, Eligio de la Garza (Texas), Manual Lujan, Jr. (New Mexico), and Matthew G. Martinez (California) were among the 11 Hispanics in the U.S. House of Representatives. Mexican-American mayors of large cities included Henry G. Cisneros in San Antonio and Federico Pena in Denver. Toney Anaya was governor of New Mexico.

Despite the political gains they had made by the late 1980s, Mexican-American leaders realized that their ethnic group had more potential political power than it was realizing. The nine states in which Hispanics are concentrated (California, Texas, New York, Florida, Illinois, New Jersey, New Mexico, Arizona, and Colorado) have 193 electoral votes, which is 71% of the 270 needed to put a presidential candidate in the White House. Yet, several factors worked against Mexican Americans realizing their potential political strength, including the low voter turnout rate among them and the fact that a significant percentage of Mexican Americans are not U.S. citizens.

Mexican Americans are a very urbanized population. About 74% of Mexican Americans were city dwellers in 1980. However, about 87% of Hispanics were urban dwellers.[18] Large populations of Mexican Americans were concentrated in such cities as Los Angeles, Houston, Dallas, Denver, and Chicago. The Mexican-American population, like the African-American population, has also become more economically stratified since the 1970s. There have always been middle-class Mexican Americans. However, a new group of middle-class Hispanics developed as a result of the economic and educational opportunities they experienced during the civil rights movement of the 1960s and 1970s.[19]

This new middle-class group of Mexican Americans are professionals and business people. They frequently work in mainstream White institutions and live in predominantly White middle-class communities, and consequently they have little contact with the Hispanic barrio or with lower- and working-class Mexican-American communities. The children of this new middle class often have little knowledge of the traditional Mexican-American culture in the United States. Acuña has pointed out that these new middle-class professionals and business people often have an identity with and use the term *Hispanic* to refer to themselves. These new middle-class Hispanics, according to Acuña, are often more interested in business development than social action and see business leaders, rather than social activists, as the important movers and shakers in the Mexican-American community.[20]

During the 1980s, which some media writers called, "The Decade of the Hispanic," the emphasis in the Mexican-American community was often on educational and economic development rather than on the kind of strident social action that characterized the civil rights movement of the 1960s and 1970s. Both Presidents Reagan and Bush appointed successful and visible Mexican Americans to important federal positions. President Reagan appointed a university president, Dr. Lauro F. Cavazos, to be Secretary of the Department of Education. Cavazos was the first Hispanic appointed to a Cabinet post. Bush kept him in that position when he was took office in 1989. In 1983, Reagan made history again when he appointed Linda Chavez to the U.S. Commission on Civil Rights. Bush also appointed a number of Hispanics to important positions in his administration.

Nativism in the 1990s: New Xenophobia

The so-called "Decade of the Hispanics" was not without its stresses and strains, emergent xenophobia (fear of foreigners), and subtle and sometimes blatant racism. The new xenophobia, nativism, and sometimes racism have been triggered by several factors, including the large influx of legal Asian and Latin-American immigrants to the United States, the nation's inability to control the large but undetermined number of undocumented or illegal immigrants (some estimates put the figure at 200,000 annually), the radical changes in the U.S. economy discussed above, and the escalating class schism in U.S. society.

Nativistic sentiments and proposals surfaced during the years of heated discussion that finally resulted in the passage of the Immigration Reform and Control Act of 1986. The act is designed to curb the rapid flow of undocumented (illegal) immigrants that enter the United States each year. It severely penalizes employers who knowingly hire undocumented workers. The enacted bill was a difficult compromise. Some of the voices heard during the strident debates over the proposed bill were decidedly anti-Hispanic in tone. The English-Only movement, which came to the forefront during the 1980s, sometimes articulates chilling language that is reminiscent of the nativistic movements at the turn of the last century. A major goal of this movement is to get enacted in as many states as possible referenda that make English the "official language." What these referenda exactly mean in a legal sense is ambiguous. However, important purposes are to halt the growth of bilingual education programs and to send the message to native speakers of languages other than English, such as Spanish, that the only language accepted in the United States is English.

The English-Only movement is fostered by U.S. English, a political action group that has a deep pocket and the endorsement of some influential Americans. The English-Only movement initially targeted states with large Hispanic populations for the passage of English-Only referenda. One of its major successes was the November 1986 passage of Proposition 63 in California. U.S. English knew that the stakes were high in California. It spent more than $700,000 to get Proposition 63 passed there.[21] By the beginning of 1990, U.S. English had been instrumental in getting English-Only referenda enacted in 16 states, including Arizona, Colorado, and Florida (see Table 10–2 for a complete list of these states).

Mexican Americans face several important challenges in the years ahead, including the need to increase the educational status of its youth, to close the income gap between Mexican Americans and the total U.S. population, and to work with other Hispanic groups to influence political elections and national

Table 10–2   *The English-Only States, with Effective Dates of Policy*

Nebraska, 1920
Illinois, 1969
Virginia, 1981
Indiana, Kentucky, and Tennessee, 1984
California and Georgia, 1986
Arkansas, Mississippi, North Carolina, North Dakota, and South Carolina, 1987
Arizona, Colorado, and Florida, 1988

Based on information in James Crawford, *Bilingual Education: History, Politics, Theory and Practice.* Trenton, N.J.: Crane Publishing Company, 1989.

policy. There are encouraging signs that the Mexican-American community will face these challenges creatively.

Teaching Strategies

To illustrate how content about Mexican Americans can be used to integrate the curriculum, three key concepts have been identified and exemplary strategies are given for teaching them. Strategies are presented for teaching *stereotype*, *immigration*, and *social protest* for the primary, intermediate and upper, and high school grades respectively.

Primary Grades

CONCEPT: Stereotypes

Generalization: People have many stereotypes about what makes a person an American. These stereotypes often cause hurt and harm.

1. Read the following story to the class and ask the questions that follow:

Child from Another Land

Manual and Maria Gonzales are descendants of Indian, Mexican, and Spanish people who have lived in the state of New Mexico for at least a century. The Gonzaleses are proud to be Americans but are just as proud of their Mexican-American heritage. In their upper-middle-class community in the Southwest, their eight-year-old son, Ramon, went to a public elementary school that had a 20% Mexican-American population. Ramon felt at home at the school and was sorry when he learned that his father, an engineer, was moving to the Midwest to accept an important job at a well-known computer company. Mrs. Gonzales, a high school English teacher, was also able to get a job in the Midwest city to which the family was moving.

   Manual and Maria were excited about the move to the Midwest because of the opportunity it offered Manual. Ramon was very sorry to leave his friends and the only home and community he had ever known. He had decided, however, that he would try to make the best of the move. Ramon was the only Mexican-American child in the third grade in his new school. There were only five Mexican-American children in the entire school. During the first several days in his new school, Ramon fared okay but felt awkward when the teacher had trouble pronouncing his name and several children asked him, "What country are you from?"

Questions

1. How do you think Ramon felt about leaving his friends?
2. How do you think he felt in his new school? Why did he feel that way? Have you ever felt that way?

3. How do you think Ramon felt when the teacher had trouble pronouncing his name?
4. Why did the children ask Ramon, "What country are you from?"
5. Why do you think the children thought Ramon was from another country?

2. Introduce the concept *stereotype* to the students. Tell the students that a stereotype is a rigid and simplified way of thinking about a group of people and that it often causes harm to individuals and groups. Explain to the students how stereotypes lead to prejudice and discrimination. Ask them to list some of the stereotypes of different groups they may have, such as stereotypes about boys, girls, rich people, poor people, and fat people.

3. Explain to the students that the children thought that Ramon was from a different country because he was a person of color who had a Spanish name. Explain that the children had a stereotypic notion of what an American is. Tell the students that Americans are of all racial, ethnic, and cultural origins. Given them several examples. Also show them pictures of African Americans, Mexican Americans, and Asian Americans. Summarize the lesson by asking the children to list the hurt and harm that stereotypes cause.

Intermediate and Upper Grades

CONCEPT: Immigration

Generalization: Social, economic, and political conditions have influenced Mexican immigration to the United States. Mexican immigrants in the United States have been the victims of racism, deportation, and labor exploitation.

1. Tell the students that about 1 million Mexican immigrants came to the United States between 1910 and 1930. Ask them to state hypotheses to explain why so many Mexicans immigrated to the United States during this period. List their responses on the board. When the students have finished stating their hypotheses, ask them to group their hypotheses into several categories, using symbols such as "×" and "+" to indicate statements that should be grouped together. When the statements have been grouped, ask the students to label the groups. The hypotheses might be grouped into such broad categories as "social reasons," "political reasons," and "economic reasons." These categories need not be mutually exclusive. In this initial exercise, you will be teaching your students how to hypothesize and conceptualize, which involves three major steps: listing, grouping, and labeling. See James A. Banks, with Ambrose A. Clegg, Jr., *Teaching Strategies for the Social Studies: Inquiry, Valuing and Decision-Making*, 4th ed. (White Plains, N.Y.: Longman, Inc., 1990), p. 95.

2. When the first exercise is completed, the students should record their hypotheses and categories in their notebooks. They will need to refer to them later in this exercise when they are tested. The students should now collect and study data to test their hypotheses. Their readings should include information on the Mexican Revolution of 1910 and the tremendous need for agricultural labor that had developed in the Southwest by the turn of the century. The Mexican Revolution caused many displaced Mexican

peasants to come to the United States looking for jobs after 1910. The wealthy farmers in the Southwest wanted a large and cheap labor supply.

3. Students should investigate the conditions of the early Mexican immigrants to the United States. Most became migrant workers who followed the seasonal crops. Many of their dreams were shattered in the United States. Their problems are vividly and poignantly revealed in Manuel Gamio, *The Life Story of the Mexican Immigrant*. Ask four students to read and dramatize to the class the accounts by these migratory laborers: Gumersindo Valdéz, Juan Berzunzolo, Elías Garza, and Nivardo del Rio. Accounts by these writers are found on pages 141–159 of the Gamio book.

4. When the Great Depression struck in 1929, a movement began to deport Mexican immigrants to Mexico. Ask a student to prepare a class presentation giving the views of the U.S. Immigration Service and another to prepare a report revealing how different segments of the Mexican-American community felt about this massive repatriation movement. The class should discuss the problem after these two presentations have been given.

5. Beginning in 1942, Mexican immigrants entered the United States under the terms of an agreement between the United States and Mexico. Ask the students to pretend that it is January 1942, and that the *bracero* bill is being debated in the U.S. Congress. Ask different members of the class to play the roles of various kinds of people in the Mexican-American community (old settlers, new immigrants, etc.), southwest agribusinessmen, and representatives of major unions in the United States. Ask the students playing the assigned roles to argue for or against the bill before the simulated Congress. The class should vote to decide the fate of the *bracero* bill of 1942 after they have heard the arguments. The class should then compare the results of their vote with the bill passed by Congress in 1942.

6. Ask several students in the class to make reports on Public Law 78, the Migratory Labor Agreement, and Operation Wetback, which began in 1954. Conduct a class discussion on the legal, social and moral implications of these two activities that were implemented by the U.S. government. Particular attention should be given to how they affected U.S. citizens of Mexican descent.

7. During the debates and discussion on the passage of the Immigration Reform and Control Act of 1986, many problems of undocumented immigrants to the United States were revealed. Ask the students to research the debates that took place when the proposed act was being discussed, to describe the main goals of the act, and to determine the extent to which the act has been successful.

8. Because of the economic problems in Mexico today, a large number of people (both documented and undocumented) are entering the United States from Mexico. In 1987, 72,400 legal Mexican immigrants entered the United States. A large but unknown number of undocumented immigrants also enter the United States each year.

Ask the students to investigate the economic conditions in Mexico today that cause large numbers of Mexicans to leave their nation and head for the United States. Unlike the past, most of these immigrants settle in large U.S. cities, such as Los Angeles, Dallas, and Houston. Ask the students to find out what kinds of jobs these immigrants obtain in U.S. cities, the problems they encounter, and their general status in U.S. society.

9. Summarize the unit by asking the students to take out the hypotheses they formulated at the beginning of this unit and evaluate them, using the information they have collected and evaluated. They should determine which hypotheses can remain as they were originally stated, which ones must be modified, and which ones must be totally rejected on the basis of the evidence collected.

10. Culminate the unit by showing and discussing a videotape or film on the experiences of Mexican Americans. See Appendix B for the descriptions and annotations of videotapes and films. In the discussion, focus on social, economic, and political conditions that have influenced Mexican immigration to the United States.

Valuing Activity

Read the following story to the class and ask the questions that follow.

The Sánchez Family and the Grape Strike

Mr. and Mrs. Sánchez and their seven children came from Mexico to live in California four years ago. Mr. Sánchez had been told by relatives who had been to the United States that he could make money very quickly if he came to California. When Mr. Sánchez arrived in California, he found that it was hard to make a living working in the fields. Since the Sánchez family has been living in California, the family has had to move many times in order to follow the crops and find work. The family has traveled as far as Texas and Michigan to work in the fields.

The work in the fields is very hard. Everyone in the family, except little Carlos, works in the fields so that the family can make enough money. Even Mrs. Sánchez, who used to stay at home and take care of the home when they lived in Mexico, now must work in the fields. The pay for the work is low. Mr. and Mrs. Sánchez find that they become further and further in debt each year.

The Sánchez family is now living in the San Joaquin Valley in California. The family went to live there to work in the grape fields. For a while everything there was okay. Recently, a lot of things have been happening in the valley that Mr. and Mrs. Sánchez do not fully understand. Most of the field workers have said that they will not go to work next week because the Mexican American Union, led by Juan Gonzalez, who is popular with the workers, has called a strike. The union is demanding that the owners of the grape fields pay the workers more money and give them better worker benefits. The workers who belong to the union are threatening to attack any worker who tries to go to work while the strike is on.

Mr. Sánchez is not a member of the union. He wants very much to go to work next week. He has many bills to pay and needs money for food and clothing. The family simply cannot get by with the small amount of money that the union has promised to give Mr. Sánchez if he joins it and refuses to work next week. Mr. Sánchez also realizes that if the grapes are not picked within the next two weeks, they will rot. He has heard that these strikes sometimes last for months. His boss told him that if he wants to go to work next Monday morning—the day the strike is to begin—he will protect him from the unionized workers. Mrs. Sánchez thinks that Mr. Sánchez should support the strike so that he can make higher wages in the future.

Questions

1. Do you think that Mr. Sánchez and his family will go to work in the fields next Monday? Why or why not?
2. If Mr. Sánchez does go to work, what do you think will happen to him and his family?
3. If Mr. Sánchez does not go to work in the grape fields next Monday, what do you think he might do to earn money?
4. What do you think Mr. Sánchez should do? Why?
5. What would you do if you were (a) Mr. Sánchez (b) Mrs. Sánchez (c) the children? Why?
6. Tell whether you agree or disagree with this statement and why: "The head of a family should never let his or her spouse and children do without the food and clothing they need."

High School Grades

CONCEPT: Social Protest

Generalization: Since the Anglo-American conquest of the Southwest, Mexican Americans have used a variety of means to resist oppression and discrimination. This resistance intensified and assumed new characteristics in the 1960s and 1970s.

1. The teacher can begin this unit by having the students read and dramatize the epic poem of the Chicano movement, *I Am Joaquín*, by Rodolfo Gonzales. This poem is a powerful statement of the history and culture of Chicanos, with emphasis on their oppression and struggle for freedom. The author draws on nearly 2,000 years of Mexican and United States history. Among the many references made in the poem related to social protest are Father Miguel Hidalgo and *El Grito de Dolores of 1810*, Cinco de Mayo, the Treaty of Guadalupe Hidalgo, and the Anglo conquest of the Southwest in the 1800s. This poem will stimulate many questions students can pursue during this study of Chicano resistance to oppression. The teacher may also want to show the film based on the poem *I Am Joaquín*.

2. References are frequently made to the Treaty of Guadalupe Hidalgo by Chicano leaders. After students have studied the events that led to the treaty, have them examine the treaty in detail and give their interpretations of it. They should compare their interpretations of the treaty with interpretations given by contemporary Chicano leaders. The complete text of the treaty is found in *A Documentary History of Mexican Americans*, edited by Moquin with Van Doren. A useful annotated copy of the treaty appears in Bill Tate's *Guadalupe Hidalgo Treaty of Peace 1848 and the Gadsden Treaty with Mexico 1853*, 5th ed., published by the Tate Gallery, P.O. Box 428, Truchas, New Mexico 87578.

3. Ask a group of students to prepare and present to the class a dramatization portraying the positions and statements of early Mexican-American militant leaders, such as Juan Patron, J. J. Herrerra, and Juan N. Cortina.

4. Some of the earliest Chicano resistance activities were unionization and strikes. Ask a group of students to prepare short reports on the various strikes and union activities during the period from 1900 to 1940. The strike in the California Imperial Valley in 1928 should be highlighted.

5. The earliest Mexican-American civil rights organizations pursued what Cuellar has called a "politics of adaptation." Mexican-American civil rights organizations became more politicized in the post–World War II period. Militant Chicano organizations emerged in the 1960s. Ask the students to research the goals, tactics, and strategies used by the following Mexican-American civil rights groups. They will discover the trends described above.

   a. Order of the Sons of America (formed in 1921)
   b. League of United Latin-American Citizens (1929)
   c. The Community Service Organization (1947)
   d. The American G.I. Forum (1948)
   e. Federal Alliance of Free Cities (1963)
   f. Crusade for Justice (1965)

6. Ask the class to research the following questions: How was the Chicano movement similar to other Mexican-American protest movements? How were its goals and strategies different? When did the movement emerge? What problems did it help to solve? What had happened to the movement by the late 1980s? Why? In what ways was the Chicano movement similar to, and different from, civil rights movements that emerged within other ethnic minority communities in the 1960s? What long-term effects do you think the Chicano movement will have on U.S. society?

7. The union activity led by Cesar Chávez during the 1960s and 1970s was an integral part of the Chicano movement. You may begin a study of these events by reading to the class the brilliant and poignant letter that Chávez wrote to E. L. Barr, Jr., president of the California Grape and Tree Fruit League, reprinted in Fusco and Horwitz, *La Causa: The California Grape Strike*. The moving photographs in this book will evoke many questions and comments about the strike. The students can also read the excellently written book on the strike by John Gregory Dunne, *Delano: The Story of the California Grape Strike*.

8. After the students have read and discussed accounts and interpretations of Mexican-American resistance and the Chicano movement, ask them to write and present a dramatization on "Mexican-American Resistance to Oppression in the United States, 1848 to the present."

Endnotes

1. U.S. Bureau of the Census, *Projections of the Population of the U.S. by Age, Sex, and Race 1983–2080* (Washington, D.C.: U.S. Government Printing Office, 1989).
2. U.S. Bureau of the Census, *Statistical Abstract of the United States: 1989*, 109th ed. (Washington, D.C.: U.S. Government Printing Office, 1989), p. 10.

3. Jack D. Forbes, *Mexican-Americans: A Handbook for Educators* (Washington, D.C.: U.S. Government Printing Office, n.d.), p. 3.

4. Carey McWilliams, *North from Mexico: The Spanish-Speaking People of the United States* (New York: Greenwood Press, 1968), p. 20.

5. John Hope Franklin and Alfred A. Moss, Jr. *From Slavery to Freedom: A History of Negro Americans.* 6th ed. (New York: Knopf, 1988).

6. McWilliams, *North from Mexico*, p. 34.

7. "The Treaty of Guadalupe Hidalgo," in *A Documentary History of Mexican Americans*, Wayne Moquin, with Charles Van Doren, eds. (New York: Bantam Books, 1971), p. 247.

8. Matt S. Meier and Feliciano Rivera, *The Chicanos: A History of Mexican Americans* (New York: Hill and Wang, 1972), p. 71.

9. Joan W. Moore, with Harry Pachon, *Mexican-Americans*, 2nd ed. (Englewood Cliffs, N.J.: Prentice-Hall, 1976), p. 36.

10. Ibid., p. 42.

11. McWilliams, *North from Mexico*, pp. 178–179.

12. Rodolfo Acuña, *Occupied America: The Chicano's Struggle toward Liberation* (San Francisco: Canfield Press, 1972), p. 77.

13. Rodolfo Acuña, *Occupied America: The Chicano's Struggle toward Liberation*, 3rd ed. (New York: Harper and Row, 1988).

14. Meier and Rivera, *The Chicanos*, p. 184.

15. Joan W. Moore, with Alfredo Cuellar, *Mexican Americans* (Englewood Cliffs, N.J.: Prentice-Hall, 1970).

16. William J. Wilson, *The Truly Disadvantaged: The Inner City, the Underclass, and Public Policy* (Chicago: The University of Chicago Press, 1987).

17. The Census data reported in this section are from U.S. Bureau of the Census, *Statistical Abstract of the United States: 1989*, 109th ed., p. 38.

18. Acuña, *Occupied America*, 3rd ed., p. 428.

19. Ibid., pp. ix–xii.

20. Ibid., p. 449.

21. James Crawford, *Bilingual Education: History, Politics, Theory and Practice* (Trenton, N.J.: Crane Publishing Company, 1989), p. 53.

Annotated Bibliography

Books for Teachers

Especially Recommended

Acuña, Rodolfo. *Occupied America: A History of Chicanos*, 3rd ed. New York: Harper and Row, 1988.

This comprehensive and readable history of Mexican Americans presents different and refreshing perspectives on their experiences in the United States. It is the most up-to-date comprehensive history of the group.

Kanellos, Nicolas. *A History of Hispanic Theatre in the United States: Origins to 1940.* Austin: University of Texas Press, 1990.

This valuable and well-researched history contains information about Hispanic plays, authors, artists, companies, houses, directors, and theatrical circuits.

Keefe, Susan E., and Padilla, Amado M. *Chicano Ethnicity.* Albuquerque: University of New Mexico Press, 1987.

This important study examines the complex relationship between ethnicity, acculturation, and assimilation among Mexican Americans.

Martinez, Julio A., and Lomeli, Francisco A., eds. *Chicano Literature: A Reference Guide.* Westport, Conn.: Greenwood Press, 1985.

This excellent and comprehensive reference book includes informative biographies of Mexican American writers, topical essays such as "Chicano Literature from 1942 to the Present" and "Chicano Poetry and Literature," as well as a useful chronology of Chicano literature.

Mirande, Alfredo. *The Chicano Experience: An Alternative Perspective.* Notre Dame, Ind.: University of Notre Dame Press, 1985.

In this interesting sociological study of Mexican Americans, the author challenges the traditional assimilationist model that is often used to study Chicanos. He describes their experiences from a different and refreshing perspective.

Rocard, Marcienne. Translated by Edward G. Brown, Jr. *The Children of the Sun: Mexican American Literature of the United States.* Tucson: The University of Arizona Press, 1989.

A scholarly literary analysis that examines works by Mexican and Mexican American authors. This important book also contains an extensive and valuable bibliography of literature by and about Mexican Americans.

San Miguel, Guadalupe, Jr. *"Let All of Them Take Heed": Mexican Americans and the Campaign for Educational Equality in Texas, 1910-1981.* Austin: University of Texas Press, 1987.

This is a scholarly, informative, and important history of the education of Mexican Americans in Texas. Their education in Texas mirrors their education in the other Southwestern states.

Other References

Abalos, David T. *Latinos in the United States: The Sacred and the Political.* Notre Dame, Ind.: University of Notre Dame Press, 1986.

The author applies a transformation theory to key aspects of the Latino experience in the United States. The book includes a chapter on Latino professionals.

Anzaldua, Gloria. *Borderlands La Frontera: The New Mestiza.* San Francisco: Spinsters/ Aunt Lute Book Company, 1987.

The author describes her childhood along the Texas-Mexico border and recounts her experiences of being an alien in both Mexican and U.S. cultures.

Bean, Frank D.; Schmandt, Jurgen; and Weintraub, Sidney, eds. *Mexican and Central American Populations and U.S. Immigration Policy.* Austin: University of Texas Press, 1989.

In this edited collection, nine academic specialists examine the demographic situations of Mexico, Central America, and the U.S. Southwest to reveal their influence on U.S. immigration and population policy.

Camarillo, Albert. *Chicanos in California: A History of Mexican Americans in California.* San Francisco: Boyd and Fraser, 1984.

This is an important and scholarly social history of Chicanos in California since the 1948 U.S. annexation.

Connor, Walker, ed. *Mexican-Americans in Comparative Perspective.* Washington, D.C.: The Urban Institute, 1985.

A useful and informative collection of scholarly essays that examine the Mexican-American experience from a comparative perspective.

Crockcroft, James D. *Outlaws in the Promised Land: Mexican Immigrant Workers and America's Future.* New York: Grove Press, 1986.

This historical and sociological study examines the role of Mexican immigrant workers in the U.S. economy.

De La Garza, Rodolfo O.; Bean, Frank D.; Bonjean, Charles M.; Romo, Ricardo; and Alvarez, Rodolfo, eds. *The Mexican American Experience: An Interdisciplinary Anthology.* Austin: University of Texas Press, 1985.

Labor problems, self-identity, political struggles, school desegregation, and language patterns are among the topics treated in this anthology.

Del Castillo, Richard Griswold. *LaFamilia: Chicano Families in the Urban Southwest, 1848 to the Present.* Notre Dame, Ind.: University of Notre Dame Press, 1984.

This book investigates the social and economic history of Mexican-American families since 1848 in Los Angeles, Tucson, Santa Fe, and San Antonio. This is a scholarly and informative source.

Fernandez, Raul A. *The Mexican-American Border Region: Issues and Trends.* Notre Dame, Ind.: University of Notre Dame Press, 1989.

The author discusses the political and economic developments related to the Mexican-U.S. border region.

Foley, Douglas E., with Mota, Clarice; Post, Donald E.; and Ignacio, Lozano. *From Peones to Politicos: Class and Ethnicity in a South Texas Town, 1900–1987.* Austin: University of Texas Press, 1988.

A scholarly study of class and ethnicity in a Texas town.

Garcia, F. Chris. *Latinos and the Political System.* Notre Dame, Ind.: University of Notre Dame Press, 1989.

This anthology consists of 28 papers that discuss both local and national developments in Latino politics.

Garcia, Mario T. *Mexican Americans: Leadership, Ideology and Identity.* New Haven: Yale University Press, 1990.

An informative and well-researched historical treatment of the first significant civil rights movement by Mexican Americans.

Jankowski, Martin Sanchez. *City Bound: Urban Life and Political Attitudes among Chicano Youth.* Albuquerque: University of New Mexico Press, 1986.

An important sociological study of the political attitudes of Mexican-American youths in selected cities. This book contains an important chapter on "Chicano Ethnicity and City Life."

Markides, Kyriakos S., and Martin, Harry W., with Gomez, Ernesto. *Older Mexican Americans: A Study in an Urban Barrio.* Austin: Center for Mexican American Studies, University of Texas, 1983.

An informative, scholarly study of older Mexican Americans.

Martinez, Oscar J. *Troublesome Border.* Tucson: The University of Arizona Press, 1988.

Using conflict as a central theme, the author examines the historical and contemporary relationships in the United States-Mexico borderlands.

Melville, Margarita B., ed. *Twice a Minority: Mexican American Women.* St. Louis: C. V. Mosby, 1980.

This book consists of a collection of scholarly papers that discuss specific topics related to Chicanos. It is a highly specialized book rather than a general introduction to the topic of Mexican-American women.

Mirandé, Alfredo. *Gringo Justice.* Notre Dame, Ind.: University of Notre Dame Press, 1987.

This is a scholarly study of the relationship of Mexican Americans to the legal and judicial system from 1848 to the present.

Mirandé, Alfredo, and Eriquez, Evangelina. *La Chicana: The Mexican-American Woman.* Chicago: The University of Chicago Press, 1979.

Viewing Mexican Americans as a colonized group, this book discusses the historical and social factors related to the experiences of Chicanas in the United States. The fresh perspectives presented in this book merit study and reflection.

Montejano, David. *Anglos and Mexicans in the Making of Texas, 1836–1986.* Austin: University of Texas Press, 1987.

This scholarly history of the Mexican in Texas won the Walter Prescott Award.

Moore, Joan W., with Pachon, Harry. *Mexican Americans,* 2d ed. Englewood Cliffs, N.J.: Prentice-Hall, 1976.

This introductory study is primarily sociological but includes a useful historical overview. Written from an assimilationist perspective, the author focuses on change, conflict, and cultural diversity.

Muller, Thomas, and Espenshade, Thomas J. *The Fourth Wave: California's Newest Immigrants.* Washington, D.C.: The Urban Institute, 1985.

A scholarly and informative treatment of the newest immigrants to our most populous state. Mexican Americans are prominent in the book.

Muñoz, Carlos, Jr. *Youth, Identity, Power: The Chicano Movement.* New York: Verso, 1989.

This book is a treatment of the rise of the Chicano movement in'the 1960s by one of its leading participants, now a professor of ethnic studies at the University of California, Berkeley.

Pena, Manuel. *The Texas-Mexican Conjunto: History of a Working Class Music.* Austin: University of Texas Press, 1985.

An informative study of conjunto, a popular and distinctive style of accordion music.

Portes, Alejandro, and Bach, Robert L. *Latin Journey: Cuban and Mexican Immigrants in the United States*. Berkeley: University of California Press, 1985.

> *An important, scholarly comparative study of Cuban and Mexican immigrants in the United States.*

Tatum, Charles M. *Chicano Literature*. Boston: Twayne Publishers, 1982.

> *This informative book on Chicano literature includes chapters on the origins and evolution of Chicano literature, Chicano theater, Chicano short story, Chicano novel, and Chicano poetry. It also includes a useful annotated bibliography and a literary chronology.*

Vasquez, Josefina Zoraida, and Meyer, Lorenzo. *The United States and Mexico*. Chicago: The University of Chicago Press, 1985.

> *An important and scholarly history of the relationship between the United States and Mexico.*

Villarreal, Roberto; Hernandez, Norma G; and Neighbor, Howard D., eds. *Latino Empowerment: Progress, Problems, and Prospects*. New York: Greenwood Press, 1988.

> *The papers that constitute this volume discuss various aspects of Latino and Mexican-American political life. Essays include "The Politics of Mexican-American Empowerment," "Structural Barriers to Chicano Empowerment," and "Latino Representation in Los Angeles."*

Virgil, James Diego. *Barrio Gangs: Street Life and Identity in Southern California*. Austin: University of Texas Press, 1988.

> *In this informative study, the author describes some major factors that give rise to gangs.*

Weyr, Thomas. *Hispanic U.S.A.: Breaking the Melting Pot*. New York: Harper and Row, 1988.

> *"Immigrants and Illegal Aliens," "Education," "Politics," and "The Hispanic Market" are among the topics discussed in this popular book. It is appropriate for high school students.*

Books for Students

Anaya, Rudolfo A. *Heart of Azlán: A Novel*. Albuquerque: University of New Mexico, 1988.

> *The reader experiences the frustration, despair, and triumphs of the Chávez family as they work to make life better for themselves and other farm laborers. (High School)*

Anderson, Joan. *Spanish Pioneers of the Southwest*. New York: Dutton, 1989.

> *This beautifully illustrated book describes the lives of the Spanish settlers who established the first colony of Europeans in what is now New Mexico. (Primary/Intermediate)*

Ashabranner, Brent. *Dark Harvest: Migrant Farmworkers in America*. New York: Dodd, Mead, 1985.

> *This book contains an intimate view of the lives of migrant workers. It reveals the reasons they become migrant workers, the injustices they suffer, and the impact of their work on their children's education. (Intermediate)*

Beatty, Patricia. *Lupita Mañana*. New York: William Morrow, 1981.

> *This novel is about thirteen-year-old Lupita, who enters the United States without legal papers and without her father after he dies in Mexico. (High School)*

Bethancourt, T. Ernesto. *The Me inside of Me*. Minneapolis: Lerner, 1987.

> *Alfredo Flores suddenly becomes rich and leaves his Mexican-American community for an elite college prep school, where he encounters prejudice. (High School)*

Brown, Tricia. *Hello Amigos*. New York: Henry Holt, 1986.

> *Readers follow Frankie Valdez and his family and friends through the day as they celebrate Frankie's birthday. (Primary)*

Christian, Rebecca. *Cooking the Spanish Way*. Minneapolis: Lerner, 1982.

> *This cookbook introduces its readers to easy-to-cook recipes and information about the history and culture of Spain. (All Ages)*

de Garza, Patricia. *Chicanos: The Story of Mexican Americans*. New York: Julian Messner, 1973.

> *This is a well-written and interesting history of Mexican Americans. The author discusses the contributions Mexican Americans have made to the United States and the problems they have encountered. (Intermediate)*

Dobrin, Arnold. *The New Life—La Vida Nueva*. New York: Dodd, Mead, 1971.

> *This illustrated book presents a panoramic view of Mexican Americans today. The author looks at their hopes, aspirations, and problems. (Intermediate)*

Editors, *Raintree Hispanic Stories*. Milwaukee: Raintree Publishers, 1990.

> *This series of sixteen books recounts key events in the lives of notable Hispanics. The beautifully illustrated books are written in English and in Spanish. Individuals such as Pedro Menéndez de Avilés, who founded settlements in Florida and North Carolina and claimed Florida for Spain, are profiled in this series. Vilma Martinez, who won the 1974 case that guaranteed the right of bilingual education to all non-English speaking children, is also profiled. Ms. Martinez also wrote the brief for the first equal employment case tried under the 1964 Civil Rights Bill before the Supreme Court. Scientists such as Luis W. Alvarez are also profiled. Dr. Alvarez won the 1968 Nobel Prize in physics and is the author of the "Big Bang" theory on the origin of our planet. (Primary/Intermediate)*

Edwards, Nicholas. *Stand and Deliver*. New York: Scholastic Books, 1989.

> *Photographs from the popular motion picture of the same name illustrate this inspirational story about a math teacher who motivates his students to master college-level calculus and to work for a better future for themselves. (Middle School/High School)*

Fincher, E. B. *Mexico and the United States: Their Linked Destinies*. New York: Thomas Y. Crowell, 1983.

> *This book explores the long standing relationship between Mexico and the United States. (Middle School)*

Fisher, Leonard Everett. *Pyramid of the Sun/Pyramid of the Moon*. New York: Macmillan, 1988.

> *This informative book describes the civilization that built two great pyramids to worship the sun and the moon. The book includes maps that show the location of*

the two pyramids in Teotihuacan. It is illustrated with black-and-white artwork with colored symbols on time charts. The time charts chronicle the history of the Toltec civilization from 150 B.C. to 1521, when it was conquered by Spanish explorers. This book can be used to help students understand the cultural heritage of Mexican Americans. (High School)

Galarza, Ernesto. *Barrio Boy*. Notre Dame, Ind.: University of Notre Dame Press, 1971.

A well-written, interesting autobiography of a noted Mexican-American scholar, this book can be used to teach the concept of acculturation. (High School)

Gonzales, Rodolfo. *I Am Joaquin*. New York: Bantam Books, 1967.

An important epic poem of the Chicano people, this book includes a useful chronology of Mexican-American history. (High School)

Haddox, John. *Los Chicanos: An Awakening People*. El Paso, Tex.: Western Press, 1970.

The author discusses self-concept, culture and the values of Chicanos and looks to the future. He writes with deep feeling. (High School)

Harlan, Judith. *Hispanic Voters*. New York: Watts, 1988.

The potential impact of Hispanics on American politics is examined in this book. (High School)

Haskins, Jim. *Count Your Way through Mexico*. Minneapolis: Lerner, 1988.

This book introduces students to the language and culture of Mexico. It is part of a series of counting books that features the languages of Africa, the Arab world, Canada, China, Japan, Korea, and the U.S.S.R. (Primary)

Hernández, Irene Beltrán. *Across the Great River*. Houston: Art Público, 1989.

A young girl becomes the leader of her family when her parents are separated from the other family members when they cross the border into the United States. (High School)

Krumgold, Joseph. *And Now Miguel*. New York: Thomas Y. Crowell, 1953.

Miguel struggles to become a man in this powerful and beautifully written Newbery Medal book. The reader experiences his conflicts and identity crisis. (Middle School)

Kurtycz, Marcos, and Kobeh, Ana García. *Tigers and Opossums: Animal Legends*. Boston: Little, Brown, 1981.

This book contains five magical folktales of ancient Mexico. (Primary)

MacMillan, Dianne, and Freeman, Dorothy. *Martha Rodriguez: Meeting a Mexican-American Family*. New York: Messner, 1986.

A young Anglo girl learns about Mexican-American foods, songs, and family events as a result of her friendship with Martha Rodriguez and her family. (Primary)

Martínez-Ostos, Susana, and Blackmore, Vivien. *Why Corn Is Golden*. Boston: Little, Brown, 1984.

These delightful stories about plants were first told by Mexican Indians in ancient times. (Primary)

Meltzer, Milton. *The Hispanic Americans.* New York: Thomas Y. Crowell, 1982.

> *The cultures, backgrounds, and social and economic problems of Mexican Americans and other Hispanic groups are discussed in this informative book. (Intermediate)*

Perl, Lila. *Pinatas and Paper Flowers/Pinatas y Flores de Papel.* New York: Clarion, 1983.

> *Written in English and Spanish, this book describes several holidays that are celebrated in North, Central, and South America. (Primary/Intermediate)*

Pinchot, Jane. *The Mexicans in America.* Minneapolis: Lerner, 1989.

> *This book provides a historical overview of Mexican Americans and their contributions to American society. (Intermediate/Middle School)*

Roberts, Maurice. *César Chávez and La Causa.* Chicago: Children's Press, 1986.

> *César Chávez's life is profiled in black-and-white photographs and an easy-to-read text. This biography is part of a series of picture-story biographies about notable Americans. Another book by Roberts is* Henry Ciseros: Mexican American Mayor *(Children's Press, 1986). (Primary/Intermediate)*

Rohmer, Harriet. *The Legend of Food Mountain.* San Francisco: Children's Book Press, 1988.

> *Adapted from the Chimalpopocatl Codice, this legend reminds the reader that human beings have a special relationship with the earth and that they must respect and care for it. Other books by Rohmer include* How We Came to the Fifth World *(Children's Book Press, 1988);* Uncle Nacho's Hat *(Children's Book Press, 1988); and* When Mr. Sugar Came to Town *(Children's Book Press, 1988). (Intermediate)*

Soto, Gary. *Living up the Street: Narrative Recollections.* San Francisco: Strawberry Hill, 1985.

> *The early years of a Mexican-American poet who grew up in Fresno is recounted in this 1985 American Book Award selection. (High School)*

Stark, William, and de Gerez, Toni. *My Song Is a Piece of Jade.* Boston: Little, Brown, 1981.

> *Originally written by the Toltec people, these poems are a tribute to the gods. They are written in English and Spanish. (Primary)*

Treviño, Lee, and Blair, Sam. *The Snake in the Sandtrap.* New York: Holt, 1985.

> *Golfers will enjoy Treviño's humorous collection of anecdotes from his golfing tours. The book is illustrated with black-and-white photographs. (High School)*

Chapter 11

Puerto Ricans

in the United States

Concepts, Strategies, and Materials

> *Among the Hispanic communities, we were not the first to establish our-selves in the northeast United States. However, it was we, the Puerto Ricans, who came in major numbers. . . . We were poor in material riches. But we were rich in faith, hopes, and spirit.*
>
> —José Lumen Roman

Introduction

Puerto Ricans are the second largest Hispanic group in the United States. Their (projected) 1990 population, about 2,666,188, is about 13% of the total popu-lation of documented Hispanics living in the United States. The Puerto Rican population increased about 32% between 1980 and 1990. This rate of growth was considerably greater than the rate of increase for the total U.S. population and for Whites but below the rate of growth for the total Hispanic population (about 50%). The 32% population increase experienced by Puerto Ricans between 1980 and 1990 was due primarily to a high birthrate rather than to migration. Puerto Rican migration to the United States peaked in 1953 with about 75,000 net arrivals. Since that time net migration between Puerto Rico and the United States has ebbed and flowed with economic conditions in the two nations (see Figure 11–1).[1]

The Puerto Rican population on the U.S. mainland is growing faster than the population in Puerto Rico. In 1988, Puerto Rico's population was about 3,359,000, compared to a mainland Puerto Rican population of about 2,522,000. The island's population increased about 5% between 1980 and 1988, whereas the Puerto Rican population on the mainland increased about 25%.[2] Not all of the people who lived on the island, however, were of Puerto

344

Figure 11–1   *Migration from Puerto Rico to the United States, 1920–1986*

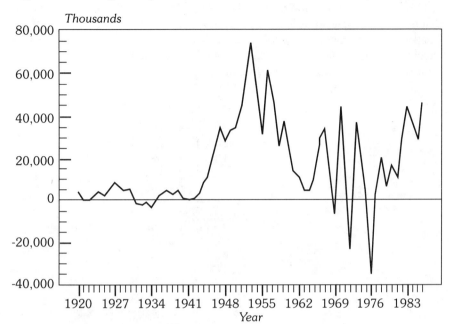

Source: Figure 1.1 from Clara E. Rodriguez, *Puerto Ricans Born in the U.S.A.* (Boston: Unwin Hyman, Inc., 1989), p. 3. © 1989 by Unwin Hyman, Inc. Reprinted with permission.

Rican descent. Puerto Rico has a sizable immigrant population. Some population experts predict that if the current disproportionate rate of population growth on the island and the mainland continues, the number of Puerto Ricans on the U.S. mainland will equal if not exceed the number on the island by the turn of the century.

Content about Puerto Ricans should be included in the mainstream curriculum because they are an integral part of U.S. society. Knowledge of their experience on the mainland can help students master important social science concepts, such as migration, cultural diversity, racism, and colonialism.

When studying about Puerto Ricans on the U.S. mainland, students can compare and contrast their experience with those of other migrant and immigrant groups. In some ways, their migration is similar to the movement of other groups to the United States. They are culturally uprooted, like European immigrants were, when they migrate to the United States. However, their migration is also unique in U.S. history. When large numbers of Puerto Ricans began to migrate to the U.S. mainland, automation had greatly decreased the need for manual labor in the United States. Puerto Ricans are U.S. citizens when they set foot on American soil. Their migration is the first "airborne migration" in U.S. history. Puerto Ricans bring racial attitudes to this country that are considerably different from those they find here. The study of the complex nature of the Puerto Rican migration and experience on the mainland provides students with excellent opportunities to formulate generalizations that are essential components of a sound multicultural curriculum.

Puerto Ricans in the United States: Historical Perspective

Important Dates

1493	Columbus landed on the island of Boriquén, November 19, 1493. Boriquén was the home of the Taíno (or Arawak) Indians, the native inhabitants of Puerto Rico.
1508	Juan Ponce de León became the governor of Puerto Rico.
1511	The Taíno Indians unsuccessfully rebelled against the Spanish system of forced labor.
1513	African slaves were introduced on Puerto Rican plantations.
1868	*El Grito De Lares:* a group of Puerto Rican revolutionaries called for independence and planned an unsuccessful revolt.
1873	Slavery was abolished in Puerto Rico.
1898	Spain ceded Puerto Rico to the United States under the terms of the Treaty of Paris, the treaty that formally ended the Spanish-American War.
1900	Under the terms of the Foraker Act, the United States established a government in Puerto Rico in which the president of the United States appointed the governor and the Executive Council. The House of Delegates and the resident commissioner were to be elected by popular vote.
1910	The U.S. Census indicated that there were 1,513 native Puerto Ricans living in the United States.
1917	The Jones Act was passed by the U.S. Congress. It made Puerto Ricans U.S. citizens and subject to the U.S. draft. The act also provided for the popular election of both houses of the Puerto Rican legislature.

Important Dates	
1920	11,811 persons born in Puerto Rico were living in the United States. That number increased to 58,200 in 1935.
1937	Twenty people were killed in a tragedy known as the "Ponce Massacre" on Palm Sunday.
1947	The U.S. Congress amended the Jones Act of 1917. Puerto Ricans were granted the right to elect their own governor. The governor was given the right to make most of the appointments for high public offices.
1948	Luis Muñoz Marin became the first elected governor of Puerto Rico. He was governor of Puerto Rico until 1964.
1952	On July 25, Governor Luis Muñoz Marin led the inaugural ceremonies establishing the Commonwealth of Puerto Rico, or the Associated Free State.
1965	With the passage of the Civil Rights Act of 1965, Puerto Ricans in the United States were no longer required to pass an English literacy test to vote in the state of New York.
1967	In a plebiscite, Puerto Ricans voted to maintain the Commonwealth status. Statehood and independence were the second and third choices, respectively.
1970	Herman Badillo was elected to the U.S. House of Representatives. He was the first mainland Puerto Rican elected to Congress. Governor Ferré and President Nixon formed an ad hoc committee to discuss the U.S. presidential vote for Puerto Rico.
1971	Cuban representatives to the United Nations proposed a resolution to have U.S. colonialism in Puerto Rico debated during a meeting of the United Nations Trusteeship Council.
1972	The Popular Democratic party was returned to power in Puerto Rico with the election of Rafael Hernandez Colón as the new governor. The United Nations Decolonization Committee declared that Puerto Rico is a colony of the United States.
1974	The legal case, *Aspira of New York, Inc. et al. v. Board of Education of the City of New York, Inc. et al.*, ended when the two parties reached an agreement, legally termed a "consent decree." The Board of Education agreed to provide bilingual instruction for Puerto Rican students.

*Important
Dates*

1990   The Puerto Rican population on the U.S. mainland in-
                       creased about 32% between 1980 and 1990, primarily
                       from new births rather than from migration.

The Island Background

Puerto Rico

Puerto Rico, called San Juan Baptista by Christopher Columbus, is a beautiful, small tropical island in the Caribbean Sea. The island, which sits on the top of a large underwater mountain, is smaller than the state of Connecticut. It is about 35 miles wide, 100 miles long, and is made up of slightly more than 3,400 square miles. Puerto Rico, which has become one of the favorite vacation places for U.S. tourists, has one of the highest population densities in the world, 362.6 persons per square kilometer in 1988. In 1988, about 3,359,000 people lived on this attractive island.

Puerto Rico's history is just as interesting as its terrain and demography. During the last four centuries, it has suffered an identity crisis and a sense of political alienation because its destiny has been determined by two faraway nations that ruled it the way absentee landlords govern a slum. Spain ruled the country from the sixteenth century up to the Spanish-American War in 1898. In 1898, the United States took control. It governed Puerto Rico awkwardly and ambiguously. Although the Commonwealth of Puerto Rico has existed since July 1952, Puerto Rico's relationship with the United States is still shaky and unclear. Puerto Rico, which is neither a state nor an independent nation, is still in search of its identity and destiny. This identity quest is likely to continue for some years to come, especially as cries for independence keep emerging in Puerto Rico, even if they are voiced only by a determined, forceful few.

Since 1917, Puerto Ricans have been U.S. citizens. In the period between the two world wars, they started migrating to the mainland in large numbers, mainly to New York City. In 1988, about 42% of all Puerto Ricans lived in the U.S. mainland. About half of the mainland Puerto Ricans were born in the United States. The number of Puerto Ricans in the United States mainland is significant and increases at every Census count. The Puerto Rican mainland population grew from 900,000 in 1960 to more than 2.5 million in 1988.

The Taíno Indians

Puerto Ricans have three major racial heritages—Indian, African, and Spanish. The island was inhabited by a group of Indians called the Taínos when the Spanish came in the fifteenth century. Because they left no written records, little is known about the Taínos, except what archaeologists have been able to detect from potsherds and skulls. Some social scientists believe that there were about 40,000 Taínos on the island when the Spanish came and that they had straight black hair and copper-colored skin.[3] Their culture was based on farming, hunting, and raising animals. Religion was also an important part of the Taíno culture. The Spaniards caught the Indians by surprise and totally without the kinds of weapons they needed to fight men who fought with swords.[4]

The Coming of the Spaniards

In search of a new route to India, Columbus arrived in the Americas in 1492. When he came back to the Americas in 1493, he landed on the island of Boriquén, home of the Taíno Indians. Columbus's arrival on the island foreshadowed the Spanish takeover. When Juan Ponce de León was made governor of the island in 1508, the Spanish occupation of Puerto Rico was well underway. From the time of the arrival of the Spanish conquistadores, life for the native Indians became increasingly more difficult. Eventually, they were almost totally exterminated. The Spanish set up a kind of forced labor, known as the *encomienda system*. Under this system, each Spanish colonizer was given a group of Indians to work for him. The Spanish colonizer was supposed to "teach" the Indians Spanish "culture" in return for their work.

At first, the Indians did not fight back. They thought that the Spaniards were immortal. Eventually, a group of Taíno Indians decided to find out if the Spanish were actually immortal. They tried to drown a young Spaniard and succeeded. Once they discovered that the Spaniards died like other men, they started fighting back. A number of Indian rebellions occurred in various parts of the island. Many Spaniards were killed in these skirmishes. The Taínos also ran away from the Spanish settlements. The conquistadores searched for them, often with little success. So many Indians were killed by the Spaniards and their diseases, and so many escaped from the island, that by 1777 they had all but disappeared from Puerto Rico.

Spanish Rule

By the late nineteenth century, Puerto Rico was one of the most neglected colonies in the Western Hemisphere. For nearly 400 years, Spain had ruled the colony from across the Atlantic like an absentee landlord and had woefully neglected it. Puerto Rico's last series of Spanish governors were incompetent and autocratic. They ineptly governed the island with an oppressive, heavy hand. When Spain and the United States entered the Spanish-American War in 1898, Spain's 400-year neglect of her small Caribbean colony was painfully visible. The masses of the people were peons, and the country's wealth was concentrated in the hands of the small upper-class. No middle-class existed. Most of the people were illiterate, and 92% of the children were not in school.

Contagious diseases were widespread. Public health facilities were almost totally absent. Nearly 80% of the draftable Puerto Rican males failed the physical test given by the U.S. military during World War I.

Spain's neglect and mistreatment of Puerto Rico had led to an aggressive movement for home rule by the 1800s. In 1868, the famous Lares Revolt occurred. A group of independence advocates took the city of Lares and proclaimed it the "Republic of Puerto Rico." The revolt failed, but the agitation for home rule continued, even though it was often sporadic and poorly organized. Eventually the movement bore fruit. On November 28, 1897, Puerto Rico was granted autonomy by Spain. This proved to be one of the shortest and most meaningless political changes in history. Barely before the new Puerto Rican government could begin to function, U.S. troops landed on the island.

The Spanish-American War

Spain declared war on the United States on April 24, 1898. A truce was signed on August 12 of that same year. Spain was a pushover for the United States. The two nations formally ended the war with the Treaty of Paris, signed on December 10, 1898. At the meeting, the United States reigned supreme. Spain ceded the Philippines and Puerto Rico to the United States and gave up rights to Cuba. The United States also acquired American Guam.

As had been the case for 400 years, nobody asked Puerto Rico about its political future. Its fate was determined by the United States and Spain. After the meeting, Puerto Rico lost the little autonomy that Spain had granted it in 1897 and became a United States possession. Puerto Rican independence leaders were shocked and dismayed. They had thought that their neighbor from the North had come to free them from colonialism. It was a rude awakening to discover that the United States, the "citadel of freedom and democracy," would also subjugate Puerto Rico just as Spain had done.

U.S. Rule

When the U.S. government took control of Puerto Rico in 1898, it had little experience in governing colonies. In fact, "self-determination of nations" had been one of the main ideas voiced by the U.S. government. However, with the emergence of the doctrine of Manifest Destiny, the United States began to go after foreign lands rather aggressively. It acquired nearly one-third of Mexico's territory in 1848 and increasingly saw how important Caribbean possessions would be to it, both financially and militarily. When the United States entered the Spanish-American War, it hoped to acquire a toehold in the Caribbean Sea.

The U.S. relationship with Puerto Rico was awkward and ambiguous during the first two years of U.S. rule. Military governors from the United States ran the island. This type of government did not prove satisfactory. Congress attempted to establish a more workable relationship with Puerto Rico in 1900. That year it passed the Foraker Act. Under the terms of this act, Puerto Rico became "the People of Porto Rico." Puerto Ricans were not U.S. citizens nor was the nation independent. The governor and the Executive Council (the Upper House) were to be appointed by the president of the United States. The House of Delegates (the Lower House) and the resident commissioner were to be chosen by popular election. The resident commissioner's job was to present the island's views on issues in the U.S. House of Representatives, although he would be unable to vote. Any action taken by the elected House of Delegates could be vetoed by the U.S. Congress. The Circuit Court of Boston was named the high court for the island. Puerto Rican leaders were shocked by this arrangement, which they interpreted as a slap in the face. They had hoped that when the United States took over the island, its people would be able to decide their own political destiny with a plebiscite. The Foraker Act shattered their hopes.

The Struggle for Self-Governance

Cries for independence were heard throughout Puerto Rico during the 16 years that the Foraker Act was in effect. Anti-U.S. feelings continued to grow and spread on the island. The island's factional parties shared the belief that Puerto Rico had been betrayed by the United States. As anti-American feelings escalated, the president and the Congress decided that action had to be taken. The then resident commissioner in Washington, Muñoz Rivera, wanted to poll Puerto Rico's citizens to determine what they felt should be the political status of the island. Muñoz's arguments were ignored. Congress decided to deal with the problem by making Puerto Ricans U.S. citizens with the Jones Act in 1917. This act only further alienated the Puerto Ricans who wanted self-governance on the island. The act not only "forced" citizenship on Puerto Ricans, but it also made them obligated to serve in the U.S. armed forces. Many Puerto Ricans resented the "forced" U.S. citizenship and the fact that they had no voice in the matter. They could resist U.S. citizenship, but resistance meant that they would lose many benefits and become aliens within their homeland. Because of the Jones Act, 140,000 Puerto Ricans fought in World War I.

The Nationalist Party

The Nationalist party, the radical party that strongly advocated the independence of Puerto Rico, emerged out of the forces that opposed how the United States was handling Puerto Rico's affairs. The party leaders felt, with some justification, that the major Puerto Rican parties were too sympathetic to American interests and that party members could not deal with the United States effectively by using traditional means such as the ballot and appealing to the U.S. conscience. Pedro Albizu Campos emerged as the militant leader of the party. A graduate of Harvard, Albizu knew U.S. politics well. The party became a target of the Puerto Rican and U.S. governments, who considered it extreme and dangerous. At a parade sponsored by the Nationalist party on Palm Sunday, March 21, 1937, a shot fired into a crowd resulted in a massacre in the streets of Ponce. In the ruckus, 20 people lost their lives and more than 100 were wounded. Liberation leaders remember this day as the "Ponce Massacre." It symbolizes the independence struggle in Puerto Rico.

Luis Muñoz Marín: Governor of Puerto Rico, 1948–1964

Between 1900 and 1946, Puerto Rico was headed by a series of 15 U.S. governors appointed by the president of the United States. With only a few exceptions, they were unimpressive men. They differed little from the Spaniards who had ruled Puerto Rico prior to 1898. Medical, educational, and economic conditions on the island reflected poor leadership. By 1940, conditions in Puerto Rico were not substantially different from conditions in 1898. Persistent expressions of dissatisfaction with the governors by Puerto Rican leaders led the United States to grant Puerto Rico the opportunity to elect its own governor in 1947. In 1948, Senator Luis Muñoz Marín was elected governor of Puerto Rico. He was the first elected governor in Puerto Rico's history.

The Commonwealth of Puerto Rico

Muñoz was destined to change decisively the course of Puerto Rican history. More changes occurred in Puerto Rico during his 16 years as governor than had taken place during the previous 4 centuries of Spanish rule. Without question, Muñoz's influence on the island was unprecedented. Like any political leader who gets things done and shapes history, he was a charismatic and controversial figure.

Once in office, Muñoz took a position on the polemical status question. He favored what later became known as the Commonwealth or the Estado Libre Asociado (Free Associated State). With this status, Puerto Rico would maintain a tie with the United States, but would have a degree of governmental autonomy. Muñoz fought hard to make the Commonwealth a reality. The people approved it in a plebiscite on June 4, 1951. Muñoz led an inauguration ceremony for the Commonwealth of Puerto Rico on July 25, 1952.

The Commonwealth did not solve the status question, and the controversy continued. Both statehood and independence advocates opposed the new status. Many people refused to go to the polls, claiming that the plebiscite was a hoax because the voters were presented with only two choices. They had to vote either to maintain the status quo or to initiate the proposed Commonwealth. Thus, the meaning of the plebiscite was bitterly debated. To this day, the status question is still one of the hottest political issues on the island. It tends to dominate and overshadow other issues.

Urbanization and Operation Bootstrap

Muñoz also set Puerto Rico on a new economic course. He felt that income from the island's three main cash crops—sugar, tobacco, and coffee—was inadequate to support Puerto Rico. Muñoz wanted to industrialize the island by luring U.S. manufacturers to set up plants in Puerto Rico. He formed "Operation Bootstrap" to attract American industry to Puerto Rico. He offered generous benefits such as lower wages and tax exemptions for up to ten years. Many U.S. companies set up plants in Puerto Rico under this program. Like most changes that Muñoz implemented, the program was both successful and controversial. The changes that Operation Bootstrap stimulated in Puerto Rico were truly amazing. By 1971, the program had recruited 2,000 plants and millions of dollars in investments. Income from manufacturing was more than three times that from agriculture, although agriculture was still important in the island's economy. The island's per capita income jumped from $188 a year in 1940 to $1,234 a year in 1969.

The Operation Bootstrap reforms and modernization of Puerto Rico that occurred during the 1940s, 1950s, and 1960s were mixed blessings. Urbanization brought the usual problems in housing and created a new poverty class: the urban poor. Although Operation Bootstrap was designed to help solve the problem of unemployment, it actually increased it. Industrialization displaced small farmers, who migrated to the cities and became unemployed. Many Puerto Ricans left the island and migrated to the U.S. mainland to look for work. Migration from the island to the United States peaked during the 1950s, at a time when Operation Bootstrap was booming.

The Puerto Rican economy remains precarious. The island has a high level of unemployment. Even when Operation Bootstrap was booming, the large numbers of Puerto Ricans who migrated to the United States each year helped maintain a healthy economy on the island. Urbanization has pulled many families to the cities looking for work and has created city slums, housing congestion, and other problems associated with urban growth. In 1987, the income per family in Puerto Rico, while high compared to Latin American nations, was about 65% of that in the U.S. mainland ($20,016 compared to $30,759).

Although urbanization created a middle class in Puerto Rico and bedroom-suburban communities, Muñoz's critics correctly note that Operation Bootstrap brought the greatest benefits to the upper-class and to U.S. industrialists. American companies take the bulk of the money they earn on the island back to the United States. Many of them are now deserting Puerto Rico for nations in Asia where they can find cheaper labor. Urbanization in Puerto Rico, like so many other developments, has done little to change the living conditions of the poor, except perhaps to show them how to live poor "urban" rather than poor "rural" style. Despite the mixed blessings of the Muñoz reforms, his 16-year reign made a tremendous difference in Puerto Rico's present and future.

Life on the Mainland

The Migration

After the United States gained control of Puerto Rico, the stage was set for the mass movement of islanders to the U.S. mainland. A few Puerto Ricans, such as cigar makers and merchant seamen, had settled in New York before the 1920s; but Puerto Ricans did not begin to migrate to the United States in significant numbers until the 1920s and 1930s. When Mills et al. published their pioneering study in 1950, most Puerto Ricans in New York City had come during the years between the two great world wars.[5] The number of Puerto Ricans migrating to the United States decreased considerably during World War II because of the closing of transportation routes between New York and Puerto Rico.

After the war, the number of Puerto Ricans migrating to the United States increased. In 1945, only 22,737 Puerto Ricans came to the United States. That number increased to 101,115 in 1947. Puerto Rican migration to the United States has always reflected economic trends. A significant number of migrants usually return to the island when the mainland economy is depressed. During the Great Depression of the 1930s, the net migration back to the island reached 8,694 people in a four-year period.[6] *Net migration* is the difference between the number of Puerto Ricans who enter the United States and the number who leave within a specific time period. It can be a positive ($+$) or a negative ($-$) figure. When the U.S. economy is booming, Puerto Rican migration usually increases and return migration decreases considerably.

Rodriguez describes three major periods of Puerto Rican migration to the U.S. mainland.[7] The first significant number of migrants arrived between 1900 and 1945. Most of these people settled in New York City. The second period of migration took place between 1946 and 1964. During this period, the largest number of migrants from Puerto Rico settled in the U.S. mainland. Rodriguez calls the third period of Puerto Rican migration, from 1965 to the present, "the revolving-door migration."[8] During this period, migration to the mainland has varied with economic developments on the island and the mainland. Migrants have also dispersed to other regions in the United States, such as New Jersey, Illinois, and Florida.

The lack of legal barriers is a major factor in Puerto Rican migration to the United States. The Jones Act of 1917 made Puerto Ricans U.S. citizens. As U.S.

citizens, they can move freely from the island to the mainland and within various parts of the United States. Their migration to the United States is not limited by restrictive quotas, as was the case in Mexico and in the various Asian nations. Many Puerto Ricans take advantage of their freedom of movement and migrate to the United States. Although the movement of Puerto Ricans to the mainland has many of the sociological characteristics of an immigration, Puerto Ricans are technically migrants rather than immigrants because they are citizens of the United States.

Easy and inexpensive transportation to the mainland also facilitates Puerto Rican migration. In the 1930s, Puerto Ricans could make a boat trip from San Juan to New York City in the relatively short period of three and a half days, and for as low as $40.[9] After World War II, plane transportation from the island became more available and inexpensive. During this period, a migrant could fly from San Juan to New York City for as low as $35.[10] Today, transportation from the island is more convenient and still inexpensive. Whereas the flight from San Juan to New York City took eight bumpy hours in the 1940s, the trip could be made as quickly as three hours and for as low as $250.00 in 1990. Convenient and inexpensive transportation has not only stimulated migration from the island to the mainland but has also helped make Puerto Ricans transients between the island and the United States. Many Puerto Ricans in New York return to the island to visit relatives, to vacation, or to take care of business for short periods.

The "Americanization" of Puerto Rico since 1898 and economic factors have played major roles in motivating Puerto Ricans to migrate to the United States. Since Puerto Rico became an American colony, U.S. culture and institutions have profoundly influenced Puerto Rican culture and life-styles. Americans forced the teaching of English in Puerto Rican schools for years and introduced textbooks that venerated George Washington and Abraham Lincoln rather than Puerto Rican leaders.[11] These books also described the United States as the neighbor to the North in which "democracy and freedom" flourished. American stores such as J. C. Penney and Sears dot the streets in San Juan as they do in Chicago.

During the period of high migration to the U.S. mainland in the 1950s, many Puerto Ricans who returned to the island told their relatives and friends about the "great" new life in New York City. The availability of jobs in New York City during periods of intensive migration and the higher pay Puerto Ricans could earn in New York, compared to San Juan, lured many Puerto Ricans from the island to the mainland.

Since the great period of migration to the U.S. mainland from Puerto Rico between 1946 and 1964, migration to and from the U.S. mainland has followed economic trends. When economic times are good on the mainland, the number of migrants from Puerto Rico increases. However, migrants tend to return to the island during economic hard times on the mainland. In 1953, migration from

Puerto Rico to the mainland peaked at 74,000. Since the mid-1960s, migration from Puerto Rico to the mainland has been fluctuating. A deep drop occurred around 1976 (see Figure 11–1).

The population increase in the Puerto Rican mainland community today results primarily from new births rather than from migration. Migration still occurs. However, much of it consists of unemployed individuals who circulate from the island to the mainland and back again. These migrants often cannot find jobs on the island or the mainland.[12]

Although the migration of Puerto Ricans from the island to the mainland is similar in many ways to other movements of peoples to the United States, it is unique in several ways. As Fitzpatrick notes, it was the first "airborne migration" in U.S. history.[13] Puerto Ricans, unlike many of the earlier immigrants, are also U.S. citizens when they arrive in the United States. They bring attitudes toward race that are different from and more complex than those in the United States. They also started migrating to the United States at a time when automation had eliminated most of the jobs requiring unskilled laborers. Most of these factors, along with the racism and discrimination they experience in the United States, have increased rather than mitigated their problems in the United States.

The Family

The family, which is important in traditional Puerto Rican culture, is experiencing tremendous changes on the island. Cultures are not static in modernized societies; they are dynamic and changing. As Puerto Rico becomes increasingly urbanized, many of its traditional rural values—including those related to the family—are changing. While the Puerto Rican family and its values are changing on the island, the family faces even more conflicts and problems when it moves to the U.S. mainland. It becomes part of a U.S. mainstream culture that is often unaware of and unsympathetic to traditional Puerto Rican values related to family and community. The racism and discrimination that the Puerto Rican family experiences in the United States also create adjustment problems.

The serious economic problems that faced the Puerto Rican community by the late 1980s affected the family. In 1987, about 39.4% of Puerto Ricans were living below the official government poverty level.[14] This percentage was greater than that of all other Hispanics and also greater than that of African Americans and Whites. Of these groups, Puerto Ricans also had the highest percentage of female-headed households in 1980, 33%, compared to 30% for African Americans and 8% for Whites.[15] A deep sense of family remains within the Puerto Rican community despite the increase in the percentage of female-headed households. In 1980, most Puerto Rican households were made up of families of more than one person, 77%, compared to 34% for African Americans and 42% for Whites.[16]

A number of values are still strongly held within Puerto Rican families, including respect for the elderly and for parents, and extremely strong bonds within the family, particularly with the mother.[17] The family, rather than the individual, tends to be the main identification focus. The extended family is important, and all family members tend to feel obligated to care for and be responsible for one another. The protection of children, especially girls, is very important to the family. This protection is often viewed as overprotection by people outside the culture. These traditional values of Puerto Rican families are being challenged by modernization, by urbanization, and by the levels of assimilation occurring among the current generation of Puerto Ricans in the United States. However, they still have a great deal of tenacity in the Puerto Rican community.

Despite the problems that they face in the United States, many Puerto Rican migrants remain in the United States. A few return to the island for many different reasons, including the lack of a job, alienation, discrimination, and longing for their homeland, family, and friends. Most Puerto Ricans who remain in the United States retain important aspects of their culture but re-create and change their culture in ways that enable them to become effective participants in U.S. society. How Puerto Ricans use language illustrates this process of cultural adaptation and change. While learning English, Puerto Ricans have held tenaciously onto Spanish and have to some extent created a Spanish that reflects their current experiences in the United States. In 1980, about 91% of Puerto Ricans in New York City spoke Spanish in the home, compared to 90% of Cubans and 64% of Mexicans.[18]

Racial Problems

Although racism exists in both Puerto Rico and the U.S. mainland, race is highly complex in Puerto Rico, and *social race* has different meanings in the two cultures. Scholars, such as Isabelo Zenón Cruz and Samuel Betances, believe that social scientists have exaggerated the differences between racism in the United States and in Puerto Rico.[19] These two researchers believe that most social scientists have underestimated the extent to which Blacks are victimized by racism in Puerto Rico. They believe that racism is an important part of Puerto Rican society. Although Zenón and Betances provide a needed perspective on race relations in Puerto Rico, social-class status in Puerto Rico interacts with race in a complex way. Upper-class Whites tend to exclude both poor Whites and poor Blacks from their social gathering. However, poor Whites and poor Blacks tend to mix more freely in Puerto Rico than in the United States. Even though Whites tend to marry other Whites in Puerto Rico, intermarriage occurs more often in Puerto Rico than in the United States.

Puerto Ricans on the U.S. mainland are forced to fit into one of two racial categories: Black or White. These categories are often less meaningful in the Puerto Rican community. Puerto Ricans, both on the island and on the mainland, recognize and use a number of different racial categories, such as *blanco* (Whites), *prieto* (dark-skinned), *negro* (Blacks), and *trigueño* (tan).[20] Other words they use to make color distinctions among themselves are *idio, grifo,* and *de color.*[21] When determining an individual's color, Puerto Ricans consider hair color and texture as well as skin color. Also, an individual's color classification is determined primarily by his or her physical traits rather than by the color of parents or relatives. Within one family there can be individuals who are considered *blanco, negro,* and *trigueño.*

The different ways in which color is recognized and treated on the mainland cause problems for the Puerto Rican migrant, especially for those who are intermediate in skin color. In their community, they are neither Black nor White; but they are often considered Black by outsiders. This causes the intermediate individual to feel alienated from both the White and Black communities in the United States. A research study in the 1950s indicated that Puerto Rican migrants who were intermediate in color experienced more adjustment problems in the United States than did individuals who were clearly identified as either Black or White.[22]

The Puerto Rican Mainland Community

When they first started migrating to the United States, most Puerto Ricans settled in New York City. However, the percentage of Puerto Rican migrants settling in New York City has steadily decreased in recent decades; the percentage settling in other mainland cities and states has increased. In 1940, 88% of the Puerto Rican population in the United States lived in New York City. By 1960, that number had declined to 69%. In 1980, 51% of Puerto Ricans lived outside of New York City.

While 60% of Puerto Ricans in the United States lived in the states of New York and New Jersey in 1980, many lived in other parts of the nation. A considerable number of Puerto Ricans (15.7%) lived in Illinois, Florida, and California. Most Puerto Ricans (76.8%) were concentrated in five states (New York, New Jersey, Illinois, Florida, and California) in 1980, and pockets of them lived in many other states, including Pennsylvania (91,802), Texas (22,938), and Washington state (5,065) (see Table 11–1).

Pockets of Puerto Ricans in U.S. cities constitute ethnic neighborhoods. The Puerto Rican community is usually a poor community, with the characteristics of people who are poor. In 1987, Puerto Ricans had the lowest median family income of the major Hispanic groups and the largest percentage of families below the poverty level.[23] The median family income was $14,584 for

Table 11–1   *Puerto Rican Population*
in Selected States (1980)

New York	986,389
New Jersey	243,540
Illinois	129,165
Florida	94,775
California	93,038
Pennsylvania	91,802
Connecticut	88,361
Massachusetts	76,450
Ohio	32,442
Texas	22,938
Hawaii	19,351
Indiana	12,683
Michigan	12,425
Wisconsin	10,483
Virginia	10,227
Maryland	9,014
Georgia	7,887
Washington	5,065
Colorado	4,246
Louisiana	4,539
Arizona	4,048

Source: Based on data in the U.S. Census, 1980

Puerto Ricans, compared to $19,326 for Mexicans, and $27,300 for Cuban Americans. In 1987, about 39.4% of Puerto Ricans lived below the poverty level, compared to 28.4% of Mexican Americans, 14% of Cubans, 31.1% of African Americans, and 11% of Whites. The educational status of Puerto Ricans was also comparatively low in 1987. Even though the percentage of Puerto Rican persons 25 years old and over who had completed four years of high school was slightly above the percentage for Mexican Americans, 31.4% compared to 27.3%, it was below the percentage for African Americans (37.1%), Whites (39.2%), and the total population, 38.7%.[24]

The sound of Spanish, bodegas, travel agencies, and Pentecostal storefront churches are familiar sounds and sights in most Puerto Rican mainland neighborhoods. Although Puerto Rican mainland culture is decidedly different from Puerto Rican culture—even the Spanish they speak is different—certain parts of the old culture are retained on the mainland. Hispanos, as many Puerto Ricans call themselves, usually speak Spanish at home and English when talking with outsiders. To obtain the foods to prepare favorite ethnic dishes, such as rice and beans, fried plaintains, or dried codfish, the family shops at the bodegas, the little corner grocery store usually run by Puerto Ricans. Herbs and plants needed to cure illnesses or to fight the "evil" can be bought at the botánicas. Tickets for an air trip back home are bought at the local travel agency, perhaps on easy terms. The Pentecostal Church, a fast-growing institution in the Puerto Rican mainland community, serves the spiritual needs of the migrants. The Puerto Rican community, with its bodegas, botánicas, and Pentecostal churches, like ethnic communities of the past, helps to ease the cultural shock for the migrants and helps them to develop roots in their new land.

The Future

On most major indices, such as occupational status, education, and income, Puerto Ricans fall far behind the general U.S. population and most other Hispanic groups. Yet, the future of the Puerto Rican community can be shaped by educational, political, and social action. Puerto Ricans in the United States are a young and growing population—they had the youngest median age, 20.7, of any Hispanic group in 1980. There are signs that the Puerto Rican community is becoming more politically and legally active than it has been in the past. By 1980, the New York Puerto Rican community had played decisive roles in one congressional and several city and state elections.

A number of Puerto Rican educational and civic organizations are working to strengthen the Puerto Rican community. These include Aspira of America, a leadership and educational development agency; the National Puerto Rican Coalition, which coordinates a group of organizations and works to improve the social and economic conditions of Puerto Ricans in the United States; and the Puerto Rican Legal Defense and Educational Fund, which litigates for Hispanics who live in the Northeast. The National Congress for Puerto Rican Rights (NCPRR) works to obtain "civil and human rights for Puerto Ricans." A report commissioned by NCPRR's Board of Directors describes social, legal, and political action being taken by Puerto Ricans today:

> Puerto Ricans around the country are today fighting in the courts, in the streets, in the migrant farm camps, in the factories, offices, unions, and schools; and increasingly the fight for our democratic rights is being fought in the voting booth. Clearly, many of the issues we confront are not just "Puerto Rican problems" and reflecting this, we are also involved in greater efforts nationwide to coalesce with Blacks and Latinos and to build unity with all those who are working for a society based on true democracy, equality, justice, and peace.[25]

The future of Puerto Ricans in the United States will be heavily influenced by political, economic, and social developments on the island. These two communities are integrally bound. Many Puerto Ricans see Puerto Ricans on the island and those on the mainland as one divided nation. Consequently, the status question that haunts the island cogently influences the ideologies, debates, and visions of mainland Puerto Ricans.

Teaching Strategies

To illustrate how content related to the Puerto Rican experience can be incorporated into a conceptual curriculum, I have identified three key concepts related to the Puerto Rican experience and sample strategies for teaching them. Strategies are presented for teaching *cultural conflict, racial categories,* and *colonialism* in the primary, intermediate and upper, and high school grades, respectively.

Primary Grades

CONCEPT: Cultural Conflict

Generalization: The Puerto Rican migrant family in the United States experiences many conflicts and problems because it encounters new norms, values, and roles on the mainland that conflict with those in Puerto Rico.

1. Read the following case study to the students and ask the questions that follow. During the discussion of the story, help the children to state the generalization in their own words.

The Ramos Family

Mr. and Mrs. Ramos and their two children, Maria, age three, and Carlos, age seven, live in New York City in an area called El Barrio. The Ramos family moved to New York two years ago from San Juan, Puerto Rico. When the family lived in San Juan, Mr. Ramos worked in a factory. Mrs. Ramos stayed at home and took care of the children and house.

Both Mr. and Mrs. Ramos were happy living in San Juan until some of their relatives moved from San Juan to New York City. First, Mrs. Ramos's two sisters, whom she liked very much, moved to New York. Later, Mr. Ramos's brother moved to New York. They missed their relatives very much. They wanted to be able to see them more often. Mr. and Mrs. Ramos decided to go to New York to pay their relatives a visit.

When Mr. and Mrs. Ramos arrived in New York to visit, their relatives were very glad to see them. Mrs. Ramos kissed her two sisters. She told them about all the news back home. Her sisters told her about New York City. They liked it very much. Mrs. Ramos became very excited about New York City as she listened to her sisters talk about it. Mr. Ramos and his brother were also glad to see each other. Mr. Ramos told his brother how the family was doing in San Juan. Mr. Ramos's brother told him about how good things were in New York. He told Mr. Ramos that he could make twice as much money in New York as he made in San Juan! Mr. and Mrs. Ramos enjoyed New York City for two weeks. When they left, they had decided that they would move to New York City as soon as they got back home.

When the Ramos family got to New York again, things were not as nice as they thought they would be. The family was not as happy as it had been in San Juan. They had to live with Mr. Ramos's brother for two months because they could not find a nice apartment right away. When they did find one, it cost much more than they had paid for rent in San Juan. Mr. Ramos looked a long time before he could find a job. To help the family pay its bills, Mrs. Ramos got a job in a garment factory. Mrs. Ramos was the only person in the family working. She began to make more and more decisions for everyone in the family.

Mr. Ramos spent most of each day looking for a job. He spoke good Spanish but many companies would not hire him because he spoke little English. Since Mrs. Ramos was working and Mr. Ramos was job hunting, Carlos and Maria had to spend a lot of time without either parent. Sometimes they would get into trouble with the neighborhood children.

Carlos became sad when he started to school. He was a top student in Puerto Rico. However, he did poorly in school in New York. He could not read English well. He fell further and further behind in school each week. The teacher called him "Charlie" instead of "Carlos." The children teased him because he spoke "funny." Carlos tried hard to speak English, even at home. His parents wanted him to speak Spanish at home so that they could understand him.

After looking for three months, Mr. Ramos found a job in a hotel. The family then moved into their own apartment. Things got better then. Mr. Ramos wanted Mrs. Ramos to quit her job and stay at home with the children. Mrs. Ramos wanted to keep working because she felt that it took more money to live in New York than in San Juan. Sometimes the family wished that they had stayed in San Juan.

The Ramos family has now been in New York City for two years. They are much happier now, but they still miss their friends and relatives in San Juan. Mr. Ramos understands why Mrs. Ramos wants to work. Carlos is speaking better English and getting better grades in school. The family is planning to visit Puerto Rico during the Christmas season. Carlos is counting the days until Christmas!

Questions

1. Why did the Ramos family move from San Juan to New York City?
2. Was New York City like the family expected it to be? Why or why not?
3. What problems did each of the family members have in New York City that he or she did not have in San Juan?
4. Which family member faced the greatest problems in New York? Why?
5. Which family member faced the fewest problems in New York? Why?
6. What problems do you think the family faced in New York City that are not brought out in the story? Why?
7. How do you think the family will feel about New York a year from now? Do you think that the family will move back to Puerto Rico? Why or why not?

Intermediate and Upper Grades

CONCEPT: Racial categories

Generalization: Racial categories differ in Puerto Rico and on the U.S. mainland. These differing racial categories make the experience of Puerto Rican migrants to the mainland more difficult.

1. Find old copies of magazines such as *Ebony, Hispanic, Essence, Black Enterprise,* and *Life.* Locate pictures of people who look (a) obviously European American, (b) obviously African American, (c) like fair-skinned African Americans. Mount these pictures on cardboard.

2. Show the students three of the pictures, one that will fit into each of the categories described above. Ask the students to name the "race" of the person in each picture. They will most likely say that one of the pictured persons is "White," and that the other two are "Black" or "African American." Ask: "Why do we use only two categories to classify the people in these pictures?" With the use of careful questions, explain that in the United States any person, regardless of his or her physical appearance, is considered "Black" or "African American" if he or she has any *known* African ancestry.

3. Show the class mounted pictures of (a) a fair-skinned African-American male adult, (b) a fair-skinned African-American female adult, (c) a dark-skinned African-American male child, (d) a female child who looks Caucasian.

4. Ask the students to name the "race" of each of the pictured persons. After discussing their responses, tell the class that the pictures represent a Puerto Rican family that recently moved from San Juan to New York City. In the pictures are mom, dad, brother, and sister. Point out that even though we may call the parents and the son "Black," Puerto Ricans have words to describe each color. Introduce these words. They would call the parents *trigueño,* the son *Negro* or *de color,* and the daughter *blanca.* Tell the students that in Puerto Rico "color" has a special meaning that is different from its meaning in the United States. Ask the students what race would the different family members belong to in the United States and why. Through questioning, bring out that all of them would be considered "Black" or "African American" and why.

5. Ask: "Now that the family is in New York City, what kinds of racial problems might they encounter?" "Why?" Through questioning, reveal that mother and father will be considered "Black" on the mainland even though they were intermediates (*trigueños*) in Puerto Rico. Discuss with the class the kinds of identity and social problems that the couple will face on the mainland and how they might cope with them. Ask the class the following questions:

   a. How do you think mother and father will feel when mainland Whites call them "Black" or "African American"?
   b. How do you think they will feel when African Americans call them "Black"? Do you think they will identify with the Black struggle for civil rights? Why or why not?
   c. Do you think they will want to be called "White" or "Black"? Why? What problems might they encounter when seeking to obtain their preferred racial identification? Why? How might they go about solving them?

6. With these and other questions, bring out the generalization that Puerto Rican migrants to the mainland who are intermediate in color have serious racial and adjustment problems because they are neither White nor Black in Puerto Rico but are forced to be "Black" on the mainland. Ask the class these valuing questions: Do you think that it is right to consider intermediates on the mainland "Blacks"? Why or why not? Do you think they should be considered "White"? Why or why not? If you were an intermediate

Puerto Rican on the mainland, would you want to be considered "White" or "Black"? Why? When asking such valuing questions, accept all responses and maintain an open classroom atmosphere.

Ask the class these questions:

a. What special identity and racial problems might the son have in his family? In school? In the community? Why? How might he deal with them?

b. What special racial and identity problems might the daughter have in the family? In school? In the community? Why? How might she deal with them?

Read the following case study to the class and ask the questions that follow.

Mr. Díaz and Mr. Seda on the Mainland

Mr. Díaz looks Caucasian. In Puerto Rico he and Mr. Seda, who is *de color,* were close friends. They both now live in New York City. When they first came to New York City, they would visit each other often, as they had done in Puerto Rico. Eventually Mr. Díaz started visiting Mr. Seda less and less and would often act unfriendly when Mr. Seda came to visit him, especially when his White friends were over. Mr. Díaz's White friends would always give Mr. Seda strange looks when he came over. Mr. Díaz began to understand that in New York City he was expected to mix socially with Whites only. Now, Mr. Díaz never visits Mr. Seda, and Mr. Seda goes to Mr. Díaz's house very seldom. When he does, he stays only a short time. The last time that Mr. Seda visited Mr. Díaz's home, Mr. Díaz left in the middle of the visit with a White American friend. He told Mr. Seda that he and his White American friend had to go out and take care of some important business.

Questions

1. What is the main problem in this case study?
2. What kind of relationship did Mr. Díaz and Mr. Seda have in Puerto Rico?
3. Why did their relationship change when they moved to the mainland?
4. If you were Mr. Díaz, would you act as he acted when he moved to the mainland? Why or why not?
5. If you were Mr. Seda, would you act as he acted when he moved to New York City? Why or why not?

Valuing Exercises

Ask the students independently to complete these open-ended sentences. After they have completed them, discuss their responses and summarize the lesson by highlighting the generalization about the racial problems Puerto Rican migrants experience on the U.S. mainland.

1. Mr. Díaz should _____ .
2. Mr. Seda should _____ .
3. Mr. Díaz values _____ more than _____ .
4. Mr. Seda values _____ more than _____ .

5. If I were Mr. Díaz, I would _____ .

6. If I were Mr. Seda, I would _____ .

High School Grades

CONCEPT: Colonialism

Generalizations: Since the late fifteenth century, Puerto Rico has been controlled by foreign powers. This has caused rebellions, political ambiguity, and instability on the island.

1. Give the students a copy of the questions below and ask them to read a selection about the Arawak Indians prior to 1493. One source is Fred Olsen, *On the Trail of the Arawaks.* Norman: University of Oklahoma Press, 1974. Tell them to be able to respond to these questions when they have finished their reading. After the students have completed the reading assignment, discuss the questions.

   a. How did the Arawaks obtain food?
   b. What kind of political system did they have?
   c. What kind of religion did they have?
   d. What was a typical day like for (1) an Arawak adult female, (2) an Arawak adult male, (3) Arawak children?
   e. What kinds of relationships did the Arawaks have with other American Indian groups?
   f. What kinds of weapons did the Arawaks use when they were at war with other Indian tribes?

2. Divide the class into research groups and ask them to prepare and give short reports on each of the following topics. They should be encouraged to present their reports to the class in the form of debates, simulations, and roleplay situations, and with the use of visual aids such as charts and graphs.

   a. Columbus's trip to North America and his relationship with the native populations.
   b. The establishment of Spanish domination in Puerto Rico in the 1500s.
   c. The *encomienda* system of forced labor that the Spanish established in Puerto Rico during the early years of domination.
   d. Ways in which the Arawaks resisted Spanish colonization by rebelling and running away.
   e. Spanish domination in Puerto Rico in the 1600s, 1700s, and 1800s.
   f. *Grito de Lares* of 1868.
   g. The political, economic, and social status of Puerto Rico in 1898.
   h. The Spanish-American War (causes and effects).
   i. The American takeover of Puerto Rico in 1898.
   j. The Treaty of Paris, 1898.

After the students have a basic understanding of Puerto Rican history up to 1898, they can then become involved in activities like those below to gain a better understanding of the island's political and economic status today.

3. Ask the students to pretend that they are members of the U.S. Congress in 1898. Spain has just ceded Puerto Rico to the United States. Their job is to decide on specific political and economic policies for their new territory. They must spell out a plan for governing the island and have it approved by majority vote. After this exercise is completed, ask the students to compare their plan with the plan the United States used to govern Puerto Rico during the first two years of U.S. rule and with the plan delineated in the Foraker Act of 1900. Ask the students to discuss the similarities and differences in the three plans and possible reasons for them.

4. Ask the students to research the positions advocated by the following political parties regarding the political status of Puerto Rico:

   a. The Independence party (Independence)
   b. The New Progressive party (Statehood)
   c. The popular party (Commonwealth)

After this research, ask three students to roleplay an advocate of each status position. The advocate of each position should argue his or her position in front of the class. The three speakers will debate the status question and answer questions posed by the class. After the debate and discussion, each class member will vote for one of the three following positions: (1) the Commonwealth, (2) statehood, or (3) independence. After the voting, conduct a class discussion in which the class will compare their choice with the choice made by the citizens of Puerto Rico in a plebiscite held in 1967. See the list of important dates at the beginning of this chapter. The students should discuss the reasons for the similarities and differences in their choice and the choice made by Puerto Rican citizens.

5. Ask a group of students to roleplay a discussion between the individuals named below about what should be the future of Puerto Rico. Conduct a class discussion about the roleplay situation when it ends.

   a. Pedro Albizu Campos
   b. Luis Muñoz Marín
   c. Luis A. Ferré
   d. Rafael Hernández Colón
   e. A U.S. businessperson who is president of a company that owns several factories in Puerto Rico.
   f. A southern U.S. senator
   g. A U.S. congressional representative from the Midwest

6. Since the Spanish colonized Puerto Rico in the sixteenth century, there have been uprisings and rebellions against oppression on the island. Ask the students to prepare a short research paper on forms of resistance to oppression in Puerto Rico since the sixteenth century. Make sure that they note resistance as exemplified by (1) the Arawak Indians, (2) the Lares Rebellion of 1868, (3) the Nationalist party, and (4) the university student uprisings in Puerto Rico in the 1960s. After the students have completed and discussed their papers, ask them to write and present a dramatization about "The Struggle for Home Rule in Puerto Rico." They can invite another class or their parents and friends to attend the presentation.

Endnotes

1. Clara E. Rodríguez, *Puerto Ricans Born in the U.S.A.* (Boston: Unwin Hyman, 1989), pp. 3–4.

2. U.S. Bureau of the Census, Supplementary Report, *Persons of Spanish Ancestry, 1980*; U.S. Bureau of the Census, *Statistical Abstract of the United States: 1989,* 109th ed. (Washington, D.C.: U.S. Government Printing Office, 1989), p. 815.

3. Maria Teresa Babín, *The Puerto Ricans' Spirit*, translated by Barry Luby (New York: Collier Books, 1971), p. 154.

4. Kal Wagenheim, *Puerto Rico: A Profile*, 2nd ed. (New York: Praeger, 1975).

5. C. Wright Mills, Clarence Senior, and Rose K. Goldsen, *The Puerto Rican Journey: New York's Newest Migrants* (New York: Russel and Russel, 1967).

6. Ibid., p. 44.

7. Rodríguez, *Puerto Ricans Born in the U.S.A.*, pp. 3–4.

8. Ibid., p. 4.

9. Lawrence R. Chenault, *The Puerto Rican Migrant in New York City* (New York: Columbia University Press, 1938), p. 56.

10. Mills, Senior, and Goldsen, *The Puerto Rican Journey*, p. 44.

11. Aida Negron de Montilla, *Americanization in Puerto Rico and the Public-School System 1900/1920* (Rio Piedras: University of Puerto Rico Press, 1975).

12. This information is from an interview by the author with Dr. Ricardo Campos, at the Centro de Estudios Puertorriqueños, Hunter College of the City University of New York, 9 January 1986.

13. Joseph P. Fitzpatrick, *Puerto Rican Americans: The Meaning of Migration to the Mainland,* 2nd ed. (Englewood Cliffs, N.J.: Prentice-Hall, 1987), p. 20.

14. U.S. Bureau of the Census, *Statistical Abstract of the United States: 1989,* 109th ed., p. 38.

15. Rodríguez, *Puerto Ricans Born in the U.S.A.*, pp. 33–34.

16. Ibid., pp. 34–35.

17. This section is based on comments prepared by Sonia Nieto on June 15, 1989, for the author in preparation for *Teaching Strategies for Ethnic Studies*, 5th ed. See also Melba Sánchez-Ayéndez, "The Puerto Rican American Family," in *Ethnic Families in America: Patterns and Variations*, 3rd ed., eds. C. H. Mindel, R. W. Haberstein, and R. Wright, Jr. (New York: Elsevier, 1988), pp. 173–195.

18. Rodríguez, *Puerto Ricans Born in the U.S.A.*, p. 30.

19. Isabelo Zenón Cruz, *Narcisco Descubre Su Trasero* (Homacao, Puerto Rico: Editorial Furidi, 1975); Samuel Betances, "The Prejudice of Having No Prejudice in Puerto Rico," Part I, *The Rican*, Winter 1972, pp. 41–52; Part II, *The Rican*, Spring 1973, pp. 22–37.

20. Wagenheim, *Puerto Rico: A Profile*, p. 147.

21. Elena Padilla, *Up from Puerto Rico* (New York: Columbia University Press, 1958), p. 76.

22. Mills, Senior, and Goldsen, *The Puerto Rican Journey*, p. 133.

23. U.S. Bureau of the Census, *Statistical Abstract of the United States: 1989,* 109th ed., p. 38.

24. Ibid.

25. *The Status of Puerto Ricans in the United States* (Philadelphia: National Congress for Puerto Rican Rights, 1 June 1985), p. 10.

Annotated Bibliography

Books for Teachers

Especially Recommended

Carr, Raymond. *Puerto Rico: A Colonial Experiment.* New York: Vintage Books, 1984.

> *Sponsored by the Twentieth Century Fund, this comprehensive history of Puerto Rico includes a list of main political parties, a chronology of key events, and a helpful select reading list.*

De Laguna, Asela Rodríguez, ed. *Images and Identities: The Puerto Rican in Two Worlds Contexts.* New Brunswick, N.J.: Transaction, 1987.

> *This anthology includes a number of informative papers, including "Self-Affirmation or Self-Destruction: The Image of Puerto Ricans in Children's Literature Written in English," by Sonia Nieto.*

Fitzpatrick, Joseph P. *Puerto Rican Americans: The Meaning of Migration to the Mainland,* 2nd edition. Englewood Cliffs, N.J.: Prentice-Hall, 1987.

> *This sociological survey of Puerto Ricans focuses on their experiences in New York City. Chapters are included on the dynamics of migration, the island background, the Puerto Rican community in New York City, the Puerto Rican family, and Puerto Ricans and the schools of New York City.*

Gonzalez, Juan D., and Ortiz, Hildamar. *The Status of Puerto Ricans in the United States.* New York: Centro de Estudios Puertorriquenos, Hunter College of the City University of New York, May 1987.

> *This report, commissioned by the National Congress for Puerto Rican Rights, is a statistical profile as well as a civil rights position statement for Puerto Ricans in the United States. Sections include "An Economic Disaster of Epic Proportions," "Official English: A Growing Menace," and "The Role of the Church in the Fight for Racial Justice."*

Padilla, Felix. *Puerto Rican Chicago.* Notre Dame, Ind.: University of Notre Dame Press, 1987.

> *An informative and comprehensive study of the Puerto Rican community in Chicago. It is a welcomed addition to the literature on Puerto Ricans, most of which focuses on their experiences in New York City.*

Rodríguez, Clara E. *Puerto Ricans Born in the U.S.A.* Boston: Unwin Hyman, 1989.

> *This is an excellent, readable, and informative introduction to the experiences of Puerto Ricans in the United States. It has an excellent chapter on race, "The Rainbow People," as well as informative chapters on "The Political-Economic Context," "Housing and the South Bronx," and "Educational Dynamics." The book focuses on the Puerto Ricans in New York City.*

Sánchez-Ayéndez, Melba. "The Puerto Rican Family." In *Ethnic Families in America: Patterns and Variations,* 3rd ed., edited by Charles H. Mindel, Robert W. Habenstein, and Roosevelt Wright, Jr. New York: Elsevier, 1988, pp. 173–195.

An excellent overview of the historical background, migration, and values of the Puerto Rican family in the United States. The list of references is a useful guide to other sources.

Other References

Acosta-Belen, Edna, ed. *The Puerto Rican Woman.* New York: Praeger, 1979.

This collection of scholarly papers focuses on the historical, socioeconomic, and cultural factors that have influenced the role of women in Puerto Rican society.

Alers-Montalvo, Manuel. *The Puerto Rican Migrants of New York City: A Study of Anomie.* New York: AMS Press, 1985.

This sociological study of Puerto Rican migrants in New York City uses the concept of anomie as the key conceptual framework.

Algarin, Miguel, and Pinero, Miguel. *Nuyorican Poetry: An Anthology of Puerto Rican Words and Feelings.* New York: William Morrow, 1975.

This collection of poetry conveys a range of feelings and moods.

Babín, María Teresa, and Steiner, Stan, eds. *Borinquén: An Anthology of Puerto Rican Literature.* New York: Vintage, 1974.

This comprehensive anthology includes more than 100 selections by poets, patriots, novelists, playwrights, and nationalists on the island and the mainland.

Bloomfield, Richard J., ed. *Puerto Rico: The Search for a National Policy.* Boulder, Colo.: Westview Press, 1985.

This scholarly collection of papers discusses the Puerto Rican status question from various perspectives and Puerto Rico's relationship to the United States.

Bonilla, Frank, and Campos, Ricardo. "Evolving Patterns of Puerto Rican Migration." In *The Americas in the New International Division of Labor,* edited by Steven E. Sanderson, pp. 177–205. New York: Holmes and Meier, 1985.

An informative historical and sociological analysis of Puerto Rican migration to the U.S. mainland.

Colón, Jesús. *A Puerto Rican in New York and Other Sketches,* 2nd ed. New York: International Publishers, 1982.

This well-written autobiographical book, first published in 1961, conveys the feelings and experiences of a Puerto Rican in New York City.

Dietz, James L. *Economic History of Puerto Rico: Institutional Change and Capitalist Development.* Princeton, N.J.: Princeton University Press, 1986.

A scholarly and informative economic history of Puerto Rico.

García-Passalacqua, Juan M. *Puerto Rico: Equality and Freedom at Issue.* New York: Praeger, 1984.

This historical study, written by a writer for the San Juan Star, includes chapters on "The Caribbean Context," "A History of the Puerto Rican People," "The Years of American Hegemony," and "The Status Question."

Jennings, James, and Rivera, Monte, eds. *Puerto Rican Politics in Urban America*. Westport, Conn.: Greenwood Press, 1984.

This informative study of Puerto Rican politics includes chapters on politics in New York City, Boston, and Chicago. The last section of the book contains a chapter that deals with politics and urban education.

Lewis, Gordon K. *Puerto Rico: Freedom and Power in the Caribbean*. New York: Monthly Review Press, 1963.

This classic history of Puerto Rico is written from a refreshingly perceptive and sympathetic point of view. It is a dated but valuable resource.

Marquez, Roberto, and Nieto, Sonia. *Literature and Society of the Puerto Rican People: A Syllabus for Secondary Schools*. New York: The Ford Foundation, 1986.

This guide, which focuses on the literature of Puerto Ricans, is designed for high school students. It includes a curriculum outline, sample lessons, and bibliographies.

Morales, Julio. *Puerto Rican Poverty and Migration: We Just Had to Try Elsewhere*. New York: Praeger, 1986.

This sociological study of Puerto Ricans focuses on their migration to New York City and other eastern regions. It also includes a chapter on Puerto Rican migration from New York to other locations.

Olivas, Michael, ed. *Latino College Students*. New York: Teachers College Press.

This collection of papers presents diverse perspectives on the experiences of Hispanic college students, including Puerto Ricans.

Perussse, Roland I. *The United States and Puerto Rico: Decolonization Options and Prospects*. Lanham, Md.: University Press of America, 1987.

The author discusses the three major options for the political status of Puerto Rico: the free association option and its prospects, the statehood option and its prospects, and the independence option and its prospects. The final chapter is "An Escape from the Colonial Dilemma."

Rodríguez, C.; Sanchez-Korrol, Viginia; and Alers, J. Oscar, eds. *The Puerto Rican Struggle: Essays on Survival in the U.S.* Maplewood, N.J.: Waterfront, 1984.

An interesting and informative collection of essays.

Sanchez-Korrol, Virginia E. *From Colonia to Community: The History of Puerto Ricans in New York, 1917–1948*. Westport, Conn.: Greenwood Press, 1983.

This is an important and informative study of early Puerto Rican migrants to New York City.

Thomas, Piri. *Savior, Savior, Hold My Hand*. Garden City, N.Y.: Doubleday, 1972.

This book is a sequel to the author's earlier book, Down These Mean Streets (Doubleday, 1967). It begins with Mr. Thomas returning to the barrio from prison. While he faces many problems,the author also discusses many pleasant memories in this part of his life, such as meeting and dating his wife.

Wagenheim, Kal, with Jiménez de Wagenheim, Olga, eds. *The Puerto Ricans: A Documentary History.* Garden City, N.Y.: Doubleday, 1973.

> *This comprehensive documentary history includes documents dealing with Puerto Rican history on the island and on the U.S. mainland.*

Books for Students

Allyn, Paul. *The Picture Life of Herman Badillo.* New York: Franklin Watts, 1972.

> *This biography of the first person of Puerto Rican ancestry elected to the U.S. Congress is readable and well illustrated. It can be an inspiration to Puerto Rican children and help other children to appreciate the contributions Puerto Ricans have made to American life. (Intermediate)*

Barth, Edna. *The Day Luis Was Lost.* Boston: Little, Brown, 1971.

> *This is a story about Luis, a young Puerto Rican boy who recently migrated to the United States, and his efforts to grow up. The story deals with how Puerto Ricans from the island have to adapt to new life-styles when they arrive in the United States. The illustrations are good. (Primary)*

Belpré, Pura. *Dance of the Animals.* New York: Frederick Warne, 1972.

> *This is a truly delightful Puerto Rican folktale about how the goat got his stump tail. It is well illustrated with color drawings. (All Levels)*

————. *Once in Puerto Rico.* New York: Frederick Warne, 1973.

> *These sixteen short, historical, magical tales reflect the fusion of Black, Spanish, and Indian cultures in Puerto Rico. (All Ages)*

————. *The Rainbow-Colored Horse.* New York: Frederick Warne, 1978.

> *This is an interesting Puerto Rican folktale for young children. (Primary)*

Bethancourt, T. Ernesto. *The Me Inside of Me.* Minneapolis, Minn.: Lerner, 1985.

> *This book tells the story of 17-year-old Alfredo Flores. He suddenly becomes a millionaire and moves from a middle-class to an affluent Puerto Rican community. (Intermediate)*

Brahs, Stuart. *An Album of Puerto Ricans in the United States.* New York: Franklin Watts, 1973.

> *This is a comprehensive treatment of Puerto Ricans on the U.S. mainland. (High School)*

Garcia, Richard. *My Aunt Otilia's Spirits.* San Francisco: Children's Book Press, 1987.

> *Written in English and Spanish, this bilingual book explores the dynamic nature of culture and shows how traditional cultural elements are sometimes viewed with discomfort. (Primary/Intermediate)*

Getz, Arthur. *Tar Beach.* New York: Dial Press, 1979.

> *This book explores some of the fun things two Puerto Rican children find to do during a hot New York summer. (Primary)*

Harlan, Judith. *Hispanic Voters: A Voice in American Politics*. New York: Franklin Watts, 1988.

   The important role of Hispanics in American politics is explored in this book. Puerto Rican leaders such as Herman Badillo are profiled and the concerns and positions of Puerto Ricans and other Hispanic groups are discussed. (Middle School/High School)

Kesselman, Wendy. *Joey*. New York: Lawrence Hill, 1972.

   This is a photographic essay about a young Puerto Rican boy's adjustment to life in New York City. (All ages)

Larsen, Ronald J. *The Puerto Ricans in America*. Minneapolis: Lerner, 1989.

   A historical overview of Puerto Rico and Puerto Rican migration to the mainland is included in this readable book. (Intermediate/Middle School)

Levoy, Myron. *A Shadow Like a Leopard*. New York: Harper and Row, 1981.

   This novel paints a poignant picture of a young Puerto Rican boy whose mother is in the hospital and father is in prison. Violence, urban blight, and crime form the backdrop for the story. Buried within this poverty-ridden setting is a story of the friendship that develops between the young boy and an older man. (High School)

Martel, Cruz. *Yagua Days*. New York: Dial Press, 1976.

   In this book, a young Puerto Rican shares his world with the reader. (Intermediate)

McKown, Robin. *The Image of Puerto Rico, Its History and Its People: On the Island—On the Mainland*. New York: McGraw-Hill, 1973.

   The author provides a historical overview of Puerto Rico and raises many important questions about its current status and the future of Puerto Ricans in the United States. (High School)

Meltzer, Milton. *The Hispanic Americans*. Boston: Thomas Y. Crowell, 1982.

   Puerto Ricans in the United States are one of the Hispanic groups discussed in this informative book about the problems facing Hispanics and the steps they have taken to solve them.

Mohr, Nicholasa. *Nilda*. New York: Harper, 1973.

   This story is about a young first-generation Puerto Rican in the United States who grows up in New York. (High School)

———. *El Bronx Remembered*. New York: Harper and Row, 1975.

   This collection of 12 stories is set in New York City. (High School)

———. *Felita*. New York: Dial Press, 1979.

   The reader explores a close-knit Puerto Rican community with an 8-year-old girl who feels a part of her community. A conflict arises when her parents want to move to a "better neighborhood." (Intermediate)

———. *In Nueva York*. New York: Dial Press, 1977.

   This collection of interrelated stories is about Puerto Ricans living in New York City. (High School)

Molnar, Joe. *Elizabeth: A Puerto Rican-American Child Tells Her Story.* New York: Franklin Watts, 1974.

This story centers around a young Puerto Rican girl in the United States who shares her thoughts on life. (Intermediate)

Newlon, Clarke. *Famous Puerto Ricans.* New York: Dodd, Mead, 1975.

This book contains a collection of short biographies of notable Puerto Ricans. (Intermediate)

Perl, Lila. *Puerto Rico: Island between Two Worlds.* New York, William Morrow, 1979.

The author presents a balanced view of Puerto Rico by describing both American and Puerto Rican perspectives. (Intermediate)

Rohmer, Harriet, and Rea, Jesus Guerrero. *Arariba and Niguayona.* San Francisco: Children's Book Press, 1987.

Full-color paintings illustrate this legend from the Taíno people of Puerto Rico and tell a universal story about love and sacrifice. (Primary/Intermediate)

Singer, Julia. *We All Come from Puerto Rico, Too.* New York: Atheneum, 1977.

This book describes Puerto Rico through the eyes of children and an older man. (Intermediate)

Tobier, Arthur. *The Puerto Ricans.* New York: Chelsea House, 1990.

This book is part of a series of books entitled "The Peoples of North America Series." The books in the series include historical overviews and information on individuals who have made significant contributions to society. (Intermediate)

Walker, Paul Robert. *Pride of Puerto Rico: The Life of Roberto Clemente.* San Diego: Harcourt Brace Jovanovich, 1988.

This book chronicles the life of Roberto Clemente, a world-famous baseball player from Puerto Rico. Clemente died on New Year's Eve, 1972, in a plane crash while trying to take relief supplies to earthquake victims in Nicaragua. (Middle School/ High School)

Chapter 12

Cuban Americans

Concepts, Strategies, and Materials

*If in things concerning my country I should be given a choice above all others
. . . this would be the good I would choose: I should want the cornerstone of
our Republic to be the devotion of Cubans to the dignity of man.*

—José Martí

Introduction

This chapter discusses the background and experience of one of the newer
major groups of Hispanics in the United States. Cubans have lived in small
communities in New York, Tampa, and Key West, Florida, since the latter part of
the nineteenth century, but large numbers did not immigrate to the United
States until after Castro assumed power in the revolution that occurred in 1959.

It would be difficult to appreciate the Cuban experience in the United
States without fully understanding the political situation that prompted them to
emigrate. The intense feelings toward the forces that caused them to leave their
homeland often surface as they adjust to life in the United States.

Yet, the experiences of immigrant and refugee groups like the Cubans, the
Jews, and the Vietnamese indicate how the United States has often been a
beacon of hope for many uprooted groups and has sometimes been the only
possibility for the realization of their dreams and aspirations. This chapter
illustrates that the American dream is far more than an abstraction for a people
who have left one homeland but gained another. The influx of Cubans on the
American scene has provided another major element among the diverse
Spanish-speaking ethnic groups in the United States, such as Mexican Americans and Puerto Ricans.

Since the 1960s, Cubans have been one of the largest groups immigrating
to the United States. Of the foreign nationals entering the United States from
Spanish-speaking nations, they have been the second largest immigrant group,
exceeded only by Mexicans. The number of Cubans immigrating to the United
States between 1971 and 1980 (276,800) was 28% larger than the number that
settled in the United States between 1951 and 1960 (78,300).[1] After the

This chapter is contributed by Carlos F. Diaz, Assistant Professor of Education, Florida
Atlantic University, Boca Raton, Florida.

374

125,000 entrants from the Mariel boatlift in 1980, Cuban immigration declined during the remainder of the decade. Immigration from Cuba has been a sporadic process since 1959, and it is difficult to predict its course for the 1990s and beyond.

Cuban Americans are a group with low visibility because their relocation has occurred almost exclusively in a few large urban areas. In 1990 they numbered more than 1 million. The largest Cuban-American community is in the greater Miami, Florida, area, and it includes more than 500,000 people. Other large concentrations are found in the New York City metropolitan area and in the greater Los Angeles area (see Table 12–1).

The Cubans' brief history on U.S. soil shares some common elements with older and more established immigrant groups. Yet, many unique differences distinguish their exodus. Most Cubans have migrated to the United States since the Castro revolution of 1959. Those who came did so primarily because they felt threatened by the political situation they experienced in Cuba. This contrasts with most other American immigrants who came to the United States searching mainly for economic promise.

Another characteristic of the Cuban influx is that those who left the island in search of a political haven are not a representative sample of the Cuban population at large. A demographic study showed that "a disproportionate number of refugees come from the middle- and upper-strata of prerevolutionary

Table 12–1   *Cuban American Population in Selected States (1980)*

Florida	470,250
New Jersey	80,860
New York	76,942
California	61,004
Illinois	19,063
Texas	14,124
Louisiana	7,970
Massachusetts	6,617
Georgia	5,863
Connecticut	5,610
Pennsylvania	5,600
Maryland	5,315
Virginia	4,958
Michigan	4,177
Nevada	3,708
Ohio	3,233
North Carolina	3,136
Indiana	1,916
South Carolina	1,665
Alabama	1,546

Source: Based on data in the U.S. Census, 1980

society."[2] People in the lower socioeconomic strata who opposed the revolution had fewer resources at their disposal to turn their dissatisfaction into some viable action.

The middle and upper strata of Cuban society were most heavily represented in the first wave of immigration during the early 1960s. As time progressed, Cuban immigration became a more representative sample of the Cuban population. However, the total number of Cuban immigrants in the United States still contains a higher proportion of business and professional persons than are present in the Cuban population.

This overrepresentation of the Cuban upper class among immigrants can be partly explained by the fact the people in this class felt particularly threatened by changes made by the government that eroded their economic position. Most Cuban Americans were never part of the elite in their homeland so their departure cannot be attributed to a loss of great wealth. They left their native land primarily because of their genuine opposition to the political system and for reasons of family reunification.

Another group that is overrepresented in the Cuban-American population is older people. Barriers to their exit from the island have been considerably fewer than those faced by younger Cubans. Another factor contributing to this demographic trend is that many Cuban families sent for their parents or grandparents after they had gained an economic foothold in the United States.

The ethnic composition of Cuban Americans is also disproportionate to the Cuban population. According to Perez, "Black Cubans were probably less likely to emigrate because of their perception that race relations in the United States are less satisfactory than they are in socialist Cuba."[3] Even though Black Cubans are underrepresented among immigrants, their numbers increased significantly after the Mariel influx in 1980. Caucasians and Chinese Cubans are found in greater proportions among Cubans in the United States than in the Cuban population. In prerevolutionary Cuba, Caucasian and Chinese Cubans were more prevalent in the middle- and upper economic strata of society. Conversely, Black Cubans were more likely to be present in the lower economic class. Most Cuban Americans of all racial and ethnic backgrounds share an opposition to the Castro regime in Cuba. Among those who immigrated as adults, it is difficult to describe the depth and emotional nature of their sentiments. The desire for political as well as economic stability has shaped the Cuban migration to the United States.

The Cuban immigrant has generally accepted and lived by the predominant American ethos that hard work will ultimately be rewarded. Considering the deprived economic conditions that most started with, the results have been notable. Their accomplishments will probably lead them to be touted as a "model minority," much like their Japanese-American counterparts. Yet the success of Cubans should not be construed to obscure the general plight of Spanish-speaking Americans. For most, this success has not occurred without hardship. Their accomplishments do not mean that Cuban Americans do not have problems. Their median income still lags behind the national average. To attain this economic level, a disproportionate number of working wives are found in Cuban-American households. Also, the cohesive nature of the Cuban family has sometimes suffered because of economic pressures.

The assimilation of Cubans has occurred at different levels among people living in various locations in the United States. Like most immigrant groups, assimilation has been less for the older segment of the population as well as in cities with large Cuban communities. The continuum of assimilation ranges from the almost perfectly integrated to those who have failed to accept the permanence of their American surroundings.

Cuban Americans: Historical Perspective

Important Dates

1959	Fidel Castro took over the reins of power in Cuba from the government of dictator Fulgencio Batista.
1961	Diplomatic relations between the United States and Cuba were severed. The Cuban exile brigade 2500 landed at the Bay of Pigs, on the southern coast of Cuba, in an ill-fated attempt to overthrow the Castro regime.
1962	Commercial air flights between the United States and Cuba were ended. Immigration to the United States became strictly clandestine. The Cuban missile crisis prompted President Kennedy to blockade Cuba. The Soviet Union eventually withdrew the missiles from Cuban soil.
1965	Beginning of the Cuban Refugee Airlift program. Flights from Cuba to Miami, Florida, were sponsored by the U.S. government.
1973	Termination of the Cuban Refugee Airlift program. Immigration to the United States returned to a clandestine status or took place through a third country, such as Spain or Mexico.
1977	Diplomatic interest sections were established by the U.S. and Cuban governments in embassies of third countries. Cuba used the Czechoslovakian embassy in Washington and the United States used the Swiss embassy in Havana. This move was strongly opposed by most Cuban Americans.

**Important
Dates**

Fidel Castro allowed U.S. citizens and their Cuban dependents living in Cuba who wished to leave to depart Cuba.

1980   125,000 Cubans arrived in the United States via a boatlift from Mariel. Reaction in the United States ranged from welcome to open hostility.

1981   Cuban activity in Central America strained Cuban relations with the United States. President Reagan moved to establish Radio Martí to broadcast programs to Cuba.

1984   The Immigration and Naturalization Service ruled that Cubans who entered the United States via Mariel with the classification of "entrant" would be permitted to apply for permanent resident status under the Cuban Refugee Readjustment Act of 1966.

1985   In response to Radio Martí broadcasts beamed at Cuba, Fidel Castro stopped familial visits of Cuban Americans and abrogated the agreement with the United States to repatriate Mariel Cubans who were being held in American jails.
Xavier Suarez was elected mayor of Miami, Florida. He was the first Cuban American to be elected to that office.

1987   Mariel refugee inmates imprisoned in Atlanta, Georgia, and Oakdale, Louisiana, rioted and took hostages on learning that they might be deported. Riots ended after the U.S. government set up a review process for anyone facing deportation.

1988   The Cuban American National Foundation began a program with U.S. immigration's approval to reunite Cubans in third countries with relatives in the United States. The foundation paid all travel and relocation costs.

1989   Rep. Ileana Ros-Lehtinen became the first Cuban-born member of the U.S. Congress in a special election to replace the late Rep. Claude Pepper.
Florida followed the precedent set in California, Illinois, and other states and voted 84% to 16% to amend the state constitution declaring English the state's official language. Cuban Americans in Florida largely opposed this measure.

Cuban Americans: Life in Cuba

On January 1, 1959, the city of Havana, Cuba, rocked with the effects of a drastic change. The regime of dictator Fulgencio Batista had been deposed by *"la Revolucion,"* led by a bearded young rebel named Fidel Castro. His triumphal entry into the capital city was seen by nearly everyone as the coming of a new messiah. His popularity was more than that of a political figure; he had all the markings of a charismatic leader.

Promises of economic prosperity and of uniting the Cuban people were among the many Fidel Castro made. The synthesis of the Cuban revolution took place in a slow, deliberate series of steps, to the delight of some and the disillusionment of others. The Agrarian Reform confiscated large holdings of land in private hands. This land became government property, and farmers became government employees.

As the course of the revolution drifted politically left, a marked polarization of Cuban society began to occur. A person either supported the revolution or was thought of as a *gusano* (worm). The latter was a parasite to progress and the revolution was better off without him or her. True to the Cuban sense of humor, the expression *abrir los ajos* (see the light) marked a person who took exception to revolutionary policies. These political divisions permeated the family unit and caused bitter disagreements between relatives who advocated the revolution and those who opposed it. Many of these rifts remain today. The Cuban revolution affected everyone, regardless of his or her place in society. Fundamental changes reached the economic, political, social, and religious sectors of Cuban life.

The educational system in Cuba was affected fundamentally by the revolution. The number of schools in rural areas was increased in a campaign to end *analfabetismo* (illiteracy). Also, new high schools were located primarily in rural areas. Many urban students had to board at school in order to obtain a secondary education. In the public schools, instruction in the humanities and the natural and physical sciences was fraught with political socialization, which placed a premium on loyalty to the revolution.

Along with expanding education in the rural areas, the Cuban government has increased the number of health facilities. Clinics are more readily available to farmers than in prerevolutionary times.

The Cuban economy today, like that of other communist nations, deemphasizes consumer goods in favor of products for export. As a result of this emphasis, as well as of production lags, rationing is fairly common. The following ration limits, obtained by interviewing an exile, were in effect in 1990:

Rice	4 pounds per month
Beans	6 ounces per month
Coffee	4 ounces per month
Meat	12 ounces per month

Chicken	6 ounces every 9 days (instead of meat)
Lard	1 pound per month
Toothpaste	1 medium tube per month for every 2 persons
Bath soap	1 bar per month
Milk	1 liter daily for children under age 7 and adults over 65

It is ironic that in the world's leading sugar-producing nation Cubans are rationed to 4 pounds per month. It should be noted that even though quantities are limited, prices on the official market are inexpensive. For years, Cubans have resorted to an illicit underground market system in which food has sold at 5 to 10 times the price of rationed items. In the past few years, the government established official free-market stores in which food items could be bought that were in excess of one's ration. However, the price in these markets was also 5 or more times that of the rationed items.

In addition to the rationing, Cubans must plan on spending a fair amount of time waiting to buy their food items. It is not an uncommon occurrence for the shopper to spend 2 hours or more per day making food purchases. Whenever something extra can be obtained, people do so for friends or relatives. Any outing from the home is a potential shopping trip. Because the availability of products is often sporadic, the shopping bag (*jaba*) is a constant companion.

Socioeconomic mobility in Cuba is accomplished by a mixture of individual talent, effort, and loyalty. The last of these factors creates some wrenching psychological dilemmas for certain individuals. To hold most of the managerial and many professional positions, the person must be a card-carrying *militante* (militant). Some people hold this status out of conviction for communist or revolutionary beliefs and others because the card is an asset for upward mobility in the society. These people must be particularly careful of their associations. Participating in religious activity would be grounds for the revocation of the militant status.

A constant dilemma for the militants of convenience is whether their activities or associations will help or hinder their image as militants. For this reason, some children have been baptized without the knowledge of one parent.

It is also assumed that people with militant status will be prepared to serve on any international mission that may be assigned. This is also true for people studying any one of the professions, particularly those in the health fields. These missions may last two or three years, and some couples are separated for that long.

Other adaptations to revolutionary society include having every salary in the nation specified by the government. The money derived from working is not sufficient to purchase most foodstuffs or consumer goods. It must be accompanied by a ration coupon permitting the purchase of specific items.

Salary laws require workers to meet a production quota of either goods or services. If this quota is not reached, the worker's salary is reduced by a proportional amount. In addition to a worker's obligatory job, there is volunteer labor available on Sundays or holidays. This volunteer work may consist of cleaning details, construction projects, or harvesting sugar cane, as well as many other tasks. Workers who want to purchase a major item such as a refrigerator often accumulate many hours of volunteer labor.

Leaving the country entails many sacrifices. Invariably relatives are left behind. This point is particularly significant when one realizes the close-knit nature of the Cuban extended family, which makes it difficult for members to break from the family unit.

Forfeiture of all possessions is another factor to consider. Everything a person has worked for in a lifetime finds its way into government hands. Also, there is the prospect of starting over in a strange environment. For most immigrants, this happens without command of the English language. Despite all these difficulties, however, nearly a million Cubans have felt compelled to leave their homeland.

Opinions about the Castro regime vary within Cuba. Supporters point out that the Cuban government has vastly expanded health care and education. Cubans on the island who are strong supporters of the Castro government and its philosophy cite wide gaps in living standards between the elite and common persons in other Latin American nations. These issues, however valid, are not salient with the Cuban-American population. For most of them, the ills perpetrated by the Castro government outweigh any of its positive measures.

In the early 1960s, the United States accepted as a political refugee any Cuban who could reach its shores. In 1966, a Congressional act gave Cuban refugees the status of parolees and allowed a change to permanent resident status after 2 years in the United States. This law also gave Cubans special immigration status so their number would not be limited or counted against the limits allowed for other nations in the Americas.

This remained U.S. policy until the Refugee Act of 1980 removed special immigration status for Cuban immigrants. In order to accommodate the influx of Cubans in 1980, President Carter created a special immigration category of entrants. People who held this entrant status remained as temporary residents of the United States until late 1984, when the Immigration and Naturalization Service decided to allow them to apply for permanent residency status. Today, Cubans as a group no longer hold officially favored immigration status.

Departure

Prohias and Casal have identified the following three stages in the migration of Cubans to the United States:

> They are as follows: A *first stage,* between January 1959 and October 1962, when commercial flights between Cuba and the United States were available; a *second stage,* between October 1962 and December 1965, with a corresponding slow-down of the migration rate as Cubans had to resort to unconventional means (small boats, rafts, etc.) or flights through third countries to come to the United

States; a *third stage,* with daily airflights between Varadero and Miami throughout most of the period.[4]

The third stage, known as the Cuban Refugee Airlift, was terminated in January 1973. From 1973 to 1980, Cubans reverted to the unconventional means of the second stage. In 1980, a temporary policy change by the Cuban government produced a fourth stage resulting in a wave of 125,000 Cubans coming by sea from Mariel to Key West, Florida. At the conclusion of this boatlift in May 1980, Cubans reverted to stage-two methods.

In 1988, the Cuban American National Foundation received permission from the Immigration and Naturalization Service to sponsor Cubans living outside of Cuba. This effort was to reunify them with relatives living in the United States. The visas granted to these individuals stipulated that their relocation would occur at no cost to the national, state, or local government.

The trauma of leaving Cuba varied greatly with the particular experience. Leaving by commercial airline in 1960 was fairly conventional. However, escaping in a small boat meant jeopardizing one's life. Also, the date of departure determined how much difficulty an exile would encounter in leaving the island. In general, the longer a family waited before making the decision to leave, the more obstacles it would have to face before it could secure permission to exit. In the early 1960s, many families sent their children out of Cuba via Catholic or other religious relief agencies in the hope that the parents could follow later. Some of these families have been reunited; others are still waiting.

Many Americans have heard of Cubans reaching U.S. shores in small boats, but little publicity is given to the fact that many never made it after encountering a patrol boat or drifting away in the Gulf Stream current.

The Mariel Immigrants of 1980

In April 1980, more than 10,000 Cubans sought political asylum in the Peruvian embassy in Havana. The Cuban government's initial response was to allow them permission to leave Cuba via Peru or other willing Latin American nations, such as Costa Rica. Within days, that policy was changed to allow the exit of those people, as well as others who had sought to immigrate, directly to the United States.

The Cuban-American community in the United States saw this temporary respite in Cuban immigration policy as an opportunity to reunite themselves with relatives whom they had been trying to join for years.

A small port city on the northern coast of Cuba, Mariel, became the staging area for people waiting for transportation to the United States. On May 5, 1980, President Carter stated that the United States would receive the refugees "with an open heart and open arms." Nine days later, a presidential order forbade boats going to Cuba to pick up refugees. By then, hundreds of boats were on their way to or waiting in Mariel. Many Cuban-American families spent their savings or pooled their earnings to pay for passage on a boat for relatives in Cuba.

The hundreds of boats that had crossed the Straits of Florida found a chaotic situation at the port of Mariel. Most boats had to anchor and wait, sometimes for weeks, until the government indicated that a group of people was ready for loading. Boat captains brought lists of people they came to transport, but often the lists were ignored or only one or two people on the list would be permitted to leave.

Meanwhile, food and supplies began to run low on board these vessels. Provisions had to be purchased from the Cuban government at three to six times their price in the United States. As time passed, tempers began to flare in the Mariel harbor.

People who had declared a willingness to leave via Mariel were gathered from all parts of Cuba. In some instances, people departing were publicly humiliated by zealous supporters of the revolution. Some people who declared a desire to leave through Mariel were not able to do so for logistical or other reasons. Their declaration caused them to lose their jobs, and many could not find other jobs.

The return crossing of the Straits of Florida was often a perilous ordeal. As a rule, boats were loaded beyond their capacity. Some captains objected to this, as well as to carrying people whom they had not come for. When the Cuban authorities insisted on both points, boat captains faced the dilemma of violating these directives or violating U.S. directives to stop the boatlift when they returned to Florida.

More than 50 people died during these crossings. Some drowned when boats capsized in heavy seas, and others succumbed to carbon monoxide fumes in the holds of overloaded vessels. A frequently repeated ritual was of Cuban refugees kissing the ground after arriving in Key West, Florida.

As the flood of refugees continued, they were housed in a variety of temporary holding centers such as the Orange Bowl in Miami, Florida. People with immediate relatives were the most likely to be released quickly. Others without relatives waited patiently for relocation in other parts of the United States.

As the numbers of refugees increased, a backlash of public opinion began. A Gallup poll conducted nationally in late May 1980 found that 59% of respondents felt that Cuban emigration was bad for the United States.[5] In the Miami area, a similar survey conducted by the *Miami Herald* in May 1980 found that 68% of the non-Latin White population and 57% of the Black population surveyed felt that the new wave of Cuban refugees would have a large negative influence on the local community.[6]

The Cuban community in Miami raised more than $2 million in cash and other assistance to help accommodate the new arrivals. Nevertheless, the size of the influx made it necessary to relocate many Cubans in holding centers outside southern Florida. As Cuban refugees were relocated on military bases in predominantly rural areas of Arkansas, Pennsylvania, Wisconsin, and Florida, residents of those areas vehemently protested the Cuban presence.

The characteristics of the Cubans who emigrated via the Mariel boatlift showed that there was a higher proportion of Black Cubans, single males, and blue-collar workers than among previous groups of Cuban immigrants. Much has been written about the undesirable or criminal element that came to the United States during the boatlift. The Cuban government seized the opportunity to rid itself of people who had committed serious crimes or suffered mental or physical problems; but people in these categories constituted less than 5% of the 125,000 entrants. Also, the fact that a person had spent time in a Cuban jail could be due either to criminal or political activity. Consequently, not all criminals would have had that label if they had been living in the United States. Most of the Mariel Cubans originally detained were eventually released. About 1,200 Mariel Cubans have remained in jail since their arrival in the United States.[7] The bulk of these prisoners have been detained at the Atlanta Federal Penitentiary.

Most Cubans who came via the 1980 boatlift were generally of humbler origins than their predecessors but just as determined to improve themselves. A few gave the term *Marielito* a pejorative connotation. Unfortunately, that connotation has sometimes tainted the majority of Mariel Cubans who have worked hard and respected the law. Today, more than a decade after their arrival, the evidence shows that Mariel Cubans have generally adjusted well to U.S. society.

Adaptation to American Life

Most immigrants to the United States have come with the unwavering conviction of making this country their permanent home. Many Cubans arrived here with the thought of returning to their homeland as soon as the political climate changed. Although grateful to the United States for their asylum, their ultimate plans were not in this country. Thus, they did not feel the need to assimilate into the mainstream culture. With the passing of time, only the most optimistic clung exclusively to this viewpoint. Because the Castro regime showed strong signs of longevity, exiles tried to adapt to their new environment.

The adaptation of Cubans to American life has often been difficult. This process has been more extensive in areas where the Cuban population is small. In a city like Miami, with its large Cuban community, it is possible to live without crossing the boundaries of the ethnic neighborhood. Assimilation is not imperative in this situation. One major change has been to forsake the more leisurely mood of the Cuban life-style. According to the *New York Times*, "Conversion to the pace of American life has threatened to disrupt the traditional Cuban way of life. The initial cultural shock was compounded by the dizzying social changes underway in this country that perplexed most Americans."[8]

The high percentage of Cuban-American working wives has had a significant social, as well as economic, impact on the Cuban community. One study found that "Resources of the wife, particularly as they compared favorably to the resources possessed by her husband, were found to be an additional influence in the absorption of a more egalitarian ideology."[9] The traditional dominant role of the husband in the Cuban household has undergone some modification, particularly in locations where families live in a largely non-Cuban community.

One problem encountered by Cuban parents was having their children adhere to Cuban values, norms, and customs. These permitted less freedom than their American peers enjoyed. This gap was felt more acutely by daughters in Cuban families than sons, since traditionally girls have been more closely supervised by parents.

The custom of having someone chaperone a date has caused conflicts in many Cuban-American families. Girls who had to abide by this custom often felt that they were at a disadvantage in their peer group. This situation does not differ significantly from those faced by other immigrant groups as their children drifted away from traditional customs. With the passage of time, fewer and fewer families still insist on a chaperone and have substituted other methods of supervision that are more prevalent in the United States.

Where Cubans resettled in large numbers, they were received in a variety of ways. A former Cuban lawyer related his impression in the following manner: "There are many people in Miami who still resent the Cubans settling here," he said, "but for the most part, since we have been the most successful immigrants in American history, Americans find it hard to look down their noses at us because we arrived here loaded with American characteristics. We are just too outgoing and enterprising and hard-working for them to stay mad at us."[10]

The reactions experienced by Cuban immigrants depended on the time and location of their immigration. People who were relocated to cities and towns with low Hispanic populations experienced little negative reaction. The influx of a few families is probably noticed little in most communities. Among Cubans who settled in areas like Miami, Florida, initial opposition to their arrival came from people in unskilled and blue-collar jobs. These new arrivals were perceived as an economic threat. People in higher economic positions were relatively unconcerned and often praised the hard-working emigrés.

With time and command of English, Cubans began to climb the socioeconomic ladder. They began to assert themselves economically and, to a lesser extent, politically. In 1969, Dade County (Miami) had 3,449 Hispanic businesses. By 1977, that figure became 8,248, and in 1985 it had grown to 15,000. The Hispanic (mostly Cuban) population of Dade County had an annual income in 1985 of $6.7 billion.[11] In 1990, the economic output of the Dade County Hispanic business community exceeded that of Hispanic businesses in Los Angeles, which has more than double the Hispanic population of Miami.

When Cubans started to become a potent economic force in Miami and in other cities where their numbers are significant, they encountered difficulties from segments of the community that traditionally held most of the economic and political influence and wanted no change. Many of these people had been relatively unconcerned a decade or two before. Today, they realize that Cuban Americans are a viable economic entity and a competitive force. Competition is not always welcomed.

Like many immigrant groups, Cuban Americans have formed their own organizations to promote common interests. Groups such as the Latin American Chamber of Commerce were formed in Miami and claim the greatest membership among Cuban-American businesspeople. While a time may come when members of this association may join the Greater Miami Chamber of Commerce in large numbers, the Latin chamber is expected to continue in the foreseeable future.

The median income of Cuban Americans is higher than that of Puerto Rican or Mexican Americans, but they rank slightly below the median income for the entire nation. Cuban median family income in 1987, at $27,300, approached the non-Hispanic median.[12] An unusually high percentage of Cuban women in the work force partly explains this comparison. The entrance of thousands of Cubans in 1980 into the labor force has reduced the median income of Cuban Americans because most new arrivals began working in the United States at low-status jobs. The effect of this group on Cuban median income is lessening with the passage of time.

When they tried to pursue their former occupations in the United States, most Cubans ran into difficulties. The main obstacle to white-collar employment was mastery of the English language, which most did not have. In the professional fields, degrees earned in Cuba were often not recognized, and individuals frequently returned to college if they wanted to obtain work related to their training in Cuba. Even though many Cubans have regained their former occupational status and some have even surpassed it, a slight loss of occupational status remains.

The typical newly arrived exile family received some assistance from the Cuban Refugee program while it existed. Afterwards, Cubans took whatever employment was immediately available, anticipating that their preferred work could be obtained later. When the concentration of Cubans in the Miami area became substantial, the government started a resettlement program. This program offered jobs and 1 month's free rent to immigrants who agreed to move outside Florida. In recent years, some Cubans who had been relocated trickled back into the South Florida area after they had achieved a financial foothold.

Many Cubans arriving via the 1980 boatlift had a more difficult time, especially single males with no family in the United States. Many waited months behind camp fences looking for an organization or person to sponsor their release. As time passed, frustration grew and even erupted into hostility at some camps. Even after being released in the care of a sponsor, some Mariel Cubans found it difficult to adjust to a competitive capitalist society with opportunities but few guarantees. After decades of working in a socialist economic system, some were unaccustomed or unsure of work patterns and habits in the United States. Others adapted quickly and easily.

A rift sometimes developed between the older, established Cuban immigrant and the Mariel emigré. The former sometimes felt that the latter were insufficiently driven to succeed or grateful for the assistance received. This situation is similar to the relationship that had developed in the latter part of the nineteenth century between the established German-American Jews and the new arrivals from Eastern Europe.

Mariel refugees have had a more difficult time adjusting to American life than their predecessors for a variety of reasons. They arrived in the midst of a recessionary economic cycle, which made obtaining the first jobs more difficult. On average, they possessed fewer marketable skills than did their predecessors. A year after their arrival, 45,000 Mariel entrants were living below the official poverty line and committing suicide at a rate seven times the U.S. average.[13] Despite difficult economic conditions and homesickness at first, both rates have diminished significantly in the years that followed.

The children who entered via Mariel also had to make major adjustments, as did the school systems that were to receive them. "In absolute numbers, the Dade County Public Schools faced integrating a school population larger than 95% of the school districts in the United States."[14] The Dade County schools enrolled more than 11,500 Cuban refugee children in the 1980–1981 school year. Students were divided between two entrant facilities established exclusively for Mariel students, and the remaining students attended special programs in schools designated as entrant centers, as well as neighborhood schools.

Along with the new language and curriculum, some students had to learn a new value system. Self-discipline was sometimes lacking, along with a concept of private property. Authority was equated with people one does not trust and taking someone else's property synonymous with "need," not "bad."[15] With time and the patience of teachers, these students have usually adjusted to the new value system and most have progressed well. It is difficult to measure their degree of academic or social integration because Mariel students were not identified beyond their initial period of adjustment.

Mariel Cubans often cite a lack of closeness and spirituality about life in the United States. Many centered their lives in Cuba around these qualities, which helped them endure hardships and privations. They see themselves as distinct from the older emigrés, some of whom they view as living in a frozen Cuban culture. This frozen culture is based solely on Cuban values, beliefs, and attitudes and to which all aspects of contemporary life are compared. These people exist as a subculture within a subculture. It will be interesting to note the degree to which Mariel Cubans will exhibit some of the characteristics of the older immigrants in the future.

The process of assimilation has been most difficult for the elderly Cuban population. They represent an unusually high percentage of the exile population because older people faced fewer restrictions in trying to leave the island. This elderly population faces the usual problems of the aged, compounded by an environment to which many cannot adapt. For those whose families have strayed from traditional Cuban customs regarding the aged, they miss being the center of the family. Elderly persons living alone are found in larger than expected numbers in the Cuban-American community. Many of the Cuban elderly who live in an extended family household provide the crucial day care function that allows many Cuban women to join the labor force.

As might be expected, the Cuban-American elderly are the least culturally assimilated segment of the Cuban community in the United States. Most speak minimal or no English and are thus limited from taking part in many facets of American life. Their children and grandchildren are often their link to the non-Cuban community. Some, though not most, of these people belong to what has been described as the frozen culture.

News from relatives in Cuba keeps Cuban Americans of all ages psychologically aware of two countries. They feel deeply the difficulties and privations that loved ones may be experiencing, and they do whatever they can to help ameliorate the circumstances. In 1979, the Cuban government decided to allow familial visits. Tens of thousands of Cubans in the United States returned to the island with suitcases bulging with clothes, food, and gifts for relatives. These visitors were described by the Cuban population as belonging to the community. The stories of their lives in the United States were sometimes exaggerated toward more affluence than truly existed, but it became evident to Cubans in Cuba that most visitors were not suffering the way the Cuban government had claimed. These visits brought badly needed foreign exchange to Cuba; therefore, they were allowed to continue for quite some time. However, the ease or difficulty of familial visits for Cubans will likely correlate with the state of political relations between the United States and Cuba for some time to come.

Politically, Cuban Americans have been in general more conservative than most recently arrived immigrants. However, this conservatism should not be equated unequivocally with American conservatism. Cuban Americans are conservative on foreign policy issues, especially if those issues concern nations with communist governments. They tend to be considerably more moderate on domestic social issues.

In the Miami metropolitan area, Cubans are becoming an increasing portion of the electorate through naturalization. In the fall of 1981, Raul Martinez was elected mayor of Hialeah, Florida, thus becoming the first Cuban-American mayor of a large American city. Until 1982, no Cuban American had been elected to the state legislature of Florida, even though Cuban Americans comprised approximately one-half of Miami's Dade County. In 1982, Florida changed from multimember to single-member legislative districts, and a number of Cuban Americans were elected to serve in the state house of representatives. The mid and late 1980s saw Xavier Suarez elected mayor of Miami and Cuban Americans also elected to the Florida state senate. In 1989, Ileana Ros-Lehtinen was elected to the U.S. House of Representatives, becoming the first Cuban-American member of Congress.

As more Cuban Americans become naturalized citizens and turn their attention to American politics, their political participation and influence should grow proportionately.

The Second Generation

The Cuban-American community has come to have a larger proportion of persons who immigrated to the United States in early childhood or who were born here. This second generation represents a unique group of English-dominant bilingual persons who function well in both the Cuban-American community and the larger society. They range approximately from age 20 to 40 and are found in nearly every walk of life.

They are sometimes referred to as YUCAS (young upwardly mobile Cuban Americans). The term has a double meaning because yucca is a starchy root that Cubans frequently eat. The perspectives of this second generation are neither those of their parents or of their American peers. One American-born young woman in her early twenties commented, "The Cubans consider me an American and the Americans consider me a Cuban." Another American-born young man observed, "I didn't realize how Cuban I was until I left South Florida for Boston to attend college." Many of these young people understand the anachronisms in Cuban-American culture but are respectful of the persons who hold them.

Cuba is not a personal experience or memory for most of these people. They know of Cuba only from their parents' accounts, which typically grow fonder with each telling. It thus is understandable that most do not hold as strong an attachment for a place and a way of life that appears mythical.

Most of this second generation is fundamentally pragmatic. They are generally less politicized and conservative than their parents, but they still see themselves as culturally distinct. Their identity as Cuban Americans does not generally include thinking of themselves as minority group members. They sometimes are surprised when they interact with other young Hispanics who do identify with minority group status.

As a rule, the YUCAs see the perpetuation of the Spanish language in their own children as a desirable goal even if some of their own command of Spanish grammar is rudimentary. If this second generation is successful in keeping Spanish fluency in their children, it will mark a significant departure from the traditional immigrant pattern of losing the immigrant language by the second generation.

This group understands and respects the sacrifices and hardships that their parents faced as a consequence of immigration. However, they are generally not preoccupied with nostalgia. They seek the best in both cultures in order to carve out their own unique identity in U.S. society.

Cuban Americans Today

Cuban Americans represent an ethnic group that, while making economic, social, and cultural contributions to the United States, also seek to maintain their cultural identity. In general, Cubans have adapted relatively well to American life.

As Prohias and Casal note, "A cursory reading of the studies surveyed seems to indicate that Cubans have adjusted well to life in the United States and that, after the initial influx which caught Miami by surprise, they have not been a social problem. Early studies found Cubans to be low in all indices of social disorganization or maladjustment."[16] Their statement suggests that the process of acculturation is slowly occurring. As in the case of the Japanese Americans, the amount of cultural assimilation has exceeded the degree of structural assimilation. Where large Cuban settlements occur, a great deal of the social and civic life still centers around the ethnic community. In Miami, theaters show films in Spanish; the city has Latin civic clubs and a Latin Chamber of Commerce. Miami has become a de facto bilingual city.

This Latinization of Miami, while a boon to economic development with Latin America, has created a discernible backlash among a significant portion of the non-Latin community. In 1980, voters in Dade County (Miami) approved a local "anti-bilingual ordinance" barring the expenditure of county taxes to use or promote any language other than English. The same community owes much, if not most, of its economic viability to Latin-American tourists and trade.

In 1989, Florida voters amended the state constitution to make English the state's official language. This amendment was overwhelmingly approved by an 84% vote of the electorate. Cuban Americans usually agree with other Hispanic groups that these efforts are lightly veiled attempts to limit the viability and options of Hispanic Americans. Cuban Americans, like their Mexican American and Puerto Rican counterparts, believe that it is imperative that people who choose to live in the United States should learn to speak English.[17] It would be almost impossible to find an individual in the Cuban community who does not want his or her children taught English. However, many Cuban Americans regard English-only legislation as emblematic of coerced assimilation. Some feel that any pressure to assimilate implies they are not acceptable as they are.

Another language-related issue with significant support among Cuban Americans is bilingual education. Most feel that bilingual education is a necessary bridge for limited and non–English-speaking students to succeed in American classrooms. Elimination of these programs would not find support among most Hispanics in this nation, including Cuban Americans.

The average Cuban immigrant has gone through a great psychological transition, the severity of which is strongly related to age at the time of leaving. Much trauma was involved. Many former professional men in Cuba had to begin in middle age as unskilled workers. This change required some mature adjustment in order to cope.

It would be conjecture to estimate how many Cubans would return to their native land if the Castro regime were replaced by a government more acceptable to them. Many have established roots in the United States that cannot be severed. Others would find the lure of a free Cuba irresistible, even though they might be well established in the United States.

Even though many Cubans are opposed to any thaw in relations between the governments of Cuba and the United States, a growing number favor accommodation, particularly if it can help bring families together. Visits of Cuban Americans to their families in Cuba have been possible in recent years after nearly 3 decades of prohibition. The intellectual and academic Cuban-American community tends to be more favorable to a less rigid policy toward Cuba than do blue-collar Cubans.

Some intellectuals in the Cuban-American community are speculating on what influence, if any, the 1989 fall of Eastern European communist regimes will have on Cuba. Cuba's greatest benefactor, the Soviet Union, is going through an internal restructuring process favoring greater openness. Meanwhile, the Castro government has maintained an orthodox communist posture. Can the Castro government maintain its traditional policies if the Soviet Union and Eastern European nations reduce their financial support of the Cuban government?

Today, Cuban Americans are the third largest Spanish-speaking group in the United States; Mexican Americans and Puerto Ricans rank first and second. The Cuban experience indicates that they have been a viable and beneficial addition to U.S. society. This pattern can be expected to continue.

Teaching Strategies

CONCEPT: Immigration

Generalization: Many Cuban immigrants found themselves unable and/or unwilling to live with the Castro government and chose to leave their homeland instead.

1. Divide your class into small groups and instruct them as follows: Your family is forced to move to a country in which the language and customs are alien. Each of you is allowed to take only a small amount of clothes. All of your possessions are left behind and forfeited, since you cannot return. Describe what your life might be like where you are going. What clothing would you take with you? Why? How well do you think your family would fare? What adjustments would all of you have to make? The students' reactions

can be taped or written. The taping would provide more spontaneous responses. Afterwards, compare and discuss reactions among groups.

2. After sufficient background information is presented, ask each student to write an essay titled, "If I Had Been a Cuban in 1959, What Would I Have Done?"

3. Organize a debate in which one side takes the position that deposing the Castro regime is feasible and the other feels it is impossible.

4. Read the following story to the class and ask the questions that follow.

The Pina Family

Ernesto Pina was a fisherman who lived in Cardenas, on the north coast of Cuba. He and his wife, Iliana, had never been wealthy, but fishing had always provided for the necessities of life. Ernesto always seemed to be able to return with fish of one type or another.

They had been happy to see the tyrant Batista deposed by the Castro revolution. Ernesto felt that Fidel Castro had the interests of the "little man" like himself at heart. One day when he returned to the fishery to sell his catch, Ernesto was informed that part of it would go to the government. Officials said that his fish would be exported and goods received in return would help the revolution. Ernesto did not want to be considered greedy, but he needed his entire catch to support his family. At the risk of being caught, he would hide some fish and sell them privately to his friends.

The family's only son, José, was 16 and had been forced to join the militia. Neither parent liked this, but it could not be helped.

One night Ernesto and Iliana were talking and she suggested going to the United States. Yet both knew that they could not depart legally, because José was of military age. Obviously, they could not leave their only son behind. So the three decided to try to escape in the fishing boat one night. They knew they would be shot in the water if discovered, but decided to take the risk anyway.

The eventful night came, and the Pina family slipped away from the harbor. Ernesto was sailing the craft because he did not want the noise of the engine to be heard. He had been quite careful to wait for the proper tide and a moonless night. After a short time, they heard an engine; the sound kept coming closer. It was the shore patrol! He lowered the sail quickly and they hid in the bottom of the boat. The patrol boat passed within fifty yards but had not spotted them. They had been saved by the darkness!

When morning came, Ernesto started his small engine because the breeze had faded. He hoped for the best because he did not have much gasoline. After two days at sea he was beginning to worry. His family was sunburned, he was out of gasoline, and he had not yet spotted the Florida coast. Yet, they kept their faith. They were lucky to be seen by a U.S. Coast Guard cutter, which towed them into port.

As the three stepped off the boat onto American soil, they each said a prayer for having been so fortunate.

Questions

1. If you had been one of the Pina family and found yourself in their circumstances, would you have taken the risk they did? Why or why not?

2. What problems did Mr. Pina encounter that made him decide to leave Cuba?
3. Why didn't the Pina family attempt to leave Cuba by legal means?
4. What kind of future do you foresee for the Pina family in the United States?
5. Have each student (either in writing or orally) describe the circumstances of a political situation in the United States that would cause him or her to escape to a foreign nation, which would involve risking his or her life.

CONCEPT: Intergenerational Conflict

Generalization: The second generation of any immigrant group is going to absorb from the larger society values, beliefs, and priorities that are sometimes at odds with their parents' beliefs.

Read the following story to the class and ask the questions that follow.

The Rodriguez Family

Carlos Rodriguez is a young, successful professional person working in the Miami branch of a major American corporation. His wife, Maria, teaches in the public schools; their daughters, Gloria and Cecilia, are ages 3 and 4.

Both Carlos and Maria's parents live within a 20-minute drive. Maria's parents provide the much-needed daycare for their granddaughters, and Carlos's parents are happy to substitute if needed. Most other family members who left Cuba are also living in the greater Miami area; family gatherings are frequent and well attended.

One day Carlos tells his wife of a possible promotion, which would involve moving to Minneapolis. Carlos can choose to accept the promotion or can stay in his current job.

Carlos and Maria informed their parents before deciding. As expected, both sets of parents were opposed to the family's moving. They pointed out that Carlos's and Maria's combined income enabled them to live comfortably and that in Minneapolis, the girls would be cared for by strangers and their contact with their grandparents would be limited. Maria's father also remarked that some things are more important than higher positions and more money, such as family.

Questions

1. What is the value system that is prompting the objections from the Rodriguez's grandparents?
2. How do the grandparents' values compare with the predominant values in American society regarding advancement and mobility?
3. When you think of the term *family*, do you think of it as a nuclear or an extended family?
4. If you think Carlos and Maria should remain in Miami, give at least three reasons.
5. If you think the Rodriguez family should move to Minneapolis, give at least three reasons.

CONCEPT: Nativism

Generalization. A new group of immigrants arriving in the United States is likely to encounter rejection from some segments of the population.

The following is an example of letters to the editor that appeared in South Florida newspapers in response to the 1980 Mariel boatlift. Read the sample letter to the students and ask the questions that follow.

South Florida Saturated

As a citizen of South Florida for the past ten years, I strongly object to the masses of Cuban refugees being dumped on our shores. I am also distressed at the lack of response by national and state elected officials to stop this alien infusion.

We are having sluggish economic times and adequate housing is scarce for American citizens. How can we continue to be "nice guys" and accept more Cubans and Haitians. We already have enough!

We, the tax paying public of Florida, are being forced to subsidize these unwanted refugees that should either stay in their own country or go elsewhere. Included among these refugees are Castro's gifts of criminals, insane, and other undesirables.

I also understand that Cubans are training military groups on Florida soil. Why can't we prosecute these people? Meanwhile, many of our own Americans around the country need the assistance being given to these people we don't want.

Why can't we take care of our own first and forget about the headaches of other nations?

Name withheld by request

Questions

1. What facts does the letter's author use to substantiate his or her positions?
2. Compare the positions in the letter with the idea that the United States is the land of immigrants.
3. Do you agree or disagree with the author's positions? Which ones? Explain the reasons for your responses.
4. As a comparative exercise where library facilities permit, ask students to look for letters to the editor in major newspapers concerning immigration around 1910. Afterwards, ask the students to compare reactions to immigration in 1910 to the letter above.

Endnotes

1. U.S. Bureau of the Census, *Statistical Abstract of the United States, 1985*, 105th ed. (Washington, D.C.: U.S. Government Printing Office, 1985), p. 86.
2. Richard R. Fagen, Richard A. Brody, and Thomas J. O'Leary, *Cubans in Exile* (Stanford, Calif.: Stanford University Press, 1968), p. 16.
3. Lisandro Perez, "Cubans," in *Harvard Encyclopedia of American Ethnic Groups,* eds. Stephan Thernstrom, Ann Orlov, and Oscar Handlin (Cambridge: Harvard University Press, 1980), p. 257.
4. Rafael J. Prohias and Lourdes Casal, *The Cuban Minority in the U.S.,* Cuban Minority Planning Study (Boca Raton: Florida Atlantic University, 1973), p. 12.

5. David Alpen, "Carter and the Cuban Influx," *Newsweek*, 26 May 1980, p. 25.

6. Richard Morin, "Dade Fears Refugee Wave, Poll Shows," *Miami Herald*, 11 May 1980, p. 1.

7. Mary Barberis, "Hispanic America," Editorial Research Reports, *Congressional Quarterly* (Washington, D.C.: U.S. Government Printing Office, 1982), p. 560.

8. *New York Times*, 16 April 1971, p. 4.

9. Marie L. Richmond, *Immigrant Adaptation and Family Structure among Cubans in Miami, Florida* (New York: Arno Press, 1980), p. 115.

10. *New York Times*, 16 April 1971, p. 4.

11. Andres Oppenheimer, "Dade's Latins Feel a Separate Economy" *Miami Herald*, 25 August 1985, p. 1.

12. Rafael Valdivieso and Cary Davis, *U.S. Hispanics: Challenging Issues for the 1990's* (Washington, D.C.: Population Reference Bureau, 1988), p. 7.

13. James Kelly, "Closing the Golden Door," *Time*, 18 May 1981, p. 27.

14. Helga Silva, *The Children of Mariel: Cuban Refugee Children in South Florida Schools* (Washington, D.C.: The Cuban American National Foundation, 1985), p. 23.

15. Ibid., p. 38.

16. Prohias and Casal, *The Cuban Minority*, p. 6.

17. William Diaz, *Hispanics: Challenges and Opportunities* (New York: Ford Foundation, 1984), p. 38.

Annotated Bibliography

Books for Teachers

A considerable amount of literature is available on Cuba and the Cuban revolution. There is less on the immigration experience of Cubans in the United States. Some of the latter is in the form of newspaper articles and unpublished theses and reports. However, the information base on Cuban Americans has been growing in recent years and some is in more available sources.

One obvious resource is to invite a Cuban American into the classroom to relate personal experiences. This possibility may depend on the geographic area in which you teach. Most of the following are easily available sources for all teachers.

Alpern, David et al. "Carter and the Cuban Influx," *Newsweek*, 26 May 1980, pp. 22–31.

This article concerns immigration policy during the 1980 Mariel boatlift.

Alvarez, Orlando. *Estudio Demografico Social y Economica de la Comunidad Latina del Condado de Dade*. Miami, Fla.: Editorial AIP, 1976. [in Spanish]

Este libro da muchas estadisticas sobre la comunidad latina de Miami.

Boswell, Thomas D., and Curtis, James R. *The Cuban-American Experience: Culture, Images and Perspectives*. Totowa, N.J.: Rowman and Allanheld, 1984.

This is a useful source for understanding the cultural adjustments Cuban immigrants have made in the United States.

Casal, Lourdes, and Hernandez, Anders. "Cubans in the U.S.: A Survey of the Literature," *Cuban Studies* 5 (July 1975): 25–51.

The authors provide an annotated bibliography and a well-documented summary of information on Cuban Americans organized by topics.

Cortes, Carlos E., ed. *Cuban Exiles in the United States.* New York: Arno Press, 1980.

A series of articles written in the early 1970s that discuss mostly the occupational adaptation of Cubans in the United States.

Fagan, Richard R.; Brody, Richard A.; and O'Leary, Thomas J. *Cubans in Exile.* Stanford, Calif.: Stanford University Press, 1968.

This is a major published source on Cubans in Miami, Florida, and their reasons for leaving Cuba. It is complete with demographic information on the Cuban exodus.

Fox, Geoffrey E. *Working-Class Emigres from Cuba.* Palo Alto, Calif.: R. E. Research Associates, 1979.

This is a sociological study of the attitudes of recently arrived blue-collar Cubans in the Chicago area toward many aspects of life in Cuba.

Gallagher, Patrick. *The Cuban Exile: A Socio-Political Analysis.* New York: Arno Press, 1980.

This source is a 1974 doctoral dissertation reprint. It concerns the political adaptation of the Cuban immigrant and describes Cuban political attitudes on a range of issues.

Gonzales, Esther B. *Annotated Bibliography on Cubans in the United States 1960–1976.* Miami: Florida International University, 1977.

This work contains published as well as unpublished sources on Cuban Americans.

Hernandez, Andres, ed. *The Cuban Minority in the U.S.,* vol. 2. New York: Arno Press, 1980.

This is a continuation of the 1973 Prohias study concentrating on educational and occupational mobility and the needs and problems of Cuban-American youth and the elderly population.

Jaffe, A. J.; Cullen, Ruth; and Boswell, Thomas. *The Changing Demography of Spanish Americans.* New York: Academic Press, 1980.

This source covers all Hispanic groups in the United States; it also contains an excellent chapter on the education, demographics, and other variables of the Cuban-American population.

Kelly, James. "Closing the Golden Door," *Time,* 18 May 1981, pp. 24–27.

This article discusses efforts to stem the tide of immigration. It contains an interesting excerpt on Cubans who have been imprisoned since they arrived on the Mariel boatlift in 1980.

Linehan, Edward J. "Cuba's Exiles Bring New Life to Miami," *National Geographic* 144 (July 1973): 68–95.

This is an excellent article with many photographs. This would be a good source for students to peruse.

Mackey, William R., and Beebe, Von N. *Bilingual Schools for a Bicultural Community.* Rowley, Mass.: Newburg House, 1977.

This work examines a variety of models used in bilingual education in Miami to accommodate students arriving from Cuba.

Masud-Piloto, Roberto. *With Open Arms: Cuban Migration to the United States.* Totowa, N.J.: Rowman and Littlefield, 1988.

This book focuses on the Cuban migration from 1959–1980. The author suggests that humanitarian concerns of either the United States or Cuba had little to do with migration. Rather, refugees became the prime weapon in the political war between the two nations.

Mindel, Charles H.; Habenstein, Robert W.; and Wright, Roosevelt, Jr., eds. *Ethnic Families in America: Patterns and Variations,* 3rd ed. New York: Elsevier, 1988.

The chapter on the Cuban American family contributed by Jose Szapocznik and Roberto Hernandez contains an insightful section explaining the West African and Iberian influences on the Cuban character and family life.

Oppenheimer, Andres. "Dade's Latins Feel a Separate Economy," *Miami Herald,* 25 August 1985, p. 1.

This newspaper article provides valuable statistics to document the size and importance of the Latin (mostly Cuban) component of the economy in Miami, Florida.

Perez, Lisandro. "Cubans." In *Harvard Encyclopedia of American Ethnic Groups,* edited by Stephen Thernstrom, Ann Orlov, and Oscar Handlin. Cambridge: Harvard University Press, 1980.

This is an excellent synopsis of the status of Cubans in the United States. However, this source does not contain information on the Mariel boatlift.

Poyo, Gerald E. *With All and for the Good of All: The Emergence of Popular Nationalism in the Cuban Communities of the United States, 1848–1898.* Durham, N.C.: Duke University Press, 1989.

An excellent source for teachers interested in examining the long-established Cuban communities in the United States. The author examines the connection between these communities and the struggle for independence in Cuba.

Prohias, Rafael J., and Casal, Lourdes. *The Cuban Minority in the U.S.,* vol. 1. New York: Arno Press, 1980.

The most comprehensive study on Cubans in the United States, this publication is based on a study completed in 1973. The demographic data relate to circumstances in the early 1970s.

Richmond, Marie L. *Immigrant Adaptation and Family Structure among Cubans in Miami, Florida.* New York: Arno Press, 1980.

This reprint of a 1974 doctoral dissertation provides the reader with considerable information on how the immigration experience affected the Cuban family.

Rogg, Eleanor Meyer. *The Assimilation of Cuban Exiles: The Role of Community and Class.* New York: Aberdeen Press, 1974.

This study is based primarily on interviews with 250 Cuban heads of households in western New York and New Jersey.

Rohter, Larry. "What Today's Cuba Is Like," *Newsweek,* 26 May 1980, pp. 32–34.

>   *This useful article could serve as a primer to acquaint the reader with conditions inside Castro's Cuba.*

Silva, Helga. *The Children of Mariel: Cuban Refugee Children in South Florida Schools.* Washington, D.C.: The Cuban American National Foundation, 1985.

>   *This report examines the programs established by the Miami (Dade Country) school system to cope with an immediate influx of more than 15,000 non–English-speaking students. Statistics abound to document funding and the nature of the academic programs offered through 1982.*

Szapocznik, Jose; Cohen, Raquel; and Hernandez, Roberto, eds. *Coping with Adolescent Refugees: The Mariel Boatlift.* New York: Praeger, 1985.

>   *This source emphasizes the psychological adaptation of young Mariel refugees, particularly during the internment camps. A mental health perspective is taken in this work.*

Thomas, Hugh. *Cuba—The Pursuit of Freedom.* New York: Harper and Row, 1971.

>   *This is the most comprehensive history of Cuba in book form. (Spanish edition available).*

Thompson, Elivia Hernandez. "Can Cuban Culture Last through the Next Generation?" *Miami Magazine,* April 1977, pp. 25–27, 54–57.

>   *An informative source on the level of cultural retention among Cuban youths in South Florida. It discusses value conflicts between assimilated Cuban youths and their more traditional parents.*

Valdivieso, Rafael, and Davis, Cary. *U.S. Hispanics: Challenging Issues for the 1990's.* Washington, D.C.: Population Reference Bureau, 1988.

>   *This source analyzes trends affecting the Hispanic community now and in the future. Cuban Americans are contrasted with other Hispanic groups in such areas as education, income, political trends, and use of the Spanish language.*

Weyr, Thomas. *Hispanic U.S.A.* New York: Harper and Row, 1988.

>   *This source contains information about Cuban-American immigration, education, politics, and economic position interwoven among similar data concerning other Hispanic groups.*

Books for Students

Curtin, Margaretta. *Cubanitos in a New Land: Cuban Children of Miami.* Hialeah, Fla.: Miami Press, 1974.

>   *This is a collection of seven stories written at about a fifth-grade reading level. (Intermediate)*

Haskins, James. *The New Americans: Cuban Boat People.* Hillside, N.J.: Enslow Publishers, 1982.

>   *The author analyzes the reasons for the Mariel boatlift of 1980. The entrance and initial adaptation of these refugees is examined. Specific cases illustrate this experi-*

ence, which gives the work a particularly human quality. (Intermediate/High School)

Philipson, Lorin, and Llerena, Rafael. *Freedom Flights.* New York: Random House, 1980.

This text is composed of a series of vignettes on how 20 different Cubans left Cuba. Some of the stories are tragic and poignant. (High School)

Part V

Asian Americans

Concepts and Strategies

art V consists of content, concepts, teaching strategies, and materials
for teaching about three of the oldest Asian groups in America—the
Chinese Americans, Japanese Americans, and Filipino Americans—and the
most recent group of Asians to settle in the United States, the Indochinese
Americans.

Asian Americans, one of the most diverse and interesting ethnic groups
in the United States, are rarely studied in the elementary and high school
grades. When discussed in textbooks and in the popular media, they are
often used to illustrate how an ethnic group of color can succeed in the
United States. Because of their tremendous educational, occupational, and
economic success, Asian Americans are often called the model minority in
the popular media. It is true that some Asian American groups are better
educated, have a higher occupational status, and earn more money than
other Americans, including White Americans. However, the model minority
concept is problematic for several reasons.

Problems with the Model Minority Concept

A focus on the economic success of Asian Americans results in several
problems. It obscures the tremendous economic diversity within Asian-
American communities and the problems Asians have. When we look only
at the group characteristics of Chinese Americans, for example, the serious
economic problems of the new immigrants are overlooked. In 1980, about
52% of the Chinese immigrants had menial service, low-skilled, and blue-
collar jobs. About 42% had managerial and technical jobs. Takaki has called
the unskilled Chinese immigrant workers "a colonized labor force."[1] Many
Chinese immigrant women work as seamstresses in San Francisco and in
New York for long hours at very low wages. The model minority concept
also obscures the stories of successful members of other ethnic groups, such
as upward mobile African Americans and Hispanics. Finally, when overly
emphasized, the model minority argument can divert attention from the
racism that Asian Americans and other people of color in the United States

still experience.² Daniels states that diverting attention from racism was one of the intents of William Peterson, the writer who invented and used the concept of "the model minority" in a 1960 *New York Times* article.³

Rapid Increases in the Asian-American Population

Asian Americans, in percentage terms, increased faster than any other U.S. ethnic group between 1970 and 1980. The number of Asians in the United States increased from 1.4 million in 1970 to 3.5 million in 1980, a 141% increase, compared to a 61% increase for Hispanics, an 18% increase for African Americans, an 11% increase for the total population, and a 6% increase for Whites. (Results of the 1990 Census are not yet available.) However, some demographers are projecting that the Asian-American population in 1990 will be about 6.53 million.⁴ The projections for the various Asian groups are presented in Table 1–3 in chapter 1 and in Table 13–2 in chapter 13.

The number of Asians immigrating to the United States has increased substantially since the Immigration Reform Act became effective in 1968. In 1965, 3,180 Filipinos immigrated to the United States; in 1987 the number rose to 50,100. Between 1981 and 1987, more immigrants to the United States came from the Philippines than from any other nation except Mexico (323,900 compared to 474,100).

The United States now has a sizable population of Vietnamese Americans, projected to be about 860,000 in 1990.⁵ They are discussed in detail in chapter 14. After U.S. participation in the Vietnam War ended (1973) and Communists took control of that nation (1975), thousands of Vietnamese refugees rushed to the United States. Only 226 Vietnamese immigrated to the United States in 1965, but more than 87,000 came to the United States in 1978. Between 1971 and 1987, 468,700 Vietnamese immigrants settled in the United States (see Table 13–1).

The number of Chinese immigrants settling in the United States from China and Hong Kong has also increased substantially since 1965. In 1965, for example, 4,769 immigrants from China settled in the United States. Between 1971 and 1987, however, 459,600 immigrants entered the United States from China and 82,900 from Hong Kong (see Table 13–1).⁶

Korean Americans

The number of Koreans and Asian Indian immigrants to the United States has also increased tremendously since the immigration act of 1965 became effective in 1968. The Korean-American population increased from 10,000 in 1960 to about one-half million in 1985.⁷ The first Koreans who came to the United States arrived in 1885. Later, between 1890 and 1905, 64 Korean students came to study in the United States.⁸ A significant number of Koreans were recruited to work in the sugar plantations in Hawaii in the early 1900s. However, few Korean immigrants settled in the United States until the 1970s. Only 6,231 Koreans immigrated to the United States between 1951 and 1960 and 34,526 between 1961 and 1970.[9] However, 237,600 immigrated to the United States between 1981 and 1987.

Korean Americans are one of the fastest growing ethnic groups in the United States today. Some demographers project that they will number about 810,000 in the 1990 Census.[10] If this happens, they will equal or slightly exceed the number of Japanese Americans in the 1990 Census. Like the new immigrants from the Philippines, most of the new Korean immigrants are college-educated professionals. Surveys conducted in New York and Los Angeles indicated that about 70% had college degrees.[11]

Asian Indian and Pakistani Immigrants

Only a small number of immigrants from India settled in the United States prior to 1965. A total of about 130,000 came during the period between 1820 and 1976.[12] Most of the immigrants who came during the nineteenth century were professionals, adventurers, merchants, and monks.[13] A few thousand agricultural workers came to California between 1904 and 1923.[14] Only 1,973 immigrants from India came to the United States between 1951 and 1960; 31,200 immigrated to United States between 1961 and 1979.[15]

Since 1971, immigrants from India have been entering the United States in substantial numbers. About 350,000 Indian immigrants settled in the United States between 1971 and 1987. A significant number of immigrants to the United States from Pakistan have also entered the United States since 1960. About 74,200 Pakistani immigrants settled in the United States between 1961 and 1987.

There were about 525,000 Asian Indians living in the United States in 1985, about 34% of whom live in the Northeast.[16] These Asian Indians are English speaking and are a highly educated group. Among the immigrants are a large number of engineers, scientists, physicians, dentists, and other kinds of professionals. Like the new Filipino immigrants, they are settling in the United States primarily because of the paucity of professional job opportunities in their native land.

Asian Americans are one of the most highly diversified ethnic groups in the United States. They vary greatly in both cultural and physical characteristics. The attitudes, values, and ethnic institutions often differ within Japanese-American, Chinese-American, Filipino-American, and Asian-Indian communities. However, the first waves of Chinese, Japanese, and Filipino immigrants had some parallel experiences in the United States. For example, their immigration began when there was a need for cheap labor, but they were harassed and demeaned, and eventually immigration laws were passed to exclude them. After the Chinese Exclusion Act was passed in 1882, there was still a desire for cheap laborers in Hawaii and California. Consequently, Japanese immigrants began arriving in California in significant numbers in the 1890s. When the Gentlemen's Agreement of 1908 and the Immigration Act of 1924 halted Japanese immigration, California farmers imported Filipinos from Hawaii and the Philippines to work in the fields. Anti-Filipino forces emerged on the West Coast and culminated in 1934, when Congress limited Filipino immigration to 50 people per year. This quota constituted, in effect, the virtual exclusion of Filipino immigrants.

Because of their tremendous diversity, similarities, and unique experiences in the United States, the study of Asian Americans can help students increase their ethnic literacy and develop a respect for cultural differences. Chapter 13 discusses Chinese Americans, Japanese Americans, and Filipino Americans. Indochinese Americans are discussed in chapter 14.

Endnotes

1. Ronald Takaki, *Strangers from a Different Shore: A History of Asian Americans* (New York: Little Brown, 1989), p. 425.

2. Ibid., p. 426.

3. Roger Daniels, *Asian America: Chinese and Japanese in the United States since 1950* (Seattle: University of Washington Press, 1988), pp. 317–322; William Petersen, "Success Story, Japanese American Style," *New York Times Magazine,* 6 January 1966, pp. 20 ff.

4. John Wright, ed., *The Universal Almanac 1990* (Kansas City, Mo.: Andrews and McMeel, 1989), p. 236.

5. Ibid., p. 236.

6. U.S. Bureau of the Census, *Statistical Abstract of the United States: 1989,* 109th ed. (Washington, D.C.: U.S. Government Printing Office, 1989), p. 10.

7. Takaki, *Strangers from a Different Shore,* p. 437.

8. Hyung-Chan Kim, "Koreans," *Harvard Encyclopedia of American Ethnic Groups,* eds. Stephan Thernstrom, Ann Orlov, and Oscar Handlin (Cambridge: Harvard University Press, 1980), p. 602.

9. U.S. Department of Justice, Immigration and Naturalization Service, *1984 Statistical Yearbook of the Immigration and Naturalization Service* (Washington, D.C.: U.S. Government Printing Office, 1986), p. 4.

10. Wright, *The Universal Almanac 1990,* p. 236.

11. Takaki, *Strangers from a Different Shore,* p. 437.

12. Joan M. Jensen, "East Indians," in *Harvard Encyclopedia of American Ethnic Groups,* p. 296.

13. Ibid.

14. Ibid.

15. *1984 Statistical Yearbook of the Immigration and Naturalization Service,* p. 4.

16. Takaki, *Strangers from a Different Shore,* p. 445.

Chapter 13

Chinese Americans,

Japanese Americans,

and Filipino Americans

Concepts, Strategies, and Materials

In America, Asian immigrants and their offspring have been actors in history. . . . Their dreams and hopes unfurled here before the wind, all of them—from the first Chinese miners sailing through the Golden Gate to the last Vietnamese boat people flying into Los Angeles International Airport— have been making history in America.

—Ronald Takaki

Introduction

This chapter discusses content, concepts, strategies, and materials for teaching about three Asian-American groups that live in the United States: the Chinese Americans, Japanese Americans, and Filipino Americans. These groups have important similarities, as well as differences. Each group came to the United States seeking the American dream, satisfied important labor needs, and became victims of an anti-Asian movement designed to prevent their further immigration to the United States. Chinese Americans, Japanese Americans, and Filipino Americans have also experienced tremendous economic, educational, and social mobility and success in U.S. society.

The number of Chinese, Japanese, and Filipino immigrants that settled in the United States between 1951 and 1960 was small compared to the number from Europe. However, the number of immigrants to the United States from China and the Philippines has increased enormously since the Immigration Reform Act of 1965 became effective in 1968. The number of Japanese

405

immigrating to the United States since 1968 has remained moderate. Between 1951 and 1960, 19,300 immigrants from the Philippines and 25,200 from China and Hong Kong settled in the United States. Between 1981 and 1987 the numbers were 323,900 from the Philippines and 292,900 from Hong Kong and China (see Table 13–1).

As a result of the increasing number of immigrants from China, Hong Kong, and the Philippines, as well as from other Asian nations, the Japanese are becoming an increasingly smaller percentage of the Asian-American population. In 1970, Japanese Americans were the largest Asian American group, followed by the Chinese and the Filipinos. By 1980, however, the Japanese were the third largest Asian-American group, exceeded in size by both the Chinese, the largest group, and the Filipinos, the second largest group (see Table 13–2).

The story of the Chinese, Japanese, and Filipinos in the United States has been largely one of success, if we measure success by the educational, income, and occupational levels these groups have attained. They have attained tremendous educational, income, and occupational success even though they have historically been the victims of racism and discrimination and are often the victims of subtle discrimination today. The stories of the Chinese, Japanese, and Filipinos in the United States can help students understand how the American dream can be pursued and attained. However, when these groups are studied, the problems that Asian Americans still face in American society, such as cultural conflict, identity, and attaining a balance between their ethnic cultures and the mainstream culture, should not be glossed over. The poverty that exists in Asian-American communities, especially in urban ethnic communities, where newly arrived immigrants settle in large numbers, should also be studied.

When studying about Asians in the United States, students should examine and analyze the new wave of racism that has been directed against Asian

Table 13–1   *Asian Immigrants to the United States (1961–1987)*

Country of Birth	1961–1970	1971–1980	1981–1987	Total
Philippines	101,500	360,200	323,900	785,600
China	96,700	202,500	257,100	556,300
Korea	35,800	272,000	237,600	545,400
Vietnam	4,600	179,700	289,000	473,300
India	31,200	176,800	173,700	381,700
Laos	100	22,600	112,000	134,700
Japan	38,500	47,900	28,200	114,600
Hong Kong	25,600	47,500	35,400	108,500
Cambodia	1,200	8,400	96,100	105,700
Thailand	5,000	44,100	39,200	88,300
Pakistan	4,900	31,200	38,100	74,200

Source: U.S. Bureau of the Census, *Statistical Abstract of the United States* (109th ed.) Washington, D.C.: U.S. Government Printing Office, 1989, p. 10.

Table 13–2 Selected Characteristics of the Japanese, Chinese, and Filipino Populations, 1979, 1980, and 1990

	Chinese	Japanese	Filipino	[Non-Spanish] Whites	African Americans	All Persons
Population (1980)	812,178	716,331	781,894	180,602,838	26,091,857	226,545,805
Projected population (1990)[a]	1,260,000	800,000	1,410,000	191,594,000	30,915,000	252,293,000
Median Household Income (1979)	$19,561	$22,517	$21,926	$17,814	$10,959	$16,841
Median Family Income (1979)	$22,559	$27,354	$23,687	$21,014	$12,627	$19,917
Percentage of High School Graduates[b] (1979)	71.3%	81.6%	74.2%	69.6%	51.2%	66.5%
Median Years of School Attended[b] (1979)	13.4	12.9	14.1	12.5	12.0	12.5

Source: Based on data in the U.S. Bureau of the Census, Vol. 1, Characteristics of the Population, *General Social and Economic Characteristics*, Part 1 (United States Summary, PC80-1-C1, December 1983).

[a]The 1990 population projections for Asian American groups are from John W. Wright, ed., *The Universal Almanac 1990*. Kansas City: Andrews and McNeel, 1990, p. 236; The 1990 projections for the other groups are from U.S. Bureau of the Census, *Projections of the Population of the U.S. by Age, Sex, and Race, 1983–2080*. Washington, D.C.: U.S. Government Printing Office, 1989.

[b]Persons 25 years or older.

Americans, as well as against other ethnic groups of color. This new wave of racism, which emerged in the 1980s, has been expressed in a number of ways, including ugly racial incidents on college campuses. The rising number of Asian students at some of the nation's most prestigious colleges and universities has evoked comments that some Asians have interpreted as a call for restrictive quotas. In 1989, Asian Americans made up about 16% of the students at Stanford, about 25% at the University of California at Berkeley, and about 11% at Harvard.[1]

Many Americans, particularly unemployed auto workers, blame Japan for the stiff competition from Japanese car manufacturers. This hostility has sometimes been directed at Japanese Americans because some Americans do not distinguish Japanese nationals and Japanese Americans. This hostility has taken diverse forms, including bumper stickers that read, "Unemployment—Made in Japan" and statements such as "Auto unemployment is an economic Pearl Harbor."[2] The most odious incident was the June 19, 1982, beating death in a Detroit suburb of Vincent Chin by an unemployed auto worker, Ronald Ebens, and his stepson. Ebens thought that Chin was a Japanese American. Despite their success—and sometimes because of it—Asian Americans are still victims of racism and discrimination. Some Americans still consider Asian Americans "strangers from a different shore."[3]

Chinese Americans: Historical Perspective

Important Dates

1850	The U.S. Census showed 450 Chinese immigrants in the United States. This number increased to 34,933 in 1860. The California legislature passed a discriminatory Foreign Miner's Tax, which forced Chinese immigrants to pay a highly disproportionate share of the state taxes.
1859	Authorities in the Guangdong Province legalized the recruitment of Chinese laborers.
1974	The U.S. Supreme Court ruled on *Lau* v. *Nichols* that the San Francisco Unified School District was denying Chinese-American students who did not speak English "a meaningful opportunity to participate in the public educational program." This ruling by the high court established a legal basis for bilingual educational programs. Such programs were later established in various parts of the nation.

Important Dates	
1980	The U.S. Census indicated that the Chinese were one of the largest groups that immigrated to the United States between 1970 and 1980. The percentage of Chinese in the United States increased 88% between 1970 and 1980, compared to 11% for the total population and 6% for Whites.
1982	Vincent Chin was beaten to death in a Detroit suburb by an unemployed auto worker and his stepson. Ronald Ebens, the unemployed auto worker, thought Chin was of Japanese descent.
1987	About 42,700 immigrants from China and Hong Kong entered the United States, making the Chinese the second largest Asian group immigrating to the United States.

The Immigration

When the news reached the Guandong Province in southeast China that there was a "Golden Mountain" across the Pacific, a number of young men violated both Chinese law and tradition and headed for the promised land. The decision to leave China for a foreign land was a serious one because it was illegal to immigrate and violators could be severely punished. Also, Confucian doctrine, which was an integral part of Chinese life during this period, taught that a young man should value his family above all else and thus should not leave it. However, both the promises of the land of the Mountain of Gold and the severe living conditions in the Toishan district in Guandong, from which most of the first Chinese immigrants hailed, helped push the young immigrants across the Pacific.

Political upheaval, famine, local warfare, excessive taxes, a severely depressed economy, and a rugged terrain in Toishan that was inimical to farming motivated young Chinese males to seek better opportunities in an unknown land where, according to a pervasive myth, one could easily strike gold and return to China a rich man. Most of the Chinese who headed for California were young married men. They were self-proclaimed "sojourners" who intended to earn their fortunes in the United States and return to their families in China. Because of tradition and the rough voyage across the Pacific, their families were left behind.

The journey across the Pacific was rugged and hazardous. On their arrival in California, the Chinese immigrants experienced a rude awakening. Although White Americans expressed little overt hostility toward the Chinese when they first started immigrating to the West Coast in substantial numbers in the 1850s, they considered them exotic, strange people. Whites thought that the Chinese were strange because of their traditional Chinese clothing, language, queue hairstyle (which Whites called pigtails), and skin color. Almost from the beginning, the Chinese were the victims of curiosity and racism. One historian has noted, "From almost the first moment the Chinese landed in San Francisco in the 1850s, they were subjected to harsh treatment. The aim was to exclude them from the United States because of basically *racist* fears and beliefs"[4] (emphasis added).

Labor

In addition to receiving a curious and strange welcome from Californians, the Chinese immigrants found that the mines in which they had to dig for gold had already been thoroughly gone over by White gold diggers. They had to dig for the scraps. However, some Chinese immigrants managed to secure respectable sums of money by re-mining White claims.

When Congress decided to build a railroad linking the Missouri River to the Pacific Coast in 1862, the Central Pacific issued a call for men to build the western portion of the railroad. Because of the back-breaking work involved in building a railroad over the rugged Western terrain, few Whites would take the work. But the Chinese took up the challenge and almost single-handedly built the Pacific portion of the transcontinental railroad. While the nation celebrated the completion of the railroad on May 10, 1869, 25,000 laborers, most of them Chinese, lost their jobs.

It was not easy for the Chinese immigrants to save money because of the large debts they had incurred when they arranged to come to California. Most of them came to the United States through a credit-ticket system, which was similar to the indenture system used to bring many European immigrants to North America. In this system, a moneyless Chinese could borrow money from a relative or fellow villager to pay for his passage to California. Chinese organizations, such as the Hui Kuan or *Landsmanner*, collected the money from the immigrant and sent it to the individuals from whom it was borrowed.

The leaders of the Hui Kuan also provided the immigrants with a place to eat and sleep on their arrival in San Francisco and sent gangs of them to work in the mines. Before the worker received his wages, the amount he owed for his passage was deducted. Because of the credit-ticket system, some immigrants ended up worse off financially than they had been before they came to California. Some found that their return to China was indefinitely delayed. What at first promised to be a nation of gold turned out, for many, to be a land of disillusionment and shattered dreams. "The Chinese existed at a poverty level, receiving low wages for their work. Even so, they gained materially a bit more than they had in China. The dream of coming to the Golden Mountain to make a fortune and return home still seemed possible to most. For many, however, this was the impossible dream."[5]

Despite the difficulties the Chinese immigrants experienced, many were able to find enough work in a wide range of occupations that most Whites found unpalatable, such as domestic work, work on railroads, and intensive farming, to save enough money to return to China to visit their families and to father children, hopefully sons. The immigrants who returned to China usually told about the promises of California but said little about its difficulties. Also, the home folks were impressed with what seemed like sizable sums of money the sojourners brought back to China. As the news about the Mountain of Gold spread, and immigrants returned home with money or sent money home to their families, the number of Chinese immigrating to California rose tremendously.

Anti-Chinese Agitation

According to the 1860 census, there were 34,933 Chinese in the United States. By 1880, that number had risen to 105,465. Although the increase was sizable, there were still few Chinese immigrating to the United States compared to the number of European immigrants. Between 1820 and 1930, 38 million immigrants entered the United States, mostly from Europe. However, many Whites became alarmed at the number of Chinese entering the United States, and a vicious movement developed to keep them out. Although leaders of the anti-Chinese movement claimed that the Chinese could not be assimilated and that they competed unfairly with Whites on the labor market, racism was one of the main forces behind the anti-Chinese movement. As Saxton has pointed out, "The Chinese inherited the long-standing hostility of White against people of color, particularly Blacks. White Californians, conditioned to the notion that Blacks were inferior persons and servile workers, easily transferred these perceptions to the Chinese."[6]

Led by Dennis Kearney and the California Workingmen's party, "The Chinese Must Go" became the rallying cry of the anti-Chinese movement. Leaders of all types joined in the movement to push the Chinese out of the West. Labor leaders were among the most staunch anti-Chinese advocates. Politicians jumped on the bandwagon in order to gain votes. As the hostility against the Chinese mounted, they became increasingly defenseless. Unlike the Japanese, they did not have a strong nation that could threaten the balance of world power when its citizens in the United States were ill treated.

The anti-Chinese movement spread as the Chinese moved to such states as Washington, Oregon, Colorado, and Wyoming. Anti-Chinese activities took the form of racist newspaper stories; violent attacks against defenseless men, women, and children; and highly discriminatory laws aimed particularly at the Chinese, such as the Queues Ordinance, the Laundry Ordinance, and the 1876 Cubic Air Law. One of the most blatantly discriminatory laws was the Foreign Miner's Tax passed by the California legislature in 1850. Applied most effectively against the Chinese, it forced them to pay a highly disproportionate share of the taxes collected under the law. Taxes paid by the Chinese largely financed the California state and county governments during this period.[7] The movement to ban the immigration of Chinese culminated with the passage of the Immigration Act of 1882. This bill stopped the immigration of Chinese laborers for a period of 10 years. A victory for the anti-Chinese leaders, it was followed by a series of similar bills that drastically reduced Chinese immigration for decades. The number of Chinese entering the United States dwindled from 39,579 in 1882 to 472 in 1893.

Violence and Riots

Violence directed against the Chinese was widespread in the late 1880s. An anti-Chinese riot occurred in San Francisco as early as 1869. A White mob in Los Angeles attacked a Chinese community in 1871. When the conflict ended, 19 Chinese Americans had been killed and their community was in shambles. Another anti-Chinese riot exploded in Denver, Colorado, in 1880. One Chinese was killed and most of the homes in the Chinese community were wrecked during the riot. A serious anti-Chinese riot occurred in Rock Springs, Wyoming, in 1885. Twenty-eight Chinese were killed, 15 were wounded, and many were driven from their homes. The property destroyed was estimated at $150,000. Most of the White aggressors in these riots went unpunished partly because testimony against a White person by a Chinese was inadmissible in the courts.

Chinatowns

The Chinese responded to this violence by moving farther eastward, to the Northeast (where they also became the victims of violence), and by retreating into ethnic communities in urban areas. "By the end of the nineteenth century, the California Chinese had, for the most part, died off, returned to China, moved eastward or settled into the ghettos of American cities referred to as 'Chinatowns.' "[8]

Despite its outer glitter, life in Chinatown was and is tough and depressing. Since most of the male immigrants did not bring their wives to California and were unable to marry Caucasians because of miscegenation laws, Chinatown was made up primarily of desperate and lonely men who sought their recreation in the form of prostitution, gambling, and opium smoking. Because of the high population of lonely and virile men, and the scarcity of females, prostitution loomed large in Chinatown in the 1800s. It was controlled by the Chinese secret societies that paid off police officials so that they could "safely" practice their business. Competition between the various Chinese societies for power, women, and money was keen, and violence between them often erupted. These conflicts were sensationalized by the White press and were popularized as "tong wars." Such stories made good copy and were eagerly sought by many journalists. These news stories played into the hands of the anti-Chinese racists and were fully exploited.

Prostitution, tong wars, gambling, and opium smoking are largely things of the past in Chinatown. However, powerful antiquated Chinese organizations that care little about the masses still exercise considerable power. Poverty, squalor, and disease are rampant in some Chinese urban communities. San Francisco's Chinatown has one of the highest population densities in the nation. Many women in San Francisco's Chinatown work in the garment industry for very low wages. Housing and education in San Francisco's Chinatown are among the worst in the nation. The power elite in Chinatown, which profits from the misery of the masses, has helped obscure its outrageous conditions and publicized its glitter. Chinatown has been described as a "gilded ghetto whose tinseled streets and brightly lit shops barely camouflage a pocket of poverty in the metropolis."[9]

Chinese Americans Today

Chinatown served as a port of entry for most of the earlier immigrants; it provided them with a sense of security, ties with the old world culture, and a partial escape from discrimination. Many Chinese Americans who are descendants of these earlier immigrants have experienced upward social and economic mobility and are leaving Chinatown. They have joined the exodus to the suburbs. However, the American Chinatowns are still viable and important communities. The newly upwardly mobile Chinese Americans who are moving to suburban communities are being replaced in Chinatown by new waves of immigrants from China and Hong Kong. In 1980, 63.3% of the Chinese Americans were foreign-born, compared to 20.7% of the Japanese. In his anthropological study of New York's Chinatown, Wong identifies four groups that live there: (1) old overseas Chinese, (2) American-born Chinese and naturalized Chinese Americans, (3) jump-ship sailors and refugees, and (4) disenchanted/disenfranchised youths.[10] The refugees from Southeast Asia face tremendous economic hardships and work long hours each day, sometimes from 18 to 20 hours.

The new immigrants who have entered the United States since the Immigration Reform Act of 1965 have been bipolar in their social class backgrounds. About half of the immigrants that came to the United States in 1980 were menial service, low-skilled, and blue-collar workers. About 42% of them were managerial and technical workers.[11] Even though the economic and educational levels of the total Chinese population is high, a large group of the new immigrants have low-paying jobs that are concentrated highly in restaurants and textile work. The bipolar nature of the Chinese community is also reflected in where they live. Many of the lower-level workers live in Chinatown, whereas many of the professional and upper-status workers live in suburban communities. By 1988,

Monterey Park, California, a suburban community of 61,000 people, had 50% Chinese residents. It had become "America's first suburban Chinatown."[12]

The social, educational, and economic characteristics of the total population of Chinese Americans in 1980 were impressive. Most Chinese Americans (about 71.3%) who were 25 years or older were high school graduates, compared to 69.6% for Whites, and 66.5% for all groups within the nation.[13] The median family income of Chinese Americans in 1980 was $22,559, compared to $21,014 for Whites, and $19,917 for all groups. Chinese Americans were also highly concentrated in managerial, professional, and technical jobs in 1980: 36% of them held managerial and professional speciality jobs, compared to 24% for Whites, and 23% for all groups within the nation. In addition, 30% of them held technical, sales, and administrative support occupations in 1980, compared to 31% of Whites, and 30% for all groups. On most leading indicators of success in 1980, the Chinese in the United States exceeded Whites, as well as most other ethnic groups for which separate data are available. Census data on these variables are not available for Jews, another successful ethnic group.

Because of the educational, occupational, and economic success of Chinese Americans, many of them have moved out of Chinatown to other areas within the city. They are still primarily urban and metropolitan dwellers. About 96% lived in metropolitan areas in 1980. Almost all poor Chinese, aged bachelors, and recent immigrants live in Chinatown. Other groups, however, also live there. Although many Chinese Americans have joined the larger society, the Chinatowns of the nation are still viable communities that satisfy important human and cultural needs. Even the highly assimilated Chinese American occasionally returns to Chinatown on the weekend for a good ethnic meal or to buy certain Chinese products unavailable in predominantly White communities.

The Chinese community has experienced an influx of immigrants since the passage of the Immigration Act of 1965, which gave a liberal quota of 170,000 to people who lived in Eastern Hemisphere nations. A chain migration has developed. Once they are in the United States and have become citizens, many Chinese send for relatives under the provisions of the immigrant act that allow families to join other family members. The process multiplies. Between 1970 and 1980, the Chinese population in the United States increased 88%, while the White population increased 6%. In 1965, only 4,769 Chinese immigrants entered the United States, whereas 42,400 persons born in China and Hong Kong immigrated to the United States in 1987. The projected population of Chinese Americans for 1990 is about 1,260,000.[14] This will make them one of the largest Asian groups in the United States.

Despite the tremendous increase in the Chinese-American population since 1965, Asians still comprised only a small percentage of the U.S. population of more than 250 million in 1990. However, the Asian population in the United States grew more rapidly than any other ethnic group between 1970 and 1980.[15] The rapid growth of the Chinese population in the United States is likely to have a number of important consequences. One possible consequence is that U.S. foreign policy will focus more on Asia.

Japanese Americans: Historical Perspective

Important Dates

1868	One hundred forty-eight Japanese contract laborers arrived in Hawaii.
1869	The unsuccessful Wakamatsu Colony, made up of Japanese immigrants, was established in California.
1906	The San Francisco Board of Education ordered all Asian children to attend a segregated Oriental school.
1907–08	The United States and Japan made the Gentlemen's Agreement, which was designed to reduce the number of Japanese immigrants entering the United States.
1913	The California legislature passed a land bill making it difficult for Japanese immigrants to lease land.
1924	An immigration bill was passed by Congress that stopped Asian immigration to the United States.
1930	The Japanese American Citizenship League was founded.
1941	Japan attacked Pearl Harbor on December 7.
1942	On February 19, President Franklin D. Roosevelt issued Executive Order 9066, which authorized the internment of Japanese Americans who lived on the West Coast.
1946	The last internment camp was closed.
1948	The Japanese American Evacuation Claims Act, signed by President Harry S Truman, authorized some compensation for the financial losses incurred by the Japanese Americans during the internment. The U.S. government eventually compensated the Japanese Americans for property loss at the rate of about 10¢ per dollar.
1952	The McCarran-Walter Immigration Act was passed by Congress. It ended the total exclusion of Asian immigrants, which had begun with the passage of the Immigration Act of 1924. Asian Americans were granted naturalization rights.

Important Dates	
1972	Statistics indicated that 47% of the Japanese Americans living in Los Angeles were married to non-Japanese spouses.
1986	A U.S. Court of Appeals reinstated the claim that the U.S. Government illegally took property from a group of Japanese interned during World War II. This case made it possible for claims by survivors to be heard in court.
1988	The American Civil Liberties bill was passed by Congress and signed by President Reagan. It provided an apology for the internment of Japanese Americans during World War II and a $20,000 payment for each survivor of the internment.

The Immigration

Because of overpopulation, depressed farming conditions, and political turmoil in Japan in the late 1800s, its citizens began immigrating to Hawaii and the U.S. mainland in search of better economic opportunities. The arrival of 148 Japanese contract laborers in Hawaii in 1868 to work on the plantations violated Japanese law. Japanese immigrants did not arrive in the United States and Hawaii in significant numbers until the Japanese government, because of internal problems, legalized immigration in 1886. There were 55 people of Japanese ancestry in the United States in 1870; 2,039 in 1890; and 111,010 in 1920.[16] The largest number of Japanese immigrants arrived in the United States between 1891 and 1924. About 200,000 came during this period.[17]

After the anti-Chinese forces had successfully stopped Chinese immigration, epitomized by the Chinese Exclusion Act of 1882, there was still a need for seasonal farm laborers in the developing West. The Japanese immigrants filled the labor void in agriculture and in other areas that had been created by the cessation of Chinese immigration. Why Whites on the West Coast halted the immigration of one group of Asians and then encouraged the coming of another is a curious and complex historical event. However, it was only a matter of time before the anti-Asian forces, already mobilized, began to attack aggressively the Japanese Americans as they had earlier attacked the Chinese.

Most of the first Japanese immigrants were young men, some of whom were married. They hoped to earn a small fortune in the United States and return to Japan. Like the Chinese, however, most of them remained in North America. There were many similarities in the experiences of Japanese and Chinese immigrants to the United States. However, there were some significant differences that influenced profoundly the development of the Chinese-

American and Japanese-American communities. Organizations emerged within the Little Tokyos of America, as in early Chinatown, to help the new immigrant secure lodging, food, and jobs.

There were also few women among the first Japanese immigrants. Like the Chinese, the men had to share the women who were available. However, the man–woman ratio never became as imbalanced within the Japanese-American community as it became in the Chinese community because the Japanese immigrants were able to marry Japanese women, despite the exclusion laws that were directed against Japanese immigrants. Although the men were in the United States and the women in Japan, marriages were arranged with photographs. The wives would later join their husbands, whom they had never seen, in the United States. These women became known as "picture brides." The picture bride custom was similar in some ways to the "tobacco bride" custom that was practiced in the Jamestown colony. The Virginia Company sent 90 European women to Virginia in the spring of 1620. Each man who married one of the women had to pay 120 pounds of the best tobacco to help pay for his bride's transportation costs from Europe. In later years, the company continued to send more "maids" to Virginia to marry the lonely male colonists.

Although the picture-bride marriage practice was opposed vigorously by anti-Japanese groups, it was consistent with Japanese custom and continued until outlawed in Japan in 1920. Many parents of second-generation Japanese Americans (Nisei) were married in a "picture" ceremony. (Japanese Americans use specific terms to designate each generation: *Issei, Nisei, Sansei,* and *Yonsei* refer to the first, second, third, and fourth generations, respectively. These terms are used throughout this book.) These marriages worked amazingly well, partly because traditionally romantic love had not been a major factor in Japanese marriages. Rather, marriages were more the joining of two families (or *ie*) than two individuals. This Japanese adage expresses cogently this attitude toward marriage: "Those who come together in passion stay together in tears."

Although most of the Issei men were much older than their picture brides, the fact that they were able to marry helped the Japanese to establish strong families in the United States. Some writers consider the Japanese family the most significant factor in the social and economic mobility of Japanese Americans. Strong families developed early in the Japanese-American community, partly because of the picture-bride custom. Because of exclusion laws that prohibited the immigration of Chinese females, family life in the Chinese-American community developed slowly. A large and assertive second generation of Japanese Americans emerged because the Issei were able to establish families in the United States. Such a generation did not develop among the Chinese for several decades because of their lack of family life. There were few Chinese women available and Chinese men were unable to marry Whites. The Chinese community, because of exclusion laws, was made up primarily of destitute, lonely, aging, and exploited men for several decades.

When they arrived on the West Coast, the Japanese immigrants worked in a variety of fields, including agriculture, the railroads, domestic work, gardening, small businesses, and industry. Because of job discrimination, they worked mainly in self-employment types of occupations. Consequently, they made their greatest impact in such fields as agriculture, gardening, and small business. Of all these areas, their accomplishments in agriculture, and especially truck farming, were the most impressive. Much of the land they were able to farm was considered unarable and largely useless by most White farmers. With a great deal of ingenuity and the use of intensive-farming techniques, the Japanese began to dominate certain areas of California truck farming. They produced 90% of the state's peppers, strawberries, celery, and snap beans in 1941. In the same year, they raised a large percentage of California's cucumbers, tomatoes, cabbage, carrots, lettuce, and onions.[18]

The Japanese immigrants were often praised for their industry and eagerness when they first arrived in California. However, their tremendous success in agriculture eventually alarmed and frightened farmers. They no longer saw the Japanese merely as ambitious workers and servants, but rather as tough competitors in the marketplace. To halt their success and to drive them out of California, White farmers and labor leaders inflamed anti-Asian feelings and warned of a new "Yellow Peril."

Some familiar faces and organizations, such as Dennis Kearney and the California newspapers, renewed their anti-Asian tactics. Anti-Japanese attitudes were pervasive on the West Coast. Almost every institution was affected. In 1906, the San Francisco Board of Education ordered all Asian-American children, including the Japanese, to attend the segregated Oriental school. Japan was upset by this order and considered it a gross insult. Because of Japan's growing military strength, President Theodore Roosevelt thought that the order might cause a serious conflict with Japan. Consequently, he intervened and persuaded the school board to rescind the order.

To help mitigate the pervasive anti-Japanese feelings on the West Coast, the United States and Japan worked out an agreement designed to reduce drastically the immigration of Japanese laborers to the United States. This agreement, which became known as the Gentlemen's Agreement, was completed in 1908. Japan agreed to halt the immigration of laborers to the United States; the United States agreed to end discrimination against the Japanese. After this agreement, the number of Japanese entering the United States was reduced drastically. However, the anti-Japanese movements continued unabated. The most extremist groups wanted nothing less than total exclusion of the Japanese.

"The Japs Must Go!" became the rallying cry of the anti-Japanese movements. Racist headlines in the press, attacks on Japanese businesses, and other forms of violence occurred. The anti-Japanese forces won a major victory when the California legislature passed the Alien Land Bill in 1913. Japanese immigrants were considered "aliens ineligible for citizenship." This bill, designed to drive the Japanese out of farming, prohibited the Issei from leasing land for more than 3 years. Although the Japanese found this law devastating, they were able, to some extent, to circumvent it. Consequently, it did not have the impact its architects had hoped. Many Issei used their children's names to secure land or obtained land with the help of White friends. In 1920, the California legislature passed a more severe law, which was destined to have the effects the legislators had hoped the 1913 law would have. This law prevented the Issei from leasing land and prohibited them from using their children's names to lease land they could not legally lease themselves. This law served as the prototype for laws later passed in such states as Arizona, New Mexico, Oregon, Utah, and Wyoming.

Although the Alien Land Law of 1920 successfully reduced the number of Japanese Americans in agriculture, the anti-Japanese movement continued in full force. The groups comprising this movement wanted a total victory, which they viewed as a complete halt of Japanese immigration to the United States and the removal of the Japanese from California. They claimed that despite the Gentlemen's Agreement, the picture brides were swelling the Japanese population in the United States and that the Japanese were having an alarming number of children. The phobia of these groups was totally unfounded. The proportion of Japanese immigrants in the United States has always been small. From 1915 to 1924, when the movement to exclude Japanese immigrants was intense, 85,197 Japanese immigrants entered the United States, which comprised only 2.16% of all immigrants who came to the United States during this period.[19] A total of 45,533,116 immigrants came to the United States between 1820 and 1971; only 370,033 of these were Japanese. In 1920, there were only 111,010 Japanese immigrants in the United States. Thus, it was clearly fiction, politics, economic competition, and racism rather than the large number of Japanese immigrants that caused alarm about the "swelling" Japanese population in the United States.

The anti-Japanese forces experienced a long-awaited victory when the Immigration Act of 1924 was passed. This act fixed quotas for European countries on the basis of the percentages of their immigrants living in the United States and prohibited the immigration of aliens ineligible for citizenship. The act, in effect, stopped Asian immigration. "The 1924 immigration act was a major victory for racists, nativists, and exclusionists, and there is little doubt that it was resented by an insulted and bewildered Japan, which having understood that she was to become an important member of the family of nations, did not now understand this slap in the face."[20]

The Internment

On December 7, 1941, Japan attacked Pearl Harbor. Hysteria emerged on the West Coast as the anti-Japanese groups spread rumors about the so-called fifth column and espionage activities among the Japanese.[21] Some Whites argued that all Japanese Americans were still loyal to their mother country; others claimed that you could not tell a "good Jap" from a "bad Jap." Rumors, which spread like wildfire, suggested that the United States was in danger of being attacked by a fleet of Japanese soldiers and that Japanese Americans were helping to plan the attack. A tremendous fear of what came to be known as the Yellow Peril haunted the Pacific Coast. Daniels notes that the fear of conquest by Japan was irrational and racist.[22] The press reinforced and perpetuated the fear by printing highly fictionalized and sensationalized news stories about the Japanese "threat."

It is significant to note that California farmers and politicians played key roles in creating and perpetuating myths about the Yellow Peril. The farmers had long wanted to drive the Japanese out of California; politicians used the issue to gain votes and to divert attention from real political and social issues. It is also worth noting that we know of no sabotage activities in which Japanese Americans were involved during the war. In his perceptive study of the internment, Daniels argues that the decision to remove the Japanese from the West Coast was a political rather than military decision. Military officials knew during the war that the Japanese on the West Coast were not a security risk. However, because anti-Japanese groups in California urged the removal of the Japanese, it was politically expedient to intern them.[23]

The uproar on the West Coast and the fear that spread throughout other parts of the nation resulted in the issuance of Executive Order No. 9066 by President Franklin D. Roosevelt on February 19, 1942. This order authorized the secretary of war to declare military areas "from which any or all persons may be excluded, and with respect to which, the right of any person to enter, remain in, or leave shall be subject to whatever restrictions the Secretary of War . . . may impose in his discretion." Although mention of the Japanese Americans by name is notably absent from the document, the order was clearly aimed at them. It authorized the secretary of war to remove Japanese Americans from the West Coast (declared a "military area") and to set up federal concentration camps to which they would be forcibly removed.

The Japanese were first sent to assembly centers, which served as temporary living quarters. Later, a total of 110,000 Japanese Americans (two-thirds of whom were citizens of the United States) were located in these 10 concentration camps: Tule Lake and Manzanar in interior California, Minidoka in Idaho, Topaz in Utah, Poston and Gila River in Arizona, Heart Mountain in Wyoming, Granada in Colorado, and Rohwer and Jerome in Arkansas. Most of the camps were located in desolate and barren areas that had hot weather in the summer and cold weather in the winter. They were fenced in with barbed wire and guarded by soldiers.

The internment had some adverse effects on the culture and life of the Japanese American. Because of the wide differences in the cultures of Japan and the United States, the Issei and Nisei had been less able to understand each other than most other immigrants and their children. The camp experience increased their alienation. The position of the Issei was further undermined in the camps because often their children, who were U.S. citizens, were able to obtain responsible jobs for which the Issei did not qualify. This was a severe blow to the self-image and confidence of the Issei male, since for centuries the oldest Japanese male had been the undisputed head of the household.

Other events undermined the strength and cogency of the Japanese family, which traditionally had been the pivotal force within the Japanese community. The female often made as much money as the male, and the family had to eat in a communal dining room. The father was unable to exercise his usual authority because of these types of situations. Consequently, family solidarity was lessened in the camps.

Widespread conflict developed within the camps over the question of loyalty. The Nisei often questioned the loyalty of the Issei. Japanese nationals accused the leaders of the Japanese American Citizenship League, who cooperated with the War Relocation Authority, of participating in the oppression of the Japanese. In their eagerness to prove their loyalty to the U.S. government, some Japanese helped federal authorities to conduct witch hunts for "suspected" Japanese. The internment showed how a dehumanizing experience could demoralize a group, which had traditionally had high group solidarity and trust, and cause mistrust and suspicion within it.

Japanese Americans Today

The U.S. Japanese population has never been very large. Japanese immigration was halted by the Immigration Act of 1924 and did not resume until the ban on Asian immigration was lifted when the McCarran-Walter Act was passed in 1952. Although this act set a quota of only 185 Japanese immigrants per year, Asian immigrants were no longer totally excluded.

Compared to the other Asian immigrant groups, few Japanese have immigrated to the United States since the passage of the Immigration Reform Act of 1965. This is because of the highly developed nature of the economy of Japan and its ability to provide jobs for large numbers of technical and professional workers. Most of the immigrants who come to the United States from nations such as the Philippines, Korea, and India—and many of those from China and Hong Kong—are professional workers who are not able to find jobs consistent with their educations in their native lands. This is not the case in Japan. Between 1981 and 1987, 28,200 immigrants came to the United States from Japan, compared to 323,900 from the Philippines, 292,500 from China and Hong Kong, 289,000 from Vietnam, 173,700 from India, and 96,100 from Cambodia (see Table 13–1).

As a result of its small immigrating population, Japanese Americans are becoming one of the smallest of the Asian-American groups and have one of the smallest foreign-born populations. In 1980, most Japanese Americans (about 72%) were U.S.-born citizens.[24]

Some demographers predict that the Japanese-American population will be about 800,000 in 1990.[25] This will make the Japanese one of the smallest of the Asian groups and also one of the slowest-growing groups. Their 1980 population was 716,331. Japanese Americans are a highly culturally assimilated group. They have a high rate of out-marriage with Whites.[26] Most Japanese also speak English. Most of the third- and fourth-generation Japanese speak only English and do not understand Japanese.

The Japanese Americans have been termed the so-called model American ethnic minority because of their success in education, social-class mobility, and low levels of crime, mental illness, and other social deviances. In 1980, the Japanese median family income was $27,354 compared to $21,014 for Whites and $19,917 for all Americans.[27] The Japanese also had high educational achievement in 1980; 81.6% of Japanese, 25 years or older, were high school graduates, compared to 69.6% for Whites and 66.5% for all persons in the United States. The Japanese were also highly concentrated in managerial, professional, and technical occupations in 1980 (employed persons age 16 and older); 28.4% of the Japanese had managerial and professional speciality occupations, compared to 24% for Whites and 23% for all persons. In addition, 34% of the Japanese had technical, sales, and administrative support occupations, compared to 31% for Whites and 30% for all persons.

According to Petersen, "By almost any criterion of good citizenship that we choose, not only are Japanese Americans better than any other segment of American society, including native Whites of native parents, but they have realized this remarkable progress by their own almost unaided effort. . . . Every attempt to hamper the progress of Japanese Americans, in short, has resulted in enhancing their determination to succeed."[28]

Breaking Silence and the Future of the Japanese in U.S. Society

The silence that many Japanese Americans had kept about their internment during World War II was broken during the hearings before the Commission on Wartime Relocation and Internment of Civilians (CWRIC). Congress created the Commission "to determine whether a wrong was committed against those American citizens and permanent residents relocated and/or interned as a result of Executive Order Numbered 9066 and other associated acts of the Federal Government, and to recommend appropriate remedies." The Commission held 20 days of hearings and took testimony from more than 750 witnesses between

July and December 1981.[29] Many people who spoke before the Commission were Japanese Americans who had been interned. They told about their experiences in poignant and moving language.

In December 1982 the Commission issued its report, *Personal Justice Denied*.[30] The report condemned the internment and in June 1983 recommended that Congress allow $1.5 billion to provide personal redress to the Japanese who were interned during the war years. The Commission stated in its report:

> *The promulgation of Executive Order 9066 was not justified by military necessity, and the decisions which followed from it—detention, ending detention and ending exclusion—were not driven by analysis of military conditions. The broad historical causes which shaped these decisions were race prejudice, war hysteria and a failure of political leadership. Widespread ignorance of Japanese Americans contributed to a policy conceived in haste and executed in an atmosphere of fear and anger at Japan. A grave injustice was done to American citizens and resident aliens of Japanese ancestry who, without individual review or any probative evidence against them, were excluded, removed and detained by the United States during World War II.[31]*

It was a long road of debate and controversy, both within and outside of Congress, between the Commission's recommendation of redress for internees in June 1983 and the enactment of the American Civil Liberties bill by Congress in August 1988. The bill offered the Japanese Americans an apology for their internment and provided a payment of $20,000 for each internee. The payments, scheduled to begin in 1990, will be made over a 10-year period, will go to older persons first, and may be made to survivors' descendants in the event of the survivor's death. Because the payment will be made over a 10-year period, many internees will die before the total payment is made. President Ronald Reagan praised the Japanese who served in World War II when he signed the bill and said that the nation was gravely wrong when it interned the Japanese Americans.

The success of the Japanese in American society is indisputable. However, the future of Japanese culture, values, and behaviors in the United States is uncertain. Their success is probably a result largely of traditional Japanese values, attitudes, and beliefs. With a high outmarriage rate and a relatively low rate of immigration, cultural and structural assimilation into the mainstream society may erode the most important values that have taken the Japanese down the road to success. However, a more hopeful possibility is that as they become structurally integrated into the mainstream society, they will enrich it with traditional Japanese values and remain to some extent culturally Japanese as they become full participants in U.S. society.

Filipino Americans:
Historical Perspective

Important Dates	
1898	The Philippine Islands were ceded to the United States under the Treaty of Paris that ended the Spanish-American War.
1907	More than 200 Filipino contract laborers were brought to Hawaii by the Hawaiian Sugar Planters Association.
1923–29	A large number of Filipinos immigrated to Hawaii and the U.S. mainland to work as field laborers.
1927	The Filipino Federation of Labor was founded in Los Angeles. Filipinos became active in the union movement and organized a number of strikes during the 1920s.
1929	An anti-Filipino riot occurred in Exeter, California, in which more than 200 Filipinos were assaulted.
1930	Fermin Tobera, who later became a Filipino martyr, was killed in an anti-Filipino riot in Watsonville, California.
1934	Congress passed the Tydings-McDuffie Act. This act promised the Philippines independence and limited Filipino immigration to the United States to 50 per year.
1935	President Franklin D. Roosevelt signed the Repatriation Act on July 11. This act offered free transportation to Filipinos who would return to the Philippines. Those who left were unable to return except under the quota system.
1940	Under the terms of the Nationality Act of 1940, Filipino immigrants to the United States could become citizens through naturalization. U.S. citizenship was extended to other categories of Filipino Americans on July 2, 1946.
1941	Japan attacked the Philippines.
1946	On July 4, 1946, the Philippines became independent.
1970	By 1970, Filipino immigration had increased substantially because of the Immigration Act of 1965. In 1965, 3,130 Filipinos immigrated to the United States, and in 1974, 32,857 came.
1980	The 1980 Census indicated that Filipinos were the second largest Asian ethnic group in the United States.
1987	About 50,100 Filipino immigrants entered the United States, making them the largest national group that entered the United States except Mexicans.

The Immigration

The magnet that pulled Filipinos to Hawaii and the United States came primarily from without rather than from within. Immigration from the Philippines during the 333 years that the islands were ruled by Spain was virtually nil. However, when the United States acquired the Philippines after the Spanish-American War in 1898, it was only a matter of time before farmers in Hawaii and the United States would successfully lure Filipinos away from the islands to work as cheap and exploited field hands. Recruiting and transportation agents lured Filipinos away from their homeland with high-pressure propaganda about the promises of Hawaii and the United States. Because of chronic unemployment and widespread poverty in the islands, thousands of Filipinos left their native land in search of the dream.

Since Chinese immigration had come to an abrupt end in 1882, Japanese immigrants had been the main source of cheap labor for plantation owners in Hawaii and big farmers on the U.S. West Coast. However, the Gentlemen's Agreement of 1907–1908 substantially reduced Japanese immigration, and the Immigration Act of 1924 virtually stopped it. When Japanese immigration ended, a new source of cheap labor was desired by farmers in Hawaii and in the United States. The United States had recently annexed both Puerto Rico and the Philippines. Each nation was regarded as a promising source of cheap labor. However, the attempt to start large-scale immigration from Puerto Rico failed, and the farmers turned to the Philippines, where they had considerable success. The powerful Hawaiian Sugar Planters Association became so alarmed when the Gentlemen's Agreement restricted Japanese immigration in 1907–1908 that it brought more than 200 Filipino workers to Hawaii that year. The association wanted to make sure that when Japanese immigration stopped there would be a new source of labor just as abundant and cheap.

Filipino immigration to Hawaii continued and escalated after 1907. However, until the 1920s, most of the Filipino immigrants remained in Hawaii and did not come to the U.S. mainland. In 1920, there were only 5,603 Filipinos in the United States. However, from 1923, when Filipino immigration to the United States gained momentum, until it reached its peak in 1929, large-scale immigration to the mainland occurred. In 1929 alone 5,795 Filipinos entered California. Between 1907 and 1910, about 150,000 immigrants left the Philippines and headed for Hawaii or the United States.

Although the highly glorified and exaggerated tales spread by recruiting and transportation agents were the magnet that pulled hundreds of Filipinos from their homeland, the letters and money sent back home by immigrants, as well as the desire to get rich quickly, helped to motivate them to leave the poverty-stricken islands.

Filipino immigrants in the United States had some unique group characteristics that were destined to make their lives on the West Coast harsh and poignant. As the third wave of Asian immigrants, they were victims of the accumulated anti-Asian racism. They were also a young group. According to McWilliams, they were the youngest group of immigrants in U.S. history. They ranged in age from about 16 to 30. Most, 84.3%, were under 30.[32] The immigrants were predominantly male. Few Filipino women immigrated because female immigration violated tradition. Also, most of the immigrants were so-journers who hoped to return to the Philippines after attaining the riches of America. Like the other Asian sojourners, the longer they stayed in the United States, the more the hope waned that they would ever be able to return home.

The sex ratio was imbalanced, as it was in early Chinese-American communities. In 1930, there was 1 woman for every 143 men. The Filipinos immigrated from a country that was a U.S. colony in which the American myth of "all men are created equal" was taught in the schools. Thus, unlike the other Asian groups, they came to the United States expecting to be treated like equals. Their acceptance of this myth made their adjustment in the United States more difficult.

Work

Like other Asian immigrants, the Filipinos came to Hawaii and the United States to do work the Whites disdained and refused to do. They were hired, usually under a contract system, to pick asparagus and lettuce and to do other kinds of "stoop" field work. In addition to farming, the Filipinos, especially after World War II, worked as domestics. They cooked, washed dishes, and worked as house servants. Some worked in the fishing industry and in canneries.

The Filipino Community

Unlike the Japanese and Chinese, the Filipinos were unable to develop tightly knit ethnic communities. The Little Manila districts in cities such as Los Angeles and San Francisco were primarily stopping places for the field hands between seasons and entertainment centers. The Filipinos could not establish highly cohesive communities because their jobs kept them moving and because, like the Chinese immigrants, they were unable to have much of a family life because of the small number of Filipino females.

The types of entertainment and recreation that emerged within Filipino-American communities reflected the sociological makeup of young, unmarried males searching for meaning in life within a hostile and racist atmosphere. Prostitution, cockfighting, and gambling were favorite pastimes for the lonely, alienated men. The Filipino-owned dance halls, in which White girls danced and sold or gave other favors to the immigrants, were popular and a source of widespread tension between Filipinos and White men. Whites passed laws prohibiting Filipinos from marrying White women. However, these laws had little effect on biological drives and mutual attraction between White women and

Filipino men. Stockton, California, was dubbed the Manila of the United States because so many Filipinos settled there. It was the site of much conflict and tension between Filipinos and Whites. Although there were few tightly organized Filipino communities, a strong sense of group solidarity and sense of people-hood emerged among Filipinos. Strong nationalism, as the gifted Filipino-American writer Carlos Bulosan epitomized,[33] was widespread among Filipinos in the United States.

Anti-Filipino Agitation

As the third wave of Asian immigrants to the West Coast, Filipinos inherited all of the anti-Asian prejudice and racism that had accumulated since the Chinese started immigrating to the United States in the 1850s. When Filipino immigration reached significant levels in the 1920s, familiar anti-Asian screams about the Yellow Peril were again heard. These anti-Asian movements were, again, led by organized labor and patriotic organizations such as the American Federation of Labor and the Native Sons of the Golden West. The arguments were identical to those that had been made against the Chinese and Japanese: the victims were different but the victimizers were the same. Labor groups claimed that Filipinos were "unfair competition"; patriotic groups argued that they were unassimilable and would pollute the "pure" White race. One exclusionist warned, "This mongrel stream is small, but when it is considered how rapidly it multiplies and grows it is clear that the tide must be stemmed before it gets beyond control."[34]

Labor and nativistic groups had succeeded in halting Chinese and Japanese immigration by urging Congress to pass exclusion laws. However, the Filipinos presented a different problem. They could not be excluded as "aliens" under the provisions of the Immigration Act of 1924 because of their peculiar and ambiguous legal status. Because the United States had annexed the Philippines in 1898, its citizens were not aliens. However, unlike Puerto Ricans, they were not citizens of the United States either. Filipinos were "nationals" or "wards" of the United States. Consequently, they could not be excluded with the immigration laws that applied to foreign nations. Representative Richard Welch of California, nevertheless, fought hard to get an outright exclusion act through Congress in 1928. The attempt failed, but Welch succeeded in rallying widespread support for the anti-Filipino cause.

The failure of the Welch bill convinced the leaders of the exclusion movement that they had to try another strategy. The desire for independence within the Philippines had become intense by the late 1920s. The Philippines' independence movement gave the exclusionists new hope for a cause that had become an obsession: to exclude and deport Filipinos. They jumped on the independence bandwagon. If the Philippines became independent, they correctly reasoned, its citizens could be excluded under the provisions of existing immigration laws. The passage of the Tydings-McDuffie Act on March 24, 1934, was a significant victory for the exclusionists.

In addition to promising the Philippines independence, the Tydings-McDuffie Act limited Filipino immigration to the United States to 50 people per year. This act, as was the intention of its architects, virtually excluded Filipino immigration to the United States. Even this bill did not totally satisfy the exclusionists. They not only wanted Filipino immigration stopped, but they also wanted Filipinos deported. They pushed the so-called Repatriation Act through Congress. President Franklin D. Roosevelt signed the act on July 11, 1935. Under the terms of the act, any Filipino could obtain free transportation back to the Philippines. However, there was an insidious catch to this inducement. Once they returned, they could not reenter the United States. Few Filipinos were seduced by this act. Only about 2,000 returned to the Philippines under its provisions.

Riots and Anti-Filipino Violence

Both before and after the Filipino exclusion and deportation acts, anti-Filipino Whites carried out a vicious and active campaign of violence against Filipinos in the western states. One of the first anti-Filipino riots broke out in Yakima, Washington, on September 19, 1928. Some of the most serious riots occurred in California, where most Filipino immigrants first settled. On October 24, 1929, Whites attacked and assaulted more than 200 Filipinos and did considerable property damage in Exeter, California. Fermin Tobera, a lettuce picker, was killed in a riot that occurred in Watsonville, California in January 1930. Tobera's murder greatly disturbed his native homeland, and a National Humiliation Day was declared in Manila. Some Filipinos felt that Tobera had been ruthlessly slain by a "mob of blood-thirsty Americans."[35] Three people were shot in a riot that occurred near Salinas, California, in August 1934. An anti-Filipino riot occurred as late as June 1939 in Lake County, California. "No reparations or indemnities were ever made for these repeated outrages; nor were the culprits ever punished."[36]

Filipino Americans Today

Between 1981 and 1987, Filipinos were the second largest group immigrating to the United States; they were exceeded only by immigrants from Mexico. The number of Filipinos entering the United States increased from 3,130 in 1965 to 50,100 in 1987. The Filipino population in the United States increased 132% in the decade between 1970 and 1980, while the White population increased by 6%. In 1980, there were about 781,984 Filipinos living in the United States. Of these, 46.2% lived in California and 17.3% lived in Hawaii. The next highest concentrations lived in Illinois (5.7%), New York (4.4%), and Washington state (3.1%). Most Filipinos lived in urban areas in 1980. Some demographers project that the Filipino population will exceed 1.4 million in the 1990 Census.[37] If this projection proves accurate, Filipinos may become the largest Asian group living in the United States.

Most Filipinos who came to the United States in the 1920s were unskilled laborers. The Immigration Act of 1965 not only significantly increased the number of Filipino immigrants to the United States but also changed the characteristics of the immigrants. The majority of the immigrants now entering the United States from the Philippines are professional, technical, and kindred workers. These immigrants come to the United States to seek jobs that are more consistent with their training than those they can obtain in the Philippines. A significant number of them are specialists in the health professions. Professional and technical workers from the Philippines have encountered some difficulties obtaining licenses to practice their crafts in the United States and have experienced language problems and discrimination. Sometimes doctors, dentists, and pharmacists must take lower-level jobs out of their fields until they can obtain the licenses needed to practice their professions in the United States. Many Filipinos who eventually practice their professions in the United States have obtained additional training in U.S. schools.

The significant number of professionally trained Filipinos who have immigrated to the United States since the Immigration Act of 1965 was enacted has changed substantially the social and demographic characteristics of the Filipino Americans. In 1980, 66.3% of Filipinos in the United States were foreign born.

Before 1970, Filipinos were heavily concentrated in the lower strata of the population on most indices, such as education, income, and job status. However, data from both the 1970 and 1980 U.S. Censuses indicate that the group characteristics of Filipino Americans—based on several criteria related to education, income, and job status—do not differ significantly from the Japanese, Chinese, and other Asian groups in the United States (see Table 13–1). Like the Chinese and Japanese, Filipinos are ahead of Whites on most of these indices. In 1980, the median family income for Filipinos was $23,687, compared to $21,014 for Whites and $19,917 for all persons in the United States. The percentage of Filipino high school graduates, 25 years or older, was 74.2%, compared to 69.6% for Whites and 66.5% for all persons in the United States.

Kim's study of Filipinos in Chicago[38] suggests why the median family income of Asian families might be higher than that of White families. In many Asian families, both parents are highly trained and have professional jobs. Kim describes the typical Filipino in her study as follows:

> *In broad terms, the Chicago Pilipino [sic] respondent can be categorized as young, well-educated, and fairly well-off financially: he is in his early thirties, has finished college, and may have a graduate or professional degree. Unlike most of the other groups in the study, it does not matter in this area whether the Pilipino respondent is male or female. In either case, the educational level and job level—skilled, white-collar, or professional—will probably be about the same. The Pilipino female will also be just about as likely as her male counterpart to have a full-time job, or to hold more than one job.[39]*

A study of the Chinese, Japanese, and Filipinos in the United States will help students to understand how these groups resisted racism and discrimination and attained success in American society. However, their success was attained and is maintained by hard work, tenacity, and the will to overcome. Despite their success in American society, Asians are still the victims of racism and discrimination—both subtle and blatant. Violent incidents against Asian Americans received national attention in 1985. A *New York Times* article was entitled "Violent Incidents against Asian-Americans Seen as Part of Racist Pattern."[40] Part of the violence may have its roots in the U.S. response to competition from the Japanese; some Americans blur the distinction between Japanese Americans and foreign Japanese. The violence may be partly a response to the significant number of Asian immigrants now entering the United States. Regardless of the cause of this new wave of anti-Asian violence, it reminds us that racism is an integral part of U.S. society that can victimize any racial or ethnic group, no matter how successful.

Teaching Strategies

Concepts such as immigration, discrimination, and cultural diversity are highlighted in the historical overviews. This part of the chapter illustrates strategies for teaching two concepts, *immigration* and *discrimination*. An infinite variety of strategies can be used to teach both concepts. However, these activities are illustrative and can serve as a guide to teacher planning. Although both concepts can and should be taught at all grade levels, we discuss strategies for teaching immigration at the primary and intermediate and upper levels, and discrimination at the high school level.

Primary Grades

CONCEPTS: Immigration

Generalization: Asian Americans immigrated to the United States to improve their economic conditions and to fulfill labor needs in Hawaii and in the continental United States.

1. Ask the students if their families have ever moved from one part of the city to another, from one city to another, or from one state to another. Also ask if any students have moved from one country to another. Record their responses on the board or butcher paper. Discuss them.

2. Ask the students *why* their families moved. List their responses on the board or butcher paper. Reasons may include "My dad had to move because he was out of work. He moved to get a new job." "We moved because we wanted a bigger house." "We moved to be closer to relatives." "We moved because the building that we were living in was being torn down." Group and classify the reasons that people move. Discuss the reasons.

3. Introduce the concept of *immigration*. Tell the students that some people not only move from one part of a city to another, or from city to city, or state to state, but also nation to nation. In fact, every group of people in our nation, except the first Americans, came to this country from another nation. Say "When people move from one nation to another we say they are *immigrating*." Write the word on the board or butcher paper. Ask the students if they have ever known a family that immigrated. If so, discuss their responses.

4. Explain to the students, using a large primary grade map, that present Americans came from many different lands, including Africa, Australia, Europe, and Asia. Say: "Today, we will discuss a family that lived in China [*show on map*] in 1847 [*explain how long ago that was*], the Wong family. Before I read the story about the Wong family, let's list some reasons we think that Mr. Wong may have wanted to leave China and come to the United States." List students' responses on the board or butcher paper.

5. Through questioning, bring out that people sometimes move from nation to nation for some of the same reasons that they move from city to city, or from state to state; for example, for work, for more money, or to live closer to relatives.

Read the following story to the class and ask the questions that follow.

The Wong Family

Many, many years ago, in 1847, there lived a family in a land far across the Pacific Ocean in a country called China. The father's name was Mr. Wong. The mother's name was Mrs. Wong. Their three children and Mr. Wong's parents lived with Mr. and Mrs. Wong. The Wongs lived in a tiny village in southern China called Toishan.

"I think that the rice crop will fail this year," said Mr. Wong to Mrs. Wong one day as they walked to the house on their way from the rice field after a hard day's work. For three years in a row floods had almost totally destroyed their rice crops. Rice was the main crop and source of food in Toishan. This year another big flood had come, and it seemed like the crop would again be nearly destroyed. Mr. and Mrs. Wong had been working in the field all day trying to save the rice crop.

Mr. and Mrs. Wong were worried about how they would harvest enough rice to feed the family and to pay the high taxes, which had become higher and higher each year. The Wongs also had other problems. Their small farm was too small for a family as large as theirs to make a good living. There were too many people in the tiny village and more and more children were born each year. The government was running the nation. They had started *rebellions*. [*Explain*]

The Wong family had just finished dinner when Mr. Chan, a family friend, stopped by the house. Mr. Chan was very excited! He was so excited that he could barely tell the good news he had heard that day in town. "We needn't worry about our crops anymore, about high taxes, or about the trouble with the government!" said Mr. Chan.

"Why, why, why?" asked Mr. Wong anxiously.

"About 7,000 miles across the ocean there is a land of a Mountain of Gold!" said Mr. Chan. Mr. Chan told Mr. and Mrs. Wong about the great land of gold, and how Mr. Wong could go there, get rich, and come back home. He then showed them a glittering gold nugget that Mr. Lee's son had brought back from the land of gold. Everyone was speechless with excitement! Mr. Chan said that if he and Mr. Wong went to the land of gold and came back, they would never again have to worry about failing crops. He told Mr. and Mrs. Wong about how much the trip cost and when the next ship would be leaving for the land of gold from Canton, a city north of Toishan.

Mr. and Mrs. Wong thought for weeks about the land of the Mountain of Gold, and how great it would be if Mr. Wong could go there and become rich! Mr. Wong did not want to tell his parents that he was thinking of leaving China because he knew that custom taught that a son should stay and take care of his family, which included a son's parents in China. Mr. and Mrs. Wong also knew that the family could not go with Mr. Wong if he went, and that Mr. Wong would be harshly punished if he was caught trying to leave the country. It was *illegal [explain]* to leave the country. They also did not know where they would obtain the money for his trip.

Nearly two months after Mr. Chan's visit, Mr. Wong, Mr. Chan, and some other men who lived in Toishan left for the land of the Mountain of Gold. The parting of the Wong family was very sad, but Mr. Wong thought that he would become rich and return home in a year or two. The three young Wong children cried when Daddy said good-bye, but they knew that he was trying to make things better for them, mother, and their grandparents.

After a rough 7,000-mile voyage across the ocean, Mr. Wong finally reached the land of the Mountain of Gold. However, when he arrived in San Francisco, the people thought that he looked strange, and would often say mean things to him. He could not find any gold and had to dig in mines that had already been dug by White men from the eastern part of the United States. Mr. Wong's dreams were shattered. He was able to send a little money home, but it was many years later before he was able to go back to China to see his family. But Mr. Wong was luckier than some of the other men who went to California from Toishan. Mr. Chan never saw his family in China again.

Questions

1. In what nation did Mr. and Mrs. Wong live? Point it out on the map.
2. What problems did the Wong family have in China? Why?
3. Why did Mr. Wong decide to come to California (show on map)?
4. Why was California known as the "land of the Mountain of Gold"?
5. What happened to Mr. Wong once he was in California? Why?
6. What do you think happened to his family back in China?
7. Summarize the lesson by saying: "Let's see if we can summarize what we have learned about why people *immigrate* and why Mr. Wong came to San Francisco." List the children's responses on the board or butcher paper.

Intermediate and Upper Grades

CONCEPT: Immigration

Generalization: Asian Americans immigrated to the United States to improve their economic conditions and to fulfill labor needs in Hawaii and in the continental United States.

1. Read to the class accounts that describe the early immigrations of Chinese, Japanese, and Filipinos to the United States (see bibliography at the end of this chapter for appropriate references).

Students should be able to answer the following questions when they have finished the readings:

    a. What economic, social, and political problems did the Chinese, Japanese, and Filipinos have in China, Japan, and the Philippines?
    b. What were the labor needs on the West Coast of the United States?
    c. Why did the immigrants leave China, Japan, and the Philippines?
    d. Was the United States what they expected? Why or why not?

2. Carefully study the historical summary on Filipino Americans in this chapter and read this article listed in the teacher bibliography of this chapter: H. Brett Melendy, "Filipinos." Prepare a two-page ditto summarizing the economic, social, and political conditions of the early Filipino immigrants who went to Hawaii and the United States. Assign this ditto to the students as a third reading.

3. After the students have read and discussed each of the three readings, have them complete Table 13–3.

4. When the students have completed the chart, have them summarize and generalize about why many Chinese, Japanese, and Filipinos immigrated to Hawaii and the United States, and about the labor needs that they satisfied there.

5. Have the students roleplay the situation below, which involves a representative of the Hawaiian Farmers Association trying to persuade a Filipino worker to go to Hawaii to work on a sugar plantation in 1910. After the roleplaying situation, ask the students the questions that follow. The role descriptions follow:

Table 13–3   *Data Retrieval Chart on Asian-American Immigrants*

	Chinese Immigrants	*Japanese Immigrants*	*Filipino Immigrants*
Economic situation in homeland when immigration began			
Political situation in homeland when immigration began			
Social conditions in homeland when immigration began			
Labor needs on U.S. mainland when immigration began			
Labor needs in Hawaii when immigration began			

Mr. Howard Smith,
the Hawaiian Sugar Planters Association Representative

Mr. Smith has been hired to recruit workers for the association. He realizes that his job depends on his success in recruiting workers. He also realizes that if he truthfully explains the situation in Hawaii, he will obtain few workers. He therefore decides to paint a rosy picture of the work on the sugar plantation in Hawaii. He explains to Mr. Ilanos that the contract is for three years and that the association will pay his transportation from the Philippines to Hawaii.

Mr. José Ilanos, a Filipino Who Lives in the Philippines

Mr. Ilanos is a young man with a wife and two children. He is a hard worker. However, in the last few years he has not been able to make enough money to support his family. He has heard about Mr. Smith and is interested in talking to him. However, his wife does not want him to leave the Philippines. Moreover, he has heard from friends that the work in Hawaii is hard and that the pay is rather low.

Questions

1. Did Mr. Smith succeed in persuading Mr. Ilanos to go to Hawaii to work? Why or why not?
2. If Mr. Ilanos decides to go to Hawaii, do you think that Mrs. Ilanos would go with him? Why or why not?
3. If Mr. Ilanos decides to go to Hawaii, what do you think will happen to him? Why? Do you think he might eventually immigrate to the United States? Why or why not?
4. If Mr. Ilanos decides to remain in the Philippines, what do you think will happen to him? Why?
5. Were there any other options open to Mr. Ilanos besides keeping his same job or going to Hawaii to work on the sugar plantations? If there were, what were they? If there were not, why?
6. If you were Mr. Ilanos would you have accepted a contract from Mr. Smith? Why or why not?

Valuing Activity

Read the following story to the class and ask the questions that follow.

Father and Son

Mr. Robert Morimoto is a second-generation Japanese American who lives in an upper-middle-class, predominantly White suburban community near Los Angeles. He is a successful businessman. Mr. Morimoto is proud to be an American and believes that even though our country has problems, any person, regardless of his or her race, can make it in the United States if he or she really tries. Mr. Morimoto does not like to talk about the years that he spent in the Heart Mountain federal concentration camp in Wyoming during World War II. The internment, he feels, is a thing of the past. Japanese Americans should not dwell on it too much today. Mr.

Morimoto is impatient with those Sansei who talk about the internment all of the time. He feels that they have had it easy and do not have much right to criticize their country the way that they do.

Mr. Morimoto and his son have many fights because of their different beliefs. Henry is a student at a local university and is president of the Asian-American Student Association on campus. Henry believes that the United States is a racist nation that oppresses all people of color, including the Japanese Americans. He often talks about the internment and harshly criticizes Japanese Americans like his father who try to "sweep it under the rug." Henry believes that all Third World people (by which he means all non-Whites) should join together to fight oppression and racism in America. When they had their last verbal fight, Henry told his father that even though he was successful in business, he had no political power in America, and was Yellow on the outside but was White on the inside. Mr. Morimoto became very upset with Henry. He told Henry that he would either have to start treating him with respect or move out of his house.

Questions

1. Why do you think Mr. Morimoto feels the way he does?
2. Why do you think Henry feels the way he does?
3. Do you think that Henry is treating Mr. Morimoto fairly?
4. Do you think that Mr. Morimoto is treating Henry fairly?
5. If you were Henry, what would you do? Why?
6. If you were Mr. Morimoto, what would you do? Why?

High School Grades

CONCEPT: Discrimination

Generalization: Asian Americans have been the victims of widespread prejudice and highly discriminatory immigration and migration laws.

Initiate this unit by showing the students a videotape about the internment such as *Family Gathering* (New Day Films). In this videotape, a granddaughter searches for facts about her Japanese family's experiences during World War II. After viewing the videotape, ask the students to write one-sentence reactions to it. Divide the class into groups of three to five to discuss their written reactions to the videotape. Each group should be asked to develop a written reaction, to be shared later with the entire class, on which all group members can agree.

1. Ask individual students or small groups of students to prepare short research reports on the following topics and present them to the class.

   a. The California Foreign Miner's Tax of 1850.
   b. Anti-Chinese riots that occurred in the 1800s.
   c. The Chinese Exclusion Act of 1882.
   d. Anti-Asian groups that developed on the West Coast in the late 1800s and continued through the 1930s, such as the Native Sons of the Golden West.

e. The California Alien Land Laws that prohibited Japanese immigrants from owning or leasing land.

f. The internment of Japanese Americans.

g. The Immigration Act of 1924.

h. Anti-Filipino riots that occurred in the 1920s and 1930s.

i. The Tydings-McDuffie Act of 1934.

j. The Repatriation Act of July 11, 1935.

2. When students share their reports, have them list on a master chart (a) ways in which all of the laws and actions were similar, (b) ways in which they were different, and (c) ways in which they discriminated against Asian Americans. Through the use of higher-level questions, help the students derive the key generalization stated previously.

3. Have your students roleplay a session of Congress in which the Chinese Exclusion Act of 1882 is debated. The entire class can participate. However, assign several specific students to lead the debates. For example, ask one student to play the role of a California senator who is anxious to be reelected, and thus is strongly in favor of the act. Ask another student to argue against the act. Before the roleplaying begins, read and discuss the act with the class. It is reprinted in *"Chink!" A Documentary History of Anti-Chinese Prejudice in America*, by Cheng-Tsu Wu. Ditto the act for the class.

When the main speakers start debating, the other class members can participate both by asking them questions and by arguing on the floor. When the discussion of the act is complete, the students should then vote on it. After the voting, the roleplaying should be discussed, as well as the actual historical events. The students should discuss why their voting results were similar to or different from that of Congress in 1882 and why. In this activity, try to help the students to create the political and social atmosphere of the late 1800s. One way this can be done is to ask each student to pretend that he or she is a senator from a specific state with a particular mandate from his or her constituency.

4. Ask a group of students to do research and complete Table 13–4. After the students have completed the table, ask them to (a) write a generalization about the percentage of Asian immigrants that came to the United States between 1861 and 1960 and the total number of immigrants that came to the United States during this period and (b) discuss, using the completed chart, whether White Americans on the West Coast had valid reasons to fear what was called the Yellow Peril. Ask them to discuss: "If Whites on the West Coast had no valid reasons to fear a Yellow Peril, why do you think that Asian Americans were the victims of so much hostility and harassment?"

5. Ask the students to read a book on the internment. Recommended books are as follows:

- Allan R. Bosworth, *America's Concentration Camps*.
- Roger Daniels, *Concentration Camps U.S.A.: Japanese Americans and World War II*.
- Audrie Girdner and Anne Loftis, *The Great Betrayal: The Evacuation of the Japanese Americans during World War II*.

6. After they have read a book on the subject, ask them to do the following:

a. Compare the interpretation of the internment in the book read with the interpretation in a high school American history textbook or some other source.

b. Discuss why they think the internment occurred.

Table 13– 4   *Asian Immigrants in the United States*

Period	Number	Percentage of all Immigrants
1861–1880		
1881–1900		
1900–1914		
1914–1925		
1925–1940		
1940–1960		
1960–1970		
1970–1980		

    c. Discuss the role of the Japanese American Citizenship League during the internment.

    d. Discuss the roles of the following men in the internment:

       (1) President Franklin D. Roosevelt
       (2) Secretary of War Henry L. Stimson
       (3) Lieutenant General John L. DeWitt
       (4) Assistant Secretary of War John J. McCloy
       (5) Colonel Karl R. Bendetsen
       (6) Major General Allen W. Gullion

    7. Roleplay a meeting of the men listed above discussing whether the Japanese should be interned during World War II.

    8. Discuss the moral implications of the internment, that is: Should the internment have occurred? Why or why not? Who was responsible for the internment? What does the internment teach us about our society? Do you believe that an ethnic minority group cold be interned today? Why or why not? Why were the Japanese interned and not the Germans?

    9. Ask the students to review the hearing and testimony made before the Commission on Wartime Relocation and Internment of Civilians and to identify the factors that resulted in the passage of the American Civil Liberties bill in 1988. The hearing and testimony are summarized in *Personal Justice Denied* (see bibliography).

    10. To summarize this activity, ask the students to write an essay on "The Meaning of the Internment—Then and Now."

    11. Asian-American authors, like other American writers, often express their reactions to and experiences with prejudice and discrimination in their writings. Literary works by Asian Americans can provide students with insights that cannot be gained from factual

sources. To help your students understand better the reactions of Asian Americans to discrimination, have the class read and discuss selections from the following books:

    a. John Okada, *No-No Boy*. This is a powerful and well-crafted novel about a Japanese American who refused to fight in World War II.

    b. Carlos Bulosan, *America Is in the Heart*. This is a poignant, beautiful, and revealing book. It can serve as an excellent springboard for a discussion about anti-Filipino discrimination in the United States.

    c. Frank Chin et al., eds. *Aiiieeeee: An Anthology of Asian-American Writers*. This anthology includes stories, poetry, and excerpts from novels.

    d. Asian Women of California, *Making Waves: An Anthology of Writings by and about Asian Women*. Part 6 of this excellent anthology is called "Thunderstorms: Injustice." The readings provide first-hand accounts of the injustice experienced by Asian-American women.

    e. Mine Okubo, *Citizen 13660*. An individual who was interned poignantly describes her experiences.

Endnotes

    1. Ronald Takaki, *Strangers from a Different Shore: A History of Asian Americans* (Boston: Little Brown, 1989), p. 4.

    2. Roger Daniels, *Asian America: Chinese and Japanese in the United States Since 1850* (Seattle: University of Washington Press, 1988), p. 342.

    3. This phrase is taken from the title of Takaki's excellent history of Asians in the United States. See Takaki, *Strangers from a Different Shore*.

    4. H. Brent Melendy, *The Oriental Americans* (New York: Hippocrene Books, 1972).

    5. Ibid., p. 20.

    6. Quoted in ibid., p. 18.

    7. Lowell K. Y. Chun-Hoon, "Teaching the Asian American Experience," in *Teaching Ethnic Studies: Concepts and Strategies*, ed. James A. Banks (Washington, D.C.: National Council for the Social Studies, 1973), p. 136.

    8. Stanford M. Lyman, *The Asian in the West* (Reno: Desert Research Institute, 1970), p. 14.

    9. Ibid., p. 8.

    10. Bernard P. Wong, *Chinatown: Economic Adaptation and Ethnic Identity in Chinatown* (New York: Holt, 1982), pp. 73–85.

    11. Takaki, *Strangers from a Different Shore*, p. 425.

    12. Ibid.

    13. All of the Census data cited in this chapter are from the U.S. Bureau of the Census, *General Social and Economic Characteristics*, Part 1, United States Summary, PC80–1C1, December 1983.

    14. John W. Wright, ed. *The Universal Almanac 1990* (Kansas City: Andrews and McMeel, 1989), p. 236.

    15. Ibid.

    16. Lyman, *The Asian in the West*, p. 66.

    17. Harry H. L. Kitano, *Japanese Americans: The Evolution of a Subculture*, 2nd ed. (Englewood Cliffs, N.J.: Prentice-Hall, 1976).

18. Melendy, *Oriental Americans*, p. 137.

19. William Petersen, *Japanese Americans* (New York: Random House, 1971), pp. 4–5.

20. Kitano, *Japanese Americans*, p. 28.

21. Roger Daniels, *Concentration Camps USA: Japanese Americans and World War II* (New York: Holt, 1971).

22. Ibid., p. 29.

23. This is the major thesis set forth in Daniels, *Concentration Camps USA*.

24. Takaki, *Strangers from a Different Shore*, p. 421.

25. Wright, *The Universal Almanac*, p. 236.

26. Harry H. L. Kitano and Roger Daniels, *Asian Americans: Emerging Minorities* (Englewood Cliffs, N.J.: Prentice-Hall, 1988).

27. U.S. Bureau of the Census, *General Social and Economic Characteristics*.

28. Petersen, *Japanese Americans*, pp. 4–5.

29. Report of the Commission on Wartime Relocation and Internment of Civilians, *Personal Justice Denied* (Washington, D.C.: U.S. Government Printing Office, December 1982).

30. Ibid.

31. Ibid., p. 18.

32. Carey McWilliams, *Brothers under the Skin* (Boston: Little, Brown, 1943), p. 232.

33. Bulosan's works are perceptively discussed in E. San Juan, Jr., *Carlos Bulosan and the Imagination of the Class Struggle* (Quezon City: Philippines Press, 1972).

34. Quoted in Robert A. Divine, *American Immigration Policy, 1924–1952* (New Haven: Yale University Press, 1957).

35. Sonia E. Wallovits, "The Filipinos in California," Master's Thesis, University of Southern California, 1966, p. 124.

36. McWilliams, *Brothers*, p. 240.

37. Wright, *The Universal Almanac*, p. 236.

38. Bok-Lim C. Kim, *The Asian Americans: Changing Patterns, Changing Needs* (Montclair, N.J.: Association of Korean Christian Scholars in North America, Inc. [AKCS], 1978).

39. Ibid., p. 172.

40. Fox Butterfield, "Violent Incidents against Asian-Americans Seen as Part of Racist Pattern," *The New York Times*, 31 August 1985.

Annotated Bibliography

Books for Teachers

Multiethnic

Amerasia Journal. Published by the Asian American Studies Center, 3232 Campbell Hall, University of California, Los Angeles, CA 90024.

> *This scholarly journal publishes papers that deal with the experiences of Asians in the United States in both the past and present.*

Asian Women United of California, eds. *Making Waves: An Anthology of Writings by and about Asian American Women.* Boston: Beacon Press, 1989.

> *This rich collection of works by and about Asian-American women includes an informative introductory essay, "General Introduction: A Woman-Centered Perspective on Asian American History." The documents in this book are a rich teaching resource.*

Bruchac, Joseph, ed. *Breaking Silence: An Anthology of Contemporary Asian American Poets.* Greenfield Center, N.Y.: The Greenfield Review Press, 1983.

> *This anthology contains poems by 50 Asian-American poets from the United States and Canada. Short biographical sketches of the poets are included.*

Cheung, King-kok, and Yoji, Stan. *Asian American Literature: An Annotated Bibliography.* New York: The Modern Language Association, 1988.

> *A comprehensive guide to Asian-American literature.*

Chin, Frank; Chan, Jeffery Paul; Inada, Lawson Fusao; and Wong, Shawn, eds. *Aiiieeeee: An Anthology of Asian-American Writers.* Washington, D.C.: Howard University Press, 1983.

> *An anthology of the writings of 14 U.S. writers of Japanese, Chinese, and Filipino descent. It includes short stories, plays, and excerpts from novels and autobiographies.*

Daniels, Roger. *Asian America: Chinese and Japanese in the United States Since 1850.* Seattle: University of Washington Press, 1988.

> *This excellent and well-researched history of the Chinese and Japanese in the United States was written by a veteran scholar who has made many distinguished contributions to the scholarship on Asian Americans. It contains an excellent and comprehensive bibliography.*

Hsia, Jayjia. *Asian Americans in Higher Education and at Work.* Hillsdale, N.J.: Lawrence Erlbaum Associates, 1988.

> *An important and informative study of Asian Americans in higher education.*

Kim, Elaine H. *Asian American Literature: An Introduction to the Writings and Their Social Context.* Philadelphia: Temple University Press, 1982.

> *This important study of literary criticism discusses works by Americans of Chinese, Japanese, Korean, and Filipino descent.*

Kim, Hyung-Chan, ed. *Dictionary of Asian American History.* New York: Greenwood Press, 1986.

> *An excellent and comprehensive guide to studying the history of Asian groups in the United States. It is broad in its conceptualization of Asian-American groups and contains detailed historical entries, historical overview essays on the various Asian-American groups, and an excellent chronology of Asian-American history.*

Kitano, Harry H. L., and Daniels, Roger. *Asian Americans: Emerging Minorities.* Englewood Cliffs, N.J.: Prentice-Hall, 1988.

> *This book consists of easy-to-read, brief historical overviews of the major Asian groups in the United States, including the Chinese, Japanese, Filipinos, Asian Indians, Koreans, Pacific Islanders, and Southeast Asians.*

Knoll, Tricia. *Becoming Americans: Asian Sojourners, Immigrants, and Refugees in the Western United States.* Portland: Coast to Coast Books, 1982.

This book contains historical accounts of a range of Asian-American groups, including the Chinese, Japanese, Filipino, Vietnamese, Laotian, and Kampuchean Americans. This is an excellent, informative, and well-written book.

Lim, Shirley Geok-lin; Tsutakawa, Mayumi; and Donnelly, Margarita, eds. *The Forbidden Stitch: An Asian American Women's Anthology.* Corvallis, Ore.: Calyx Books, 1989.

Poetry, essays, photographs, and other literary forms are used in this interesting and informative book to empower the voices and reveal the diverse and complex cultures of Asian-American women. The book contains an excellent section of book reviews.

McKay, Sandra Lee, and Wong, Sau-ling Cynthia, eds. *Language Diversity: Problem or Resource, a Social and Educational Perspective on Language Minorities in the United States.* New York: Harper and Row, 1988.

This informative collection of papers deals with language diversity in the United States.

Takaki, Ronald. *Strangers from a Different Shore: A History of Asian Americans.* Boston: Little, Brown, 1989.

This is the best general history of Asians in the United States. Written by a veteran scholar in ethnic studies, it is comprehensive in the groups included and is extremely well written. The author interlaces stories of people with major historical events in describing the saga of the Asians in the United States. Nominated for the 1990 Pulitzer Prize in History.

Tsang, Sau-Lim, and Wing, Linda C. *Beyond Angel Island: The Education of Asian-Americans.* New York: Institute for Urban and Minority Education, Teachers College, Columbia University, 1985.

This is an informative reference on the education of Asian Americans.

Chinese Americans

Arkuch, R. David, and Lee, Leo O., eds. *Land without Ghosts: Chinese Impressions of America from the Mid-Nineteenth Century to the Present.* Berkeley: University of California Press, 1989.

The selections that make up this book include accounts by writers, travelers, diplomats, and scholars.

Chan, Sucheng. *This Bittersweet Soil: The Chinese in California, 1850–1910.* Berkeley: The University of California Press, 1986.

An important scholarly study of the early Chinese immigrants to California.

Chinn, Thomas W. *Bridging the Pacific: San Francisco Chinatown and Its People.* San Francisco: Chinese Historical Society of America, 1989.

This informative book is illustrated with more than 100 photographs.

Cohen, Lucy M. *Chinese in the Post-Civil War South: A People without a History.* Baton Rouge: Louisiana State University Press, 1984.

This is a carefully researched history of the Chinese who came to the South during Reconstruction. Many were recruited to do the work previously done by slaves.

Gillenkirk, Jeff, and Motlow, James. *Bitter Melon: Stories from the Last Rural Chinese Town in America.* Seattle: University of Washington Press, 1987.

Words and photographs from Locke, a town built by the Chinese in the Mississippi delta, are contained in this book. This book is appealing and informative.

Guthrie, Grace Pung. *A School Divided: An Ethnography of Bilingual Education in a Chinese Community.* Hillsdale, N.J.: Lawrence Erlbaum Associates, 1985.

This is an ethnography of a Chinese bilingual-education program in a public school in the heart of a Chinatown in California. It reveals the conflicting expectations of a bilingual program held by immigrant and English-speaking parents.

Kwong, Peter. *The New Chinatown.* New York: The Noonday Press (Farrar, Straus and Giroux), 1987.

A study of the new Chinatown that has come to life since the large immigration of the Chinese that began after 1965. The author focuses on New York's Chinatown.

McCunn, Ruthanne Lum. *Chinese American Portraits: Personal Histories 1828–1988.* San Francisco: Chronicle Books, 1988.

This interesting book includes biographical profiles of individuals and generations. It is illustrated with captivating photographs.

Sung, Betty Lee. *Chinese Immigrant Children in New York City: The Experience of Adjustment.* New York: Center for Migration Studies, 1987.

An informative study of the adjustment of Chinese immigrant children in New York City by a veteran writer and observer of the Chinese in the United States. Also see her book The Story of the Chinese in America (New York: Macmillan, 1967).

Tsai, Shih-Shan Henry. *The Chinese Experience in America.* Bloomington: Indiana University Press, 1986.

A scholarly chronological history of the Chinese in the United States that includes a chapter on "Contemporary Chinese-American Society." Among the topics discussed are new Chinese immigrants since 1965 and Chinese women in a changing American society.

Yung, Judy. *Chinese Women in American Society: A Pictorial History.* Seattle: University of Washington Press, 1986.

This informative pictorial history reveals, through photographs and an interesting text, the sojourn of Chinese women in the United States from 1834 to the 1980s.

Japanese Americans

Armor, John, and Wright, Peter. *Manzanar.* Photographs by Ansel Adams. Commentary by John Hersey. New York: Vintage, 1988.

This comprehensive account of life at Manzanar, a Japanese-American internment camp during World War II, is illustrated with excellent photographs.

Daniels, Roger; Taylor, Sandra C.; and Kitano, Harry H. L., eds. *Japanese Americans: From Relocation to Redress.* Salt Lake City: University of Utah Press, 1986.

The essays in this anthology are comprehensive and informative.

Ichioka, Juji. *The Issei: The World of the First Generation Japanese Immigrants 1885– 1924.* New York: The Free Press, 1988.

A well-researched history of the first generation of Japanese immigrants to the United States and the difficulties they experienced.

Irons, Peter, ed. *Justice Delayed: The Record of the Japanese Internment Cases.* Middletown, Conn.: Wesleyan University Press, 1989.

This book contains the historical records and documents related to the internment of the Japanese Americans during World War II.

James, Thomas. *Exile within: The Schooling of Japanese Americans 1942–1945.* Cambridge: Harvard University Press, 1987.

A scholarly account of schooling in the camps in which the Japanese Americans were interned during World War II.

Kikumura, Akemi. *Through Harsh Winters: The Life of a Japanese Immigrant Woman.* Novato, Calif.: Chandler and Sharp Publishers, 1981.

This biography tells the story of a Japanese woman who came to America in the early 1900s. It chronicles her life through World War II and into old age.

Kitano, Harry H. L. *Japanese Americans: The Evolution of a Subculture,* 2nd ed. Englewood Cliffs, N.J.: Prentice-Hall, 1976.

This is a useful and informative historical and sociological overview of Japanese Americans by a well-known expert in race relations. The second edition includes an important chapter on the Japanese Americans in Hawaii.

Kogawa, Joy. *Obasan: A Novel.* Boston: David R. Godine, 1982.

This first novel by a Nisei tells what happened to her, her family, and her people in Canada during World War II.

Masaoka, Mike, with Hosokawa, Bill. *They Call Me Moses Masaoka: An American Saga.* New York: William Morrow and Company, 1987.

The biography of a Japanese American who had an influential voice in the effort to formulate a liberal policy toward Japan at the end of World War II.

Okada, John. *No-No-Boy.* San Francisco: The Combined Asian American Resources Project, Inc., 1976.

This is a powerfully written and sophisticated novel about a young Japanese American who refused to fight in World War II and the reactions of his family and community to his refusal to go to war. In this skillfully crafted novel, the reader shares the author's despair, frustrations, and hope.

Okubo, Miné. *Citizen 13660.* Seattle: University of Washington Press, 1983.

This poignantly written and illustrated memoir of life in an internment camp was first published in 1946. It has been re-issued with a new preface by the author.

Sarasohn, Eileen S., ed. *The Issei, Portrait of a Pioneer: An Oral History.* Palo Alto, Calif.: Pacific Books, 1983.

This book documents the collective experiences of the first-generation Japanese from early life in Japan to their journey and life in the United States.

Sone, Monica. *Nisei Daughter.* Seattle: University of Washington Press, 1979 (reprint).

In this autobiography, a Japanese woman describes growing up in an immigrant family in Seattle. It was originally published in 1953.

Uchida, Yoshiko. *Desert Exile: The Uprooting of a Japanese American Family.* Seattle: University of Washington Press, 1982.

A well-known writer tells the personal story of the internment of her family during World War II in this moving and powerful book.

Wilson, Robert A., and Hosokawa, Bill. *East to America: A History of the Japanese in the United States.* New York: William Morrow, 1980.

This is an informative, readable, and comprehensive history of the Japanese in the United States by a journalist and a historian. This book is one of the important products of the Japanese American Research Project sponsored by the Japanese American Citizens League (JACL) and UCLA.

Yamamoto, Hisaye. *Seventeen Syllables and Other Stories.* Lathan, N.Y.: Kitchen Table Press, 1988.

A collection of short stories by an important Asian-American writer.

Yanagisako, Sylvia Junko. *Transforming the Past: Tradition and Kinship among Japanese Americans.* Stanford: Stanford University Press, 1985.

This study of first- and second-generation Japanese in Seattle is scholarly and revealing.

Filipino Americans

Bay Area Pilipino American Writers. *Without Names: A Collection of Poems.* San Francisco: Kearny Street Workshop, 827 Pacific Street, Box 3, San Francisco, CA 94133, 1985.

Poems by 15 Filipino American writers are contained in this anthology.

Bulosan, Carlos. *America Is in the Heart.* Seattle: University of Washington Press, 1973.

This is a powerful and extremely well written personal history by one of the most talented modern American writers.

———. *Sound of Falling Light: Letters in Exile.* Edited by Dolores S. Feria. Quezon City: published by the editor, 1960.

This is a perceptive and deeply moving collection of letters and previously unpublished poems by one of the most gifted writers of this century.

Cordova, Fred. *Filipinos: Forgotten Asian Americans.* Dubuque, Ia.: Kendall/Hunt Publishing Company, 1983.

This interesting and informative book on the Filipino saga in the United States is based on oral history interviews and includes a gold mine of photographs that can be used to teach effectively about Filipinos in the United States.

"Filipinos in American Life." *Amerasia Journal*, special issue, Vol. 13, No. 1, 1986–87. Available from JACP Incorporated, 414 East Third Avenue, P.O. Box 367, San Mateo, CA 94401.

This 195-page special issue includes scholarly papers that focus on the historical and contemporary experiences of Filipinos in the United States. Labor, education, the economy, literature, and folklore are some of the topics discussed.

Garcia, Mila Astorga; Lanot, Marra PL.; and Santiago, Lilia Quindoza, eds. *Filipina.* Quezon City: New Day Publishers, Vol. I, 1984; Vol. II, 1985.

This anthology contains literary works written by women in the Philippines.

Lasker, Bruno. *Filipino Immigration to Continental United States and Hawaii.* Chicago: University of Chicago Press, 1931.

Although this book is dated, it is still valuable for the teacher who needs basic information about the early immigration of Filipinos to Hawaii and the U.S. mainland.

Melendy, H. Brett. "Filipinos." In *Harvard Encyclopedia of American Ethnic Groups*, edited by Stephan Thernstrom, Ann Orlov, and Oscar Handlin. Cambridge: Harvard University Press 1980.

This is a useful, brief, but informative historical overview of the experience of Filipinos in the United States.

Morantte, P. C. *Remembering Carlos Bulosan.* Quezon City: New Day Publishers, 1984.

A personal memoir of the famous writer.

Pido, Antonio J. A. *The Pilipinos in America: Macro/Micro Dimensions of Immigration and Integration.* New York: Center for Migration Studies, 1986.

An important theoretical study of Filipino immigration to the United States.

San Juan, Epifanio, Jr. *Carlos Bulosan and the Imagination of the Class Struggle.* Quezon City: University of the Philippines Press, 1972.

A brilliant and perceptive study of the writings of the gifted Filipino-American writer. This study is especially important because it treats the writing of one of the most talented, yet sadly neglected, twentieth-century writers.

———, ed. *If You Want to Know What We Are: A Carlos Bulosan Reader.* Minneapolis: West End Press, 1983.

Essays, poetry, and short stories by the noted author are included in this anthology.

Santos, Bienvenido N. Edited by Leonard Casper. *Distances In Time.* Manila: Ateneo de Manila Press, 1983.

A collection of poetry by the established author.

———. *Dwell in the Wilderness: Selected Short Stories.* Quezon City: New Day Publishers, 1985.

A collection of 18 short stories by the noted author.

———. *Scent of Apples: A Collection of Stories.* Seattle: University of Washington Press, 1979.

This collection of 16 short stories deals with the lives of Filipinos in the United States: barbers, cooks, munitions workers, college students, and aging Pinoys.

Vallangca, Caridad Concepcion. *The Second Wave: Pinay and Pinoy (1945–1960)*. San Francisco: Strawberry Hill Press, 2594 15th Avenue, 94127, 1987.

> *A historical treatment of the Filipinos who immigrated to the United States between 1945 and 1960. The book is rich in first-hand accounts by immigrants. These accounts are good teaching sources.*

Vallangca, Roberto V. *Pinoy, The First Wave, 1898–1941*. San Francisco: Strawberry Hill Press, 1977 [address in entry above].

> *A historical treatment of the Filipinos who immigrated to the United States between 1898 and 1941.*

Books for Students

Multiethnic

Asian Writers' Project/Asian Media Project. *Sojourner I, II, III, and IV*. Berkeley: Unified School District, 1972, 1973, 1974.

> *This is a collection of original prose, poetry, photographs, and drawings by Asian-American students. Four books are in the series. (High School)*

Goldberg, George. *East Meets West: The Story of the Chinese and Japanese in California*. New York: Harcourt, 1970.

> *This is a well-written and perceptive account of the Chinese and Japanese in America. (Intermediate)*

Hsu, Kai-yu, and Palubinskas, Helen, eds. *Asian-American Authors*. Boston: Houghton Mifflin, 1972.

> *This anthology contains literary selections written by Japanese, Chinese, and Filipino authors and a useful chronology of each group. (High School)*

Perrin, Linda. *Coming to America: Immigrants from the Far East*. New York: Delacorte, 1980.

> *This book tells the story of the Chinese, Japanese, Filipinos, and Vietnamese in the United States. (High School)*

Wong, Diane Yen-Men. *Dear Diane: Letters from Our Daughters*. Oakland: Asian Women United of California, 1983.

> *This book uses a question-and-answer format to explore a wide range of topics identified by more than 600 Asian-American girls who answered survey questions on a variety of subjects including their relationships with peers, teachers, and parents. (High School)*

Chinese Americans

Brown, Trica. *Chinese New Year*. New York: Henry Holt, 1987.

> *The Chinese New Year is a 5,000-year-old festival that is celebrated in Chinese-American communities throughout the United States. This book explains how the celebration began and describes the symbols and traditions associated with it. (Primary)*

Brownstone, David M. *The Chinese-American Heritage.* New York: Facts on File, 1988.

> *The experiences of Chinese Americans in Hawaii and on the mainland are profiled in this comprehensive history of Chinese Americans. (Middle School)*

Bunting, Eve. *The Happy Funeral.* New York: Harper and Row, 1982.

> *Laura learns more about Chinese-American culture as she and her family make funeral preparations for her grandfather. (Primary)*

Fyson, Nance Lui, and Greenhill, Richard. *A Family in China.* Minneapolis: Lerner, 1985.

> *This book describes the daily activities of a 12-year-old girl who lives in rural northeast China. (Intermediate/Middle School)*

Jones, Clarie. *The Chinese in America.* Minneapolis, Minn.: Lerner, 1972.

> *This book provides the reader with background information on life in China, reasons immigrants left China, the problems that Chinese immigrants have encountered, and the contributions they have made to U.S. society. (Intermediate)*

Lord, Bette Bao. *In the Year of the Boar and Jackie Robinson.* New York: Harper and Row, 1984.

> *Shirley Temple Wong, the main character in this story, came to the United States in 1947 and learned a new language, made friends, and learned to play baseball. (Intermediate)*

Louie, Ai-Ling, as retold by. *Yeh-Shen: A Cinderella Story from China.* New York: Putnam, 1988.

> *Ed Young's beautiful illustrations evoke mystical images of the past in this Chinese Cinderella story. (Primary)*

McKenna, Nancy Durrell. *A Family in Hong Kong.* Minneapolis: Lerner, 1987.

> *The reader learns about the social life and customs of Hong Kong through Tse Yik Ming, a 10-year-old boy who lives in an apartment building in Hong Kong. (Intermediate/Middle School)*

Meltzer, Milton. *The Chinese Americans.* New York: Thomas Y. Crowell, 1980.

> *This well-crafted history of the Chinese Americans received the Carter G. Woodson Award from the National Council for the Social Studies. (Intermediate)*

Sung, Betty Lee. *An Album of Chinese Americans.* New York: Franklin Watts, 1977.

> *This general history of Chinese Americans includes information on immigrants from Hong Kong. Another book by Sung is The Chinese in America (Macmillan, 1972). (Middle School)*

Suyin, Han. *Han Suyin's China.* New York: Universe, 1988.

> *The more remote areas of China including Tibet, Xinjiang, and Gansu, as well as the more familiar areas such as Beijing and Shanghai, are pictured and discussed in this book. (All Ages)*

Wong, Don, and Collier, Irene Dea. *Chinese Americans Past and Present: A Collection of Chinese American Readings and Learning Activities.* San Francisco: The Association of Chinese Teachers, 1977.

> *This interesting history of Chinese Americans is presented in short readings. A series of questions and activities follows each reading selection. (High School)*

Yee, Paul. *Tales from Gold Mountain.* New York: Macmillan, 1990.

> *The adventures of young Chinese immigrants who came to the United States at the turn of the century and worked in salmon fisheries, farms, railway camps, and canneries are told in this provocative book. (High School)*

Yep, Laurence. *Mountain Light.* New York: Harper and Row, 1985.

> *Through the words of Squeaky Lau, the main character in this book, the reader experiences the hopes, joys, and failed promises of Chinese immigrants who traveled far from home to the California gold fields in the 1800s. Other books by Yep include* Child of the Owl *(Harper and Row, 1977);* Dragon Steel *(Harper and Row, 1985);* Dragonwings *(Harper and Row, 1975).*

Ying, Pan Cai. *Monkey Creates Havoc in Heaven.* New York: Viking, 1987.

> *Vivid color paintings illustrate this story about the activities of a monkey king that led to his imprisonment in a mountain. (Primary)*

Yung, Judy. *Chinese Women in America: A Pictorial History.* Seattle: University of Washington Press, 1986.

> *The experiences of Chinese American women from 1834 to 1985 are chronicled in rich and vivid photographs. (All Ages)*

Filipino Americans

Buaken, Manuel. *I Have Lived with the American People.* Caxton Printers, 1948.

> *This interesting personal account of the author's experiences in the United States raises and answers a number of powerful questions about Filipino Americans. (High School)*

Bulosan, Carlos. *The Laughter of My Father.* New York: Harcourt, 1942.

> *In this collection of vignettes about his family, the author discusses poignant events in a lighthearted manner. (High School)*

————. *America Is in the Heart.* Seattle: University of Washington Press, 1973.

> *This beautiful, poignant book is about a young man trying to survive in a hostile land. In this autobiography, Mr. Bulosan illuminates the culture of his people in both the Philippines and the United States. (High School)*

Cordova, Fred. *Filipinos: Forgotten Asian Americans.* Dubuque, Ia: Kendall/Hunt Publishing Co., 1983.

> *This book presents an illustrated historical overview of the Filipino experience in the United States. (High School)*

Crouchett, Lorraine Jacobs. *Filipinos in California: From the Days of the Galleons to the Present.* El Cerrito, Calif.: Downey Place Publishing House, 1982.

> *The contributions of Filipinos who work in many areas are discussed in this book. (High School)*

Evangelista, Susan. *Carlos Bulosan and His Poetry: A Biography and Anthology.* Seattle: University of Washington Press, 1985.

> *This book contains biographical material on Bulosan, as well as samples of his writings. (High School)*

Hieb, Harley F. *Heart of Iron.* Lodi, Calif.: Pacifica Publishers, 1987.

> *The experiences of a Filipino soldier who served during World War II are chronicled in this book. (High School)*

Robles, Al. *Looking for Ifugao Mountain.* San Francisco: Children's Book Press, 1977.

> *Kayumanggi, a young Filipino-American man, searches for his ancestral roots by embarking on a mystical journey. This is a bilingual book. (All Ages)*

Taruc, Luis. *Born of the People.* New York: International Publishers, 1953.

> *This touching book is about life in the Philippines and the conditions that lead to a fight for liberation. (High School)*

Teodoro, Luis V., Jr. *Out of This Struggle: The Filipinos in Hawaii 1906–1981.* Honolulu: The University Press of Hawaii, 1981.

> *This is an overview of the Filipino experience in Hawaii. (High School)*

Stern, Jennifer. *The Filipino Americans.* New York: Chelsea House Publishers, 1989.

> *This is a comprehensive and interesting account of the experience of Filipinos in the United States. (Middle school/High School)*

Winter, Frank. *The Filipinos in America.* Minneapolis: Lerner, 1988.

> *The experiences of Filipino immigrants to the United States and the contributions Filipinos have made to American life are discussed in this book. (Middle School)*

Japanese Americans

Bryan, Ashley. *Sh-Ko and His Eight Wicked Brothers.* New York: Atheneum, 1988.

> *The reader will enjoy reading about the exploits of Sh-Ko and his wicked brothers as they try to decide which of them is the most handsome. (Primary)*

Elkin, Judith. *A Family in Japan.* Minneapolis: Lerner, 1986.

> *The daily activities of a young boy and his family who live in a town near Tokyo are described in this book. (Intermediate/Middle School)*

Friedman, Ina R. *How My Parents Learned to Eat.* Boston: Houghton Mifflin, 1984.

> *A Japanese girl and an American sailor learn each other's way of eating. (Primary)*

Goodsell, Jane. *Daniel Inouye.* New York: Thomas Y. Crowell, 1977.

> *This is an interesting biography of a Japanese-American U.S. senator. (Intermediate)*

Hamanaka, Sheila. *The Journey.* New York: Orchard, 1990.

> *The illustrations and the text of this book paint a vivid picture of Japanese-American history and the personal experiences of the author's family. (All Ages)*

Houston, Jeanne Wakatsuki, and Houston, James. *Farewell to Manzanar.* Boston: Houghton Mifflin, 1973.

> *This true story focuses on the period during and after World War II. (High School)*

Irwin, Hadley. *Kim/Kimi.* New York: Macmillan, 1987.

> *Sixteen-year-old Kimi feels a need to find out about her Japanese-American father, whom she never knew. (High School)*

Japanese American Curriculum Project. *The Japanese American Journey.* San Mateo, Calif.: JACP, 1985.

> *Historical and biographical essays are included in this excellent resource book for students in grade 5 through 8. It also includes three well-crafted short stories. (Intermediate)*

Leathers, Noel L. *The Japanese in America.* Minneapolis: Lerner, 1982.

> *This history of Japanese Americans explores the background of Japanese immigrants, their contributions, and the discrimination they have experienced. (Intermediate)*

Meyer, Carolyn. *A Voice from Japan: An Outsider Looks In.* San Diego: Harcourt Brace Jovanovich, 1988.

> *This book provides information on how Japanese teenagers relate to each other, their parents, schools, and society. (Middle School)*

Tobias, Tobi. *Isamu Noguchi: The Life of a Sculptor.* New York: Thomas Y. Crowell, 1974.

> *This is a succinct biography of one of America's most gifted artists. The book is filled with black-and-white photographs of Noguchi's work. (Intermediate)*

Tsutsui, Yoriko. *Anna in Charge.* New York: Viking, 1979.

> *Illustrated with beautiful color paintings, this book tells about how Anna searched for her missing sister. (Primary)*

Uchida, Yoshiko. *The Happiest Ending.* New York: Atheneum, 1985.

> *Rinko Tsujimura learns a valuable lesson when she rejects arranged marriages and tries to bring two people together who she thinks would make the perfect couple. (Intermediate). Other books by Uchida include* The Best Bad Thing *(Atheneum, 1983);* A Jar of Dreams *(Atheneum, 1982); and* Journey to Topaz *(Atheneum, 1985).*

Weston, Reiko. *Cooking the Japanese Way.* Minneapolis: Lerner, 1983.

> *This book features easy-to-cook recipes for soups, appetizers, and main dishes and describes how to set a Japanese table and how to eat with chopsticks. (All Ages)*

Chapter 14

Indochinese Americans

Concepts, Strategies, and Materials

In Vietnam traditional values have deep roots. When the heavy winds blow reeds bend, but when the winds cease, they once again stand straight and tall.

—Vuong G. Thuy

Introduction

In the decade before 1975, only about 20,000 Vietnamese immigrated to the United States.[1] It is not known how many immigrants came from Laos and Kampuchea (Cambodia) during this period. The first refugees from Indochina fled to the United States in 1975. Their journey to America was directly related to the ending of the Vietnam War and the resulting communist governments in Vietnam, Laos, and Kampuchea.

The Indochinese, like the Cuban refugees from 1959 to 1962, sought refuge in the United States when communist governments came to power in their homelands. A large number of Indochinese refugees were resettled in the United States between mid-May 1975 and December 31, 1978. This was one of the largest emergency resettlement programs in the nation's history.

The number of Vietnamese, Laotians, and Kampucheans in the United States grew significantly between 1981 and 1987. Vietnam was one of the 10 nations that sent the most legal immigrants to the United States during this period. It ranked fifth and was exceeded only by Mexico, the Philippines, South Korea, and China. Nearly one-half million (497,100) immigrants from Vietnam, Laos, and Kumpuchea settled in the United States between 1981 and 1987 (see Table 14–1). Most of these immigrants (58%) came from Vietnam.

The Vietnamese population in the United States is one of the nation's fasting growing populations. There were about 245,025 Vietnamese living in the United States in 1970. Some demographers have projected that there will be about 860,000 Vietnamese in the United States when data from the 1990 Census are compiled.[2] If this projection proves accurate, the Vietnamese will be

Table 14–1   Immigrants from Vietnam, Laos, and Kampuchea, 1961–1987

Nation	1961–1970	1971–1980	1981–1987	Total
Vietnam	4,600	179,700	289,000	473,300
Kampuchea	1,200	8,400	96,100	105,700
Laos	100	22,600	112,000	134,700
Total from all nations				713,700

Source: U.S. Bureau of the Census, *Statistical Abstract of the United States: 1989*, 109th ed. Washington, D.C.: U.S. Government Printing Office, 1989, p. 10.

one of the largest Asian-American populations. Table 14–2 shows the population of the Vietnamese, Laotians, and Kampucheans in the United States in 1980 and their estimated population in 1985.

A number of developments have contributed to the rapid growth in the Indochinese population in the United States. Indochinese refugees continued to come to the United States from refugee camps in Southeast Asia between 1981 and 1989. Many Vietnamese, including Amerasian children (children of American fathers and Vietnamese mothers) and their close relatives have been permitted to immigrate to the United States by federal policies designed to facilitate family reunification. About 10,000 Amerasian children were scheduled for resettlement in the United States in 1989.

The Indochinese came to the United States for many different reasons. Singular political, economic, or personal concerns motivated some of the refugees to leave their homelands. Others were motivated by many factors. Many of the Indochinese refugees had been directly touched by the trauma of the Vietnam War (1954–1975) or its aftermath. The Indochinese left their nations as refugees and are now in the process of becoming Americans. To understand their story fully, we must begin where it started—in Indochina.

Table 14–2   Population of the Vietnamese, Laotians, and Kampucheans in the United States in 1980; Estimated Population in 1985

Group	1980	1985 (Est.)
Vietnamese	245,025	634,200
Laotians	47,683	218,400
Kampucheans	16,044	160,800

Based on U.S. Bureau of the Census, 1980 Census of Population, PC80 1–B1, *General Population Characteristics*; Robert W. Gardner, Bryant Robey, and Peter C. Smith, *Asian Americans: Growth, Change, and Diversity*. Washington, D.C.: Population Reference Bureau, Inc., 1985, p. 5.

Indochinese Americans:
Historical Perspective

*Important
Dates*

111 B.C.   China began a 1,000-year hegemony in Vietnam.

939 A.D.   The Vietnamese drove the Chinese out of Vietnam and began a period of 900 years of independence.

1883   Vietnam signed a treaty with France that made Vietnam a French protectorate.

1945   Ho Chi Minh took advantage of the Japanese occupation of Vietnam during World War II and began an insurrection against France. He declared Vietnam the Democratic Republic of Vietnam.

1946   France signed an agreement recognizing Ho Chi Minh's Vietnam Independence League as the only legitimate native political regime in Vietnam.

1946–1954   The French-Indochina War occurred. Fighting broke out between France and Vietnam when the two nations could not reconcile their differences regarding the rights France would exercise in Vietnam.

1947   The Front of the National Union was founded in Saigon. This anti-Communist organization later became involved in Vietnam's war for independence.

1953   The United States signed the Korean Armistice ending the Korean War. Fearing a Communist takeover in the rest of Asia, the United States increased its aid to the French, who were fighting in Vietnam. By 1954, the United States was supporting about 80% of France's war effort in Vietnam.

1954   The French Army was defeated at Dien Bien Phu, North Vietnam. The Geneva Agreement of 1954 ended the French-Indochina War. Vietnam was divided along the 17th parallel: the North under the Communist rule of Ho Chi Minh and the South under the anti-Communist rule of Ngo Dinh Diem. Both the North and South claimed to be the legitimate government of Vietnam and wanted to control and consolidate Vietnam.

1963   The Diem regime was overthrown, and President Ngo Dinh Diem was killed.

1964   The Johnson administration began the covert bombing of Laos. The Gulf of Tonkin Resolution was passed.

Important Dates	
1965	184,000 U.S. troops were stationed in Vietnam.
1973	The United States signed a peace accord with North Vietnam. The last U.S. combat troops left Vietnam.
April 1975	Phnom Penh, the capital of Cambodia, fell to the Khmer Rouge. The nation was renamed Kampuchea. Parole was authorized for Vietnamese dependents of U.S. citizens. President Ford established an Interagency Task Force (IATF) to coordinate the activities of 12 federal agencies concerned with the evacuation and resettlement of Vietnamese refugees. The U.S. government evacuated American and Vietnamese individuals from Saigon in Operation Frequent Wind. Saigon fell to the Vietnam People's Army (North Vietnamese Army). Camp Pendleton, California, prepared to accept Indochinese refugees.
May 1975	A refugee center opened at Fort Chaffee, Arkansas. A refugee center opened at Eglin Air Force Base, Florida. The Indochina Migration and Refugee Assistance Act was enacted by Congress. A refugee center opened at Fort Indian Town Gap, Pennsylvania.
September 1975	The refugee center at Eglin Air Force Base, Florida, closed.
October 1975	The refugee center at Camp Pendleton, California, closed.
December 1975	All Indochinese refugees left the resettlement centers and the centers were closed. The Interagency Task Force responsible for the evacuation and resettlement of the refugees was terminated. The HEW Refugee Task Force assumed the responsibility for resettling the refugees in the United States.
September 1976	The Indochina Refugee Children Assistance Act was enacted by Congress.
October 1977	Public Law 95-135, authorizing Indochinese refugees to become permanent residents of the United States, was enacted by Congress.

Important Dates	
1977–1980	Additional Indochinese refugees arrived in the United States. These refugees included ethnic Chinese, Hmong, Kampucheans, and Vietnamese. The Refugee Act of 1980 was passed.
1981–1989	Refugees continued to come to the United States from camps in Southeast Asia.

The Peoples and Cultures of Indochina

The word *Indochina* was first used by Europeans to describe a geographical area in southeast Asia that had historically been influenced by India and China. Three contiguous nations—Vietnam, Kampuchea (Cambodia), and Laos—make up Indochina (see Figure 14–1).

France became interested in Indochina in the nineteenth century. In 1887, France consolidated Cochin China (southern portion of Vietnam), Cambodia, Annam (central portion of Vietnam), and Tonkin (northern portion of Vietnam) into the French Indochinese Union. Laos joined the Union in 1893. French control of Indochina ended in 1954.

Each nation in Indochina has its own unique sociocultural traditions and political structures. However, even though there is diversity within Indochina, the people of these nations share many characteristics. All the nations in Indochina have been strongly and deeply influenced by both Chinese and Indian cultures. These influences have taken many forms. Vietnam has been traditionally associated with China, whereas Laos and Cambodia (Kampuchea) have been closely associated with Indian civilization. These influences are seen in many aspects of Indochinese life, including art, music, government, food, literature, and religion.

Religion

With French support and encouragement, the Catholic Church expanded its missionary work in Indochina. There are also a small number of Protestant religions in Indochina. Animism, ancestor worship, and Taoist-Confucianist beliefs and rituals are also practiced by the Indochinese. Most Indochinese, however, are Buddhists.

A specific religious affiliation in Indochina does not always limit the day-to-day religious practices and beliefs of individuals. In general, most Indochinese do not see a conflict in practicing rituals and/or accepting the beliefs of more than

Figure 14–1   Indochina

one religion. Taoist-Confucianist beliefs are accepted and practiced by many Buddhist, as well as Catholic, Vietnamese.

Education

Education in Indochina, like religion, reflects an integration of foreign and indigenous influences. Chinese, French, and Vietnamese influences can be seen in Vietnamese schools. The Chinese helped shape an appreciation for knowledge during their long contact with the Vietnamese. Within traditional Chinese culture, there is great respect for scholarship. The Vietnamese, like the Chinese, view education as an important part of life.

The French also influenced Indochinese education during their years of rule in Indochina. The French established schools that had French teachers and administrators. The French introduced their educational philosophy, curricula, methods, language, and values to the Indochinese elite in these schools. Few Vietnamese were allowed to attend the French schools. They were established and operated to benefit an elite group of Indochinese society.

After Vietnam declared its independence from France in 1945, a number of schools were established by the Vietnamese. Many of these schools were based on the strict and classical orientation of the French educational system. These schools helped to expand educational opportunities in Vietnam.

The Vietnamese people were able to influence their schools directly after they gained independence from France in 1954. After independence, the South Vietnamese government increased the number of public schools. The government's goals were to eliminate illiteracy and to improve the education of the Vietnamese population. It increased the number of schools, hired Vietnamese teachers and administrators, and used Vietnamese teaching materials. The books used in the schools were written in Vietnamese, not French. The schools gradually began to reflect Vietnamese culture and values.

The Evacuation

Events Preceding the Vietnamese Evacuation

On January 27, 1973, a formal peace accord was signed in Paris by the United States, North Vietnam, South Vietnam, and the National Liberation Front, a group that also fought against South Vietnam. This document was an attempt to resolve a number of war-related issues, including the withdrawal of U.S. troops from Vietnam. In March 1973, the last U.S. combat troops left South Vietnam.

The war had left deep scars and bitter memories in the American people. Not since the Civil War had the nation been so divided on a war effort. Nearly 57,000 American soldiers had died, 900 soldiers were listed as missing in action, and $150 billion had been spent on the war. It was an unpopular war that many Americans had never understood. When it was over, many simply wanted to forget it.

The fighting in Vietnam, however, was not over. North and South Vietnamese forces continued to fight after 1973. However, the South Vietnamese were now fighting alone. The South Vietnamese continued fighting into 1975. In the spring of 1975, the South Vietnamese were forced to evacuate several provinces. At that time, the U.S. government did not have a well-coordinated plan for the evacuation of the Americans and South Vietnamese who would need to leave the country in the event of a North Vietnamese victory. Both the South Vietnamese and the U.S. governments believed that the Saigon government would be able to hold off defeat for at least several more months. The focus in Vietnam was on securing additional U.S. economic and military aid for the South Vietnamese government, not on evacuation. However, as it became increasingly clear that the fall of the Saigon government was imminent, plans for evacuation were developed hastily.

The Vietnamese Evacuation

The evacuation was characterized by confusion. The war was still underway. Rumors were rampant. There were fears of death lists and potential atrocities. A few Vietnamese were trying to leave Vietnam in any way that was possible. This included marrying foreigners and bribing officials. Because of the atmosphere surrounding the evacuation and the haste with which it occurred, some South Vietnamese had little time to think about where they would go and what they would do when they resettled. Many did not realize that they were leaving their homeland forever. A survey of the Vietnamese refugees arriving in the United States in 1975 revealed that 41% of the heads of households planned to return to Vietnam.[3]

The evacuation almost reached a panic level in its last days. A startled American public watched the evening news and saw Americans and South Vietnamese fleeing from Saigon one step ahead of the North Vietnamese army. More than 7,000 people were evacuated from Saigon during those last hours. However, not everyone was evacuated. A few Americans were left behind. Most of them were newspaper correspondents and missionaries. Also left behind were thousands of South Vietnamese who had been closely associated with the Americans and the Saigon government. In the months and years to come, many of these individuals would find their own ways to leave Vietnam.

The Refugees Enter the United States

The U.S. government had originally planned to admit only those Vietnamese who worked for the U.S. government or who were dependents of U.S. citizens. However, four days before the Saigon government fell, the U.S. government agreed to expand the criteria used for determining who would be evacuated. Those people whose lives would be endangered if they remained in Vietnam were allowed to enter the United States. In the end, however, the population of Indochinese refugees admitted to the United States reflected other factors more than they reflected government admission criteria. The individual decisions of refugees to leave their homelands and their ingenuity in finding ways to leave determined the refugee population more decisively than did official government criteria.

By mid-May 1975, about 130,000 refugees had entered the United States or U.S. territory. Most of them were Vietnamese. The others were Laotians, Hmong (the tribespeople of Laos), and a few Cambodians. In the fall of 1975, an additional 10,000 Vietnamese refugees were admitted to the United States. The Indochinese refugees entered the United States under the Indochinese Refugee Act of 1975. This act allowed the U.S. attorney general to grant *parole* status to Vietnamese refugees. The refugees were allowed to enter the United States, but they were not eligible to become permanent residents. Subsequently, Public Law 95-145, effective October 28, 1977, allowed refugees to change their status from parolees to permanent residents after a two-year residency in the United States.

The 1975 Refugees

For many of the Vietnamese refugees, this was not their first experience as refugees.[4] Many refugees had been born in North Vietnam and fled to the South as refugees after the 1954 defeat of the French. Many of these refugees were Catholic. The Catholic religious affiliation is also reflected in the current Indochinese refugee population. For example, 40% of the Vietnamese refugees who came to the United States were Catholic. Less than 10% of the Vietnamese population is Catholic.

Most of the refugees came to the United States as part of a family group. Households with more than 5 persons represented 62% of all the refugees. Sixty-two families had 17 or more members of their family with them. Many of the refugees were young. More than 45% of the refugees were under 18 at the time of their arrival in the United States. More than 700 children came unaccompanied by adults or relatives.[5]

A wide range of socioeconomic levels was represented in the group. A few refugees brought gold and/or jewelry with them to the United States. Others owned only the clothes they wore. There was also a wide range of educational levels among the refugees. The group included scholars, professionals, and skilled workers. More than 27% of the heads of households had some university training. Other refugees were illiterate. Eighteen percent had no formal education or had only completed some elementary school.[6] The refugees also varied in their experiences with urban and Western life-styles. Some had lived in Saigon or other Vietnamese cities and had experienced daily contact with U.S. citizens. They were well acquainted with urban living and Western life-styles. Others, particularly Indochinese fishermen and farmers and Hmong and Laotian peasants, were unaware of many aspects of Western and urban life. It was apparent that a transition period was needed to help the refuges integrate into American society. Refugee camps were established to process the refugees for admission to the United States and to provide a transition period.

Refugee Camps

When Saigon fell in April 1975, the refugees who were evacuated did not come directly to the United States. They went to U.S. bases overseas. Two such bases were Utapo in Thailand and Subic Bay in the Philippines. From there, they were sent to receiving stations on Wake or Guam Island. When additional bases were needed to process the refugees, four relocation stations were opened on the mainland at Camp Pendleton outside San Diego, Fort Chaffee in Arkansas, Eglin Air Force Base in Florida, and Fort Indian Town Gap near Harrisburg, Pennsylvania.

The centers were run by the Interagency Task Force (IATF) and the military. The IATF was a conglomeration of 12 federal agencies established on April 18, 1975, by President Ford. Its job was to coordinate the evacuation and resettlement of the Indochinese refugees. The funds for the resettlement program were provided by the Indochina Migration and Refugee Assistance Act. This act was passed by Congress on May 24, 1975. The IATF contracted 9 voluntary agencies known as VOLAGS to handle the relocation of the refugees. These agencies were given funds ($500 for each refugee) to help with the resettlement expenses. The VOLAGS dispensed the money in a variety of ways. In some cases, the money was given in part or total to the refugee, and in other cases it was given to the refugee's sponsor. A portion of the money was usually retained by the VOLAGS to cover administrative costs.

When the refugees arrived at the refugee camps, they were given temporary housing, food, clothing, and any needed medical assistance. They were interviewed and underwent security checks conducted by the Immigration and Naturalization Service, the CIA, the Department of Defense, the Department of the Treasury, and in some cases the FBI. The refugees were given medical examinations and Social Security numbers. They registered with American agencies such as the Department of Commerce and were further introduced to American culture through movies, schools, newspapers, and other means.

One major goal of the refugee camps was the rapid assimilation of the refugees into American society. The emphasis on assimilation was resented by some Indochinese refugees. They felt they were being forced to replace their cultural traditions with American life-styles.[7]

English as a second language programs (ESL) were used to teach the refugees English. In some cases, the refugees were not allowed to use their native languages during school hours. A number of teachers in these programs did not speak an Indochinese language. Most of the Indochinese refugees spoke little, if any, English.

Individual states had different responses to the refugees. Some states provided services at the resettlement centers. At Fort Indian Town Gap, Pennsylvania, the state provided educational services for both children and adults. This center's staff also conducted special programs for women and registered the adult refugees for employment. Other states tried to discourage refugees from settling within them. Some state officials voiced concerns about their states' becoming centers for Indochinese resettlement. These states did not send officials to register the refugees for employment.

Leaving the Refugee Camps

There were four ways for refugees to leave the resettlement centers. They could return to Indochina, immigrate to another nation, demonstrate their ability to be self-supporting, or find an American sponsor.[8] Each method was used by the refugees. By October 1975, 1,546 Vietnamese refugees had returned to their homeland. Some of them were low-ranking military personnel who happened to be on ships or planes when their commanders ordered them to leave Vietnam. Some had families in Vietnam and did not want to leave them. By December 1975, an additional 403 Vietnamese had asked to be returned to their homeland.

Refugees who had marketable skills had little trouble finding sponsors in the United States. Nebraska, for example, offered to pay a yearly salary to refugees who were doctors while they studied for their medical examinations. These doctors were required to promise that they would practice in Nebraska for 10 years. A few families were able to leave the refugee camps by showing that they were self-supporting. In 1975, a refugee family was considered self-supporting if the family could show proof of having at least $4,000 per family member.[9]

The majority of the Vietnamese left the resettlement centers with U.S. sponsors. The VOLAGS were contracted by the IATF to find sponsors for the refugees. Becoming a sponsor was a major responsibility. The sponsor not only provided economic assistance, including medical care if needed, but also helped the head of the household to find a job, enroll the children in school, and helped the family adjust to the new community. Moreover, since family problems, illness, or unemployment could occur, sponsorship was seen as a long-term commitment.[10] However, if the sponsorship did not work out, the VOLAG was responsible for trying to find a second sponsor. Some sponsors were relatives of the refugees who were already living in the United States. Church congregations and other voluntary organizations also served as sponsors. Five states—Washington, Iowa, New Mexico, Oklahoma, and Maine—provided sponsorship to the Indochinese refugees.

Some employers were also sponsors. However, initially employers were not considered for sponsorships because VOLAG personnel were concerned about a possible conflict of interest. Some of the employment/sponsor offers appeared to be motivated by a desire for cheap labor, domestic help, or the fulfillment of personal desires. However, as the VOLAGS encountered more pressure to process the refugees in 45 days, employment-related sponsorship was viewed more positively.

The refugees were able to reject offers of sponsorship freely until late August 1975. After that date, rejecting sponsorships was strongly discouraged. By September, refugees were allowed to turn down no more than two offers of sponsorship. The refugees had many reasons for rejecting sponsorships. They included fear of isolation and separation from family members, and fear of exploitation. However, the most-often-stated reasons for rejecting a sponsorship at Fort Indian Town Gap were the cold climate of places like Maine and fear of racial prejudice.[11]

All the refugees had left the refugee camps and the camps were closed by late December 1975. The government's overriding purpose in resettlement was to prevent large populations of Indochinese from settling in any one location or in areas of high unemployment. In this way, the federal government hoped to prevent potential political problems or economic burdens for state and local governments. The government succeeded in dispersing the Indochinese into various parts of the nation with no large concentrations in any single area. In 1975, more than 50% of the Vietnamese were located in states where the total number of Indochinese was under 3,000.

The Refugees after 1975

Indochinese refugees came to the United States in two major groups. The first group arrived in 1975. After 1975, events in Indochina caused a large number of ethnic Chinese, Vietnamese, Laotians, Hmong, and Kampucheans to leave their homelands. These peoples comprised the second group of refugees who came to the United States. The second group of refugees, like the first group, were motivated to leave Indochina for various economic, political, and personal reasons.

Food had become increasingly difficult to obtain in the refugees' homelands. Inflation had driven the price of goods and services to very high levels. There were increasing shortages of most goods, including medicines. Political reprisals were occurring. In Vietnam, many people who had supported the Saigon government were sent away to re-education camps. The free enterprise economies of the nations of Indochina had been replaced by economies governed by communist ideology. In addition, fighting had continued in many parts of Indochina. Vietnam was at war with China and Kampuchea. The ethnic Chinese in Vietnam were viewed by some Vietnamese as China loyalists.

The ethnic Chinese felt that their loyalty was in question. Some of the ethnic Chinese felt it was no longer safe for them to remain in Vietnam. Additionally, as middlepeople in the urban economy, their commercial and financial interests were uncertain.

Many Kampucheans also began to feel it was unsafe for them to remain in Kampuchea. The Communists, under the leadership of Pol Pot, took control of Cambodia in April 1975. The name of the country was changed from Cambodia to Kampuchea. Thousands of supporters of the former leader, Lon Nol, were killed. Many other Kampucheans died during the forced evacuation of the capital city of Phnom Penh and during the ongoing war with Vietnam. There was widespread starvation. The Laotian government fell in 1975. The Laotians, like the other Indochinese refugees, felt they had to leave their homeland because of fear of reprisals, political unheaval, and the uncertain future of Laos.

These ethnic Chinese, Laotians, Hmong, Kampucheans, and Vietnamese used their own resources to leave Indochina. Some paid large sums of money to escape in fishing boats. The boats were small, poorly constructed, and unsuitable for travel on the high seas. The refugees sailed to places as near as Thailand and as far away as Australia. The journeys were long, tiring, and dangerous with the threat of unpredictable weather, pirates, and mechanical breakdowns. If the refugees survived the sea journey, they often faced hardships in refugee camps in the Far East. Many of these refugees were called boat people by the press. Their journey to the United States and their experiences in the United States have been difficult. It is believed that sometimes as many as 50% of them perished on the perilous journey to America.

In the spring of 1976, 11,000 Indochinese, mostly Laotians, were admitted to the United States. By the end of 1976, 144,100 Indochinese had been admitted to the United States. In 1977, 4,300 Indochinese were admitted to the United States under President Carter's administration. In 1978, 27,900 additional Indochinese were authorized to enter the United States. There were an estimated 1,013,400 Vietnamese, Laotians, and Kampucheans in the United States by September 30, 1985.[12]

Even though there was some diversity within the second group of refugees, it was a more homogeneous group than the refugees who came to the United States in 1975. Most refugees who came after 1975 were not highly educated. Most of them did not speak English or have marketable skills. As a group, they were neither urbanized nor Westernized. Their expectations in terms of jobs and resettlement services tended to be lower than those of refugees who came in 1975. This group of refugees had a larger number of severe health problems than did the 1975 refugees. Many had suffered trauma as a result of their escape from Indochina and had been living in difficult circumstances in refugee camps in the Far East. Health examinations revealed cases of tuberculosis, infections, and a few cases of diphtheria.[13] These refugees were not as financially well off as some of the 1975 refugees.

Compared to the 1975 refugees, the refugees who came after 1975 received less government support for their resettlement. Refugees who received government help with their airfare to the United States had to sign a promissory note to repay a portion of that expense. Private volunteer agencies responsible for finding sponsors for them received a grant of $300 per refugee, compared to $500 per refugee for resettling the 1975 refugees. In addition, these refugees did not go to resettlement centers. Some Vietnamese refugees were able to join their relatives in newly formed Vietnamese communities in cities such as Los Angeles, Chicago, New Orleans, Dallas, and Houston. This gave them an advantage that the first refugees did not have. They were able to depend on the support of thriving Vietnamese communities to help them bridge the gap between the old and familiar Vietnamese culture and the new and sometimes baffling American life-styles and values.

Adjusting to Life in the United States

The Indochinese refugees have had varying experiences in the United States. Some of the refugees have more than adjusted to life in the United States; they have also prospered. In 1979, the median family income for Vietnamese families was $12,840, compared to $21,014 for Whites, $12,627 for African Americans, and $19,917 for all persons in the United States. Slightly more than 13% of Vietnamese (employed persons age 16 and over) held managerial and professional specialty jobs, compared to 24% for Whites and 14% for African Americans. About 27% of them held technical, sales, and administrative support occupations, compared to 31% for Whites, 25% for African Americans, and 30% for the total U.S. population. A significant percentage of Vietnamese workers were operators, fabricators, and laborers, 29.3%, compared to 16.7% for Whites, 26.6% for African Americans, and 18.2% for all persons in the United States.[14]

The success of some of the refugees is undoubtedly related to many factors, including hard work, thrift, family support, and the middle-class socio-economic and educational backgrounds of some of the families. In 1980, 62.2% of the Vietnamese who were 25 years or older were high school graduates, compared to 69.6% for Whites, 66.5% for all persons in the United States, and 51.2% for African Americans.[15] The government provided support by trying to create a sympathetic and supportive atmosphere for the refugees, as well as providing both economic support and education programs. High government officials, including two presidents, strongly encouraged the nation to welcome the Indochinese refugees. In addition, the government spent more than one-half billion dollars in refugee assistance. Some of the refugees, particularly those who were educated and middle-class, were prepared to take advantage of employment and/or educational opportunities as they became available. These individuals are well on their way to achieving the American dream. Their experience, however, has not been representative of the total refugee population. Many Indochinese refugees have found adjusting to life and making a living in the United States difficult. Thirty-five percent of Vietnamese families in the United States had incomes below the poverty level in 1979, compared to 4.2% for the Japanese, 6.6% for Whites, 26.4% for African Americans, and 9.6% for all persons in the United States.[16]

Many Indochinese refugees have had to make a number of psychological, social, and economic adjustments. Their arrival in the United States was filled with traumatic and emotional circumstances associated with the war and evacuation. The uncertainty of refugee status itself can cause psychological stress. Many refugees had to leave family members in Indochina; in some cases, this has resulted in long-term depression. Some refugees have not made the adjustment to life in the United States. A few have taken their own lives; many have been divorced. Traditionally, divorce was not common in their homelands.

The cultural shock of being thrust almost overnight into a new and different environment has jolted many refugees. This relocation has meant exposure to a new language, values, life-styles, and statuses. Most of the Indochinese left nations where they were part of the ethnic majority. They now have to adjust to being ethnic and racial minorities.

While some refugees have been able to maintain or even improve their economic statuses, many have had to experience dramatic downward economic mobility. For refugees who were middle-class, adjusting to a lower-status job can be difficult. Many people who were professionals in Indochina have had to take jobs that do not in any way reflect their training or former status. There are Indochinese lawyers working as busboys or in factories, and doctors who are unable to practice medicine because of their lack of facility with English and their inability to meet professional requirements due to the language barrier and past training. In some families in which the father has traditionally been a high wage earner, the wife or children now earn more money than he. In such situations the father may see his role as head of the family threatened. This can lead to a stressful situation for the entire family.

The tensions involved in downward economic and social mobility were not always understood by sponsors and sometimes led to conflict. Sponsors, who were keenly aware of their financial responsibilities and the difficulty with finding jobs, sometimes found it hard to understand why a refugee would not take a particular job or how the family could ask for more financial support.[17]

Conflicts also resulted from the values the children learned at school and the behavior parents expected at home. In traditional Indochinese cultures children are expected to respect older people. They demonstrate that respect by being quiet, polite, modest, and humble. These behaviors are often viewed negatively by teachers and school administrators. The American school tries to help children become more independent, vocal, and assertive. The conflicting behavioral expectations of the home and school sometimes confuse children and put them in the position of choosing one set of behaviors rather than the other. This choice devalues one set of behaviors and exalts the other.

The Development of the Indochinese Community

The stresses that resulted from psychological, social, and economic adjustments were often faced within the family because the refugees were isolated from other Indochinese families. The Indochinese refugees increasingly began to feel a need for an ethnic community that could help bridge the gap between life in

Indochina and life in the United States. A significant number of refugees began moving from their original settlement sites. Within 6 months of their assignment to a sponsor, the Indochinese refugees began to establish and move to Vietnamese communities, primarily in California and Texas. By 1978, about half of the refugees had moved from their original locations. In 1975, about 20% of the refugees lived in California. By 1985, about 40% lived there. Table 14–3 identifies the location of the estimated population of the Indochinese refugees in selected states as of January 31, 1985. Although such movements were sometimes viewed as ingratitude by sponsors, the refugees felt that their new communities fulfilled needs that could not be met outside their ethnic communities.

The ethnic communities provided newspapers, employment services, and social clubs. Perhaps most important, they provided a link with the life the refugees had left in Indochina. When the refugees left their original settlement sites, they were rejecting their ethnic isolation and perhaps their relegation to lower-class status. The cities provided them with opportunities to live in ethnic communities with psychological support systems and familiar cultural components. Even though moving meant the loss of sponsorship, the refugees were able to participate in a number of government-sponsored educational and social service programs in their new communities.

American Reactions to the Indochinese Refugees

When the first large numbers of Indochinese started settling in the United States, the nation was experiencing one of its severest economic recessions. Unemployment had soared: more than 8 million Americans were out of work.

More and more Americans were receiving government assistance. A Harris poll taken in May 1975 indicated that only 36% of the American public felt the Vietnamese should be admitted to the United States; 54% felt that they should be excluded.[18] The economic condition of the nation was a factor in anti-Indochinese feelings; nativism and racism were also important factors. Arguing against U.S. acceptance of the Indochinese refugees, one California congressman said that feelings among his constituents could be summed up as, "Damn it, we have too many Orientals."

Ugly incidents occurred in some cities in which the Indochinese settled. About 120 Vietnamese settled in Seadrift, a small town in Texas. Seadrift had a population of 1,000. Initially, the Indochinese worked in crab-processing plants. However, they eventually were able to purchase fishing boats and become fishermen. Disputes between the local fishermen and the Indochinese fishermen developed over their different fishing practices. The disputes were not resolved, and violence broke out. Three boats belonging to the Indochinese were burned, the home of an Indochinese family was firebombed, and the Ku Klux Klan began harassing the refugees.

Ethnic minority leaders have consistently spoken out for the rights of the Indochinese. However, limited resources and what was perceived as favoritism

Table 14–3   *The Population of Indochinese Refugees in Selected States (January 1985)*

State	Estimated Population
California	290,200
Texas	52,500
Washington	33,300
New York	25,500
Pennsylvania	24,300
Illinois	24,000
Minnesota	23,000
Virginia	21,400
Massachusetts	20,100
Oregon	17,400
Louisiana	13,800
Florida	11,800
Colorado	10,800
Wisconsin	10,500
Michigan	10,100
Ohio	9,900

Source: Office of Refugee Resettlement.

have resulted in a few isolated incidents between the Indochinese and other ethnic minority groups. American ethnic minorities and the Indochinese refugees have often competed for the same low-cost housing, jobs, and government assistance. Some ethnic minorities felt that the Indochinese refugees were given preferential treatment in several areas. Some suspected Whites of using Indochinese refugees to meet government guidelines related to housing and affirmative action, while denying housing and job opportunities to native minorities such as African Americans and Mexican Americans.

Americans did not seem to respond to the Indochinese based on their political orientations. Opposition to, as well as support for, the Indochinese refugees came from both political liberals and conservatives. Some conservatives argued against admitting the refugees because they believed that there were too many unscrupulous generals and businesspeople among them who had been able to force or bribe their way out of Vietnam. Other conservatives supported admitting the refugees because they felt that they would work for low wages and take jobs that Americans would not accept. Some liberals maintained that the refugees should be admitted to the United States because of our role in Vietnam. Like many other Americans, they felt that the United States had a moral obligation to the Indochinese refugees because of the role of our nation in the Vietnam War.

While the reaction to the refugees has been mixed, most Americans welcomed the Indochinese refugees into their communities. The Indochinese will continue their adjustment to their new homeland. They are now in the process of moving from refugees to immigrants and becoming full-fledged Americans. They have already demonstrated that they have the will and determination to become full and active participants in American society.

Teaching Strategies

Primary Grades

CONCEPT: Names (Similarities and Differences)

Generalization: We all have names. However, our different names often give other people clues about our different origins, cultures, and experiences.

Introduction

Similarities and *differences* are two concepts that can be effectively taught in the primary grades. These concepts can be understood by young children when they are taught with concrete examples. A unit on names can help primary grade children learn that even though we all have names (a similarity), our names often give other people clues about our different origins, experiences, and cultural backgrounds. It is appropriate to help children better understand the nature and origins of names when they are studying about the Indochinese because teachers and students often find Vietnamese names difficult to pronounce and understand.

1. Begin this unit by telling the class that the people who live in our nation, the United States [point it out to the children on a primary globe], came from many different nations and lands. Ask the students: "Can you name some of the nations from which the people in the United States came?" Record accurate responses on the board or butcher paper.

Using a primary globe, show the students some of the nations and continents from which immigrants to the United States came. Ask the students if any of them have ever traveled to any of these nations and continents. If any of them have, ask them to tell briefly about their trips.

Say to the class: "The ancestors of American Indians came to what is now the United States thousands of years ago. The ancestors of many Jews and Italians came to the United States almost 100 years ago. Other Americans, such as many Cubans and Vietnamese, have lived in the United States for fewer than 20 years. People from different parts of the world have many different ways of living, often believe different things, eat different kinds of food, and have different religions. Often people from various nations keep some of their differences after they have lived in the United States for many years. People in various nations often have different kinds of names. Many Americans, whose ancestors came from many different nations or who came from different nations themselves, have names that sound and look different from the names of other groups. These different kinds of names give us clues about the homelands of their ancestors or about their homelands, and about their ways of life and beliefs."

Write the following names on the board or butcher paper:

Susan Schmidt
Juan Rivera Sanchez
Jennifer Kim
Patrick O'Shea
Ito Matsuda
Wing Chu
Katherine Ann Shilenski
Hoang Hy Vinh

Say to the class: "Here are the names of eight of the children in Mrs. Gonzales's third-grade class in a school in Los Angeles. Do their names give us any clues about where their ancestors came from, about what foods they might eat, and about which holidays they might celebrate?"

After giving the students an opportunity to state their ideas about what the children's names reveal about them, tell them a little about each of the eight students in Mrs. Gonzales's class. A brief description of each student follows.

Susan Schmidt. Susan's ancestors came to the United States from Germany in the 1820s. However, Susan says she is a *complete* American. She has no German characteristics that she knows about.

Ask the class: "Why do you think Susan has an American, rather than a German, given name? Why does she consider herself completely American rather than part German? Do any of you have German names? If so, do you feel totally American or part German? Why?"

Juan Rivera Sanchez. Juan was born in Mexico and moved to Los Angeles last year. Unlike Susan's name, Juan's name includes both his father's surname (Rivera), and his mother's maiden surname (Sanchez). This is a common practice in Spanish-speaking nations. In Mexico, it is correct to call Juan, "Mr. Rivera."

Ask the class: "Why do you think that in Spanish-speaking nations children's names often include both their father's surname and their mother's surname before marriage? If your name included both of your parents' surnames (and not just your father's), how would your name be written? If you don't know your mother's surname before she married, ask a parent tonight and be prepared to share your name written with your father's surname and your mother's surname before she married." (*Note*: Some of the children's mothers might use their maiden surnames, rather than the surnames of their spouses. Some of them may also be single parents who have never used any other surname.)

Jennifer Kim. Jennifer's grandparents came to the United States during the Korean War in 1952. Jennifer does not speak Korean but enjoys Korean foods. She also likes to visit her relatives who speak Korean and talk about what life was like in Korea.

Ask the class: "Why do you think Jennifer has an American, rather than a Korean, given name? Do you think Jennifer feels like a total American, or part Korean and part American? Why do you think she feels this way?"

Patrick O'Shea. Patrick's great-grandparents came to the United States from Ireland. He thinks of himself as both Irish and American—as an "Irish American."

Ask the class: "Why do you think Patrick feels more Irish than Susan feels German?"

Ito Matsuda. Ito was born in Japan and came to the United States when he was 2 years old. Ito speaks Japanese and English. He feels that he is both Japanese and American. At home, the Matsuda family usually eats Japanese, rather than American, food. Most of the time the Matsudas speak Japanese, rather than English, when talking to each other.

Ask the class: "Why do you think Ito is more Japanese than Jennifer is Korean?"

Wing Chu. Wing's family moved from China to the United States last year. Wing is still learning to speak English. Most of his family's friends are Chinese. He lives in a Chinese neighborhood.

Ask the class: "Do you think Wing feels Chinese and American, or Chinese? Why do you think he feels this way?"

Katherine Ann Shilenski. Katherine's grandparents came to the United States from Poland before her parents were born. Katherine does not speak Polish. She knows only a little about the Polish culture. She has often heard her parents talk about the problems of the people in Poland. Katherine is interested in learning more about the culture and language of her ancestors. She hopes to visit Poland someday.

Ask the class: "Why do you think Katherine feels more Polish than Susan feels German?"

Hoang Hy Vinh. Vinh came to the United States with his parents from Vietnam three years ago. Vinh's name is different in one important way from the names of his classmates. His surname (Hoang) is written first, his middle name (Hy) next, and his first or given name last (Vinh). Because of respect for him and his ancestors, the people in Vietnam would not address Vinh by his surname.[19] Rather, they would call him "Vinh" or "Mr. Vinh." Point out to the class how Susan's, Jennifer's, Juan's, and Patrick's names, and most of their names, are written differently from Vinh's. Ask the students to write their names in the Vietnamese way and read them aloud.

Ask the class: "What problems do you think Vinh's teachers and classmates might have with his name? How do you think these problems make Vinh feel? If you moved to Vietnam and went to school, what do you think the teachers and students would call you? Why? How do you think this would make you feel?"

2. Tell the students to ask their parents to tell them the national origins of their surnames. End this unit by making a chart on butcher paper (or on the board) that shows each student's surname and the nation from which it came. Ask the children to tell as much as they can about the nations from which their surnames came, and whether their families eat foods, celebrate holidays, or have customs related to those nations. Second

and third grade students can do research on these nations using a source such as *Britannica Junior.*

Note: Some children in your class might not be able to find out the nations from which their surnames came. It is difficult, for example, for many Blacks to find out the national origins of their surnames. In these cases, label their names *American* on the class chart and ask these students to tell what American customs their families practice.

Intermediate and Upper Grades

CONCEPT: Refugee

Generalization. Refugees are individuals and groups who leave their homelands to settle in other nations in order to escape expulsion or persecution that results from political changes.

Give the students copies of the following statements and ask them to study them carefully.

1. The Jews and the Moors were forced to leave Spain in the late fifteenth century.
2. During the Russian Revolution of 1917, about one and one-half million people who opposed communism left Russia because they believed their lives were endangered.
3. On June 25, 1950, North Korean troops invaded South Korea and captured the city of Seoul. Because of the war that resulted, 9 million people who opposed communism left Korea and settled in other nations. The Korean War lasted from June 25, 1950, to July 27, 1953.
4. About 190,000 Hungarians fled their country after a revolution against communism occurred there in 1956, and 21,000 of these Hungarians were airlifted to New Jersey.
5. In 1959, Fidel Castro overthrew the government of Fulgencio Batista in Cuba. More than 155,000 Cubans came to the United States between January 1959 and 1962. They came to the United States because they did not want to live under the newly established Cuban communist government.
6. In 1975, thousands of people fled Vietnam, Laos, and Kampuchea because of the communist takeover in these Indochinese nations. Most of these individuals opposed the communist government and economic system that were being established in Indochina.

After the students have carefully studied each example, ask them: "How are these examples alike? How are they different? What are the most important characteristics that these examples have in common? What words or phrases can be used to describe these statements as a group?"

On the board, list the words and phrases the students provide. The students might offer words and phrases such as *forced immigrants, uprooted immigrants,* and *political immigrants.* Tell the students that words such as these are accurate, but that social scientists usually use the concept *refugee* to describe the individuals and groups in these examples.

Through further discussion of the above examples of refugees and others that you and the students might provide, help the students formulate the following characteristics of refugees:

1. Their movements tend to be motivated primarily by political developments rather than by multiple factors, as is the case with most other immigrants. However, point out to the students that during the movements of political refugees, some individuals within these groups immigrate, in part, for economic reasons. This was especially true during the immigration of the Indochinese refugees to the United States in the 1970s. Often the individuals who come to the United States as political refugees believe that the new political orders in their native lands will be harmful to their economic statuses and to their political lives.

2. Refugees do not usually freely choose the nations into which they immigrate, as do most other immigrants. Rather, they settle in nations that are willing to accept them as political refugees. There is less volunteerism in their movements than in the movements of most other immigrant groups.

3. Refugees often perceive their stay in their new nations as temporary and usually plan to return to their native lands as soon as there are changes in the political statuses of these nations. Often, however, political refugees, such as many Cubans and Vietnamese in the United States, gradually begin to perceive themselves as permanent residents of their new nations as the possibility of political changes in their homelands becomes increasingly remote. They also begin to assimilate into the cultures and to adopt the values and ways of life of the new nations. Their children are likely to have little interest in their parents' homelands and to share many cultural characteristics with the native residents of the new nations.

4. The movement of refugees into new nations tends to be highly concentrated in time and numbers, as opposed to the more gradual coming of other immigrants who arrive during a longer period of time. Between 1965 and 1970, 300,000 Cubans were airlifted to the United States. After the fall of Saigon in 1975, about 120,000 Vietnamese arrived in the United States by air within 2 weeks.

5. Refugees often view the situations in their original homelands as life-threatening. Their movements and adjustments in their new nations tend to be traumatic and sudden, and to result in moral and psychological disorientation.

6. The criteria for determining whether individuals and groups are political refugees often become difficult to develop and implement and thus capricious. In 1980, between January and August, more than 14,000 Haitians entered the United States. An acid debate developed over whether they should be considered political refugees. Some leaders argued that the Haitians were coming to the United States to escape poverty (Haiti is the poorest nation in the Western Hemisphere) and not political persecution. Other leaders maintained that the Haitians should be considered political refugees and that they were denied that classification because they were Black.

Assign six groups of students to (1) gather more information about the refugees described in the earlier examples, (2) test the six generalizations above about refugees using the information they gather, (3) derive further generalizations about refugees that do not appear above, and (4) extend the definition of refugee given in the generalization that appears at the beginning of this exercise (the definitional generalization on page 471). When the students have finished their research, ask them to share the information they have gathered with the rest of the class in the form of oral reports, simulated television programs, roleplaying, and other creative ways. The students can use the data retrieval chart illustrated in Table 14–4 to guide their research and to organize their reports.

Enrichment Activity

During their study of refugees, some of your more able students might be interested in examining the *process* by which refugees change their psychological and cultural status from *refugees*, to *immigrants*, to *ethnic Americans*. Give the students the diagram in Figure 14–2 and the definitions below (in more simplified language). Ask them to apply these definitions to the study of several different groups that came to the United States as refugees, such as the Hungarians and the Indochinese, and to determine which of the three stages they are in today and why.

Definitions

Refugee: The refugee enters the new nation because of political changes and hopes to return to his or her homeland as soon as a new political order is established there. Refugees do not usually freely choose their new nations.

Immigrant: The immigrant has accepted the new nation as his or her permanent home. However, the immigrant still has strong personal and psychological attachments to the original homeland.

Ethnic American: The ethnic American considers his or her first identity as American and does not have strong psychological and personal attachments to the ancestral homeland. The ethnic traits and characteristics of the ethnic American are strongly influenced by his or her experiences and socialization in the United States.

Valuing Activity

Tuyen's Decision

Tuyen knew that the war was going badly for South Vietnam. As a South Vietnamese pilot who had participated in several bombings of North Vietnam, he

Table 14–4 *Refugees in Various Historical Periods*

	Jewish-Spanish Refugees (15th century)	Moorish-Spanish Refugees (15th century)	Russian Refugees (1917)	Korean Refugees (1950–1953)	Hungarian Refugees (1956)	Cuban Refugees (1959–1960)	Indochinese Refugees (1975–1978)
Why did they leave their homelands?							
In what nations did they settle?							
How many returned to their homelands?							
What is the political status of their homelands today?							
What is their political status in their new nations today?							
What is their economic status in their new nations today?							

Figure 14–2 *From Refugee to Ethnic American*

Refugees arrive at their new nations hoping to return as soon as the political orders in these nations change. They become immigrants when they accept their new nations as permanent homes and voluntarily choose to stay. Immigrants become ethnic Americans when their primary identity is American rather than foreign. The expanding sizes of the circles indicate that refugees become increasingly more American as they move from refugee to ethnic American status.

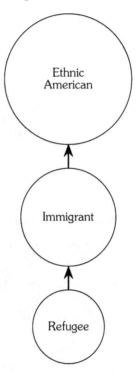

believed he would be killed if the North Vietnamese took over Vietnam. Several of his friends talked about flying their planes to Thailand if a North Vietnamese victory was announced.

Tuyen began to make plans to leave Vietnam. He talked to all 16 members of his family and told them to be prepared to leave Vietnam when he sent them word. They would meet at his uncle's home. His uncle lived in a small village a few hours from Saigon. They would go to his plane and fly to Thailand from there.

On April 27, 1975, with North Vietnamese soldiers on the outskirts of Saigon, Tuyen sent word to his family to meet him the next day and be prepared to leave Vietnam. When Tuyen arrived at his uncle's home, several members of his family were crying. There was much sadness. All of the family members were there. However, his father-in-law, Thuy, refused to leave Vietnam. He was ill and expected to die within the year. More than anything else, Thuy did not want to die in a strange land. He said he wanted his bones to rest in the land of his ancestors. Tuyen's mother-in-law would not leave her husband. Tuyen's wife, Thanh, was sad because if she left Vietnam, there wouldn't be anyone left to care for her elderly parents. She wanted her parents with her. To leave them would be like leaving a part of herself. Thanh also knew that if she stayed in Vietnam, Tuyen would find it painful to leave. He would not want to dishonor himself by leaving his wife. However, if Tuyen stayed in Vietnam, he believed he would be killed.

A decision had to be made quickly. If they did not leave within the hour, Tuyen would not be able to get to his plane and they would all have to stay in Vietnam.

Questions

1. What is the main problem in this situation?
2. What do you think Thuy should do? Why?
3. What do you think Thanh should do? Why?
4. What is the most important thing an individual owes his or her family?
5. What should Tuyen do? Why?

High School Grades

CONCEPT: Cultural Differences and Similarities

Generalization: There are important similarities and differences within and between ethnic group cultures in the United States.

The study of the Indochinese in the United States provides an excellent opportunity to help students better understand the similarities and differences between and within various ethnic cultures in the United States. The most important variables that distinguish one culture from another are not concrete cultural artifacts, such as ways of dressing and foods. Life-styles, values, and attitudes are the important variables that distinguish one culture from another, or that join them together.

A careful study of Asian values and attitudes in the United States will reveal that there are important values and attitudes that Asian-American cultures share. However, there are important differences in the ways in which these values and attitudes are manifested. The different histories of Asian nations such as China, Japan, and Vietnam are an important source of the diversity within Asian cultures. Novak recommends the cross-cultural study of ethnic groups and suggests eight important attitudes that students can examine when comparing cultures.[20]

1. Attitudes toward the divine, the sacred, or the holy.
2. Attitudes toward nature, history, and moral striving.
3. Attitudes toward intelligence, learning, and ideas.

4. Attitudes toward the rein to be given passion and emotion, and in which respects.
5. Attitudes toward authority, the past, tradition.
6. Attitudes toward the individuality or the communality of human living, toward solitude and solidarity, self, and family.
7. Attitudes toward masculinity and fathering: toward femininity and mothering.
8. Attitudes toward the power of goodness and the power of evil in human affairs.

Writes Novak, "Cultures, like individuals, differ remarkably from one another in such matters. One might turn to rites of passage, to sports, to ceremonies of birth, and marriage and death, and to other locations in each culture for clues as to how the above-mentioned attitudes are passed on to new generations. There are many methods for studying such attitudes."[21]

High school students can gain valuable insights into different Asian cultures, into other American ethnic cultures, and into their own ethnic cultures by examining the expression of the attitudes identified by Novak within the Vietnamese, Japanese, Chinese, Jewish, and Anglo-American communities. Jewish culture is an interesting one to examine while studying Asian cultures because both Jews and Asians are economically and educationally successful ethnic groups. Many Anglo-American Protestant values contrast sharply with some traditional Asian values. In Anglo-American culture, individualism and attachment to a nuclear family are highly valued. However, within many Asian cultures, group rights are more important than individual rights, and attachment to family is primarily to the extended family. Studying the Anglo-American culture is important while studying Asian cultures not only because much of it contrasts with Asian cultures, but also because most American students are Anglo-Americans. Consequently, many students will be able to study their own culture in juxtaposition with several Asian cultures and with Jewish culture.

Reference materials exist that able high school readers can use successfully to complete this unit. The students will encounter one serious problem: Writers tend to describe the traditional values of ethnic groups without indicating how these values are changing or have changed among highly assimilated and urbanized members of these groups. Highly assimilated and urbanized Vietnamese-American individuals are likely to have more commitment to their nuclear than to their extended families. Consequently, in the data retrieval chart in Table 14–5, which students can use as a guide for studying the values of these ethnic groups, the students are asked to indicate how the values of these groups are expressed in their *original* and *Americanized* forms of these cultures.

Students can be divided into five groups to study these cultures (with one group studying both the original and Americanized forms of each culture). When their research is complete, the students should share their findings with their classmates. At that time, the class can collectively insert the necessary information in the data retrieval chart in Table 14–5.

Table 14–5 *Data Retrieval Chart: The Attitudes of Ethnic Groups*

Attitudes	Vietnamese		Japanese		Chinese		Jewish		Anglo-Saxon	
	Original	American	Original	American	Original	American	Original	American	Original	American
The divine, the sacred, or the holy										
Nature, history, and moral striving										
Intelligence, learning, and ideas										
Passion and emotion										
Authority, the past, and tradition										
Individuality or communality of human living (self, family)										
Masculinity and femininity										
Power of goodness and evil										

When initiating this study of cultures, the teacher should begin the unit by helping students to develop specific and clear definitions of each concept identified by Novak. The teacher should also make sure that the students can identify and recognize examples of each of these types of values. A high value is placed on learning and education in traditional Vietnamese and Jewish cultures. The Vietnamese have a strong loyalty to family, which they value more than individuality, whereas in Anglo-American culture individuality is highly valued. In Japanese culture, self-needs are considered less important than group needs. However, the values of these ethnic groups are mediated as they become more assimilated members of American society.

The teacher can effectively conclude this unit by asking each student to use the eight values identified by Novak to write a description of his or her own family and community culture. These papers should be submitted to the teacher for evaluation. However, the students should be able to decide whether they want to share them with their classmates.

Endnotes

1. Mary Brown Wright, "Indochinese," *Harvard Encyclopedia of American Ethnic Groups*, eds. Stephan Thernstrom, Ann Orlov, and Oscar Handlin (Cambridge: Harvard University Press, 1980), p. 508.

2. John W. Wright, *The Universal Almanac 1990* (Kansas City: Andrews and McMeel, 1989), p. 236.

3. Kenneth A. Skinner, "Vietnamese in America: Diversity in Adaptation," *California Sociologist 3* (Summer 1980): 102–125.

4. Gail Paradise Kelly, *From Vietnam to America: A Chronicle of Vietnamese Immigration to the United States* (Boulder, Colo.: Westview Press, 1977).

5. Ibid., p. 47.

6. Ibid., p. 48.

7. Wright, "Indochinese," p. 510.

8. Kelly, *From Vietnam to America*, p. 129.

9. Darrel Montero, *Vietnamese Americans: Patterns of Resettlement and Socio-economic Adaptation in the United States* (Boulder, Colo.: Westview Press, 1979), p. 27.

10. "Report of Interagency Task Force on Indochina Refugees Transmitted to the Congress," *Department of State Bulletin*, 28 July 1975, p. 136.

11. Kelly, *From Vietnam to America*, p. 139.

12. Robert W. Gardner, Bryant Robey, and Peter C. Smith, *Asian Americans: Growth, Change, and Diversity* (Washington, D.C.: Population Reference Bureau, Inc., 1985), p.5.

13. Kelly, *From Vietnam to America*, p. 139.

14. U.S. Bureau of the Census, *General Social and Economic Characteristics*, Part 1, United States Summary, PC80–1–C1.

15. Ibid.

16. Ibid.

17. Skinner, "Vietnamese in America," p. 112.

18. "A Cool and Wary Reception," *Time*, 12 May 1975, p. 24.

19. Duong Thanh Binh, *A Handbook for Teachers of Vietnamese Students: Hints for Dealing with Cultural Differences in Schools* (Arlington, Va.: Center for Applied Linguistics, 1975), p. 9.

20. Michael Novak, "Pluralism: A Humanistic Perspective," in *Harvard Encyclopedia of American Ethnic Groups*, eds. Stephan Thernstrom, Ann Orlov, and Oscar Handlin (Cambridge: Harvard University Press, 1980), p. 780.

21. Ibid.

Annotated Bibliography

Books for Teachers

Bannerian, James, ed. *Vietnamese Short Stories: An Introduction*. Phoenix: Sphinx, 1986.

These short stories will help students understand the culture of the Vietnamese in their homeland.

Caplan, Nathan; Whitmore, John K.; and Choy, Marcella H. *The Boat People and Achievement in America: A Study of Family Life, Hard Work, and Cultural Values.* Ann Arbor: The University of Michigan Press, 1989.

The cultural values, family factors, and psychological factors that explain the academic success of Indochinese students are discussed in this research report. This study is based on data collected over a 5-year period from surveys in Boston, Chicago, Houston, Seattle, and Orange County, California.

Edelman, Bernard, ed. *Dear America: Letters Home from Vietnam*. New York: Pocket Books, 1985.

This book contains 208 letters written by 125 men and women to spouses, friends, and lovers at home in the United States. The letters chill and pain but also inform.

Fawcett, James T., and Carino, Benjamin V., eds. *Pacific Bridges: The New Immigration from Asia and the Pacific Islands*. Staten Island, N.Y.: Center for Migration Studies, 1987.

This book, which presents perspectives from both the sending and receiving nations involved in Asian immigration, includes a chapter on "Southeast Asian Refugee Migration to the United States."

Freeman, James M. *Hearts of Sorrow: Vietnamese American Lives*. Stanford, Calif.: Stanford University Press, 1989.

Fourteen Vietnamese refugees tell about their journeys in Vietnam and America.

Haines, David W., ed. *Refugees as Immigrants: Cambodians, Laotians, and Vietnamese in America*. Totowa, N.J.: Rowman and Littlefield, 1989.

This book consists of a collection of research-based papers that discuss various aspects of the experiences of Indochinese Americans. "National Surveys of Southeast Asian Refugees: Methods, Findings, Issues" and "Differential Reference Group Assimilation among Refugees" are among the papers included.

—. *Refugees in the United States: A Reference Handbook.* Westport, Conn.: Greenwood Press, 1985.

A useful and informative reference book.

Hawthorne, Lesleyanne, ed. *Refugee: The Vietnamese Experience.* New York: Oxford University Press, 1982.

Twenty Vietnamese refugees who settled in Australia tell their stories in this book. This book can help teachers deal with ethnic-related issues in world studies units and courses.

Hayslip, Le Lay, with Wurts, Jay. *When Heaven and Earth Changed Places: A Vietnamese Woman's Journey from War to Peace.* New York: Doubleday, 1989.

A powerful and moving account of a woman's experiences in war-torn Vietnam and her experiences in the United States.

Hendricks, Glenn L.; Downing, Bruce T.; and Deinard, Amos, eds. *The Hmong in Transition.* Staten Island, N.Y.: Center for Migration Studies, 1986.

This collection of 25 papers discusses physical and mental health issues of the Hmong. Agency assistance problems, economic and development issues, religion, and female adaptation are among the topics discussed.

Huynh Dinh Te. *The Indochinese and Their Cultures.* Sacramento: California State Department of Education, 1987.

This teacher's aid book describes the peoples and cultures of Indochina.

—. *Introduction to Vietnamese Culture.* Sacramento: California State Department of Education, 1987.

The language, religion, and values system of the Vietnamese culture are among the topics discussed in this useful book for teachers.

—. *Selected Vietnamese Proverbs.* Oakland, Calif.: Center for International Communication and Development, 1988. (Order from JACP, P.O. Box 367, San Mateo, CA 94401)

These proverbs are in both English and Vietnamese.

Kelly, Gail Paradise. *From Vietnam to America: A Chronicle of Vietnamese Immigration to the United States.* Boulder, Colo.: Westview Press, 1977.

This is one of the most comprehensive and informative studies of the Vietnamese refugees. It focuses on the experiences of the refugees at Fort Indian Town Gap, Pennsylvania. However, much of this information is generalizable to most of the Indochinese refugees. This book contains interviews with refugees, observations made by the author at Fort Indian Town Gap, and statistics on many aspects of the refugees' lives.

—. "Southeast Asians in the United States." In *Dictionary of Asian American History,* edited by Hyung-Chan Kim. New York: Greenwood Press, 1986, pp. 39–49.

A readable and brief historical overview of the experience of Southeast Asian refugees in the United States.

Knoll, Tricia. *Becoming Americans: Asian Sojourners, Immigrants, and Refugees in the Western United States.* Portland, Ore.: Coast to Coast Books, 1982.

This book includes informative chapters on Vietnamese Americans, Laotian Americans, Kampuchean Americans, and the ethnic Chinese.

The National Coalition of Advocates for Students. *New Voices: Immigrant Students in U.S. Public Schools.* Boston: The National Coalition, 1988.

This book contains some useful information and guidelines for working with immigrant students in U.S. schools.

Special Service for Groups. *Bridging Cultures: Southeast Asian Refugees in America.* Los Angeles: Asian American Community Mental Health Training Center, 1983.

The informative papers that constitute this book include a range of articles that will help teachers understand the values and cultures of Southeast Asian refugees. Contains a helpful bibliography.

Strand, Paul J., and Jones, Woodrow J. *Indochinese Refugees in America: Problems of Adaptation and Assimilation.* Durham, N.C.: Duke University Press, 1985.

This excellent and well-researched book describes the nature and characteristics of the Indochinese refugees in the United States, as well as reports the findings of a study of refugees conducted in the San Diego, California, area.

Ta Van Tai. *The Vietnamese Tradition of Human Rights.* Berkeley: Institute of East Asian Studies, University of California, 1989.

Justice, equity, and respect for the integrity of individuals, as well as other values implicit in the Vietnamese tradition of human rights, are discussed in this book.

Vuong G. Thuy. *Getting to Know the Vietnamese and Their Culture.* New York: Frederick Ungar, 1976.

This informative and lucid book discusses the cultural background of the Vietnamese, their values and characteristics, and education in Vietnam. It is an excellent introductory source for teachers and high school students.

———— "The Indochinese in America: Who Are They and How Are They Doing?" In *The Education of Asian and Pacific Americans,* edited by Don T. Nakanishi. Phoenix: Oryx Press, 1983.

This article presents an overview of the experience and problems of Indochinese refugees in U.S. society and the schools.

Books for Students

Chi Nguyen and Monroe, Judy. *Cooking the Vietnamese Way.* Minneapolis: Learner, 1985.

A guide to cooking delicious Vietnamese foods. Illustrated with color photographs. (All Ages)

Coutant, Helen. *First Snow*. Illustrated by Vo Dinh. New York: Alfred A. Knopf, 1975.

> *A gentle story about a Vietnamese girl who tries to understand why her grandmother is dying. One of the few books for young children about the Vietnamese in the United States. This book is designed for primary grade children. (Primary)*

Goldfarb, Mace. *Fighters, Refugees, Immigrants: A Story of the Hmong*. Minneapolis: Carolrhoda Books, Inc., 1982.

> *The author, a medical doctor who went to Thailand to work with refugees, describes life at Ban Vinai, a Thai refugee camp. Illustrated with photographs. (Intermediate)*

Haskins, James. *The New Americans: Vietnamese Boat People*. Hillside, N.J.: Enslow Publishers, 1980.

> *This is an interesting and informative account of the settlement of the Vietnamese boat people for young readers. Illustrated with photographs. (Primary)*

Karnow, Stanley. *Vietnam: A History*. New York: Penguin Books, 1984.

> *A popular, highly readable, and comprehensive history, this book gives a complete account of the Vietnam War and its aftermath. It was a companion to the Public Broadcasting System (PBS) series on Vietnam. (High School)*

Lee, Jeanne M. *Toad Is the Uncle of Heaven*. New York: Holt, 1985.

> *Young readers will enjoy this delightful and colorful Vietnamese folktale about how Toad goes to heaven with several other animals to persuade the king to send rain to the dry earth. (Primary)*

Rutledge, Paul. *The Vietnamese in America*. Minneapolis: Lerner, 1987.

> *An informative historical account of the journey of the Vietnamese to the United States and their experiences in their new land. Illustrated with photographs. Includes a chapter on "Some Notable Vietnamese Americans." (Intermediate/Middle School)*

Trân-Khán-Tuyêt. Illustrations by Nancy Hom. *The Little Weaver of Thai-Yen Village*, rev. ed. San Francisco: Children's Book Press, 1987.

> *A true story about a young Vietnamese girl who is brought to the United States after her parents are killed in the war. Bilingual: Vietnamese/English. (Primary)*

Wartski, Maureen Crane. *A Boat to Nowhere*. Philadelphia: Westminster Press, 1980.

> *This story tells how a young boy faces the dangers of the sea in an attempt to find freedom. (Intermediate)*

———. *A Long Way from Home*. Philadelphia: Westminster Press, 1980.

> *Kien, a Vietnamese teenager, has difficulty adapting to his new life in the United States. He leaves the home of his adoptive parents and goes to live in a Vietnamese fishing village. (Middle School)*

Willcox, Don. *Hmong Folklife*. Penland: Hmong Natural Association of North Carolina, 1986. (Order from JACP, P.O. Box 367, San Mateo, CA 94401)

> *Hmong language, music, religion, clothing, courtship, marriage, and children and their games are among the topics discussed in this informative book about the culture of the Hmong. (All Ages)*

Part VI

Multicultural

Units and

Evaluation

Part I discusses the goals and trends in the multicultural curriculum, key concepts, and ways to organize and plan the multicultural curriculum. Parts II through V present content about ethnic groups and strategies and materials that can be incorporated into the school curriculum. Part VI highlights and summarizes the major points discussed in the previous chapters and illustrates how you can use the information and strategies in Parts I through V to develop and teach multicultural units and curricula that focus on several different ethnic and cultural groups. The major components of a sample multicultural unit are presented in the first part of chapter 15, the chapter that constitutes Part VI. The second part of the chapter highlights the need for planned evaluation within an effective multicultural curriculum and discusses strategies for evaluating the components of decision making and the total school environment.

Chapter 15

Multicultural Units

and Evaluation

Strategies

Identifying Key Concepts

When planning a multicultural unit, you should first decide which key concepts you will use to organize the unit. As stated in chapter 3, these concepts should be higher-level ones that are capable of encompassing a wide range of data and information. Concepts chosen for the multicultural unit should also be inter-disciplinary. Interdisciplinary concepts are capable of encompassing facts, gener-alizations, and examples from several disciplines and content areas. Concepts drawn from the various behavioral sciences, such as culture, social protest, and intercultural communication, can be used effectively to organize interdisciplinary units and lessons. The rationale for an interdisciplinary curriculum is presented in chapter 3. I have selected the following key concepts for the sample unit discussed in this chapter:

Key Concept	*Discipline*
cultural assimilation	anthropology
economic status	economics
ethnic community	geography
immigration	geography–history
social protest	political science
identity	psychology
discrimination	sociology

Identifying Key
and Intermediate-Level Generalizations

After you have identified organizing concepts, key generalizations related to each of the concepts should be chosen. Ideally, you should identify a key or universal generalization for each concept and then an intermediate-level gener-alization for each concept. A universal generalization applies to all cultures, times, and peoples (see pages 45–46). An intermediate-level generalization is limited in its application to a particular nation, subculture, or time period. Thus, a generalization that applies only to the United States is an intermediate-level generalization. In the following examples, I identify a universal generalization and an intermediate-level generalization for the first concept, *cultural assimilation*, but only intermediate-level generalizations for the other key concepts.

KEY CONCEPT: Cultural Assimilation

Key or Universal Generalization: Whenever a minority group comes into contact with a dominant culture, it is usually expected to acquire the culture and values of the dominant group.

Intermediate-Level Generalization: In the United States, ethnic minority groups are expected to acquire the culture and values of the mainstream American culture.

KEY CONCEPT: Economic Status

Intermediate-Level Generalization: Because of racial discrimination and other factors, members of U.S. minority groups are often paid low wages for their work. Consequently, most of them are members of the lower socio-economic classes.

KEY CONCEPT: Ethnic Community

Intermediate-Level Generalization: U.S. ethnic groups that have strong ethnic identities and characteristics often live in ethnic neighborhoods and communities.

KEY CONCEPT: Immigration

Intermediate-Level Generalization: Most ethnic groups came to the United States or moved within it to improve their economic conditions. However, some ethnic groups were either forced to come to the United States or were forced to move from one region of it to another.

KEY CONCEPT: Social Protest

Intermediate-Level Generalization: Throughout their experiences in the United States, ethnic minorities have resisted discrimination and oppression in various ways.

KEY CONCEPT: Identity

Intermediate-Level Generalization: During the 1960s and 1970s, ethnic groups in the United States became increasingly aware of their ethnic identities and expressed them in various ways.

KEY CONCEPT: Discrimination

Intermediate-Level Generalization: Most ethnic groups in the United States have been the victims of various kinds of discrimination. Ethnic groups of color still experience discrimination in contemporary U.S. society.

Determining Which Ethnic Groups to Include in the Unit

After the key and intermediate-level generalizations have been identified, you should decide which ethnic groups will be included in the unit. It is neither possible nor desirable to include every U.S. ethnic group within a particular unit or curriculum. For each unit, you should select several ethnic groups that best illustrate the particular concepts you are trying to teach. *In conceptual teaching, the major goal is to help students master higher-level concepts and generalizations.* Which particular ethnic groups are selected to illustrate the concepts chosen for study is a secondary but important consideration.

As pointed out earlier, it is essential that certain concepts be taught in an effective multicultural curriculum. These concepts include racism, discrimination, prejudice, social protest, and culture. In each unit, you should not only include groups that best exemplify particular concepts but should also be sure that a *range* of ethnic groups is selected for study. Groups that vary in cultural characteristics, geographical location, socioeconomic status, racial characteristics, history, and level of assimilation should be selected for study. During the course of the year, a variety of ethnic groups should be studied, although only several will be studied within a particular unit. In one unit, for example, you may wish to focus on African Americans, Anglo-Americans, Chinese Americans, and Jewish Americans. In another, the focus may be on Mexican Americans, Anglo-Americans, Japanese Americans, and Polish Americans. I am including African Americans, Mexican Americans, Puerto Ricans, Jewish Americans, and American Indians in the exemplary unit outlined in this chapter.

Identifying Low-Level Generalizations

After the ethnic groups to be included in the unit have been identified, you should then identify low-level generalizations (see Table 4–2) related to each key concept and to each ethnic group chosen for study. Low-level generalizations are low-level statements that explain how the experiences of specific groups are related to the key concepts and generalizations. In the examples below, I have identified low-level generalizations for each of the key concepts as they relate to African Americans, one ethnic group chosen for study in our sample unit. However, in an actual unit, you should identify low-level generalizations for each group chosen for study.

Ethnic Group: African Americans

Cultural Assimilation: To attain economic and social mobility, African Americans must usually acquire the behavior, values, and norms of the dominant middle-class culture in the United States.

Economic Status: Because of job discrimination, low educational levels, and other factors, most African Americans are members of the lower socio-economic classes. However, there is a significant Black middle class.

Ethnic Community: Many African Americans live in ethnic communities called "ghettos" by the dominant society. However, as individual African Americans attain higher social status and higher levels of cultural assimilation, they tend to move out of their ethnic communities.

Immigration: Ethnic groups who immigrated to America came voluntarily to improve their economic conditions; most African Americans were forced to come to America as slaves.

Social Protest: Since they were first captured on the west coast of Africa, African Americans have systematically protested against oppression and discrimination. Their forms of protest have reflected the times in which they occurred.

Identity: In the 1960s, African Americans attempted to shape a new identity and to reject the view of themselves that had been perpetuated by the dominant society.

Discrimination: Since they landed in America, African Americans have been the victims of racism and discrimination. Discrimination against African Americans has taken different forms in various historical periods.

Developing Teaching Strategies

When the low-level generalizations for each ethnic group have been identified, you are then ready to write the strategies and identify the materials for teaching each of the low-level generalizations. One helpful format is for you to divide a sheet of paper as illustrated in Table 15–1 and list the concepts and generalizations on one side and the activities and materials on the other. In the lesson plan in Table 15–1, I illustrate how content about Mexican Americans, one of the ethnic groups chosen for study in our sample unit, can be used to teach the concept of social protest at the senior high school level.

Helping Students to Derive
the Key Generalizations

In order to formulate the key generalizations in the unit, the students must be given opportunities to compare and contrast the experiences of different ethnic groups. Students cannot derive key generalizations by studying one ethnic group. Rather, high-level generalizations can be derived only when students use data from several groups. At various points during the teaching of multicultural units, the teacher should give the students ample opportunities to compare and contrast the experiences of various ethnic groups and to formulate the key generalizations.

Table 15–1 *Key Ideas and Teaching Strategies*

Key Ideas	*Activities*

KEY CONCEPT: Social Protest
Key Generalization: When individuals and groups are victims of oppression and discrimination, they tend to protest against their situation in various ways.
 	
Intermediate-Level Generalization: Throughout their experiences in the United States, ethnic minorities have resisted discrimination and oppression in various ways.
 	
Low-Level Generalization: Mexican Americans have resisted Anglo discrimination and oppression since Anglo-Americans conquered and occupied the Southwest.
	1. To give the students a general overview of Mexican-American history, show them a videotape, such as *Mexican People and Culture*, a videotape in *The Hispanic Culture Series* distributed by Zenger Video (see Appendix B). After showing the videotape, ask the students to discuss the questions:
	
	  a. What major problems have Mexican Americans experienced in the United States?
	  b. What actions have been taken by Mexican-American individuals and groups to eliminate the discrimination they have experienced?
	
	2. Ask a group of students to prepare reports that reveal the ways in which the following men led organized resistance to Anglo-Americans in the 1800s:
	
	  Juan N. Cortina
	  Juan Jose Herrera
	  Juan Patron
	
	The class should discuss these men when the reports are presented. A good reference for this activity is Rodolfo Acuña, *Occupied America: A History of Chicanos*, 3rd ed.
	
	3. Ask a group of students to prepare a report to be presented in class that describes Chicano involvement in strikes and unions between 1900 and 1940. When this report is presented, the students should discuss ways in which strikes and union activities were forms of organized resistance.
	
	4. Ask the students to research the goals, tactics, and strategies used by the following Mexican-American civil rights groups: Order of the Sons of America, League of United Latin-American Citizens, The Community Service Organization, The American G.I. Forum, Federal Alliance of Free Cities, and Crusade for Justice. Ask the students to write several generalizations about the activities of these groups.
	
	(continued)

Table 15–1 *Continued*

Key Ideas	Activities
	5. Ask the students to research the following questions:
	a. How is the "Chicano" movement similar to other Mexican-American protest movements?
	b. How are its goals and strategies different?
	c. When did the movement emerge?
	d. What long-range effects do you think the movement will have? Why?
	6. Ask the students to read and dramatize the epic poem of the Chicano movement, *I Am Joaquin*, by Rodolfo Gonzales.
	7. Ask the students questions that will enable them to summarize and generalize about how Mexican Americans have resisted Anglo discrimination and oppression in both the past and in contemporary American society.
	8. Conclude the unit by viewing and discussing the film *I Am Joaquin*, distributed by El Teatro Campesino, San Juan Bautisa, CA.

A simple device that enables students to compare and contrast the experiences of various ethnic groups and to derive key generalizations is the data retrieval chart. This device allows students to log in the data they have found in answer to a series of questions related to the key concepts in the unit. Its chief value is that it can be easily expanded to include two or more data samples. The data retrieval chart enables students to ask the same kinds of questions about a number of ethnic groups. Thus, comparisons and contrasts can be readily made. A data retrieval chart related to our sample unit is presented in Table 15–2.

Determining Unit Objectives

Multicultural units should have clearly stated objectives so that the teacher can effectively evaluate instruction and student learning. Multicultural units should have two major kinds of objectives, *cognitive* and *affective*. Cognitive objectives are related to the mastery of knowledge. Affective objectives are related to student attitudes and values. Multicultural units should also have objectives that

Table 15-2 *Comparative Study of Ethnic Groups*

Key Concepts and Questions	American Indians	Mexican Americans	African Americans	Jewish Americans	Puerto Ricans
Cultural Assimilation Level: Within group?					
Economic Status: High or low?					
Ethnic Community: To what extent?					
Immigration: Reasons?					
Social Protest: Forms?					
Identity: Kinds of expressions?					
Discrimination: What kinds does group experience?					

are related to the student's ability to relate knowledge and values when making decisions on ethnic and other social issues. I call these kinds of objectives *synthesis* objectives.

Writing Cognitive Objectives

Throughout this book, I recommend the conceptual approach to instruction, in which the teacher determines the key concepts and generalizations to be taught and then selects content related to ethnic groups to be used in teaching the concepts and generalizations. In the conceptual approach, the teacher emphasizes the mastery of concepts and generalizations rather than the mastery of specific facts. Facts are important only to the extent that they are necessary to help students learn key concepts and generalizations.

When you identify the key concepts and generalizations for a unit, you have already largely determined the cognitive objectives of the unit, although they have not been specifically stated. In the sample unit discussed in this chapter, the key concepts chosen for study are cultural assimilation, economic status, ethnic community, immigration, social protest, identity, and discrimination. A major objective of this unit is for the students to demonstrate their understandings of each of these concepts. However, because *understanding* is a word that means different things to different people, we must state the objective in *behavioral* terms so that its meaning will be more precise. To do this, we use an action word in the objective. Action words often used in behavioral objectives include the following:

recall	analyze
identify	describe
apply	contrast
recite	observe
compare	

Our two conceptual objectives for this unit can be stated as follows:

1. The student will be able to identify examples and nonexamples of the key concepts in the unit.
2. The student will be able to state examples and nonexamples of the key concepts in the unit.

Other major unit objectives relate to the key generalizations in the unit and the method of inquiry used to derive them. At the conclusion of the unit, the students should be able to state or write the key generalizations in their own words, as well as to use the method of scientific inquiry to derive them. The objective related to the method of inquiry is a skill objective. The method of inquiry involves the following five basic steps:[1]

1. Problem statement.
2. Statement of hypotheses.
3. Definition of terms (conceptualization).
4. Evaluation and analysis of data.
5. Testing hypotheses (deriving generalizations).

You can write objectives that relate to any or all of the skills involved in the process of inquiry. Presented below are objectives related to the basic steps of scientific inquiry.

When presented a problem such as, "What are the basic causes of racial and ethnic discrimination?" the student will be able to do the following:

1. State relevant hypotheses.
2. Collect pertinent data.
3. Evaluate the data (tell whether it is valid and reliable; state whether it is related to the problem).
4. Write a tentative generalization.
5. Revise the generalization when presented with additional data related to the problem.

Writing Affective Objectives

Objectives related to feelings, attitudes, and values pose special problems for the teacher. Although teachers in traditional classrooms usually had as one major objective the development of democratic attitudes in students, current theory and research about value teaching and learning have raised some serious questions about traditional approaches to value education.[2] Contemporary value education theorists argue that traditional approaches to value education have not been successful in helping students attain a system of clarified beliefs on which they are willing to act.[3]

Most students have many negative, confused, and/or conflicting feelings and attitudes toward racial and ethnic groups. The goals of the affective component of the multicultural curriculum should be to help students determine how their values conflict, to identify value alternatives, to predict the consequences of alternative values, to freely choose a set of values on which they are willing to act, and to learn how to defend their moral choices reflectively.

Like cognitive objectives, affective objectives should be stated in behavioral terms so that they can be evaluated successfully. The following nine value objectives are based on the author's valuing model that is presented in outline form in chapter 4.[4]

1. The students will be able to define and recognize value problems.
2. The students will be able to describe value-relevant behavior.
3. The students will be able to list values exemplified by behavior described.
4. The students will be able to identify conflicting values in behavior described.
5. The students will be able to state hypotheses about the sources of values analyzed.

6. The students will be able to list alternative values to those exemplified by behavior observed.
7. The students will be able to state hypotheses about the possible consequences of the values analyzed.
8. The students will be able to state value preferences.
9. The students will be able to state reasons, sources, and possible consequences of their value choices.

Writing Synthesis Objectives

Synthesis objectives are designed to increase the student's ability to use knowledge (facts, concepts, generalizations, and theories) to identify alternative courses of action, predict the possible consequences of each alternative, order those alternatives according to personal values, and take effective action consistent with his or her value positions. Examples of synthesis objectives follow.

An open-ended story like "Boycott, Yes or No" can be used to attain synthesis objectives. In this story Judy, age 16, tries to convince her family to stop buying lettuce after hearing an emotional and effective speech by Juan Garcia, a Mexican-American social activist, at school earlier that day. Garcia told the students that people who refused to join the lettuce boycott were helping to exploit Mexican-American field workers. Unable to convince her family to stop buying lettuce, the story ends with Judy frustrated and about to cry. When given such a story, the student will be able to do the following:

1. Identify and state the decision problem that Judy faces in the story.
2. State what courses of action Judy might take to solve her problem.
3. State the possible consequences of each course of action stated in objective 2.
4. State the facts, concepts, and generalizations that will help the student predict the possible consequences of each course of action stated in objective 2.
5. State the values that would play a part in each possible course of action.
6. State which course of action the student would take if he or she were Judy and *why*.
7. State how the action the student would take relates to personal values (whether it is consistent or inconsistent with the values he or she professes).

Using Multimedia Resources

Previous chapters stress the use of written materials in the exemplary teaching because books are the easiest resources for most teachers to obtain. However, whenever possible, you should use other media when teaching ethnic content, such as records, films, videotapes, photographs, and slides. Many multimedia materials are available that can be used to teach ethnic content. Many professional organizations, as well as commercial publishers, issue catalogs that list, and often annotate, available multimedia resources related to ethnic groups. The Educational Materials and Service Center (in Edmonds, Washington) publishes a periodic catalog of multicultural materials for students and teachers as well as a quarterly newsletter, *Multicultural Leader,* that describes books and materials. The Anti-Defamation League of B'nai B'rith publishes an annual catalog that includes audiovisual materials. This publication can be obtained free from either the national office or a regional office of the League. The National Education Association also publishes a list of multimedia resources it produces. Some excellent multimedia resources are listed in the catalogs of commercial firms. The Social Studies School Service (Culver City, California) publishes an annual catalog that contains an excellent selection of multiethnic audiovisual materials. The Council on Interracial Books for Children also produces and distributes audiovisual materials, most of which are designed to help students and teachers to develop more democratic attitudes and values toward various cultural and racial groups. The Japanese American Curriculum Project (JACP) publishes a comprehensive catalog annually that includes multimedia materials for teaching about Asian Americans (JACP, P.O. Box 367, San Mateo, CA 94401). An annotated list of videotapes and films is found in Appendix B.

Even though catalogs and bibliographies are helpful in locating multimedia resources, it is essential that you preview multimedia materials before using them in class. Most commercial firms will send materials for examination on a trial basis. Previewing multimedia resources is a time-consuming task. Unfortunately, however, there is no other way to make sure that they will contribute to your instructional goals and depict ethnic groups accurately and sensitively. Multimedia resources are often expensive to rent or purchase and are frequently difficult to obtain when they are needed by the teacher. However, in most metropolitan areas there is at least one good public library that has an excellent collection of audiovisual materials that can be borrowed without charge. You should take advantage of the many excellent services provided by the public libraries in your community. Photographs are usually easier to obtain than films, videotapes, and sound recordings. They can be cut from magazines such as *Ebony, Black Enterprise, Essence,* and *Hispanic,* and can be purchased from publishers for a reasonable price. There are many sets of commercial photographs available that include American ethnic groups.

Using Community Resources

Every community has resources you can use to enrich the multicultural curriculum. One of the most helpful community resources is the ethnic organization. Ethnic organizations such as the Anti-Defamation League of B'nai B'rith, the National Association for the Advancement of Colored People, the Japanese American Citizenship League, and the Puerto Rican Forum provide services, many of them without charge, that can help enrich your curriculum. These organizations issue publications that describe and annotate teaching materials (usually available free on request) and will often provide speakers for a class or school who are specialists on particular ethnic groups.

Some ethnic organizations, such as the Japanese American Curriculum Project, Inc., and the Indian Historian Press, exist solely for the purpose of developing books and other materials that can be used as teacher references and as student resources. Materials published by ethnic organizations, and annotated bibliographies issued by them, merit special attention in the multicultural curriculum. Within every ethnic community, there is a wide diversity of opinions and attitudes. However, there are certain feelings and points of view that are usually shared within the ethnic community but that are frequently unknown by authors of books about ethnic groups or by librarians and teachers who select books for the school or public library. Paying close attention to the publications issued by ethnic organizations can enable you to select books and materials that reflect ethnic cultures and perspectives.[5]

There are other community resources you should use when teaching ethnic content. Many colleges and universities have academic programs that focus on particular ethnic groups such as African Americans, Mexican Americans, Puerto Ricans, and Asian Americans. The professors who teach in these types of programs are academic specialists on the various ethnic groups and are often persons of color. You can draw on the services of these specialists when planning and teaching ethnic content. They are an important human resource that should not be overlooked. Heads of ethnic organizations, who are social activists, can also be invited to speak to the class or the school. They can present knowledge and points of view that are essential in a sound multicultural curriculum.

Evaluating Cognitive and Affective Outcomes

If both the cognitive and affective objectives have been stated in behavioral terms, the evaluation of multicultural units will be greatly facilitated. To determine whether students can recognize examples and nonexamples of such concepts as racial discrimination and social protest, you can give the students lists containing examples and nonexamples of discrimination and social protest and ask them to indicate which are examples of the concepts and which are nonexamples. Below is a list containing examples and nonexamples of racial discrimination. Note that the student must have a mastery of factual knowledge about the court cases and events in order to be able to determine which items on the list are examples and nonexamples of racial discrimination. However, the major goal of the exercise is to test the student's ability to recognize examples and nonexamples of one key concept, racial discrimination.

Directions

Below are some events and court cases we have studied. Indicate those that are examples of racial discrimination by placing an "X" in front of them. Mark those which are nonexamples of discrimination with "N."

———— the Civil Rights Act of 1964

———— the *Plessy* v. *Ferguson* decision, 1896

———— the March on Washington, 1963

———— Jim Crow laws

———— the Brown decision, 1954

———— the Detroit race riot, 1943

———— the Immigration Act of 1924

———— the Civil Liberties Act of 1988

To determine whether students can use the method of social inquiry to derive key generalizations related to such concepts as immigration, social protest, and ethnic community, you can give them graphs, statistics, maps, selected readings, and other kinds of data and ask the students key questions that will enable them to formulate and write generalizations.

Many types of sources and exercises, a number of which are described in the books by Simon et al. and Raths et al.,[6] can be used to determine whether students are able to recognize value problems, to identify value conflicts, and to state their own values. These include the valuing sheet, the values grid, the value survey, roleplaying exercises, literary selections, photographs, open-ended stories, and essays written by the students. Some of these types of materials and exercises are discussed in chapter 4 in the section dealing with valuing goals and strategies.

Evaluating Decision-Making and Social Action Skills

To evaluate the students' abilities to make decisions and to plan effective social action, they can be given a case study that presents an unresolved problem related to race and ethnicity and asked to do the following:

1. List the facts, concepts, and generalizations needed to make a sound decision regarding the issue.
2. List alternative values that are related to the issue, and the values that the student would endorse.
3. List alternative courses of action that could be taken regarding the issue, and their possible consequences (data should support each alternative listed).
4. Order the alternatives in a way most consistent with his or her values identified earlier.
5. List the course of action he or she would take on the issue.
6. State the possible consequences of taking that particular action.

In their book *Role Playing in the Curriculum*, Fannie and George Shaftel present several open-ended stories related to racial and ethnic problems.[7] These stories can be used to help students develop decision-making and social-action skills, as well as to test their mastery of these skills. "No Trespassing" deals with a situation in which a boy is the victim of anti-Semitism. However, the story can be adapted to relate to problems encountered by other ethnic individuals. In "Second Prize," a donor of a school prize wants to withdraw it when he learns that the winner of the prize is African American. A Mexican-American girl faces a personal dilemma when an Anglo boy asks her for a date in "Josefina."

Some of the open-ended stories in previous chapters of this book can be used successfully to evaluate decision making and the skill to develop social-action plans, especially "Trying to Buy a Home in Lakewood Island," "Father and Son," and "Mr. Diaz and Mr. Seda on the Mainland." You can also use pictures without captions, as well as case studies related to racial and ethnic incidents that have occurred within your school or community.

In a testing situation, you can ask the students to read "Trying to Buy a Home in Lakewood Island" (see page 200), and to respond briefly to each of the following questions.

1. What knowledge (facts, concepts, generalizations, and theories) would the Greens need in order to make an effective decision in this case?
2. What are some values that are involved in the case? What value do you think should guide the Greens' decision? What is the most important value to you in this case?
3. What are possible actions that the Greens can take? What are the possible consequences of each possible course of action?
4. Which of the courses of action you identified above are most consistent with your own values?
5. What should the Greens do? If you were the Greens, what would you do? Why?
6. What are some of the possible consequences that might result from the course of action that you would take? Are you willing to accept them?

When you evaluate a student's response to a decision-making testing exercise, such as the one above, you should determine whether the knowledge the student identifies is accurate and whether it is related to the particular case study. Knowledge about prejudice, discrimination, civil rights laws, and how real estate is traditionally sold will help the Greens make a reflective decision in the case in our example. You should also determine how well the student can identify values implicit in the case. This case, for example, raises two conflicting values—the rights of the property owner versus the rights of the buyer. You should determine how well the student can identify and state realistic alternatives and their possible consequences. The students should also be judged on how well they can state and defend a personal value position.

Evaluating the Total School Environment

Multicultural teaching can best occur within an educational environment that has institutional norms that recognize and are sensitive to cultural and ethnic diversity. Thus, to change the school climate so that the school reinforces and promotes the concept of cultural diversity, changes must occur in all the major variables of the school environment, including teacher attitudes and expectations, the "hidden curriculum," school policy, the counseling program, and the assessment and testing procedures. Figure 15–1 illustrates these and other variables that must be reformed in order to make the school a multicultural institution. In other words, effective multicultural teaching can best occur within a multicultural school environment.

When trying to determine the quality of multicultural education in their school, the instructional and administrative staffs can use the rating scale in Table 15–3. When completed, this scale will give the staff a rough estimate of the general quality of the school's multicultural education program. This information will enable the staff to identify recommendations that will guide actions to make the school environment more culturally pluralistic. In areas where the school program is already outstanding, the findings derived by using the scale can provide the staff with needed positive reinforcement.

Schools or districts that wish to use a more detailed evaluation instrument may use the *Multiethnic Education Program Evaluation Checklist* developed by the National Council for the Social Studies Task Force on Ethnic Studies Curriculum Guidelines. It is designed to encourage and assist in the assessment of specific school environments to determine the extent to which they reflect the standards for multiethnic education presented in the Task Force's publication, *Curriculum Guidelines for Multiethnic Education.*[8] This publication was issued as a position statement by the National Council for the Social Studies.

The Teacher and the Multicultural Curriculum

The teacher is the most important variable in the multicultural curriculum. His or her attitudes toward ethnic content and ethnic cultures are crucial. Many teachers, especially mainstream American teachers, may fear teaching ethnic content, particularly if their classes include students of color. This problem might be compounded if minority students in their classes express or show negative attitudes toward learning about their cultural heritages, which sometimes happens. Teachers might also be intimidated by those who argue that White teachers cannot and should not teach about African Americans, American Indians, and Mexican Americans, and that they can never know the experiences of people of color who are victims of institutional racism in America.

The teacher should clarify his or her attitudes toward people of color before attempting to teach about them. Teachers who have negative or condescending attitudes toward people of color may do more harm than good when they teach ethnic content. Research suggests that teacher attitudes are revealed to students even when teachers are unaware of their negative feelings.[9] Teachers who are unsure about their racial and ethnic attitudes should test them by reading some of the books recommended in earlier chapters and by enrolling in a human relations or multicultural education workshop. If local workshops are

Figure 15–1 *The Total School Environment*

In this figure, the total school environment is conceptualized as a system that consists of a number of major identifiable factors, such as school policy, the institutionalized norms, and the formalized curriculum or course of study. In the ideal multicultural school, each factor reflects ethnic pluralism. Even though any one factor may be the focus of initial school reform, changes must occur in each of them to create and sustain an effective multicultural educational environment.

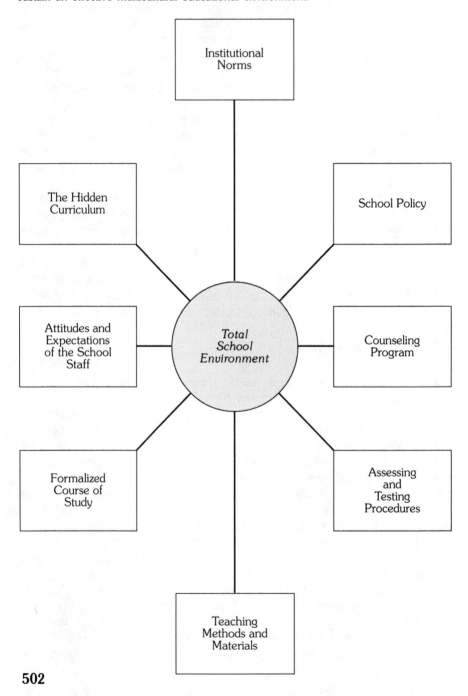

Table 15–3 *Evaluating the Total Multicultural Program*

Directions for using this rating scale:
Check "NA" if the answer to the question is "not at all." Check "1" if the answer is "yes but very little." Check "5" if the answer is "yes, that aspect of our program is outstanding." Check the numbers from 2 to 4 if the response is somewhere between the extremes. By adding the points when you have finished rating your school, you can obtain a rough estimate of the general quality of your total multicultural educational program ("NA" = 0 points). The total number of points possible is 90.

1. Is information about U.S. ethnic groups included in *all* the courses in the school, including social studies, English, literature, physical education, home economics, and science?	NA	1	2	3	4	5
2. Is there a procedure for evaluating the treatment of ethnic groups in textbooks before they are adopted for use in the school? If so, to what extent is it effective?	NA	1	2	3	4	5
3. Are there pictures of minority groups in the classrooms and in the halls of the schools?	NA	1	2	3	4	5
4. Do the calendars in the school include information about ethnic holidays and outstanding Americans of ethnic origin?	NA	1	2	3	4	5
5. Do the foods served in the school cafeteria reflect the ethnic diversity of American life? If so, in what ways?	NA	1	2	3	4	5
6. Do school assemblies and plays reflect the ethnic diversity of American life? If so, to what extent?	NA	1	2	3	4	5
7. Are the teachers and administrators provided in-service workshops and activities where they can acquire content about American ethnic cultures and ways to teach about them?	NA	1	2	3	4	5
8. Does the school's professional library include books about American ethnic groups and ways to teach about them?	NA	1	2	3	4	5
9. Does the school's library include an ample number of books about American ethnic groups for all grade levels? If so, have the books been evaluated for their sensitivity to ethnic groups?	NA	1	2	3	4	5
10. Does the school library subscribe to ethnic magazines such as *Ebony, Indian Historian, Amerasia Journal, Hispanic,* and *El Grito?*	NA	1	2	3	4	5

(continued)

503

Table 15–3 (continued)

11. Is there, or has there been a curriculum committee created to devise ways to integrate the entire school curriculum with ethnic content? If so, did the committee solicit the help of specialists in ethnic studies?	NA	1	2	3	4	5
12. Are individuals from the various ethnic organizations within the community or in nearby communities frequently invited to speak to classes and in school assemblies?	NA	1	2	3	4	5
13. Does the school offer elective courses in ethnic studies? If so, what are they? _____ Do they provide the student with a range of courses that include information about all American ethnic groups, including Puerto Ricans, Filipino Americans, Cuban Americans, and Mexican Americans?	NA	1	2	3	4	5
14. Do school holidays and celebrations reflect the ethnic diversity of American life? If so, what specific ethnic holidays are celebrated? _____ How are they celebrated? _____	NA	1	2	3	4	5
15. Do bulletin boards and other displays in the school reflect the ethnic diversity of American life? If so, in what ways? _____	NA	1	2	3	4	5
16. Does the school district have an ample supply of films, videotapes, records, and other multimedia resources on American ethnic groups? If so, have they been evaluated for ethnic sensitivity?	NA	1	2	3	4	5
17. Has the school (or the school district) developed and implemented a policy to hire staff members who represent a range of racial and ethnic groups?	NA	1	2	3	4	5
18. Does the school encourage and support dialect and language diversity?	NA	1	2	3	4	5

Total School Score _____
Recommended Actions:
1.
2.
3.
4.
5.

not available, the teacher should take a course in ethnic studies at a local college or university. A human relations workshop or an ethnic studies course will give the teacher the opportunity to express personal feelings and perceptions, compare them with the attitudes of other teachers, and clarify racial feelings.

Once a teacher is keenly aware of personal racial attitudes and is satisfied that they are basically positive toward people of color, that teacher should staunchly defend his or her right and responsibility to teach ethnic content. It is true that White teachers will never fully know what it means to be African American, Puerto Rican, or Indian in contemporary American society, just as members of these groups will never fully know what it means to be White. It is also true that teachers of color can present students with perspectives and points of view that the White teacher will be unable to present to them. However, ethnic content is legitimate knowledge that should be taught in the school. We should approach the teaching of ethnic content the way in which we approach the teaching of other content in the social sciences and humanities. We do not assume that a teacher must have lived during medieval times in order to teach medieval history effectively, or that a teacher has to be Italian in order to teach about the Renaissance in Italy. African American teachers have successfully taught European history for many years. Likewise, we are not justified in arguing that only African Americans can teach about Blacks or that only Chicanos can teach about Mexican Americans. Although it is desirable, for many reasons, for school districts to recruit and hire as many teachers of color as possible, White teachers, as well as African-American and Mexican-American teachers, have a professional and, I feel, moral responsibility to teach about American ethnic groups and to integrate ethnic content into their regular curricula and courses.

A teacher who is sensitive and knowledgeable, regardless of his or her ethnic or racial group, can teach any subject effectively. *However, it is important for students to be exposed to the points of view and perceptions of members of the various ethnic groups.* This can be done by selecting sensitive and powerful teaching materials written by ethnic authors and using the types of community resources discussed earlier in this chapter. Many excellent books written by authors of color are annotated in chapters 5 through 14. Records, films, videotapes, and ethnic periodicals can also be used to present the perspectives of ethnic groups to students. Knowledgeable and informed teachers can also interpret many of these viewpoints to students. However, there is no substitute for students' reading and listening to such viewpoints themselves.

Sensitive and knowledgeable teachers who approach teaching with integrity and openness can defend their right to teach ethnic content to any individual or group. Such teachers can convince ethnic students that they have a right and a responsibility to teach about ethnic cultures. When a teacher claims that ethnic content is being resisted by students of color, it is usually because the teacher has presented ethnic content in a condescending way, has not clarified his or her feelings toward groups of color, or has not established a norm in the classroom that respects and tolerates cultural and ethnic differences. It is unrealistic to expect minority group students to be eager to study and examine their cultural heritages in a school and classroom atmosphere in which the mainstream American culture is held up as the ideal and in which their cultures are demeaned in subtle or overt ways.

The need for teachers to be intellectually competent before they embark on teaching ethnic content cannot be overemphasized. The teacher who is serious about wanting to teach ethnic content should read at least one book on each major American ethnic group and one general source on ethnicity in American society. Every school should have a multicultural library for its professional staff.

I do not mean to suggest that teachers can read a few books and become experts in ethnic studies or specialists on a particular ethnic group. Becoming an ethnic studies specialist, in any sense, takes many years of study, research, and reflection. Even though I am recommending that all classroom teachers integrate ethnic content into their regular courses, I feel that specialized courses on ethnic groups or particular ethnic groups, such as a Black studies course or a Chicano studies course, should be taught only by a teacher who has specialized in ethnic studies. A person who has successfully functioned within an ethnic culture is more likely to have the kind of sensitivity needed to teach a specialized ethnic studies course effectively.

The Challenge of Ethnic Studies

No one who has seriously studied American ethnic groups can underestimate the difficulties involved in learning about them. Trying to learn the truth about American ethnic groups involves much unlearning of facts and interpretations that we learned in school and much new learning. A good part of the knowledge that most of us learned in school contained myths created by social scientists and historians who strongly identified with the mainstream culture and who felt a need, whether conscious or not, to justify the discrimination and racism that groups of color in the United States experienced. Studying and teaching about ethnic cultures will involve, for most teachers, intellectual and emotional confrontations with many of the feelings and beliefs they cherish about U.S. society.

To understand fully the nature of American society and the role that ethnicity plays within it, teachers will have to reconceptualize their views of America. For example, the United States is usually studied as an extension of European social and political institutions. However, American Indians were in America centuries before Columbus. To view America merely as an extension of European institutions ignores American Indian institutions and cultures. Ethnic studies demands that teachers and students reconceptualize their views of the winning of the West, the meaning of slavery, the purpose of American expansion in the late 1800s, and the nature of democracy as it is practiced in contemporary American society.

The intellectual and emotional confrontations that ethnic studies will require of teachers and students will help them attain more humanistic views of people of color and break out of their own ethnic encapsulations. Ethnic studies will teach them that there are other ways of living and being, and that to be racially and ethnically different does not mean that one is inferior or superior. More humanistic views of other cultures are imperative within our increasingly interdependent and ethnically polarized world. Humanistic views of other groups and cultures may help to create the kind of racial and ethnic harmony that our society must have to survive and prosper in the twenty-first century.

Endnotes

1. James A. Banks, with Ambrose A. Clegg, Jr., *Teaching Strategies for the Social Studies*, 4th ed. (New York: Longman, Inc., 1990).
2. James P. Shaver and William Strong, *Facing Value Decisions: Rationale-Building for Teachers*, 2nd ed. (New York: Teachers College Press, 1982).
3. Jack R. Fraenkel, *How to Teach about Values: An Analytic Approach* (Englewood Cliffs, N.J.: Prentice-Hall, 1977); Lawrence Kohlberg, "The Child as a Moral Philosopher," *Psychology Today 2*, No. 4 (September 1968): 24–30; Shaver and Strong, *Facing Value Decisions: Rationale-Building for Teachers*.
4. Banks, with Clegg, *Teaching Strategies*, pp. 435–448.
5. A list of minority group publishers and their current addresses can be obtained from the Council on Interracial Books for Children, 1841 Broadway, New York, NY 10023. *The Bulletin*, published periodically by the Council, is an excellent source of information about books written by ethnic minorities.
6. Sidney B. Simon, Leland W. Howe, and Howard Kirschenbaum, *Values Clarification: A Handbook of Practical Strategies for Teachers and Students* (New York: Hart Publishing Company, 1972); Louis E. Raths, Merrill Harmin, and Sidney B. Simon, *Values and Teaching: Working with Values in the Classroom*, 2nd ed. (Columbus, Oh.: Charles E. Merrill, 1978).
7. Fannie R. Shaftel and George Shaftel, *Role Playing in the Curriculum*, 2nd ed. (Englewood Cliffs, N.J.: Prentice-Hall, 1982).
8. The NCSS Task Force on Ethnic Studies Curriculum Guidelines (James A. Banks, Carlos E. Cortés, Ricardo L. Garcia, Geneva Gay, and Anna S. Ochoa), *Curriculum Guidelines for Multiethnic Education* (Washington, D.C.: National Council for the Social Studies, 1976).
9. James A. Banks, "Racial Prejudice and the Black Self-Concept," in *Black Self-Concept: Implications for Education and Social Science*, eds. James A. Banks and Jean D. Grambs (New York: McGraw-Hill, 1972), pp. 5–35. For suggested strategies for examining and changing racial attitudes, see George Henderson, *Human Relations: From Theory to Practice* (Norman: University of Oklahoma, 1974).

Annotated Bibliography

Books for Teachers

Banks, James. A. *Multiethnic Education: Theory and Practice*, 2nd ed. Boston: Allyn and Bacon, 1988.

> *The author describes theories, paradigms, and strategies for implementing multicultural education.*

Banks, James A., and Banks, Cherry A. McGee, eds. *Multicultural Education: Issues and Perspectives.* Boston: Allyn and Bacon, 1989.

> *Nineteen experts in multicultural education provide diverse perspectives and conceptual frameworks for implementing multicultural education in educational institutions.*

The Commission on Minority Participation in Education and American Life. *One-Third of a Nation.* Washington, D.C.: American Council on Education, 1988.

> *An important report that predicts that one out of three Americans will be a person of color by the year 2000.*

Derman-Sparks, Louise, and the A.B.C. Task Force. *Anti-Bias Curriculum: Tools for Empowering Young Children.* Washington, D.C.: National Association for the Education of Young Children, 1989.

> *A book of resources and activities for helping young children to develop positive intergroup attitudes.*

Dinnerstein, Leonard; Nichols, Roger L.; and Reimers, David M. *Native and Strangers: Blacks, Indians, and Immigrants in America,* 2nd ed. New York: Oxford University Press, 1990.

> *A highly readable historical account of ethnic groups in the United States. The authors blend the diverse ethnic histories into an interesting narrative.*

Jiobu, Robert M. *Ethnicity and Assimilation.* Albany: State University of New York Press, 1988.

> *Blacks, Chinese, Filipinos, Japanese, Koreans, Mexicans, Vietnamese, and Whites are the focus in this sociological treatment of ethnic groups in the United States.*

Lieberson, Stanley, and Waters, Mary C. *From Many Strands: Ethnic and Racial Groups in Contemporary America.* New York: Russell Sage Foundation, 1988.

> *This is one volume in "The Population of the United States in the 1980s," a Census monograph series published by the Russell Sage Foundation. Other titles in the series include Frank D. Bean and Marta Tienda,* The Hispanic Population of the United States *(1988); C. Matthew Snipp,* American Indians: The First of This Land *(1989); Peter C. Xenos et al.,* Asian and Pacific Americans *(1989).*

Nash, Gary B. *Red, White and Black: The Peoples of Early America.* Englewood Cliffs, N.J.: Prentice-Hall, 1974.

> *An excellent history of ethnic and cultural diversity in early U.S. history.*

Quality Education for Minorities Project. *Education That Works: An Action Plan for the Education of Minorities.* Cambridge: The Project, 1990. (Available from The Quality Education for Minorities Project, Room 26–157, the Massachusetts Institute of Technology, Cambridge, MA 02139)

> *This report sets forth specific goals and actions that various groups can take to increase the academic achievement of students of color. Actions are suggested for minority families, teachers and administrators, higher education, state governments, and the federal government.*

Reimers, David M. *Still the Golden Door: The Third World Comes to America.* New York: Columbia University Press, 1985.

> *A scholarly history of the immigrants and refugees who have settled in the United States since the Immigration Act of 1965 was enacted.*

University Committee on Minority Issues. *Building a Multiracial, Multicultural University Community.* Stanford, Calif.: Stanford University, March 1990.

This ambitious and comprehensive 240-page report was written by a Stanford Committee to guide the university in its efforts to create a more culturally sensitive environment. Other universities will find much to emulate in the report, especially the statement that opens the document: "Building a Multiracial, Multicultural University Community: A Vision for Stanford."

Wasserman, Paul, and Kennington, Alice E. *Ethnic Information Sources of the United States,* 2nd ed. Vols. 1 and 2. Detroit: Gale Research Company, 1983.

A comprehensive listing of organizations, agencies, foundations, institutions, and media that focus on ethnic groups in the United States.

Books for Students

Ashabranner, Brent. Photographs by Paul Conklin. *The New Americans: Changing Patterns of U.S. Immigration.* New York: Dodd, Mead, 1983.

This book focuses on the new immigrants and refugees who are coming to the United States primarily from Asia and Latin America.

Bode, Janet. *Different Worlds: Interracial and Cross-Cultural Dating.* New York: Franklin Watts, 1989.

The author tells the stories of teen-agers who date across racial and cultural lines.

————. *New Kids on the Block: Oral Histories of Immigrant Teens.* New York: Franklin Watts, 1989.

Eleven teen-age immigrants to the United States tell their stories.

Hamilton, Virginia. Illustrated by Barry Moser. *In the Beginning: Creation Stories from around the World.* New York: Harcourt Brace, 1988.

A collection of 25 creation stories from cultures in different parts of the world.

Kosof, Anna. *The Civil Rights Movement and Its Legacy.* New York: Franklin Watts, 1989.

This historical account of the civil rights movement starts with the Brown decision of 1954 and ends with Jesse Jackson's 1988 presidential campaign.

McKissack, Patricia, and McKissack, Frederick. *Taking a Stand against Racism and Discrimination.* New York: Franklin Watts, 1990.

An informative book that discusses racism in both the past and present and the need to take a stand against it.

Rosenberg, Maxine B. Photographs by George Ancona. *Making a New Home in America.* New York: Lothrop, Lee and Shepard, 1986.

The stories of four children who have immigrated to the United States from different lands are told in this book.

Spier, Peter. *People.* New York: Doubleday, 1980.

This book, illustrated by the author and designed for primary grade children, tells how people throughout the world both are similar and different.

Walton, Darwin. Photographs by Hal Franklin. *What Color Are You?* Chicago: Johnson Publishing Company, 1973. Reprinted 1985.

   Illustrated with color photographs, this book helps young children understand the scientific basis of skin color differences.

Woods, Geraldine. *Affirmative Action.* New York: Franklin Watts, 1989.

   The author helps young people understand the complex and controversial issue of affirmative action.

Appendix A

Ethnic Groups

in U.S. History

A Chronology of Key Events

*Indicates an important immigration act.

Date	Event
1513	Juan Ponce de León landed on the Florida peninsula while on route from Puerto Rico. The relationship between Europeans and Indians north of Mexico began.
1519	Hernán Cortéz, the Spanish conquistador, and a group of Spaniards arrived in the region that is now Mexico.
1565	The Spaniards established the St. Augustine colony in Florida, the first settlement organized by Europeans in present-day United States.
1619	The first Africans arrived in the English North American colonies.
1620	The Pilgrims came to America from England on the *Mayflower* and established a settlement at Plymouth, Massachusetts.
1637	More than 500 American Indians were killed by the colonists in a massacre known as the Pequot War.
1654	The first Jewish immigrants to North America settled in New Amsterdam to escape persecution in Brazil.
1683	German immigrants settled in Pennsylvania.
1718	The Scots-Irish began immigrating to North America in large numbers.
1754–63	The French and Indian War occurred.
1798	A Federalist-dominated Congress enacted the Alien and Sedition Acts to crush the Republican party and to harass aliens.
1812	The War of 1812, a war between the United States and Britain, caused deep factions among the Indian tribes because of their different allegiances.
1815	The first mass immigrations from Europe to North America began.

Date	Event
Date	*Event*
1830	Congress passed a Removal Act, which authorized the removal of Indians from east to west of the Mississippi.
1831	Nat Turner led a slave revolt in which nearly 60 Whites were killed.
1836	Mexico's President Santa Anna and his troops defeated the Texans at the Alamo. Six weeks later Santa Anna was defeated by Sam Houston and his Texan troops at San Jacinto.
1845	The United States annexed Texas, which had declared itself independent from Mexico in 1836. This was one key event that led to the Mexican-American War.
1846–48	A series of potato blights in Ireland caused thousands of its citizens to immigrate to the United States.
1846	On May 13, 1846, the United States declared war on Mexico and the Mexican-American War began.
1848	The United States and Mexico signed the Treaty of Guadalupe Hidalgo that ended the Mexican-American War. Mexico lost nearly one-third of its territory, and the United States acquired most of the territory that comprises its southwestern states.
1850	The California legislature passed a discriminatory Foreign Miner's Tax that forced Chinese immigrants to pay a highly disproportionate share of the state taxes.
1855	Castle Garden, an immigration station, opened in New York City. The antiforeign Know-Nothing Movement reached its zenith and had a number of political successes in the 1855 elections. The movement rapidly declined after 1855.
1859	Juan N. Cortina, who became a U.S. citizen under the provisions of the Treaty of Guadalupe Hidalgo, led a series of rebellions against Anglo-Americans in the Southwest.
1863	On January 1, 1863, President Abraham Lincoln issued the Emancipation Proclamation, which freed slaves in those states still fighting the Union.
1864	Nearly 300 Cheyennes were killed in a surprise attack at Sand Creek, Colorado. This event is known as the Sand Creek Massacre.
1869	The transcontinental railroad, linking the West to the East, was completed. Chinese laborers did most of the work on the Pacific portion of the railroad. The unsuccessful Wakamatsu Colony, made up of Japanese immigrants, was established in California.
1871	A White mob in Los Angeles attacked a Chinese community. When the conflict ended, 19 Chinese were killed and their community was in shambles.

Date	Event
1876	In the disputed Hayes-Tilden election, the Democrats and Republicans made a political bargain that symbolized the extent to which northern Whites had abandoned southern Blacks.
	Sioux tribes, under the leadership of Sitting Bull, wiped out Custer's Seventh Cavalry at Little Big Horn. This was one of the last victories for American Indian tribes.
* 1882	The Chinese Exclusion Act was enacted by Congress.
	Another congressional immigration act established a head tax of fifty cents and excluded lunatics, convicts, idiots, and those likely to become public charges.
1885	A serious anti-Chinese riot occurred in Rock Springs, Wyoming. Twenty-eight Chinese were killed, and many others were wounded and driven from their homes.
1886	The Apache warrior Geronimo surrendered to U.S. forces in September 1886. His surrender marked the defeat of the Southwest tribes.
	The Haymarket Affair in Chicago increased the fear of foreign "radicals" and stimulated the growth of nativistic sentiments in the United States.
	The Statue of Liberty was dedicated as nativism soared in the United States.
1887	Congress passed the Dawes Severalty Act, which was designed to terminate partially the Indian's special relationship with the U.S. government.
1888	The Scott Act prohibited the immigration of Chinese laborers and permitted only officials, teachers, students, merchants, and travelers from China to enter the United States.
1890	Three hundred Sioux were killed in a conflict at Wounded Knee Creek in South Dakota.
1891	Eleven Italian Americans were lynched in New Orleans during the height of American nativism, after being accused of murdering a police superintendent.
1892	Ellis Island opened and replaced Castle Garden as the main port of entry for European immigrants.
1893	Queen Liliuokalani of Hawaii was overthrown in a bloodless revolution led by American planters.
	The Republic of Hawaii was established, with Stanford B. Dole as president.
1896	In a historic decision, *Plessy* v. *Ferguson*, the Supreme Court ruled that "separate but equal" facilities were constitutional.
1898	Hawaii was annexed to the United States.
	Under the terms of the Treaty of Paris, the treaty that ended the Spanish-American War, the United States acquired Puerto Rico, Guam, and the Philippines. Cuba became independent of Spain but was placed under U.S. tutelage.

Date	Event
1900	With the Foraker Act, the United States established a government in Puerto Rico to which the president of the United States appointed the governor and the Executive Council.
1901–10	Almost 9 million immigrants entered the United States, most of whom came from southern and eastern Europe.
1908	The United States and Japan made the Gentlemen's Agreement, which was designed to reduce the number of Japanese immigrants entering the United States.
1910	The National Association for the Advancement of Colored People (NAACP) was organized. A Mexican revolution caused many Mexican peasants to immigrate to the United States looking for jobs. Other immigrants came to escape political turmoil and persecution.
1913	The California legislature passed a land bill that made it difficult for Japanese immigrants to lease land.
* 1917	Thirty-nine African Americans were killed in a bloody riot in East St. Louis, Missouri. A comprehensive immigration bill was enacted that established a literacy test for entering immigrants. The Jones Act was passed by the U.S. Congress. It made Puerto Ricans U.S. citizens and subject to the U.S. draft.
1920	The Hawaiian Homes Commission was started to benefit the native Hawaiian. Very little of the land involved was used for its stated purpose. The number of persons born in Puerto Rico and living in the United States was 11,811. That number increased to 58,200 in the year 1935.
* 1924	The Johnson-Reed Act established extreme quotas on immigration and blatantly discriminated against southern and eastern European and non-White nations.
1925	A large number of Filipinos began to immigrate to Hawaii and the U.S. mainland to work as field laborers.
1927	The Filipino Federation of Labor was organized in Los Angeles.
1928	The League of United Latin American Citizens was formed in Harlingen, Texas.
1929	An anti-Filipino riot occurred in Exeter, California, in which more than 200 Filipinos were assaulted.
1930	The Japanese American Citizenship League was organized.
* 1934	Congress passed the Tydings-McDuffie Act. This act promised the Philippines independence and limited Filipino immigration to the United States to 50 per year.
1935	President Franklin D. Roosevelt signed the Repatriation Act. The act offered free transportation to Filipinos who would return to the Philip-

Date	*Event*

pines. Those who left were unable to return to the United States except under a severe quota system.

1942 On February 19, 1942, President Franklin D. Roosevelt issued Executive Order 9066, which authorized the internment of Japanese Americans who lived on the West Coast.

The United States and Mexico made an agreement that authorized Mexican immigrants to work temporarily in the United States. This project is known as the *bracero* program.

1943 White violence directed at African Americans led to a serious riot in Detroit, in which 34 people were killed.

The anti-Mexican zoot suit riots occurred in Los Angeles during the summer.

1946 On July 4, 1946, the Philippines became independent.

*1952 The McCarran-Walter Immigration and Nationality Act was passed by Congress. It eliminated race as a factor in immigration. However, the national origins quota system remained but was liberalized.

1954 The Refugee Relief Act permitted 5,000 Hungarian refugees to enter the United States.

In a landmark decision, *Brown* v. *Board of Education,* the Supreme Court ruled that school segregation was inherently unequal.

The U.S. Immigration and Naturalization Service began Operation Wetback, a massive program to deport illegal Mexican immigrants.

1959 Fidel Castro took over the reins of power in Cuba from the government of Fulgencio Batista. After this revolution, many Cuban refugees entered the United States.

Hawaii became the fiftieth state of the United States.

1960 On February 1, 1960, the sit-in movement, which desegregated public accommodation facilities throughout the South, began in Greensboro, North Carolina.

1961 The National Indian Youth Council was organized.

1962 Commercial air flights between the United States and Cuba ended. Immigration from Cuba to the United States became strictly clandestine.

1963 More than 200,000 people participated in a "March on Washington for Freedom and Jobs."

1964 The Civil Rights Act of 1964, the most comprehensive civil rights bill in American history, was enacted by Congress and signed by President Lyndon B. Johnson.

1965 With the passage of the Civil Rights Act of 1965, Puerto Ricans were no longer required to pass an English literacy test to vote in New York state.

*The Immigration Reform Act of 1965 was passed by Congress. This act, which became effective in 1968, abolished the national origins

Date	*Event*

quota system and liberalized American immigration policy. Immigration from Asia and Latin America increased after this act was passed.

A grape strike led by César Chávez and the National Farm Workers Association began in Delano, California, a town in the San Joaquin Valley.

Rodolfo "Corkey" Gonzales formed the Crusade for Justice in Denver. This important civil rights organization epitomized the Chicano movement that emerged in the 1960s.

The Cuban Refugee Airlift program began. Flights from Cuba to Miami, Florida, were sponsored by the U.S. government. The program was terminated in 1973.

1965–68   A series of riots occurred in American cities in which African Americans expressed their frustrations and discontent.

1966   Stokely Carmichael issued a call for Black Power during a civil rights demonstration in Greenwood, Mississippi.

1970   Herman Badillo was elected to the U.S. House of Representatives. He was the first Puerto Rican elected to Congress.

1973   African Americans were elected mayors in Detroit, Atlanta, Los Angeles, and other cities.

1974   The U.S. Supreme Court ruled in the *Lau* v. *Nichols* case that schools should provide students with instruction in their native language. This ruling gave bilingual-bicultural education in the United States a tremendous boost.

1975   U.S. participation in the Vietnam War had ended (1973), and communist governments took control of Vietnam and Cambodia (Kampuchea). Many Indochinese refugees settled in the United States. Between 1971 and 1978, 110,200 Vietnamese refugees immigrated to the United States.

1976   Jerry Apodaca and Raul Castro were elected governors of New Mexico and Arizona, respectively.

1978   In the case of *Regents of the University of California* v. *Bakke,* the Supreme Court of the United States upheld the idea of affirmative action but ruled against strict racial quotas. The Court concluded that the affirmative action program at the Medical School of the University of California at Davis was unconstitutional.

1980   The 1980 U.S. Census indicated that the population of some ethnic groups in the United States increased dramatically in the decade between 1970 and 1980. Mexicans, Koreans, and Chinese were among the groups whose population increased the most. While the White population increased only 6% between 1970 and 1980, the population of Asian and Pacific islanders more than doubled (from 1.5 million to 3.5 million) and the Hispanic population increased more than 60%.

The Refugee Relief Act of 1980 was enacted. It enabled more refugees to enter the United States.

Date	Event
1986	The U.S. Senate approved an international treaty that outlaws genocide and that makes it an international crime to kill or injure members of national, racial, or ethnic groups. The treaty, approved by 69 other nations, was written after Jews became victims of the Nazi holocaust.
	*The Immigration Reform and Control Act of 1986 was passed by Congress and became law. The act imposed severe penalties on employers who knowingly hired illegal immigrants, and it gave amnesty to many illegal immigrants who had been living in the United States since January 1, 1982.
1988	The Civil Liberties Act of 1988 was passed by Congress and signed by President Ronald Reagan. The act provided compensation for the Japanese Americans and the Aleuts of the Pribilof Islands and the Aleutian Islands for the losses they incurred for being forcibly relocated during World War II.

Appendix B

Videotapes and Films

on U.S. Ethnic Groups

Videotapes

Becoming Bilingual. Producer/Distributor: Extension Media Center, University of California, 2176 Shattuck Avenue, Berkeley, CA 94704. Telephone: 415–642–0460.

> *This two-part documentary describes the experiences of limited English proficient students in bilingual programs in New York City Schools. Part I, Ambos a Dos, tells the story of a third-grade student from Puerto Rico. Part II, Newtown High, describes the experiences of students at a high school in Queens.*

Black in White America. Producer/Distributor: Capital Cities/ABC Enterprises, Inc., 825 Seventh Avenue, New York, NY 10019. Telephone: 212–887–1725.

> *This excellent video presentation, which originally appeared as a special on ABC television, sensitively discusses and illustrates the issues related to being Black in the United States today.*

Chinese Gold. Producer/Distributor: One West Media.*

> *The history and contemporary experiences of Chinese Americans are explored in this 40-minute videotape.*

Ethnic Notions. Producer: California Newsreel, San Francisco. Rental Agent: Instructional Media Services, University of Washington.*

> *This video presents a historical treatment of the stereotypic images of African Americans that have fueled and supported prejudice against Blacks.*

Eyes on the Prize: America's Civil Rights Years. Series I and II. Producer/Distributor: PBS Video.*

> *This is an outstanding series of 57-minute color videotapes that cover the civil rights movement in-depth from 1954 through the mid-1980s. Part I (6 videotapes) covers the period from 1954 to 1965. Part II (8 videotapes) covers the period from 1965 through the mid-1980s. Every school system, as well as college and university media centers, should purchase this outstanding series.*

The Golden Door: Our Nation of Immigrants. Distributor: Zenger Video.*

> *This 19-minute video presentation tells the story of immigration to the United States, both in the past and in contemporary times.*

*See list of addresses and telephone numbers on p. 521.

518

Hispanic Culture Series. Distributor: Zenger Video.*

> *The history, culture, and society of Hispanics are the focus in this series of 8 videotapes. Videotape titles include* History and Culture of Puerto Rico, Mexican People *and* Culture, Bilingual Americans, *and* The Spanish Language. *Each videotape is presented in both English and Spanish.*

In the Shadow of the Law. Producer/Distributor: One West Media.*

> *This 1-hour videotape presents the story of four immigrant families who have lived illegally in the United States for many years.*

Lean on Me. Producer/Distributor: Warner Communications Company, 400 Warner Blvd., Burbank, CA 91522.

> *In this powerful video, an authoritarian principal transforms an inner-city school that is in disarray and teaches the students to believe in themselves. The methods used by the principal can provoke discussion as well as controversy.*

Miles from the Border: A Portrait of a Mexican-American Family Caught between Cultures. Producer/Distributor: New Day Films.*

> *This videotape documents the experiences of the Aparicio family from their rural village in Mexico to their struggles and successes in California.*

Racism 101. Producer/Distributor: PBS Video.*

> *This 57-minute color video explores the reasons for the racial unrest that flared up on many college and university campuses during the 1980s. It is from the PBS program "Frontline."*

Sharing Legends at Upper Skagit. Producer/Distributor: Vi Hilbert, Seattle, WA. Rental agent: Instructional Media Services, University of Washington.*

> *The elders from seven Indian tribes in the Pacific Northwest tell ancient stories of their cultures.*

Stand and Deliver. Producer: Warner Home Video, Inc. Rental agent: Zenger Video.*

> *A gifted and talented mathematics teacher motivates and inspires his Hispanic students to succeed in calculus at a Los Angeles high school. This is a moving and inspiring video about the power of a talented and caring teacher.*

Topaz. Producer/Distributor: One West Media.*

> *This videotape documents the experiences of the Japanese Americans who were interned at the Topaz camp during World War II.*

Weave of Time: The Story of a Navajo Family 1938–1986. Producer: Direct Cinema Ltd., P.O. Box 69589, Los Angeles, CA 90069. Telephone: 213–656–4700.

> *Four generations of change in one Navajo family are depicted in this videotape.*

Films

Becoming Americans. Producer/Distributor: Ken Levine, P.O. Box 689, Kalahoe, HI 96741. Telephone: 808–332–9624.

> *This one-hour documentary film focuses on the Hmong refugees from Laos.*

Family Gathering. Producer/Distributor: New Day Films.*

> *The granddaughter of a Japanese American interned during World War II searches for her family's past during the war.*

Guilty by Reason of Race. Producer/Distributor: NBC Educational Enterprises, New York.

> *This is an award-winning TV documentary film about the problems of Japanese Americans during and after World War II.*

Hopi: Songs of the Fourth World. Producer/Distributor: New Day Films.*

> *The deep spirituality of the Hopi people is captured in this 58-minute color film.*

How the West Was Won . . . and Honor Lost. Producer/Distributor: CRM Films, 2233 Farday, Suite F, Carlsbad, CA 92008. Telephone: 800–421–0833

> *This is a powerful film presentation of the betrayal of the Indian through broken treaties and removal.*

Island in America. Producer/Distributor: Anti-Defamation League of B'nai B'rith, New York.*

> *The cultural, social, and economic life of mainland Puerto Ricans is the subject of this film.*

Manzanar. Distributor: JACP Incorporated, P.O. Box 367, San Mateo, CA 94401. Telephone: 415–343–9408

> *In this 16-minute film, a Nisei (second-generation Japanese American) recalls his boyhood in a concentration camp during World War II.*

Of Black America Series: Black History: Lost, Stolen or Strayed. Producer/Distributor: BFA Educational Media, 470 Park Ave. South, Santa Monica, CA 90016

> *A revealing film about Black-White relations in America that is skillfully narrated by Bill Cosby. This film is now an important historical document.*

The Prejudice Film. Distributor: Motivational Media, 6855 South Monica Blvd., Los Angeles, CA 90038

> *This is an extremely popular film. It is a good film to use to stimulate discussion, but it has some serious weaknesses in the way it treats and explains the nature of prejudice. A student might view this film and conclude that institutionalized racism and individual prejudice are identical.*

The Victims. Producer/Distributor: Anti-Defamation League of B'nai B'rith, New York.*

> *In this 48-minute black-and-white film Dr. Benjamin Spock, author, teacher, and pediatrician, discusses the causes of prejudice in children. Winner of the International Film and TV Festival Gold Medal.*

Wataridori: Birds of Passage. Rental agent: University of Washington.*

> *Three first-generation Japanese Americans talk about their lives in this film.*

Yo Soy. Rental Agent: University of Washington.*

> *Depicts the experience of Mexican Americans during the last two decades.*

Addresses and Telephone Numbers

Anti-Defamation League of B'nai B'rith, 823 United Nations Plaza, New York, NY 10017, Telephone: 212–490–2525

New Day Films, 853 Broadway, Suite 1210, New York, NY 10003, Telephone: 212–477–4604

One West Media, P.O. Box 5766, Santa Fe, NM 87502–5766, Telephone: 505–983–8685

PBS Video, 1320 Braddock Place, Alexandria, VA 22314–1698, Telephone: 1–800–424–7963

University of Washington, Instructional Media Services (DG–10), 35 Kane Hall, Seattle, WA 98195, Telephone: 206–543–9909

Zenger Video, 10200 Jefferson Blvd., P.O. Box 802, Culver City, CA 90232–0802, Telephone: 1–800–421–4246

Appendix C

Books about

Women of Color

Allen, Paula G. *The Sacred Hoop: Recovering the Feminine in American Indian Tradition.* Boston: Beacon Press, 1987.

Anzaldúa, Gloria, ed. *Making Face, Making Soul: Creative and Critical Perspectives by Women of Color.* San Francisco: Aunt Lute Foundation Books, 1990.

Anzaldúa, Gloria, and Moraga, Cherrie, eds. *This Bridge Called My Back: Writings by Radical Women of Color.* New York: Kitchen Table, Women of Color Press, 1983.

Asian Women United of California, eds. *Making Waves: An Anthology of Writings by and about Asian American Women.* Boston: Beacon Press, 1989.

Bell, Roseann P.; Parker, Betty J.; and Guy-Sheftall, Beverly. *Sturdy Black Bridges: Visions of Black Women in Literature.* New York: Avon Books, 1979.

Butler, Johnnella E. "Transforming the Curriculum: Teaching about Women of Color," in James A. Banks and Cherry A. Banks, eds., *Multicultural Education: Issues and Perspectives.* Boston: Allyn and Bacon, 1989.

Cole, Johnnetta, ed. *All American Women: Lines That Divide, Ties That Bind.* New York: Free Press, 1986.

DuBois, Ellen C., and Ruiz, Vicki L., eds. *Unequal Sisters: A Multicultural Reader in U.S. Women's History.* New York: Routledge, 1990.

Evans, Mari, ed. *Black Women Writers (1950–1980): A Critical Evaluation.* Garden City, N.Y.: Anchor Press/Doubleday, 1984.

Fisher, Dexter, ed. *The Third Woman: Minority Women Writers of the United States.* Boston: Houghton Mifflin Company, 1980.

Giddings, Paula. *When and Where I Enter: The Impact of Black Women on Race and Sex in America.* New York: Bantam Books, 1984.

Jackson, George F. *Black Women Makers of History: A Portrait.* Oakland, Calif.: GRT Book Printing, 1975.

Jones, Jacqueline. *Labor of Love, Labor of Sorrow: Black Women, Work, and the Family from Slavery to the Present.* New York: Vintage/Random House, 1985.

Kikumura, Akemi. *Through Harsh Winters: The Life of Japanese Immigrant Women.* Novato, Calif.: Chandler & Sharp, 1981.

Lerner, Gerda, ed. *Black Women in White America: A Documentary History.* New York: Vintage/Random House, 1972.

Lim, Shirley Geok-lin; Tsutakawa, Mayumi; and Donnelly, Margarita, eds. *The Forbidden Stitch: An Asian American Women's Anthology.* Corvallis, Ore.: Calyx Books, 1989.

Melville, Margarita B., ed. *Twice a Minority: Mexican American Woman.* St. Louis, Mo.: C.V. Mosby, 1980.

Mirande, Alfredo, and Enriquez, Evangelina. *La Chicana: The Mexican-American Woman.* Chicago: University of Chicago Press, 1981.

Mona, Magdalena, and Del Castillo, Adelaida, ed. *Mexican Women in the United States: Struggles Past and Present.* Los Angeles: UCLA Chicano Studies Center, 1980.

Moutoussamy-Ashe, Jeanne. *Viewfinders: Black Women Photographers.* New York: Dodd, Mead & Company, 1986.

Niethammer, Carolyn. *Daughters of the Earth: The Lives and Legends of American Indian Women.* New York: Macmillan, 1977.

Romero, Patricia W. *A Black Woman's Civil War Memoirs: Susie King Taylor.* New York: Markus Wiener, 1988.

Sone, Monica. *Nisei Daughter.* Seattle: University of Washington Press, 1979.

Steady, Filomina, ed. *The Black Women Cross-Culturally.* Cambridge, Mass.: Schenkman, 1981.

Sterling, Dorothy. *Black Foremothers: Three Lives.* Old Westbury, N.Y.: The Feminist Press, 1979.

———— *We Are Your Sisters: Black Women in the Nineteenth Century.* New York: W.W. Norton, 1985.

Tsuchida, Nobuya, ed. *Asian and Pacific American Experiences: Women's Perspectives.* Minneapolis: University of Minnesota Press, 1982.

Walker, Alice. *In Search of Our Mother's Gardens: Womanist Prose.* New York: Harcourt, Brace, Jovanovich, 1983.

Washington, Mary H. *Invented Lives: Narratives of Black Women 1860–1960.* New York: Doubleday, 1987.

Wolf, Beverly H. *The Ways of My Grandmothers.* New York: Morrow, 1981.

Yung, Judy. *Chinese Women of America: A Pictorial History.* Seattle: University of Washington Press, 1986.

Appendix D

The Carter G. Woodson

Award Books

The Carter G. Woodson Award is presented each year by the National Council for the Social Studies in honor of the distinguished Black historian and educator who wrote books for adults and young people, founded and edited the *Journal of Negro History*, and contributed in many significant ways to interracial understanding. The Award is designed to "encourage the writing, publishing, and dissemination of outstanding social science books for young readers that treat topics related to ethnic minorities and race relations sensitively and accurately."

1974
Eloise Greenfield, *Rosa Parks* (New York: Thomas Y. Crowell).

1975
Jesse Jackson, *Make a Joyful Noise unto the Lord: The Life of Mahalia Jackson* (New York: Thomas Y. Crowell).

1976
Laurence Yep, *Dragonwings* (New York: Harper and Row).

1977
Dorothy Sterling, *The Trouble They Seen* (Garden City, N.Y.: Doubleday).

1978
Jane Goodsell, *The Biography of Daniel Inouye* (New York: Thomas Y. Crowell).

1979
Peter Nabokov, *Native American Testimony* (New York: Thomas Y. Crowell).

1980
Nancy Wood, *War Cry on a Prayer Feather* (Garden City, N.Y.: Doubleday).
Outstanding Merit Books:
John Bierhorst, *A Cry from the Earth: Music of North American Indians* (New York: Four Winds Press).
Jim Haskins, *James Van Derzee: The Picture Takin' Man.* (New York: Dodd, Mead).
Eloise Greenfield and Lessie Jones Little, *Childtimes: A Three Generation Memoir* (New York: Harper and Row).

1981
Milton Meltzer, *The Chinese Americans* (New York: Thomas Y. Crowell).
Outstanding Merit Book:
Pamela Bullard and Judith Stoia, *The Hardest Lesson: Personal Accounts of a School Desegregation Crisis* (Boston: Little, Brown).

1982

Susan Carver and Paula McGuire, *Coming to North America from Mexico, Cuba and Puerto Rico* (New York: Delacorte Press).

1983

Brent Ashabranner, *Morning Star, Black Sun: The Northern Cheyenne Indians and America's Energy Crisis* (New York: Dodd, Mead).

1984

E. B. Fincher, *Mexico and the United States* (New York: Thomas Y. Crowell).

1985

Brent Ashabranner, *To Live in Two Worlds: American Indian Youth Today* (New York: Dodd, Mead).

Outstanding Merit Book:

David Adler, *Our Golda: The Story of Golda Meir* (New York: Viking).

1986

Brent Ashabranner, *Dark Harvest: Migrant Farm Workers in America* (New York: Dodd, Mead).

Outstanding Merit Book:

Elaine Pascoe, *Racial Prejudice: Issues in American History* (New York: Franklin Watts).

1987

Arlene Hirschfelder, *Happily May I Walk* (New York: Scribner's & Sons).

Outstanding Merit Book:

Brent Ashabranner, *Children of the Maya* (New York: Dodd, Mead).

Maxine B. Rosenberg, *Living in Two Worlds* (New York: Lothrop Publishers).

1988

James Haskins, *Black Music in America: A History through Its People* (New York: Harper and Row).

1989

Jeri Ferris, *Walking the Road to Freedom* (Minneapolis: Carolrhoda Books, Inc.). Elementary category

Charles Patterson, *Marian Anderson* (New York: Franklin Watts). Secondary category

Outstanding Merit Books:

Russell Freedman, *Buffalo Hunt* (New York: Holiday House). Elementary

Judith Harlan, *Hispanic Voters* (New York: Franklin Watts). Secondary

Pride against Prejudice: The Biography of Larry Dobbs. (New York: Praeger). Secondary

Appendix E

Twenty Classic

and Landmark Books

in Ethnic Literature

Adamic, Louis. *Laughing in the Jungle: The Autobiography of an Immigrant in America.* New York: Harper and Brothers, 1932. (Slavic American)

Anaya, Rudolfo A. *Bless Me, Ultima.* Berkeley, Calif.: Tonatiuh International, 1972. (Mexican American)

Bulosan, Carlos. *America Is in the Heart.* Seattle: University of Washington Press, 1973. (Filipino American)

Ellison, Ralph. *Invisible Man.* New York: New American Library, 1952. (African American)

Galarza, Ernesto. *Barrio Boy.* Notre Dame, Ind.: University of Notre Dame Press, 1971. (Mexican American)

Glazer, Nathan, and Moynihan, Daniel P. *Beyond the Melting Pot: The Negroes, Puerto Ricans, Jews, Italians and Irish of New York City,* 2nd ed. Cambridge, Mass.: The M.I.T. Press, 1970. (Multiethnic)

Haley, Alex. *Roots: The Saga of an American Family.* Garden City, N.Y.: Doubleday, 1976. (African American)

Handlin, Oscar. *The Uprooted: The Epic Story of the Great Migrations That Made the American People.* New York: Grosset and Dunlap, 1951. (European American)

Howe, Irving. *World of Our Fathers: The Journey of the Jews to America and the Life They Found and Made.* New York: Simon and Schuster, 1976. (Jewish American)

Hughes, Langston. *The Best of Simple.* New York: Hill and Wang, 1961. (African American)

Kingston, Maxine Hong. *The Woman Warrior: Memories of a Girlhood among Ghosts.* New York: Vintage, 1976. (Chinese American)

Momaday, N. Scott. *House Made of Dawn.* New York: Signet, 1966. (American Indian)

Novak, Michael.*The Rise of the Unmeltable Ethnics.* New York: Macmillan, 1973. (European American)

Okada, John. *No-No Boy.* San Francisco: Combined Asian American Resources Project, Inc., 1976. (Japanese American)

Rolvaag, O. E. *Giants in the Earth: A Saga of the Prairie.* New York: Harper and Row, 1927. (Norwegian American)

Sandoz, Mari. *Old Jules.* Boston: Little, Brown, 1935. (Norwegian American)

Takaki, Ronald. *Strangers from a Different Shore: A History of Asian Americans.* Boston: Little Brown, 1989. (Asian American)

Walker, Alice. *The Color Purple.* New York: Harcourt Brace, 1982. (African American)

Wong, Jade Snow. *Fifth Chinese Daughter.* New York: Harper and Row, 1945. (Chinese American)

Wright, Richard. *Black Boy: A Record of Childhood and Youth.* New York: Harper and Row, 1966. (African American)

Index